Journal of the Early Book Society

for the study of manuscripts and printing history

Edited by Martha W. Driver
Volume 17, 2014

ISBN: 978-0-944473-30-6
ISSN: 1525-6790

Member

Council of Editors of Learned Journals

The *Journal of the Early Book Society* is published annually. *JEBS* invites longer articles on manuscripts and/or printed books produced between 1350 and 1550. Special consideration will be given to essays exploring the period of transition from manuscript to print. Authors are asked to follow *The Chicago Manual of Style*. A Works Cited list at the end of the text should include city, publisher, and date. Manuscripts are to be sent, in triplicate, along with an abstract of up to 150 words, to Martha Driver, Early Book Society, Department of English, Pace University, 41 Park Row, New York, New York 10038. Only materials accompanied by a self-addressed, stamped envelope (or international reply coupon) will be returned. Members of the Early Book Society who are recent authors may send review books for consideration to Susan Powell, Reviews Editor, School of English, Sociology, Politics and Contemporary History (ESPaCH), University of Salford, Salford M5 4WT UK. Brief notes on recent discoveries, highlighting little-known or recently uncovered texts and/or images, may be sent to Linne R. Mooney, Centre for Medieval Studies, King's Manor, University of York, York YO1 2EP UK. Subscription information may be obtained from Martha Driver or from Pace University Press.

Those interested in joining the Early Book Society or with editorial inquiries may contact Martha Driver by post or e-mail (MDriver@Pace.edu). Information may also be found at <www.nyu.edu/projects/EBS>. For ordering information, call Pace University Press at 212-346-1405 or visit http://www.pace.edu/press. Institutions and libraries may purchase copies directly from Ingram Library Services (1-800-937-5300).

The editor wishes to thank Gill Kent, Alex Grover, and Genevieve Goldleaf for their help and advice on this issue.

Journal of the Early Book Society

for the study of manuscripts and printing history

Editor:
Martha W. Driver, *Pace University*

Associate Editors:
Linne R. Mooney, *University of York*
Susan Powell, *University of Salford*

Editorial Board:
Matthew Balensuela, *DePauw University*
Julia Boffey, *Queen Mary, University of London*
Cynthia J. Brown, *University of California, Santa Barbara*
Richard F. M. Byrn, *University of Leeds*
James Carley, *York University*
Joyce Coleman, *University of Oklahoma*
Margaret Connolly, *University of St Andrews*
Susanna Fein, *Kent State University*
Alexandra Gillespie, *University of Toronto*
Vincent Gillespie, *Lady Margaret Hall, Oxford University*
Stanley S. Hussey, *Lancaster University*
Ann M. Hutchison, *Pontifical Institute of Mediaeval Studies* and *York University*
Michael Kuczynski, *Tulane University*
William Marx, *University of Wales, Lampeter*
Carol M. Meale, *Bristol University*
Charlotte C. Morse, *Virginia Commonwealth University*
Daniel W. Mosser, *Virginia Polytechnic Institute and State University*
Ann Eljenholm Nichols, *Winona State University*
Judy Oliver, *Colgate University*
Michael Orr, *Lawrence University*
Steven Partridge, *University of British Columbia*
Derek Pearsall, *Harvard University*
Pamela Sheingorn, *Baruch College* and *The City University of New York Graduate School and University Center*
Alison Smith, *Wagner College*
Toshiyuki Takamiya, *Keio University*
Andrew Taylor, *University of Ottawa*
John Thompson, *Queen's University, Belfast*
Ronald Waldron, *King's College, University of London*
Edward Wheatley, *Loyola University*
Mary Beth Winn, *SUNY Albany*

Contents

Descriptive Reviews

The Clerical Proletariat: The Underemployed Scribe and Vocational Crisis

KATHRYN KERBY-FULTON

Among the unsung heroes of the resurgence of writing in English in the thirteenth and fourteenth centuries are the unbeneficed—that is, unemployed or underemployed—clergy, many of whom earned full or partial livings in various mundane ecclesiastical jobs, in administrative writing offices, or as freelance scribes Twentieth-century scholars of church history referred to these unbeneficed clergy as the "clerical proletariat": a "submerged" class of clergy who had only their daily labor to live upon and whose competence was almost always underestimated.[1] In one sense they were a "proletariat," but in another sense the Marxist analogy breaks down for the Middle Ages, because their scribal work gave them a certain access to a "means of production": in this case, the power to wield the pen, —and many of them did so in the service of various kinds of protest literature and, more generally, writing for hitherto neglected vernacular audiences.[2]

Whether it is accurate to say that they created these new audiences or that the audiences were already eager for vernacular texts and they merely obliged—or some combination of both—their agency was by any measure a critical factor in the rise of English literature. Since a great deal of Middle English literature was anonymously authored and copied, getting at the evidence for the role of this clerical underclass is not easy. But the fingerprints of the "clerical proletariat" at work in Middle English book production often appear both internally in texts and outwardly in the manuscripts themselves, leaving a trail of clues for us to follow.

Historically, the sheer numbers of clerical proletarians are such that we cannot afford to ignore them. For instance, in "Careers and Disappointments in the Late Medieval Church," Alison K. McHardy studies the demographics of the unbeneficed clergy in statistics from the three poll taxes of 1377, 1379, and 1381. Taking statistics from just three of the cities cited in her extensive sample, we learn that "71% [of clergy] in Stamford, 77% in Lincoln, and 82% in London" were unbeneficed.[3] These are startling numbers; they reveal that although London's percentage is high, it is by no means extraordinary nationwide. "Their duties might be primarily legal, secretarial, administrative or advisory," she notes, and their ranks included a small number of clerks who were now in alternative careers, such as "doctors, astrologers, and entertainers" (e.g., working as musicians in a lord's household).[4] Many were parish clerks (an office that allowed marriage); still more "clerks" or "chaplains" did not make their living primarily as ecclesiastics but rather "as notaries, schoolmasters, choristers, or even members of less likely trades, such as blacksmiths and archers."[5]

Though McHardy's list is not meant to be exhaustive, Middle English scholars will already be struck by the numbers of literary works we have that deal with some of these professions, whether by chance or not, lyrics, such as "Chorister's Lament," "The Blacksmiths," "In the Ecclesiastical Courts," to name but a few, or longer poems that take up issues connected with such jobs. *Piers Plowman*, for instance, is rife with concerns about legal, scribal, choral, schoolroom, and courtroom issues and also heavily preoccupied with minstrels (especially in the C-text). Moreover, passages unique to the Z-text (a version of the poem, I suggest elsewhere, redacted in a proletarian setting) deal, for example, unusually positively with doctors and show much more interest in notaries than even the A-, B-, or C-texts.[6] Z also shows a strong sense of crisis in clerical vocation, compounding Langland's own sense of vocational crisis, itself imitated by Thomas Usk, Thomas Hoccleve, and others.[7]

What all these texts speak to in some way is the fact that the unbeneficed clergy found themselves in circumstances that forced them to be *dependent on the laity* for their livelihood. As McHardy notes, "The unbeneficed had to attract the goodwill and enthusiasm of the laity who were buying their ministry, so we must enquire how well they were able to retain the loyalty of laity."[8] Historians have long talked about this dilemma for the unbeneficed, but scholars of medieval English literary culture have as yet fully to grasp its implications. This essay attempts, in the small space available here, to offer some suggestive examples and future directions.

How do we identify the clerical proletariat? First it is important to note that career status could be a moving target: an individual might begin as a promising schoolboy, chorister, or undergraduate, then fall short of a benefice, become underemployed, and work, for instance, as a chaplain, schoolmaster, university lecturer, vicar choral, scribe, scrivener, or secretary for a household—and then, perhaps, but more often *not,* finally come to a church position.[9] During this process he might delay ordination indefinitely. T. A. R. Evans notes, for instance, that ordinations of some fourteenth-century Oxford university men were put off even into as late as their forties, or never undertaken at all if the right type of employment did not appear. Even if ordained, a clerk might never achieve a position higher than chantry priest; the poet John Audelay spoke openly of being "ner a parsun or a vecory," having gotten a chantry only late in life and after household service that included a range of secular and religious duties, even working as a kind of musician.[10] As Susanna Fein notes, Audelay was embroiled in public scandal during his earlier service to Lord Richard Lestrange and had to take part in a ritual of penitence alongside him after Lestrange provoked a violent London brawl in 1417.

In Audelay, one is forcibly reminded of the range of secular duties and even risks underemployment could carry with it in a hierarchical society. Some unbeneficed clergy, of course, might have preferred "free-lancing," and some landed on their feet in quite respectable non-ecclesiastical jobs: Hoccleve, despite his grumbling, was clearly a valued member of the king's service in the Office of the Privy Seal.[11] But the unbeneficed more often appear as an economically disadvantaged group who, as Robert Swanson writes, lived "if not from hand to mouth, then from death to death, literally singing for their suppers."[12] But lest we assume that such clergy were the dregs of the profession, Tim Cooper notes:

> the extensive production of Latin clerical manuals to aid them, and the fact that they were often featured more significantly in their parishioners' wills than beneficed incumbents, or were more often entrusted with the care of children of dead parishioners, suggests rather that these men were the backbone of clerical service work, be it in praying for the living or dead, ministering in church services or in other small ways that their literacy skills offered: drawing up documents, carrying out ad hoc scribal commissions, and more.[13]

Given that no more than 15 percent of the stipendiary clergy got benefices, and that, as Cooper also notes, "possession of a benefice could only be gained by attracting the attention of a patron, and normally getting a university degree ... for those without such intellectual attainments, employment mobility was likely to be geographical but not economic."[14]

In fact, even the assumption that a university degree ensured upward mobility is likely overoptimistic. Studies tracing the careers of Oxford and

Cambridge men in the fourteenth century show little evidence that even a university education helped one to acquire a benefice until the end of the fifteenth century. Royal patronage or powerful networks of influence of any sort often trumped university learning. As Evans starkly concludes from demographic studies, "only a small proportion of the parish clergy was trained in a university and most university men did not obtain a parochial cure."[15] Many could not afford to finish their studies, and even among those who did, Evans suggests, perhaps as few as 11 percent were beneficed. Historians often cite the "autobiographical passage" in Langland's *Piers Plowman* as accurately portraying the plight of the unbeneficed and, more specifically, those without patronage for study. In this textbook portrait of underemployment, Will reflects on a time when he was young and benefice-less but unwilling to give up the clerical *habitus*:

> When Y yong was, many yer hennes,
> My fader and my frendes foende [provided for] me
> to scole
> Tyl Y wyste witterly what holy writ menede....
> And foend Y nere, in fayth, seth my frendes deyede,
> Lyf that me lykede but in this longe clothes.
> (*Piers Plowman*, C.V. 35–41, with omissions)[16]

Medieval university students were supported by patrons (both ecclesiastical and lay) but most often by their families ("frendes" here can mean relatives, too). Having been trained as a clerk and having fallen on hard times since the death of his patrons for university study ("scole"), Will still refuses to support himself by doing agricultural labor:

> "Sertes," Y sayde, "and so me god helpe,
> Y am to wayke to worche with sykel or with sythe
> And to long, lef me lowe to stoupe,
> To wurche as a werkeman eny while to duyren."

Rather, he says:

> "And yf Y be labour sholde lyuen and lyflode
> [livelihood] deseruen,
> That laboure þat Y lerned best þerwith lyuen Y
> sholde:
> *In eadem vocacione qua vocati estis, &c.*
> And so Y leue in London and opelond bothe:
> The lomes [tools] þat Y labore with and lyflode

> deserue
> Is *pater-noster* and my prymer, *placebo* and *dirige,*
> And my sauter som tyme and my seuene psalmes.
> Thus y synge for here soules of suche as me helpeth
> . . .
> . . . on this wyse y begge
> Withoute bagge or botel but my wombe one.
> (*Piers Plowman,* C.V. 22–52, with omissions)

Instead, the tools that he labors with are those available to a clerk in minor orders: his *pater noster* and primer, especially the Seven Penitential Psalms and the Office for the Dead, by which he lives (to quote Swanson again) "if not from hand to mouth, then from death to death."[17]

In fact, as often as this passage has been analyzed as self-deprecatory, scholars have not really appreciated that what Langland says here is also historically accurate for a certain class of those "left behind."[18] In the later Middle Ages, losing one's university patrons, most often family members, was a life crisis—not only did it drive one into proletarian status, dependent on daily or hourly work, but it could also drive one to a form of officially sanctioned begging. In such cases, Oxford university authorities could deliver sealed testimonial letters declaring the student legally "able to seek alms"—an administrative category.[19] Poor students might also be expected to live by menial labor working for their colleges or halls, sometimes even by agricultural labor (e.g., there are records of indigent students paid to work in the gardens at King's Hall, Cambridge, or paid to help build the new library at Merton College, Oxford in the 1370s).[20] Oxford and Cambridge also had to adhere to the repulsive (to us) rules enforced by lords against bondsmen or the "unfree" becoming clerics; in such cases, admission to university was technically against the law because their labor was "owned" elsewhere. Fines were amerced fairly often on bondsmen for sending sons to Oxford, which, however financially troublesome, did frequently provide a means of access to university education, because the "unfree" (paradoxically) could be financially better off than free tenants might be.[21] This unwelcome competition for already scarce jobs is also deplored in Langland's C.V. *apologia,* for which modern scholars have often maligned him as a social elitist:

> And also moreouer me thynketh, syre Resoun,
> Me [Men] sholde constrayne no clerc to no knaues
> werkes,
> For by the law of *Leuyticy* that oure lord ordeynede
> Clerkes ycrouned . . .
> Sholde nother swynke ne swete ne swerien at

enquestes
Ne fyhte . . .
For hit ben eyres of heuene . . .
Domininus pars hereditatis mee, &c . . .
For sholde no clerke be crouned but yf he come
were
Of frankeleynes and fre men and of folke ywedded.
(C.V. 53–67)

In fact, depressing as these views are to us, Langland is actually describing state, ecclesiastical and university regulations about who may study, how much they can pay, and who may ultimately be ordained.[22] Like the later Audelay, what Langland is really embittered about here is the intervention of a new free-market economy in the *buying* of opportunities, benefices, and other types of office by the illiterate and unqualified, which finally, for Langland, ends in "pore gentel blood [being] refused" (*Piers Plowman*, C.V. 78).[23] Competition is especially unwelcome when there is already so little to go around.

I leave aside for now as too complex a problem for the space allotted here the intriguing questions this raises about Langland's biography and whether he himself had a university education, even a partial one.[24] Suffice it to say that poetic portraits of the clerical proletariat such as Langland's were repeated in Ricardian and Lancastrian writing. The same repertoire of "labouring" psalms, of course, was famously used in the chronicle account of another one-time scrivener we normally think of as a secular, Usk, as he was being drawn to his execution in 1388, and praying this professional repertoire with great devotion: "dicensque cum traheretur valde devote Placebo et Dirige, vij. Psalmos Penitenciales, Te Deum laudamus, Nunc dimittis, Quicumque vult, et alios in articulo mortis tangentes."[25]

Hoccleve also uses the motif of being unable to work agriculturally in his own "autobiographical" Prologue to the *Regiment of Princes*:

With plow can y noght medle ne with harrow
Ne wote noght what londe gode is for corne
And forto laude a Cart or fille a barow
To wiche y neuer vsid whas to forne
My bak vnbuxum' hathe swych swynk for sworne.
(Hoccleve, *Regiment*, ll. 983–987)[26]

Here (and elsewhere) Hoccleve has Langlandian proclivities, but the trope predates Langland as a longtime scribal complaint,[27] and the motif about being too weak to work agriculturally and reluctant to beg ultimately de-

scends from the parable of the unjust steward in the Gospel of Luke, a job
to which many medieval underemployed clerics, it turns out, could relate.
There the steward, on the verge of losing his job, says:

> What shall I do seeing that my master is taking away
> the stewardship from me? <u>To dig I am not able</u>; <u>to</u>
> <u>beg I am ashamed</u>
> [Quid faciam quia dominus meus aufert a me
> vilicationem? <u>Fodere non valeo</u>, <u>mendicare</u>
> <u>erubesco</u>.]
> (Luke 16:3, my emphasis)

The parable, I argue here, was very popular among clerical proletariat writers,
in part because it portrays a bookkeeper's vocational crisis, with which such
a group might readily identify. In fact, as is discussed in more detail below, it
appears in a macaronic line unique to the Z version of *Piers Plowman*: "For
fodere non valeo [to dig I am not able], so feble ar my bones" (*Piers Plowman,
Z Version* V. 141).[28]

And a related form of the trope even crops up in the self-deprecatory
prologue to the *Orchard of Syon*, written by the anonymous English translator of a Latin version of Catherine of Siena's Italian *Dialogo* : "Grete laborer
was I never, bodili ne gostli. I had never greate strengthe myghtli to laboure
with spade ne with schovel. Therfore now, devoute sustren, helpeth me with
preiers, for me lackith kunnynge, ayens my grete febelnes."[29]The use of the
motif here, though possibly just rhetorical, hints at something more: where
scholars have routinely assumed monastic authorship and copying of late
medieval devotional works like the *Orchard*, unbeneficed workers are also
possible candidates and are documented on both sides of the monastic wall.
Scribal evidence of several books of monastic provenance points to the involvement of such hired labor, especially in urban monasteries, while former
scribes also sometimes joined religious orders.[30]

In addition to piecework in education and book production, clerical
proletarians are best known to us from their donkey work in documentary
and writing office capacities. Hoccleve, who worked for the King's Office of
the Privy Seal, tells us explicitly that he gave up waiting for a benefice and
married ("I gasyd longe ... / After some benefice; and whan non cam, / By
process I me weddid atte laste").[31] Many gave up the wait for a benefice, and
with odds of less than 15 percent, who can wonder. But what modern scholarship most underestimates is how many clerical proletariat thinkers never
discarded their past or training: Usk, whom we think of as a man of political
factionalism, interwove extensive material from Anselm's *De Concordia* into
his text; he also, as Melinda Nielsen shows, made unexpectedly extensive use

of university logic texts.[32] So, too, Hoccleve, whom we think of as a largely secular poet, brought to his poetry a distinctively pastoral sensibility, as, for instance, his "Lerne to Die" shows. Hoccleve's modern editor, Charles Blyth, expressed surprise over the amount of quotation from canon law in Hoccleve's *Regiment*.[33] But we should not be surprised about any of these cases; these men were amphibians—pastoral passion informs their political thought, and politics informs their ecclesiastical views. Poised between two worlds, they composed and copied works that both taught the laity and engaged the literate—and raised the bar in vernacular writing, which was still scarce at the onset of Richard II's reign in 1377.

Only slowly have I begun to realize that much of the literature composed, copied, or redacted by proletarian clerics is, like the passages above, *about vocational crisis* of one sort or another. We have seen Langland describe what it meant socially to lose one's university patronage and career prospects midstream, and what living at the edge of clerical status meant, vocationally and socially. So, too, Usk, who, though he rose from scrivener to sergeant-at-arms, only ever comes to us in writing when he is in crisis: first in his *Appeal*, then in his *Testament*, and is finally chronicled as he approaches execution, clinging to his clerical status to the last. And Hoccleve, though he rose from benefice-less clerk to be a significant employee of the Privy Seal,[34] is always in vocational crisis or financial need or both. In what space remains, I focus on further evidence, often anonymous—sometimes glimpsed through fissures or unexpected cracks in scribal professional work—that a scribe may be "underemployed," given his degree of learning. These clues, along with evidence of a certain distinctive hybridity of the "religious" and the "secular," are suggestive of proletarian productions. Many of our writers and scribes, then, are more sophisticated than we think. Many of our anonymous (and not so anonymous) writers are more *religious* in their training than we think, while the secularity of religious men can surprise us elsewhere, as we see below.

Case Study 1: An Underemployed Vernacular Scribe, More Clerically Trained Than We Thought

My first example of an apparently underemployed scribe is the copyist and annotator of Oxford, Oriel College, MS 79 ("O"), a text of *Piers Plowman*.[35] A small sample of his marginal annotations appears in the chart below alongside the parallel ones found in Cambridge, University Library Ll.iv.14 ("C²"), both manuscripts of the B-text. This is a unique marginal cycle, shared only by O and C² (O predates C² and was perhaps the exemplar for it).[36] Like most B-text notes, these are terse and, as their modern editor, David Benson, complains, not usually interpretively illuminating.[37] But they can tell us more than we might realize about the scribes who copied or created them. Take, for instance, the annotations to the B-text Pardon episode that so fascinates modern readers. These notes highlight only telegraphically the topics of merchants, begging, and almsgiving, and both sets entirely skip over the *Tearing* of the Pardon (*Piers Plowman*, B.VII.115–138).[38]

O	C²
30r / B.VII.18 Marchauntis	34r / B.VII.18 March[a]undis
30r / .26 how þu schalt do | þin almes	34r / .26 How þu shalt do | þin almes
30v / .72 catoun of | almes dedis	35r / .72 Caton of | almes dedis
30v / .83 Of falcse beggeris	35r / .83 ffalse beggers
31r / .99 [written in red] þe pardoun | of peris | Plowman	———
32r / .192 Of pardoun	36v / .192 of pardon

These notes, all too representative of B-text marginalia, are the opposite of the learned, lengthy Latin source glosses that are common in *Canterbury Tales* and *Confessio amantis* manuscripts but virtually never appear in *Piers Plowman*. But I would note that this does not necessarily mean that *Piers* scribes (or any vernacular scribes, for that matter) could not *produce* learned glosses if needed. So, for instance, at the very end of the annotation cycle, O suddenly sprouts a highly learned gloss (see Fig. 1) in the last passus, where Will falls asleep and dreams of the arrival of a seductive Antichrist who "in mannes foorme" will appear to "spedde mennys nedis" even while uprooting truth, "as he a god were" (fol. 84r; cf. B.XX.53ff.).[39] Having originally written only a one-word note here ("Antecrist"), the annotator later came back to add an uncharacteristically long and exegetical gloss in heavily abbreviated Latin:

> Ieronimus super illud Danielis .12. Beatus qui expectat & peruenit usque ad dies .1335. Beatus inquit, qui interfecto antichristo . dies supra numerum perfinitum .45 .prestolatur: quibus & dominus Saluator in sua magestate venturus est.
> [Jerome on Daniel 12, "Blessed is he who waits and comes through [perseveres] until 1335 days have

> passed. Blessed," he says, "is he who, after the death
> of Antichrist, remains for forty-five days beyond the
> aforementioned number, when the Lord Saviour is
> about to come in his majesty."]
> (fol. 84r, note to B.XX.53)

He had initially, however, merely contented himself with the simple English annotation ("Antecrist"), just like the others in O's cycle and at the very same line (XX.53). The longer gloss is written in the same hand but in different ink and is fitted awkwardly around the original "Antecrist" note, even extending down to surround the second original terse note ("ffreris"). The long gloss was, then, an *afterthought* and absolutely unusual in this cycle. The new gloss encourages the reader to be among the "blessed" who persevere through this terrible period to see Antichrist's death. And the gloss reassures the reader that the period of pain will have a specific numerical end, that the real messiah, *dominus Saluator*, is coming in majesty, and that there will be a brief period (45 days) of blessedness after the death of Antichrist.

Some years ago Wendy Scase suggested that the gloss might refer to disputes over Joachite doctrine. In fact, there is no indication what its composer thought of Joachimism, if anything (its origin is Jerome), but I would suggest that what unnerved the annotator and caused him to spring into action was something textual: in an unnoticed error in O's main text a few lines below, fools (that is, "fools for Christ"), the only ones not taken in by Antichrist's deceptions, would rather die than live "Lenger þan lenten .~ to be so rebuked" (line 63). In fact "lenten" (Lent), a period of forty days (not the eschatological forty-five days), is a misreading in O for "leute."[40] In most manuscripts, B.XX.62–63 reads: "Whiche fooles were wel gladdere to deye / Than to lyve lenger sith Leute was so rebuked." But O mistakenly invokes Lent: "Lenger þan lenten .~ to be so rebuked" (my emphasis).

Realizing that this did not add up, the annotator (I would guess) decided that more authoritative information—and better math!—were urgently needed. But whatever his theological reason, the heavily abbreviated Latin gloss supplies a valuable piece of evidence to us that the normally telegraphic, mainly *vernacular* annotators of the B-text tradition were neither monolingual nor unlearned—nor did they expect their readers to be.

In material terms, O is a modest manuscript, and the annotating scribe's work has all the hallmarks of a member of the clerical proletariat.[41] For instance, at 11.281, he supplies the technical term "Of annuelerie preestis" in a passage advocating for poor priests. He beefs up references to other chantry priest matters (e.g., 11.149, "nota | þe ground of trentalis"), to legal genres (e.g., "Carta" at 2.75), and everywhere to merchants, a key group for scribes, poorly paid chaplains, and freelance liturgical workers.[42] The swelling ranks

of the unbeneficed clergy were dependent on the laity for their funding—
something that was slowly changing the dynamics of English society and
vernacular literature.

Case Study 2: More Secular Than We Imagined: The Chantry Chaplain's Accounts Roll and "A Bird of Bishopswood"

I would like now to look at another proletarian case that reveals the opposite kind of reversal of expectations; if the O annotator is more learnedly
religious than we might imagine, this next proletarian is more secular than
we might think, given his job description. John Tyckhill was a rent collector
(*collector reddituum*) and chantry chaplain at St. Paul's, London, likely though
not certainly ordained when he composed an alliterative poem now called
"A Bird of Bishopswood."[43] It was written down on that most bureaucratic of
writing surfaces, a roll, in fact a St. Paul's rent roll for 1396–1397 maintained
by Tyckhill himself (see Fig. 2). The poem, like *Piers Plowman*, employs the
May morning trope of the *chanson d'aventure*, but it is also semi-erotic, even
a touch Chaucerian. Despite its quality and Ruth Kennedy's good edition,
it has not been much studied, though Ralph Hanna astutely mentions its St.
Paul's context as "provocative" in relation to *St. Erkenwald*.[44] It manages to
capture a compelling sense of interiority, almost *apologia*, with, I would note,
a surprisingly Hocclevian air of melancholy or depression for its early date.
Implicitly, it laments a kind of clerical loneliness during the spring season of
love, which is also, fittingly for the poet's mood, the period of Lent:

> And I had lenyd me long al a Lentyn tyme
> In vnlust of my lyf and lost al my joye . . .
> As a I welk þus and wandryd, wery of myself.
> ("Bird in Bishopswood," ll. 12–13.17).

He sees a beautiful bird, "sade in al semblant," who neither "chauntyd ne
chatryd," and it seems to the narrator that that she "Myssyd a make [mate]
myrth for to mak here" (30). He fears to go near her in case she flees, and he
laments his own lack of wings and perhaps lack of something else:

> For sche had wengys at her wylle and wantyd neuer
> a fethyr
> And I vnlyght of my lymus and lyme had I none . . .
> Ne couth noght cheuysch me with charmys ne
> chauntyng of bryddys.
> ("Bird in Bishopswood," ll. 34–36)

He ends the poem with erotic wordplay and love-longing—especially poignant if the author is indeed a fully ordained chantry chaplain: not only does he lack a "lyme" (a pun meaning both "limb" and "bait"), but he admits that he lacks the ability to chant like a bird (that is, literally, like a bird catcher) a metaphor that speaks volumes in relation to the author's vocation.[45]

The St. Paul's poem is a real treasure, and it opens up a crack through which we can learn about the opposite end of proletarian vocational crisis and perhaps even the loneliness of clerical life in that liminal religious status. The poem is almost certainly both written out and composed by Tyckhill, whose corrections to it appear in the same hand as the draft itself (evident in Fig. 2). Each collector kept his own roll (the St. Paul's rolls are cut and sewn together chancery style), apparently in his lodgings. Tyckhill's rolls themselves tell us a great deal: he also wrote Latin scientific prose into one of them, passages of which also show some sort of active revisions.[46] His is not, according to Malcolm Parkes, the hand of an Oxford or Cambridge student, nor is it really an ecclesiastical hand.[47] Rather, Parkes compares it professionally to the type of hand of the *Equatorie of the Planets*, which many scholars have attributed to Chaucer: practiced, lay, functional. And like Chaucer, Tyckhill was learned; his ability to compose in Latin, French, and English made him stand out among his chantry colleagues and may explain his promotion at last to a real benefice: a rectorship of St. Gregory's, a church by St. Paul's, in 1398.[48]

Ruth Kennedy assumes, reasonably enough, that Tyckhill was ordained, despite some conflicting evidence, at the time he wrote the poem. But we cannot be certain, since his first benefice came along only upon his leaving St. Paul's, and whether Tyckhill was among them or not, many clerks waited to be sure of beneficed church employment before fully committing to ordination and celibacy. Moreover, as the extensive entries in his rent rolls show, Tyckhill's day job involved a great deal of association with the laity. At the time of writing the poem, then, Tyckhill was one of the many clerks inhabiting the liminal world between the lay and the clerical. If so, the topic of the poem appears slightly poignant, especially if one thinks of Hoccleve, who at roughly the same time and in the same city waited decades for a benefice and eventually decided to marry.

Of course, the May morning encounter with a bird that leaves the speaker loveless, sexless ("without a limb"), and alone may simply be a diverting piece of creative fantasy for an otherwise pious churchman to amuse himself with on his days off. But even if that is all it is, it reminds us of the real humanity of proletarians, even those perched (whether Tyckhill knew it or not) on the edge of career success (he would be beneficed by 1398). Kennedy is at pains to separate him from the "chantry priests of ill repute" in contemporary satires. But his life was not wholly smooth: in 1394 he was part of a group of about twelve chaplains accused of intimidating ("averring threats" against) three other named chaplains.[49]

The character of his accounting activities has not really been studied, and what follows suggests only the tip of an iceberg, but there are some important, unnoticed clues to be found in them: the rent rolls he kept show that he dealt daily with people from all walks of life. St. Paul's was a landowner on a large scale, and he managed financial transactions with not only clergy of all ranks but laity of all kinds, including sheriffs, Guildhall officials, and others.[50] Whatever his reasons for crafting the poem, it gives us hitherto underappreciated evidence of a St. Paul's proletarian of the 1390s already deeply steeped in the latest London vernacular styles. The alliterative nature of the poem, its *chanson d'aventure* style, and its skilled use of the poetic "I" sound at different times Chaucerian, Langlandian, or Hocclevian by turn. As I suggest elsewhere, Hoccleve indulges in alliteration in just such Langlandian moments as his own *apologia* poetry[51]—and Hoccleve certainly did not learn the art of proletarian melancholy from Chaucer.

This much we can intuit from the literary parallels in the poem, but there are two rather compelling pieces of new evidence I would like to mention here that suggest Tyckhill might well have been *actually* connected with Middle English literary circles. One is that Tyckhill's service at St. Paul's in the 1390s overlapped with that of another chantry chaplain well known to Langland scholars, William Palmer (d. 1400): Palmer bequeathed a copy of *Piers Plowman* to a woman of his parish, Agnes Eggesfield, giving us evidence of Langland's earliest female reader. William died as rector of St. Alphage in London, but apparently served as a St. Paul's chantry priest in the 1390s.[52] In the rather tight-knit community of St. Paul's chaplains, it is not hard to imagine that ideas and texts were shared (several records survive of their book bequests to one another).[53]

A second piece of evidence is the fact that on the dorse of the rent roll that contains Tyckhill's poem there are several Latin account entries involving payments to a "Joh*annis* Merchaunt [or M*a*rchaunt]" (Fig. 3). These occur amidst other accounts sporadically relating to the London Guildhall (spelled variously, e.g., "in Gyldhalda" or "ad Gildhaldam"). Take, for instance, one that can be easily found in Figure 3, by counting six lines above the seam on the roll, and reading, "Item soluitur Johanni Marchaunt pro precepto eiusdem vicecomitis," indicating that Marchaunt drafted a writ for a previously named sheriff. John Marchaunt, assuming, as seems likely from the context, it is the same man, is the person Mooney and Stubbs have just recently identified as having held various Guildhall posts as an attorney in the city's courts between about 1380 and 1417 , and as Doyle and Parkes's Scribe D, the most prolific known London scribe of Middle English literature in this period.[54] Scribe D, of course, copied early and important manuscripts with works by Langland, Chaucer, Gower, and other vernacular writers and worked alongside Hoccleve himself on the Trinity Gower (Trinity College, Cambridge MS R.3.2).[55] John Marchaunt, as Mooney and Stubbs demonstrate, was also known to Usk.

Assuming this is also the Marchaunt of Tyckhill's roll accounts, it would appear that Tyckhill might easily have had access to any number of London writers' works in the 1390s, if not before. Since his poem is dateable to before 1398, when he resigned his St. Paul's collectorship to take up a benefice, he was certainly among the very earliest readers of Chaucer, Langland, and perhaps even Hoccleve. And, if Mooney's and Stubbs' identification is correct, he apparently handled some business with the most prolific of their scribes, John Marchaunt.

Proletarians like Tyckhill exemplify perfectly a type of conjunction that is foreign to us, where poetry, account-keeping, and liturgical training converge. To underline the latter, we should conclude by mentioning that Tyckhill's poem is written out in prose, as Kennedy notes, with great attention to punctuation for enhancing oral performance. This is exactly what a trained liturgist might do: he supplies metrical cues where space is too short to copy in verse, very like the punctuation in the more famous alliterative poem "The Blacksmiths," also copied out in prose, in British Library MS Arundel 292. Like "A Bird in Bishopswood," "Blacksmiths," as I suggest elsewhere, is elaborately punctuated for meticulous performance using the *punctus elevatus*, the *punctus versus*, and the *virgula suspensiva*, not only to mark off the alliterative line units, but to indicate intonation patterns (Fig. 4).[56]

Arundel 292 is another manuscript that has been somewhat misjudged as purely religious, even monastic in purpose. But Arundel 292 is actually more likely to have been used by non-monastic clergy at Norwich Cathedral Priory, and in a circumstance very like Tyckhill's liminal situation at St. Paul's.[57] Arundel 292 captures this amphibious clerical culture well, especially in two poems entered into the manuscript at later dates, "Chorister's Lament" (ca. 1350), and "Blacksmiths" (ca. 1400–1450).

"Blacksmiths" straddles the lay and the clerical world in unexpected ways.[58] Ostensibly written against the policy of allowing smiths to work at night (an issue of city ordinances of a type that Guildhall scribes dealt with daily), the poem in fact luxuriates in the very sounds of the smithy, which it seeks to imitate in exuberantly over-alliterated lines. "Blacksmiths" has been compared by Elizabeth Salter to the "urban disturbance" genres of Horace, Juvenal, and Martial, so, I would suggest, its origins in schoolboy rhetorical exercises and its careful punctuating for voicing link it culturally to the song school, and with its earlier companion, "Choristers."[59] Made of often misshapen parchment, Arundel 292 was a working volume for basic pastoral care or lay teaching and its blank pages became something of a log for complaint verse that resonated with clerks caught in dead-end choral or schoolmaster positions. Proletarians appear to have spoken the same language in more ways than one, and they brought a set of liturgical skills to their vernacular writing, which is somehow married up with their more secular work in day jobs like Tyckhill's account-keeping. We turn next to their frequent identity as account-keepers, real and metaphorical.

Case Study 3: "Render an Account of Your Stewardship": White-Collar Vocational Crisis and the Clerical Proletariat in the Z-Text of *Piers Plowman*

We have seen that proletarians were amphibians who moved between two worlds, often between some form of secular office life and liturgical practice. But only slowly have I come to understand exactly why one particular metaphor, that of "rendering accounts," seems to crop up so often in proletarian texts. In this section, with Tyckhill's literal account-keeping vividly before us, we explore the use of this motif in the biblical Parable of the Unjust Steward and its interpolation into *Piers Plowman* in the redaction known as the Z-text. And this brings us to another dimension of proletarian book producers: their incredible sense of freedom, not to say entitlement, about *meddling* in book production. The reason for this is not far to seek: with so many underemployed clerically trained copyists, well versed in both church and government matters, scribal intervention in texts is confident and often highly intelligent—to the extent that it can be difficult for modern editors to tell scribes from authors.

One of the best examples of this I know is the Z-text redaction of *Piers*, which is awash in unique lines added to further emphasize and augment clerical proletarian concerns (a topic Langland himself had already found compelling), especially scribal and notarial life. Take this example from Z, with its unique additions bolded:

> Sire Simonye ys ofsent to sele the chartres
> **Ant alle the notaryes by name, that they noen fayle,**
> **To sette on here sygnes as Symonye wyl bydde**.
> (Z.II.39–41; see also II.99ff. and 119ff.)

Likely, though not certainly, a Londoner, from a similar proletarian background as Langland himself, the Z redactor seems to have known and had access to all three versions of the poem, though it was an A-text he chose to "improve."[60] In the short space left here, we will examine:

1. The Z redactor's fascination with the Parable of the Unjust Steward, which, as we saw at the outset, resonated deeply with multiple proletarian writers in the Ricardian period.

2. The redactor's fascination with Langland's special treatment of merchants among the three social groups (merchants, lawyers, and beggars) in the Pardon scene, three groups that is, of real importance to proletarian thinkers, such as we have also just seen picked out for attention in the laconic marginal notes of Oriel 79 (O).

To begin with the parable: the biblical steward was denounced to his master (*diffamatus est*) for dissipating his goods—we never know whether in fact he is guilty. His master then asks him to "render an account of his stewardship" (*redde rationem villicationis tuae*; Luke 16:2). Middle English scholars know this as the famous theme of Wimbledon's popular 1388 sermon, written about the same time as the Z redaction. But as we saw above, in the parable's key passage the steward, on the verge of being fired, asks himself (*ait . . . intra se*) "what shall I do seeing that my master is taking away the stewardship from me? To dig I am not able; to beg I am ashamed" (*quid faciam quia dominus meus aufert a me villicationem? fodere non valeo; mendicare erubesco*; Luke 16:3). The parable describes, then, in modern terms, a crisis of *white-collar* unemployment. As such, it seems to have caught the attention of Langland, the Z redactor, Wimbledon, and, as we saw earlier, Hoccleve, and the *Orchard of Syon* author.

Langland's interest, though most evident in the C.V. *apologia*, goes back to the A- and B-texts, in which Robert the Robber (one of the voices of Sloth in the Seven Deadly Sins' confessions) also has a remarkable moment of interiority that explicitly invokes the parable's accounting moment (*redde rationem villicationis tuae*):

> Robert þe robbour on reddite[61] lokide,
> Ac for þere was nou3t wherewith he wepte swiþe sore.
> And 3et þe sinful shrewe seide to hymselue.
> (A.V. 233ff)

Invoking the good thief crucified alongside Christ (an emblem of salvational hope for the desperate), Robert prays for mercy, stressing the accounting theme again:

> So rewe on þis Robert þat red[dere] ne hauiþ,
> Ne neuere wen[e] to wynne wiþ craft þat [I owe].
> (A.V. 240–241)

That is, "have pity on this Rob(b)er(t) who does not have the means to pay back, nor [do I] ever think to earn that which I owe with any craft."[62] The lines are poignant, and Langland would return to them in complex ways, especially in the C-text and latently in the C.V. *apologia*—not so latently, however, that a fellow proletarian did not see the connections. In the Z-text, the A-text lines above are mysteriously augmented with unique Latin lines of the redactor's own composition, directly quoting the Parable of the Unjust Steward that is unobtrusively foundational—for the biblically alert—to Langland's C.V. autobiographical passage:

> So rewe on me, Robert, for *reddere* ne habbe
> Ne nere wene to wynne *wyth* craft that Y knowe . . .
> **For *fodere non valeo*, so feble ar my bones:**
> **Caucyon, ant Y couthe, *caute* wolde Y make**
> **That Y ne begged ne borwed ne in despeyr deyde.**
> (Z.V. 142–143)

In their note to this passage (Z.V. 142), Rigg and Brewer translate these rather difficult last two lines as follows:

> For I cannot dig, so feeble are my bones. If I could,
> I would prudently [caute] make a down payment
> [caucyon],* in order not to beg or borrow or die in
> despair.
> *"caucyon" can mean "surety, bond" given against
> a loan.

To understand this challenging interpolation, one has to know a little bit about loans and bonds, some biblical Latin, and the parable of the Unjust Steward—in short, the kind of mixture of knowledge a proletarian would have. Faced with his white-collar unemployment crisis and unpalatable blue-collar options, the steward comes up with a shrewd plan to call in his master's debtors for payment of at least part of their debt, apparently forgiving them the rest of the debt: thus one debtor who owes a hundred jars of oil is told "accipe cautionem tuam et sede cito scribe quinquaginta" [Take thy bond and sit down at once and write fifty] (Luke 16:6). In this way he pleases his master by prudently (*prudenter*) gathering in his debts, if at a loss (Luke 16:8). In a parable already laden with ambiguities, the questionable nature of the steward's remedy was not lost on medieval commentators, and it was not lost on Christ himself, who ends with this cryptic comment: "quia filii huius saeculi prudentiores filiis lucis in generatione sua sunt" [for the children of this world, in relation to their own generation, are more prudent than the children of the light] (Luke 16:8).[63]

The parable's central character, a minor bureaucrat down on his luck, demonstrates a strange mix of interiority, audacious entrepreneurialism, self-interest, and ingenuity. Utilizing a language of law and accountancy, the parable must have struck a chord with many who worked in writing offices that dealt with debt (such as the Exchequer, Privy Seal, or even a proletarian St. Paul's rent collector). Apparently Robert the Robber's "*reddere*" in the A-text sparked off an association with the "*redde rationem vilicationis*" of the parable, so the Z redactor inserted the "*fodere*" passage to cement the allusion. And by then he was really having fun with his embellishments. He could not have actually been Langland, by the way, because the interpolation does not make much poetic sense in its context, but he was eager to impress. He came up with the punning next line, "Caucyon, ant Y couthe, *caute* wolde Y make" (Z.V. 143), by borrowing the word *cautionem* (bond) from the parable. Then, like a math genius wanting to show not only that he can solve a problem but that he can also skip whole steps while doing it, there is a kind of showing-off quality here (an attempt to "out-Langland" Langland).

The maneuver served mainly to stake out membership in a sophisticated club.[64] One has to have agile Latin grammar to get this, and the Z redactor must have found irresistible the opportunity to play similarly with the Luke parable to evoke the legal language of financial offices and places where employment crises were rife. Hoccleve made a poetic career of writing about such crises in his begging poems. For instance, in *La Male Regle* he confesses that he dare not "stele, for the guerdoun is so keene, / Ne darst . . .nat, ne begge also for shame" (367–368); even Chaucer's "Complaint to His Purse" fits into just such a genre of white-collar employment crisis. And then there is the C.V. *apologia* itself, in which the dreamer renders his own account of slightly dubious stewardship in the language of business:

> Ac yut Y hope, as he that ofte hath ychaffared
> And ay loste and loste and at the laste hym happed
> A bouhte such a bargain he was the bet euere
> And sette al his los at leef. . . .
> So hope Y to haue of hym that is almighty
> A gobet of his grace.
> (*Piers Plowman*, C.V. 94–100, with omissions)

Members of the clerical proletariat, then, seem to speak the same language and furthermore to serve a very specific set of clientele. Among the strikingly proletarian features of the Z-text that I discuss elsewhere is his special attention to Piers's Pardon from Truth, in which Langland innovatively tried to bring new social groups (merchants, lawyers, and beggars) into the salvational covenant, finding loopholes for them under certain moral conditions.[65] The Z redactor warmly approves of Langland's efforts and embellishes them lovingly wherever he can, for instance, in his emphasis on the physical documentary nature of the Pardon from Truth. Whereas in the A-text beggars are not allowed directly into Piers's "bull" unless they meet certain criteria, Z rather amusingly shifts them quite physically "to the dorse" (**"in the bak halfe"**) of the document:

> Beggaueres ne byddares ne but nat in the bulle
> **But yt be in the bak half** [dorse] **wythouten, by hemsilue**
> [outside by themselves]
> (Z.VIII.68–69)

The three "newer" groups Langland is so keen to find a place for in Truth's Pardon, the merchants, lawyers, and beggars, are also social groups highly relevant to writing office life and freelance documentary work. Langland had squeezed the merchants into Truth's Pardon (*Piers* C.IX.22–24 and 27) by giving them a clause in the *margin* of the "bull," thus emphasizing their "marginality" in the Church's schema but slyly claiming they are covered under God's "secrete (or privy) seal." This brings a powerful, surprisingly emotional response from the merchants—the only group allowed the distinction of being able respond to Truth's offer in the poem itself:

> Tho were marchauntes mury; many wopen for ioye
> And preyed for Peres the plouhman þat purchased hem þis bulles.
> (C.IX.41–2)

But in the A-text and in Z, these lines run very differently:

> þanne were marchauntis merye: many wepe for ioye,
> And 3af wille for his writing wollene cloþis;
> For he co[pie]de þus here clause þei [couden] hym gret mede.
> (A.VIII.42–44)

In A and Z, Will (not, as in BC, Piers) is the agent of the merchant's joy via his scribal work. Z is even more pointed:

> And yeuen Wylle for **thys** wrytyng wollen clothus
> For he coped thus here clause, couth hym gret mede.
> (Z.VIII.43–44).

Interestingly "copiede" (which as Kane points out in his note to A.VIII.44 is quite a new verb) is "coped" in Z, a delightful pun on the idea of clothing the words in ecclesiastical garb, the "bull" itself. One cannot help but see in A's (and Z's) version a moment of writerly vocation, indeed, even mission. In Z it is emphatically "thys" writing, and the act of copying the "clause" is both allegorized and sanctified quite cleverly.

Why should merchants have such a special role? One pertinent factor may be, as many historians and codicologists have shown, that scribes and scriveners did much of their daily work for merchants and lawyers. The Church regarded the rising merchant class as a gray area in canon law; someone like Langland must have found this intolerable, or at least unsatisfactory. Langland's move is avant-garde here, and theologically progressive. As I show elsewhere, though the Z redactor is more conservative than Langland on many ecclesiastical issues,[66] his redaction evokes scribal culture even more, and he followed Langland in this inclusiveness wholeheartedly. The Z redactor felt that Langland's innovations to the Pardon system to include these groups were so crucial that he even suppressed the Tearing of the Pardon to make sure that the inclusion was not undermined.[67] It is no wonder. Merchants, as I need not explain to readers of this journal, were an important early readership for English literature. From the thirteenth-century evidence of the clientele of poetic competitions like the London Puy, to Linne Mooney and Estelle Stubbs's Guildhall discoveries, to fifteenth-century evidence offered by the scribe-anthologist, John Shirley, merchants loom large.[68] The clerical proletariat, as we saw above in McHardy's researches, are clerics who now work for the laity

To conclude, the latest poem we have looked at here in any detail is the 1396–1397 "Bird in Bishopswood," and perhaps it is not by chance that this poem is the most poignantly uncertain about the clerical life. In the Ricardian period there began to be a steep drop in requests for ordination, as bureaucratic culture found ways other than the benefice to fund itself directly, and by the early fifteenth century the symbiosis that had existed between church and state was partly dissolved, or at least unmoored, as fewer amphibians were forced to tread the road of disappointment.[69] The popular writers of the mid- to late fifteenth century are not so much clerical proletariat civil servants and chantry priests but members of religious orders (like John Lydgate, John Walton, John Capgrave, and Osbern Bokenham). Increasingly in the fifteenth century large numbers of benefices were appropriated to the monastic houses (a shift still not fully taken account of in scholarship), while in the other direction the civil service laicized at a terrific rate.[70]

In such an environment, binaries like secular and religious, heresy and orthodoxy, clerical and lay, and other oppositions are bound to rigidify more than they did in the fourteenth century. I would suggest that some of the more judgmental, platitudinous, or "orthodox" tones we sense in fifteenth-century English writing[71] stem in part from such demographic shifts—not so much from growing "anticlericalism" or post-Arundel censorship, but a shift of tone arising rather, as the number of ordained religious in the civil service dropped off and the numbers of the "clerical proletariat" melted away into a growing laicization of the writing offices—with the loss of their unique, vocationally troubled voices.

University of Notre Dame

Acknowledgments

This essay is dedicated with gratitude to the memory of Malcolm Parkes, who taught generations of us to prepare our earliest "questions to ask the manuscript." I would also like to thank Derek Pearsall, Martha Driver, Linne Mooney, Estelle Stubbs and Katherine Zieman for their helpful readings of this paper. I am grateful also for stimulating questions in response to an oral version given for the English Faculty at Cambridge (May 2014), and for the 2013 Early Book Society conference audience in St. Andrews, where this paper was first delivered as a plenary.

NOTES

1. See, e.g., the introduction in J. F. Goodridge, *Piers the Ploughman* (London: Penguin, 1959), 9, citing W. A. Pantin's comments on the "clerical proletariat" as a social and economic underclass: "though the case of Langland shows us that a more or less submerged cleric might be the intellectual equal of anybody." Among recent studies, see especially Tim Cooper, *The Last Generation of English Catholic Clergy: Parish Priests in the Diocese of Coventry and Lichfield in the Early Sixteenth Century* (Woodbridge, UK: Boydell and Brewer, 1999); and T. A. R. Evans, "The Numbers, Origin and Careers of Scholars," in *The History of the University of Oxford*, vol. 2, *Late Medieval Oxford*, ed. J. I. Catto and Ralph Evans (Oxford: Clarendon, 1992), 485–538; Alison K. McHardy, "Careers and Disappointments in the Late Medieval Church," *Studies in Church History* 26 (1989): 111–130. I use the term "proletariat" not in the pejorative sense of scholars like Pantin, but in the "reclaimed" sense fostered by Marxist scholarship and in recent histories such as Cooper, *Last Generation*.
2. These two categories of writing are, of course, both large and distinct, though sometimes overlapping. The treatment of protest literature especially is beyond the scope of this essay, but for a learned recent analysis of its connections with legal genres, see Wendy Scase, *Literature and Complaint in England, 1272–1553* (Oxford: Oxford University Press, 2007). Also beyond the scope of this essay is whether proletarians espoused or came to espouse

Wycliffism, but it is worth noting that the young Wyclif was bitterly disappointed when he was passed over for a prebend in 1375; see Barrie Dobson, "The English Vicars Choral: An Introduction," in *Vicars Choral at English Cathedrals*, ed. Richard Hall and David Stocker (Oxford: Oxbow Press, 2005), 4. For a classic account of the development of Marxist theory in twentieth-century scholarship, see Lee Patterson, "Historical Criticism and the Claims of Humanism," in *Negotiating the Past: The Historical Understanding of Medieval Literature* (Madison: University of Wisconsin Press, 1987), 41–76. Of course many of these clerks were trilingual and also served new audiences in French and Latin.

3. McHardy, "Careers," 113.

4. Ibid., 118.

5. Ibid., 127.

6. Kathryn Kerby-Fulton, "Confronting the Scribe-Poet Binary: The Z Text, Writing Office Redaction and Oxford Reading Circles," in *New Directions in Manuscript Studies and Reading Practices: Essays in Honour of Derek Pearsall*, ed. Kathryn Kerby-Fulton, John Thompson, and Sarah Baechle (Notre Dame, IN: University of Notre Dame Press, forthcoming 2014). 189 515 On no taries and "poor clerks," see Beverly Brian Gilbert, "'Civil' and the Notaries in *Piers Plowman*," *Medium Aevum* 50 (1981): 49–63.

7. Kathryn Kerby-Fulton, "Professional Readers of Langland at Home and Abroad: New Directions in the Political and Bureaucratic Codicology of *Piers Plowman*," in *New Directions in Later Medieval Manuscript Studies: Essays from the 1998 Harvard Conference*, ed. Derek Pearsall (Woodbridge, UK: Boydell and Brewer, 2000), 103–129.

8. McHardy, "Careers," 119. For detailed analysis showing that the unbeneficed were underpaid chaplains in charge of about half the parish churches in Norwich, but often able to supplement their incomes via the chantries endowed by the laity, see Norman P. Tanner, *The Church in Late Medieval Norwich, 1370-1532* (Toronto: PIMS, 1989), 47-51.

9. For scribe attorneys and other writing office profiles, see Linne R. Mooney and Estelle Stubbs, *Scribes and the City: London Guildhall Clerks and the Dissemination of Middle English Literature, 1375–1425* (York, UK: York Medieval Press, 2013). For university and educational professional careers, see Evans, "Numbers." On careers as vicars choral, see Barrie Dobson, "The English Vicars Choral: an Introduction," in *Vicars Choral at English Cathedrals*, ed. Richard Hall and David Stocker (Oxford: Oxbow Press, 2005), 1–10. Tanner, *The Church*, 47-8, notes the rarity of upward mobility to a benefice in his Norwich data.

10. See Evans, "Numbers," 534–535, on the late careers of Hoccleve and Audelay; for Audelay's career disappointments, see McHardy, "Careers," 127–128, citing this passage; and on Audelay's biography, see the introduction in Susanna Fein, ed., *John the Blind Audelay, Poems and Carols (Oxford, Bodleian Library MS Douce 302)* (Kalamazoo, MI: TEAMS, 2009).

11. Linne R. Mooney, "Some New Light on Thomas Hoccleve," *Studies in the Age of Chaucer* 29 (2007): 293–340. See Tanner, *The Church*, 51, for evidence that most Norwich unbeneficed lived above mere subsistence levels, and some might have preferred "free-lancing" for lay chantries as decently lucrative and less burdensome.

12. Robert Swanson, *Church and Society* (Oxford: Blackwells, 1989), 62.

13. Cooper, *Last Generation*, 127.

14. Ibid.

15. Evans, "Numbers," 538.

16. Derek Pearsall, ed., *William Langland: Piers Plowman. A New Annotated Edition of the C-Text* (Exeter, UK: University of Exeter Press, 2008).

17. Swanson, *Church and Society*, 62.

18. For a summary of scholarship on C.V., see Pearsall, *William Langland*, 21, and his notes to V. ll. 1–108.

19. Evans, "Numbers," 509–511, and 511 n. 84, citing H. E. Salter, ed., *Registrum cancellarii Oxoniensis 1434–69*, Oxford Historical Society, XCIII–IV (Oxford: Clarendon, 1932), ii: 40, as an example in which the chancellor provided letters authorizing begging.

20. These are referred to in records as *batellarii*. See Evans, "Numbers," 509, for these examples.

21. Ibid., 515, noting that unfree tenants were often wealthier than free ones.

22. On ordination regulations, which Langland faithfully mirrors here, see H. S. Bennett, "Medieval Ordination Lists in the English Episcopal Records," *Studies Presented to Hilary Jenkinson*, ed. J. Conway-Davies (London: Oxford University Press, 1957), 20–34.

23. McHardy, "Careers," 128 on Audelay.

24. On Langland's life, see most recently, if speculatively, Robert Adams, *Langland and the Rokele Family: The Gentry Background to Piers Plowman* (Dublin: Four Courts, 2013).

25. L. C. Hector and Barbara F. Harvey, ed. and trans., *Westminster Chronicle 1381–1394* (Oxford: Clarendon, 1982), 314–315; see also Paul Strohm, "Politics and Poetics," in *Literary Practice and Social Change in Britain, 1380–1530*, ed. Lee Patterson (Berkeley: University of California Press, 1990), 89. For liturgical practices, see Katherine Zieman, *Singing the New Song: Literacy and Liturgy in Late Medieval England* (Philadelphia: University of Pennsylvania Press, 2008).

26. Thomas Hoccleve, *The Regiment of Princes*, ed. Charles R. Blyth (Kalamazoo, MI: TEAMS, 1999). On Hoccleve and Langland, see Kathryn Kerby-Fulton, Linda Olson, and Maidie Hilmo, *Opening Up Middle English Manuscripts: Literary and Visual Approaches* (Ithaca, NY: Cornell University Press, 2012), 87–90.

27. Kerby-Fulton, et al., *Opening Up*.

28. A. G. Rigg and Charlotte Brewer, *Piers Plowman: The Z Version* (Toronto: Pontifical Institute of Medieval Studies, 1983). I retain Rigg and Brewer's use of bolded text for lines unique to Z.

29. Jocelyn Wogan-Browne, Nicholas Watson, Andrew Taylor, and Ruth Evans, eds., *The Idea of the Vernacular: An Anthology of Middle English Literary Theory, 1280–1520* (University Park: Pennsylvania State University Press, 1999), 237, and notes 45, on the translator's comment that he completed this during leisure time, and 47 on the translator's possible Carthusian status.

30. See Margaret Connolly, "Mapping Manuscripts and Readers of *Contemplations of the Dread and Love of God*," in *Design and Distribution of Late Medieval Manuscripts*, ed. Margaret Connolly and Linne R. Mooney (Woodbridge, UK: Boydell, 2008).

31. Hoccleve, *Regiment of Princes*, ll. 1451–1453; see also McHardy, "Careers," 127.

32. Melinda Nielsen, "Scholastic Persuasion in Thomas Usk's *Testament of Love*," *Viator* 42 (2011): 183–204. Nielsen traces the pragmatic and theological kinds of learning available to a man like Usk, who was clearly intellectually ambitious, and concludes, "From grammar school to university connections, apprenticeship to involvement in documentary London, possibilities abound for how a London scrivener could develop and gratify his taste to imitate Boethius, translate Anselm, allude to Trevisa, adapt scholastic logic, and pioneer English prose" (186); see also R. Allen Shoaf, ed., *Thomas Usk: The Testament of Love,* Robbins Library Digital Projects (Kalamazoo, MI: TEAMS, 1998), http://d.lib.rochester.edu/teams/text/shoaf-usk-testament-of-love-introduction#sources.

33. Hoccleve, *Regiment of Princes*, 12; see also Kerby-Fulton, et al., *Opening Up*, 89–90.

34. Mooney, "Some New Light."

35. Katherine Heinrichs, ed., *The Piers Plowman Electronic Archive*, vol. 3, *Oxford, Oriel College, MS 79 (O)* (Medieval Academy of America and SEENET by Boydell and Brewer, Woodbridge, U.K., 2004): "The main scribe has written, in addition to the text, marginal glosses, corrections, *notae*, and . . .parasigns"; Introduction, Section I.6, "Handwriting," 6.

36. See C. David Benson and Lynne Blanchfield, *The Manuscripts of Piers Plowman: The B Version* (Woodbridge, UK: Boydell and Brewer, 1997), 20.

37. Benson writes, "Unlike proper medieval glosses, they do not analyze, comment on, or elucidate the text at any length. [They] . . .are almost always brief and often not more than a single word—*nota* . . .Each scribe apparently produced his own, . . .with the exception of two groups of closely affiliated MSS." Ibid., 20. O and C^2 form one such group.

38. Proletarian disapproval of this episode is discussed in more detail below, as well as in Kerby-Fulton, "Confronting."

39. George Kane and E. T. Donaldson, *Piers Plowman: The B Version* (London: Athlone Press, 1978).
40. See Wendy Scase, *Piers Plowman and the New Anticlericalism* (Cambridge, UK: Cambridge University Press, 1989), 116–117.
41. In addition to copying the *Piers* text and annotations in Oriel 79, this scribe also copied the last eight lines of a Latin poem on fol. 1r. Kathryn Heinrichs, who transcribed Oriel 79 as the third volume for the *Piers Plowman Electronic Archive*, writes in the description posted on the *Archive*'s project site, "The manuscript is a professional production, written in a small, regular *anglicana formata* by a scribe of North Hertfordshire whose language is almost perfectly consistent. The quality of the vellum is poor, and the manuscript is only modestly ornamented." http://piers.iath.virginia.edu/manuscripts/B/b0Ackn.html.
42. Mooney and Stubbs, *Scribes and the City*. We cannot know for certain whether the O scribe is creating or copying the marginal cycle, but his is the earliest manuscript with the cycle. At the very least, we know he approved enough of the annotations to copy them.
43. Ruth Kennedy, "'A Bird in Bishopswood': Some Newly-Discovered Lines of Alliterative Verse from the Late Fourteenth Century," in *Medieval Literature and Antiquities: Studies in Honour of Basil Cottle*, ed. Myra Stokes and T. L. Burton (Cambridge, UK: D. S. Brewer, 1987), 71–87.
44. See Hanna, "Alliterative Poetry," in Wallace, *Cambridge History*, 510.
45. See the *Middle English Dictionary* online for definitions of birdlime: "brid ~ [see brid 5. (a)]; (b) *fig.* something that entraps [birds]; (c)?glue; (d)?mineral pitch, bitumen; (e) mud, slime." http://quod.lib.umich.edu/cgi/m/mec/med-idx?type=id&id=MED6006
46. London Metropolitan Archives (formerly Guildhall Library) 25125/34. On the scientific writings, see Kennedy, "Bird," 73–74; they are on the face, with accounts on the dorse.
47. Parkes, cited in Kennedy, "Bird," 74. Parkes drew Kennedy's attention here to the professional, non-ecclesiastical type of hand in Cambridge University Library MS Peterhouse 75 (containing the *Equatorie of the Planets*) as a parallel to Tykhill's hand. Parkes' points remain pertinent whether or not Chaucer proves to be the scribe of Peterhouse 75, though Linne Mooney and Estelle Stubbs kindly inform me that Kari Ann Schmidt has unpublished evidence that the scribe was not Chaucer.
48. For this theory, see Marie-Hélène Rousseau, *Saving the Souls of Medieval London: Perpetual Chantries at St. Paul's, c. 1200–1548* (Farnham, UK: Ashgate, 2011), 115–116.
49. Kennedy, "Bird," 76–77.
50. I have had a chance to examine only two of the rent rolls held at the London Metropolitan Archives in any detail: formerly Guildhall Library MS 25125/32 and 25125/34.

51. Kerby-Fulton, et al., *Opening Up*, 87–90.
52. Rousseau, *Saving the Souls*, 116. On Palmer, see Kerby-Fulton, "The Women Readers in Langland's Earliest Audience: Some Codicological Evidence," in *Learning and Literacy in Medieval England and Abroad*, ed. Sarah Rees-Jones (Turnhout, Belgium: Brepols, 2002), 121–134.
53. Rousseau, *Saving the Souls*, 115–116.
54. Ian Doyle and M. B. Parkes, "The Production of Copies of the Canterbury Tales," in *Medieval Scribes, Manuscripts and Libraries: Essays Presented to N.R. Ker*, ed. M.B. Parkes and Andrew Watson (London: Scolar Books, 1978) 163-212.
55. For the fullest recent list of English manuscripts attributed to Scribe D, see Mooney and Stubbs, *Scribes and the City*, 38, and for his employment history, 56–57.
56. Ibid., 329–330; see Jane Roberts, *Guide to Scripts Used in English Writings up to 1500* (London: British Library, 2005), xiii, for the types of punctuation. And see Kerby-Fulton, et al., *Opening Up*, 45, for their use in "Blacksmiths."
57. See Susan Boynton and Eric Rice, eds., *Young Choristers, 650–1700* (Woodbridge, UK: Boydell and Brewer, 2008), 14ff, on Norwich's almonry school for boys of all ages and choirmasters appointed from outside the monastery. On "Blacksmiths" and "Choristers," see Kerby-Fulton, et al., *Opening Up*, 42–43. For a more detailed study of the musicology of "Choristers," see Anna de Bakker's forthcoming article on the vocabulary of the poem and medieval chorister training.
58. It is written into Arundel 292 on fol. 71v, just after a text on what to do if, as a priest, one has an accident with the host ("Si aperta quod absit neglicencia de corpore aut sanguine Christi acciderit")
59. Especially like those found in Geoffrey de Vinsauf's *Poetria nova*. See Elizabeth Salter, *English and International: Studies in the Literature, Art and Patronage of Medieval England*, ed. Derek Pearsall and Nicolette Zeeman (Cambridge, UK: Cambridge University Press, 1988), 211–213.
60. See Kerby-Fulton, "Confronting." The London scribe who made the copy of *Piers Plowman* in Huntington Library HM 114 similarly had access to all three versions of the poem. See Kerby-Fulton, et al., *Opening Up*, 70.
61. I.e., "render" or "pay back"; the line also echoes Rom. 13:7.
62. A. G. Kane, *Piers Plowman: The A Version* (London: Athlone, 1960), see variants to A.V. 241, but sixteen manuscripts read some form of "any craft that I *know*"; three MSS read "redde" at 240.
63. The exegetical interpretations of the passage, too complex for discussion here, enrich interpretations of Z, as redactors and imitators of Langland knew well. See Stephen Wailes, *Medieval Allegories of Jesus' Parables* (Berkeley: University of California Press, 1987), 245ff. As Augustine noted, "not all aspects of the steward praised by the lord are to be imitated" (247), and

the inability to dig signifies the inability to do penance, thus clarifying Langland's invocation of the parable in relation to Sloth and unrestituted robbery.
64. For a genuine Langlandian example, see Pearsall's note to C.V. 86–87.
65. Kerby-Fulton, "Confronting."
66. For a list of passages in Z, see Kathryn Kerby-Fulton, "Piers Plowman," in *The Cambridge History of Medieval English Literature*, ed. David Wallace (Cambridge, UK: Cambridge University Press, 1999), 513–538; and see also Karrie Fuller, "The Craft of the Z- Maker: Reading the Z Text's Unique Lines in Context," *Yearbook of Langland Studies* 28 (2014) 15-30.
67. For the evidence of this case, see Kerby-Fulton, "Confronting." The term "merchants" is used in this paragraph as a convenient shorthand, just as Langland employs it. However, Linne Mooney has suggested to me (in private correspondence, Aug. 12, 2014) that the term "is now not used by historians for a general term for members of the great livery companies in London, since it has connotations of Mercers or trading companies." She suggests instead "some term like 'members of London's craft companies, members of London's livery companies, or the craft oligarchy of London, rather than 'merchants.'" Langland, however, uses the term "marchauntis" (e.g. A.VIII.42) in the general sense I use it here.
68. Ralph Hanna, *London Literature, 1300–1380* (Cambridge, UK: Cambridge University Press, 2005), 126–129; Mooney and Stubbs, *Scribes and the City*, for recent discussion of the London Puy (128–129) and Shirley (69–71).
69. See Evans, "Numbers," 531, on the drop in requests for ordination.
70. Evans notes that "The number of rectories available in England was significantly reduced in the later Middle Ages by the appropriation of livings, especially to monasteries. . . . It has been estimated that the number of appropriated rectories in England rose from about 1,500 in 1291 to about 3,300 in 1535." Ibid., 533.
71. Most recently, see Vincent Gillespie and Kantik Ghosh, *After Arundel: Religious Writing in Fifteenth-Century England* (Turnhout, Belgium: Brepols, 2011).

WORKS CITED

Adams, Robert. *Langland and the Rokele Family: The Gentry Background to Piers Plowman*. Dublin: Four Courts, 2013.
Bennett, H. S. "Medieval Ordination Lists in the English Episcopal Records." In *Studies Presented to Hilary Jenkinson*, ed. J. Conway-Davies, 20–34. London: Oxford University Press, 1957.
Benson, C. David, and Lynne Blanchfield. *The Manuscripts of Piers Plowman: The B Version*. Woodbridge, UK: Boydell and Brewer, 1997.

Boynton, Susan. "Boy Singers in Medieval Monasteries and Cathedrals." In *Young Choristers, 650–1700*, ed. Susan Boynton and Eric Rice, 37–48. Woodbridge, UK: Boydell and Brewer, 2008.

Boynton, Susan, and Eric Rice, eds. *Young Choristers, 650–1700*. Woodbridge, UK: Boydell and Brewer, 2008.

Connolly, Margaret. "Mapping Manuscripts and Readers of *Contemplations of the Dread and Love of God*." In *Design and Distribution of Late Medieval Manuscripts*, ed. Margaret Connolly and Linne R. Mooney, 261–278. Woodbridge, UK: Boydell, 2008.

Cooper, Tim. *The Last Generation of English Catholic Clergy: Parish Priests in the Diocese of Coventry and Lichfield in the Early Sixteenth Century*. Woodbridge, UK: Boydell and Brewer, 1999.

Dobson, Barrie. "The English Vicars Choral: An Introduction." In *Vicars Choral at English Cathedrals*, ed. Richard Hall and David Stocker, 1–10. Oxford: Oxbow Press, 2005.

Evans, T. A. R. "The Numbers, Origin and Careers of Scholars." In *The History of the University of Oxford*. Vol. 2, *Late Medieval Oxford*, ed. J. I. Catto and Ralph Evans, 485–538. Oxford, Clarendon, 1992.

Fein, Susanna, ed. *John the Blind Audelay, Poems and Carols (Oxford, Bodleian Library MS Douce 302)*. Kalamazoo, MI: TEAMS, 2009.

———. *Studies in the Harley Lyrics*. Kalamazoo, MI: TEAMS, 2000.

Fuller, Karrie. "The Craft of the Z-Maker: Reading the Z Text's Unique Lines in Context," *Yearbook of Langland Studies* 28 (2014) 15-30.

Gilbert, Beverly Bryan. "'Civil' and the Notaries in *Piers Plowman*," *Medium Aevum* 50 (1981): 49–63.

Gillespie, Vincent, and Kantik Ghosh. *After Arundel: Religious Writing in Fifteenth-Century England*. Turnhout, Belgium: Brepols, 2011.

Goodridge, J. F. *Piers the Ploughman*. London: Penguin, 1959.

Hanna, Ralph. *London Literature, 1300–1380*. Cambridge, UK: Cambridge University Press, 2005.

Hector, L. C., and Barbara F. Harvey, ed. and trans. *Westminster Chronicle 1381–1394*. Oxford: Clarendon, 1982.

Heinrichs, Katherine, ed. *The Piers Plowman Electronic Archive*. Vol. 3, *Oxford, Oriel College, MS 79 (O)*. Published for Medieval Academy of America and SEENET by Boydell and Brewer, 2004.

Hoccleve, Thomas. *The Regiment of Princes*, ed. Charles R. Blyth. Kalamazoo, MI: TEAMS, 1999.

Holsinger, Bruce. "Langland's Musical Reader: Liturgy, Law, and the Constraints of Performance." *Studies in the Age of Chaucer* 21 (1999): 99–141.

Kane, A. G. *Piers Plowman: The A Version*. London: Athlone, 1960.

Kennedy, Ruth. "'A Bird in Bishopswood': Some Newly-Discovered Lines of Alliterative Verse from the Late Fourteenth Century." In *Medieval*

Literature and Antiquities: Studies in Honour of Basil Cottle, ed. Myra Stokes and T. L. Burton, 71–87. Cambridge, UK: D. S. Brewer, 1987.

Ker, N. R. *Medieval Libraries of Great Britain: A List of Surviving Books*. 2nd ed. London: Royal Historical Society, 1964.

Kerby-Fulton, Kathryn. "Confronting the Scribe-Poet Binary: The Z Text, Writing Office Redaction and Oxford Reading Circles." In *New Directions in Manuscript Studies and Reading Practices: Essays in Honour of Derek Pearsall*, ed. Kathryn Kerby-Fulton, John Thompson, and Sarah Baechle. Notre Dame, IN: University of Notre Dame Press, forthcoming 2014. 489-515.

———. "Piers Plowman." In *The Cambridge History of Medieval English Literature*, ed. David Wallace, 513–538. Cambridge, UK: Cambridge University Press, 1999.

———. "Professional Readers of Langland at Home and Abroad: New Directions in the Political and Bureaucratic Codicology of *Piers Plowman*." In *New Directions in Later Medieval Manuscript Studies: Essays from the 1998 Harvard Conference*, ed. Derek Pearsall, 103–129. Woodbridge, UK: Boydell and Brewer, 2000.

———. "The Women Readers in Langland's Earliest Audience: Some Codicological Evidence." In *Learning and Literacy in Medieval England and Abroad*, ed. Sarah Rees-Jones, 121–134. Turnhout, Belgium: Brepols, 2002.

Kerby-Fulton, Kathryn, Linda Olson, and Maidie Hilmo. *Opening Up Middle English Manuscripts: Literary and Visual Approaches*. Ithaca, NY: Cornell University Press, 2012.

McHardy, Alison K. "Careers and Disappointments in the Late Medieval Church." *Studies in Church History* 26 (1989): 111–130.

Mooney, Linne R. "Some New Light on Thomas Hoccleve." *Studies in the Age of Chaucer* 29 (2007): 293–340.

Mooney, Linne R., and Estelle Stubbs. *Scribes and the City: London Guildhall Clerks and the Dissemination of Middle English Literature, 1375–1425*. York, UK: York Medieval Press, 2013.

Nielsen, Melinda. "Scholastic Persuasion in Thomas Usk's *Testament of Love*." *Viator* 42 (2011): 183–204.

Orme, Nicholas. *Medieval Schools from Roman Britain to Renaissance England*. New Haven, CT: Yale University Press, 2006.

Pantin, W. A. *The English Church in the Fourteenth Century*. New York: Cambridge University Press, 1955.

Patterson, Lee. "Historical Criticism and the Claims of Humanism," In *Negotiating the Past: The Historical Understanding of Medieval Literature*. 41–76. Madison: University of Wisconsin Press, 1987.

Pearsall, Derek, ed. *William Langland: Piers Plowman. A New Annotated Edition of the C-Text*. Exeter, UK: University of Exeter Press, 2008.

Rigg, A. G., and Charlotte Brewer. *Piers Plowman: The Z Version*. Toronto: Pontifical Institute of Medieval Studies, 1983.

Roberts, Jane. *Guide to Scripts Used in English Writings up to 1500*. London: British Library, 2005.

Rousseau, Marie-Hélène. *Saving the Souls of Medieval London: Perpetual Chantries at St. Paul's, c. 1200–1548*. Farnham, UK: Ashgate, 2011.

Salter, Elizabeth. *English and International: Studies in the Literature, Art and Patronage of Medieval England*, ed. Derek Pearsall and Nicolette Zeeman. Cambridge, UK: Cambridge University Press, 1988.

Salter, H. E., ed. *Registrum cancellarii Oxoniensis 1434–69*. Oxford Historical Society, XCIII–IV. Oxford: Clarendon, 1932.

Scase, Wendy. *Piers Plowman and the New Anticlericalism*. Cambridge, UK: Cambridge University Press, 1989.

———. *Literature and Complaint in England, 1272–1553*. Oxford: Oxford University Press, 2007.

Shoaf, R. Allen, ed. *Thomas Usk: The Testament of Love*. Robbins Library Digital Projects, Kalamazoo, MI: TEAMS, 1998. http://d.lib.rochester.edu/teams/text/shoaf-usk-testament-of-love-introduction#sources.

Sisam, Celia, and Kenneth Sisam, eds. *Oxford Book of Medieval English Verse*. Oxford: Clarendon, 1970.

Strohm, Paul. "Politics and Poetics." In *Literary Practice and Social Change in Britain, 1380–1530*, ed. Lee Patterson, 83–112. Berkeley: University of California Press, 1990.

Swanson, Robert. *Church and Society in Late Medieval England*. Oxford: Blackwells, 1989.

Tanner, Norman P. *The Church in Late Medieval Norwich, 1370-1532*. Toronto: PIMS, 1989.

Veeman, Kathryn. "'Sende þis booke ageyne hoome to Shirley': John Shirley and the Circulation of Manuscripts in Fifteenth-Century England." Ph.D. dissertation, University of Notre Dame, 2010.

Wailes, Stephen. *Medieval Allegories of Jesus' Parables*. Berkeley: University of California Press, 1987.

Wirtjes, Hanneke, ed. *The Middle English Physiologus*. EETS o.s. 299. Oxford: Oxford University Press, 1991.

Wogan-Browne, Jocelyn, Nicholas Watson, Andrew Taylor, and Ruth Evans, eds. *The Idea of the Vernacular: An Anthology of Middle English Literary Theory, 1280–1520*. University Park: Pennsylvania State University Press, 1999.

Zieman, Katherine. *Singing the New Song: Literacy and Liturgy in Late Medieval England*. Philadelphia: University of Pennsylvania Press, 2008.

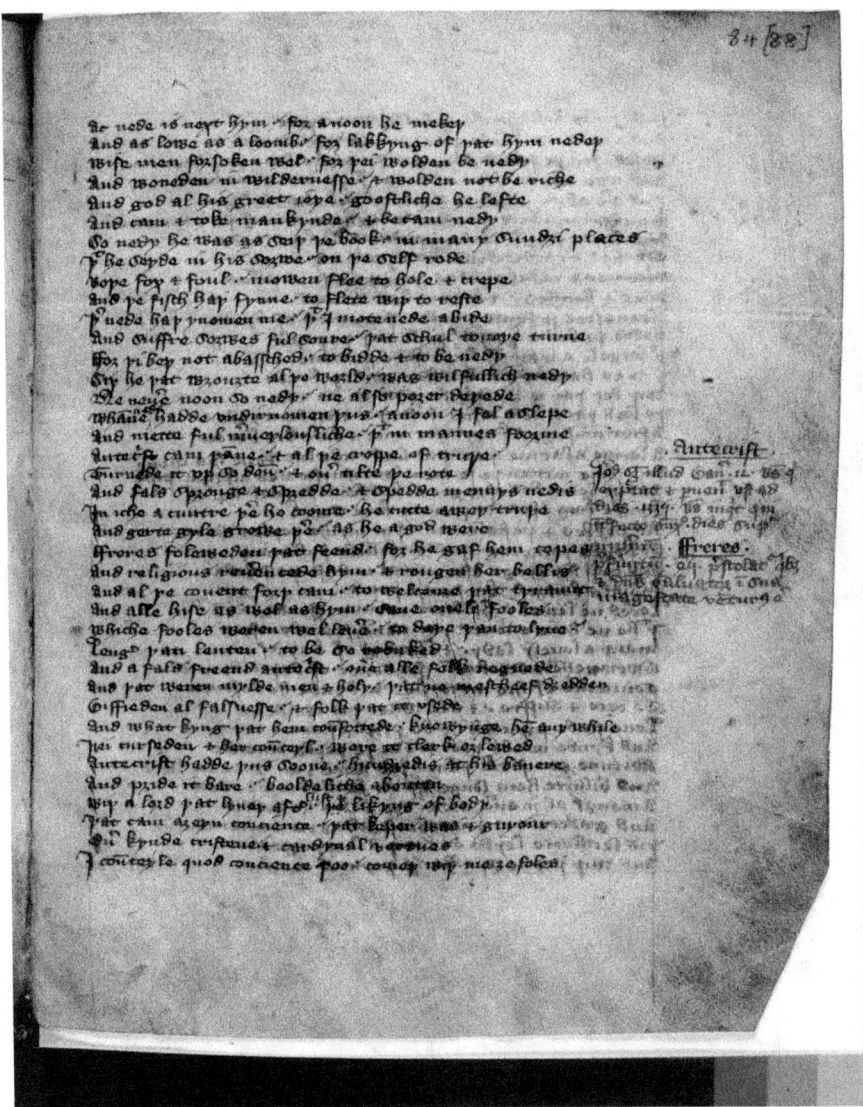

Figure 1. A lengthy gloss on Antichrist added later by the same annotator who wrote the two brief notes in the *Piers Plowman* text of Oxford MS Oriel College 79 (sigil: "O"), fol. 84r.

Figure 2. "A Bird of Bishopswood," an alliterative poem in hand of John Tyckhil, London Metropolitan Archives (formerly Guildhall Library) 25125/ 32 (face), a St. Paul's rent roll maintained by Tyckhill, 1395-6, dated as the 19th year of Richard II's reign.

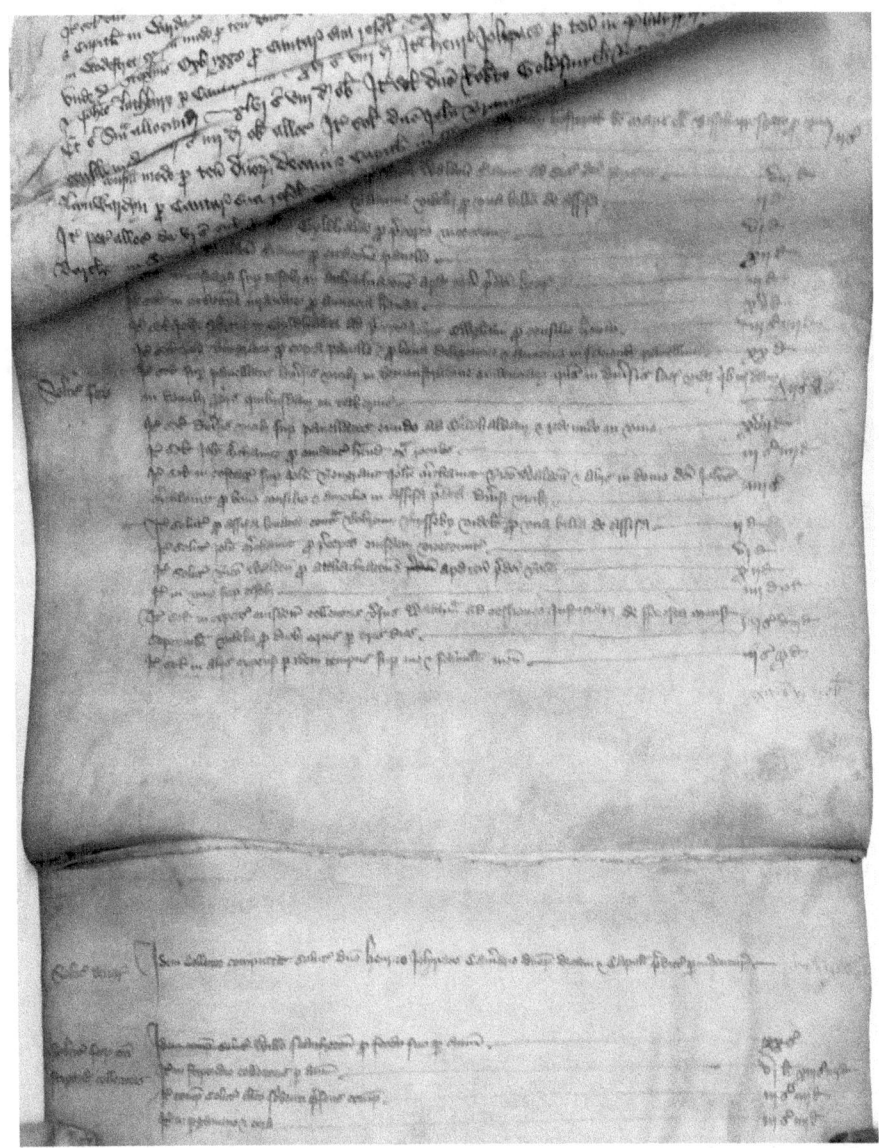

Figure 3. London Metropolitan Archives (formerly Guildhall Library) 25125/ 32 (dorse), showing a section of accounts that name "Johanni[s] Merchaunt" in four different transactions. For instance, the one that appears six lines above the seam on the roll reads: "Item soluitur Johanni Marchaunt pro precepto eiusdem vicecomitis" indicating that Marchaunt drafted a writ for a previously named sheriff. Nearby are other entries pertaining to the Guildhall.

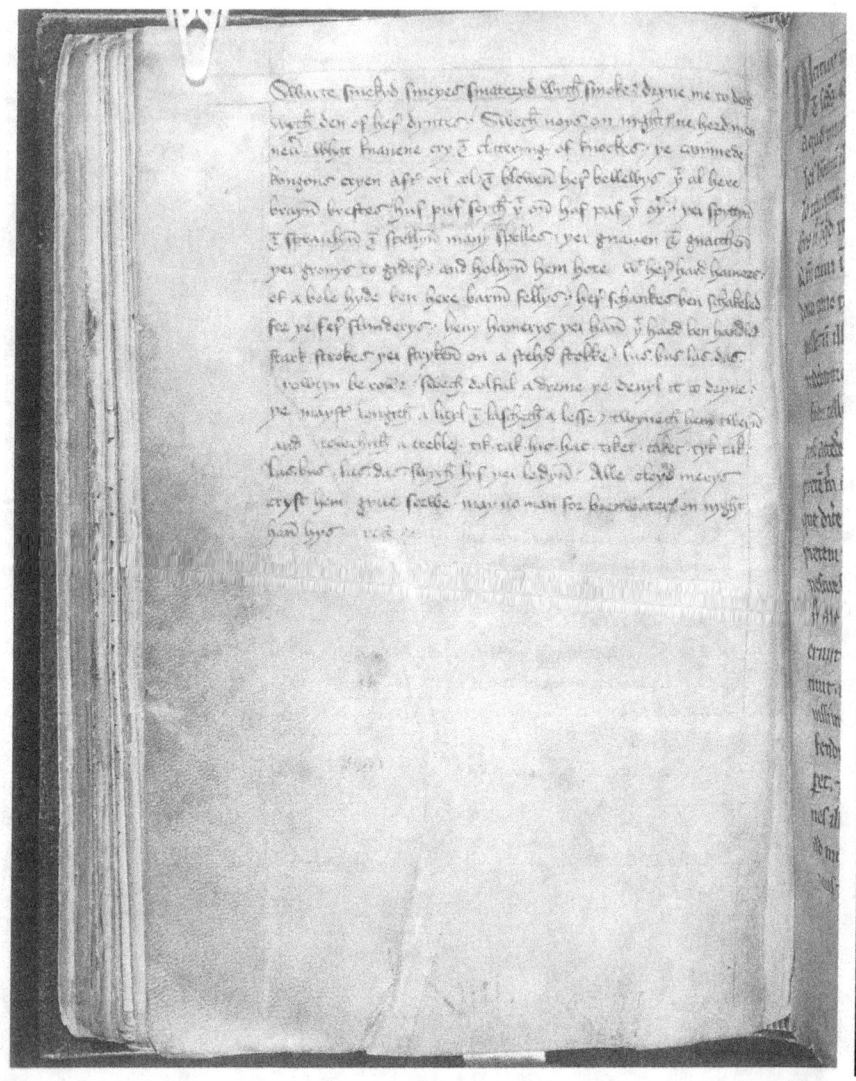

Figure 4. The alliterative poem now known as "The Blacksmiths" in its unique copy, London, © The British Library Board, Arundel 292, col 71v, carefully punctuated.

Werewolf Transformation in the Manuscript Era

JOHN BLOCK FRIEDMAN

I

In the Renaissance there was a great outpouring of engraved and wood-cut images by French and German humanist and polymath writers on demonology depicting what we might call broadly witchcraft and demonic possession. Some of this art appeared in books, and some was in anonymous broadsheets relating to Inquisitorial trials like those of the French were-wolves Pierre Burgot and Michel Verdun and the German Stubbe Peeter.[1] The most important of these books were Jean Bodin's (1530–1596) *De la démonomanie des sorciers* (1580); Claude Prieur's (d. ca. 1596) *Dialogue de lycanthropie, ou transformation d'hommes en loups* (1595); Jean de Nynauld's *De la lycanthropie, transformation et extase des sorciers* (1615); and Beauvois de Chauvincourt's *Discours de la lycanthropie, ou de la transformation des hommes en loups* (1599), as well as the arch collector of lycanthropic tales, Henri Boguet of Saint-Claude, in Burgundy's *Discors exécrable des sorciers* (1602) and the German Johannes Weyer's (1515–1558) *De Praestigiis daemonum et incantationibus*. All were especially fascinated by werewolves, among other instances of the demonic irrupting into human life.[2]

As part of this Renaissance humanist interest in demonology and in portents (such as comets and monstrous births), werewolves naturally received the attentions of woodcut artists and engravers. For example, lycanthropic trials, human-werewolf encounters, and even transformations were often shown in broadsheets, pamphlets, and books. These images ranged widely in character. For example, in 1508 the Swiss humanist Johannes Geiler von

Kaiserberg (1445–1510) preached in Strasbourg Cathedral on the third Sunday in Lent a sermon on superstitions in which he mentioned, among several other examples, werewolves and quoted Vincent of Beauvais and William of Auvergne; this sermon was later published, probably from memory, by another writer, Johannes Pauli, in *Die Emeis* (*The Ants*, 1516). It featured a dramatic woodcut by Hans Weiditz of an urban werewolf attack (see Fig. 1).[3]

A similar but far more gory scene appeared in the work of Lucas Cranach the Elder (1472–1553) (who, incidentally, did a very fine portrait of Geiler). His woodcut of 1512, now in the New York Metropolitan Museum, shows a werewolf devouring his prey in a field of ravaged bodies, presenting him as a still-human figure in an animal posture (see Fig. 2). Werewolves even appeared among depictions of the monstrous races from Pliny's *Natural History*, such as pygmies, anthropophagi, cynocephali, Arimaspians, Blemmyae, Essedones, and Hyperboreans in the German *Esopi appologi siue mythologi cum quibusdam carminum et fabularum additionibus Sebastiani Brant*, a collection whose second part gives a variety of fables, proverbs, riddles, and portents adapted from classical and folk sources, each with an accompanying woodcut (see Fig. 3).[4] One such fable shows the story of certain Arcadians of the Xanthus family chosen by drawing lots and turned into werewolves after hanging their clothes in trees and swimming across a pond during the ancient festival of Lykaia. Their story will occupy us shortly.

The rich interchange among certain French manuscript painters of the mid- to late fifteenth century, chiefly the eminent Valois court artist Robinet Testard, and Continental engravers like the Housebook Master, as well as various playing card makers, woodcut artists, and printmakers, is well known. Indeed, manuscript painters in France and elsewhere borrowed from graphic media and were borrowed from: scenes, architectural elements, iconographic topoi such as the World Upside Down, and images of animals, birds, and flowers moved freely between the works of such painters as Testard or the anonymous but witty and ingenious French illustrator of the *Livre des simples médicines*, now Brussels, Bibliothèque Royale MS IV. 1024, and graphic media artists such as Israhel van Meckenem and the Initial Masters.[5]

Given this pattern of cross-fertilization between manuscript artists and those working in graphic media, one would expect to see evidence of copying of medieval lycanthropic miniatures by the woodcut makers and engravers just mentioned. Thus a significant question for students of the early book, especially in France, is why the many depictions of werewolves in the early to mid-sixteenth century are not based on any late-medieval manuscript miniatures or other representations of werewolves,[6] but rather appear to have been created from whole cloth. Surely so fascinating a visual moment as a man's transformation into a werewolf begged for depiction as much before the age of print as after it.

To judge from recent scholarship on lycanthropy,[7] moreover, seemingly no encounter with a medieval werewolf, no transformation, no ecclesiastical trial was depicted by medieval artists with the exception of the werewolves of Ossory in Gerald of Wales's *Topographia Hibernica* from around 1220, illustrated in a British Library codex, MS Royal 13.B.viii, fol. 18r (see Fig. 4), and its Bury copy from around 1320 in Cambridge University Library MS Ff.I.27. This story, in brief, tells of a priest traveling to Ulster who meets a distraught male werewolf in the woods who still retains reason, speech, and even religious faith. The werewolf asks him to give the Eucharist to an aged, dying female werewolf, who is human under her wolf skin and utters human cries. The gift of the Eucharist returns the woman to her human condition.[8] Significantly, no werewolf image made before the sixteenth century appears in the illustrations for Gaël Milin's extensive *Les chiens de Dieu*, cited in note 1, and chapter 3 of Milin's book. "Images médiévales du loup-garou" does not refer to a single manuscript, or indeed, intend the word "images" to mean visual representations. In short, werewolves seem absent from the visual history of the handmade book.

II

Werewolves do appear in the illustrations of an anonymous Middle French translation of the lengthy *Reductorium morale* by the Benedictine and humanist Pierre Bersuire. Begun in 1320 and largely finished by 1343, the *Reductorium* in sixteen books was a preachers' encyclopedia intended to help clerics compose sermons by supplying instructive and attention-getting stories drawn from a variety of learned and traditional folkloric sources as well as from personal experience and hearsay. It gives classical myths, marvels, and wonders a moralizing or allegorical slant, tying them to the Bible and to various works of spirituality. Thus each element of a myth or marvel is examined *in bono* and *in malo*, producing a work of very considerable length.[9]

Its fourteenth book, treating marvels and wonders found in fifty-six different geographic regions and countries and in the natural and created world—for example, birds, bodies of water, and buildings—was excerpted (or may have been found as an excerpt) and put into French about 1390 by a clerical translator. Three of the four known luxurious manuscripts of this treatise, copied between 1427 and 1485, and sometimes titled *Livre des merveilles du monde* or more commonly *Secrets de l'histoire naturelle* (here called *Secrets of Natural History*), and treating countries and regions arranged alphabetically, depict werewolves and their transformation, although, as mentioned above, the pictures have not been treated by modern students of lycanthropy. These artistic treatments of the werewolf's transformative moment and how they go far beyond the theological comfort level of the written text they illustrate are my subject here. By making these miniatures and their cultural context more available to scholars, I hope to right the present imbalance between the primarily textual treatments of medieval lycanthropy and the possibilities for equally fascinating iconographic ones and show the bold and innovative character of the artists who painted these werewolves.

Learned and theological debate over the likelihood of human transformation into wolves—or other nonhuman forms—extends from the ninth-century *Canones episcopi* attributed to Regino of Prum, and its elaborations in book 19 of Burchard of Worms's (965–1025) *Corrector sive medicus*, through works by Gerald of Wales (1146–1223), Gervaise of Tilbury (1150–1228), and William of Auvergne's *De Universo* (1180–1249), and on into the books of the sixteenth- and seventeenth-century humanists mentioned above; it even finds its way into rabbinical commentaries of the late Middle Ages, such as that of Eleazar ben Judah of Worms. Indeed, at least with regard to Gerald, Gervaise, and William, Manfred Bambeck can justly speak of a sort of twelfth-century werewolf Renaissance among speculative writers as well as poets.[10]

The orthodox Christian (and to some degree rabbinic) position—so ably charted by Caroline Walker Bynum in her insightful study *Metamorphosis and Identity*—was that such transformation is impossible and that both the person who believes he is a werewolf and those who claim to see him as such are victims of diabolic illusion or of a willing pact with the Devil.[11] A minority popular or folkloric view that such transformations can and do happen—often through *lunatio* or lunar power—was codified by Gervaise in his *Otia imperialia* (1214) who was the source for much of Bersuire's werewolf lore.[12] Narrative treatments of werewolves, such as Marie de France's *Bisclavret* and its variants, admitting such transformations' apparent existence but without speculating further, also attribute them to enchantment.[13]

In this context, it may be useful to offer some background on Pierre Bersuire's life and times in order to explain his fascination with metamorphosis generally and werewolf legends in particular. He was probably born about 1290 in Saint-Pierre-du-Chemin, in the modern Department of the Vendée in Western France in the region of Pays de la Loire, and died in 1362.[14] As his family was noble but without fortune, Bersuire entered religious life early, as was customary for landless sons, apparently first joining the Franciscans and then transferring through papal dispensation to the Benedictines.[15] Recognized by his contemporaries as a monk, he is shown as tonsured in an author portrait in a manuscript of his works, for example, in a deluxe copy of his French translation of Livy, now in Australia, made from Francesco Petrarch's (1307–1374) reconstruction of the Latin text.[16] He speaks of his birthplace reverently and often in his works (*"in mea vero patria Pictavia"*),[17] and he is fond of anecdotes about its folklore, its marsh birds, its weather, and its bell towers. It would be only natural for him to be particularly responsive to Gervaise of Tilbury's retelling of folktales from the

Auvergne about werewolves and particularly to one such tale heard directly from an Auvergnat informant.[18]

By about 1320, Bersuire was associated with the newly formed papal court at Avignon. As a humanist it was natural that he would gravitate to the papal palace, rich in books and a gathering place for cultivated men, where he remained active in the papal curia as a scholar for a good part of his life and where he wrote his chief works. Of particular importance with regard to the papal palace at Avignon was the prevalence of protohumanist thought and the congregation there of poets, artists, and scholars with humanistic interests, especially related to Ovid's *Metamorphoses*.

At the Avignon court, Bersuire was the protégé and a member of the household of the humanist Pierre des Prés (d. 1361), a papal vice-chancellor and later a cardinal. Other important humanist contacts at the papal court and outside it were the bibliophile Richard de Bury and the classicizing writers, mythographers, and poets Thomas Waleys, Louis Heilingen, Phillipe de Vitry, and Francesco Petrarch, who gathered in Avignon in part to use the magnificent papal library.[19]

As was common among churchmen during this period, Bersuire eagerly sought benefices for their income, and after receiving several minor ones, in 1349, he was preferred to the important office of chamberer of Notre Dame de Colombes in the diocese of Chartres, bringing him closer to Paris, where he finally moved. There was trouble, however, almost immediately over the revenues of this benefice, because the incumbent, one Gauthier, a vindictive and conservative cleric, had arranged for his cousin to have the income, and eventually Bersuire found himself accused of and for a period imprisoned and tortured for heresy in 1350 and 1351. Though the precise nature of these accusations of heresy is not clear, it is probable that Gauthier and his ally, the bishop of Paris, used Bersuire's open fascination with Greek and Roman myth and ancient philosophic writing as well as his close ties with contemporary classicizing humanists against him. The actual charges seem to have involved Bersuire's interest in "forbidden sciences" and magic.

Were the bishop of Paris to have looked carefully into book 14 of Bersuire's *Reductorium*, he would have found support for the charges, for there are numerous examples of magical and Ovidian transformation, in addition to stories of werewolves. Bersuire discusses in considerable detail various forms of transformation in chapter 3, on England, chapter 9, on Brittany, and chapter 18, on Ethiopia, as well as in chapter 57, on the human body (although he usually cautiously dissociates himself from the reality of such bodily changes). In England, for instance, the sea is translated to the heavens, and Merlin turns stones into dancers. In Brittany, men turn themselves into beasts, while in Ethiopia men become storks. In chapter 57, men are physically changed to women and women to men.

Bersuire was particularly vulnerable to episcopal charges of excess interest in the pagan gods and their deeds, because book 15 of the *Reductorium* was a reworking of Ovid's *Metamorphoses*, which recounts, as the word "metamorphoses" suggests, the transformations of gods and mortals into animal or other nonhuman shapes.[20] For example, in book 1, Ovid describes how the god Jupiter's omniscience was tested while visiting the palace of Lycaon, king of Arcadia. After being served a dinner of the flesh of a hostage, Jupiter turned Lycaon into a wolf as punishment, and Lycaon roamed the world ravening and howling unceasingly.[21]

We can, then, situate Bersuire's stories of werewolves against the background of the charges of heresy made against him and in relation to a lengthy career as a translator of the Roman historian Livy and as a reteller of Ovidian myth. Indeed, in *Secrets of Natural History*, Bersuire's interest in antique gods, myths, religious practices, and transformations is everywhere apparent, though the translator of his work into French has skipped many of these passages in the Latin original, perhaps because he felt ill at ease with Bersuire's classicizing humanism. Nonetheless, there are fifteen places in the text where Ovid's myths and stories of transformation are offered in illustration of a point, and there are many other neutrally presented references to the worship of pagan deities in various temples in Greece and Rome.

Just as fascinated by and uneasy about the possibility of werewolf transformation as any of the later humanists mentioned at the beginning of this article, Bersuire grappled strenuously with the orthodoxy of their putative existence. He was torn between the popular or folkloric belief in the actual transformation, as described, for example, in Ovid's *Metamorphoses*, and the "official" philosophic and religious denial of human-into-nonhuman transformation.

Bersuire's detailed accounts of werewolves occurring throughout the *Secrets*—as they were filtered through his translator—show a striking tension between his humanistic fascination with pagan antiquity and his Christian concern as a Benedictine monk for the inviolability of human status and the criteria distinguishing man from animals. Ultimately, however, he could not accept the reality of werewolf transformation, though one of his three main sources for book 14, Gervaise of Tilbury's *Otia imperialia*, did. The illustrators, showing remarkable artistic freedom, apparently followed Gervaise and popular or folkloric accounts when conceiving and painting their miniatures in some of the manuscripts of the *Secrets of Natural History* rather than be bound by Christian orthodoxy.

Bersuire signals his particular interest in werewolf transformation openly elsewhere in the *Reductorium*. Though Ovid's *Metamorphoses* may seem at first unlikely material for a preaching aid, book 15 of the *Reductorium* is devoted to its fables. As mentioned above, in his book 15, Bersuire opens with his own moral interpretation of the ur-werewolf Lycaon, whose fable serves as prologue to the stories of human-animal transformations in the *Metamorphoses*. Lycaon, turned into a werewolf by Jove, represents the Jews whom God made fugitives, eternally wandering the earth because of their sins against the flesh of Christ during the Passion and Crucifixion. Significantly, by means of this Christian moralization, Bersuire avoids committing himself to the truth or falsity of Lycaon's very realistically described transformation yet retells the story with considerable detail.

He was more specific in book 14 of the *Reductorium*. Throughout its seventy-five chapters (one topic Bersuire treated in two chapters is made one chapter by the French translator), werewolves are discussed more frequently and in greater detail than any creature save the lion and the elephant, and the stories are longer than those of the transformations already mentioned in England, Brittany, and Ethiopia. And he brings these stories very close to home by situating three of them in his own region of France.

III

Let us then consider these stories in detail, with some comparison between Bersuire's Latin, his source for some of the stories in Gervaise of Tilbury's *Otia imperialia*, and the French translator's changes to these to see the raw material that the artists had to work with and to guide them in their depictions. Three werewolf narratives occur in book 14 of the *Secrets*, chapter 22, on Gaul. Apparently quoting from memory or using notes rather than referring to a manuscript copy of Gervaise's work, Bersuire retells two contemporary werewolf stories from the *Otia* and one unfamiliar popular or folkloric narrative of an entire werewolf family gathered from an informant. He implies that he is picking these stories from among an array of similar examples known to him: "*infinita alia sunt exempla,*" he says (book 14, 599).

The first werewolf story mentions an actual historical person, Pons de Chepteuil or de Capdeuil, a crusader and troubadour, who possibly died in 1227, not so distant from Gervaise's lifetime:

> Gervaise says that in Auvergne are some men who are of very strange condition. For at certain times of the year they are transformed into enraged and hungry wolves. And Isidore alleges and claims in his book on transformations that it is possible that certain men by real transformation, and not by fantastic fiction and melancholy imagination, sometimes lose their human estate and are mutated and changed into the size, manner, and condition of a wolf and ravenous beast, losing the noble condition of sweet human nature. Isidore recounts just such a case that happened in the Auvergne in

the Diocese of Clermont. And he says that in this country was conceived and born a most noble and worthy knight named Rambault de Pulet, who was ruined and disinherited from his lands as much by the power of men at arms as by force of law, through another knight who was his enemy, who was called Ponce de Capitol. But because of the great grief and desolation that this noble knight experienced when he saw himself thus banished and deprived of his lands and his honor, he felt such despair and such heaviness of heart that he fled in the dark of night through the wastelands and thickets and through the high mountains, to the point that he forgot that he was a rational human being. And he was transformed into a ravenous, greedy wolf, and he strangled small children, and he did the same to grown men when he could overcome them. And because of the great cruelty of this wolf, the good men of the lowlands left their dwellings and went away with their children and all their goods, to live in strong-walled towns. And then it happened about this time that the wolf attacked a carpenter in the woods. And the carpenter fought back so fiercely that he cut off one of the wolf's feet. Then, when this wolf saw his foot cut off in this way and the great quantity of blood which gushed from his body, at this very hour he regained his human form and his original nature and condition and was a man just as before, and most humbly he thanked the carpenter, telling him that by him he was delivered from his wretched wolf nature and that he had come back to the state of the noble disposition and condition of a human being. And this knight said to the carpenter that for all those who have been transformed into the form of a wolf, it is their sovereign remedy to suffer the cutting of one or another of their members and to render a great spilling of their blood, and by this they would lose the nature and form of a wolf and regain their proper human nature.[22]

The second story in chapter 22 also concerns a named person, one Calcevayra—whose name is corrupted from the name of the castle in Gervaise's Latin, though it seems to go back to an antique lycanthropic tale in Petronius's *Satyricon* (para. 62). This story of a sunbather turned into a werewolf through the loss of his clothing—a topos common to many stories of werewolf creation—offers a different explanation for transformation than the familiar one of lunar causation:

Gervaise gives us another example on this subject and says that near a castle called Calcebara, which is near Viviers, it happened that there was a man of the region who was accustomed at certain times to strip himself nude at the foot of a mountain and leave his clothing there, and then lie totally naked in the sand, and there he would turn and toast himself in this sand. And in doing this he lost his human form and was transmuted and transformed into a wolf.[23]

In the third story of French werewolves—which has no literary source—we learn that

> it came about in Auvergne that a knight who was passing through a wood was attacked by an old wolf and two young cubs. It so happened that in defending himself, he killed the old wolf, and he continued onward and went on his way, and at the edge of the woods he met an old woman who was carrying some raw meat and other foods in her apron. The knight recounted his adventure to this woman with good will and with the intention that she should avoid the path of the two cubs. Then the good woman began to weep in great sorrow. And she said to the knight that this wolf he had killed was her husband and that the two cubs were her two children. And she said that at certain times they became wolves, as he had seen, to whom she would bring some food to eat.[24]

Other, less detailed and contemporary stories occur in the rest of the *Secrets*. A legend in chapter 47 of the *Secrets* derived from Solinus and Pomponius Mela, about the mysterious region of Scythia, or inner Asia, involves werewolf transformation by or near water, a common, liminal feature of such stories, where water was a type of frontier separating two worlds or two species, animal and human, in this case human and wolf:

> Solinus says that in Scythia, among the other nations of people in the region, there is a province called Neutrie through which flows the river Borriscenes, and on the banks of this river live people who are of such nature that on certain days of the summertime, when they pass through the waters of this river, they are transfigured and become wolves and live only on raw flesh. And they remain in this state for a certain period of time and then, when their term is finished and completed, they return and regain their human face and condition.[25]

In chapter 73 of the *Secrets*, on Portents, men swimming across a pond as part of the *Lykaia* festival were ritually transformed into werewolves in Arcadia, again, as in the previous example, for a limited period of time:

> Pliny says that in Arcadia there was a pool. And when some men were led beyond this pool and were, by chance, lying about and wallowing in the sands, they were changed and transfigured into the shape of wolves. And if for a period of nine years they refrained from eating human flesh, after the ninth year they reverted to their own human nature and condition.[26]

This material is followed by a lengthy discussion of how Christians should interpret the transformations:

> With regard to this, Saint Augustine speaks in . . .*The City of God* . . ..And he says that the Arcadians foolishly believed that men who went beyond the lake mentioned above were changed and converted into wolves. But St. Augustine, through a long argument, shows these opinions to be the work of the Devil and contrary to all reason, without finding there any appearance of truth. But it is all full of fantastic and damnable illusion, as has been said and told above in the chapter on Gaul . . . .And as to the responses that could be offered regarding the stories just given, the chief response that comes to mind and pertains is this one: that the Devil obscured their vision and deceived them in order that they not see clearly, to make them fall into diverse errors.[27]

In one way or another, Bersuire's five lycanthropic marvels all treat some of the subject's major motifs, such as full-time and part-time werewolves. The naturalistic explanation of temporary werewolves assumes that their condition results from some tremendous mental shock such as loss of loved ones or economic disaster that changes the genetic makeup, we might say, of the subject. The three Auvergnat narratives also contain other, equally familiar and intertwined motifs: the werewolf Rambault's madness because of his neighbor's malign actions, his original noble nature, his return to human form, speech, and penitent state of mind through a wound accompanied by the loss of a large quantity of blood, the Auvergnat sunbather's loss of human clothing, which distinguishes men from animals, leading to a loss of humanity, and the werewolf family's seasonal, perhaps lunar transformation, a cause as old as Propertius's *Elegies*. The word "*lunatio,*" or its Old French counterpart "*lunaison,*" seems to indicate the power of the moon over humans on certain critical days during the new and full moons. For example, Milin mentions such lunar transformation in the *Vita* of the Breton saint Ronan, where the saint is accused of transforming himself "*per interlunia*" into a werewolf. There the word seems to mean "at the moment of the new moon" or "under the new moon's influence."[28]

We see, then, that a thematically linked collection of stories, contemporary and ancient, leads to Bersuire's consideration of the problems of orthodoxy that these accounts raise and offers an opportunity for novel artistic renderings of werewolves. Since the human forms of these werewolves were in flux, whatever the cause, lunar or other, they were ideal and highly dramatic subject matter for the artistic depiction of transformation as the artists responded to the Middle French text of the *Secrets* either directly or, more probably, through notes and other indications made on the parchment by the manuscripts' designers, or by a mix of both methods.

IV

For this reason, the translator of Bersuire's book 14 is also important to my argument, since in the act of translation he often subtly imposes his own responses to Bersuire's Latin on the question of human-to-animal transformation. Accordingly, his changes show us the state of late fourteenth- or early fifteenth-century attitudes toward lycanthropy. For this translator does not merely put Bersuire's Latin into French, but in a positive way he often adds personal predilections, idiomatic phrasings, and features that make him as much an adapter as a translator of the original Latin. And in a negative way, his omissions and often willful changes to the original are also a sign of his sensibility and result in a different text in some respects from the one that would have been before the eyes of a reader of Bersuire's Latin. Thus, as we see below, while the translator's French may not add significant details to the stories of transformation in the *Secrets*, by the simple fact of putting the marvels in relief, largely free of comment, and focusing on what is concrete and dramatic in them, he sets the stage for the artists' rendering of these events for a secular audience desiring primarily titillation and visual gratification rather than morally improving matter.

Moreover, this translator is of considerable interest in the history of the French translations of scientific, ethical, historical, and other Latin works that came about through the patronage of Charles V of France (1338–1380).[29] Under his aegis the royal library of over 1,200 volumes was gathered and made easily accessible to members of his administration.[30] In fact, Charles was very partial to luxuriously illustrated versions of these translated texts of exactly the sort that the French *Secrets* is, with its fifty-six large "menu" style miniatures. Menu pictures give synopses of the contents of the chapters they illustrate, showing by an assortment, usually in a landscape, of animals, people or natural phenomena, the marvels discussed in the chapter.

Although Jean de Vignay (1283–1340) set a precedent for books such as the *Secrets* with his translations of the *Golden Legend,* Vincent of Beauvais's *Speculum maius,* the *Itinerarium* of Odoric de Pordenone, and the *Chess Book* of Jacobo de Cessolis, the great wave of translation activity came toward the end of the fourteenth century, and it is there we should probably place our translator.

Besides the better-known translators most closely associated with Charles, such as Nicole Oresme (1320–1382),[31] Raoul de Presles (1316–1382), and Jean Corbechon, who translated the *De proprietatibus rerum* of Bartholomaeus Anglicus in 1372 in a magnificently illustrated manuscript, there were others, less eminent, but the range of their work is significant for the wide vernacular interests of the period. Among these can be mentioned Jacques Bauchant (d. 1396), who translated the pseudo-Senecan *Remedies of Fortune,* Denis Foulechat, who translated John of Salisbury's *Polycraticus* in 1372, Jean Daudin (d. 1386), who translated Petrarch's *Remedies of Fortune* in 1372, Jean Golein (1325–1403), who translated among other works Durandus's *Rationale,* and Simon Hesdin (d. 1383), who was responsible for an enormously popular translation of Valerius Maximus's *Dicta and Sayings of the Philosophers.*[32] As Aden Kumler notes, "Aided by such talented translators . . . Charles V initiated an unprecedented program of translations from Latin to the vernacular."[33]

It is in the immediate historical aftermath of this program that we must situate the translator of the *Secrets.* Unfortunately for students of medieval translation, he says very little about himself. His dates of activity must lie between 1343, when Bersuire's Latin text was completed and circulating, and the appearance of the first extant manuscript of the *Secrets* in 1427. Linguistically, the style and orthography of the French point to a date late in the fourteenth or early in the fifteenth centuries, and this translator cites no author later than those used by Bersuire.

Thus, absent any personal comments, our knowledge of this translator and his attitude to the Latin source, especially as expressed in Bersuire's werewolf stories, comes from a brief Prologue that appears only in New York, Pierpont Morgan Library MS M.461, a version of the *Secrets* copied about 1460, midway between the earliest extant manuscript in 1427 and the latest in 1485,[34] and from the way the translator's French reshapes the Latin original. Let us, then, spend a moment with this Prologue for the light it can shed on the purpose of the *Secrets* as a compilation and for the translator's attitudes toward Bersuire's text, as these factors may have influenced his reworking of the werewolf material.

It is possible that this Prologue was not the work of the translator but was created in the Master of the Geneva Boccaccio's workshop around 1460 to amplify a deluxe copy of the work. The Prologue does not appear in the earliest manuscript, Paris, Bibliothèque nationale de France MS fr. 1377-1379, nor in the early printed editions of the *Secrets*. (Stubs of excised matter appear in the quiring of the latest manuscript of the *Secrets*, and the book has no index, which may indicate that the Prologue and Index were originally there). Against these points must be set the fact that the author of the Prologue, whoever he was, had a clear sense of the alphabetically arranged content of the *Secrets* and knew that it abridged the extensive moralizations of the Latin original.

The author of the Pierpont Morgan Library Prologue never alludes to Bersuire by name or to his source, the *Reductorium morale*. Yet in a key sentence he does indicate that he is radically shortening a homiletic Christian work and that his own version differs markedly in content and emphasis from the original: "Et selon le texte de la lettre a lentencion des acteurs *en delaissant la morale exposicion qui est plainne dannuieuse prolixite.*" (And [they are presented] according to the literal text intended by the authors, leaving aside the moral exposition [of Bersuire] which is full of tedious prolixity; my translation, Morgan MS M. 461, fol. 2v).

We can also add to our store of information about the translator a passage in the Prologue relating to his motivation and trepidation in undertaking the work:

> Et jassoit ce que ceste charge me soit assez pesante
> a porter. Touteffoiz quant je considere le fait qu[e]
> ce peut ensuivir, charite a esmeu mon couraige a
> translater ce petit livre de Latin en Francois affin
> que les lisans puissent avoir congnoissance des
> merveilles et diversites de ce monde.
> [And I have come to believe that this will be a heavy
> charge that I must bear. Yet when I consider the
> effect that can follow, charity has roused my courage
> to translate this small book from Latin into French
> in order that those reading it can have knowledge of
> the marvels and the diversity of this world.]
> (Morgan MS M.461, fol. 2v)

Suggestively, the phrase "small book" indicates the translator may have been using an independent copy of book 14 rather than consulting book 14 of an entire manuscript of the enormous *Reductorium*, and so may have known little or nothing about the scope and purpose of Bersuire's work. Moreover, the remark about abridging his Latin original because of its "tedious prolixity" has a concreteness and edge that does suggest a genuine voice and view of a specific audience clearly not that of preachers.

Just as the translator feels he is in a position to modify or abridge his original according to his own lights, he also feels free to show a certain skepticism about the material he is translating, and often reveals a degree of discomfort about Bersuire's stories of bodily transformation; in chapter 3, on England, after the particularly amazing story of transformation of the sea to the heavens cited above, he adds his own view that the marvel can perhaps be attributed to the illusory work of devils.

Sometimes he inserts personal opinions into Bersuire's text without comment, and this is apparent only by direct comparison of the Latin and French. The most extended expression of such views—and possibly a subtle rebuke of what he regarded as the excesses of Bersuire's classical humanism and apparent naturalism—comes in chapter 67, on the Wonders of Herbs:

> Item dit Plinius que ung docteur appelle Paniche le grant hystorien allegue et dit que les anciens et loppinion des philozophes les predecesseurs fut aveugle qui disoient quil nestoit chose possible ou faisible sur terre qui par force derbes ne ne puent faire et acomplir qui auroit la congnoissance des herbes ad ce propres et convenables. Et quant a moy il me semble que ceste oppinion pas nest creable, mais est tres predjudiciable a la verite de nostre seigneur, foy, et creance. Toutesfoiz ledit Paniche le Grant nous met avant aucuns cas qui advindrent selon celle folle oppinion par la vertu et force de certaines herbes. Et dist quil est une herbe appellee baalan pour la vertu de laquelle herbe ung petit dragon qui estoit octis et mort seulement par la touchment dicelle herbe fut ressuscite et revint de mort a vie.
>
> [Pliny says that the learned man called Paniche the Great Historian alleges and says that the ancients and the opinion of the philosopher who preceded him were blind when they said that there was nothing possible or feasible on earth that could not be done or accomplished by the power of herbs, by one who would have the applicable and appropriate knowledge of herbs. *And as for me, it seems to me that this opinion is not credible, but is very prejudicial to the truth of our Lord, faith, and belief.* Nevertheless, the said Paniche the Great puts before us some cases that occurred, *according to this foolish opinion,* by

virtue and force of certain herbs. And he says that
there is an herb called Balaan by whose power a
small dragon, which had been killed and had died,
was resuscitated and came back to life from death,
by means of only a touch of this herb.]
(Paris, Bibliothèque nationale de France MS fr.
22971, fol. 87; my translation and emphasis.)

There is no such botanist mentioned by Pliny, and Bersuire actually attributes the idea that herbs have divine powers to Xanthus, one of Pliny's
botanical sources. Elsewhere in book 25 of Pliny's *Natural History*, mention
is made of both a plant named *panaces*, and Panacia, Asclepius's daughter,
though not in the section from which Bersuire is working.

Paniche, then, seems a constructed voice; the idea for the name probably
derives from Panacia and relates to the idea of panacea or all-healing. Apparently the translator, dismayed by a naturalistic "folle oppinion" that could
diminish God's power, adds this story and, not content with what he found
in Bersuire, may have searched the *Natural History* for help in making it up.
Thus Paniche, the translator's creation, dramatizes his negative response to
Bersuire's discussion of the absolute power of herbs by presenting an artificial
buffer figure, one that historicizes and paganizes Bersuire's contemporary
view, rhetorically weakening its authority.

I mention above as a motive for deletions of details and insertions of
opinion the translator's suspicion of his author's classical humanism, especially as it relates to bodily transformations. His practice of removing most
traces of Bersuire's personality and asseverations of direct experience may
relate to this desire, coming partly from a belief in impersonality and anonymity as Christian and clerical virtues and partly from a desire to keep certain
of Bersuire's wonders at the level of hearsay rather than objective truth and
so to diminish their power.

For example, in the following case relating to gender transformation,
the translator is as much an adapter as he is translator. In chapter 59 of Bersuire's book 14, which differs in number slightly from the position of the
corresponding chapter in the *Secrets*, the Benedictine attests, as he often
does, to the truth of a marvel he has heard, in this case from a Dominican,
who vouches for the event, where a girl changes gender and lives a long time
that way after being married (book 14, ch. 59, 636). The translator makes
the subject of the impersonal verb "*dit*" Gaius Julius Solinus (mid 3rd century
AD) and one of Bersuire's three main authorities, who has been mentioned
in connection with an earlier item in the paragraph instead of the Dominican friar. Thus, in the French there is no longer Bersuire's contemporary
and direct source to attest to the truth of the story. It is possible that the

translator wished to dissociate this story from the Dominican order. But the willful shift in grammatical subject is consistent with his practice in the Paniche quotation of associating transformation stories with antique rather than contemporary sources in order to detract from their reality.

With these sorts of changes and truncations in mind, let us see how the translator alters the werewolf stories in Bersuire. The first of the Auvergnat stories in book 14, chapter 22, that of Rambault de Pulet, is introduced in the Latin by the general belief ("*ponit Gervasius*") that certain men at certain times change into wolves. Bersuire skips Gervaise's attestation of veracity and adds a reference to Isidore of Seville's *Etymologiae*, book 11, chapter 4, "*de transformatis*," on men changing into werewolves not in fiction but in fact. This is the story later told in chapter 73 of men turned into werewolves during the Arcadian festival of *Lykaia*. The Isidore reference, however, is not in Gervaise. Bersuire then moves, as does Gervaise, to the story of Rambault, and follows Gervaise detail by detail, through Rambault's madness and rapine, the villagers' response, the meeting with the woodcutter, the loss of the paw, and the general claim that werewolves are changed back into human form by such mutilation. The wording, however, differs enough to suggest he was not quoting from direct consultation of the relevant passage.

Bersuire introduces the Auvergnat sunbather story as a concrete illustration of his elaboration of Isidore of Seville's remarks, for after the remark about "quidam homines, non fantastica fictione, sed vera & formali transmutatione, transmutantur in lupus" (certain men, not in the fictions of fantasists, but truly in bodily form are changed into wolves; 14:599), he cites the *Otia* ("Gervasius hic ponit exemplum; Gervaise gives an example here") and tells the story. Gervaise adds the detail that this transformation occurs whenever there is a "new moon," but Bersuire says more vaguely, "certo tempore," "in a certain time."

Bersuire next introduces the story of the werewolf family with the assertion in his own voice: "infinita alia sunt exempla nam & ego audiui a quodam Arvernigena" (infinite are the number of other examples which could be offered, and I have heard from a certain Auvergnat; 14:599). After the story of this family, he again speaks in his own voice: "igitur cum per haec & alia exempla dicta mutatio appareat esse vera, therefore by this and other examples the said transformation appears to be true." The translator, however, blunts the vividness of Bersuire's language ("Gervaise tells us of another example on this subject"), without offering a clear sense of just what aspect of the subject he means, reducing the sharpness of Bersuire's account of transformation in general.

In rendering these three stories, the translator makes a number of interesting changes to them. He adds the general claim about the residents of the Auvergne ("there are some men who are of very strange condition"), attributing this to Gervaise. Neither he nor Bersuire invokes the moon as a traditional cause of transformation, though Gervaise clearly gives this ("perlunationes mutantur"). As noted above, of particular significance is the extensive pseudo-Isidorean addition made by Bersuire and followed by the translator, though Bersuire correctly identifies the passage in the *Etymologiae* as a chapter and the translator calls it a "*livre*." Isidore's *Etymologiae* often circulated in extract form, so it is possible that the translator recalled a book of Isidorean extracts on transformation. All Isidore says in the chapter is that certain men who swim across a marsh in Arcadia are changed into wolves. Bersuire adds the idea of "real transformation," which the translator amplifies to a far greater degree.

In chapter 22, on Gaul, before telling the story of the Auvergnat sunbather werewolf, as we saw above, Bersuire pauses for a moment, summing up his view of the number of werewolf narratives (14:599), though he does not commit to the absolute veracity of such transformations. Moving into his final story of French werewolves,[37] the translator adds the detail about the woman's apron and fleshes out the story with a more logical explanation for their conversation, the knight's desire to warn her about wolves in the woods (not in the Latin original), and the final detail that she brought food to the werewolf family. Significantly, the translator deletes from the second French tale the claim of apparent truth, the entire remark about the infinite number of examples, and the Auvergnat source that introduce the third example.

Similar changes occur in chapter 47, on Scythia (chapter 48 in Bersuire), with a slight elaboration of Bersuire's details. For example, Bersuire says the transformations occur "in certain times of the year," which the translator renders more concretely as "summer time." And Bersuire says that for a "specific period" they are wolves and then recover their original form. This, however, is much amplified with the addition of the werewolves eating flesh, a detail not found in Bersuire, and of an increase in the length of time the Scythians stay as werewolves.

In chapter 73, on Portents (in Bersuire, this is chapter 75), men crossing over water as part of the Arcadian *Lykaia* festival are transformed into werewolves, for a limited time, as in the previous example. The translator improves the story with small details of a realistic sort. He adds the phrases "by chance" and "lying about," but he drops altogether Bersuire's more fairy-talelike "pristinis vestibus . . . vestiebantur, in their original garments" (14:668).

Bersuire introduces this section on the Arcadian werewolves with a lengthy moralization on the life of man compared to rivers. He then cites Pliny, book 8, chapter 22 (correctly 8:34) in the general discussion of wolves among many other animal as support for how human transformation into wolves should not be believed in, referring the reader to "what I had said above," in chapter 22. He then offers the Arcadian story, speaking of the men's transformation "in luporum *effigiem*" (14:668; emphasis added). Bersuire gives a detailed retelling of the Plinean story, mentioning the nine-year period of abstention from human flesh, after which the werewolves are returned to their original human state and even find their original clothes in the trees where they had left them. Bersuire abridges Pliny considerably, for the Roman author notes such details as how the person is chosen by lots, as well as the species of tree on which the clothes are hung. Bersuire continues on with more material from Pliny about the *Lykaia*, until he moves to the discussion paraphrased from Saint Augustine.

Both Bersuire and the translator give the same story, ascribing it to the *Vita* of Saint Hilary of Poitiers, to illustrate more fully with a hagiographic exemplum this issue of demonic deception at work in apparent bodily transformations. The exemplum offered by the translator, however, is considerably more detailed than that given by Bersuire, as if the translator went to a different source from the one Bersuire used:

> A story is told that is written in the life of Saint Hilary, where he says there was a father who led his daughter to this holy man and said to him, "Sire, see my daughter who has become a mare by my enemies' power of enchantment. Thus I beg you of your grace that it might please you to pray to God for her, that she might be returned to her original human condition." For the father and mother and all the girl's companions believed she had become a mare. Then the saint said to them, "I do not see a mare here, but I see a beautiful girl." And the father and all the others said that they did not see a young girl but saw a mare. For the Devil had enchanted their eyes in this way by a strong dose of faerie. Then the holy man prayed God that he would illuminate their eyes with clear faith and pure understanding. And immediately they saw quite clearly and recognized their daughter, who was in her proper state of womanhood and not a mare.[35]

This story seems intended both to illustrate Saint Augustine's remarks on diabolic deception and to rebut other, more contemporary claims of human transformation, in this case those of Gervaise of Tilbury. "Demonic possession" explanations for transformation, however, were popular among sixteenth-century authors.

Since Bersuire makes Gervaise one of the three "doctors," along with Pliny and Solinus, on which the fourteenth book of the *Reductorium* is based, it is obviously awkward that Gervaise believes in the reality of human-animal transformation and attests to it from his own experience: "in England we have often seen men change into wolves according to the phases of the moon. . . . One thing I know to be of daily occurrence among the people of our country, certain men are changed into wolves according to the cycles of the moon." Bersuire, however, offers an argument from antique and Patristic authority, citing, in addition to Saint Augustine, the irrefutable Pliny, who said that it is impossible for a man to be changed into an animal. Thus there are two lines of argument that Bersuire and later his translator lay out: the reality of transformation as exemplified by the stories borrowed from Gervaise, and the contrary and orthodox idea that it is a diabolically induced illusion.

Bersuire, followed by his translator, attempts to refute Gervaise, at least in the matter of transformations. We recall that Gervaise of Tilbury is the source for the marvel of the sea translated to the heavens in Bersuire's book 14, chapter 3, on England. Bersuire takes issue with Gervaise as he does with that author's belief in the reality of werewolves:

> For truly, saving the honor of this very learned doctor Gervaise, according to nature it is impossible to believe in these two marvelous occurrences mentioned above. For even Aristotle in his authoritative experience does not recite or touch upon similar cases, but it could well be that by chance those to whom these marvelous things happened were deceived by some diabolical illusions or something similar.[36.]

That Bersuire and his translator were troubled by the truth of these werewolf legends is clear from the story in chapter 22, introducing several points of view about them and trying to mediate among these. The textual explanation is in keeping with Bersuire's humanistic approach to other mythological themes:

> Pliny addresses this question of transformation . . . entirely rebuking, reprehending, and dismissing Gervaise's opinion; he says that it is impossible for a man to be changed from a man into an animal. Thus the aforesaid [Lykaian] transformation does not occur in a physical sense, but it occurs in a moral sense to many who ought to live reasonably as men but instead live like wolves or dogs. Cicero speaks of this in his book of offices and asks what difference there is between men who are changed and transformed into beasts

and men who have bestial morals and manners. And he says that the men who have human faces and forms, and who forget reason and abandon all the virtues of good morals in order to obey the dictates of sin, behave like gluttons and gourmands who live only to fill their bellies. And such men are regarded as wolves and pigs; the overproud become lions; the greedy become leopards; the lustful are monkeys.[37]

By this moral and metaphoric explanation, Bersuire is able to use his love of classical learning and retain his Christian principles in dealing with the clearly fascinating (to him) topic of human-into-animal transformation.

The translator follows Bersuire's attitudes toward this topic closely, but is considerably more insistent than Bersuire on the fabulous quality of some of the stories. Moreover, by removing Bersuire's assurances of truth from many stories and assigning the authority for such stories to a pagan, non-contemporary, or nonreligious source, he diminishes the validity of many of the marvels and wonders in Bersuire's book 14. In small ways, then, the translation makes these tales more dramatic (the woman's apron full of food) and interesting to the reader, while at the same time undercutting the truth of transformation.

On the basis of these changes, it seems that the French translator of book 14 of Bersuire's *Reductorium* largely differs from his Latin original in writing for a bourgeois elite or aristocratic audience rather than for an ecclesiastical one. To appeal to a secular audience, he strips from Bersuire's chapters on wonders and natural history all of the extensive moralization the Benedictine added so lovingly and which made the *Reductorium* useful to preachers; instead the French translator strives for a more dramatic and human-centered work of interest to the armchair traveler, though still with an improving purpose, as his attitude toward Bersuire's naturalism makes clear.

It is evident from this discussion that though the translator did not significantly alter the stories of transformation in the *Secrets*, by the addition of a number of concrete and dramatic details, which may have come naturally through the flexibility of the vernacular, he prepares for the artistic treatment of transformation aimed at a secular audience desiring titillation and visual gratification and not much concerned with subtle questions of scholastic orthodoxy.

V

The four known manuscripts of the *Secrets* were illustrated by three eminent court artists, the Master of Marguerite d'Orléans, The Master of the Geneva Boccaccio (who did two of them, one possibly for King René d'Anjou), and Robinet Testard (for Louise de Savoie.) Their large miniatures illustrate the geographical portions (56 chapters of the work's 73; the last 17 being devoted to wonders of nature), so there is no artistic rendering of chapter 73's Arcadian werewolf transformation and related discussion. As Testard did not include werewolves in his pictures at all, the following remarks pertain only to the Master of Marguerite d'Orléans and the Master of the Geneva Boccaccio.

Since the manuscripts and artists of the *Secrets of Natural History* are relatively little known, it may be useful to give a brief account of them. Eberhard König attributes the banner-like ink and watercolor drawings of the oldest example, Paris, Bibliothèque nationale de France MS fr. 1377-1379, to a master who was named after his main work, the magnificent Book of Hours once in the possession of Marguerite d'Orléans, now Paris, Bibliothèque nationale de France MS lat. 1156B.[38] This *Horae*, painted around 1430, is well known for its extraordinary scenic borders. Indeed, certain features of this artist's paintings for the *Secrets*, such as the camels of the miniature for the chapter on Egypt (fol. 30v), were exported with relatively little change to that *Horae* in the border of the depiction of Saint Marguerite (fol. 176). Likewise, the miniature showing the war between the Pigmies and the cranes in the chapter on Pygmee (fol. 33) also corresponds to the scene of the Mission of the Apostles in the same *Horae* (fol. 148).

As a relatively cosmopolitan traveling artist, the Master of Marguerite d'Orléans was active in different cities: probably in Paris about 1425, in Bourges, where he illuminated the *Secrets* around 1427, in Rennes, about 1430, probably in Angers about 1440, in Poitiers about 1450, and again in Angers about 1460. From his more than thirty-year period of creativity, eleven of his manuscripts are currently known.[39]

The second artist was responsible for the conception and much of the execution of the two copies of Bibliothèque nationale de France MS fr. 1377-1379. These are the much more luxuriously produced New York, Pierpont Morgan Library MS M. 461 and a fragmentary codex of the *Secrets* once owned (or perhaps still owned) by the Charnacé family of Paris. In recent years this artist has received considerable attention.[40] This master is named after a copy of Giovanni Boccaccio's *De casibus virorum illustrium* in the French translation of Laurent de Premierfait, illuminated about 1460 and preserved today as MS fr. 191 in the Geneva Public and University Library under the title *Des cas des nobles hommes et femmes*.[41] In 1955 Jean Porcher offered the name Master of the Geneva Boccaccio for the artist, an attribution that has now been widely accepted.[42] At present twenty-seven manuscripts can be attributed to him.[43]

There is much evidence that the Master of the Geneva Boccaccio was theologically sophisticated and fully aware of Christian orthodoxy. For example, he was involved in the decoration of several liturgical books, such as Paris, Bibliothèque nationale de France MS fr. 166, a *Bible moralisée*.[44] He was just as adept at depicting pagan legends, as indicated by the derivation of his name from a work describing famous persons, both historical and mythical.

How do the two artists of the three manuscripts with werewolf illustrations, the Master of Marguerite d'Orléans and the Master of the Geneva Boccaccio, handle transformations? Though the Auvergnat and Scythian werewolf stories occupy a considerable part of their respective chapters, the two miniaturists who illustrated these legends did not treat them proportionately, though this may have been owing to the pressures of the "menu" picture style format more than anything else.

Because of the length of the chapter on Gaul and the number of marvels discussed, the menu pictures of the two artists would be overburdened if each event were equally touched upon. Accordingly, the miniature for Gaul in the earliest known copy of the *Secrets,* Paris, Bibliothèque nationale de France MS fr. 1377-1379, reflects interesting choices among the three Auvergnat stories, showing the fact but not the process of transformation (see Figs. 5 and 6). The Master of Marguerite d'Orléans paints a more or less human but semi-erect, hairy and wolf-headed man on a crag who must be the dispossessed knight Rambault de l'ulot of the first story.

As can be seen in Figure 6 detail, clearly this master is sensitive to Rambault's mixed nature as described in the details of the chapter's story, for his werewolf haunts the margins of civilization in moody isolation. Such werewolves seem modeled on the madman in the woods whom we meet in contemporary romances such as Chrétien de Troyes's *Lancelot* and *Yvain,* for the story of Rambault follows the romance pattern, with loss of human identity and attendant self-awareness, apparent loss of language (since Rambault speaks to the woodcutter only after his paw is cut off and he is returned to a human state), eating raw meat, no longer walking erect, and losing the use of tools such as his chivalric weapons. These factors, as much as his madness, remove him from his former chivalric culture, hinted at by the background of spires and other architectural features that contrast with his mountainous habitat. This mix of locales, then, must figure both his savage behavior and his later repentance after losing his paw. No transformation is shown, either of Rambault becoming a wolf or of his returning to human status. The conception of this portion of the miniature is entirely in the present moment; Rambault has neither past nor future.

Surprisingly, in Pierpont Morgan Library MS M.461 (Fig. 7), painted by the Master of the Geneva Boccaccio, a much more sophisticated manuscript in all respects than the one from which it was copied, the artist depicts in his menu painting not the Rambault story but only a somewhat generic wolf in the Auvergnat tale of the knight who kills the werewolf in the forest whose cubs flee. Unlike the creature in the previous image, the animal painted does not stand erect or show any human traits at all.

It appears then, that the French werewolf stories did not especially exercise the artists' imaginations with their possibilities for the representation of man becoming wolf or wolf becoming man. Since these key transformative moments were clearly stated in the chapter's text and formed a considerable part of the story, it is hard to see why they were ignored and the werewolves treated in a pedestrian manner, unless the large number of marvels in the chapter simply required a greater simplicity of treatment for each.

In contrast, the werewolves in chapter 47, on the mysterious region of Scythia or Inner Asia, are far more imaginatively handled by both artists than those in the Auvergne (see Figs. 8 and 9 detail). The artists of the three *Secrets* manuscripts with werewolves depicted this marvel before and after, following the actual process of transformation in a dramatic way. The copy done by the Master of Marguerite d'Orléans shows men on the far bank of the river in ordinary clothes but in animal poses, biting or eating a human victim. They are presumably in the earliest stage of transformation and, like the figure in the Cranach scene (see Fig. 2), still retain their human form, while on the near bank their werewolf counterparts are shown as an ordinary wolf and a human-headed wolf in the process of transformation back to human status. The detail shown in Figure 9 gives a better sense of the werewolves' appearance. Presumably, depicting one werewolf with an animal head and one with a human head shows the temporal process of return from animal to human status. Since there are numerous men becoming werewolves in Scythia, the painter can show each in a different state without implying that the illustration is more than a snapshot of one moment in time.

As noted above, we know of two manuscripts of the *Secrets* illustrated by the Master of the Geneva Boccaccio. The second copy (see Fig. 10), once in the possession of the Charnacé family of Paris, is now of uncertain whereabouts and deserves a moment's discussion. In its early sale history, it was defective at front and rear, consisting of sixty-five leaves, and had only twenty-three of the original fifty-six miniatures remaining, done in a pale watercolor or wash. When I photographed it at the home of the then-owner, Baron Jean de Charnacé, at Chateau d'Aulnoy, Coulommiers, Seine-et-Marne, in the region of Île de France in 1973, it measured 300.5 x 230 mm and consisted of folios 32 to 97, with more lacking of the beginning than of the end. Thus the codex contained only chapters 23 to 54, covering Germany to Thrace.

Although the manuscript was shown publicly at the Paris Exhibition of 1955, there is not a great deal known about it. At one time it had a Breton connection; on folio 87 it bears a name, "Jehan Bregerault," apparently that of an early owner, possibly a cleric living in Rennes in the sixteenth century. A search of the Schoenberg Database of Manuscripts at the University of Pennsylvania adds no information to this.

In 1897 the manuscript was sold with the collection of the Parisian architect Pierre Henri Gélis-Didot. Later, it formed part of the collection of the art historian Comte Paul Durrieu and came into the possession of the Charnacé family through the marriage of Durrieu's daughter Gabrielle to Baron Gautier de Charnacé. His descendant, Jean de Charnacé, was the owner in 1973.

At the death of Baron Jean de Charnacé in 2004, according to someone familiar with the contemporary manuscript market who wishes to remain anonymous, the codex, along with other manuscripts from the collection, seems to have passed into the possession of a consortium of American dealers headed by Bruce Ferrini of Akron, Ohio, which attempted to sell the work at auction. Ferrini filed for bankruptcy in 2005 and died in May 2010. Ferrini was familiar to rare book dealers and museum curators as someone who bought manuscripts or acquired them on speculation and then broke them up, selling the individual leaves (for example, leaves of the Coptic Gospel of Judas) on eBay and in other places; consequently, the chances of the Charnacé *Secrets* remaining whole at the present time may not be good, unless it was returned to the Charnacé family. Another opinion is that it did not go to Ferrini for sale with the other Charnacé manuscripts but stayed with a branch of the Charnacé family, where it may remain.[45]

The Scythian werewolves of the Charnacé manuscript closely resemble, as do those of Morgan M.461, those of its model, Bibliothèque nationale de France MS fr. 1377-1379; in an unusual development one of the riverine figures wears a hairy or wolf-skin-like jerkin that is still distinctively a piece of human costume, as is also the case in the other copy, the Morgan *Secrets*. This animal jacket illustrates the artist's perception of the dual nature of the werewolf; he has not lost his humanity entirely nor has he yet fully assumed his animal condition during transformation; his animal nature, as with the Ossory werewolf mentioned at the beginning of this article, can be taken on or off like a garment and is figured by the jerkin.[46]

Given the fact that there are many treatments of werewolves in the late Middle Ages, ranging from William of Auvergne's extended theoretical one in *De universo* (*Qualiter maligni spiritus vexant et decipiunt homines*) down to the narratives *Bisclavret, Melion, Arthur and Gorlagon,*[47] and others, all unillustrated as if not to commit to the reality of the story, it is remarkable that the artists of the *Secrets* not only accepted the existence of werewolves but boldly went so far as to assert the reality of their transformation by depicting it. It could, of course, be argued that as artists they did not know of or did not care about Christian orthodox views of werewolf transformation, or possibly had some oral knowledge of Gervaise of Tilbury's view of werewolves and were willing to go far beyond the author of the *Secrets* in accepting the truth of human-animal transformation for the purposes of creating a dramatic miniature. Certainly, it is fortunate for the history of the early book that they decided to defy the strictures of the author they were illustrating and to paint werewolves at all.

As noted above, both the exclusively medieval textual focus on were-wolves, their appearance in *lais*, romances, and the like, and the discussion in modern lycanthropic scholarship have largely obscured their iconographical importance. The existence of these hitherto unknown (or perhaps under-known) werewolf depictions suggests that already in the fifteenth century illustrators were considering the problem of human-to-animal transformation. Presenting these unusual werewolf miniatures to a wider scholarly audience will certainly create a more balanced and nuanced knowledge of the artistic and literary medieval treatments of this fascinating topic.

Center for Medieval and Renaissance Studies, The Ohio State University

Acknowledgments
It is a pleasure to thank Robert Bartlett, Kristen Figg, Kathrin Giogoli, Richard F. Green, Laurence Harf-Lancner, Jason Kalman of Hebrew Union College, South Africa, Jacqueline Leclercq-Marx, Asa Mittman, Aleksandra Pfau, Lynn Ransom, Kimberly Rivers, Amelia Sargent, Susan Small, Lorraine Stock, Michael Twomey, Chet Van Duzer, and Renee Ward for advice and information. I am very grateful to Eric Johnson and the staff of the Special Collections Department of Ohio State University for generously providing me with materials for my research. Somewhat different versions of this article were presented as a lecture to the Medieval Studies Program of Wilfrid Laurier University, Waterloo, Ontario, Canada, and as the Joseph S. Schick Memorial Lecture at Indiana State University, Terre Haute.

NOTES

1. A good account in English of some of these trials with, in some cases, trial documents, is in Charlotte F. Otten, ed., *A Lycanthropy Reader: Werewolves in Western Culture* (Syracuse, NY: Syracuse University Press, 1986), 45–91; and in greater detail in Gaël Milin, *Les chiens de Dieu: La représentation du loup-garou en occident (XIe–XIX siècles)*, Centre de Recherche Bretonne et Celtique: Cahiers de Bretagne Occidentale 13 (Brest, France: Université de Bretagne Occidentale 1993), 117–166.
2. On these French lycanthropists, see Nicole Jacques-Lefèvre, "Such an Impure, Cruel and Savage Beast . . .: Images of the Werewolf in Demono-logical Works," in *Werewolves, Witches, and Wandering Spirits: Traditional Belief in Folklore in Early Modern Europe*, ed. Kathryn A. Edwards, 181–197 (Kirksville, MO: Truman State University Press, 2002); and Caroline Oates, "Démonologues et lycanthropes: Les théories de la métamorphose au XVI siècle," in *Métamorphose et bestiaire fantastique au Moyen Âge*, ed. Laurence Harf-Lancner, 71–105, Collection de l'École Normale Supérieure de Jeunes

Filles 28 (Paris: École Normale Supérieure de Jeunes Filles, 1985). For modern editions of Bodin, Nynauld, Boguet, and Weyer, see Jean Bodin, *De la démonomanie des sorciers* (NP: Gutenberg Reprints, 1979), reprinted as Randy A. Scott, trans., *On the Demon-Mania of Witches* (Toronto: Centre for Reformation and Renaissance Studies, 1995); Jean de Nynauld, *De la lycan-thropie, transformation et extase des sorciers (1615), édition critique augmentée d'études sur les lycanthropes et les loups garous*, ed. Nicole Jacques-Chaquin and Maxime Préaud (Paris: Frénésie, 1990); Henri Boguet, *Discours exécrable des sorciers: Ensemble leur procez, faits depuis 2 ans en ca en divers endroicts de la France*, ed. Maxime Préaud (Marseille, France: Lafitte, 1979); Benjamin C. Kohl and H. C. Erik Midelfort, eds. and trans., *On Witchcraft: An Abridged Translation of Johannes Weyer's De praesigiis daemonum* (Asheville: University of North Carolina at Asheville and Pegasus Press,1998); and Thibaut Maus de Rolley, "La part du diable: Jean Wier et la fabrique de l'illusion diabolique," *Tracés, Revue de Sciences Humaines* 8 (2005): 29–46. The *Malleus maleficarum* (1486), attributed variously to Jacob Sprenger and Heinrich Kramer by both date and contents, does not, strictly speaking, belong with the works mentioned here, but it is profoundly concerned with the role of diabolic illusion and quotes the key passage of William of Auvergne on this topic, applying it to a discussion of one who thinks he has become a werewolf. See Christopher S. Mackay, ed. and trans., *Malleus maleficarum*, 2 vols. (Cambridge, UK: Cambridge University Press, 2006).

3. See, on this author, E. Jane Dempsey Douglass, *Justification in Late Medieval Preaching: A Study of John Geiler of Kaiserberg* (New York and Leiden, Holland: Brill, 1989). *Die Emeis: Die ist das buch von der Omelissen* was published in Strasbourg by Johannes Greininger in 1516. The werewolf image shown here is on fol. XLI and is in the public domain.

4. This work was published in Basle by Jacob de Phortzheim in 1501. The image appears on p. 360. A copy of the book from which this image comes is held in the Library of Congress, and the picture shown here is in the public domain.

5. On this topic and on the artist Robinet Testard, see Kathrin Giogoli and John Block Friedman, "Robinet Testard: Court Illuminator, His Manuscripts and His Debt to the Graphic Arts," *Journal of the Early Book Society* 8 (2005): 152–196. The subject of Testard's borrowings from graphic media is much more thoroughly discussed in John Block Friedman with Kristen Figg and Kathrin Giogoli, *Libro de las maravillas del mundo* (Burgos, Spain: Siloé, in press, 2015). This work is an edition of, translation of, and commentary on the *Secrets de l'histoire naturelle*, a Middle French geographical and encyclo-pedic compendium, referred to throughout this article as *Secrets of Natural History*. The anonymous illustrator of Brussels, Bibliothèque Royale MS IV.1024 is discussed in John Block Friedman, "The Humour and Folly of the

World in Odd Places: A Fifteenth-Century Manuscript Herbal," in *Science and Literature at the Crossroads: Papers from the 34th CEMERS Interdisciplinary Conference,* ed. Dana Stewart, *Mediaevalia* 29.1 (2008): 207–235.

6. Intriguing references to a medieval wall painting of three werewolves holding knives, reputed to have been in the Dominican Church at Poligny in the Jura, seem traceable only as far back as Boguet, *Discours exécrable,* 123, though it could, of course, have been in the church at one time.

7. This scholarship is extensive and of uneven quality. I give here only more recent titles that have proven useful for this article or which are generally relevant to France. See Mihaela Bacou, "De quelques loups-garous," in *Métamorphose et bestiaire fantastique au Moyen Âge,* ed. Laurence Harf-Lancner, Collection de l'École Normale Supérieure de Jeunes Filles 28 (Paris: École Normale Supérieure de Jeunes Filles, 1985), 29–50; Phillip A. Bernhardt-House, *Werewolves, Magical Hounds, and Dog-Headed Men in Celtic Literature: A Typological Study of Shape-Shifting* (Lewiston, New York and Queenston, Ontario, Canada: Edwin Mellen Press, 2010); and Willem de Bécort, "'I would have eaten you too': Werewolf Legends in the Flemish, Dutch, and German Area," *Folklore* 118 (April, 2007): 23-43. Adam Douglas, *The Beast Within: A History of the Werewolf* New York: Avon, 1992); Laurence Harf-Lancner, "La métamorphose illusoire: Des théories chrétiennes de la métamorphose aux images médiévales du loup-garou," *Annales Economies Societés Civilisations* 40 (1985): 208–226; Sophie Houdard, "Le loup-garou ou les limites de l'animalité," in Jean de Nynauld, *De la lycanthropie, transformation et extase des sorciers (1615), édition critique augmentée d'études sur les lycanthropes et les loups garous,* ed. Nicole Jacques-Chaquin and Maxime Préaud (Paris: Frénésie, 1990), 189–196; Dennis M. Kratz, "Fictus Lupus: The Werewolf in Christian Thought," *Classical Folia: Studies in the Christian Perpetuation of the Classics* 30.1 (1976): 57–80; Philippe Ménard, "Les histoires de loup-garou au Moyen Âge," in *Symposium in honorem prof. M. de Riquer* (Barcelona: Universitat de Barcelona Quaderns Crema, 1984), 209–238; Michel Meurger, "L'homme-loup et son témoin: Construction d'une factualité lycanthropique," in Jean de Nynauld, *De la lycanthropie, transformation et extase des sorciers (1615), édition critique augmentée d'études sur les lycanthropes et les loups garous,* ed. Nicole Jacques-Chaquin and Maxime Préaud (Paris: Frénésie, 1990), 143–179; Sophie Quénet, "Mises en récit d'une métamorphose: Le loup-garou," in *Le merveilleux et la magie dans la littérature,* ed. Gérard Chandes, CERMEIL 2 (Amsterdam: Rodopi, 1992), 137–163; Leslie A. Sconduto, *Metamorphoses of the Werewolf: A Literary Study from Antiquity through the Renaissance* (Jefferson, NC: McFarland, 2008); Susan Small, "The Medieval Werewolf Model of Reading Skin," in *Reading Skin in Medieval Literature and Culture,* ed. Katie Walter, The New Middle Ages (New York: Palgrave, 2013), 81–97; and Jan R.Veenstra, "The

Ever-Changing Nature of the Beast: Cultural Change, Lycanthropy, and the Question of Substantial Transformation (from Petronius to Del Rio)," in *The Metamorphosis of Magic from Late Antiquity to the Early Modern Period*, ed. Jan N.Bremer and Jan R. Veenstra (Leuven, Belgium: Peeters, 2002), 133-166.
8. On British Library MS Royal 13.B.viii, see Michelle P. Brown, "Marvels of the West: Giraldus Cambrensis and the Role of the Author in the Development of Marginal Illustration," in *English Manuscript Studies*, vol. 10, *Decoration and Illustration in Medieval English Manuscripts*, ed. A. S. G. Edwards (London: British Library, 2002), 34–59. Gerald's first version of the story was published in John J. O'Meara, "Geraldus Cambrensis in *Topographia Hibernica*: Text of the First Recension," *Proceedings of the Royal Irish Academy* 52, sec. C.4 (1949), 143–145. Note that the widely cited Penguin translation of Gerald offers this shorter first version, not the later and much reworked one with additions to the story. There are five recensions of Gerald's tale of the priest and the werewolves of Ossory. The second, done before July 1189, is considerably more philosophical and nearly three times as long as the first. Caroline Walker Bynum, *Metamorphosis and Identity* (New York: Zone, 2001), 16, calls "that addition ... an explicit and complex discussion of what it means for something to become something else." See Gerald of Wales, *Topographia Hibernica*, dist. 2, ch. 19, in *Giraldi Cambrensis opera*, ed. J. S. Brewer, et al., Rerum Britannicum Medii Aevi Scriptores 21 (London: Longman, 1861–1891; rpt. Nendeln, Liechtenstein: Kraus, 1964–1966), 5:101–107. The most recent discussion of these versions of the *Topographia* is that of Amelia Sargent, "Gerald of Wales's *Topographia Hibernica*: Dates, Versions, Readers," *Viator* 43.1 (2012): 241–261. Sargent, 259–160, dates version 1 to 1185–1186, version 2 to 1189, version 3 probably to 1193, version 4 to 1196–1198, and version 5 before 1209. She discusses the Ossory story very briefly on 253. On Gerald's account of werewolves, see Bynum, *Metamorphosis and Identity*, 15–18, 106–108. Additional studies of the priest and the werewolves of Ossory are Ménard, "Histoires de loup-garou," 215–216; Jeanne-Marie Boivin, "Le prêtre et les loups-garous: Un épisode de la *Topographia Hibernica* de Giraud de Barri," in *Métamorphose et bestiaire fantastique au Moyen Âge*, ed. Laurence Harf-Lancner, Collection de l'École Normale Supérieure de Jeunes Filles 28 (Paris: École Normale Supérieure de Jeunes Filles, 1985), 51–69; John Carey, "Werewolves of Medieval Ireland," *Cambrian Medieval Celtic Studies* 44 (2002): 37–72; Catherine E. Kharkov, "Tales of the Ancients: Colonial Werewolves and the Mapping of Postcolonial Ireland," in *Postcolonial Moves: Medieval through Modern*, ed. Patricia Clare Ingham and Michelle R. Warren (New York: Palgrave Macmillan, 2003) 93-109; Rhonda Knight, "Werewolves, Monsters, and Miracles: Representing Colonial Fantasies in Gerald of Wales *Topographia Hibernica*," *Studies in Iconography* 22 (2001):55-86; and Susan Small, "Medieval Werewolf Model,"

87. The most thorough study of Gerald of Wales is that of Robert Bartlett, *Gerald of Wales, 1146–1223* (Oxford: Clarendon, 1982). That the Irish were thought to have more werewolves than other nations by a kind of ancestral predisposition seems to be a common idea and appears in the thirteenth-century Latin hexameter poem "De hominibus qui se vertunt in lupos," translated with bibliography in Montague Summers, *The Werewolf in Lore and Legend* (New York: Dover, 2003), 206–207. See also Ménard, "Histoires de loup-garou," 224–225; and Milin, *Les chiens de Dieu*, 70.

9. The literature on exempla and preaching handbooks, *artes praedicandi*, is vast. Some recent works are Olga Weijers, *Dictionnaires et répertoires au Moyen Âge: Une étude du vocabulaire* (Turnhout, Belgium: Brepols, 1991); Claude Bremond, et al., *L'exemplum*, Typologie des Sources du Moyen Âge Occidental 40 (Turnhout, Belgium: Brepols, 1982); Jacques Berlioz and Marie Anne Polo de Beaulieu, eds., *Les exempla médiévaux: Introduction à la recherche: Suivie des tables critiques de l'index exemplorum de Frederic C. Tubach* (Carcassone, France: GARAE/Hesiode, 1992); Thomas Amos, et al., eds., *De ore domini: Preacher and Word in the Middle Ages* (Kalamazoo, MI: Medieval Institute Publications, 1989); Marianne Briscoe and Barbara H. Jaye, *Artes praedicandi and Artes orandi*, Typologie des Sources du Moyen Âge Occidental 61 (Turnhout, Belgium: Brepols, 1992); Donald L. d'Avray, *The Preaching of the Friars: Sermons Diffused from Paris before 1300* (Oxford and New York: Clarendon, 1985); Roger Andersson, ed., *Constructing the Medieval Sermon* (Turnhout, Belgium: Brepols, 2008); Richard Rouse and Mary Rouse, *Preachers, Florilegia, and Sermons: Studies on the "Manipulus florum" of Thomas of Ireland* (Toronto: Pontifical Institute, 1979); Franco Morenzoni, *Des écoles aux paroisses: Thomas de Chobham et la promotion de la prédication au début du XIIIe siècle* (Paris: Institut des Études Augustiniennes, 1995); Jenny Swanson, *John of Wales: A Study of the Works and Ideas of a Thirteenth-Century Friar*, Cambridge Studies in Medieval Life and Thought, 4th series (Cambridge, UK: Cambridge University Press, 2002); and Carlo Delcorno, *Quasi quidam cantus: Studi sulla predicazione medievale* (Florence, Italy: L. S. Olschki, 2009). I am grateful to Claire M. Waters for suggestions on this topic.

10. Manfred Bambeck, "Das Werewolfsmotiv im 'Bisclavret,'" *Zeitschrift für Romanische Philologie* 89 (1973): 123–147, esp. 146. The twelfth- and thirteenth-century fascination with tales of werewolves is also noted in Ménard, "Histoires de loup-garou," 20; and Joyce E. Salisbury, *The Beast Within: Animals in the Middle Ages* (London: Routledge, 1994).

11. The group of penitential texts associated with the *Canones*—including that of Bartholomew Iscanus, Bishop of Exeter, d. 1184—is briefly discussed and quoted in Summers, *Werewolf in Lore*, 185; and, more recently and with better documentation and translation, treated in Kratz, "Fictus Lupus,"

63; and Sconduto, *Metamorphoses*, 19–21. On Burchard's Latin text about werewolves, see J.-P. Migne, ed., *Patrologia Latina* 140, 950–1071; and for a translation, see Cyrille Vogel, *Le pécheur et la pénitence au Moyen Âge* (Paris: Éditions du Cerf, 1982), 104; and Cyrille Vogel, "Pratiques superstitieuses au début du XIe siècle d'après le *Corrector sive medicus* de Burchard, évêque de Worms (965–1025)," *Études de civilisation médiévale, IXe–XIIe siècles: Mélanges offerts à Edmond-René Labande à l'occasion de son départ à la retraite et du XXe anniversaire du C.É.S.C.M. par ses amis, ses collègues, ses élèves* (Poitiers, France: C.É.S.C.M., 1974), 751–761, esp. 759. For discussion, see Ménard, "Histoires de loup-garou," 217–218; and Salisbury, *Beast Within*.

12. See S. E. Banks and Jonathan W. Binns, eds. and trans., *Gervase of Tilbury Otia Imperialia: Recreations for an Emperor* (Oxford: Oxford University Press, 2002), 3:120, 813–814.

13. The poets' point of view, as best expressed by Jean d'Arras's *Melusine* and by Marie de France's *Bisclavret*, held that the transformation of the human body into that of another species was the result of sorcery but did not go deeply into the question. As no medieval literary text treating werewolves was illustrated, I give here only a few titles relating to transformation in those works that seem especially relevant to my topic. On *Melusine*, see Donald Maddox and Sara Sturm-Maddox, eds., *Melusine of Lusignan: Founding Fiction in Late Medieval France* (Athens, GA: University of Georgia Press, 1996); and Donald Maddox and Sara Sturm-Maddox, trans., *Melusine or the Noble History of Lusignan* (University Park: Pennsylvania State University Press, 2012). For Marie, see Bynum, *Metamorphosis*, 170–173; and Sconduto, *Metamorphoses*, 39–56; Edith Benkov, "The Naked Beast: Clothing and Humanity in Bisclavret," *Chimères* 19 (1988): 27–43; Carine Bouillot, "Quand l'homme se fait animal, deux cas de métamorphose chez Marie de France: Yonec et Bisclavret," in *Magie et illusion au Moyen Âge*, Senefiance 42 (Aix-en-Provence, France: CUERMA, 1999), 65–78; Matilda T. Bruckner, "Of Men and Beasts in Bisclavret," *Romanic Review* 81.3 (1991): 251–269; M. Faure, "Le *Bisclavret* de Marie de France: Une histoire suspecte de loup-garou," *Revues des Langues Romanes* 83 (1978): 345–356; and François Suard, "Bisclavret et les contes du loup-garou: Essai d'interprétation," *Marche Romane* 30 (1980): 267–276. As with Christian exegesis and narrative literature of the same period, rabbinical commentary held that such transformation was an illusion on the part of the beholder or only a metaphor. There were, of course, certain passages in the Old Testament, such as the account of Nebuchadnezzar in Daniel 4:28–30, where such a transformation is hinted at or claimed. Commentators such as Abraham ibn Ezra (1092–1157) specifically repudiated transformation. See, for example, Abraham ibn Ezra on Daniel 4:28–30. See also Henry John Mathews, "Abraham ibn Ezra's Short Commentary on Daniel," *Miscellany of Hebrew Literature* 2 (1887): 257–276; and Aharon Mondschein,

"R. Abraham ibn Ezra: The Short Commentary on Daniel" (Hebrew; MA thesis, Bar Ilan University, 1977). See generally, Ariel Toaff, *Mostri giudei: L'immaginario ebraico dal medioevo alla prima età moderna* (Bologna, Italy: Il Mulino, 1996).

14. Fundamental to the study of Bersuire's life and work is Charles Samaran and Jacques Monfrin, "Pierre Bersuire, prieur de St. Eloi de Paris," *Histoire Littéraire de France* 39 (Paris: Imprimerie Nationale, 1900; rpt. 1962), 259–450. Biographical information here is largely drawn from pp. 259–301 of this work and is not further documented. See also Joseph Engels, "Berchoriana I: Notice bibliographique sur Pierre Bersuire, supplément au *Repertorium biblicum medii aevi*," *Vivarium* 2 (1964): 62–124. Studies focusing on Bersure's classical humanism include René-Adrien Meunier, "L'humaniste Pierre Bersuire (fin du XIIIe siècle–1362)," *Bulletin de la Société des Antiquaires de l'Ouest* (1948): 511–532; and Jane Chance, *Medieval Mythography from the School of Chartres to the Court at Avignon 1177–1350* (Gainesville: University of Florida Press, 2000). Chance offers an extensive bibliography, primarily relating to Bersuire's book 15 of the *Reductorium morale*. See Kimberly Rivers, "Another Look at the Career of Pierre Bersuire O. S. B.," *Revue Bénédictine* 116 (2006): 92–100; and Kimberly Rivers, *Preaching the Memory of Virtue and Vice: Memory, Images, and Preaching in the Late Middle Ages* (Turnhout, Belgium: Brepols, 2010), ch. 7. For the *Reductorium*, see Ralph Hexter, "The *Allegari* of Pierre Bersuire: Interpretation and the *Reductorium morale*," *Allegorica* 10 (1989): 51–84; Marie-Hélène Tesnière, "Le *Reductorium morale* de Pierre Bersuire," in *L'enciclopedismo medievale: Actes du colloque international San Gimignano, 8–10 octobre 1992*, ed. Michelangelo Picone (Ravenna: Longo, 1993), 225–242; and Marie-Hélène Tesnière, "Pierre Bersuire, un encyclopédiste au XIVe siècle," *Plein Chant* 69–70 (2000): 7–15. No mention of Bersuire appears in Anne-Caroline Beaugendre, *Les merveilles du monde ou Les secrets de l'histoire naturelle* (Paris: Anthèse, 1996), who calls *Secrets* the work of "un auteur anonyme du XVe siècle," and says that "la personnalité de l'auteur, malgré de rares indications, continue à nous échapper," 80, 83, though it is possible that Bersuire's connection with *Secrets* is noted in her earlier doctoral dissertation, Anne-Caroline Beaugendre, "Le 'livre des merveilles du monde' ou 'Secret de l'histoire naturelle,' premier tiers du XVe siècle, édition critique" (PhD diss., Paris, École Nationale des Chartes, 1992), 5 vols., a work that was unavailable to me. Since Beaugendre apparently did not realize that *Secrets of Natural History* was a translation of Bersuire's *Reductorium morale*, book 14, most of what she says about the translator's possible sources in Beaugendre, *Les merveilles du monde*, 83–85, is either incorrect or suspect.

15. Chance, *Medieval Mythography*, 322; and William D. Reynolds, "Sources, Nature, and Influence of the *Ovidius moralizatus* of Pierre Bersuire," in

The Mythographic Art: Classical Fable and the Rise of the Vernacular in Early France and England, ed. Jane Chance (Gainesville: University of Florida Press, 1990), 86. Both mention that Bersuire was early a Franciscan; a more detailed recent discussion is that of Rivers, "Another Look," 93–96; the document relating to this event is on 94.

16. The portrait of Bersuire tonsured is in the Livy manuscript, now in the Felton Collection of the National Gallery of Victoria, Australia, published in Margaret Manion, *The Felton Illuminated Manuscripts in the National Gallery of Victoria* (Melbourne, Australia: Macmillan Art Publishing and the National Gallery of Victoria, 2005), 271–272, 285. On this codex, see also Keith Val Sinclair, *The Melbourne Livy. A Study of Bersuire's Translation Based on the Manuscript in the Collection of the National Gallery in Victoria, Melbourne*, Melbourne University Press Monographs 7 (Melbourne: University Press for Australian Humanities Research Council, 1961). For a list of the Livy translation manuscripts, see Inge Zacher, "Die Livius-Illustration in der Pariser Buchmalerei (1370–1420)," PhD diss., Berlin, Freie Universität, rpt. 1974. On Bersuire's Livy translation generally, see Jean Rychner, "Observations sur la traduction de Tite Live par Pierre Bersuire (1354–1356)," in *"L'humanisme médiéval dans les littératures romanes du XIIe au XIVe siècle. Colloque organisé par le Centre de Philologie et Littératures Romanes de l'Université de Strasbourg du 29 janvier au 2 février 1962*, ed. Anthime Fourrier (Paris: Klincksieck, 1964), 167–192; Marie-Hélène Tesnière, "À propos de la traduction de Tite-Live par Pierre Bersuire: Le manuscrit d'Oxford, Bibliothèque bodléienne, Rawlinson C. 447," *Romania* 118 (2000): 449–498; and Marie-Hélène Tesnière, "Un manuscrit exceptionnel des *Décades* de Tite-Live traduites par Pierre Bersuire," in *La traduction vers le moyen français: Actes du IIe colloque de l'AIEMF, Poitiers, 27–29 avril 2006*, ed. Claudio Galderisi and Cinzia Pignatelli, Traduire au Moyen Âge 11 (Turnhout, Belgium: Brepols, 2007), 125–147.

17. All quotations from Pierre Bersuire's work are drawn from Pierre Bersuire, *Petri Berchorii opera omnia: Reductorium morale super totam bibliam* (Mainz, Germany: Antonii Hierati, 1609), vol. 1, Prologue to book 14, 586. Further quotations are given by book and page number of this edition.

18. For Bersuire's preoccupation with the Auvergne, e.g., his stories of werewolves encountered there, see René-Adrien Meunier, "Le fonds auvergnat, provençal et alpestre dans les '*Récréations impériales*' de Gervais de Tilbury et le '*Réductoire morale*' de Pierre Bersuire," *Annales de l'Université de Poitiers* (1952–1954): 151–161; René-Adrien Meunier, "Le livre des merveilles de Pierre Bersuire," *Annuaire de l'Université de Poitiers* 2nd ser., 3 (1951): 1–8; and Denis Hüe, "Espace et paysage chez Pierre Bersuire et quelques Avignonnais," *Cahiers de recherches médiévales* 6 (1999): 41–57.

19. See, e.g., Aldo S. Bernardo, ed. and trans., *Francesco Petrarch, Letters on Familiar Matters: Rerum familiarium libri* (New York: Italica Press, 2005), 22.13.

See generally Edward H. R. Tatham, *Francesco Petrarca, the First Modern Man of Letters: His Life and Correspondence* (London: Sheldon Press, 1925–1926); and Ernest H. Wilkins, *Life of Petrarch* (Chicago and London: University of Chicago Press, 1961). See Maurice Faucon, *La librairie des papes d'Avignon, sa formation, sa composition, ses catalogues (1316–1420) d'après les registres de comptes et d'inventaires des archives vaticanes*, Bibliothèque des écoles françaises d'Athènes et de Rome, fascicules 43,50 (Paris: E. Thorin, 1886–1887). See also Marie-Henriette Jullien de Pommerol and Jacques Monfrin, *La bibliothèque pontificale à Avignon et à Peñiscola pendant le grand schisme d'occident et sa dispersion: Inventaires et concordances*, Collection de l'École Française de Rome 141 (Rome: École Française, 1991), 2 vols.; and Pierre Pansier, *Histoire du livre et de l'imprimerie à Avignon du XIVe au XVIe siècle* (Avignon: Aubanel Frères, 1922), vol. 1.

20. Book 15 of the *Reductorium* has been much studied by scholars interested in medieval mythography. The most important of these works are Joseph Engels, ed., *De formis figurisque deorum: Reductorium morale, liber XV, cap. 1:1* (Utrecht, Holland: Institut voor Laat Latijn der Rijksuniversiteit, 1966); Joseph Engels, ed., *Reductorium morale, liber XV, cap. ii–xv: Ovidius moralizatus* (Utrecht, Holland: Institut voor Laat Latijn der Rijksuniversiteit, 1966); Joseph Engels, "L'édition critique de l'*Ovidius moralizatus* de Bersuire," *Vivarium* 9 (1971): 19–24; Frank T. Coulson, "A Checklist of Newly Discovered Manuscripts of Pierre Bersuire's *Ovidius moralizatus*," *Scriptorium* 51.1 (1997): 164–186; and Robert Levine, "Exploiting Ovid: Medieval Allegorizations of the *Metamorphoses*," *Medioevo Romanzo* 14 (1989): 197–213.

21. See Engels, *De formis figurisque deorum*, fable 4, sig. b. That Bersuire's interpretation of Lycaon's fate is original to him is clear from looking at the story in John of Garland's *Integumenta* or in the Three Vatican Mythographers, where it does not receive a Christian or moral interpretation. See Lester K. Born, "The *Integumenta* of the *Metamorphoses* of Ovid of John of Garland" (PhD diss., University of Chicago, 1929), 66; and Ronald E. Pepin, trans., *The Vatican Mythographers* (New York: Fordham University Press, 2008), First Vatican Mythographer, 17, 20, and Third Vatican Mythographer, 76, 130. The story is told in detail in Pausanias, *Description of Greece*, trans. W. H. S. Jones, 8.58.5 (London: Loeb Classical Library, 1977), 3:350–353. The fullest discussion is in Milin, *Les chiens de Dieu*, 10–14.

22. Paris, Bibliothèque nationale de France MS fr. 22971, ch. 22, fol. 26v, my translation. Boguet, *Discours exécrable*, identifies Rambault as Raimbaud de Pinetum, an actual Auvergnat place name, and tells essentially the same story. This story from Gervaise is discussed in Small, "Medieval Werewolf Model," 88. More is known about Rambault's adversary, Pons de Chepteuil, who came from Le Puy and who did indeed seem to have dispossessed someone of a castle. But the castle belonged not to a knight but to a bishop, Robert

of Clermont. See Jean Perrel, "Le troubadour Pons, seigneur de Chapteuil et de Vertaizon: Son temps, sa vie, son oeuvre," *Revue d'Auvergne* 90.2–3 (1976): 89–199.

23. Paris, Bibliothèque nationale de France MS fr. 22971, ch. 22, fol. 26v, my translation. For a full discussion of the loss-of-clothes motif, which can be traced to the *Satyricon* of Petronius, see Ménard, "Histoires de loup-garou," 211–213, 219–221.

24. Paris, Bibliothèque nationale de France MS fr. 22971, ch. 22, fol. 26v, my translation.

25. Paris, Bibliothèque nationale de France MS fr. 22971, ch. 47, fol. 54v, my translation. The story of the Scythian werewolves goes back to Herodotus, *Histories*, book 4.

26. Paris, Bibliothèque nationale de France MS fr. 22971, ch. 73, fol. 93v, my translation. The motifs in this story in Gervaise are discussed in detail in Ménard, "Histoires de loup-garou," 226–227.

27. Paris, Bibliothèque nationale de France MS fr. 22971, ch. 73, fol. 93v, my translation.

28. See Propertius, *Elegies*, "Audax cantatae leges imponere Lunae. Et sub nocturno fallere terga lupo," book 4, elegy 5, 13–14. On the "lunar" cause of werewolf transformation, see Ménard, "Histoires de loup-garou," 222–223; and Milin, *Les chiens de Dieu*, 46–52; for a brief discussion of the *Vita Ronani*, see Milin, *Les chiens de Dieu*, 46–47 and notes. A fuller treatment is in Gaël Milin, "La *Vita Ronani* et les contes de loup-garou aux XIIe et XIIIe siècles," *Moyen Âge* 97 (1991): 259–273. For the *Vita Ronani*, see Charles de Smedt, *Catalogus codicum hagiographicum qui asservantur in Bibliotheca Nationali Parisiensi* (Brussels: Société des Bollandistes, 1889), vol. 1, 438–458, esp. 442.

29. Though Aden Kumler's study is not specifically of Charles' translators, her discussion and bibliography are relatively recent and very helpful. See Aden Kumler, "Faire translater, faire historier: Charles V's *Bible historiale* (Houghton Library, MS Typ. 555) and the Visual Rhetoric of Vernacular Sapience," *Studies in Iconography* 29 (2008): 90–135. See also Michèle Goyens, et al., *Science Translated: Latin and Vernacular Translations of Scientific Treatises in Medieval Europe* (Leuven, Belgium: Leuven University Press, 2008); Joan Cadden, "Charles V, Nicole Oresme, and Christine de Pizan: Unities and Uses of Knowledge in Fourteenth-Century France," in *Texts and Contexts in Ancient and Medieval Science: Studies on the Occasion of John E. Murdoch's Seventieth Birthday*, ed. Edith Sylla and Michael McVaugh (Leiden, Holland: Brill, 1997), 208–244; Léopold Delisle, *Recherches sur la librairie de Charles V* (Paris: H. Champion,1907); Jacques Monfrin, "Humanisme et traductions au Moyen Âge," *Journal des Savants* (1963): 161–190; and Jacques Monfrin, "Les traducteurs et leur public en France au Moyen Âge," *Journal des Savants* (1964): 5–20. Both of Monfrin's articles are reprinted in Jacques

Monfrin, *Études de philologie romane*, Publications Romanes et Françaises 230 (Geneva: Droz 2001). See also Thelma Fenster, "'Perdre son latin': Christine de Pizan and Vernacular Humanism," in *Christine de Pizan and the Categories of Difference*, ed. Marilynn Desmond (Minneapolis: University of Minnesota Press, 1998), 91–107; Sue Ellen Holbrook, "The Properties of Things and Textual Power: Illustrating the French Translation of *De proprietatibus rerum* and a Latin Precursor," in *Patrons, Authors, and Workshops: Books and Book Production in Paris*, ed. Godfried Croenen and Peter Ainsworth (Leuven, Belgium: Peeters, 2006), 367–404; Serge Lusignan, *La langue des rois au Moyen Âge: Le français en France et en Angleterre* (Paris: Presses Universitaires de France, 2004); Serge Lusignan, "Langue française et société du XIIIe au XVe siècle," in *Nouvelle histoire de la langue française*, ed. Jacques Chaurand (Paris: Éditions du Seuil, 1999), 91–143; Serge Lusignan, "Parler vulgairement: Les intellectuels et la langue française au XIIIe et XIVe siècles," in *Études médiévales*, ed. Pierre Boglioni (Montreal, Canada: Presses de l'Université de Montréal, 1987); Nicole Pons, "L'historiographie chez les premiers humanistes français," in *L'aube de la Renaissance: Pour la dixième anniversaire de la disparition de Franco Simone*, ed. Dario Cecchetti, L. Sozzi, and L. Terreaux (Geneva: Slatkine, 1991), 103–122; Alex Schutz, *Vernacular Books in Parisian Public Libraries* (Chapel Hill: University of North Carolina Press, 1965); Claire Richter Sherman, *Imaging Aristotle: Verbal and Visual Representation in Fourteenth-Century France* (Berkeley: University of California Press, 1995); and Claire Richter Sherman, "Les thèmes humanistes dans le programme de traduction de Charles V: Compilation des textes et illustrations," in *Pratiques de la culture écrite en France au XVe siècle, Actes du colloque international du CNRS, Paris, 16–18 mai 1992, organisé en l'honneur de Gilbert Ouy par l'unité de recherche "Culture écrite du Moyen Âge tardif,"* ed. Monique Ornato and Nicole Pons, Textes et Études du Moyen Âge 2 (Louvain-la-Neuve, Belgium: Fédération Internationale des Instituts d'Études Médiévales, 1995), 527–537. For a discussion of the work of the translator Evrart de Conty, some of whose works were illuminated by Robinet Testard, see Françoise Guichard-Tesson, "Le métier de traducteur de commentateur au XIVe siècle d'après Evrart de Conty," *Moyen Français* 24–25 (1989): 131–167.

30. On Charles V's royal library, see François Avril and Jean Lafaurie, eds., *La librairie de Charles V* (Paris: Bibliothèque nationale de France, 1968); and Marie-Hélène Tesnière, "La librairie modèle," in *Paris et Charles V: Arts et architecture*, ed. Frédéric Pleybert, Collection Paris et son Patrimoine (Paris: Action Artistique de la Ville de Paris, 2001), 225–233, esp. 225.

31. For Nicole Oresme as a translator, see Susan M. Babbitt, "Oresme's *Livre de politiques* and the France of Charles V," in *Transactions of the American Philosophical Society* 75, pt. 1 (Philadelphia, PA: American Philosophical Society,

1985); Serge Lusignan, "Le Latin était la langue maternelle des Romains: La fortune d'un argument à la fin du Moyen Âge," in *Préludes à la Renaissance: Aspects de la vie intellectuelle en France au XVe siècle*, ed. Carla Bozzolo and Ezio Ornato (Paris: Éditions du CNRS, 1992), 265–282; Serge Lusignan, "Lire, indexer et gloser: Nicole Oresme et la 'Politique' d'Aristote," in *L'écrit dans la société médiévale: Divers aspects de sa pratique du XIe au XVe siècle: Textes en hommage à Lucie Fossier*, ed. Caroline Bourlet and Annie Dufour (Paris: CNRS, 1991), 167–181; and Jeannine Quillet, "Nicole Oresme et le français médiéval," in *Figures de l'écrivain au Moyen Âge: Actes du colloque du Centre d'Études Médiévales de l'Université de Picardie, Amiens, 18–20 mars 1988*, ed. Danielle Bushinger, Göppinger Arbeiten zur Germanistik 510 (Göppingen, Germany: Kümmerle, 1991), 235–243.

32. See generally P. Chavy, *Traducteurs d'autrefois: Moyen Âge et Renaissance, dictionnaire des traducteurs et de la littérature traduite en ancien et moyen français 842–1600* (Paris and Geneva: Champion-Slatkine, 1988); and A. Vitale Brovarone, "Notes sur la traduction de Valère Maxime par Simon de Hesdin," in *"Pour acquerir honneur et pris," mélanges de moyen français offerts à Giuseppe Di Stefano*, ed. Maria Colombo Timelli and Claudio Galderisi (Montreal, Canada: Ceres, 2004), 183–191.

33. Kumler, "Faire translater," 121.

34. On New York, Pierpont Morgan Library MS M.461, which many scholars now believe was made for King René d'Anjou or for his affinity, as his arms appear in some of the miniatures, see Christian de Mérindol, *Le roi René et la seconde maison d'Anjou: emblematique art histoire* (Paris: Léopard d'Or, 1987), 340; and François Avril and Nicole Reynaud, *Les manuscrits à peintures en France 1440–1520*, exhibition catalogue (Paris: Flammarion, 1993), 404. See Eberhard König, "Le livre des secrets d'histoire naturelle," in *Splendeur de l'enluminure: Le roi René et les livres*, ed. Marc-Édouard Gautier (Angers, France: Actes Sud, 2009), no. 35, 324. In Eberhard König, *Das Provost-Stundenbuch: Der Meister der Marguerite d'Orléans und die Buchmalerei in Angers*, Illuminationen. Studien und Monographien, ed. Heribert Tenschert, IV (Ramsen, Switzerland, and Rotthalmünster, Germany: Antiquariat Bibermühle AG, 2002), 184, König now dates Morgan MS M.461 a little later, about 1460–1470. On the painter now called the Master of the Geneva Boccaccio, see König, "Maître de Boccacce de Genève," in *Splendeur de l'enluminure: Le roi René et les livres*, ed. Marc-Édouard Gautier (Angers, France: Actes Sud, 2009), 133–143. See also Eberhard König, *Das liebentbrannte Herz: der Wiener Codex und der Maler Barthélemy d'Eyck* (Graz, Austria: Akademische Druck- und Verlagsanstalt, 1996), esp. 103–115.

35. The story does not in fact appear in Venantius Fortunatus' life of St. Hilary of Poitiers, ed. J.-P. Migne, *Patrologia Latina* (Rpt.Turnhout, Belgium: Brepols, 1969), 88, 437ff. It may be Bersuire's variant of one told in the life

of the fifth-century Saint Macarius of Alexandria, where a man, wishing to seduce a married woman, had a magician seem to change her into a mare. See *Vita abbatis Macarii Aegyptii, Vitae Patrum*, ed. J.-P. Migne, *Patrologia Latina* (Rpt. Turnhout, Belgium: Brepols, 1969), 7, 1110 ff.; and more conveniently Robert T. Meyer, trans., *Palladius: The Lausiac History* (Westminster, MD: Newman Press, 1965), ch. 18. For a comparison between this passage and the one by William of Auvergne, in *De universo in Opera Omnia* (Orleans and Paris: F. Hotot, and Andraea Pralard, 1674, Rpt Frankfurt-am-Main, Germany: Minerva, 1963), II.iii, c. 13. pp. 1042ff, see the convenient presentation of William's text in Milin, *Les chiens de Dieu*, 66, n. 91, with a French translation on 66–67.

36. Paris, Bibliothèque nationale de France MS fr. 22971, fol. 5, my translation.

37. Paris, Bibliothèque nationale de France MS fr. 22971, fol. 26v-27, my translation.

38. On Paris, Bibliothèque nationale de France MS lat. 1156B, see Eberhard König, *Les Heures de Marguerite d'Orléans: Reproduction intégrale du calendrier et des images du manuscrit latin 1156B de la Bibliothèque nationale* (Paris: Éditions du Cerf, Bibliothèque nationale, 1991), esp. 83–86; and Avril and Reynaud, *Manuscrits à peintures*, 28–29. For a detailed description of the style of this master, see König, *Provost-Stundenbuch*. Earlier accounts of the illuminator are in Victor Leroquais, *Les livres d'heures: Manuscrits de la Bibliothèque nationale, I–III* (Mâcon, France: Protat Frères, 1927); and Victor Leroquais, *Supplement* (Mâcon, France: Protat Frères, 1943), no. 21 I, 67–70. See also Eberhard König, *Französische Buchmalerei um 1450, der Jouvenel-Maler, der Maler des Genfer Boccaccio und die Anfänge Jean Fouquets* (Berlin: Mann, 1982), esp. 22, 108, and 226–231; Eberhard König, "Die Très Belles Heures de Notre Dame, eine datierte Handschrift aus der Zeit nach 1404," in *Flanders in a European Perspective: Manuscript Illumination around 1400 in Flanders and Abroad: Proceedings of the International Colloquium, Leuven, 7–10 September 1993*, ed. Maurits Smeyers and Bert Cardon (Leuven, Belgium: Peeters, 1995), 41–61; and remarks in Marc-Édouard Gautier, *Splendeur de l'enluminure: Le roi René et les livres* (Angers, France: Actes Sud, 2009), no. 35, 324.

39. König, *Heures de Marguerite d'Orléans*, esp. 95–104.

40. A list of these manuscripts in chronological order and with bibliographical notes is in König, *Provost-Stundenbuch*, 105–106.

41. See König, "Maître de Boccacce de Genève," 133–143, as well as descriptions of some manuscripts by this master, especially nos. 21, 33–42, and 48. See also König, *Liebentbrannte Herz*, esp. 103–115. Avril and Reynaud supply an overview of the current state of research, based on König, *Französische Buchmalerei*, and Eberhard König, "Un atelier d'enluminure à Nantes et l'art

du temps de Fouquet," *Revue de l'Art* 35 (1977): 64–73; see Avril and Reynaud, *Les manuscrits à peintures*, 106, and 109–119; see also François Avril, "À propos d'un livre d'heures français de la Biblioteca Forteguerriana de Pistoia," in *Von Kunst und Temperament: Festschrift für Eberhard König*, ed. Caroline Zöhl and Mara Hofmann (Turnhout, Belgium: Brepols, 2007), 36–43.

42. See Hippolyte Aubert, *Notices sur les manuscrits Petau conservés à la bibliothèque de Genève (fonds Ami Lullin)* (Paris: Daupeley-Gouverneur, 1911), 586–591; and Eberhard König, "Le Livre des cas des nobles hommes et femmes, traduit en français par Laurent de Premierfait," in *Splendeur de l'enluminure: Le roi René et les livres*, ed. Marc-Édouard Gautier (Angers, France: Actes Sud, 2009), no. 38, 332–335; and Paule Hochuli-Dubuis, *Catalogue des manuscrits français 1–198*, 5th ed. (Geneva: Odyssée/ BGE, 2011), 354–355.

43. See Jean Porcher, *Les manuscrits à peintures en France du XIII au XVI siècle*, exhibition catalog (Paris: A. Tournon, 1955), nos. 274–290; and Jean Porcher, *L'enluminure française* (Paris: Arts & Métiers Graphiques, 1959), 87.

44. These are treated by Eberhard König and John Lowden, *La Biblia moralizada de los Limbourg: De los hermanos Limbourg à George Trubert, Facsimile commentary* (Valencia, Spain: Patrimonio, 2010).

45. The sale catalogue of Gélis-Didot incorrectly claims the manuscript has fifty-five leaves but also indicates that it was already defective. See *Catalogue de manuscrits et miniatures du XIe au XVIIe siècles: Ouvrages d'ornementation des XVIIe et XVIIIe siècles. Estampes composant la collection de M. P. Gélis-Didot*, no. 14, 12 (Paris: Théophile Bélin Libraire, 1897), http://gallica.bnf.fr/ark:/12148/bpt6k371357v/f11.image.52. For scholarly comment, see Porcher, *Manuscrits à peintures*, no. 274, 131; Carl Nordenfalk, "Französische Buchmalerei 1200–1599," *Kunstchronik* 9.7 (1956): 179–189; and Patricia C. Craig, et al., "A Finding Aid to the Jacques Seligman & Co. Records 1904–1978, Bulk 1913–1974," in Collectors' Files, 1908, 1917–1977: Collectors: Charnacé, Baron Gautier de and Baronne, née Gabrielle Durrieu 1954–1957, box 179, folder 27, Archives of American Art, ser. 2, Smithsonian Institution. http://www.aaa.si.edu/collections/container/viewer/Charnacé-Baron-Gautier-de-and Baronne-née-Gabrielle Durrieu-291128.

46. With regard to these jackets, see the fascinating discussion of the "innerness" and "outerness" of the werewolf's skin in Small, "Medieval Werewolf Model," 83.

47. See Noah D. Guynn, "Hybridity, Ethics and Gender in Two Old French Werewolf Tales," in E. Jane Burns and Peggy McCracken, eds., *From Beasts to Souls: Gender and Embodiment in Medieval Europe* (Notre Dame, IN: Notre Dame University Press, 2013, pp.157-185.

WORKS CITED

Amos, Thomas, et al., eds. *De ore domini: Preacher and Word in the Middle Ages.* Kalamazoo, MI: Medieval Institute Publications, 1989.

Andersson, Roger, ed. *Constructing the Medieval Sermon.* Turnhout, Belgium: Brepols, 2008.

Aubert, Hippolyte. *Notices sur les manuscrits Petau conservés à la bibliothèque de Genève (fonds Ami Lullin).* Paris: Daupeley-Gouverneur, 1911.

Avril, François. "À propos d'un livre d'heures français de la Biblioteca Forteguerriana de Pistoia." In *Von Kunst und Temperament: Festschrift für Eberhard König,* edited by Caroline Zöhl and Mara Hofmann, 36–43. Turnhout, Belgium: Brepols, 2007.

Avril, François, and Jean Lafaurie, eds. *La librairie de Charles V.* Paris: Bibliothèque nationale de France, 1968.

Avril, François, and Nicole Reynaud. *Les manuscrits à peintures en France 1440–1520.* Exhibition catalog. Paris: Flammarion, 1993.

Babbitt, Susan M. "Oresme's *Livre de politiques* and the France of Charles V." In *Transactions of the American Philosophical Society* 75, pt. 1. Philadelphia, PA: American Philosophical Society, 1985.

Bacou, Mihaela. "De quelques loups-garous." In *Métamorphose et bestiaire fantastique au Moyen Âge,* edited by Laurence Harf-Lancner, 29–50. Collection de l'École Normale Supérieure de Jeunes Filles 28. Paris: École Normale Supérieure de Jeunes Filles, 1985.

Bambeck, Manfred. "Das Werewolfsmotiv im 'Bisclavret.'" *Zeitschrift für Romanische Philologie* 89 (1973): 123–147.

Banks, S. E., and Jonathan W. Binns, eds. and trans. *Gervase of Tilbury Otia Imperialia: Recreations for an Emperor.* Oxford: Oxford University Press, 2002.

Bartlett, Robert. *Gerald of Wales, 1146–1223.* Oxford: Clarendon, 1982.

Beaugendre, Anne-Caroline. *Les merveilles du monde ou Les secrets de l'histoire naturelle.* Paris: Anthèse, 1996.

———. "Le '*Livre des merveilles du monde*' ou '*Secret de l'histoire naturelle,*' premier tiers du XVe siècle, édition critique." PhD diss., Paris, École Nationale des Chartes, 1992.

Benkov, Edith. "The Naked Beast: Clothing and Humanity in Bisclavret." *Chimères* 19 (1988): 27–43.

Berlioz, Jacques, and Marie Anne Polo de Beaulieu, eds. *Les exempla médiévaux: Introduction à la recherche: Suivie des tables critiques de l'index exemplorum de Frederic C. Tubach.* Carcassone, France: GARAE/Hesiode, 1992.

Bernardo, Aldo S., ed. and trans. *Francesco Petrarch, Letters on Familiar Matters: Rerum familiarium libri.* New York: Italica Press, 2005.

Bernhardt-House, Phillip A. *Werewolves, Magical Hounds, and Dog-Headed Men in Celtic Literature: A Typological Study of Shape-Shifting*. Lewiston, New York and Queenston, Ontario, Canada: Edwin Mellen Press, 2010.

Bersuire, Pierre. *Petri Berchorii opera omnia: Reductorium morale super totam bibliam*. Mainz, Germany: Antonii Hierati, 1609.

Bodin, Jean. *De la démonomanie des sorciers*. Rpt. NP: Gutenberg Reprints, 1979. Reprinted as Randy A. Scott, trans. *On the Demon-Mania of Witches*. Toronto: Centre for Reformation and Renaissance Studies, 1995.

Boivin, Jeanne-Marie. "Le prêtre et les loups-garous: Un épisode de la *Topographia Hibernica* de Giraud de Barri." In *Métamorphose et bestiaire fantastique au Moyen Âge*, edited by Laurence Harf-Lancner, 51–69. Collection de l'École Normale Supérieure de Jeunes Filles 28. Paris: École Normale Supérieure de Jeunes Filles, 1985.

Born, Lester K. "The *Integumenta* of the *Metamorphoses* of Ovid of John of Garland." PhD diss., University of Chicago, 1929.

Boguet, Henri. *Discours exécrable des sorciers: Ensemble leur procez, faits depuis 2 ans en ca en divers endroicts de la France*, edited by Maxime Préaud Marseille, Françoi Lafitte, 1979.

Bouillot, Carine. "Quand l'homme se fait animal, deux cas de métamorphose chez Marie de France: Yonec et Bisclavret." In *Magie et illusion au Moyen Âge*, 65–78. Senefiance 42. Aix-en-Provence, France: CUERMA, 1999.

Bremond, Claude, et al., *L'exemplum*. Typologie des Sources du Moyen Âge Occidental 40. Turnhout, Belgium: Brepols, 1982.

Brewer, J. S., et al., eds. *Giraldi Cambrensis opera*. Rerum Britannicum Medii Aevi Scriptores 21. London: Longman, 1861–1891; rpt. Nendeln, Liechtenstein: Kraus, 1964–1966.

Briscoe, Marianne, and Barbara H. Jaye. *Artes praedicandi and Artes orandi*. Typologie des Sources du Moyen Âge Occidental 61. Turnhout, Belgium: Brepols, 1992.

Brovarone, A. Vitale. "Notes sur la traduction de Valère Maxime par Simon de Hesdin." In *"Pour acquerir honneur et pris," mélanges de moyen français offerts à Giuseppe di Stefano*, edited by Maria Colombo Timelli and Claudio Galderisi, 183–191. Montreal, Canada: Ceres, 2004.

Brown, Michelle P. "Marvels of the West: Giraldus Cambrensis and the Role of the Author in the Development of Marginal Illustration." In *English Manuscript Studies*. Vol. 10, *Decoration and Illustration in Medieval English Manuscripts*, edited by A. S. G. Edwards, 34–59. London: British Library, 2002.

Bruckner, Matilda T. "Of Men and Beasts in Bisclavret." *Romanic Review* 81.3 (1991): 251–269.

Bynum, Caroline Walker. *Metamorphosis and Identity*. New York: Zone, 2001.

Caciola, Nancy. *Discerning Spirits: Divine and Demonic Possession in the Middle Ages*. Ithaca, NY: Cornell University Press, 2003.

Cadden, Joan. "Charles V, Nicole Oresme, and Christine de Pizan: Unities and Uses of Knowledge in Fourteenth-Century France." In *Texts and Contexts in Ancient and Medieval Science: Studies on the Occasion of John E. Murdoch's Seventieth Birthday*, edited by Edith Sylla and Michael McVaugh, 208–244. Leiden, Holland: Brill, 1997.

Carey, John. "Werewolves of Medieval Ireland." *Cambrian Medieval Celtic Studies* 44 (2002): 37–72.

Catalogue de manuscrits et miniatures du XIe au XVIIe siècles: Ouvrages d'ornementation des XVIIe et XVIIIe siècles. Estampes composant la collection de M. P. Gélis-Didot, no. 14, 12. Paris: Théophile Bélin Libraire, 1897. http://gallica.bnf.fr/ark:/12148/bpt6k371357v/f11.image.52.

Chance, Jane. *Medieval Mythography from the School of Chartres to the Court at Avignon 1177–1350*. Gainesville: University of Florida Press, 2000.

Chavy, P. *Traducteurs d'autrefois: Moyen Âge et Renaissance, dictionnaire des traducteurs et de la littérature traduite en ancien et moyen français 842–1600*. Paris and Geneva: Champion-Slatkine, 1988.

Coulson, Frank T. "A Checklist of Newly Discovered Manuscripts of Pierre Bersuire's *Ovidius moralizatus*." *Scriptorium* 51.1 (1997): 164–186.

Craig, Patricia C., et al. "A Finding Aid to the Jacques Seligman & Co. Records 1904–1978, Bulk 1913–1974." In Collectors' Files, 1908, 1917–1977: Collectors. Charnacé, Baron Gautier de and Baronne, née Gabrielle Durrieu 1954–1957, box 179, folder 27. Archives of American Art, series 2. Smithsonian Institution. http://www.aaa.si.edu/collections/container/viewer/Charnacé-Baron-Gautier-de-and Baronne-née-Gabrielle Durrieu-291128.

d'Arras, Jean. *Melusine or the Noble History of Lusignan*, translated with an introduction by Donald Maddox and Sara Sturm-Maddox. University Park: Pennsylvania State University Press, 2012.

d'Avray, Donald L. *The Preaching of the Friars: Sermons Diffused from Paris before 1300*. Oxford and New York: Clarendon, 1985.

Delcorno, Carlo. *Quasi quidam cantus: Studi sulla predicazione medievale*. Florence, Italy: L. S. Olschki, 2009.

Delisle, Léopold. *Recherches sur la librairie de Charles V*. Paris: H. Champion, 1907.

de Bécort, Willem. "'I would have eaten you too':Werewolf Legends in the Flemish, Dutch and German Area." *Folklore* 118 (April, 2007): 23-43.

de Nynauld, Jean. *De la lycanthropie, transformation et extase des sorciers (1615), édition critique augmentée d'études sur les lycanthropes et les loups garous*, edited by Nicole Jacques-Chaquin and Maxime Préaud. Paris: Frénésie, 1990.

de Mérindol, Christian. *Le roi René et la seconde maison d'Anjou: Emblematique art histoire*. Paris: Léopard d'Or, 1987.

de Rolley, Thibaut Maus. "La part du diable: Jean Wier et la fabrique de l'illusion diabolique." *Tracés, Revue de Sciences Humaines* 8 (2005): 29–46.

de Smedt, Charles. *Catalogus codicum hagiographicum qui asservantur in Bibliotheca Nationali Parisiensi*. Brussels: Société des Bollandistes, 1889.

Douglas, Adam. *The Beast Within: A History of the Werewolf*. New York: Avon, 1992.

Douglass, E. Jane Dempsey. *Justification in Late Medieval Preaching: A Study of John Geiler of Kaiserberg*. New York and Leiden, Holland: Brill, 1989.

Engels, Joseph, ed. *De formis figurisque deorum. Reductorium morale, liber XV, cap. 1:1*. Utrecht, Holland: Institut voor Laat Latijn der Rijksuniversiteit, 1966.

———. *Reductorium morale, liber XV, cap. ii–xv: Ovidius moralizatus*. Utrecht, Holland: Institut voor Laat Latijn der Rijksuniversiteit, 1966.

———. "L'édition critique de l'*Ovidius moralizatus* de Bersuire." *Vivarium* 9 (1971): 19–24.

———. "Borchoriana I. Notice bibliographique sur Pierre Bersuire, supplément au *Repertorium biblicum medii aevi*." *Vivarium* 2 (1964): 62–124.

Faucon, Maurice. *La librairie des papes d'Avignon, sa formation, sa composition, ses catalogues (1316–1420) d'après les registres de comptes et d'inventaires des archives vaticanes*. Bibliothèque des Écoles Françaises d'Athènes et de Rome, fascicules 43,50. Paris: E. Thorin, 1886–1887.

Faure, M. "Le *Bisclavret* de Marie de France: Une histoire suspecte de loup-garou." *Revues des Langues Romanes* 83 (1978): 345–356.

Fenster, Thelma. "'Perdre son latin': Christine de Pizan and Vernacular Humanism." In *Christine de Pizan and the Categories of Difference*, edited by Marilynn Desmond, 91–107. Minneapolis: University of Minnesota Press, 1998.

Friedman, John Block. "The Humour and Folly of the World in Odd Places: A Fifteenth-Century Manuscript Herbal." In *Science and Literature at the Crossroads: Papers from the 34th CEMERS Interdisciplinary Conference*, edited by Dana Stewart. *Mediaevalia* 29.1 (2008): 207–235.

Friedman, John Block, with Kristen Figg and Kathrin Giogoli. *Libro de las maravillas del mundo*. Burgos, Spain: Siloé, in press, 2015.

Gautier, Marc-Édouard. *Splendeur de l'enluminure: Le roi René et les livres*. Angers, France: Actes Sud, 2009.

Gerald of Wales. *Topographia Hibernica*. In *Giraldi Cambrensis opera*, edited by J. S. Brewer, et al., 5:101–107. Rerum Britannicum Medii Aevi Scriptores 21. London: Longman, 1861–1891; rpt. Nendeln, Liechtenstein: Kraus, 1964–1966.

Giogoli, Kathrin, and John Block Friedman. "Robinet Testard: Court Illuminator, His Manuscripts and His Debt to the Graphic Arts." *Journal of the Early Book Society* 8 (2005): 152–196.

Goyens, Michèle, et al. *Science Translated: Latin and Vernacular Translations of Scientific Treatises in Medieval Europe.* Leuven, Belgium: Leuven University Press, 2008.

Guichard-Tesson, Françoise. "Le métier de traducteur de commentateur au XIVe siècle d'après Evrart de Conty." *Moyen Français* 24–25 (1989): 131–167.

Guynn, Noah D. "Hybridity, Ethics and Gender in Two Old French Werewolf Tales." In *From Beasts to Souls: Gender and Embodiment in Medieval Europe,* edited by E. Jane Burns and Peggy McCracken, 157-185. Notre Dame, IN: Notre Dame University Press, 2013,

Harf-Lancner, Laurence. "La métamorphose illusoire: Des théories chrétiennes de la métamorphose aux images médiévales du loup-garou." *Annales Economies Societés Civilisations* 40 (1985): 208–226.

Hexter, Ralph. "The *Allegari* of Pierre Bersuire: Interpretation and the *Reductorium morale.*" *Allegorica* 10 (1989): 51–84.

Hochuli-Dubuis, Paule. *Catalogue des manuscrits français 1–198.* 5th ed. Geneva: Odyssée/ BGE, 2011.

Holbrook, Sue Ellen. "The Properties of Things and Textual Power: Illustrating the French Translation of *De proprietatibus rerum* and a Latin Precursor." In *Patrons, Authors, and Workshops: Books and Book Production in Paris,* edited by Godfried Croenen and Peter Ainsworth, 367–404. Leuven, Belgium: Peeters, 2006.

Houdard, Sophie. "Le loup-garou ou les limites de l'animalité." In Jean de Nynauld, *De la lycanthropie, transformation et extase des sorciers (1615), édition critique augmentée d'études sur les lycanthropes et les loups garous,* edited by Nicole Jacques-Chaquin and Maxime Préaud, 189–196. Paris: Frénésie, 1990.

Hüe, Denis. "Espace et paysage chez Pierre Bersuire et quelques Avignonnais." *Cahiers de Recherches Médiévales* 6 (1999): 41–57.

Jacques-Lefèvre, Nicole. "Such an Impure, Cruel and Savage Beast...: Images of the Werewolf in Demonological Works." In *Werewolves, Witches, and Wandering Spirits: Traditional Belief in Folklore in Early Modern Europe,* edited by Kathryn A. Edwards, 181–197. Kirksville, MO: Truman State University Press, 2002.

Jullien de Pommerol, Marie-Henriette, and Jacques Monfrin. *La bibliothèque pontificale à Avignon et à Peñiscola pendant le grand schisme d'occident et sa dispersion: Inventaires et concordances.* Collection de l'École Française de Rome 141. Rome: École Française, 1991.

Kharkov, Catherine E. "Tales of the Ancients: Colonial Werewolves and the Mapping of Postcolonial Ireland." In *Postcolonial Moves: Medieval through Modern*, edited by Patricia Clare Ingham and Michelle R. Warren, 93-109. New York: Palgrave Macmillan, 2003.

Knight, Rhonda, "Werewolves, Monsters, and Miracles: Representing Colonial Fantasies in Gerald of Wales *Topographia Hibernica*," *Studies in Iconography* 22 (2001):55-86.

Kohl, Benjamin C., and H. C. Erik Midelfort, eds. and trans. *On Witchcraft: An Abridged Translation of Johannes Weyer's De praesigiis daemonum*. Asheville: University of North Carolina at Asheville and Pegasus Press, 1998.

König, Eberhard. "Le livre des secrets d'histoire naturelle." In *Splendeur de l'enluminure: Le roi René et les livres*, edited by Marc-Édouard Gautier. Angers, France: Actes Sud, 2009.

——. *Das Provost-Stundenbuch: Der Meister der Marguerite d'Orléans und die Buchmalerei in Angers*. Illuminationen. Studien und Monographien, ed. Heribert Tenschert, IV. Ramsen, Switzerland, and Rotthalmünster, Germany: Antiquariat Bibermuhle AG, 2002.

——. "Le Maître de Boccacce de Genève." In *Splendeur de l'enluminure: Le roi René et les livres*, edited by Marc-Édouard Gautier, 133–143. Angers, France: Actes Sud, 2009.

——. *Das liebentbrannte Herz: Der Wiener Codex und der Maler Barthélemy d'Eyck*. Graz, Austria: Akademische Druck- und Verlagsanstalt, 1996.

——. *Französische Buchmalerei um 1450, der Jouvenel-Maler, der Maler des Genfer Boccaccio und die Anfänge Jean Fouquets*. Berlin: Mann, 1982.

——. "Die *Très Belles Heures de Notre Dame*, eine datierte Handschrift aus der Zeit nach 1404." In *Flanders in a European Perspective: Manuscript Illumination around 1400 in Flanders and Abroad: Proceedings of the International Colloquium, Leuven, 7–10 September 1993*, edited by Maurits Smeyers and Bert Cardon, 41–61. Leuven, Belgium: Peeters, 1995.

——. "Un atelier d'enluminure à Nantes et l'art du temps de Fouquet." *Revue de l'Art* 35 (1977): 64–73.

——. "Le livre des cas des nobles hommes et femmes, traduit en français par Laurent de Premierfait." In *Splendeur de l'enluminure: Le roi René et les livres*, edited by Marc-Édouard Gautier, 332–335. Angers, France: Actes Sud, 2009.

——. *Les Heures de Marguerite d'Orléans: Reproduction intégrale du calendrier et des images du manuscrit latin 1156B de la Bibliothèque nationale*. Paris: Éditions du Cerf, Bibliothèque nationale, 1991.

König, Eberhard, and John Lowden, *La biblia moralizada de los Limbourg: De los hermanos Limbourg à George Trubert, Facsimile commentary*. Valencia, Spain: Patrimonio, 2010.

Kratz, Dennis M. "Fictus Lupus: The Werewolf in Christian Thought." *Classical Folia: Studies in the Christian Perpetuation of the Classics* 30.1 (1976): 57–80.

Kumler, Aden. "Faire translater, faire historier: Charles V's *Bible historiale* (Houghton Library, MS Typ. 555) and the Visual Rhetoric of Vernacular Sapience." *Studies in Iconography* 29 (2008): 90–135.

Leroquais, Victor. *Les livres d'heures: Manuscrits de la Bibliothèque nationale, I–III*. Mâcon, France: Protat Frères, 1927.

———. *Supplement*. Mâcon: Protat Frères, 1943.

Levine, Robert. "Exploiting Ovid: Medieval Allegorizations of the *Metamorphoses*." *Medioevo Romanzo* 14 (1989): 197–213.

Lusignan, Serge. "Le latin était la langue maternelle des Romains: La fortune d'un argument à la fin du Moyen Âge." In *Préludes à la Renaissance: Aspects de la vie intellectuelle en France au XVe siècle*, edited by Carla Bozzolo and Ezio Ornato, 265–282. Paris: Éditions du CNRS, 1992.

———. "Lire, indexer et gloser: Nicole Oresme et la 'Politique' d'Aristote." In *L'écrit dans la société médiévale: Divers aspects de sa pratique du XIe au XVe siècle: Textes en hommage à Lucie Fossier*, edited by Caroline Bourlet and Annie Dufour, 167–181. Paris: CNRS, 1991.

———. *La langue des rois au Moyen Âge: Le français en France et en Angleterre*. Paris: Presses Universitaires de France, 2004.

———. "Langue française et société du XIIIe au XVe siècle." In *Nouvelle histoire de la langue française*, edited by Jacques Chaurand, 91–143. Paris: Éditions du Seuil, 1999.

———. "Parler vulgairement: Les intellectuels et la langue française au XIIIe et XIVe siècles." In *Études médiévales*, edited by Pierre Boglioni. Montreal, Canada: Presses de l'Université de Montréal, 1987.

Mackay, Christopher S., ed. and trans. *Malleus maleficarum*. Cambridge, UK: Cambridge University Press, 2006.

Maddox, Donald, and Sara Sturm-Maddox, eds. *Melusine of Lusignan: Founding Fiction in Late Medieval France*. Athens, GA: University of Georgia Press, 1996.

———, trans. *Melusine or the Noble History of Lusignan*. University Park: Pennsylvania State University Press, 2012.

Manion, Margaret. *The Felton Illuminated Manuscripts in the National Gallery of Victoria*. Melbourne, Australia: Macmillan Art Publishing and the National Gallery of Victoria, 2005.

Mathews, Henry John. "Abraham ibn Ezra's Short Commentary on Daniel." *Miscellany of Hebrew Literature* 2 (1887): 257–276.

Ménard, Philippe. "Les histoires de loup-garou au Moyen Âge." In *Symposium in honorem prof. M. de Riquer*, 209–238. Barcelona: Universitat de Barcelona, Quaderns Crema, 1984.

Meunier, René-Adrien. "Le fonds auvergnat, provençal et alpestre dans les 'Récréations impériales' de Gervais de Tilbury et le 'Réductoire morale' de Pierre Bersuire." Annales de l'Université de Poitiers (1952–1954): 151–161.

———. "Le livre des merveilles de Pierre Bersuire." Annuaire de l'Université de Poitiers 2nd ser., 3 (1951): 1–8.

———. "L'humaniste Pierre Bersuire (fin du XIIIe siècle–1362)." Bulletin de la Société des Antiquaires de l'Ouest (1948): 511–532.

Meurger, Michel. "L'homme-loup et son témoin: Construction d'une factualité lycanthropique." In Jean de Nynauld, De la lycanthropie, transformation et extase des sorciers (1615), édition critique augmentée d'études sur les lycanthropes et les loups garous, edited by Nicole Jacques-Chaquin and Maxime Préaud, 143–179. Paris: Frénésie, 1990.

Meyer, Robert T., trans. Palladius: The Lausiac History. Westminster, MD: Newman Press, 1965.

Milin, Gaël. Les chiens de Dieu: La représentation du loup-garou en occident (XIe–XIX siècles). Centre de Recherche Bretonne et Celtique: Cahiers de Bretagne Occidentale 13, Diest, France: Université de Bretagne Occidentale, 1993.

———. "La Vita Ronani et les contes de loup-garou aux XIIe et XIIIe siècles." Moyen Âge 97 (1991): 259–273.

Mondschein, Aharon. "R. Abraham ibn Ezra: The Short Commentary on Daniel." (Hebrew) MA thesis, Bar Ilan University, 1977.

Monfrin, Jacques. "Humanisme et traductions au Moyen Âge." Journal des Savants (1963): 161–190.

———. "Les traducteurs et leur public en France au Moyen Âge." Journal des Savants (1964): 5–20.

———. Études de philologie romane. Publications Romanes et Françaises 230. Geneva: Droz 2001.

Morenzoni, Franco. Des écoles aux paroisses: Thomas de Chobham et la promotion de la prédication au début du XIIIe siècle. Paris: Institut des Études Augustiniennes, 1995.

Nordenfalk, Carl. "Französische Buchmalerei 1200–1599." Kunstchronik 9.7 (1956): 179–189.

Oates, Caroline. "Démonologues et lycanthropes: Les théories de la métamorphose au XVI siècle." In Métamorphose et bestiaire fantastique au Moyen Âge, edited by Laurence Harf-Lancner, 71–105. Collection de l'École Normale Supérieure de Jeunes Filles 28. Paris: École Normale Supérieure de Jeunes Filles, 1985.

O'Meara, John J. "Geraldus Cambrensis in Topographia Hibernica: Text of the First Recension." Proceedings of the Royal Irish Academy 52, sec. C.4 (1949): 143–145.

Otten, Charlotte F., ed. *A Lycanthropy Reader: Werewolves in Western Culture.* Syracuse, NY: Syracuse University Press, 1986.

Pansier, Pierre. *Histoire du livre et de l'imprimerie à Avignon du XIVe au XVIe siècle.* Avignon, France: Aubanel Frères, 1922.

Pausanias. *Description of Greece,* trans. W. H. S. Jones. London: Loeb Classical Library, 1977.

Pepin, Ronald E., trans. *The Vatican Mythographers.* New York: Fordham University Press, 2008.

Perrel, Jean. "Le troubadour Pons, seigneur de Chapteuil et de Vertaizon: Son temps, sa vie, son oeuvre." *Revue d'Auvergne* 90.2–3 (1976): 89–199.

Pons, Nicole. "L'historiographie chez les premiers humanistes français." In *L'aube de la Renaissance: Pour la dixième anniversaire de la disparition de Franco Simone,* edited by Dario Cecchetti, L. Sozzi, and L. Terreaux, 103–122. Geneva: Slatkine, 1991.

Porcher, Jean. *Les manuscrits à peintures en France du XIII au XVI siècle.* Exhibition catalog. Paris: A. Tournon, 1955.

———. *L'enluminure française.* Paris: Arts & Métiers Graphiques, 1959.

Quénet, Sophie. "Mises en récit d'une métamorphose: Le loup-garou." In *Le merveilleux et la magie dans la littérature,* edited by Gérard Chandes, 137–163. CERMEIL 2. Amsterdam: Rodopi, 1992.

Quillet, Jeannine. "Nicole Oresme et le français médiéval." In *Figures de l'écrivain au Moyen Âge: Actes du colloque du Centre d'Études Médiévales de l'Université de Picardie, Amiens, 18–20 mars 1988,* edited by Danielle Bushinger, 235–243. Göppinger Arbeiten zur Germanistik 510. Göppingen, Germany: Kümmerle, 1991.

Reynolds, William D. "Sources, Nature, and Influence of the *Ovidius moralizatus* of Pierre Bersuire." In *The Mythographic Art: Classical Fable and the Rise of the Vernacular in Early France and England,* edited by Jane Chance, 83–99. Gainesville: University of Florida Press, 1990.

Rivers, Kimberly. "Another Look at the Career of Pierre Bersuire O. S. B." *Revue Bénédictine* 116 (2006): 92–100.

———. *Preaching the Memory of Virtue and Vice: Memory, Images, and Preaching in the Late Middle Ages.* Turnhout, Belgium: Brepols, 2010.

Rouse, Richard, and Mary Rouse. *Preachers, Florilegia, and Sermons: Studies on the "Manipulus florum" of Thomas of Ireland.* Toronto: Pontifical Institute, 1979.

Rychner, Jean. "Observations sur la traduction de Tite-Live par Pierre Bersuire (1354–1356)." In *L'humanisme médiéval dans les littératures romanes du XIIe au XIVe siècle: Colloque organisé par le Centre de Philologie et Littératures Romanes de l'Université de Strasbourg du 29 janvier au 2 février 1962,* edited by Anthime Fourrier, 167–192. Paris: Klincksieck, 1964.

Salisbury, Joyce E. *The Beast Within: Animals in the Middle Ages*. London: Routledge, 1994.

Samaran, Charles, and Jacques Monfrin. "Pierre Bersuire, prieur de St. Eloi de Paris." *Histoire littéraire de France* 39, 259–450. Paris: Imprimerie Nationale, 1900. Rpt. 1962.

Sargent, Amelia. "Gerald of Wales's *Topographia Hibernica*: Dates, Versions, Readers." *Viator* 43.1 (2012): 241–261.

Schutz, Alex. *Vernacular Books in Parisian Public Libraries*. Chapel Hill: University of North Carolina Press, 1965.

Sconduto, Leslie A. *Metamorphoses of the Werewolf: A Literary Study from Antiquity through the Renaissance*. Jefferson, NC: McFarland, 2008.

Sherman, Claire Richter. *Imaging Aristotle: Verbal and Visual Representation in Fourteenth-Century France*. Berkeley: University of California Press, 1995.

———. "Les thèmes humanistes dans le programme de traduction de Charles V: Compilation des textes et illustrations." In *Pratiques de la culture écrite en France au XVe siècle, Actes du colloque international du CNRS, Paris, 16–18 mai 1992, organisé en l'honneur de Gilbert Ouy par l'unité de recherche "Culture écrite du Moyen Âge tardif,"* edited by Monique Ornato and Nicole Pons, 527–537. Textes et Études du Moyen Âge 2. Louvain-la-Neuve, Belgium: Fédération Internationale des Instituts d'Études Médiévales, 1995.

Sinclair, Keith Val. *The Melbourne Livy. A Study of Bersuire's Translation Based on the Manuscript in the Collection of the National Gallery in Victoria, Melbourne*. Melbourne University Press Monographs 7. Melbourne: University Press for Australian Humanities Research Council, 1961.

Small, Susan. "The Medieval Werewolf Model of Reading Skin." In *Reading Skin in Medieval Literature and Culture*, edited by Katie Walter, 81–97. New York: Palgrave, 2013.

Suard, François. "Bisclavret et les contes du loup-garou: Essai d'interpretation." *Marche Romane* 30 (1980): 267–276.

Summers, Montague. *The Werewolf in Lore and Legend*. New York: Dover, 2003.

Swanson, Jenny. *John of Wales: A Study of the Works and Ideas of a Thirteenth-Century Friar*. Cambridge Studies in Medieval Life and Thought, 4th series. Cambridge, UK: Cambridge University Press, 2002.

Tatham, Edward H. R. *Francesco Petrarca, the First Modern Man of Letters: His Life and Correspondence*. London: Sheldon Press, 1925–1926.

Tesnière, Marie-Hélène. "Le *Reductorium morale* de Pierre Bersuire." In *L'enciclopedismo medievale: Actes du colloque international San Gimignano, 8–10 octobre 1992*, edited by Michelangelo Picone, 225–242. Ravenna, Italy: Longo, 1993.

————. "Pierre Bersuire, un encyclopédiste au XIVe siècle." *Plein Chant* 69–70 (2000): 7–15.

————. "À propos de la traduction de Tite-Live par Pierre Bersuire: Le manuscrit d'Oxford, Bibliothèque bodléienne, Rawlinson C. 447." *Romania* 118 (2000): 449–498.

————. "Un manuscrit exceptionnel des *Décades* de Tite-Live traduites par Pierre Bersuire." In *La traduction vers le moyen français: Actes du IIe colloque de l'AIEMF, Poitiers, 27–29 avril 2006*, edited by Claudio Galderisi and Cinzia Pignatelli, 125–147. Traduire au Moyen Âge 11. Turnhout, Belgium: Brepols, 2007.

————. "La librairie modèle." In *Paris et Charles V: Arts et architecture*, edited by Frédéric Pleybert, 225–233. Collection Paris et son Patrimoine. Paris: Action Artistique de la Ville de Paris, 2001.

Toaff, Ariel. *Mostri giudei: L'immaginario ebraico dal medioevo alla prima età moderna*. Bologna, Italy: II Mulino, 1996.

Veenstra, Jan R. "The Ever-Changing Nature of the Beast: Cultural Change, Lycanthropy, and the Question of Substantial Transformation (from Petronius to Del Rio)." In *The Metamorphosis of Magic from Late Antiquity to the Early Modern Period*, edited by Jan N. Bremer and Jan R. Veenstra. 133-166. Leuven, Belgium: Peeters, 2002,

Venantius Fortunatus, *Vita* of Hilary of Poitiers *PL* 88.

Vita abbatis Macarii Aegyptii, Vitae Patrum. In J.-P. Migne, ed., *Patrologia Latina*. Vol. 73. Rpt. Turnhout, Belgium: Brepols, 1969.

Vogel, Cyrille. *Le pécheur et la pénitence au Moyen Âge*. Paris: Éditions du Cerf, 1982.

————. "Pratiques superstitieuses au début du XIe siècle d'après le *Corrector sive medicus* de Burchard, évêque de Worms (965–1025)." In *Études de civilisation médiévale, IXe–XIIe siècles: Mélanges offerts à Edmond-René Labande à l'occasion de son départ à la retraite et du XXe anniversaire du C.É.S.C.M. par ses amis, ses collègues, ses élèves*, 751–761. Poitiers, France: C.É.S.C.M., 1974.

Weijers, Olga. *Dictionnaires et répertoires au Moyen Âge: Une étude du vocabulaire*. Turnhout, Belgium: Brepols, 1991.

Wilkins, Ernest H. *Life of Petrarch*. Chicago and London: University of Chicago Press, 1961.

William of Auvergne, *De universo*. In *Opera Omnia*. Orléans and Paris: F. Hotot and Andraea Pralard, 1674; Rpt. Frankfurt –am- Main, Germany: Minerva, 1963.

Zacher, Inge. "Die Livius-Illustration in der Pariser Buchmalerei (1370–1420)." PhD diss., Berlin, Freie Universität, 1974.

Figure 1. Hans Weiditz, scene of an urban werewolf attack. Johannes Geiler von Kaiserberg, *Die Emeis:*
Die ist das buch von der Omelissen (The Ants), 1516. Public domain.

Figure 2. Lucas Cranach the Elder, Rural werewolf attack. 1512. Courtesy New York, Metropolitan Museum.

Figure 3. Werewolves of Arcadia. *Esopi appologi siue mythologi cum quibusdam carminum et fabularum additionibus Sebastiani Brant,* 1501, 301. Public domain.

Figure 4. Werewolves of Ossory. Gerald of Wales, *Topographica Hibernica*, London, © The British Library Board, Royal 13.B. viii, folio 18r, ca. 1196–1223. Courtesy British Library.

Figure 5. Master of Marguerite d'Orléans, werewolves of France. *Secrets de l'histoire naturelle*, ch. 22, Paris, Bibliothèque nationale de France MS fr. 1378, fol. 2v, 1427. Courtesy Bibliothèque nationale de France.

Figure 6. Detail, Master of Marguerite d'Orléans, werewolves of France. *Secrets de l'histoire naturelle*, ch. 22, Paris, Bibliothèque nationale de France MS fr. 1378, fol. 2v, 1427. Courtesy Bibliothèque nationale de France.

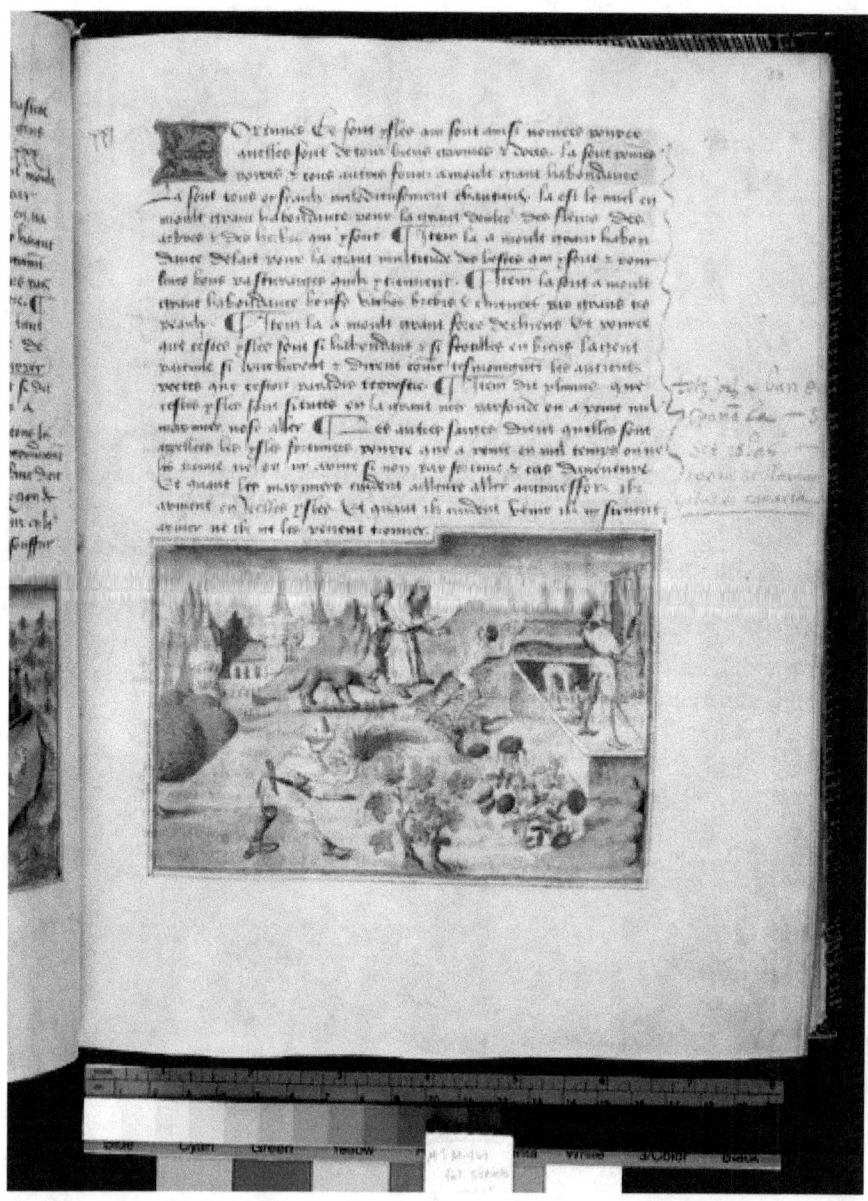

Figure 7. Master of the Geneva Boccaccio, werewolves of France. *Secrets de l'histoire naturelle*, ch. 22, The Pierpont Morgan Library, New York. MS M.461. Purchased by J. Pierpont Morgan (1837–1913) in 1911.

Figure 8. Master of Marguerite d'Orléans, werewolves of Scythia. *Secrets de l'histoire naturelle*, ch. 47, Paris, Bibliothèque nationale de France MS fr. 1379, fol. 70r, 1427. Courtesy Bibliothèque nationale de France.

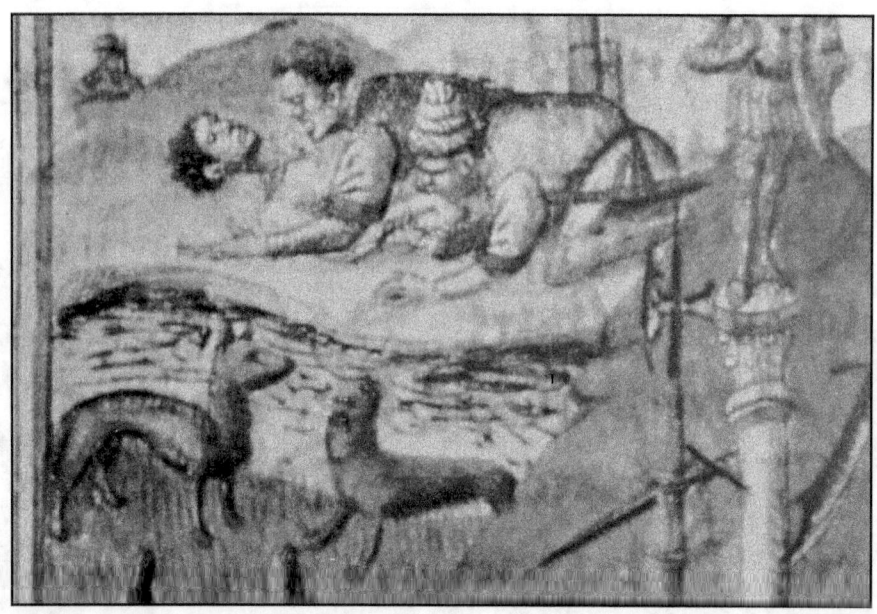

Figure 9. Detail, Master of Marguerite d'Orléans, werewolves of Scythia. *Secrets de l'histoire naturelle,* ch. 47, Paris, Bibliothèque nationale de France MS fr. 1379, fol. 70r, 1427. Courtesy Bibliothèque nationale de France.

Figure 10. Werewolves of Scythia. *Secrets de l'histoire naturelle*, ch. 47, fol. 62, 1450–1460. Formerly in the collection of Baron Jean de Charnacé, Chateau d'Aulnoy, Coulommiers, Seine-et-Marne. Present whereabouts unknown. Photograph and copyright by author.

William Peto, O.F.M.Obs., and the 1556 Edition of *The folowinge of Chryste*: Background and Context

JAMES P. CARLEY AND ANN M. HUTCHISON

I. Background and Context

In 1529, Sir Thomas More's *A dyaloge . . .touching the pestylent sect of Luther and Tyndale* was printed by John Rastell (STC 18084), and in 1531 the exiled reformer and Bible translator William Tyndale responded with *An answere vnto sir Thomas Mores dialoge*, printed in Antwerp by Simon Cock (STC 24437). The first part of More's *The confutacyon of Tyndales answere* appeared in 1532, printed by William Rastell (STC 18079).[1] In the preface to *The confutacyon*, More states that sincere Christians, especially "people vnlerned," should avoid heretical books being put forth by individuals such as Martin Luther and William Tyndale, and should

> occupye them selfe besyde theyr other busynesse in prayour, good medytacyon and redynge of suche *englysshe* bookes as moste may norysshe and encrease deuocyon. Of whyche kynde is Bonauenture of the lyfe of Cryste, Gerson of the folowynge of Cryste, and the deuoute contemplatyue booke of *Scala perfectionis* wyth suche other lyke. (emphasis added)[2]

The books recommended by More were Nicholas Love's translation of pseudo-Bonaventure's *Meditationes Vitae Christi* as *The Mirror of the Blessed*

Life of Jesus Christ;[3] Thomas à Kempis's *Imitatio Christi*, here attributed to Jean Gerson; and Walter Hilton's *The Scale of Perfection*.[4] In the case of the *Imitatio Christi*, as Roger Lovatt points out, More was "almost certainly" referring "to the third English translation of the work which was published c. 1531" by the London printer Robert Wyer (STC 23961).[5]

Even though the first three books of the *Imitatio* had already been translated into English from Latin by William Atkinson (d. 1509), and the fourth from French by Lady Margaret Beaufort (d. 1509) specifically for print, the author of the introduction to the ca. 1531 text justified a new translation on the grounds that the earlier one—albeit "ryght well and deuoutly translatyd into Englysshe"—was not altogether accurate in the first three books, and the fourth was derived from French.[6] (There was an earlier English translation of the first three books undertaken in the mid-fifteenth century which survives in four manuscripts, but it appears to have had a very limited circulation and did not find its way into print until 1997).[7]

Wyer's edition encompassed all four books of the *Imitatio*, although the fourth, "whiche treatyth most specyally of the sacrament of the aulter" (Bk. 4, sig. A.ir), was set in different type deriving from the Southwark house of Peter Treveris. Soon afterwards, Wyer brought out an edition of the fourth book only, making use of his own type (STC 23962).[8] Thomas Godfray's edition of all four books appeared around 1531/32 (STC 23963). Godfray improved on some of Wyer's readings, and Edward J. Klein "speculates" that these improvements may have been introduced by the author, whom he identifies as Richard Whitford, Bridgettine priest-brother, translator, and prolific author of devotional treatises.[9] Godfray also added other texts: after *The folowyng of Chryste* comes a translation of St. Bernard of Clairvaux's *Epistola de perfectione uitae* as the *Golden Epistle* (STC 1915), and four of the *Revelations* of St. Bridget of Sweden.[10]

Godfray explained that he had appended the *Golden Epistle* to *The folowyng* "to the encrease of the deuotion of them that can rede Englyshe and understande nat the latyn tonge"—that is, precisely the audience to whom More directed his remarks.[11] He also observed that the *Golden Epistle* "is in some bokes imprinted in the later ende of the boke called in latyn Imitatio Christi that is to say in Englisshe the folowyng of Christ."[12] The introduction to Wyer's edition opens with precisely the same phrase—"Hereafter folowyth a boke callyd in latyn Imitacio Cristi, that is to say in englysshe the folowynge of Cryst"—and one would assume that Godfray was making an allusion to this edition, except for the fact that it does not contain a copy of the *Golden Epistle* or the selection from the *Revelations*.[13]

In 1530, Wynkyn de Worde had issued a different English translation of the *Golden Epistle*, this one by Richard Whitford (STC 1912). In his short epilogue to the text, Whitford claimed that he had been brought "an olde translacyon rugh and rude"—probably that of Thomas Betson, deacon-broth-er at Syon Abbey, who died in 1516—which he was required to "amende."[14] Although Wyer printed this translation in 1531 as a separate tract (STC 1914), he did not include it with the *The folowynge* in either of his surviving editions. What, then, are the "some bokes" containing both *The folowynge* and the *Golden Epistle* to which Godfray is referring and which he is imitat-ing?[15] It is a problem to which we shall return.

This little group of translations forms part of a cluster of devotional ma-terials appearing in the early 1530s, some first written many years earlier, as part of the campaign, to which More referred, to combat the heretical texts that were corrupting English readers.[16] Whitford's statement in the preface to *The Pype, or Tonne, of the Lyfe of Perfection* published by Redman in 1532 (STC 25421) is representative: "This worke was wrytten yeres ago. And nowe thought necessarye to be sende forth: bycause of these newe fangle persones whiche in dede ben heretykes all though they wyll nat so be called."[17] In re-sponse to the heretical texts, with their emphasis on solifidianism, there was a committed program of publication advocating the traditional devotional life and the role within it of laymen as well as of religious.[18]

In spite of valiant efforts made by traditionalists, Henry did break de-finitively with Rome in 1534. Over the next six years monastic life in Eng-land came to an abrupt end: proto-Lutheranism seems to have triumphed. Some of the religious, such as John Bale, had already become disaffected with their vocation and switched allegiance; some, such as the Dominicans William Peryn and Robert Buckenham, fled abroad; and some, such as the three Carthusian priors who were martyred on May 4, 1535, along with the Bridgettine brother Richard Reynolds and John Hale, a secular priest and vicar of Isleworth, gave up their lives for their faith.[19] There was a brief return to a more conservative religious policy toward the end of Henry's reign, when Peryn, for example, came back to England for a time, but things became even more difficult under Edward VI, when there was a concerted attempt to purge both "superstitiouse bookes" and adherents of the Old Faith.

When Mary came to the throne in 1553, some religious returned from abroad and others came out of hiding, leaving the clandestine cells in which they had carried on their devotional practices for the previous decade and a half. During the next five years, houses were refounded by at least five orders: the Benedictines at Westminster; the Bridgettines at Isleworth; the Carthu-sians at Sheen; the Dominicans at St Bartholomew's, Smithfield; the Do-minican nuns at Dartford; and the Observant Franciscans at Greenwich and Southampton.[20] Apart from service books, these refounded houses required books of the sort earlier recommended by More. So, too, did layfolk who were being reintroduced to the devotional life that had gone underground more than twenty years earlier. It is in this context that we should examine the new edition of *The folowinge of Chryste* brought out by the Queen's printer John Cawood, who had been appointed to this position in 1556 primarily as a result of his religious credentials (STC 23966).[21]

Although the translator of the third version has long been identified as Richard Whitford, his name does not appear in any of the editions issued in the 1530s: as early as 1932, Albert Owen Evans pointed out that "It was only in 1556 that the name of Richard Whitford appeared for the first time as translator."[22] Does it in fact appear in this edition? As was the case with earlier versions, the 1556 edition includes the *Golden Epistle* after *The folowynge* (although it omits the Bridgettine texts). It is, however, Whitford's translation of the *Golden Epistle* earlier printed as a discrete entity by de Worde and Wyer, rather than the "anonymous" translation brought out by Godfray and Redman, that is appended. The 1556 edition includes, moreover, Whitford's brief epilogue to his translation of the *Golden Epistle*, describing the genesis of the project and concluding with his request that his readers "praye for the olde wretched brother of Syon Rycharde Whytforde." This is followed by Cawood's "Finis" for the whole book—both *The folowinge* and the *Golden Epistle*—and the publication information. This mise-en-page thus creates an unintentionally misleading situation. For a reader unaware that the epilogue was copied verbatim from the earlier editions of the *Golden Epistle*, it would seem natural to assume that Whitford's claim of authorship must apply to both works. This is not necessarily what was meant, however, and there is no internal evidence that Whitford was the translator of this version of *The folowinge of Chryste*. Certainly Whitford, who almost invariably acknowledged books he had written, never laid claim to it.[23]

After his replication of the original introduction, the individual who commissioned the Cawood version but who did not identify himself added his own preface, explaining that it was his admiration for *The folowinge* that led him to request "the Quenes highnes printer to take the paines eftsones to emprint it, seing the other is worne away, which was very faultye in many places, and in this he hath done his diligence in correction thereof as you shal wel perceiue in conferring them together."[24] In fact, the text is taken more or less verbatim from the Wyer edition, which the compositor has followed in extraordinary detail, trying to match both pagination and lineation. The only significant change occurs in the introduction itself, where "Kyng Henry the ,vii. father unto our *late* soueraigne lord king Henry the viii." is substituted for "Henry the .vii. father unto our soueraine lorde the kyng that *now* is kyng Henry the .viii." (emphasis added).[25] After *The folowinge* comes the *Golden Epistle* in the Whitford translation, which, as we point out above, does not occur in Wyer's surviving earlier editions. Given that Cawood's is a virtual replication of the Wyer edition, this provides strong evidence that there was another Wyer edition, now lost, containing both texts, and it was this that

Cawood used as his base text.[26] This is no doubt confirmed by Godfray's statement that his was not the first version to bring them together (even if with differing translations of the *Golden Epistle*).

In the 1530s, then, the Whitford translation of the *Golden Epistle*, as well as St. German's, must have been circulating in conjunction with *The folowynge*.[27] This stands as a reminder both that these sorts of devotional books may have been read more widely than surviving exemplars indicate and that they would have been particularly prone to destruction in the years after the break with Rome. The lost edition may also strengthen the argument that Whitford was the author of this translation of the *Imitatio* as well as the *Golden Epistle*, and that Wyer combined the two since they were by the same author.[28] On the other hand, Whitford was concerned about the dangers of print: he realized that texts could appear authoritative when they were not and that information could be disseminated under false attributions.[29] Almost inevitably, therefore, he named himself in his writings: "Richard Whytford, the wreche of Syon," "the sayd wreched brother of Syon," "the olde wreched brother of Syon," "the former wrecche of Syon," or variants thereof. The lack of self identification in this translation is, therefore, at least suspicious.

II

One of those who showed himself loyal to Catherine of Aragon when Henry set about repudiating her for the younger and evangelically inclined Anne Boleyn was William Peto (ca. 1485–1558), the English Provincial of the Observant Franciscans and possibly Catherine's confessor.[30] An outspoken and active advocate for her cause, he preached a powerful sermon against the divorce on Easter Sunday 1532 in the presence of the king.[31] This led to a brief imprisonment and a flight to Antwerp, where he was accused of writing books against the king's second marriage.[32] Described in 1533 by the royal agent Stephen Vaughan as "an ipocrite knave . . .a wolff, a tyger cladd in a shepes skyn . . .a perilous knave, a reyser of sedycon, an evyll reporter of the kynges heighnes,"[33] he later became associated with Henry VIII's renegade cousin Reginald Pole. In 1539, he was included in the Act of Attainder against Pole and his friends, and he spent the next fifteen years in Italy. During Mary's reign, he returned to England.

According to the *Revised Short Title Catalogue*, Peto was behind the 1556 edition of *The folowinge of Chryste*—"[Ed. W. Peto]." No explanation is given—his name appears nowhere in the printed text—and, although generally accepted, this identification has not been confirmed elsewhere.[34] Six copies of this edition are known to survive, one imperfect and another a fragment. In a copy now in the British Library (C.122.c.29), there are two handwritten statements of ownership in differing hands, each inscribed twice, at the beginning and the end of the book.[35] The first, which appears in the upper margin of the title page and in the same hand in the lower margin on the penultimate page of text, reads "Libellus Dominae Elizabetae uxoris Thomae Pope militis ex dono patris Peto Grenwycensis."[36] The second inscription, in a different hand, found in the lower margin of the title page and the lower margin of the final page of text, has "Liber uxoris Thome Pope militis ex dono patris Iohannis Casei fratris Grenewichensis."[37] In the first instance, "Iohannis Casei" has been deleted, and the whole inscription crossed out. John Case does not appear among the list of brothers who entered the refounded convent at Greenwich, but it is possible that Case was a pseudonym for Peto, although the name does not appear elsewhere.[38]

Elizabeth Pope (d. 1593), the recipient of the book, was the third (or possibly second) wife of Sir Thomas Pope, the founder of Trinity College, Oxford, and the daughter of Walter Blount of Blount's Hall, Staffordshire. A conservative in religion, Sir Thomas died in 1559.[39] Toward the end of 1560, Elizabeth married Sir Hugh Paulet, and after Paulet's death in 1573, she revealed herself to be an unregenerate Catholic.[40] Even after Pope died she retained an interest in the college, where she had been recognized as foundress, and in 1583 she introduced her nephew Richard Blount into a fellowship. He left almost immediately for the Continent, however, was ordained in Rome, and eventually became a Jesuit provincial.[41]

The volume in the British Library shows that Elizabeth's strong and conservative piety dated to Pope's lifetime. On sig. Aiir, following the introduction, there is a hand-written note, no doubt to Elizabeth, then Lady Pope, from Peto:

> Jhesus be euer with vs in all our // doynges &
> workys. // Madam, / y sende here by þis berer //
> to your ladyscipe ii bookes of þe // folowynge of
> Chryst, / oone for // youe, and þe oder for your
> ow[n] // syster / wyche / yff hit please your //
> ladyscipe to reed aduysedly euer[y] // day one
> chapyter you schale ha[ue] //gret[42] spirituale
> cumforte of // your sowle, as you schale percey[ue]
> // in þe preface, in þe turning of þis // 1 leafe, which
> y made of late // in þe newe prynting of þis bo[ke].
> // Your beadman / [ ] Peto.[43]

By "turning of þis 1 leafe," the reader is led to the statement in the preface to the effect that "euerye good chrysten reader, who wil set his mynde earnestly to folow christ his stepes, let them proue by readyng euerye day a chapter, whan they haue best layser." With the statement "which y made of late in þe new prynting of þis boke," the note confirms that Peto was the author of the preface and commissioner of the edition. It is also clear that he considered this to be a text that pious readers should read and reread. The need for constant consultation would explain, moreover, how his own copy, like others, had become "worne away" during his years on the Continent.

After he was exiled in late 1532, Peto maintained close ties with More, who sent him a copy of his *The confutacyon of Tyndales answere*, in which, as has been noted, More recommended that in order to resist heresy, unlearned (i.e., non-Latinate) people should spend their leisure in "redynge of suche englysshe bookes as moste may norysshe and encrease deuocyon," including *The folowynge of Chryste*. What Peto and his contemporaries had seen after More's death was a long period when heresy had triumphed, when the people were denied exposure to these sorts of books, and he must have been anxious that they be made available now that orthodoxy had been revived.[44] As he observed in his preface, there had been many treatises put out in this perilous world "to seduce the symple people, and to bryng them from the unitie of the catholyke church into peruerse and abhominable errours"—that is, the religion of King Edward VI under Thomas Cranmer's stewardship— but there had also been good treatises made "in tyme past before" which "yf men woulde haue ben so *diligent* to loke upon, as they were *curious* to loke on the other, they shuld not haue fallen so sone from the true knowledge of Chrystes doctryne and the ryght sence of holy scrypture" (emphasis added). Reading the wrong sort of books out of curiosity, just as Whitford, More, and others had feared, had precipitated the fall into heresy that had overwhelmed England. And the way to combat this and to cement the reconciliation of the English Church to Rome was through a concerted effort to reissue the books recommended earlier in the century, books that taught the importance of individual meditation and showed the function of the religious orders in the life of the realm.[45] It was part of the Counter-Reformation policy adopted in Mary's England of favoring the "devout heart" over the "inquisitive head" among the laity.[46]

Peto's associations with Reginald Pole, Queen Mary's cousin and her archbishop of Canterbury, go back at least to 1537, when Peto was involved in Pole's first English legation and covered Pole's tracks after the latter's recall by the pope. By 1538, Peto was in the Observant Convent in Venice "by Mr Pole's means."[47] Later he was a *camerarius* and then *custos* of the English Hospice in Rome, where Pole himself had been elected *custos* in 1538.[48] For a number of years, he alternated in this position with Thomas Goldwell, Pole's chaplain and bishop of St. Asaph under Queen Mary. He departed in 1553, and by 1554 he was in the Franciscan house in Mantua. Soon afterwards he followed Pole to England, where he was one of the twenty-five friars who established themselves at the restored convent at Greenwich. He may also have been confessor to the queen.

Pole, educated by the Carthusians of Sheen, would have been introduced to the *Imitatio Christi* before he left England in 1532, that is, shortly after the "Whitford" translation appeared in print. In Italy, moreover, the *Imitatio* had been enthusiastically espoused by the Cassinese Benedictines. In Pole's household in Viterbo, established in 1541, it was especially venerated, and its influence was "immense," Pole's intimate, the poet and spiritual writer Marcantonio Flaminio, stating in a letter to Carlo Gualteruzzi that "I can't recommend any book—setting aside the scriptures—that could be more useful to you."[49] For both Pole and Peto, then, this book would have seemed a major desideratum once they were back in England, and it was a natural choice for publication. It was part, in other words, of a calculated policy.[50] It complements neatly, for example, *A bouclier of the catholike fayth* (STC 22816; 1554) written by Richard Smith, whose mission was "not to enstruct the learned in Divinitie, whiche nede not much my teachyng, but to teach the unlearned, to stay and establish the waueryng, to assure and certify the doubtfull of the trouth, to bryng them agayne vnto the trouth of the catholike churche, whiche were disceaued through ignoraunce."[51]

Another book to be reissued in Mary's reign was John Fisher's *This treatyse concernynge the fruytfull sayinges of Dauyd*, printed by Thomas Marshe in 1555 (STC 10908).[52] This survives in multiple copies, one of which has been bound with the only recorded copy of Cawood's 1566 edition of the Peto text, now Washington, Folger Library (STC 23967.5). After Elizabeth came to the throne in 1558, Cawood was replaced as royal printer by Richard Jugge, but he was soon reinstated in conjunction with Jugge. There is no definitive proof of Cawood's religious position in Elizabeth's reign, but he had acquaintances among known Catholics, and his son Gabriel, who succeeded him in his business after his death in 1572, certainly supported recusants. By 1566, publication of the fourth book in particular would have been a dangerous undertaking, and Cawood must have known the risks he was incurring.[53]

In the following year, Henry Denham published a new translation by Edward Hake of the first three books only (STC 23969), which was decidedly Protestant in its orientation.[54] With the elimination of Book Four (as was the case in all Protestant translations), moreover, "the spirituality of the *Imitatio* remained focused entirely upon interior renewal without any allusion to the sacraments."[55] It is just possible that Cawood was aware that the Hake edition was about to appear— "Seene and allowed according to the order appointed," as was stated on the title page—and wished to put forth an edition including the fourth book before it became entirely impossible to do so.[56] Be that as it may, Cawood's edition would have appealed almost exclusively to Catholics, and that the only surviving copy has been placed with Fisher's *Treatise* in a contemporary binding provides evidence for the religious allegiance of the original readership.[57]

In its new Protestant manifestation, the *Imitatio* found a wide market, and Denham commissioned a new version by the religious controversialist and translator Thomas Rogers, which was first printed in 1580 (STC 23973).[58] Neither Hake's nor Rogers's versions were palatable to Catholic readers, of course, and Cawood's former apprentice, the future martyr William Carter, issued a new edition of the "Whitford" translation, including Peto's preface, under a false imprint (that of the 1556 edition) after Cawood's death in 1572 (STC 23967).[59] One of the known surviving copies is found in Lambeth Palace Library, now ZZ1556.1. In this copy, there is an inscription: "Thys is Dorothe Este Booke. Pray for her all that herein dothe loke." There is also some annotation and underlining. Dorothy East was the only daughter and heiress of Edward East of Bledlow, Buckinghamshire. In 1580, she married Thomas Fitzherbert (1552–1640), who had been imprisoned for recusancy in 1572, after he had been at Oxford University (in 1568) and come under the influence of Edmund Campion.[60] Soon after Campion's execution in 1581, Dorothy and her husband prudently migrated to France.

Dorothy died in 1588, and Thomas then moved to Spain and subsequently to Rome, where he was ordained a priest in 1602. In 1615, he joined the Jesuits. Dorothy's copy of *The Folovving of Christ* passed to Richard Bancroft's collection and is found in the inventory of his books drawn up after his death in 1610: "Gersons imitation of Christ. 8°."[61] How it got to Bancroft is not certain—it does not seem to derive from his principal source for printed books, that is, the library of his predecessor as archbishop, John Whitgift—but it was probably left behind when the Fitzherberts migrated to France. The markings make it clear that this was a book that Dorothy treasured greatly, and it is ironic that its subsequent owners were not the individuals whose prayers she desired.

Conclusion

Much has been written about Thomas Cromwell's use of the printing press as an "agent of change" (Elizabeth Eisenstein's term) in the 1530s through the publication of selected works, including *The Defence of Peace*, William Marshall's translation of *Defensor pacis* by Marsilius of Padua, printed by Wyer in 1535.[62] What we see in the case of the *Imitation of Christ* is precisely the same policy, although from the opposite end of the religious spectrum.[63] It is a point articulated very clearly by Pole when he wrote to Bartolomé Carranza, archbishop of Toledo, that "just as people have been corrupted here even more by books than by the spoken word, so they must be recalled to life through the written word."[64]

In 1557, Peto was nominated by Pope Paul IV as a cardinal, and the pope also transferred Pole's legation to Peto, by now a very elderly man. Mary, however, did not wish Pole to lose his legateship, and Peto wrote to the pope rejecting this appointment. He was summoned to Rome later in the year and may have formally resigned his title to the bishopric of Salisbury (to which he had been nominated as early as 1543) shortly before his death, probably toward the end of 1558, while he was still in England. Peto would thus have had no time to continue with his publishing program after 1556, but no doubt he would have wished for those books recommended by More to have been brought out, as well as other books of a similar nature. For Peto and his like, then, the mid-1550s presented a mirror image of the early 1530s, and they were determined to find their way back through the looking glass by means of a concerted program of publication.[65] That there was so little time and so few individuals of the stature of Whitford (who died in the 1540s) to continue the work doomed the attempt—like that of the refoundation of religious houses[66]—to failure in the long run, even if *The folowinge of Chryste* did nourish, as Peto stated it would, select individuals such as Elizabeth Pope and Dorothy East, into whose willing hands it was directed.

When the Bridgettine nun Mary Champney was dying in London in 1580, George Gilbert came to see her, promising to pay for the reprinting of *The Scale of Perfection* "which is *an other* of their bookes as needefull to be renewed for the mendynge of the olde printe" (emphasis added).[67] The parallels with Peto's description of why the *Imitation of Christ* needed to be reprinted are extraordinarily close. Once again, it was books like the ones recommended by More at the beginning of the troubles, then, that kept the Catholic fires burning within the hearts of the recusants and allowed them to maintain their belief that someday England would be brought back into the Roman fold.

Pontifical Institute of Mediaeval Studies, Toronto, and the University of Kent at Canterbury

Pontifical Institute of Mediaeval Studies and York University

Acknowledgments

The original research for this paper was undertaken when we were preparing our chapter for *The Cambridge Companion to Medieval English Mysticism*, ed. Samuel Fanous and Vincent Gillespie (Cambridge, UK: Cambridge University Press, 2011), 225–248. JPC has given two conference presentations on the topic: the first on July 27, 2007, at the Harlaxton Medieval Symposium; and the second on June 11, 2010, at the conference on "Mapping Late Medieval Lives of Christ" at Queen's University, Belfast. AMH has published a related article on "Richard Whitford's *The Pype, or Tonne, of the Lyfe of Perfection*: Pastoral Care, or Political Manifesto?" in *Saint Birgitta, Syon and Vadstena: Papers from a Symposium in Stockholm 4–6 October*

2007, ed. Claes Gejrot, Sara Risberg, and Mia Åkestam (Stockholm: Royal Academy of Letters, History, and Antiquities, 2010), 89–103. We are grateful to Tom Betteridge, Peter Blaney, Tom Freeman, Max von Habsburg, Giles Mandelbrote, Anne Overell, Ryan Perry, Sue Powell, Mark Rankin, Ryan Stafford, and Georgianna Ziegler for their helpful comments on specific and general points. We also thank Lucy Wooding for showing us her essay on "Catholicism, the Printed Book and the Marian Restoration" in advance of publication.

NOTES

1. On More's antiheretical writings, see Thomas Betteridge, *Writing Faith and Telling Tales: Literature, Politics, and Religion in the Work of Thomas More* (South Bend, IN: University of Notre Dame Press, 2013).

2. *The confutacyon of Tyndales answere*, sig. Ee iiir. On this list, see Roger Lovatt, "The *Imitation of Christ* in Late Medieval England," *Transactions of the Royal Historical Society* 5th ser., 18 (1968): 97–98. The case for learned readers was different: these More taught "how to read heresy, to recognize its tricks and wiles, and to spot its baneful effects—the subversion and spoliation of all textual, religious and social boundaries"; Betteridge, *Writing Faith*, 122.

3. This was first printed by William Caxton in 1484 (STC 3259), and there were subsequent editions by Richard Pynson and Wynkyn de Worde, the last of which appeared in 1530 (STC 3267). The next, produced for the recusant market, appeared at Douai ca. 1606 (STC 3268).

4. First printed by de Worde in 1494 (STC 14042). The last sixteenth-century edition was in 1533 (STC 14045).

5. Lovatt, "*Imitation of Christ*," 98. The title of this translation was *The folowynge of Cryste*, whereas the second was printed as *A full deuout and gostely treatyse of the imytacyon and folowynge the blessed lyfe of our moste mercyfull sauyour cryste*. In the introduction to the third translation, it is observed that "some men afferme [the *Imitatio Christi*] was fyrst made and compylyd in latyn by the famous clerke mayster Johan Gerson Chauncellour of Parrys" and, as Lovatt notes, "Since 1483, when the name of Gerson had appeared on the title page of the great Venetian edition of the *Imitatio Christi*, this attribution had secured extensive acceptance"; "*Imitation of Christ*," 98. The authorship is now generally attributed to Thomas à Kempis: see *The Imitation of Christ: The First English Translation of the Imitatio Christi*, ed. B. J. H. Biggs, EETS os. 309 (Oxford and New York: Oxford University Press for the Early English Text Society, 1997), xxx–xxxv. For a general discussion of translations into English, see Maximilian von Habsburg, *Catholic and Protestant Translations of the Imitatio Christi, 1425–1650* (Farnham, UK: Ashgate, 2011), 89–105,

279–282. (Throughout our paper we use the orthography of the particular edition we are citing in our references to the title.)

6. "[I]n dyuers places," so he states, the former "lefte out moche parte of some of the chapytres and somtyme varyed fro the letter." Concerning the latter, he adds, "for as moche as it was translatyd by the sayd noble prynces out of frenche it coulde not folowe the latyn so nyghe ne soo dyrectely as yf it had ben translatyd out of latyn." Atkinson's translation of the first three books was printed by Richard Pynson in 1503, and that of the fourth book in 1504 (STC 23954.7). There were subsequent editions of this version, the last of which, brought out by Wynkyn de Worde and containing the first three books only, was printed in 1528? (STC 23960).

7. See Thomas à Kempis, *Imitation of Christ*, ed. Biggs.

8. On the dating of these two, see P. B. Tracy, "Robert Wyer: A Brief Analysis of His Types and a Suggested Chronology for the Output of His Press," *The Library* 6th ser., 2 (1980): 297–298 (nos. 17–18). See the introduction to Thomas à Kempis, *The Imitation of Christ: From the First Edition of an English Translation Made c. 1530 by Richard Whitford*, ed. Edward J. Klein (New York and London: Harper and Bros, 1941), for a detailed discussion of the sequence of printings of the third translation in general. James Hogg summarizes Klein's arguments and gives his own account of the place of *The Imitation* in Whitford's works in *Richard Whytford's* The Pype or Tonne of the Lyfe of Perfection: *With an Introductory Study of Whytford's Works*, ed. James Hogg, 1/2 (Salzburg, Austria: Institut für Anglistik und Amerikanistik, Universität Salzburg, 1989), 79–99.

9. Thomas à Kempis, *Imitation of Christ*, ed. Klein, xxxviii. On Whitford and this translation, see below.

10. These are taken from the *Revelations,* Book VI, 50, 65, 83, and the conclusion of 41. Richard Rex, "New Additions on Christopher St German: Law, Politics and Propaganda in the 1530s," *Journal of Ecclesiastical History* 59 (2008): 283–284, argues convincingly that the legal writer Christopher St. German (ca. 1460–1540/41) was the translator.

11. Rex points out that both the *Golden Epistle* and the selections from the *Revelations* were pertinent during this period of questioning of aspects of traditional religious life; the revelations chosen by St. German, for example, "concerned the love of God, the active and the contemplative life, the conversion of the infidel, and advice for those planning pilgrimages to the Holy Land"; "New Additions," 283.

12. The text of *The folowyng* ends on a verso with information that it was "Printed at London at Temple Barre by Thomas Godfray. Cum priuilegio a rege indulto" (fol. 167v). On the succeeding unnumbered recto comes Godfray's explanation for printing the added texts; the verso has a woodcut of the "Image of Pity," on which see Edward Hodnett, *English Woodcuts 1480–1535*

(Oxford: Oxford University Press, 1973), no. 2062. The *Golden Epistle* begins on sig. A.iir and is printed in a different font. In spite of the typographical hints that the two texts may originally have been separate, Rex maintains that this translation of the *Golden Epistle* was produced to accompany *The folowyng* and was only later issued separately.

13. The next edition of *The folowing* seems to be that of Robert Redman, ca. 1531, which, poorly typeset, also contains the two supplementary texts along with the introductory justification (STC 23964). Redman reset it ca. 1531 using the same type (STC 23964.3), and then he issued it again ca. 1535 (STC 23964.7).

14. See A. I. Doyle, "Thomas Betson of Syon Abbey," *The Library* 5th ser., 11 (1956): 117–118. According to Doyle, Whitford "displayed a consider-able development of critical sense and taste, worthy of the correspondent of Erasmus, not only in choosing to retranslate 'the golden epistle' almost totally but also by prefixing remarks on its authenticity, and by adapting it rather for general than for specifically religious readers."

15. In his edition of Whitford's *A werke of preparacion, vnto communion, or howsolyng* (London, 1531, STC 25412), Robert Redman printed both ver-sions of the *Golden Epistle* (as well as the excerpts from the *Revelations*), stat-ing "We haue prynted this golden pystle agayn / bycause þe other before is nat of the translation nor edicion of this auctor" (sig. Lviiiv).

16. Matters were made more critical at this time because Anne Boleyn and her circle were actively supporting the dissemination of proto-Lutheran writings in the vernacular.

17. Whitford, *Pype*, fol. 1v. See also his comment concerning the recent ap-pearance of "diuers werkes in latyn sende out openly in prynte agayne all maner of religion" by "the great heretyke Luther with all his discyples" (fol. 3r). In his writings he was providing answers so that his readers would have "some reasons and trouthes redy to auoyde the perylous poyson of suche blaterers" (fol. 3r-v).

18. On this topic see Alexandra da Costa, *Reforming Printing: Syon Abbey's Defence of Orthodoxy, 1525–1534* (Oxford: Oxford University Press, 2012), 94, who argues that the *Pype*, like More's *Confutacyon*, shows a new stage in the confrontation of heresy, by "reveal[ing] the falseness of the evangelicals' arguments directly." Lucy Wooding, "Catholicism, the Printed Book and the Marian Restoration," in *A Companion to the Early Printed Book in Brit-ain 1476–1558*, ed. Vincent Gillespie and Susan Powell (Cambridge: D. S. Brewer, 2014), 308, points out that "A failure to appreciate [the] breadth in religious media has sometimes led to criticism of Catholics for not making sufficient use of the printing press, but in fact the new technology was es-sential to Catholics and Protestants alike."

19. See James P. Carley and Ann M. Hutchison, "1534–1550s: Culture and History," in *The Cambridge Companion to Medieval English Mysticism*, ed.

Samuel Fanous and Vincent Gillespie (Cambridge, UK: Cambridge University Press, 2011), 228–229.

20. See ibid., 236–237. William Wizeman, *The Theology and Spirituality of Mary Tudor's Church* (Aldershot, UK: Ashgate, 2006), 140–141, suggests that there may have been another Franciscan house in Cambridge and that Franciscans returned to Guernsey. He also observes that two former Dominicans became bishops under Mary.

21. Wizeman, who mistakenly states that the fourth book was not printed until 1556, notes that it was particularly suitable in Marian England, where there was a strong emphasis on the Eucharist, with a "growing call for more frequent communion by a number of its leading authors and churchmen"; *Theology and Spirituality*, 34. On the increased sacramental devotion of the Marian Church see also Eamon Duffy, *Fires of Faith: Catholic England under Mary Tudor* (New Haven, CT, and London: Yale University Press, 2009), 192–193.

22. Albert Owen Evans, "Thomas a Kempis and Wales," *Journal of the Welsh Bibliographical Society* 4:1 (1932): 12. See also James Hogg, "Richard Whytford: A Forgotten Spiritual Guide," *Studies in Spirituality* 15 (2005): 136.

23. By his own account, Glanmor Williams was the first to question the attribution to Whitford; "Two Neglected London-Welsh Clerics: Richard Whitford and Richard Gwent," *Transactions of the Honourable Society of Cymmrodorion* 1961, pt 1: 23–44. Williams notes that Cawood's was the earliest edition of *The folowinge* to use Whitford's translation of the *Golden Epistle* and realizes that "Later readers, seeing the ascription of the *Epistola* to Whitford, also attributed, erroneously, the *Imitatio* to his pen"; ibid., 31. In spite of Williams's assertions, David Crane maintains that the attribution to Whitford can be "strongly argued"; "English Translations of the *Imitatio Christi* in the Sixteenth and Seventeenth Centuries," *Recusant History* 13:2 (1975): 95, nn. 7, 11. Likewise, Wizeman accepts the attribution; *Theology and Spirituality*, 33–34. As Hogg points out in *Richard Whytford's The Pype or Tonne of the Lyfe of Perfection*, 98–99, there may be a further complication as a result of Whitford's statement at the end of *The Pype* that "I am required to translate one lytell worke of a great clerke called mayster Iohan Gerson which worke can nat be made redy to be prynted at this tyme" (fol. 237v). On the other hand, Veronica Lawrence observes that there is no evidence that by "one lytell worke" Whitford meant the *Imitatio*; "Richard Whitford and Translation," in *The Medieval Translator* 4, ed. Roger Ellis and Ruth Evans (Binghamton: State University of New York, 1994), 137. Nor do stylistic issues get us very far. Owens, for example, considers it to be the "the *facile princeps* of all English editions … the strength and beauty of Whitford's translation lie in the fact that he had caught rightly the spirit of the original" (Owens, "Thomas a Kempis and Wales," 13), and R[onald] B[ayne] in his

entry for Whitford in the original *Dictionary of National Biography* 61, ed. Sidney Lee (London: Smith, Elder & Co., 1900), 126–27 states that "It is Whitford's most remarkable work, and may claim to be in style and feeling the finest rendering into English of the famous original." Others, such as Williams, take the opposite point of view.

24. See also the title page, which describes the edition as "newly corrected and amended." During the more conservative final years of Henry's reign, William Middleton, who succeeded to Redman's business, published an edition, making corrections as well as introducing new errors (STC 23965). Some of his changes reflect the post-Supremacy religious climate. As Klein points out, "the words *prince* and *bishop* are substituted for *pope*; *purging* or *hell*, for *purgatory*; *spiritual*, for *religious*; *spirituality*, for *religion*"; Kempis, *Imitation of Christ*, ed. Klein, xxxix, n. 1.

25. There are also a few small emendations based on other editions. At fol. 85r, for example, the Cawood edition reads "fulfyllynge in that most specy-ally the *wyll* of thy father," as does the Redman edition (fol. 84r), but Wyer has "wye" (fol. 85r), as does Godfray's edition (fol.79v). In the Cambridge copy of the latter, "way" has been corrected to "will" in a marginal note.

26. Collation of the Cawood edition against earlier texts indicates that in this putative lost edition Wyer must have turned to the second Wynkyn de Worde edition of the *Golden Epistle* (STC 1913) rather than simply replicating his own print (STC 1914) of the Wynkyn de Worde first edition (STC 1912).

27. Klein speculates that "there were other editions that have disappeared altogether . . .one may surmise that there may have been as many as thirteen or fourteen editions of Whitford's translation in the decade before 1541"; Kempis, *Imitation of Christ*, ed. Klein, xxxvi.

28. David Crane makes a similar point when he states that:

> one part of the argument for the attribution to Whitford of this version of the *Imitatio* is its appearance here [in the edition printed in Rouen in 1585 perhaps under the sponsorship of the exiled Bridgettine nuns] with a translation undeniably Whitford's [the *Golden Epistle*], in such a way as to suggest that the whole volume was his work, and in a place where there were many people who would know the truth of the matter.

(Crane, "English Translations," 96, n. 11.) In a slightly different context, J. T. Rhodes notes that texts by Whitford were printed in identical format so they could easily be bound together; "Syon Abbey and Its Religious Publications in the Sixteenth Century," *Journal of Ecclesiastical History* 44 (1993): 24.

29. For examples where he complained about heretical texts having been circulated under his name, see Hutchison, "Richard Whitford's *The Pype*,"

91. Apart from his anxiety to guide readers away from heresy, Whitford also took care to identify his writings out of modesty and concern to let readers know that he was willing to be corrected. As he states in his address "Unto the deuoute readers" at the beginning of *The Pype*:

> Here is somwhat spoken in our commune tonge, that all you may knowe all their false and subtyll deceites, and the rather beware of them. I beseche you applie all vnto the best, and I most mekely do submitte my selfe vuto charitable correction. And that is the veray and only cause (as oft we haue shewed) that we done sette forth our name. The olde wreched brother of Syon, Richarde Whytforde. (sig. A.iv)

30. On Peto, see T. F. Mayer, *Reginald Pole: Prince and Prophet* (Cambridge, UK: Cambridge University Press, 2000), 286, 313–314; also Peter Marshall, "Catholic Exiles," in *Religious Identities in Henry VIII's England* (Aldershot, UK: Ashgate, 2006), 230, 242, 243, 247–248, 250, 251, 255, 259, 261.
31. He also smuggled manuscripts out of England to be published abroad, including perhaps John Fisher's *De Causa matrimonia*, as well as *Parasceve*, a response to *A Glasse of the Truthe*; Marshall, "Catholic Exiles," 230.
32. The London merchant Antonio Bonvisi (1470/5–1558), a close friend of Thomas More's, helped Peto after his sermon and flight abroad. See C. T. Martin, *rev.* Basil Morgan, "Bonvisi, Antonio (1470x75–1558)," in *Oxford Dictionary of National Biography* (Oxford University Press, 2004), http://www.oxforddnb.com/view/article/2860.
33. Quoted in Marshall, "Catholic Exiles," 243.
34. Crane, "English Translations," 96, n. 10, observes that, "An unsupported manuscript note in the British Museum catalogue attributes the new preface to William Peto, later chosen, though not appointed, Papal Legate in England." The note is found in British Library IX. Eng. 126, a copy of a false imprint issued by the recusant printer and former apprentice to Cawood, William Carter, ca. 1575, on which see below.
35. A later hand, simulating black-letter type, has written in pencil on the title page "By Rycharde Whytforde" and "Rycharde Whytforde" after the introduction.
36. "Grinwycensis" in the lower margin of the penultimate page of text.
37. "Grenewychensis" in the lower margin of the final page of text.
38. In a tipped-in note, Reverend Richard Paget, fellow of Magdalen College, Oxford, brother of a later owner of the book, John Paget of Newbury House, Somerset (whose signature is accompanied with the date 1790), suggested

that Peto and Case were the same person, citing Anthony Wood's assertion that Peto took degrees at Oxford under some other name, "which perhaps was Case." There are other ownership inscriptions: "Marie Manxell [Maunsell]" (deleted); "Edward Ragnall his Booke 1642"; "[] Woolmer, Exeter, 1790." One early owner has expunged all references to saints and purgatory and has made a number of substitutions, such as "house" for "cell," "repentance" for "penance," "go to prayer" for "go to masse," and "sacrament" for "sacryfyce." Not surprisingly, the fourth book, particularly chapters 5, 6 and 7 are defaced, with references to mass and consecration, for example, expunged and longer passages entirely crossed out.

39. Among many other bequests, Pope left money to the nuns of Syon and the friars of Smithfield; T. F. T. Baker, "Thomas Pope," in *The History of Parliament: The House of Commons 1509–1558*, ed. S. T. Bindoff, 3 vols. (London: Secker and Warburg for the History of Parliament Trust, 1982), 3:133.

40. In 1578, for example, she was accused of having mass regularly said in her Clerkenwell house, which no doubt is the house where Pope died and which he left to her (*Calendar of State Papers, Domestic, Addit.*, 551). See also *Calendar of State Papers, Domestic, 1547–80, 567* (described as a recusant in 1577); and *Calendar of State Papers, Domestic, 1581–90*, 287 (denies being a recusant in 1585).

41. See Clare Hopkins, *Trinity: 450 Years of an Oxford College Community* (Oxford: Oxford University Press, 2005), 53–55.

42. "spirtu" has been deleted after "gret."

43. The signature has been cropped and all that is now visible are the ascenders for William (or an abbreviation thereof), but before the volume was rebound, Richard Paget was able to read "Peto." An original letter in Latin in Peto's hand is found in British Library, MS Cotton Cleop. E.iv, fol. 11. This appears to have been written much earlier, with a quite different pen and in a different script, but there are resemblances between letter forms.

44. It was not only the conservatives who made use of "Whitford's" translation. As Andrew Hiscock notes:

> In 1545, two years after [Catherine Parr became] queen, *Prayers or medytacions, wherin the mind is stirred paciently to suffre all afflictions here, to sette at naught the vaine prosperitee of this worlde, and alwaie to long for the eveclasting [sic] felicitee: collected out of certayne holy workes by the moste vertuous and gracious Princes Catharine, Quene of Englande, France and Irelande* was published. The first section was ordered into 288 short verses and was followed by another which contained prayers. The first drew substantially upon material from Richard Whitford's translation of *The Imitation of*

Christ by Thomas à Kempis. His translation appeared under the title *The Folwynge of Christ* (1530/31?) and Parr concentrated her attention upon Book Three (chapters 15–50) in which a contemplative's communion with Christ is enacted.

(Andrew Hiscock, "'A supernal liuely fayth': Katherine Parr and the Authoring of Devotion," *Women's Writing* 9:2 [2002]: 184.) See also Katherine Parr, *Complete Works and Correspondence*, ed. Janel Mueller (Chicago: Chicago University Press, 2011), 372, 374–382. Mueller considers that, "Through Parr's systematic selections and alterations, the connotations of spirituality are wrenched from a perceptibly traditional to an emergently Reformist cast"; ibid., 377. Noting the borrowings from *The Imitation of Christ*, John Edwards, on the other hand, maintains that "in the main [Catherine's] devotional collection represented a certain kind of mainstream Catholic spirituality. In this, Mary herself was deeply involved." *Mary I: England's Catholic Queen* (New Haven, CT, and London: Yale University Press, 2011), 230.
45. See Wizeman, *Theology and Spirituality*, 118, who noted that Peto's concern with the Holy Spirit as a guide to doctrine tied in with the manner in which the Marian Church "pursued the direction of Fisher's reprinted 1521 sermon against Luther." (The sermon was reprinted in 1554 [STC 10896] and 1556 [STC 10897].)
46. See Duffy, *Fires of Faith*, 191. Concerning the *Spirituall exercyses and goostly meditacions, and a neare waye to come to perfection and lyfe contemplatyve*, written by Peryn, at the time prior of the London Dominicans, and printed in 1557 (STC 19784), Wizeman observes, "Peryn's *Exercyses* presented to devout religious and laity a series of meditations that he hoped would lead them to union with God through the mediation of an affective relationship with Christ"; ibid., 216.
47. See T. F. Mayer, "Peto, William (c. 1485–1558)," *Oxford Dictionary of National Biography* (Oxford University Press, 2004), http://www.oxforddnb.com/view/article/22043.
48. Pole's agent and Peto's kinsman Michael Throckmorton was also resident in the hospice when he was in Rome. On Throckmorton, see Anne Overell, "Cardinal Pole's Special Agent: Michael Throckmorton, c. 1503–1558," *History* 94 (2009): 265–278. For books he owned, including the *Imitatio Christi*, see M. Anne Overell and James M. W. Willoughby, "Books from the Circle of Cardinal Pole: The Italian Library of Michael Throckmorton," *Journal of the Warburg and Courtauld Institutes* 75 (2012): 111–140. Peto's mother was Goditha Throckmorton, who owned BL, MS Additional 37787 and his aunt was Elizabeth Throckmorton, abbess of the Cambridgeshire house of Poor Clares: see Mary Erler, *Women, Reading, and Piety in Late Medieval England* (Cambridge: Cambridge University Press, 2002), 113-14.

49. Quoted in M. Anne Overell, "Pole's Piety? The Devotional Reading of Reginald Pole and His Friends," *Journal of Ecclesiastical History* 63 (2012): 468. As she points out, "In Pole's households the *Imitation* was often read aloud and his close friend Alvise Priuli tried insistently to introduce the text to others in their circle"; ibid., 467.

50. Likewise, the *Imitatio* was important to Jesuit spirituality: "The privileged place that the *Imitation* enjoyed in the *Exercises* as the only work besides the New Testament and the life of Christ recommended for reading during their course very much inclined them to the book"; John W. O'Malley, *The First Jesuits* (Cambridge, MA: Harvard University Press, 1993), 264. This stands in contrast to the Tridentine and Marian response to Nicholas Love's translation of the *Meditationes vitae Christi* as the *Mirror of the Blessed Life of Jesus Christ*, another of the books recommended by More, which virtually disappeared from sight and was not reprinted during Mary's reign. On other Marian authors apart from Peto who "were prepared to deploy both the wisdom of the past and the rhetorical techniques of their own time to achieve their ends," see Wooding, "Catholicism," 318–321.

51. *Bouchier*, sig. C.viir. Quoted in Wooding, "Catholicism," 318. Our transcription is a diplomatic one.

52. As we observe above, Fisher's 1521 sermon against Luther was also reprinted twice. Like the edition of Thomas More's English works in 1557, these reprints were, Wooding points out, "of great importance for English Catholic identity"; ibid., 319.

53. Although Crane argues (unconvincingly) that Peto's preface could be "just sufficiently interpretable, no doubt, in Protestant terms," he does acknowledge that it was somewhat audacious of Cawood to reprint the Marian edition in Elizabeth's reign; "English Translations," 80.

54. On Denham and Hake, see von Habsburg, *Catholic and Protestant Translations*, 118, 122, 130, 132, 144, 159–162. Robert M. Cummings singles out translations of the *Imitatio* as being "at the centre of an ongoing struggle for the ownership of modern devotional piety"; "Translation of Philosophical Prose in Britain," in *Übersetzung: Ein internationales Handbuch zur Übersetzungsforschung*, ed. Harald Kittel et al., 3 vols. (Berlin and New York: W. de Gruyter, 2004–2011), 3:1826.

55. See von Habsburg, *Catholic and Protestant Translations*, 128. He also notes that apart from the suppression of Book Four, the Protestant translations share the following characteristics: "the removal of all references to monasticism; the exclusion of intercessory prayers to, and veneration of, the saints, and the insertion of a more emphatic Christocentricity; the omission of any references to purgatory; and the presentation of a devotional language more suited to the Protestant reader"; ibid., 128–129.

56. We thank Peter Blayney for suggesting this possibility.

57. The binding is calf, with the initials "E" "K" flanking a gilt fleuron.

58. See von Habsburg, *Catholic and Protestant Translations*, 118–120. As von Habsburg observes, "Rogers's edition of the *Imitatio* was one of the most popular translations of any religious work from the late sixteenth century through to the Civil War"; ibid., 120. In his preface, Rogers pointed out that he had included everything apart from "what might be offensiue to the godlie," i.e., the fourth book in particular.

59. In 1575, Carter and another of Cawood's former apprentices, John Lyon, were recruited by George Gilbert and Stephen Brinkley, members of an association of young Catholics that would be blessed by Pope Gregory XIII in 1580, to establish a clandestine press in London; I. Gadd, "Carter, William (b. in or before 1549, d. 1584)," *Oxford Dictionary of National Biography* (Oxford University Press, 2004), http://www.oxforddnb.com/view/article/4802.

60. See Thomas H. Clancy, "Fitzherbert, Thomas (1552–1640)," *Oxford Dictionary of National Biography* (Oxford University Press, 2004), http://www.oxforddnb.com/view/article/9605.

61. Lambeth Palace Library, LR/F/1, fol. 4v. In preparation for the move of the library to Cambridge during the Commonwealth, a catalogue was drawn up in 1647, and *The Folovving of Christ* was listed in it (Oxford, Bodleian Library, MS Arch. Selden B.5, fol. 35r) but the wrong publication date (i.e., 1561) was given. (The cataloguers misread a Roman V for an X.) After the Lambeth collection reached Cambridge, another catalogue was produced based on the earlier one, often including its errors, as in the publication date of this book; then shelfmarks were added, in this case C zeta 53 (CUL MS Oo.7.51, fol. 43v). The Cambridge shelfmark still survives in ZZ 1556.1, and so it can be definitively identified as the Bancroft acquisition.

62. See William Underwood, "Thomas Cromwell and William Marshall's Protestant Books," *Historical Journal* 47 (2004): 517–539; see also Wooding, "Catholicism," 314.

63. On the importance of the printing press in Mary's reign, see Jennifer Loach, "The Marian Establishment and the Printing Press," *English Historical Review* 101 (1986): 135–148; also Alexandra Walsham, "'Domme Preachers'? Post-Reformation English Catholicism and the Culture of Print," *Past and Present* 168 (2000): 72–123. For an earlier view, now discredited, see J. W. Martin, "The Marian Regime's Failure to Understand the Importance of Printing," *Huntington Library Quarterly* 44 (1981): 231–247. The most recent discussions are found in Duffy, *Fires of Faith*, 57–78; and Wooding, "Catholicism," 317ff.

64. Quoted in Wizeman, *Theology and Spirituality*, 1. Wizeman gives other examples, concluding that "most authors expressed a desire to aid the renewal of the Catholic church in England, and in their dedications stated the belief that their writings would serve this cause"; ibid., 47. See also his "Martyrs

and Anti-Martyrs and Mary Tudor's Church," in *Martyrs and Martyrdom in England, c. 1400–1700*, ed. Thomas S. Freeman and Thomas F. Mayer (Woodbridge, UK: Boydell Press, 2007), 166: "An important part of that attempt [to renew Catholicism in England] was the printing of numerous catechetical, devotional, and polemical works to inculcate and explicate Catholic belief and practice, after twenty years of officially sponsored excoriation."

65. Wizeman points out that "Pole and his fellow adherents of the Catholic faith viewed the production of texts of doctrine, sermon, polemic and piety as essential to the revitalization or recalling to life of Mary Tudor's church, so that it would become an animating force in the life of a people 'corrupted' by heresy"; *Theology and Spirituality*, 1. In Wizeman's view, Marian authors were deeply influenced by the apologists of the 1520s and 1530s.

66. For difficulties in regaining ecclesiastical land, see Ethan Shagan, "Confronting Compromise: The Schism and Its Legacy in Mid-Tudor England," in *Catholics and the "Protestant Nation": Religious Politics and Identity in Early Modern England*, ed. Ethan Shagan (Manchester, UK: Manchester University Press, 2005), 61–65.

67. See Ann M. Hutchison, ed., *The Life and Good End of Sister Marie, Birgittiana* 13 (2002): 77. On the widespread reading of *The Scale of Perfection* by the nuns, see Carley and Hutchison, "1534–1550s," 238.

WORKS CITED

Primary Printed Sources

Bernard of Clairvaux, St. *Epistola de perfectione uitae*. Trans. Richard Whitford. London: Wynkyn de Worde, 1530 (STC 1912). London: Wynkyn de Worde [1531?] (STC 1913). London: Robert Wyer, 1531 (STC 1914). London: Robert Redman, 1531 (STC 25412). London: John Cawood, 1556 (STC 23966). London: John Cawood 1566 (STC 23967.5). London: John Cawood [i.e. William Carter], 1556 [i.e. post 1572] (STC 23967).

———. Trans. [Christopher St German]. London: Thomas Godfray, [1531?] (STC 1915). [London: Robert Redman, 1531?] (STC 23964). [London: Robert Redman, 1531?] (STC 23964.3). [London: Robert Redman, 1535?] (STC 23964.7). London: Robert Redman, 1531 (STC 25412). London: Thomas Godfray [ca. 1535] (STC 1915.5). London: W. Myddylton [1545?] (STC 23965).

Bridget of Sweden, St. *Revelaciones*, VI, 50, 65, 83, 41 (conclusion). Trans. [Christopher St German] London: Thomas Godfray [1531?] (STC 1915). [London: Robert Redman, 1531?] (STC 23964). [London: Robert Redman, 1531?] (STC 23964.3). London: Robert Redman, 1531 (STC 25412). London: Thomas Godfray [ca. 1535] (STC 1915.5).

Fisher, John. *This treatyse concernynge the fruytfull sayinges of Dauyd*. London: Thomas Marshe, 1555 (STC 10908).
Kempis, Thomas à. *Imitatio Christi*. Trans. [Richard Whitford?]. London: Robert Wyer, [1531?] (STC 23961). London: Robert Wyer [1531?] (Bk 4 only) (STC 23962). London: Thomas Godfray, [1531?] (STC 23963). [London: Robert Redman, 1531?] (STC 23964). [London: Robert Redman, 1531?] (STC 23964.3). [London: Robert Redman, 1535] (STC 23964.7). London: W. Myddylton [1545?] (STC 23965). London: John Cawood, 1556 (STC 23966). London: John Cawood 1566 (STC 23967.5). London: John Cawood [i.e. William Carter], 1556 [i.e. post 1572] (STC 23967).
———. Trans. Edward Hake. London: Henry Denham, 1567 (Bks 1–3 only) (STC 23969).
———. Trans. Thomas Rogers. London: Henry Denham, 1580 (Bks 1–3 only) (STC 23973).
The Life and Good End of Sister Marie, ed. Ann M. Hutchison. In *Birgittiana* 13 (2002): 33–85.
More, Thomas. *A dyaloge...touching the pestylent sect of Luther and Tyndale*. London: John Rastell, 1529 (STC 18084).
———. *The confutacyon of Tyndales answere*. London: William Rastell, 1532 (STC 18079).
Smith, Richard. *A bouclier of the catholike fayth of Christes church conteynyng diuers matters now of late called into controuersy, by the newe gospellers*. London: Richard Tottell, 1554 (STC 22816).
Tyndale, William. *An answere vnto sir Thomas Mores dialoge*. Antwerp: Simon Cock, 1531 (STC 24437).
Whitford, Richard. *A werke of preparacion, vnto communion, or howselyng*. London: Robert Redman, 1531 (STC 25412).
———. *The Pype, or tonne, of the lyfe of perfection*. London: Robert Redman, 1532 (STC 25421).

Secondary Sources
Baker, T. F. T. "Thomas Pope." In *The History of Parliament: the House of Commons 1509–1558*, ed. S. T. Bindoff, 3 vols. London: Secker and Warburg for the History of Parliament Trust, 1982, 3:131–134.
B[ayne], R[onald]. "Whitford, or Whytford, Richard (fl. 1495–1555)." In *Dictionary of National Biography* 61, ed. Sidney Lee. London: Smith, Elder & Co., 1900, 125–127.
Betteridge, Thomas. *Writing Faith and Telling Tales: Literature, Politics, and Religion in the Work of Thomas More*. South Bend, IN: University of Notre Dame Press, 2013.

Biggs, B. J. H., ed. *The Imitation of Christ: The First English Translation of the Imitatio Christi*. EETS os. 309. Oxford and New York: Oxford University Press for the Early English Text Society, 1997.

Carley, James P., and Ann M. Hutchison. "1534–1550s: Culture and History." In *The Cambridge Companion to Medieval English Mysticism*, ed. Samuel Fanous and Vincent Gillespie. Cambridge, UK: Cambridge University Press, 2011, 225–248.

Clancy, Thomas H. "Fitzherbert, Thomas (1552–1640)." In *Oxford Dictionary of National Biography*. Oxford University Press, 2004. http://www.oxforddnb.com/view/article/9605.

Crane, David. "English Translations of the *Imitatio Christi* in the Sixteenth and Seventeenth Centuries." *Recusant History* 13:2 (1975): 79–100.

Cummings, Robert M. "Translation of Philosophical Prose in Britain." In *Übersetzung: Ein internationales Handbuch zur Übersetzungsforschung*, ed. Harald Kittel et al., 3 vols. Berlin and New York: W. de Gruyter, 2004–2011, 3:1820–1837.

da Costa, Alexandra. *Reforming Printing: Syon Abbey's Defence of Orthodoxy, 1525–1534*. Oxford: Oxford University Press, 2012.

Doyle, A. I. "Thomas Betson of Syon Abbey." *The Library* 5th ser., 11 (1956): 115–118.

Duffy, Eamon. *Fires of Faith: Catholic England under Mary Tudor*. New Haven, CT, and London: Yale University Press, 2009.

Edwards, John. *Mary I: England's Catholic Queen*. New Haven, CT, and London: Yale University Press, 2011.

Erler, Mary. *Women, Reading, and Piety in Late Medieval England* (Cambridge: Cambridge University Press, 2002).

Evans, Albert Owen. "Thomas a Kempis and Wales." *Journal of the Welsh Bibliographical Society* 4:1 (1932): 5–32.

Gadd, Ian. "Carter, William (b. in or before 1549, d. 1584)." In *Oxford Dictionary of National Biography*. Oxford University Press, 2004. http://www.oxforddnb.com/view/article/4802.

Hiscock, Andrew. "'A supernal liuely fayth': Katherine Parr and the Authoring of Devotion." *Women's Writing* 9:2 (2002): 177–198.

Hodnett, Edward. *English Woodcuts 1480–1535*. Oxford: Oxford University Press, 1973.

Hogg, James. "Richard Whytford: A Forgotten Spiritual Guide." *Studies in Spirituality* 15 (2005): 129–142.

Hogg, James, ed. *Richard Whytford's The Pype or Tonne of the Lyfe of Perfection: with an Introductory Study of Whytford's Works*, 5 vols in 6 parts. Salzburg Austria: Institut für Anglistik und Amerikanistik, Universität Salzburg; 1989.

Hopkins, Clare. *Trinity: 450 Years of an Oxford College Community.* Oxford: Oxford University Press, 2005.

Hutchison, Ann M. "Richard Whitford's *The Pype, or Tonne, of the Lyfe of Perfection*: Pastoral Care, or Political Manifesto?" In *Saint Birgitta, Syon and Vadstena. Papers from a Symposium in Stockholm 4–6 October 2007,* ed. Claes Gejrot, Sara Risberg, and Mia Åkestam. Stockholm: Royal Academy of Letters, History and Antiquities, 2010, 89–103.

Klein, Edward J., ed. *The Imitation of Christ: From the First Edition of an English Translation Made c. 1530 by Richard Whitford.* New York and London: Harper and Bros, 1941.

Lawrence, Veronica. "Richard Whitford and Translation." In *The Medieval Translator* 4, ed. Roger Ellis and Ruth Evans. Binghamton: State University of New York, 1994, 136–152.

Loach, Jennifer. "The Marian Establishment and the Printing Press." *English Historical Review* 101 (1986): 135–148.

Lovatt, Roger. "The *Imitation of Christ* in Late Medieval England." *Transactions of the Royal Historical Society* 5th ser., 18 (1968): 97–121.

Marshall, Peter. "Catholic Exiles." In *Religious Identities in Henry VIII's England.* Aldershot, UK: Ashgate, 2006, 227–276.

Martin, C. T. "Bonvisi, Antonio (1470x75–1558)," rev. Basil Morgan. In *Oxford Dictionary of National Biography.* Oxford University Press, 2004. http://www.oxforddnb.com/view/article/2860.

Martin, J. W. "The Marian Regime's Failure to Understand the Importance of Printing." *Huntington Library Quarterly* 44 (1981): 231–247.

Mayer, T. F. *Reginald Pole: Prince and Prophet.* Cambridge, UK: Cambridge University Press, 2000.

———. "Peto, William (c. 1485–1558)." In *Oxford Dictionary of National Biography.* Oxford University Press, 2004. http://www.oxforddnb.com/view/article/22043.

Mueller, Janel, ed. Katherine Parr. *Complete Works and Correspondence.* Chicago University Press, 2011.

O'Malley, John W. *The First Jesuits.* Cambridge, MA: Harvard University Press, 1993.

Overell, Anne. "Cardinal Pole's Special Agent: Michael Throckmorton, c. 1503–1558." *History* 94 (2009): 265–278.

———. "Pole's Piety? The Devotional Reading of Reginald Pole and His Friends." *Journal of Ecclesiastical History* 63 (2012): 458–474.

Overell, M. Anne, and James M. W. Willoughby. "Books from the Circle of Cardinal Pole: The Italian Library of Michael Throckmorton." *Journal of the Warburg and Courtauld Institutes* 75 (2012): 111–140.

Rex, Richard. "New Additions on Christopher St. German: Law, Politics and Propaganda in the 1530s." *Journal of Ecclesiastical History* 59 (2008): 281–300.

Rhodes, J. T. "Syon Abbey and Its Religious Publications in the Sixteenth Century." *Journal of Ecclesiastical History* 44 (1993): 11–25.

Shagan, Ethan. "Confronting Compromise: The Schism and Its Legacy in Mid-Tudor England." In *Catholics and the "Protestant Nation": Religious Politics and Identity in Early Modern England,* ed. Ethan Shagan. Manchester, UK: Manchester University Press, 2005, 49–85.

Tracy, P. B. "Robert Wyer: A Brief Analysis of His Types and a Suggested Chronology for the Output of His Press." *The Library* 6th ser., 2 (1980): 293–303.

Underwood, William. "Thomas Cromwell and William Marshall's Protestant Books." *Historical Journal* 47 (2004): 517–539.

von Habsburg, Maximilian. *Catholic and Protestant Translations of the* Imitatio Christi, *1425–1650.* Farnham, UK: Ashgate, 2011.

Walsham, Alexandra. "'Domme Preachers'? Post-Reformation English Catholicism and the Culture of Print." *Past and Present* 168 (2000): 72–123.

Williams, Glanmor. "Two Neglected London-Welsh Clerics: Richard Whitford and Richard Gwent." *Transactions of the Honourable Society of Cymmrodorion* 1961, pt 1: 23–44.

Wizeman, William. *The Theology and Spirituality of Mary Tudor's Church.* Aldershot, UK: Ashgate, 2006.

———. "Martyrs and Anti-Martyrs and Mary Tudor's Church." In *Martyrs and Martyrdom in England, c. 1400–1700,* ed. Thomas S. Freeman and Thomas F. Mayer. Woodbridge, UK: Boydell Press, 2007, 166–179.

Wooding, Lucy. "Catholicism, the Printed Book and the Marian Restoration." In *A Companion to the Early Printed Book in Britain 1476–1558,* ed. Vincent Gillespie and Susan Powell. Cambridge, UK: D. S. Brewer, 2014, 307–324.

Four Fragments in the Folger Shakespeare Library

JOSEPH J. GWARA

A notable feature of early English printing is the relatively large number of editions that survive solely in fragments. In 1906, E. Gordon Duff declared that for the fifteenth century, at least fifty-three books printed in England or elsewhere for the English market were known only from scraps recovered from bindings.[1] Over the past hundred years this total has changed very little. The 2009 revised edition of Duff's *Fifteenth Century English Books*, first published in 1917, lists, by my count, forty-nine STC items known only from fragments (mostly removed from bindings), representing about 11 percent of an approximate total of 435 books and broadsides.[2] To this number we should add the eighteen unique fragments of forty-one pre-1501 STC items discovered since the publication of Duff's catalogue, raising the survival rate of such items to about 14 percent.[3]

Comparable statistics exist for the corpus of English printing from 1501 to 1535. My list of unique sixteenth-century Wynkyn de Worde fragments includes ninety-five items, representing more than 12 percent of de Worde's total post-incunabular output, estimated to be 755 books and broadsides.[4] The items printed by de Worde's ex-apprentices and employees show an even higher rate of loss, perhaps because the so-called third generation of English printers was largely engaged in the retail book trade and printed only occasionally. Three of the four books known to have been printed by Hugh Goes, who founded a press in York in 1504, exist only in fragments: STC 1987, 13689.3, and 13829.7.[5] Mutilated fragments of four leaves from STC 11562.7 [*ca.* 1512] are all that survive from the Charing Cross partnership that Goes formed around 1510 with Henry Watson, de Worde's first London apprentice. These items, together with other important early printed fragments, were rescued in the 1930s from the contemporary panel-stamped binding of a 1535 volume in the library of Westminster Abbey.[6] Similarly, of the eleven pre-1525 books printed by (or for) Henry Pepwell, four are fragments of no more than two folios: STC 23154.3 (1519), 170.3 [1520?], 10450.3 (1520), and 25502.5 (Id. Feb. 1523).

In contrast, almost all the books printed by Robert Copland, de Worde's most famous apprentice, survive in at least one complete (or nearly complete) copy. Recently, however, the discovery of a single leaf from a previously unknown edition of a prose romance translated by Copland from the French and printed by him around 1532 (ESTC S123134) suggests that a sizeable amount of his output has been lost.[7] By my calculations, this book alone would account for more than 20 percent of the total number of edition-sheets that Copland printed between 1528 and 1532.[8] Setting aside the fact that many "duplicate copies" of sixteenth-century books survive only as fragments, we must acknowledge the grim reality that binding scraps often constitute the only physical evidence of a once popular edition or text. As such, they can—and frequently do—provide critical insights into the origin and development of the early English book trade.[9]

In the present study, I describe and contextualize four binding fragments of early English printing in the Folger Shakespeare Library. Three were printed by (or for) Wynkyn de Worde between 1525 and 1535; the fourth comes from the Southwark press of Peter Treveris, one of de Worde's competitors. Although most of these fragments derive from books already familiar to scholars, one likely represents a new addition to STC. An analysis of these items casts light on key aspects of textual consumption in the early sixteenth century, revealing how a fairly recent for-profit technology responded to traditional activities like elementary education, private devotion, and public worship. Broadly speaking, these typographical treasures, once considered trash, allow us to piece together a more detailed picture of print culture during a period of profound change in England.

1. Folger Shelfmark: STC 2866

The First Tome or Volume of the Paraphrases of Erasmus vpon the Newe Testament, 2 vols. (London: Edward Whitchurch, 1551). Folio. See Fig. 1.

The Folger catalogue notes that volume 1 of this book is "bound in leather and paste paper over boards" but does not mention that the binding also contains remnants of English printed waste. This waste consists of two fragments—still glued to the inside of both boards but badly damaged by a clumsy attempt to remove them—of STC 18528.5, an edition of *Saynt Nycholas of Tollentyne* printed by Wynkyn de Worde around 1525. This edition, a quarto of eight leaves signed A, is known from only one other copy, likewise a fragment (though more extensive), preserved in the British Library (shelfmark C.40.d.64).[10] The British Library also owns a complete copy of a different edition (STC 18528), fairly close in date (shelfmark C.40.c.15).

In the Folger volume, the remnant covering the inside back board, which occupies an approximate area of 205×125mm, is part of an uncut inner sheet (sigs. A3, 4, 5, 6) with portions of sigs. A5v and A6r visible. The front remnant, by contrast, has only "[h]ad taken vpon" in the upper right-hand corner alongside the gutter margin, with two letters about ten lines down on the opposite side of the gutter: "w" and "s" (?). In STC 18528, the sequence "had taken vpon" occurs at the end of line 31 on sig. A3r (the second line from the bottom), but these words clearly end the first line of a verso in the Folger fragment, probably sig. A3v. This discrepancy suggests a displacement of two lines between STC 18528 and STC 18528.5, a number consistent with other setting differences between the two editions. The Folger fragments thus consist of two separate copies of the inner sheet of STC 18528.5, assuming, of course, the correct imposition of the formes.

The publication of an English hagiographic text about Saint Nicholas of Tolentino in the mid-1520s requires some explanation. An Italian, Nicholas of Tolentino (*ca.* 1245–September 10, 1306) was canonized in 1446, becoming the first Augustinian saint 140 years after his death and 185 years after entering the Order of St. Augustine at the age of sixteen.[11] Aside from his abstinence and severe mortifications, his reputation for holiness was founded on a series of visions—of Christ, the Virgin Mary, Saint Augustine, souls in torment, demons, and so on—all duly recounted in de Worde's pamphlet. Unlike his namesake Saint Nicholas of Myra (Bari), Saint Nicholas of Tolentino was virtually unknown in England except in Augustinian circles. It is likely, therefore, that *Saynt Nycholas of Tollentyne* was intended for the English Augustinians, perhaps a particular community. Circumstantial evidence leads me to think that de Worde's target audience was Syon Abbey, the Bridgettine house in Isleworth that nominally followed the Augustinian rule. Famous for its bookish brand of piety, the abbey embarked on an ambitious publication program of quasi-liturgical and devotional works in the mid-1520s, beginning with a de Worde edition of the Augustinian rule in English (STC 922.3). Although no direct evidence proves that *Saynt Nycholas of Tollentyne* was a Syon Abbey commission, its commercial and religious contexts point to a Syon connection of some kind.

The close working relationship between Wynkyn de Worde and Syon Abbey, especially from 1525 to 1533, is a matter of record. From the 1490s until the mid-1530s (at least), the abbey cultivated the Westminster and London stationers, turning to de Worde as their printer of choice for devotional material.[12] In Table 1, I list all the de Worde books with a Syon Abbey connection, whether explicit or circumstantial.[13] As we can see, several Syon nuns owned copies of de Worde's books, some of which were obviously produced for the abbey (or for high-profile members of the community).[14] De Worde's close ties to Syon Abbey are also suggested by his donation of two books to the brothers' library: one copy each of the 1500 edition of the *Ortus vocabulorum* (STC 13829) and the 1516 edition of the *Nova legenda Anglie* (STC 4601).[15] More important for our present purposes is the comparatively large number of books that de Worde is known to have printed for Syon Abbey between 1525 and 1533, most of which were edited and/ or translated by the Syon brothers Richard Whitford and William Bonde: STC 922.3 (28 Nov. 1525), 17532 (15 Feb. 1526), 6836 (6 Aug. 1527), 922.4 (8 Oct. 1527), 1912 (23 Nov. 1530), 25422 (20 Dec. 1530), 1913 [1531?], 3278 (23 Feb. 1531), 3273.5 (1532), 25421.6 (1532), and 25423 (2 May 1533).[16]

In terms of raw output, in fact, de Worde's only rival for Syon Abbey printing was Robert Redman, who took over Richard Pynson's shop at the Sign of the George in late 1530. Redman issued at least eleven Syon-related editions—primarily of Whitford's works—in the early 1530s, many of which were routinely reprinted: STC 25421.8 [1530?], 23964 [1531?], 23964.3 [1531?], 25412 [1531?], 25421.5 (1531), 25422.5 (19 Aug. 1531), 25421 (23 March 1532), one copy of which was owned by a Syon nun, Eleanor Fettyplace (Bodleian Library, 4° W.2.Th.Seld.), 25423.5 (14 Oct. 1533), 14553 (12 Dec. 1534), one copy of which was owned by a Syon nun, Magdalene Boeria (John Rylands University Library of Manchester, R143800), 25413.7 [1534?], and 20193.5 [1535?].[17]

As scholars have observed, Syon's commercial ties to de Worde probably grew out of an earlier relationship with William Caxton's Westminster printing office, which de Worde moved to London in late 1500 or early 1501 and turned into a highly profitable consortium of former apprentices and employees. A number of Caxton's later books have likely associations with Syon Abbey, the majority reflecting Bridgettine devotional thought and practice.[18] Their publication may have been due to the agency of Lady Margaret Beaufort, mother of Henry VII, who counted Bridgettine intellectuals among her circle of intimates and who commissioned devotional books from the early printers.[19] At the other end of this Syon/Caxton/de Worde publishing axis stood Robert Copland, who also printed books and pious images for Syon Abbey, including *A Deuout Treatyse Called the Tree and .xii. Frutes of the Holy Goost* (STC 13608) and two indulgenced images of pity (STC 14077c.11A, STC 14077c.17A), both of which appeared in the 1528 edition of *The Pomander of Prayer* (STC 25421.2), another book with likely Syon connections.[20]

The large quantity of de Worde items with links to Syon hints at the possibility that more books printed for the abbey have gone unnoticed. Indeed, if we compare the early Bridgettine corpus (1490–1501) with the books that de Worde issued at the height of the abbey's publishing program (1525–1533), we can discern a pattern of reprints pointing to a resurgence of interest in older Bridgettine material: 1) the 1525 edition of *The Medytacyons of Saint Bernarde* (STC 1918); 2) the *ca.* 1529 reissue of the *Vitas patrum* (STC 14507); 3) the *ca.* 1531 edition of *The Abbey of the Holy Ghost* (recently recovered in fragments: ESTC S498386); and 4) the 1526 edition of *The Thre Kynges of Coleyne* (STC 5575).[21] Considering that none of these books except *The Thre Kynges of Coleyne* had been reprinted since the fifteenth century, the timing of de Worde's editions seems meaningful.

By the same token, the post-1524 reprints of Bridgettine "standards"— Nicholas Love's English translation of the *Vita Christi* (STC 3266, 7 Sept. 1525; STC 3267, 8 Feb. 1530), Walter Hilton's *Scala perfectionis* in English (STC 14044, 31 March 1525; STC 14045, 27 May 1533), *The Rote or Myrour of Consolacyon & Conforte* (STC 21337, 23 March 1530), *The Remedy ayenst the Troubles of Temptacyons*, commonly attributed to Richard Rolle (STC 20876.5, *ca.* 1525), and William Atkinson's translation of the *Imitatio Christi* (STC 23960, *ca.* 1528), later reworked by Whitford—suggest that Syon had an enormous literary orbit that encompassed a substantial lay audience.[22] It seems very likely, in fact, that de Worde sold books in bulk to the nuns at Syon Abbey while simultaneously marketing the same titles to lay readers who sought to imitate the community's devotional habits.[23] All too often, however, the connection between de Worde and Syon is circumstantial, based on the probable Bridgettine appeal of a particular text or an isolated ownership inscription in a de Worde book.

In fundamental ways, *Saynt Nycholas of Tollentyne* is typical of the books that de Worde printed for the Bridgettine nuns. Although the text looks like a conventional saint's life, it is actually an English translation of the breviary lessons for the observances devoted to this Augustinian mystic.[24] The book has three sets of six lessons, the first unassigned and the second and third designated "*Feria .ii.*" (sig. A5r) and "*Feria .iii.*" (sig. A6v), respectively.[25] Two final lessons are headed by the rubric "*In translatio sancti Nicolai*" (sig. A8r). This structure indicates that the English Augustinians celebrated the principal feast day of St. Nicholas of Tolentino (September 10) plus the first two weekdays of the Octave with six (of nine) lessons at Matins and that they further observed his Translation with two lessons (of perhaps three or six).[26] The use of the vernacular suggests that the breviary text was translated for an audience unskilled in Latin, perhaps a group of nuns. As we have seen, Syon Abbey's later publishing program included English translations of standard monastic and liturgical works.

The textual pillars of this program, executed by Richard Whitford and John Fewterer with the approval of Abbess Agnes Jordan (abbess 1520–1546), were: 1) Whitford's translation of the Augustinian rule with his own English commentary as well as his English translation of Hugh of St. Victor's *Expositio in regulam beati Augustini* (STC 922.3; repr. STC 922.4); 2) an English version of the Sarum Martyrology as read at Syon (STC 17532); and 3) an English version of the Bridgettine Breviary (minus the Psalms) together with the Masses of Our Lady, accompanied by analysis and commentary (STC 17542).[27] Broadly speaking, these translations gave the sisters access to the liturgical texts that they read daily in Latin but could not understand.[28] As well as making worship intelligible to Syon's female community, the texts offered spiritual counsel and enlightenment, becoming de facto manuals of private devotion and meditation.

The same goal of accessibility via the vernacular can be detected in de Worde's lessons on St. Nicholas. Admittedly, no evidence proves that St. Nicholas of Tolentino was venerated at Syon. His name does not appear in the *Martiloge*, nor was it added to any of the Bridgettine Breviary manuscripts.[29] Nevertheless, it is conceivable that de Worde's text was adapted for the Syon nuns from the Office as used at an Augustinian house that observed his cult.[30] Certainly, the mystical character of St. Nicholas of Tolentino would have appealed to the Bridgettines, and the sisters would likely have appreciated the fact that nearly all of St. Nicholas's miracles—described in lessons 2 to 6 for the second weekday Office (sigs. A6v–A8r)—concern the salvation of women. Equally important, de Worde's work presents St. Nicholas as a "true relygyous keper" (sig. A2r), reflecting the fundamental reformist goals set by Richard Whitford for the Bridgettine sisters in the mid-1520s. In a sense, St. Nicholas is co-opted as the Augustinian exemplar of pure monasticism that Whitford earnestly sought for Syon.[31]

The male counterpart to St. Bridget, St. Nicholas would have provided the abbey's double community with a complementary model of masculine monastic virtue. Like many of Syon Abbey's books, *Saynt Nycholas of Tollentyne* would have appealed to a wider lay audience—perhaps as part of a broad attempt to promote his cult at the abbey—but the presentation of the saint as the embodiment of monastic perfection would have resonated most strongly within a reform-minded Augustinian community fighting allegations of corruption and decay. Whether de Worde's book was actually commissioned by Syon Abbey remains speculative, but the Bridgettines are plausible consumers of such a text at a time when the abbey was promoting its spiritual renewal through the medium of print.

Table 1. Wynkyn de Worde Books with Syon Abbey Associations

STC	Author/Title	Notes
24766 [1492?]	*The Lyf of Saint Katherin of Senis*	1. No direct Syon connection, but Saint Catherine's mystical writings had strong Bridgettine appeal.
		2. De Worde reissue with some sheets reset: STC 24766.3 [1500?].
5065 [1493]	*The Chastysing of Goddes Chyldern*	1. Sidney Sussex College, Cambridge, Bb.2.14, once owned by Edith Morepath and Katherine Palmer, both Syon nuns.
		2. Göttingen University Library, 4° Theol. Mor. 138/53 Inc., once owned by Awdry Daly and Mary Nevell, both Syon nuns.
		3. Possibly issued with STC 24234.
14508 [1493]	Simon Winter, *The Lyf of Saint Ierom*	1. Winter was a Syon brother.
		2. The text is found in two Bridgettine anthologies (Lambeth MS 432, Beinecke MS 317).
15875 [1493?]	[*Horae ad vsum Sarum*]	1. Bodleian Library, Arch.G e.43, exhibiting the Syon Library fore-edge tabs.
		2. Has Hodnett no. 374 (Crucifixion).
24234 [1493]	*This Tretyse Is of Loue*	1. Göttingen University Library, 4 Theol. Mor. 138/53 Inc., once owned by Awdry Daly and Mary Nevell, both Syon nuns.
		2. Possibly issued with STC 5065.
——— [ca. 1493–1494]	[*Horae ad vsum Sarum*]	1. Lambeth Palace Library, 1494.6, possibly owned by Margaret Beaufort.
		2. Contains a separate devotional engraving of Bridgettine origin.
		3. Has Hodnett no. 374 (Crucifixion).
3261 (1494)	*Speculum vite Cristi*, trans. Nicholas Love	1. De Worde reprint of STC 3260 [1490].
		2. Has Hodnett no. 374 (Crucifixion).
		3. Later de Worde editions: STC 3263.5 [1507?], 3264 (4 March 1517), 3266 (7 Sept. 1525), 3267 (8 Feb. 1530).

14042 (1494)	Walter Hilton, *Scala perfeccionis* (English)	1. Cambridge University Library, Inc. 3.J.1.2 [3545], once owned by Katherine Palmer, a Syon nun.
		2. Rosenbach Library, Philadelphia, Inc. H491, once owned by Joan (Joanna) Sewell, a Syon nun.
		3. Printed for Lady Margaret Beaufort.
		4. Later de Worde editions: STC 14043.5 (3 Jan. 1519), 14044 (31 March 1525), 14045 (27 May 1533).
21334 [*ca.* 1494]	*The Rote or Myrour of Consolacyon & Conforte*	1. Later de Worde editions: STC 21335 [1500], 21336 (1511), 21337 (23 March 1530).
		2. STC 21334 and 21335 have Hodnett no. 374 (Crucifixion).
14507 (1495)	*Vitas patrum*	1. John Rylands University Library of Manchester 16111, once owned by Agnes Regent, a Syon nun.
		2. Reissued *ca.* 1529, with some sheets reprinted, for Syon Abbey?
17723 (1495)	Clement Maydeston, [*Directorium sacerdotum*]	1. Maydeston was a Syon author, but it is unclear that the edition was a Syon commission.
		2. Later de Worde editions: STC 17726 [1499], 17728.3 (23 Feb. 1504).
1916 (9 March 1496)	*Medytacions of Saynt Bernarde*	1. Translated by Richard Whitford?
		2. Later de Worde editions: STC 1917 [1498–1499], 1918 (19 Sept. 1525).
		3. Has Hodnett no. 374 (Crucifixion).
5572 [1496]	*The Lyfe of the Thre Kynges of Coleyne*	1. Later de Worde editions: STC 5573 [1499], 5574 (1511), 5575 (1526).
		2. STC 5573 has Hodnett no. 374 (Crucifixion).
13608.7 [*ca.* Sept. 1496]	*Abbey of the Holy Ghost; The Charter of the Abbey of the Holy Ghost*	1. A possible Syon text, found in at least one Bridgettine anthology (Lambeth MS 432).

		2. Later de Worde editions: STC 13609 [1497?], 13610 [1500?], and fragments of a *ca.* 1531 edition.
		2. STC 13609 and 13610 have Hodnett no. 374 (Crucifixion).
787 [1497–1498]	*Ars moriendi*	1. Reprint of STC 786, with likely Syon connections.
		2. Later de Worde edition: STC 788 (1506).
		3. STC 787 has Hodnett no. 374 (Crucifixion).
1978 [1500]	Thomas Betson, *A Ryght Profytable Treatyse*	1. A Syon commission.
		2. Betson was keeper of the brothers' library.
13829 (1500)	*Ortus vocabulorum*	1. One copy donated by de Worde to the brothers' library at Syon Abbey.
14924 [1501]	Margery Kempe, *A Shorte Treatyse of Contemplacyon*	1. A connection to Syon Abbey and Lady Margaret Beaufort has been suggested but not proved.
		2. Has Hodnett no. 374 (Crucifixion).
22557 (1514)	Simon Appulby, *The Fruyte of Redempcyon*	1. The connection to Syon is circumstantial and disputed, but the work seems to have received the abbey's endorsement.
		2. Later de Worde editions: STC 22558 (1517), 22559 (21 May 1530), 22560 (1532).
		3. Another edition by Robert Redman: STC 22559.5 (1531).
4601 (27 Feb. 1516)	*Noua legenda Anglie*	1. One copy donated by de Worde to the brothers' library at Syon Abbey.
4815 (28 Sept. 1519)	Raymond of Capua, *The Orcharde of Syon*	1. A Syon commission.
		2. New York Public Library, Spencer Coll., Eng. 1519, once owned by Elizabeth Stryckland, a Syon nun.
6833 (20 Nov. 1520)	*The Dyetary of Ghostly Helthe*	1. A possible Syon commission.

		2. Later de Worde edition: STC 6836 (6 Aug. 1527).
		3. Both de Worde editions have Hodnett no. 457 (St. Bridget of Sweden).
		4. Editions printed by others: STC 6834 (Henry Pepwell, 15 Nov. 1521), 6835 (Robert Copland for Henry Pepwell, *ca.* 1523).
922.3 (28 Nov. 1525)	Richard Whitford, trans., *The Rule of Saynt Augustyne*	1. A Syon commission.
		2. Later de Worde edition: STC 922.4 (8 Oct. 1527).
		3. Both editions have Hodnett no. 457 (St. Bridget of Sweden).
21471.5 (7 Oct. 1525)	John Ryckes, *The Ymage of Loue*	1. Sixty copies were sold in Syon Abbey (one for each of the sisters?) and an equal number to the public. All were ordered recalled due to their suspect content.
		2. Later de Worde edition (for John Gough): STC 21472 [1532?].
17532 (15 Feb. 1526)	Richard Whitford, trans., *The Martiloge in Englysshe after the Vse of the Chirche of Salisbury / & as It Is Redde in Syon / with Addicyons*	1. A Syon commission.
		2. Has Hodnett no. 457 (St. Bridget of Sweden).
1912 (23 Nov. 1530)	Richard Whitford, ed., *The Golden Pystle*	1. A likely Syon commission. Whitford edited an older text.
		2. Later de Worde edition: STC 1913 [1531?].
		3. Edition printed by Robert Wyer: STC 1914 (1531).
25422 (20 Dec. 1530)	Richard Whitford, *A Werke for Housholders*	1. A Syon commission.
		2. Later de Worde edition: STC 25423 (2 May 1533).

		3. Both de Worde editions have Hodnett no. 457 (St. Bridget of Sweden).
		4. Editions printed by others: STC 25421.8 [1530?], 25422.3 [1531?], 25422.5 (19 Aug. 1531), 25423.5 (14 Oct. 1533), 25425 (8 Nov. 1537), 25425.5 (1537).
		5. STC 25422.5 has Hodnett no. 457 (St. Bridget of Sweden).
3278 (23 Feb. 1531)	William Bonde, *The Pilgrymage of Perfeccyon*	1. A Syon commission.
		2. Edition by Richard Pynson: STC 3277 (1526).
		3. The de Worde and Pynson editions have Hodnett no. 457 (St. Bridget of Sweden).
3273.5 (1532)	Richard Whitford, trans., *The Crosrowe, or A, B, C*	1. A possible Syon commission.
		2. Translated and edited by Richard Whitford.
		3. Edition by Richard Fawkes: STC 3273.3 [1530?].
25421.6 (1532)	[Richard Whitford, ed.,] *The Pomander of Prayer*	1. A possible Syon commission.
		2. Though not the author, Whitford likely edited the text.
		3. Editions by Robert Copland: STC 25421.2 (24 Dec. 1528), 25421.3 (31 Oct. 1530).
		4. The de Worde and Copland editions have Hodnett no. 457 (St. Bridget of Sweden).
		5. Edition by Robert Redman: STC 25421.5 (1531).

2. Folger Shelfmark: STC 12201

Dionis Gray, *The Store-House of Breuitie in VVoorkes of Arithemetike, Containyng Aswell the Soundrie Partes of the Science in Whole and Broken Numbers* (London: John Kingston for William Norton and John Harrison, 1577). Octavo. See Fig. 2.

The Folger catalogue notes that "fragments from [an] unidentified grammatical text of Robert Whittinton [*sic*], possibly printed by de Worde, were moved to [the] end of [the] text when [the] volume was rebound." Although de Worde was unarguably the most prolific printer of Whittington's grammars, these fragments—two halves of a single leaf signed C2, each measuring 141×90mm (trimmed)—actually come from a quarto edition of Whittington's *Verborum praeterita et supina* printed by Peter Treveris around 1531 (STC 25566.7).[32] Five copies of this edition are reported in collections in Great Britain and the United States: 1) British Library, C.122.d.15 (lacks G6); 2) Bodleian Library, Douce WW 73/2; 3) Cambridge University Library, Sel. 5.153/1 (lacks G3–6); 4) Henry E. Huntington Library, 61700; and 5) University of Illinois Library, IUA13093. The two fonts employed in the book—a 93mm roman and a 54mm rotunda with s³—were introduced in 1527 (STC 15574, 25489.7), providing a reliable *terminus post quem*. The date of printing, however, cannot be refined on the basis of the book's typography alone, since Treveris used the same types continuously until 1532.

Aside from its bibliographical significance, the Folger fragment is a tangible reminder of the feud that erupted between Treveris and de Worde over the printing of Robert Whittington's Latin grammars, a corner of the market that de Worde had dominated since 1510. For the first few years of his short printing career (1525–1532), Treveris appears to have collaborated with de Worde, borrowing material from him until about 1530.[33] That year, however, their relationship soured, evidently because Whittington had decided to employ Treveris as his contract printer. As illustrated in Table 2, de Worde's production of Whittington grammars declined significantly in 1530, coming to a sudden halt in 1532. Between 1530 and 1532, in contrast, Treveris issued twice as many Whittington editions as de Worde, a surprising statistic given the huge quantity of Whittingtons that de Worde had printed throughout the 1520s.[34] Doubtless de Worde blamed Treveris for poaching his best-selling author, but the elder London printer eventually regained Whittington's custom. In 1533, the year after Treveris ceased printing, de Worde issued eleven Whittington grammars, three of which contain prefatory material by Whittington—in both prose and verse—denouncing Treveris for his ignorance and carelessness (STC 25477, 25493.3, 25507.5). From Whittington's side of the story, then, it would appear that he and Treveris had their own falling-out over the German's shoddy workmanship.[35]

Ironically, historical circumstances would make this dispute seem like a schoolyard scuffle. Around 1540, Henry VIII authorized a national Latin grammar derived mostly from the work of William Lily; he simultaneously barred the publication of all other elementary Latin textbooks, including those of Robert Whittington.[36] In this historical context, the rivalries among de Worde, Treveris, and Whittington—put on ugly display less than a decade before—come across as trivial and shortsighted. The newly adopted Lily grammar meant that all Whittingtons, no matter who printed them, became obsolete virtually overnight. Many copies ended up in the hands of binders, who used them to fabricate boards and flyleaves, exactly as illustrated by the fragments discussed here.

Table 2. Editions (and Reissues) of Whittington's Works Printed by Wynkyn de Worde, 1521–1535; Peter Treveris, 1525–1533; and Richard Pynson, 1521–1529

Date	De Worde	Treveris	Pynson
1521	17	—	1
1522	12	—	3
1523	6	—	7
1524	11	—	1
1525	9	0	4
1526	6	0	1
1527	9	3	3
1528	4	2	0
1529	8	4	0
1530	1	3	—
1531	4	7	—
1532	0	0	—
1533	11	0	—
1534	1	—	—
1535	0	—	—

3. Folger Shelfmark: STC 19906

William Langland, *The Vision of Pierce Plowman* (London: Richard Grafton for Robert Crowley, 1550). Quarto. See Fig. 3.

The Folger catalogue describes the flyleaves of this volume as "Latin printed music." More specifically, these two fragments (192×270mm), representing a single folio leaf cut in half horizontally and folded once to make two conjugate pairs of quarto flyleaves, comprise sig. r1 (f. 129) of STC 15863: *Graduale secundum morem et consuetudinem preclare ecclesie Sarum* (Paris: Nicolas Prévost for Wynkyn de Worde, John Reynes, and Lewis Suethon [Sutton], 17 Cal. Jan. 1527). The upper portion of the recto contains the end of the mass for Rogation Monday, including the last two staves of music for the Offertory *Confitebor Domino*, a rubric for an optional sermon, and the Communion *Petite et accipietis*. This section is immediately followed by a long rubric with instructions for the procession and mass on Rogation Tuesday. The mass for the Vigil of the Ascension (Wednesday of the Rogation days) is then given as follows: 1) Introit *Omnes gentes* (verse: Psalm 46:4); 2) a rubric for the Collect *Presta quaesumus*, for Memorials of the Virgin and All Saints, and for the New Testament Epistle *Multitudinis* (Acts 4:32–35); 3) an Alleluia and (sig. r1v) versicle; 4) a rubric for the Gospel Lesson *Sublevatis* (John 17:1–11); 5) Offertory *Viri galilei*; 6) a prompt for the ferial preface; and 7) the first three staves of the Communion *Pater cum essem* (which ends at the top of sig. r2r). The music corresponds precisely to that in the *Liber usualis*.[37]

According to STC, two complete or nearly complete copies of this edition are known, one in Christ Church, Oxford (Arch. Inf. Subt. K.2) and the other in the Bodleian Library, Oxford (Gough Missals 35). From my notes, I can also report the existence of fragments in two British institutional collections: 1) Bodleian Library, 5 delta 285(6), sigs. F4, 6, 7, 9; and 2) Westminster Abbey Library, Printed Fragment 23, seventeen substantially complete folios (sigs. p1–3, p6–8, q2–7, D1–2, E7–8, F1) plus one fragment removed from an octavo binding (part of sig. F7).[38]

As illustrated by this gradual, the early English printers rarely printed the large Sarum service books, a part of the English book market dominated by foreigners. With the notable exception of Richard Pynson—who printed a two-volume edition of the Sarum Breviary in 1507 (STC 15806a, 15807), a Sarum Manual in 1506 (STC 16140), four editions of the Sarum Missal between 1500 and 1520 (STC 16173, 16179, 16190, 16202), and two editions of the Sarum Processional in 1501–1502 (STC 16232.6, 16232.8)—England's resident printers almost invariably outsourced such books to printing houses on the Continent, generally in Paris.[39] Competition aside, technical limitations explain the practice. A book like STC 15863, in addition to its huge size (300 leaves of Royal paper), required the intricate setting of music and text (the latter in various fonts) plus printing in two colors.[40] Although de Worde routinely produced two-color printing, he is not known to have printed music except in an improvised form and in an isolated typographical context (STC 13439, sig. n5r).[41] A gradual, in short, would have pushed de Worde's resources far beyond their limits, and it is clear why he engaged a Paris press to produce this imposing book.

In farming out STC 15863 to Nicolas Prévost, de Worde was following in the footsteps of William Bretton, who in 1507–1508 commissioned a Sarum Gradual from Wolfgang Hopyl in Paris, partnering with the London booksellers Henry Jacobi and Joyce Pelgrim (see Table 3).[42] How Bretton divided the expenses and profits with his partners is unknown, but he was heavily involved in their sprawling business, presumably as an investor, until 1514. Twenty years later de Worde followed a similar investment model, splitting the costs and profits of his gradual with the booksellers John Reynes and Lewis Sutton, both established figures in the London book trade.[43] The practice was likewise adopted by François Regnault, who partnered with the London printer-bookseller Robert Redman in marketing STC 15865 (1532), the last Sarum Gradual printed before the Reformation.

That de Worde chose Prévost as the printer of his gradual comes as no surprise. Prévost was Hopyl's son-in-law, and he inherited the family business, along with its reputation for producing high-quality liturgical books, after 1522. Perhaps de Worde also knew of Prévost through his long-standing Paris contacts. At least eleven books bearing de Worde's name were actually printed for him in Paris, including editions of the York Manual, Sarum Breviary, and Sarum Missal: STC 16169 (2 Jan. 1497), 23885.3 (15 July 1504), 15805.5 (17 Jan. 1506), 15806 (11 Cal. July 1507), 16182a.5 (27 April 1508), 15808 (11 Kal. Jan. 1509), 16160 (4 Id. Feb. 1509), 1966 (22 Aug. 1511), 16189 (6 Kal. May 1511), 23427a.3 (4 Non. April 1511), and 24827.5 [ca. 1525]. In the end, though, the success of STC 15863 was short-lived. The Reformation saw the mutilation or outright destruction of countless liturgical books. For many, copies of de Worde's magnificent commission became, like the Folger fragment discussed here, nothing more than waste paper.

Table 3. Sarum Graduals Printed for the English Market

STC	Printer	Notes
15862 (4 Id. April 1507; 1508)	Paris: Wolfgang Hopyl for William Bretton	Sold in London by Henry Jacobi and Joyce Pelgrim.
15863 (17 Cal. Jan. 1527)	Paris: Nicolas Prévost for Wynkyn de Worde, John Reynes, and Lewis Sutton	De Worde was presumably the principal investor.
15864 (6 Cal. July 1528)	Paris: Nicolas Prévost for Franz (Francis) Birckman	Sold in London by Birckman.

15865 (6 Cal. July 1532)	Paris: Nicolas Prévost for François Regnault	Sold in London by Robert Redman and in Paris by Regnault. The last Sarum Gradual printed before the Reformation.

4. Folger Shelfmark: STC 3803 copy 1

John le Breton, *Britton* (London: Robert Redman, 1533?). Octavo. See Fig. 4.

The Folger catalogue reports that this book's sixteenth-century London binding now has its original endpapers bound in at the back: "leaves E1, 2, 7 & 8 from a Primer."[44] More precisely, these leaves—all silked, evidently in 1955, when the book was rebound and conserved—come from an unfoliated twenty-line octavo edition of an intercalated Sarum Book of Hours printed in or after 1525 by Wynkyn de Worde. The leaves measure 144×94/95mm. The text, which occupies a printed area of 112×76mm, is printed in black in one of de Worde's two Great Primer fonts, a 112mm textura, with headlines, rubrics, and Lombard initials in red. Also printed in red are three four-line stanzas of English verse (E1v, E2r, E8v), all set in Duff 8, a 95mm textura. Given that this fragment is unknown to scholarship and possibly a new addition to STC, I provide a complete description of its structure and contents:

> E1r: End of Prime/Hours of the Virgin (ll. 1–20)
> 1. ll. 1–5. Antiphon: *O admirabile.*
> 2. ll. 5–10. Chapter: *In omnibus requiem.*
> 3. ll. 10–19. Responsory.
> 4. ll. 19–20. Collect: *Concede nos famulos tuos.*
> 5. l. 20. Rubric for Prime/Short Hours of the Cross.
> *Notes:* No illustrations. The antiphon and chapter confirm Sarum Use.
>
> E1v: Prime/Short Hours of the Cross (ll. 1–14). Beginning of Prime/Hours of the Compassion of Our Lady (ll. 15–20)
> 1. ll. 1–4. English verse (in red):
>
> ¶How Iesu Chryst was taken at pryme
> And before Pylate bounden presented
> Whiche in hym founde no maner cryme
> Although that he was straytly examined.
>
> 2. ll. 5–10. Hymn: *Hora prima ductus est iesus ad pylatum,* accompanied by a five-line woodcut illustration of the Betrayal (Hodnett no. 559, from

26×20mm series).
3. ll. 11–13. Versicle and response.
4. ll. 13–14. Collect: *Domine iesu xpe.*
5. ll. 15–19. Hymn: *Hora prima domina videns,* for the Hours of the Compassion of Our Lady.
6. ll. 19–20. Versicle, followed by rubric for response.

E2r: End of Prime/Hours of the Compassion of Our Lady (ll. 1–3). Beginning of Terce/Hours of the Virgin (ll. 3–20)
1. ll. 1–2. Response.
2. ll. 2–3. Collect: *Domine sancte iesu fili.*
3. l. 3. Rubric for Terce/Hours of the Virgin.
4. ll. 4–7. English verse (in red):

¶How an aungell appered in the morne
Syngynge (Gloria in excelsis deo)
Sayenge the sone of god is borne
Ye shepeherdes to Bethleem ye may go.

5. ll. 8–14. Opening versicle and response, accompanied by a nine-line illustration (metal-cut) of the Annunciation to the Shepherds (Hodnett no. 626, from 47×32mm series).
6. ll. 14–15. Hymn: *Veni creator spiritus.*
7. ll. 15–16. Antiphon: *Quando natus es,* followed by the rubric for Psalm 119.
8. ll. 16–20. Beginning of Psalm 119.

E2v: Continuation of Terce/Hours of the Virgin (ll. 1–20)
1. ll. 1–10. Conclusion of Psalm 119.
2. ll. 10–20. Beginning of Psalm 120.
Notes: No illustrations. Lacking E3–6, containing the conclusion of Terce/Hours of the Virgin, all of Terce/Short Hours of the Cross and Terce/Hours of the Compassion of Our Lady, plus Sext for all three offices.

E7r: None/Hours of the Virgin (ll. 1–20)
1. ll. 1–9. Opening versicle and response, accompanied by a nine-line illustration (metal-

cut) of the Presentation in the Temple (Hodnett no. 628, identified as the Circumcision, from 47×32mm series).
2. ll. 9–10. Hymn: *Veni creator spiritus.*
3. l. 10. Antiphon: *Germinavit*, followed by the rubric for Psalm 125.
4. ll. 10–20. Beginning of Psalm 125.

E7v: Continuation of None/Hours of the Virgin (ll. 1–20)
1. ll. 1–5. Conclusion of Psalm 125, followed by the rubric for Psalm 126.
2. ll. 5–19. Psalm 126, followed by the rubric for Psalm 127.
3. ll. 19–20. Beginning of Psalm 127.
Note: No illustrations.

E8r: Continuation of None/Hours of the Virgin (ll. 1–20)
1. ll. 1–11. Conclusion of Psalm 127.
2. ll. 11–14. Antiphon: *Germinavit.*
3. ll. 14–18. Chapter: *Et radicavi.*
4. ll. 19–20. Beginning of responsory.
Notes: No illustrations. The antiphon and chapter confirm Sarum Use.

E8v: Conclusion of None/Hours of the Virgin (ll. 1–6). Beginning of None/Short Hours of the Cross (ll. 6–20)
1. ll. 1–5. Conclusion of responsory.
2. ll. 5–6. Prayer: *Concede nos famulos tuos*, followed by the rubric for None/Short Hours of the Cross.
3. ll. 7–10. English verse (in red):

¶A[t] the houre of none Chryste his lyfe lefte
And to his father his soule he behyght
Graues opened / the temple veyle clefte
The erth shoke / the sonne lost his lyght.

4. ll. 11–17. Hymn: *Hora nona*, accompanied by a six-line woodcut illustration of the Crucifixion

(Hodnett no. 603 or 604, from 32×25mm series).
5. ll. 17–18. Versicle and response.
6. ll. 19–20. Prayer: *Domine iesu christe.*

As indicated in Table 4, twenty Sarum Books of Hours printed by de Worde have survived for the thirty-five-year period from 1493 to 1528.[45] Since six editions are known only from fragments and almost all the others exist in unique copies, it is safe to assume that many other de Worde primer editions have disappeared without trace. The Folger fragment is most closely related to one of several items catalogued under STC 15932.5, an assortment of fragments—six sheets and two half-sheets—representing three or more octavo editions recovered from a binding at the College of Arms (see Table 4 for details).[46] One of these sheets, fortuitously, consists of E1, 2, 7, 8 with the same material as the Folger fragment but in a different typesetting (see Fig. 5). The English verse is printed in black with red paraphs (instead of red with black paraphs), but otherwise the text and illustrations are identical. Both the Folger and College of Arms fragments date from 1525 or later, but the order of the editions remains unclear. Given the state of the surviving copies, we can only be certain that the Folger fragment does not come from any of the first three editions listed under STC 15932.5 in Table 4. It may belong, however, to one of the editions represented by the remaining three full sheets or the two half-sheets, assuming that these fragments do not themselves derive from the three variously signed E and F.

In the absence of complete information about STC 15901.5 (which I have not examined), the characteristics of de Worde's later octavo primers must be extrapolated from STC 15898 as collated with the quartos and duodecimos. A comparison of the Folger fragment with these sources shows that both the choice and the order of the intercalated texts in the Little Office of Our Lady (i.e., each of the daily Offices followed by the corresponding Office from the Short Hours of the Cross and the Hours of the Compassion of Our Lady) conform to the model used in de Worde's shop from at least 1493–1494, the date assigned to the reprint of STC 15875 in Lambeth Palace Library.[47] In every edition, considerations of space must have guided editorial decisions about abbreviation, layout, and decoration. The octavo fragments, for example, have only the incipits to the hymns and collects—at least for the three Short Hours that survive (Prime, Terce, and None)—whereas STC 15898 (and the Lambeth Palace reprint of STC 15875) gives the collects in full but supplies only the incipits when the hymns are repeated. After 1502, evidently, the octavos provided only the incipits following the first full citation of the recurrent hymns and collects, a pattern seen in STC 15919. By contrast, all the quartos and one of the duodecimos (STC 15936) print the full text of both the hymns and collects.

Another form of compression in the octavos concerns the layout of the Psalms. In the small format editions (and the Lambeth Palace incunable), the verses of the Psalms are continuous, with a red Lombard capital or ornamental initial marking the beginning of each. STC 15898 and the duodecimos follow this basic pattern, but the post-1500 quartos start each verse on a separate line and add ornamental fillers when necessary—a more luxurious use of the space.

The choice of illustrations in the primers necessarily reflects the limitations of the books' format, but the octavos manage to a certain extent to replicate the visual impact of the quartos by pairing medium-sized cuts with a Great Primer font. The two octavo illustrations from de Worde's 47×32mm metal-cut series (Hodnett nos. 626 and 628) are documented in three other primers, STC 15898, 15908.5, and 15919, all of which incorporate additional cuts from the same set.[48] In STC 15919, a duodecimo, nine of the twelve illustrations come from the 47×32mm series (Hodnett nos. 624–632); they introduce each of the Hours of the Virgin and the Seven Penitential Psalms. None of the cuts from this set, however, makes an appearance in the later duodecimos—STC 15936 and, by inference, STC 15941—which take all but one of their illustrations from de Worde's smaller and less sophisticated French *Horae* border series (Hodnett nos. 539–622).[49] Since the duodecimos are also set in de Worde's 53mm textura, they convey a greater sense of economy than the octavos, whose traditional Great Primer font exaggerates the scale of the otherwise mid-sized illustrations. Of course, the quartos, capable of accommodating full-page cuts, ornamental borders, and a profusion of smaller images and decorative initials, remained the gold standard for printed Books of Hours. De Worde filled this market niche until at least 1526 (STC 15948).

The Folger and College of Arms fragments differ from de Worde's other primers in their incorporation of English quatrains before each of the Hours of the Virgin and Short Hours of the Cross. The quatrain accompanying Terce for the Hours of the Virgin describes the Annunciation to the Shepherds, the Gospel event conventionally associated with that Office. In a sense, the stanza serves as a caption to the illustration. By contrast, the quatrains for the two surviving Hours of the Cross (Prime and None) appear to be either approximate translations of stanzas 2 and 5 of *Patris sapientia veritas divina*, the hymn on which the Short Hours are based, or translations of an unidentified adaptation of the same hymn.[50] The exact source and diffusion pattern of these English quatrains remain unclear, but the de Worde fragments allow us to propose a series of working hypotheses. As Mary C. Erler pointed out in 1984, the Parisian printer-publisher François Regnault started issuing primers for export to England in early 1526.[51] He began with three editions in quick succession—STC 15943 (11 Jan. 1526), 15944 (1 March 1526), and 15945 (17 March 1526)—and followed up with at least four more a year later: STC 15949 (17 March 1527), 15950–52 (27 June 1527), 15954 (10 Oct. 1527), and 15955 (13 Dec. 1527).[52] Erler explains that beginning with STC 15954, Regnault headed each of the Hours of the Virgin with an English quatrain, a feature that appeared in all the primers that he later printed for English readers.[53] Regnault's likely model for these verses, according to Erler, was a French primer like STC 15943 (11 Jan. 1526), which contains a handful of four-line stanzas in French.[54]

The information in Table 5 shows that English quatrains first appeared in Continental Sarum Primers no later than October 10, 1527 (STC 15954), and probably no earlier.[55] The use of such verse is fairly extensive. Stanzas figure in many core sections of the primer—the Calendar, Gospel Lessons, Hours of the Virgin, Short Hours of the Cross, Seven Penitential Psalms, and Office of the Dead—although not consistently in every edition. For instance, the first Regnault primer to include English quatrains for all the Short Hours of the Cross is STC 15955 (13 Dec. 1527). For our present purposes, however, the most important observation is that the three surviving quatrains in de Worde's octavo fragments belong to the same textual tradition as those in Regnault's primers.[56] Given that de Worde's last dated Book of Hours (STC 15948) does not include the English verse, we can deduce that the quatrains became part of the vulgate Sarum primer text between 4 Non. August 1526, when STC 15948 was completed, and late 1527, when Regnault published STC 15954 and STC 15955.

Pending the determination of a more accurate date for the octavo fragments, we cannot credit de Worde or Regnault with this innovation, but the fragments raise the possibility that Regnault copied a lost de Worde primer from 1526 or 1527 that contained the verse in question. Judging from STC 15957 (2 Sept. 1528) and STC 15958 [1528]—the first non-Regnault primers to incorporate the same English quatrains—it took about six months for other printers to plagiarize the textual innovations of their competitors. Hence, if Regnault had obtained a de Worde primer with the English verse in late 1526 or early 1527, he would have had plenty of time to integrate its stanzas into his own primer text, adding them gradually to successive editions of the work.

At the same time, no stretch of the imagination is required to believe that de Worde copied his English verses from Regnault. I agree with Erler that the ultimate source of the English quatrains is probably French and that STC 15943 (11 Jan. 1526), Regnault's first known attempt at a Sarum Primer, offers an approximate model.[57] This unusual primer has Latin quatrains in the Calendar, the Hours of the Virgin (except Matins and Prime), and the Short Hours of the Cross (except None) in addition to four Latin and three French quatrains in the Seven Penitential Psalms and nine Latin and two French quatrains in the Office of the Dead. With its mix of Latin and French verse, STC 15943 seems to preserve an intermediate stage in the development of the primer text in which Latin verse was being gradually adapted into French quatrains. (The adaptation would have had to have been extremely liberal, as the later English quatrains have very little in common with the Latin.) Toward the end of 1527, this French verse would have been fully translated into English, appearing in Regnault's primers in October and December. Yet the random appearance of French quatrains among a series of Latin stanzas could also suggest that Regnault was plundering a different source with all French verse—perhaps a *Horae* of Paris Use—to supply occasional lacunae in STC 15943. We cannot rule out the possibility, therefore, that the English quatrains ultimately derive from a common French source used independently by both Regnault and our anonymous English versifier.

A final consideration lends weight to the hypothesis that the English quatrains traveled from London to Paris, though not necessarily from de Worde directly to Regnault. As Erler points out, Regnault included Robert Copland's *Maner to Lyue Well*, a twelve-hundred-word devotional treatise, in all his primer editions beginning in 1529 (STC 15961.3).[] Similarly, Yolande Bonhomme, widow of the Paris printer Thielman Kerver, had incorporated Copland's *Psalter of Jesus*—STC 14563 (1529)—into a primer by August 1532 (STC 15978). Clearly, then, Copland's short devotional translations had become popular additions to the Latin texts of the Sarum Primer on the Continent.

This coincidence leads me to think that Regnault may have plagiarized his English verse from a Copland book. Admittedly, Copland could have worked on commission for de Worde, supplying his former master with English quatrains for a new line of octavo primers; in this case, Regnault could have obtained Copland's verse indirectly, via de Worde.[59] It is no less feasible, however, that Copland wrote the English verses for his own devotional pamphlets, miniature books like STC 14552.7 [1533?], a rhymed life of Christ with woodcut images and verse captions.[60] Under these circumstances, both de Worde and Regnault could have obtained their English verse from a common source—a lost Copland book published around 1526. Whatever the case, Copland's source for the quatrains would have been a text with all French verse. Strictly a translator of French, Copland is unlikely to have tackled the Latin verse in STC 15943. As the Folger and College of Arms fragments show, therefore, the textual transmission of the primer quatrains is far less straightforward than previously suspected. These scraps offer new evidence about the competition between London and Paris to supply English readers with primer material in the vernacular when Latin was under assault as the predominant language of private devotion.

Table 4. Sarum Primers Printed by Wynkyn de Worde

Note: Items marked with an asterisk (*) have not been examined.

STC	Format/Collation	Notes
15875 [1493?]	4°: A⁶a–t⁸v⁶	1. Copies: 1) British Library, IA.55260 (gathering A only); 2) Bodleian Library, Arch. G e.43 (lacks a8, c3–4, f7, g7, i8, l6, o3, p4–5, v6); 3, 4) Cambridge University Library, Inc. 4.J.1.2 [3570, 3571] (both imperfect).
		2. 22 ll. per page.
15876 [1493?]	4°: [ ]⁶a–t⁸v⁶ [?]	1. Copy: British Library, IA.55169 (lacks gatherings a–b, q–v; 1, 6 [?] of calendar; c1, c3–6, c8, g1, g6–8, i1–2, i7–8, k1, o3, o6, p4, p7–8).
		2. 22 ll. per page.
——— [ca. 1493–1494]	4°: A⁶a–t⁸v⁶	1. Copy: Lambeth Palace Library, 1494.6.
		2. This edition was apparently printed after STC 15876. The calendar is in the same typesetting as STC 15875, but the rest of the book is a paginary reprint of STC 15875.
		3. 22 ll. per page.
		4. *Equivalent text:* c8r4–d1v18, d5v1–d7r4.
15878 [1494?]	8°: ?	1. Copy: Corpus Christi College, Oxford, Φ.c.1.3 (y1–2, y7; fragments of y3–4, y6; stubs of y5, y8).
		2. 17 ll. per page.
		3. *No equivalent text.*
15898 (1502)	8°: a⁸A⁶B–T⁸V⁶ [?]	1. Copy: Bodleian Library, Arch. G e.39 (lacks gathering A; a1, a3–7).
		2. 26 ll. per page.
		3. Other copy: Corpus Christi College, Oxford, WP.iii.29(1) (fragments of H5–6 only).
		4. *Equivalent text:* D3v20–D5r16; D8r9–E1v1.

15899 (31 July 1503)	4°: a⁸b⁶A⁶B–S⁸2a⁶	1. Copy: British Library C.41.e.8 (lacks B8, O3). Gathering 2a is an appendix with the Office of the Holy Name of Jesus.
		2. *Equivalent text*: C5v2–C7r6; D2r1–D3r25.
15901.5 [*ca.* 1503]*	8°: ?	1. Copy: Lincoln Cathedral Library, RR.5.32 (lacks first A1).
		2. Printed on vellum in de Worde's 112mm Great Primer font.
		3. 26 ll. per page.
15908 [1508?]	8°: ?	1. Copy: Cambridge University Library, Rit.d.350.5 (four leaves plus fragments of four others only: parts of the calendar, the four Gospel lessons, and a prayer to the Holy Trinity beginning "*Auxiliatrix sis*").
		2. 19 ll. per page.
		3. *No equivalent text.*
15908.5 (1510)	4°: a⁸A⁶B–X⁸; A–B⁸C⁶	1. Copy: British Library, C.123.d.32 (D3–6 in manuscript with hand-stamped illustrations; C1 and ²B8 mutilated). The collation assumes that a2 and a4 are mis-signed a1 and a3. It is possible, however, that the calendar was printed separately and inserted into a fold, as follows: π² (π1+a⁶).
		2. *Equivalent text*: D7r2–D8v18; E4r17–E6r5.
15914 (1513)	4°: a⁸A⁶B–X⁸; A–B⁸C⁶	1. Copy: British Library, C.35.e.7 (lacks gatherings B–G; a1, 8). The collation assumes that a2–4 are mis-signed a1, a2, and a3. It is possible, however, that the calendar was printed separately and inserted into a fold, as follows: π² (π1+a⁶).
		2. *No equivalent text.*
15919 (24 July 1514)	12°: a–i¹²k⁶	1. Copy: Cambridge University Library, Syn.8.51.13 (lacks e1, e12, i7).
		2. *Equivalent text*: b12r26–c1r25; c3v1–c4r28.

15922 (1519)	4°: A–X^{8}y–z^8[et]^8	1. Copy: Cambridge University Library, SSS.29.10 (lacks gathering A; B1, B8, C4–5, H8, [et]3–8).
		2. Other copies: British Library, C.25.f.17 (lacks A1, 8); Houghton Library, Harvard University, STC 16266 (upper half of N8 used as front pastedown).
		3. *Equivalent text*: E5v12–E7r27; F2v3–F4r11.
15932.5 [after 1521]	8°: ?	1. Copy: College of Arms, London.
		2. Fragments of six sheets and two half-sheets representing several editions, as follows: 1) one sheet signed E and ending with Terce/Short Hours of the Cross; 2) one signed E and ending with None/Short Hours of the Cross; 3) one signed F and beginning with the Salve Regina; 4) one sheet signed N; 5) one sheet signed o; 6) one unsigned sheet; 7) one half-sheet consisting of S2, 3, 6, 7; 8) one half-sheet consisting of T1, 4, 5, 8.
15934 (20 Nov. 1523)	4°: A–X^{8}y–z^8 [et]^8[con]^6	1. Copy: British Library, C.36.e.15 (lacks D1, D3–6, D8, E1, E3–6, K3, K6; K1, L6, T4 mutilated).
		2. Other copies: Salisbury Cathedral (imperfect); Salisbury Library (imperfect).
		3. *Equivalent text*: E7v2–F1r16; F4v1–F6r10.
15941 [1524?]	12°: A–M^{12} [?]	1. Copy: Cambridge University Library, Rit.e.352.1 (lacks gatherings A–C, L, M; F6–7, G1, G3–4, I6–7, K6–7).
		2. *No equivalent text.*
15936 [1525?]	12°: A–M^{12}	1. Copy: Emmanuel College, Cambridge (first and last gatherings mutilated).
		2. *Equivalent text*: C1r9–C2v12; C5v1–C6v32.
15948 (4 Non. Aug. 1526)	4°: A–X^{8}y–z^8 [et]^8[con]^6	1. Copy: Lambeth Palace Library, 1526.2 (lacks [con]1, 2, 5, 6).

		2. Other copy: Bodleian Library, Vet. A1 e.127 (imperfect).
		3. *Equivalent text*: E7v2–F1r16; F4v1–F6r10.
———— [1528?]	12°: A–M¹² [?]	1. Copy: British Library, C.161.f.2(98) (gathering D only from an edition paginary with STC 15936).
		2. *No equivalent text.*

Table 5. Verse in the Hours of the Virgin and Short Hours of the Cross, Sarum Primers, 1519–1534

Note: The following index is based on an examination of readily available copies, many of which are imperfect. I list only the verse that appears, even when missing folios likely contain additional quatrains. Items marked with an asterisk (*) have not been examined. The individual Hours marked with a dagger symbol (+) have the same verse as is found in de Worde's octavo fragments

STC	Printer (Format)	Hours of the Virgin	Hours of the Cross
15923 (14 April 1519)	Paris: ? (4°)	No verse	No verse
15924 (24 Oct. 1519)	Paris: N. Higman (4°)	No verse	No verse
15925 (14 June 1520)	Paris: ? (4°)	No verse	No verse
15926 [1520?]	Paris: N. Higman (4°)	No verse	No verse
15926.5 [1520?]	Paris? (4°)	No verse	No verse
15928 [1520?]	Rouen: ? (12°)	English verse: Lauds, Prime, Terce+, Sext, None, Vespers, Compline	English verse: Matins, Prime+, Terce, Sext, Vespers
15929 [1520?]	Paris? (64°)	No verse	No verse
15930 (Jan. 1521)	Paris: for F. Birckman (4°)	No verse	No verse

15931 (9 April 1521)	Paris: T. Kerver (4°)	No verse	No verse
15932 [1521?]	Paris: J. Bignon (12°)	No verse	No verse
15933 (18 Jan. 1522)	London: R. Pynson (8°)	No verse	No verse
15935 [1523?]	Antwerp: C. van Ruremond (4°)	No verse	No verse
15937 (19 Aug. 1524)*	Antwerp: C. van Ruremond (4°)	Not examined	
15938 (22 Nov. 1524)	Antwerp: C. van Ruremond (12°?)	N/A (fragment)	
15938.5 (27 Nov. 1524)*	Antwerp: C. van Ruremond (4°)	Not examined	
15939 (May 1525)	Antwerp: C. van Ruremond (4°)	No verse	No verse
15940 (28 July 1525)	Rouen: ? (12°)	No verse	No verse
15943 (11 Jan. 1526)	Paris: F. Regnault (8°)	Latin quatrains: Terce, Sext, None, Vespers, Compline	Latin quatrains: Matins, Prime, Terce, Sext, Vespers, Compline
15944 (1 March 1526)	Paris: F. Regnault (4°)	No verse	No verse
15945 (17 March 1526)	Paris: F. Regnault (4°)	No verse	Latin quatrains: Matins, Prime, Terce, Sext, None, Vespers, Compline
15946 (1 Aug. 1526)*	Rouen: for J. Cousin (4°)	Not examined	

15946.5 (14 Oct. 1526)*	Paris: J. Prével (64°)	Not examined	
15949 (17 March 1527)	Paris: F. Regnault (4°)	No verse	No verse
15950 (27 June 1527)	Paris: F. Regnault (4°)	No verse	No verse
15951 (27 June 1527)	Paris: F. Regnault (4°)	English quatrains: Lauds, Terce†, Sext, None (= STC 15954?)	No verse
15952 (27 June 1527)	Paris: F. Regnault (4°)	No verse	No verse
15953 (19 July 1527)	Paris: N. Prévost (4°)	No verse	No verse
15953.5 (26 July 1527)*	Paris: N. Prévost (4°)	Not examined	
15954 (10 Oct. 1527)	Paris: F. Regnault (4°)	English quatrains: Lauds, Prime, Terce†, Sext, None, Vespers, Compline	English quatrain: Matins
15955 (13 Dec. 1527)	Paris: F. Regnault (8°)	English quatrains: Terce†, Sext, None, Vespers, Compline	English quatrains: Matins, Prime†, Terce, Sext, Vespers, Compline
15956 (1527)	Paris: Y. Kerver (32°)	No verse	No verse
15957 (2 Sept. 1528)	Paris: Y. Kerver (16°)	English quatrains: Lauds, Prime, Terce†, Sext, None, Vespers, Compline	English quatrains: Matins, Prime†, Terce, Sext, None, Vespers, Compline

15958 [1528]	Rouen: N. le Roux (12°)	English quatrains: Lauds, Prime, Terce†, Sext, None, Vespers, Compline	English quatrains: Matins, Prime†, Terce, Sext, Vespers
15959 [1528?]	Paris: G. Hardouyn (8°)	No verse	No verse
15961 [1528?]	Paris: F. Regnault (4°)	N/A (fragment)	
15961.3 (1529)*	Paris: F. Regnault (8°)	Not examined	
15961.5 (30 April 1529)	Paris: F. Regnault (16°)	N/A (imperfect)	
15962 (Jan. 1530)	Antwerp: C. van Ruremond (4°)	No verse	No verse
15963 (30 April 1530)	Paris: F. Regnault (4°)	No verse	No verse
15964 (30 April 1530)*	Paris: F. Regnault (16°)	Not examined	
15965 (11 May 1530)	Paris: G. Hardouyn (8°)	English quatrains: Lauds, Prime, Terce†, Sext, None, Vespers, Compline	English quatrains: Matins, Prime†, Terce, Sext, None, Vespers, Compline
15966 (Oct. 1530; 1531)	Antwerp: C. van Ruremond (4°)	No verse	No verse
15968 (1530)	Paris: F. Regnault (4°)	English quatrains: Lauds, Prime, Terce†, Sext, None, Vespers, Compline	English quatrain: Matins
15969 (14 May 1531)	Antwerp: C. van Ruremond (4°)	No verse	No verse

15970 (10 June 1531)	Paris: F. Regnault (16°)	English quatrains: Prime, Tercet, Sext, None, Vespers, Compline	English quatrains: Matins, Primet, Terce, Sext, Nonet, Compline
15971 (30 June 1531)	Paris: F. Regnault (8°)	English quatrains: Lauds, Prime, Tercet, Sext, None, Vespers, Compline	English quatrains: Matins, Primet, Terce, Sext, Nonet, Vespers, Compline
15973 (1531)	Paris: F. Regnault (8°)	English quatrains: Lauds, Prime, Tercet, Sext, None, Vespers, Compline	English quatrains: Matins, Primet, Terce, Sext, Nonet, Vespers, Compline
15974 [1531]	Paris: F. Regnault (8°)	English quatrains: Lauds, Prime, Tercet, Sext, None, Vespers, Compline	English quatrains: Matins, Primet, Terce, Sext, Nonet, Vespers, Compline
15975 [1531?]	Paris: F. Regnault (8°)	English quatrains: Lauds, Prime, Tercet, Sext, None, Vespers, Compline	English quatrains: Matins, Primet, Terce, Sext, Nonet, Vespers, Compline
15977 (7 Aug. 1532)	Paris: F. Regnault (16°)	English quatrains: Lauds, Prime, Tercet, Sext, None, Vespers, Compline	English quatrains: Matins, Primet, Terce, Sext, Nonet, Vespers, Compline
15978 (Aug. 1532)	Paris: Y. Kerver (16°)	English quatrains: Lauds, Prime, Tercet, Sext, None, Vespers, Compline	English quatrains: Matins, Primet, Terce, Sext, Vespers, Compline
15979 (Aug. 1532)	Paris: Y. Kerver (16°)	English quatrains: Prime, Tercet, Sext, None, Vespers, Compline	English quatrains: Matins, Primet, Terce, Sext, Vespers, Compline

15980 (31 Oct. 1532)	Paris: F. Regnault (8°)	English quatrains: Lauds, Prime, Terce†, Sext, None, Vespers, Compline	English quatrains: Matins, Prime†, Terce, Sext, None†, Vespers, Compline
15981 (4 Nov. 1533)	Paris: F. Regnault (16°)	English quatrains: Lauds, Prime, Terce†, Sext, None, Vespers, Compline	English quatrains: Matins, Prime†, Terce, Sext, None†, Vespers, Compline
15981a [1533?]	Paris: F. Regnault (16°)	English quatrains: Lauds, Prime, Terce†, Sext, None, Vespers, Compline	English quatrains: Prime†, Sext, Vespers, Compline
15982 [1533?]	Paris: G. Hardouyn (8°)	No verse	No verse
15983 [1533?]	London: R. Wyer (8°)	English quatrains: Lauds, Prime, Terce†, Sext, None, Vespers, Compline	English quatrains: Matins, Prime†, Terce, Sext, Vespers, Compline
15984 (1534)	Paris: F. Regnault (4°)	English quatrains: Lauds, Prime, Terce†, Sext, None, Vespers, Compline	English quatrain: Matins
ESTC S126806 (1534)	Paris: F. Regnault (4°)	English quatrains: Lauds, Prime, Terce†, Sext, None, Vespers, Compline	English quatrain: Matins
15985 (1534)	Paris: Y. Kerver (16°)	English quatrains: Lauds, Prime, Terce†, Sext, None, Vespers, Compline	English quatrains: Matins, Prime†, Terce, Sext, None†, Vespers, Compline
15985a [1534?]	Rouen: N. le Roux (8°)	English quatrains: Lauds, Prime, Terce†, Sext, None, Vespers, Compline	English quatrains: Matins, Prime†, Terce, Sext, None†, Vespers, Compline

15985a.5 [1534; 1535]	Paris: F. Regnault (16°)	English quatrains: Lauds, Prime, Terce†, Sext, None, Vespers, Compline	English quatrain: Matins

The existence of English printed fragments reflects, to a large extent, shifting political and religious trends as well as the evolution of popular taste. In the fifteenth century, the two main categories of English fragments are Catholic books—liturgical and devotional—and elementary Latin grammars; in the sixteenth century, popular romances become a prominent subcategory of survivors. Like many other printed scraps, the Folger fragments discussed here have a common origin in the uncompromising will of Henry VIII. The English Reformation led to the destruction of countless Catholic books—antiphonals, graduals, missals, primers, and so on—many of which were produced during the first decades of English printing. Hundreds of thousands of books must have been destroyed, sold on the Continent, or recycled as waste paper. No less harmful to English books was Henry's educational reform. His promulgation of the Lily grammar led to the abandonment of thousands of Whittingtons and other texts that generations of British boys had once used to learn their Latin. The fortuitous survival of complete books has, of course, afforded scholars generous insights into the complex and tumultuous Tudor age. The recovery of more nuanced views, however, remains an ongoing salvage operation in which England's cultural heritage must be reassembled one piece at a time.

Acknowledgments

A preliminary version of this paper was presented at the Eleventh Biennial Conference of the Early Book Society, Exeter, England, on July 12, 2009. For their assistance with the present revision, I am grateful to I. A. Doyle (Durham), Martha W. Driver (Pace University), Scott Gwara (University of South Carolina, Columbia), Stephen Tabor (Huntington Library), and Tony Trowles (Westminster Abbey Library).

NOTES

1. E. Gordon Duff, *The Printers, Stationers and Bookbinders of Westminster and London from 1476 to 1535*, Sandars Lectures in Bibliography 1899 and 1904 (Cambridge, UK: Cambridge University Press, 1906; repr. New York: Benjamin Blom, 1971), 124–125. Although Duff refers specifically to books, he seems to include broadsides in his count. See also E. Gordon Duff, *Early Printed Books* (London: Kegan Paul, Trench, Trübner, & Co., 1893; repr.

New York: Haskell House, 1968), 194–199, where he claims that "of books printed in England before 1530 more than ten per cent. are only known [from fragments rescued from bindings]"; Duff, *Early Printed Books*, 196. Throughout this article, I cite books by their entry number in *A Short-Title Catalogue of Books Printed in England, Scotland, and Ireland and of English Books Printed Abroad, 1475–1640*, first compiled by A. W. Pollard and G. R. Redgrave, 2nd ed. begun by W. A. Jackson and F. S. Ferguson, completed by Katharine F. Pantzer, 3 vols. (London: Bibliographical Society, 1976–1991), hereafter abbreviated as STC.

2. Lotte Hellinga, ed., *Printing in England in the Fifteenth Century: E. Gordon Duff's Bibliography with Supplementary Descriptions, Chronologies and a Census of Copies* (London: Bibliographical Society; British Library, 2009), 6 (no. 22 = STC 315), 8 (no. 28 = STC 695), 15 (no. 54 = STC 3304), 17 (no. 60 = STC 15794; no. 62 = STC 15801.5), 18 (no. 66 = STC 15800), 30 (no. 104 = STC 5312), 33 (no. 116 = STC 13922), 36 (nos. 128–130 = STC 7014.5, 7013, 7014), 37 (no. 135 = STC 7541), 41 (nos. 148–149 = STC 15848, 15849), 46 (nos. 169–171 = STC 12477, 12540, 12541), 47 (no. 175 = STC 15868), 48–49 (nos. 177–181 = STC 15870, 15871, 15872, 15873, 15874), 49 (no. 184 = STC 15877), 49–50 (no. 185 = STC 15878), 50 (nos. 188–190 = STC 15882, 15883, 15884), 52 (nos. 197–201 = STC 15891, 15892, 15893, 15894, 15895), 54 (no. 206 = STC 14077c. 109), 55 (no. 207 = STC 14077c.110), 55–56 (no. 209 = 14077c.112), 56 (no. 210 = STC 14077c.113), 61 (no. 221 = STC 14077c.148), 63–64 (no. 229 = STC 14098, 14098.5), 67 (no. 239–240 = STC 23163.13, 23163.8), 81 (no. 289 = STC 17325), 94 (no. 336 = STC 16228), 97 (nos. 349–350 = STC 385.7, 385.3), 100 (no. 362 = STC 13688), 102–03 (no. 370 = STC 21297), 107 (no. 387 = STC 9332). In estimating the total number of surviving editions, I include Duff nos. 123a (STC 6827), 266a (STC 17024), and 403a (STC 24766.3) but exclude nos. 44 (STC 1987, printed by Hugh Goes), 64 (like no. 63, a fragment of STC 15797), 158 (no known copy), 356 (printed *ca.* 1502), 361 (STC 13689.3, also printed by Goes), and 413 (printed *ca.* 1502). It should be noted that many single Duff entries have two STC numbers and that, conversely, one STC number often refers to two Duff entries. Sixteen Duff items are not considered STC books: nos. 25, 39, 108, 118 (2 editions), 119–122, 153–155, 159, 243–244, and 311.

3. Hellinga, *Printing in England*, 120–145. I ignore nos. 10, 25, 30, and 34, which replace Duff's original entries, and 36 (STC 21070), which was actually printed around 1502. My count includes supplement nos. 2 (STC 14077c.100), 3 (STC 317.5), 4 (STC 1987.5), 5–6 (STC 4814), 8–9 (STC 15872, note), 12 (STC 15873.5), 16 (14077c.83G), 20 (indulgence, not in STC), 23 (STC 14077c.140A), 28 (STC 17037.5), 29 (STC 17840.7), 33 (STC 16172.5), 38 (STC 23154.5), 39 (STC 23163.16), 43 (STC 23885,

note), and 44 (STC 23939.5). Some of these items are offsets or faint impressions of lost books.

4. I base this total on the STC index, which lists 741 books and broadsides printed by (or for) de Worde between 1501 and 1535. From this number, I have subtracted five items: 1) STC 14077c.81 (printed by Hugh Goes); 2) STC 13075 (printed by Richard Pynson); 3) STC 14077c.17 (no copy traced); 4) STC 20439.5 (printed by de Worde in 1497–1498); and 5) STC 6897.5 (a copy of STC 6897 sophisticated with sheets from STC 6895). At the same time, I have added the following nineteen items: 1) STC 20878 (printed *ca.* 1502); 2) STC 24224 (printed *ca.* 1502); 3) ESTC S504194 (a fragment of an unrecorded edition of Donatus, *Ars minor, ca.* 1505); 4) fragments of an unrecorded 1506 edition of the *Thre Kynges of Coleyne*, discovered by Martha W. Driver, "Ideas of Order: Wynkyn de Worde and the Title Page," in *Texts and Their Contexts: Papers from the Early Book Society*, ed. John Scattergood and Julia Boffey (Dublin: Four Courts Press, 1997), 87–149, 112–113, 146–149, rev. repr. in Martha W. Driver, *The Image in Print: Book Illustration in Late Medieval England and Its Sources* (London: British Library, 2004), 77–114, 111–112; 5) STC 14505.5 (attributed to Pynson but actually printed by de Worde in 1506); 6) a variant setting (reissue?) of STC 22270.5 [1506] in the Württemburgische Landesbibliothek in Stuttgart (shelfmark Inc.qt.8979), reported in Otto Leuze, "Zwei unbekannte Drucke des Wynkyn de Worde (1506)," *Zeitschrift für Bücherfreunde* n.s., 22 (1930): 101–104, where he also describes a second copy of STC 12412.5 [1506] in the same institution; 7–8) a *ca.* 1509 indulgence (too fragmentary to catalogue) and two leaves of a duodecimo primer, both reported in Charles Sayle, "Cambridge Fragments," *The Library* 3rd ser., 2 (1911): 338–355, 349–350; 9) STC 14077c.116 (misattributed to Pynson); 10) STC 14077c.117 (misattributed to Pynson); 11) four leaves from an edition of Alexander de Villa Dei, *Doctrinale*, differing from STC 319.7 [1515?]; 12) STC 14077c.82 (misattributed to Pynson); 13) ESTC T301183 (an unrecorded edition of Sulpitius, *Stans puer ad mensam*, printed after 1515); 14) ESTC S498654, a previously unnoticed edition of St. Peter of Luxembourg, *The Next Way to Heuen* [1520?]; 15) fragments of a *ca.* 1520 edition of *A Treatise of a Galaunt* in Cambridge University Library (shelfmark Pet.F.5.29), reported in STC addenda, 3:313; 16) ESTC S498386, fragments of a *ca.* 1531 edition of *The Abbey of the Holy Ghost* (discussed below); and 17–19) three Bandinel fragments: a) sigs. B3–4 of *Everyman* (attributed to Pynson, *ca.* 1518, but actually printed by de Worde, *ca.* 1508 or possibly 1511–1513); b) sigs. EE1–5 of an edition of *Carta feodi simplicis* [*ca.* 1512?] and c) sigs. A3–4 of a Life of St. Catherine of Alexandria [*ca.* 1515], all described in Arthur Freeman, "*Everyman* and Others, Part II: The Bandinel Fragments," *The Library* 7th ser., 9 (2008): 397–427, 416–418 (nos. 1, 8, and 15). (Since I have not seen the

four Whittington fragments catalogued as no. 9, I am unable to say if any is unique.) For the time being, I ignore the speculations in STC that sigs. b3, 4 in 4° Rawl.598(9) of the Bodleian Library, Oxford, and sig. B2 in the Harvard University copy of STC 25560.7 (1522) may come from editions other than STC 7016.4 [1508–1509] and STC 25464.5 (Id. March 1522), respectively. The 1518 edition of *Ortus vocabulorum* at the Newberry Library (shelfmark Case X 9892.34) appears to differ from STC 13834 (22 Oct. 1518) and may be an unrecorded edition with a repeated colophon date. Pending further investigation, however, I likewise ignore this matter.

5. The fourth book, which survives in two nearly complete copies, is STC 16232.4 (18 Feb. 1509), an edition of the York Ordinal. Goes also printed two indulgences—STC 14077c.81 [1505] and 14077c.63 [1506]—as well as patterned wallpaper. On the latter, see Sayle, "Cambridge Fragments," 339–344, and A. E. Shipley, "The Master's Lodgings, Christ's College, Cambridge," *Country Life* 40,1030 (30 Sept. 1916): 378–385; 40,1031 (7 Oct. 1916): 406–412.

6. For details, see Franklin B. Williams, Jr., ed., *"The Gardyners Passetaunce"* (*c. 1512*), with notes by Howard M. Nixon (London: Roxburghe Club, 1985), 43–50, 53–56, 65–75. A manuscript note in British Library Harl.5974(95) refers to a *Donatus cum Remigio* also printed by Goes and Watson, but the book does not survive. The other items removed from the Westminster Abbey binding are: 1) two leaves of the Medius part of STC 22924 (10 Oct. 1530); 2) a fragment of a Sarum Book of Hours (not in STC and, to my knowledge, still unidentified); 3) two leaves of STC 14280.5 [*ca.* 1530], a quarto edition of *Sir Isumbras* printed by John Skot; 4) two leaves of STC 11691a.5 [*ca.* 1530], a quarto edition of *The Jest of Sir Gawaine*, printed for John Butler; and 5) part of sheet B of Christoph Hegendorff, *De instituenda vita et moribus corrigendis juventutis paræneses* (Paris: Christian Wechel, 1529).

7. The romance in question is *Le Iugement d'amour*, a French translation of *La historia de Grisel y Mirabella* (*ca.* 1475) by the Spanish writer Juan de Flores. On the discovery, see Frank Stubbings, "A New Manuscript of *Generydes,*" *Transactions of the Cambridge Bibliographical Society* 10,3 (1993): 317–339, 331–332, 339; Dennis E. Rhodes, "A Lost Romance Printed by Wynkyn de Worde," *Transactions of the Cambridge Bibliographical Society* 11,4 (1999): 463–467; and Joyce Boro, "A Source and Date for the Fragment of *Grisel y Mirabella* Found in the Binding of Emmanuel College 338.5.43," *Transactions of the Cambridge Bibliographical Society* 12,4 (2003 [2005]): 422–436. The authors of these studies mistakenly attribute the fragment to de Worde.

8. Joseph J. Gwara, "Three Forms of w and Four English Printers: Robert Copland, Henry Pepwell, Henry Watson, and Wynkyn de Worde," *Papers of the Bibliographical Society of America* 106 (2012): 141–230, 180, 195.

9. For a thorough and informative account of early English fragment collections, see Arthur Freeman, "*Everyman* and Others, Part I: Some Fragments of Early English Printing, and their Preservers," *The Library* 7th ser., 9 (2008): 267–305.

10. This fragment consists of portions of sigs. A5 and A6 plus most of sigs. A7 and A8 (both trimmed at the bottom). Given the similar damage patterns, I suspect that the British Library leaves also come from the Folger binding. If so, they must have been removed before 1973, when the Folger Library acquired the volume at an auction of books belonging to George Goyder; *Catalogue of Valuable Printed Books, Autograph Letters and Historical Documents (8–9 October 1973)* (London: Sotheby & Co., 1973), lot 62. The only information on the provenance of the British Library fragment is that it was purchased on March 5, 1929, and rebound in the same year. The name "Ch. Croftes" appears above de Worde's device on sig. A8v. It should be noted that fifty copies of STC 18528.5 were apparently among the unsold stock at the Sign of the George, Richard Pynson's former printing office, in 1553; Peter W. M. Blayney, "The Site of the Sign of the Sun," in *The London Book Trade: Topographies of Print in the Metropolis from the Sixteenth Century*, ed. Robin Myers, Michael Harris, and Giles Mandelbrote (New Castle, DE: Oak Knoll Press; London: British Library, 2003), 1–20, 20 n. 55.

11. For a modern study of his canonization process (July 20–September 28, 1325), see Sari Katajala-Peltomaa, *Gender, Miracles, and Daily Life: The Evidence of Fourteenth-Century Canonization Processes*, History of Daily Life 1 (Turnhout, Belgium: Brepols, 2009), with primary sources in both manuscript and print on 301.

12. On printing by the religious orders, see James G. Clark, "Print and Pre-Reformation Religion: The Benedictines and the Press, *c.* 1470–*c.* 1550," in *The Uses of Script and Print, 1300–1700*, ed. Julia Crick and Alexandra Walsham (Cambridge, UK: Cambridge University Press, 2004), 71–92. For general information on the culture of printed books at Syon, I have consulted the following three studies: Vincent Gillespie, "The Book and the Brotherhood: Reflections on the Lost Library of Syon Abbey," in *The English Medieval Book: Studies in Memory of Jeremy Griffiths*, ed. A. S. G. Edwards, Vincent Gillespie, and Ralph Hanna (London: British Library, 2000), 185–208; Vincent Gillespie, "Dial M for Mystic: Mystical Texts in the Library of Syon Abbey and the Spirituality of the Syon Brethren," in *The Medieval Mystical Tradition in England, Ireland and Wales: Exeter Symposium VI: Papers Read at Charney Manor, July 1999*, ed. Marion Glasscoe (Cambridge, UK: D. S. Brewer, 1999), 241–268, repr. in Vincent Gillespie, *Looking in Holy Books: Essays on Late Medieval Religious Writing in England*, Brepols Collected Essays in European Culture 3 (Turnhout, Belgium: Brepols, 2011), 175–207; and Vincent Gillespie, "Syon and the English Market for Continental Printed

Books: The Incunable Phase," *Religion & Literature* 37,2 (Summer 2005): 27–49, rev. repr. in *Syon Abbey and Its Books: Reading, Writing and Religion, c. 1400–1700*, ed. E. A. Jones and Alexandra Walsham, Studies in Modern British Religious History 24 (Woodbridge, UK: Boydell Press, 2010), 104–128.
13. This table, maximally inclusive, has been compiled from the following sources (pages are noted only when they refer to specific books): David N. Bell, *What Nuns Read: Books and Libraries in Medieval English Nunneries*, Cistercian Studies Series 158 (Kalamazoo, MI; Spencer, MA: Cistercian Publications, 1995), 182–183 (STC 5065, 14042), 187 (STC 5065, 24234), 192–193 (STC 4815),198 (STC 14042); N. F. Blake, "Wynkyn de Worde: The Later Years," *Gutenberg-Jahrbuch* (1972): 128–138, 132–134; Alexandra da Costa, "The King's Great Matter: Writing under Censure at Syon Abbey 1532–1534," *Review of English Studies* n.s., 62 (2010): 15–29; Alexandra da Costa, *Reforming Printing: Syon Abbey's Defence of Orthodoxy, 1525–1534* (Oxford: Oxford University Press, 2012), esp. 10–13, 33–38, 41–42, 171–172; Christopher de Hamel, *Syon Abbey: The Library of the Bridgettine Nuns and Their Peregrinations after the Reformation*, introduction by John Martin Robinson (n.p.: Roxburghe Club, 1991), 72 (STC 17532), 84 (STC 1978), 98 (STC 14042), 101 (STC 1978, 4815, 17532, 25422–23, 3278, 25421.6), 112 (STC 4815), 126 (STC 5065); Mary Denise, "The Orchard of Syon: An Introduction," *Traditio* 14 (1958): 269–293, 269, 272–275 (STC 4815); A. I. Doyle, "Book Production by the Monastic Orders in England (*c.* 1375–1530): Assessing the Evidence," in *Medieval Book Production: Assessing the Evidence: Proceedings of the Second Conference of the Seminar in the History of the Book to 1500, Oxford, July 1988*, ed. Linda L. Brownrigg (Los Altos Hills, CA: Anderson-Lovelace, Red Gull Press, 1990), 1–19, 15 (STC 1978); Mary C. Erler, "A London Anchorite, Simon Appulby: His *Fruyte of Redempcyon* and Its Milieu," *Viator* 29 (1998): 227–239, 230–231, 238 (STC 22557–60); Mary C. Erler, *Reading and Writing during the Dissolution: Monks, Friars, and Nuns, 1530–1558* (Cambridge, UK: Cambridge University Press, 2013), 26–32 (STC 22557–60), 126–143; Mary C. Erler, *Women, Reading, and Piety in Late Medieval England* (Cambridge, UK: Cambridge University Press, 2002), 118–119 (Lambeth Palace Library, 1494.6; STC 15875), 121–122 (STC 14042), 125 (STC 5065), 126 (STC 14507), 141 (STC 14507), 148 (STC 5065, 14042), 192 n. 34 (STC 14507 reissue); C. Annette Grisé, "'Moche Profitable unto Religious Persones, Gathered by a Brother of Syon': Syon Abbey and English Books," in *Syon Abbey and Its Books: Reading, Writing and Religion, c. 1400–1700*, ed. E. A. Jones and Alexandra Walsham, Studies in Modern British Religious History 24 (Woodbridge, UK: Boydell Press, 2010), 129–154; James Hogg, "The Contribution of the Brigittine Order to Late Medieval English Spirituality," *Spiritualität Heute und Gestern, Analecta Cartusiana* 35,3 (1983): 153–174;

James Hogg, "Richard Whytford," in *Studies in St. Birgitta and the Brigittine Order 2, Analecta Cartusiana, Spiritualität Heute und Gestern* 35,19 (1993): 254–266; Sue Ellen Holbrook, "Margery Kempe and Wynkyn de Worde," in *The Medieval Mystical Tradition in England: Exeter Symposium IV: Papers Read at Dartington Hall, July 1987*, ed. Marion Glasscoe (Cambridge, UK: D. S. Brewer, 1987), 27–46 (STC 14924); Robert A. Horsfield, "*The Pomander of Prayer*: Aspects of Late Medieval English Carthusian Spirituality and Its Lay Audience," in *"De Cella in Seculum": Religious and Secular Life and Devotion in Late Medieval England: An Interdisciplinary Conference in Celebration of the Eighth Centenary of the Consecration of St Hugh of Avalon Bishop of Lincoln, 20–22 July, 1986*, ed. Michael G. Sargent (Cambridge, UK: D. S. Brewer, 1989), 205–213 (STC 25421.2, etc.); Ann M. Hutchison, "What the Nuns Read: Literary Evidence from the English Bridgettine House, Syon Abbey," *Mediaeval Studies* 57 (1995): 205–222; George R. Keiser, "The Mystics and the Early English Printers: The Economics of Devotionalism," in *The Medieval Mystical Tradition in England: Exeter Symposium IV: Papers Read at Dartington Hall, July 1987*, ed. Marion Glasscoe (Cambridge, UK: D. S. Brewer, 1987), 9–26; George R. Keiser, "Patronage and Piety in Fifteenth-Century England: Margaret, Duchess of Clarence, Symon Wynter and Beinecke MS 317," *Yale University Library Gazette* 60 (1985): 32–46, 43–45 (STC 14508); Domenico Pezzini, "'The Meditacion of Oure Lordis Passyon' and Other Bridgettine Texts in MS Lambeth 432," in *Studies in St. Birgitta and the Brigittine Order*, vol. 1, *Spiritualität Heute und Gestern, Analecta Cartusiana* 35,19 (1993): 276–295 (STC 14508, 13608.7); Henry R. Plomer, *Wynkyn de Worde & His Contemporaries from the Death of Caxton to 1535: A Chapter in English Printing* (London: Grafton & Co., 1925), 90–94 (STC 21471.5); Susan Powell, "What Caxton Did to the *Festial*," *Journal of the Early Book Society* 1 (1997): 48–77, 56–58; A. W. Reed, *Early Tudor Drama: Medwall, the Rastells, Heywood, and the More Circle* (London: Methuen & Co., 1926), 166–169 (STC 21471.5); Arthur W. Reed, "The Regulation of the Book Trade before the Proclamation of 1538," *Transactions of the Bibliographical Society* 15 (1917–1919): 157–184, 163–166 (STC 21471.5); J. T. Rhodes, "Religious Instruction at Syon in the Early Sixteenth Century," in *Studies in St. Birgitta and the Brigittine Order*, vol. 2, *Spiritualität Heute und Gestern, Analecta Cartusiana* 35,19 (1993): 151–169; J. T. Rhodes, "Syon Abbey and Its Religious Publications in the Sixteenth Century," *Journal of Ecclesiastical History* 44 (1993): 11–25; Michael G. Sargent, "Walter Hilton's *Scale of Perfection*: The London Manuscript Group Reconsidered," *Medium Ævum* 52 (1983): 189–216 (STC 14042).

14. De Worde also printed at least one devotional image of the Five Wounds of Christ (STC 14077c.15, *ca*. 1505) for the Carthusian Charterhouse at Sheen, Syon Abbey's spiritual and intellectual partner. A second pious image

from Syon, Christ Enthroned at the Last Judgment (STC 14077c.18, *ca.* 1510), is traditionally ascribed to Richard Pynson, but the leaf is just as likely to have been printed by de Worde.

15. Mary Bateson, *Catalogue of the Library of Syon Monastery, Isleworth* (Cambridge, UK: Cambridge University Press, 1898), xxvii, 9, 103; *Corpus of British Medieval Library Catalogues*, vol. 9, *Syon Abbey*, ed. Vincent Gillespie, with *The Libraries of the Carthusians*, ed. A. I. Doyle (London: British Library in association with British Academy, 2001), 24 (no. 75), 229 (no. 763), with another copy of STC 4601 donated by William Barnarde (228–229, no. 761). See also de Hamel, *Syon Abbey*, 102. De Hamel observes that several Syon bindings, on both manuscripts and printed books, emanated from the Caxton bindery, which de Worde inherited (de Hamel, *Syon Abbey*, 102–103).

16. Except for STC 1912, 1913, and 3273.5, these editions also have de Worde's famous woodcut of St. Bridget of Sweden; Edward Hodnett, *English Woodcuts, 1480–1535*, rev. ed. (London: Oxford University Press for Bibliographical Society, 1973), 177–178 (no. 457, measuring 123×91mm), hereafter abbreviated as "Hodnett." As Martha W. Driver shows, this cut likely signals Syon Abbey's endorsement of the works in which they appear; Martha W. Driver, "Nuns as Patrons, Artists, Readers: Bridgettine Woodcuts in Printed Books Produced for the English Market," in *Art into Life: Collected Papers from the Kresge Art Museum Medieval Symposia*, ed. Carol Garrett Fisher and Kathleen L. Scott (East Lansing: Michigan State University Press, 1995), 237–267, 249–252; Martha W. Driver, "Pictures in Print: Late Fifteenth- and Early Sixteenth-Century English Religious Books for Lay Readers," in *"De Cella in Seculum": Religious and Secular Life and Devotion in Late Medieval England: An Interdisciplinary Conference in Celebration of the Eighth Centenary of the Consecration of St Hugh of Avalon Bishop of Lincoln, 20–22 July, 1986*, ed. Michael G. Sargent (Cambridge, UK: D. S. Brewer, 1989), 229–244, 243–244; and Driver, *Image in Print*, 146–149. The St. Bridget cut was also used in STC 6833 (20 Nov. 1520), a likely Syon book, and in de Worde's three quarto primers from 1519 and later, where it accompanies the *Fifteen Oes*, traditionally ascribed to St. Bridget: STC 15922 (1519), 15934 (20 Nov. 1523), and 15948 (4 Non. Aug. 1526). (The block was too large to be used in octavo and duodecimo primers.) The promiscuous use of this block by other Syon printers—Lawrence Andrewe, Richard Fawkes, Richard Pynson, and Robert Redman—suggests that de Worde routinely lent (or leased) it to his fellow craftsmen, perhaps acting as the abbey's agent. Driver further argues that another woodcut illustration, Caxton's Crucifixion scene (Hodnett no. 374, measuring 119×82mm) from the Flemish *Fifteen Oes* series, may also indicate a Syon Abbey connection (Driver, "Nuns as Patrons, Artists, Readers," 258–260). The cut appears in at least twenty-nine Caxton and de Worde editions before 1503, thirteen of which have concrete

or circumstantial links to Syon: STC 20195 [1491], 15875 [1493?], Lambeth Palace reprint of STC 15875 [*ca.* 1493–1494], 3261 (1494), 21334 [*ca.* 1494], 1916 (9 March 1496), 787 [1497–1498], 13609 [1497?], 5573 [1499], 1978 [1500], 13610 [1500?], 21335 [1500], and 14924 [1501].

17. Several of these books were reprinted after 1534, often in revised or modified form: STC 23964.7 [1535?], 25413 [1537?], 25425 (8 Nov. 1537), and 25415 [1538?]. Many books with documented or possible links to Syon Abbey were printed by others: STC 17542 (Richard Fawkes, 4 Nov. 1530), 3273.3 (Richard Fawkes, [1530?]), 1914 (Robert Wyer, 1531), 1915 (Thomas Godfray, [1531?]), 25422.3 (Peter Treveris, [1531?]), 1915.5 (Thomas Godfray, [*ca.* 1535]), 3274.5 (Lawrence Andrewe, [1527]), 3275 (Michael Fawkes, [1534?]), 3276 (Michael Fawkes, [1534?]), 25413.5 (John Wayland, 1537), 25414 (John Wayland, 1537), 25425.5 (John Wayland, 1537), and 25420 (William Middleton, 1541).

18. Caxton books with Syon connections include: 1) the 1490 edition of Nicholas Love, *The Myrroure of the Blessed Lyf of Ihesu Cryste* (STC 3260), one copy of which (British Library, shelfmark IB 55119) was once owned by Susan Purlerave (Purlefeyo, Purefoy), a Syon nun; 2) the 1491 edition of the *Fifteen Oes* (STC 20195), printed at the behest of Lady Margaret Beaufort and Queen Elizabeth, her daughter-in-law; 3) two editions of the *Quattuor sermones* (STC 17957) plus the 1491 edition of Mirk's *Festial* (STC 17959); 4) the two editions (*ca.* 1484, 1489) of Clement Maydeston's *Directorium sacerdotum* (STC 17720, 17722); and 5) the *Ars moriendi* (STC 786), quoted by Thomas Betson in STC 1978 (although STC 787, de Worde's 1497–1498 reprint of Caxton's edition, is an equally plausible source). On these items, see Bell, *What Nuns Read*, 190–191; H. S. Bennett, "Notes on Two Incunables: *The Abbey of the Holy Ghost* and *A Ryght Profytable Treatyse*," *The Library* 5th ser., 10 (1955): 120–121; de Hamel, *Syon Abbey*, 126; Erler, *Women, Reading, and Piety*, 118, 124–125; Keiser, "Mystics," 11–12; Keiser, "Patronage and Piety," 44–46; Susan Powell, "Preaching at Syon Abbey," *Leeds Studies in English* n.s., 31 (2000): 229–267, 240–244; Susan Powell, "Syon, Caxton, and the *Festial*," *Birgittiana* 2 (1996): 187–207; and Susan Powell, "What Caxton Did to the *Festial*," 56–58.

19. Keiser, "Mystics," 11–13, 24–25; Keiser, "Patronage and Piety," 43–46; Powell, "Syon, Caxton, and the *Festial*," 204–207; Susan Powell, "Lady Margaret Beaufort and Her Books," *The Library* 6th ser., 20 (1998): 197–240, 211–221; Susan Powell, "Syon Abbey and the Mother of King Henry VII: The Relationship of Lady Margaret Beaufort with the English Birgittines," *Birgittiana* 19 (2005): 211–224; Michael G. Sargent, "The Transmission by the English Carthusians of Some Late Medieval Spiritual Writings," *Journal of Ecclesiastical History* 27 (1976): 225–240, 239–240.

20. Both Copland editions of *The Pomander of Prayer* also have Hodnett no. 457 (St. Bridget of Sweden), emphasizing the Syon link. A copy of STC 13608 at Ampleforth Abbey (shelfmark C.V.130) once belonged to Dorothy Codrington, a Syon nun, and a second copy, at Trinity College, Cambridge (shelfmark C.7.12), was owned by Margaret Windsor, prioress of Syon in 1518 and 1539. According to Erler, *Women, Reading, and Piety*, 97, these two books plus one other—Folger Shakespeare Library STC 13608—were corrected against British Library Add. MS 24192, a Syon manuscript that may have served as printer's copy. These circumstances suggest that the abbey commissioned Copland to print STC 13608 from its own manuscript and that the sisters later corrected their copies against this source. For background information, see Bell, *What Nuns Read*, 176, 183; de Hamel, *Syon Abbey*, 97; Erler, *Women, Reading, and Piety*, 96–98, 149; and J. J. Vaissier, ed., *"A Deuout Treatyse Called the Tree & xii. Frutes of the Holy Goost" Edited from MS. McClean 132, Fitzwilliam Museum, Cambridge* (Groningen, Holland: J. B. Wolters, 1960), xxiv–xxix, xxxii–xxxiii, xxxvi–xxxviii. On the Image of Pity woodcuts, see Mary C. Erler, "Pasted-In Embellishments in English Manuscripts and Printed Books, c. 1480–1533," *The Library* 6th Series 14 (1992): 185–206, 188. Copland also printed two other devotional works with possible—but disputed—Syon connections: the 1531 edition of *The Golden Letany in Englysshe* (STC 15707) and the 1529 edition of *The Psalter of Jesus* (STC 14563).

21. On the *Abbey of the Holy Ghost*, see Julia Boffey, "Conflations of the Abbey of the Holy Ghost and the Charter of the Abbey of the Holy Ghost in Manuscript and Print," in *The Medieval Book and a Modern Collector: Essays in Honour of Toshiyuki Takamiya*, ed. Takami Matsuda, Richard A. Linenthal, and John Scahill (Cambridge, UK: D. S. Brewer; Tokyo: Yushodo Press, 2004), 245–254, 251–252. A 1530 edition of *The Thre Kynges of Coleyne* signed by Richard Whitford was reported in Thomas Frognall Dibdin, ed., *Typographical Antiquities; or the History of Printing in England, Scotland and Ireland: Containing Memoirs of Our Ancient Printers, and a Register of the Books Printed by Them, Begun by Joseph Ames and Augmented by William Herbert*, 4 vols. (London: William Miller, 1810–1812 [vols. 1, 2]; London: John Murray, 1816 [vol. 3]; London: Longman, Hurst, Rees, Orme, and Brown, 1819 [vol. 4]), 2:167–268 (no. 230). However, Martha W. Driver dismisses this book as a probable ghost (Driver, "Nuns as Patrons, Artists, Readers," 266 n. 46). As mentioned in note 10, unsold copies of de Worde's books are listed in a 1553 inventory of goods at the sign of the George. Almost all of these remainders date from the 1520s and early 1530s, with one noticeable exception—the twelve (?) copies of Betson's *A Ryght Profytable Treatyse* [1500]. In my view, the remainders of Betson's treatise are likely to belong to a lost *ca.* 1530 reprint of this book, another sign of renewed interest in older Bridgettine texts at de Worde's shop.

22. Mary C. Erler, "Devotional Literature," in *The Cambridge History of the Book in Britain* 3: *1400–1557*, ed. Lotte Hellinga and J. B. Trapp (Cambridge, UK: Cambridge University Press, 1999), 495–525, 516–521.

23. The best-known illustration of this practice is STC 21471.5 (7 Oct. 1525), an edition of *The Image of Loue* by John Rickes. According to testimony given on December 19, 1525, de Worde sold sixty copies of this book to Syon Abbey, presumably one for each of the nuns, and an equal number to the public; Reed, "Regulation of the Book Trade," 163–166. Other evidence of bulk book purchases by Syon is slight. As discussed by Mary C. Erler, two copies of the same 1532 edition of a Sarum Primer have a Syon provenance, suggesting that they were acquired together, perhaps as part of a block purchase of new primers for the community; Erler, "Pasted-In Embellishments," 194–201. Presumably, books in frequent use would have been replaced at regular intervals, perhaps every generation.

24. For background information, see Francis Roth, *The English Austin Friars, 1249–1538*, vol. 1, *History*, vol. 2, *Sources*, Cassiciacum: Studies in St. Augustine and the Augustinian Order 6–7 (American Series) (New York: Augustinian Historical Institute, 1961 [vol. 2], 1966 [vol. 1]), 1:597, commenting that "[t]he life consists of short chapters apparently taken from the lessons of the breviary." It should be noted that the titles of all individual saints' lives printed in England before 1536 invariably begin (or include) the words "The lyf(e) of." The fact that de Worde's title lacks this phrase indicates that the work was understood as something other than a standard saint's life.

25. Quotations come from STC 18528, which preserves the complete text of the work. Where possible, I have checked the readings of this edition against those of STC 18528.5.

26. In all likelihood, the remaining lessons would have been devoted to the Octave of the Nativity of the Virgin (September 8). I am grateful to Sherry L. Reames (University of Wisconsin, Madison) for her expert guidance on these matters.

27. A likely fourth volume is *The Pype or Tonne of the Lyfe of Perfection*, revised by Whitford in 1525 to accompany his Augustinian rule in English; see P. G. Caraman "An English Monastic Reformer of the Sixteenth Century," *Clergy Review* n.s., 28 (1947): 1–16, 4, 14. Caraman's conclusion is accepted by da Costa, "King's Great Matter," 22–23; and da Costa, *Reforming Printing*, 18; and by Erler, *Reading and Writing*, 126, 130–131, who suggests that the work may have been written as early as 1518.

28. Aside from their daily performance of the Divine Office, the sisters read selections from the martyrology every day after Terce, plus, weekly at refectory, the Rule of St. Augustine, the constitutions of Bridgettine Order (the *Regula Sancti Salvatoris*), and selections from the Additions for the Sisters. For general comments, see John Henry Blunt, ed., *The Myroure of Oure Ladye,*

Containing a Devotional Treatise on Divine Service, with a Translation of the Offices used by the Sisters of the Brigittine Monastery of Sion, at Isleworth, during the Fifteenth and Sixteenth Centuries, Early English Text Society, Extra Series 19 (London: N. Trübner for the Early English Text Society, 1873; repr. Millwood, NY: Kraus Reprint Co., 1973), xxxiii, xxxvi–xl, xlv–xlvi; A. Jefferies Collins, ed., *The Bridgettine Breviary of Syon Abbey from the MS. with English Rubrics F.4.11 at Magdalene College, Cambridge,* Henry Bradshaw Society 96 (Worcester, UK: Henry Bradshaw Society, 1969), xvii, xxxii, xxxvi–xl; de Hamel, *Syon Abbey,* 71–72, remarking that the martyrology was read daily after Prime; Claes Gejrot, "The Syon Martiloge," in *Syon Abbey and Its Books: Reading, Writing and Religion, c. 1400–1700,* ed. E. A. Jones and Alexandra Walsham, Studies in Modern British Religious History 24 (Woodbridge, UK: Boydell Press, 2010), 203–227, 205–208; C. Annette Grisé, "'In the Blessid Vyneȝerd of Oure Holy Saueour': Female Religious Readers and Textual Reception in the *Myroure of Oure Ladye* and the *Orcherd of Syon,*" in *The Medieval Mystical Tradition in England, Ireland and Wales: Exeter Symposium VI: Papers Read at Charney Manor, July 1999,* ed. Marion Glasscoe (Cambridge, UK: D. S. Brewer, 1999), 193–211; Ann M. Hutchison, "Devotional Reading in the Monastery and in the Late Medieval Household," in *"De Cella in Seculum": Religious and Secular Life and Devotion in Late Medieval England: An Interdisciplinary Conference in Celebration of the Eighth Centenary of the Consecration of St Hugh of Avalon Bishop of Lincoln, 20–22 July, 1986,* ed. Michael G. Sargent (Cambridge, UK: D. S. Brewer, 1989), 215–227, 219–223; Ann M. Hutchison, "*The Myroure of Oure Ladye:* A Medieval Guide for Contemplatives," in *Studies in St. Birgitta and the Brigittine Order,* vol. 2, *Spiritualität Heute und Gestern, Analecta Cartusiana* 35,19 (1993): 215–227, 220–221, 224–225; Ann M. Hutchison, "What the Nuns Read," 208–209; Susan Powell, "Cox Manuscript 39: A Rare Survival of Sermons Preached at Syon Abbey?" *Medieval Sermon Studies* 52 (2008): 42–62, 53–54; and F. Procter and E. S. Dewick, eds., *The Martiloge in Englysshe after the Vse of the Chirche of Salisbury and as It Is Redde in Syon with Addicyons: Printed by Wynkyn de Worde in 1526,* Henry Bradshaw Society 3 (London: Henry Bradshaw Society, 1893).

29. Procter and Dewick, *Martiloge in Englysshe,* 143–144 (September 10), with no reference to St. Nicholas of Tolentino but with entries elsewhere for St. Nicholas of Myra (72, 85, 189), St. Nicholas the Pilgrim (88), and Pope Nicholas I (189); Collins, *Bridgettine Breviary,* xli–li; and de Hamel, *Syon Abbey,* 62–77, 91–94, with a list of the surviving manuscripts on 114–124.

30. Only one other book associated with the Augustinians was published in England in the early sixteenth century, a Latin *comedia* about St. Nicholas of Tolentino (STC 19816, *ca.* 1510). Roth, *English Austin Friars,* 1:209–210, describes this work as "Monks' Theatre," intended strictly for the instruction

of the novices. A Middle English Life of St. Nicholas of Tolentino is found in a fifteenth-century manuscript probably from Clare Priory; Simon Horobin, "A Manuscript Found in the Library of Abbotsford House and the Lost Legendary of Osbern Bokenham," in *English Manuscript Studies 1100–1700*, vol. 14, *Regional Manuscripts 1200–1700*, ed. A. S. G. Edwards (London: British Library, 2008), 130–162, 141. The importance of de Worde's text is underscored by the extreme rarity of materials documenting the liturgy of the Austin Friars in England; see Richard W. Pfaff, *The Liturgy in Medieval England: A History* (Cambridge, UK: Cambridge University Press, 2009), 338–340.

31. Caraman, "English Monastic Reformer," 1, 3–4, 7, 13–16; da Costa, *Reforming Printing*, 1–2, 13–17; Erler, *Reading and Writing*, 126, 128–131.

32. By all appearances, Treveris was a German immigrant, perhaps from Trier (Eng. Treves). The location of his printing office in Southwark, which had a large Northern European immigrant community, supports this deduction; see Matthew Groom, "John Siberch (d. 1554), the First Cambridge Printer: New Findings from English Records," *Transactions of the Cambridge Bibliographical Society* 12,4 (2003 [2005])· 403 413, 107 400.

33. For evidence of this relationship, see Joseph J. Gwara and Mary Morse, "A Birth Girdle Printed by Wynkyn de Worde," *The Library* 7th ser., 13 (2012): 33–62, 54–55.

34. The only other important printer of Whittingtons was Richard Pynson, who issued twenty editions between 1521 and 1530, the year of his death. For purposes of comparison, I also include Pynson's annual output in Table 2. Aside from de Worde, Pynson, and Treveris, only Henry Pepwell is known to have printed a Whittington grammar after 1520, a single edition of *De octo partibus* (STC 25502.5, Id. Feb. 1523).

35. This interpretation of events, which I find convincing, comes from Nicholas Orme, "Whittington, Robert (c. 1480–1553?)," *Oxford Dictionary of National Biography* (Oxford: Oxford University Press, 2004), http://www.oxforddnb.com/ view/article/29331 (accessed September 9, 2013). David R. Carlson, *English Humanist Books: Writers and Patrons, Manuscript and Print, 1475–1525* (Toronto: University of Toronto Press, 1993), asserts that Treveris merely pirated Whittington's editions (225 n.6). To my knowledge, the faults for which Whittington criticized Treveris have not been identified.

36. Hedwig Gwosdek, ed., *Lily's Grammar of Latin in English: "An Introduction of the Eyght Partes of Speche, and the Construction of the Same"* (Oxford: Oxford University Press, 2013), 6–10, 83–88. The earliest edition of the Latin part is STC 15610.5 (London: Thomas Berthelet, 1540); the earliest surviving edition of the English part, which contains the royal proclamation authorizing the Lily text and banning all other grammars, is STC 15610.6 (London: Thomas Berthelet, 1542). Both parts were likely prescribed for

British students in 1540 or shortly before. See also Nicholas Orme, *Medieval Schools from Roman Britain to Renaissance England* (New Haven, CT: Yale University Press, 2006), 308–309.

37. *Liber usualis missae et officii pro dominicis et festis I. vel II. classis cum cantu gregoriano* (Paris: Typ. Soc. S. Joannis Evang., Desclée, 1928), 739–740, 743.

38. Associated fragments at Westminster Abbey include parts of sigs. x1–2 and y7–8 of STC 15865 (6 Cal. July 1532), now Printed Fragment 26, and parts of sigs. 2a2 and 2a3 of STC 15790 (1519), Printed Fragment 27. The fragments of STC 15863 reported at Corpus Christi College, Oxford, appear to come from STC 15865; twenty-one folios survive, shelved at WP.vi.3: nine complete folios (sigs. l7; o3, o6; v1, 2, 7, 8; ^{2}F3, ^{2}F6) and parts of twelve others (C3–6; D1, 2, 7, 8; E2, 3, 6, 7). I thank Julie Blyth for identifying these items for me.

39. For a summary discussion of this phenomenon, see George D. Painter, Dennis E. Rhodes, and Howard M. Nixon, "Two Missals Printed for Wynkyn de Worde," *British Library Journal* 2 (1976): 159–171, esp. 159–161. Painter claims that de Worde printed a Sarum Missal in 1508 (ibid., 160), but the book in question (STC 16182a.5) was actually printed for him in Paris. An apparently perfect copy of STC 16182a.5, formerly in the collection of Jean-Baptiste Colbert (1619–1683), is in the National Library of Russia; see Olga Frolova, "Sixteenth-Century English Books in the National Library of Russia: The Editions Published by Wynkyn de Worde," in *Studies in Variation, Contacts and Change in English*, vol. 9, *Western European Manuscripts and Early Printed Books in Russia: Delving into the Collections of the Libraries of St Petersburg and Oxford*, ed. Leena Kahlas-Tarkka & Matti Kilpiö, Research Unit for Variation, Contacts and Change in English (VARIENG), University of Helsinki, 2012, http://www.helsinki.fi/varieng/series/volumes/09/frolova/. See also H. S. Bennett, *English Books & Readers, 1475 to 1557: Being a Study in the History of the Book Trade from Caxton to the Incorporation of the Stationers' Company*, 2nd ed. (Cambridge, UK: Cambridge University Press, 1969), 65–66.

40. On paper sizes, I have consulted Paul Needham, "*Res papirea*: Sizes and Formats of the Late Medieval Book," in *Rationalisierung der Buchherstellung im Mittelalter und in der frühen Neuzeit: Ergebnisse eines buchgeschichtlichen Seminars, Wolfenbüttel 12.–14. November 1990*, ed. Peter Rück and Martin Borghardt, Elementa Diplomatica 2 (Marburg an der Lahn, Germany: Institut für Historische Hilfswissenschaften, 1994), 123–145, 125. The estimated sheet dimensions of the Folger fragment are 384×540mm, too large for Chancery and Median paper. With maximum dimensions of 355×230mm, the Westminster Abbey folios have been more severely trimmed.

41. Robert Steele, *The Earliest English Music Printing: A Description and Bibliography of English Printed Music to the Close of the Sixteenth Century*, Illustrated

Monographs 11 (London: Bibliographical Society, 1903; repr. Mansfield Centre, CT: Martino, 2005), credits de Worde with STC 22924 (10 Oct. 1530), the earliest English vocal part book (5, 9–10, 36, Fig. 6). This book is now assigned to an unknown London printer operating at Sign of the Black Morens (Blackamoor).

42. Anne F. Sutton, "William Bretton, Publisher of Fine Books, 1506–10," *The Library* 7th ser., 14 (2013): 3–17, 9–14. Bretton invested in high-quality books for a clientele of wealthy clerics. Six of his seven known editions were printed by Hopyl.

43. E. Gordon Duff, *A Century of the English Book Trade: Short Notices of All Printers, Stationers, Book-Binders, and Others Connected with It from the Issue of the First Dated Book in 1457 to the Incorporation of the Company of Stationers in 1557* (London: Bibliographical Society, 1905), 135–136 (Reynes) and 153 (Sutton). Although his name appears only in STC 15863, Sutton was Warden of the Stationers' Company in 1526.

44. The binding—erroneously described as bearing "the royal arms blind-stamped on both covers"—is in fact the unrecognized work of Martin Dature [Datur, Deyter, Dulier] (d. September 1563). The panels are HE.6: Royal Arms (front cover) and ST.46: St. Paul and Evangelistic Symbols (back cover), as discussed and illustrated in J. Basil Oldham, *Blind Panels of English Binders* (Cambridge, UK: Cambridge University Press, 1958), 23, 43; plates XVI, LV. See also G. D. Hobson, *Blind-Stamped Panels in the English Book-Trade, c. 1485–1555*, Transactions of the Bibliographical Society, Supplement 17 (London: Bibliographical Society, 1944), 41, 45–46. On Dature's will, see Wayne H. Phelps, "Some Sixteenth-Century Stationers' Wills," *Studies in Bibliography* 32 (1979): 48–59, 50–51. Additional information is provided by Patrick King, "Martin Dature: London Bookbinder, 1526–1556," *Antiquarian Book Monthly Review* 5, 2, 46 (February 1978): 59–61. The Folger has two other examples of Dature's work: pressmarks STC 3039 [*ca.* 1547] and STC 10484 [*ca.* 1544]; for details on the former (plus an image), see Frederick A. Bearman, et al., *Fine and Historic Bookbindings from the Folger Shakespeare Library* (Washington, DC: Folger Shakespeare Library, Harry N. Abrams, 1992), 79. Images of the bindings of STC 3803, STC 3039, and STC 10484 can be accessed through the Folger Bindings Image Collection at http://www.folger.edu/Content/Collection/Folger-Bindings-Image-Collection/.

45. In addition to STC, I have compiled Table 4 from the following sources: Alan Coates, et al., *A Catalogue of Books Printed in the Fifteenth Century Now in the Bodleian Library, Oxford,* 6 vols. (Oxford: Oxford University Press, 2005), 3:1387–1389 (H-184 = STC 15875); Lotte Hellinga, ed., *Catalogue of Books Printed in the XVth Century Now in the British Library,* vol. 11, *England* ('t Goy-Houten, Holland: Hes & De Graaf, 2007), 186–188 (STC 15875, 15876); and Lotte Hellinga, ed., *Printing in England,* 49–50 (nos.

182–183, 185), 123–125 (suppls. 10–11). I count STC 15932.5 as three separate editions and include all fragments except that in Christ's College, Cambridge (see note 4). In several cases, the published collations strike me as dubious. For some primers, it appears that the calendars were printed in larger quantities in regularly signed gatherings of six leaves and that each gathering was inserted into an unsigned fold between the title page and the Easter table. This structure would have allowed de Worde to update the title page and the Easter table for later reissues of the same book without having to reprint the calendars.

46. Apparently discovered around 1960, the fragments came from the binding of the *Ordinary of the Whyte Book of Trykes* of Christopher Barker (d. 1550), Garter King of Arms. The original binding is preserved at the College of Arms. I thank Dr. Lynsey Darby, Archivist of the College of Arms, for this information.

47. On the Hours of the Compassion of Our Lady, which consists of eight stanzas of the hymn *Matris cor virgineum* inserted after each of the Short Hours of the Cross, see R. W. Pfaff, *New Liturgical Feasts in Later Medieval England* (Oxford: Clarendon Press, 1970), 103 n. 1. The hymn text is in Clemens Blume and Guido M. Dreves, ed., *Analecta hymnica Medii Aevi*, vol. 30, *Pia dictamina: Reimgebete und Leselieder des Mittelalters*, 3rd ser., *Stunden- und Glossen-Lieder*, ed. Guido Maria Dreves (Leipzig, Germany: O. R. Reisland, 1898), 106–107.

48. According to Hodnett, *English Woodcuts*, 17, these metal-cuts, of French origin, are first seen in STC 15898. Although no. 626 is found only in primers, no. 628 was used in several other de Worde books, specifically the successive editions of *The Festyuall* (STC 17971–75), *The Fruyte of Redempcyon* (STC 22557–60), and the English translation of the *Legenda aurea* (STC 24878.3–80). Hodnett further observes that with the exception of one woodcut—no. 338 (Madonna and Child, measuring *ca.* 51×*ca.* 40mm)—all the illustrations in STC 15899 are actually illuminations (ibid., 18).

49. The exception is Hodnett no. 405 (Dream of Jesse), measuring 50×37mm, which appears on sig. K6r in STC 15936. For comments on the origin and function of these illustrations, see Hodnett, *English Woodcuts*, 31. The two small woodcuts in the Folger fragment—Hodnett nos. 559 and 603 (or 604)—also belong to the French *Horae* border series. They appear in only three other books, all primers: STC 15934, 15936, and 15948.

50. For the hymn text, see Blume and Dreves, ed., *Analecta hymnica*, 32–35.

51. Mary C. Erler, "*The Maner to Lyue Well* and the Coming of English in François Regnault's Primers of the 1520s and 1530s," *The Library* 6th ser., 6 (1984): 229–243. See also, more generally, Erler, "Devotional Literature," 502–504.

52. STC 15951 (27 June 1527) is apparently a reissue, with the first gathering reprinted, of STC 15950, while the only known copy of STC 15952 appears to be made up of sheets from STC 15950 and 15951. The purported copy of STC 15951 at the Library of Congress (shelfmark BX2090.A2 1527 English Print) seems to be a duplicate of STC 15954; it lacks, among many other leaves, the first gathering and the colophon leaf.

53. Erler, "*Maner to Lyue Well*," 232.

54. Ibid., 232.

55. The quatrains also appear in STC 15928 [1520?], but the date conjectured for this book by STC is too early. Since I have been unable to examine all surviving primers, the date when these English quatrains first appeared in print must remain provisional.

56. The de Worde fragments transmit a metrically defective version of line 3 of the stanza for Terce/Hours of the Virgin: "Sayenge the sone of god is borne" (sig. E2r); in contrast, STC 15954 has "Sayng the veray sone of god is borne" (sig. E3r). Unless "veray" is an ad hoc correction, we must conclude that a word was accidentally dropped from the de Worde text at a later stage of transmission.

57. Erler, "*Maner to Lyue Well*," 232.

58. Ibid., 230–231; Erler, "Devotional Literature," 503–504.

59. Erler, "Devotional Literature," 503, speculated that de Worde and Regnault had a formal business arrangement concerning the production and distribution of primers, suggesting a possible way for Copland's text to have reached Paris. That Regnault chose to partner with Redman for his 1532 gradual (STC 15865) speaks against this hypothesis.

60. It is tempting to think that *The Maner to Lyue Well* also circulated as a separate book, perhaps similar to one of the nine devotional sextodecimos that Copland printed during his career: STC 14552 (1522), 23707 (1522), 14563 (1529), 20196 (1529), 22141 (20 Sept. 1529), 6933 (28 Sept. 1529), 17545 (1531), 15707 (19 June 1531), and 14552.7 [1533?].

WORKS CITED

Bateson, Mary. *Catalogue of the Library of Syon Monastery, Isleworth.* Cambridge, UK: Cambridge University Press, 1898.

Bearman, Frederick A., et al. *Fine and Historic Bookbindings from the Folger Shakespeare Library.* Washington, DC: Folger Shakespeare Library; Harry N. Abrams, 1992.

Bell, David N. *What Nuns Read: Books and Libraries in Medieval English Nunneries.* Cistercian Studies Series 158. Kalamazoo, MI; Spencer, MA: Cistercian Publications, 1995.

Bennett, H. S. *English Books & Readers, 1475 to 1557: Being a Study in the History of the Book Trade from Caxton to the Incorporation of the Stationers' Company.* 2nd ed. Cambridge, UK: Cambridge University Press, 1969. Orig. publ. 1952.

————. "Notes on Two Incunables: *The Abbey of the Holy Ghost* and *A Ryght Profytable Treatyse.*" *The Library* 5th ser., 10 (1955): 120–121.

Blake, N. F. "Wynkyn de Worde: The Later Years." *Gutenberg-Jahrbuch* (1972): 128–138.

Blayney, Peter W. M. "The Site of the Sign of the Sun." In *The London Book Trade: Topographies of Print in the Metropolis from the Sixteenth Century,* edited by Robin Myers, Michael Harris, and Giles Mandelbrote, 1–20. New Castle, DE: Oak Knoll Press; London: British Library, 2003.

Blume, Clemens, and Guido M. Dreves, eds. *Analecta hymnica Medii Aevi.* Vol. 30, *Pia dictamina: Reimgebete und Leselieder des Mittelalters.* 3rd ser., *Stunden- und Glossen-Lieder,* edited by Guido Maria Dreves. Leipzig, Germany: O. R. Reisland, 1898.

Blunt, John Henry, ed. *The Myroure of oure Ladye, Containing a Devotional Treatise on Divine Service, with a Translation of the Offices used by the Sisters of the Brigittine Monastery of Sion, at Isleworth, during the Fifteenth and Sixteenth Centuries.* Early English Text Society, Extra Series 19. London: N. Trübner for the Early English Text Society, 1873. Repr. Millwood, NY: Kraus Reprint Co., 1973.

Boffey, Julia. "Conflations of the *Abbey of the Holy Ghost* and the *Charter of the Abbey of the Holy Ghost* in Manuscript and Print." In *The Medieval Book and a Modern Collector: Essays in Honour of Toshiyuki Takamiya,* edited by Takami Matsuda, Richard A. Linenthal, and John Scahill, 245–254. Cambridge, UK: D. S. Brewer; Tokyo: Yushodo Press, 2004.

Boro, Joyce. "A Source and Date for the Fragment of *Grisel y Mirabella* Found in the Binding of Emmanuel College 338.5.43." *Transactions of the Cambridge Bibliographical Society* 12,4 (2003): 422–436.

Caraman, P. G. "An English Monastic Reformer of the Sixteenth Century." *Clergy Review* n.s., 28 (1947): 1–16.

Carlson, David R. *English Humanist Books: Writers and Patrons, Manuscript and Print, 1475–1525.* Toronto: University of Toronto Press, 1993.

Catalogue of Valuable Printed Books, Autograph Letters and Historical Documents (8–9 October 1973). London: Sotheby & Co., 1973.

Clark, James G. "Print and Pre-Reformation Religion: The Benedictines and the Press, c. 1470–c. 1550." In *The Uses of Script and Print, 1300–1700,* edited by Julia Crick and Alexandra Walsham, 71–92. Cambridge, UK: Cambridge University Press, 2004.

Coates, Alan, et al. *A Catalogue of Books Printed in the Fifteenth Century Now in the Bodleian Library, Oxford.* 6 vols. Oxford: Oxford University Press, 2005.

Collins, A. Jefferies, ed. *The Bridgettine Breviary of Syon Abbey from the MS. with English Rubrics F.4.11 at Magdalene College, Cambridge.* Henry Bradshaw Society 96. Worcester, UK: Henry Bradshaw Society, 1969.

Corpus of British Medieval Library Catalogues. Vol. 9, *Syon Abbey*, edited by Vincent Gillespie, with *The Libraries of the Carthusians*, edited by A. I. Doyle. London: British Library in association with British Academy, 2001.

da Costa, Alexandra. "The King's Great Matter: Writing under Censure at Syon Abbey 1532–1534." *Review of English Studies* n.s., 62 (2010): 15–29.

———. *Reforming Printing: Syon Abbey's Defence of Orthodoxy, 1525–1534.* Oxford: Oxford University Press, 2012.

de Hamel, Christopher. *Syon Abbey: The Library of the Bridgettine Nuns and Their Peregrinations after the Reformation.* Introduction by John Martin Robinson. N.p.: Roxburghe Club, 1991.

Denise, Mary. "The Orchard of Syon: An Introduction." *Traditio* 14 (1958): 269–293.

Dibdin, Thomas Frognall, ed. *Typographical Antiquities; or the History of Printing in England, Scotland and Ireland: Containing Memoirs of our Ancient Printers, and a Register of the Books Printed by Them*, begun by Joseph Ames and augmented by William Herbert. 4 vols. London: William Miller, 1810–1812 (vols. 1, 2); London: John Murray, 1816 (vol. 3); London: Longman, Hurst, Rees, Orme, and Brown, 1819 (vol. 4).

Doyle, A. I. "Book Production by the Monastic Orders in England (*c.* 1375–1530): Assessing the Evidence." In *Medieval Book Production: Assessing the Evidence: Proceedings of the Second Conference of The Seminar in the History of the Book to 1500, Oxford, July 1988*, edited by Linda L. Brownrigg, 1–19. Los Altos Hills, CA: Anderson-Lovelace, Red Gull Press, 1990.

Driver, Martha W. "Ideas of Order: Wynkyn de Worde and the Title Page." In *Texts and Their Contexts: Papers from the Early Book Society*, edited by John Scattergood and Julia Boffey, 87–149. Dublin: Four Courts Press, 1997.

———. *The Image in Print: Book Illustration in Late Medieval England and Its Sources.* London: British Library, 2004.

———. "Nuns as Patrons, Artists, Readers: Bridgettine Woodcuts in Printed Books Produced for the English Market." In *Art into Life: Collected Papers from the Kresge Art Museum Medieval Symposia*, edited by Carol Garrett Fisher and Kathleen L. Scott, 237–267. East Lansing: Michigan State University Press, 1995.

———. "Pictures in Print: Late Fifteenth- and Early Sixteenth-Century English Religious Books for Lay Readers." In *"De Cella in Seculum": Religious and Secular Life and Devotion in Late Medieval England: An*

Interdisciplinary Conference in Celebration of the Eighth Centenary of the Consecration of St Hugh of Avalon Bishop of Lincoln, 20–22 July, 1986, edited by Michael G. Sargent, 229–244. Cambridge, UK: D. S. Brewer, 1989.

Duff, E. Gordon. *A Century of the English Book Trade: Short Notices of All Printers, Stationers, Book-Binders, and Others Connected with It from the Issue of the First Dated Book in 1457 to the Incorporation of the Company of Stationers in 1557*. London: Bibliographical Society, 1905.

————. *Early Printed Books*. London: Kegan Paul, Trench, Trübner, & Co., 1893. Repr. New York: Haskell House, 1968.

————. *The Printers, Stationers and Bookbinders of Westminster and London from 1476 to 1535*. Sandars Lectures in Bibliography 1899 and 1904. Cambridge, UK: Cambridge University Press, 1906. Repr. New York: Benjamin Blom, 1971.

Erler, Mary C. "Devotional Literature." In *The Cambridge History of the Book in Britain* 3: *1400–1557*, edited by Lotte Hellinga and J. B. Trapp, 495–525. Cambridge, UK: Cambridge University Press, 1999.

————. "A London Anchorite, Simon Appulby: His *Fruyte of Redempcyon* and Its Milieu." *Viator* 29 (1998): 227–239.

————. "*The Maner to Lyue Well* and the Coming of English in François Regnault's Primers of the 1520s and 1530s." *The Library* 6th ser., 6 (1984): 229–243.

————. "Pasted-In Embellishments in English Manuscripts and Printed Books, c. 1480–1533." *The Library* 6th ser., 14 (1992): 185–206.

————. *Reading and Writing during the Dissolution: Monks, Friars, and Nuns, 1530–1558*. Cambridge, UK: Cambridge University Press, 2013.

————. *Women, Reading, and Piety in Late Medieval England*. Cambridge, UK: Cambridge University Press, 2002.

Freeman, Arthur. "*Everyman* and Others, Part I: Some Fragments of Early English Printing, and Their Preservers." *The Library* 7th ser., 9 (2008): 267–305.

————. "*Everyman* and Others, Part II: The Bandinel Fragments." *The Library* 7th ser., 9 (2008): 397–427.

Frolova, Olga. "Sixteenth-Century English Books in the National Library of Russia: The Editions Published by Wynkyn de Worde." In *Studies in Variation, Contacts and Change in English*. Vol. 9, *Western European Manuscripts and Early Printed Books in Russia: Delving into the Collections of the Libraries of St Petersburg and Oxford*, edited by Leena Kahlas-Tarkka & Matti Kilpiö. Research Unit for Variation, Contacts and Change in English (VARIENG), University of Helsinki, 2012. http://www.helsinki.fi/varieng/series/volumes/09/frolova/.

Gejrot, Claes. "The Syon Martiloge." In *Syon Abbey and Its Books: Reading, Writing and Religion, c. 1400–1700*, edited by E. A. Jones and Alexandra Walsham, 203–227. Studies in Modern British Religious History 24. Woodbridge, UK: Boydell Press, 2010.

Gillespie, Vincent. "The Book and the Brotherhood: Reflections on the Lost Library of Syon Abbey." In *The English Medieval Book: Studies in Memory of Jeremy Griffiths*, edited by A. S. G. Edwards, Vincent Gillespie, and Ralph Hanna, 185–208. London: British Library, 2000.

———. "Dial M for Mystic: Mystical Texts in the Library of Syon Abbey and the Spirituality of the Syon Brethren." In *The Medieval Mystical Tradition in England, Ireland and Wales: Exeter Symposium VI: Papers Read at Charney Manor, July 1999*, edited by Marion Glasscoe, 241–268. Cambridge, UK: D.S. Brewer, 1999. Repr. in Vincent Gillespie, *Looking in Holy Books: Essays on Late Medieval Religious Writing in England*, 175–207. Brepols Collected Essays in European Culture 3. Turnhout, Belgium: Brepols, 2011.

———. "Syon and the English Market for Continental Printed Books, The Incunable Phase." *Religion & Literature* 37,2 (Summer 2005): 27–49. Rev. repr. in *Syon Abbey and Its Books: Reading, Writing and Religion, c. 1400–1700*, edited by E. A. Jones and Alexandra Walsham, 104–128. Studies in Modern British Religious History 24. Woodbridge, UK: Boydell Press, 2010.

Grisé, C. Annette. "'In the Blessid Vyneȝerd of Oure Holy Saueour': Female Religious Readers and Textual Reception in the *Myroure of Oure Ladye* and the *Orcherd of Syon*." In *The Medieval Mystical Tradition in England, Ireland and Wales: Exeter Symposium VI: Papers Read at Charney Manor, July 1999*, edited by Marion Glasscoe, 193–211. Cambridge, UK: D. S. Brewer, 1999.

———. "'Moche Profitable unto Religious Persones, Gathered by a Brother of Syon': Syon Abbey and English Books." In *Syon Abbey and Its Books: Reading, Writing and Religion, c. 1400–1700*, edited by E. A. Jones and Alexandra Walsham, 129–154. Studies in Modern British Religious History 24. Woodbridge, UK: Boydell Press, 2010.

Groom, Matthew. "John Siberch (d. 1554), the First Cambridge Printer: New Findings from English Records." *Transactions of the Cambridge Bibliographical Society* 12,4 (2003): 403–413.

Gwara, Joseph J. "Three Forms of w and Four English Printers: Robert Copland, Henry Pepwell, Henry Watson, and Wynkyn de Worde." *Papers of the Bibliographical Society of America* 106 (2012): 141–230.

———, and Mary Morse. "A Birth Girdle Printed by Wynkyn de Worde." *The Library* 7th ser., 13 (2012): 33–62.

Gwosdek, Hedwig, ed. *Lily's Grammar of Latin in English: "An Introduction of the Eyght Partes of Speche, and the Construction of the Same."* Oxford: Oxford University Press, 2013.

Hellinga, Lotte, ed. *Catalogue of Books Printed in the XVth Century Now in the British Library.* Vol. 11, *England.* 't Goy-Houten, Holland: Hes & De Graaf, 2007.

———, ed. *Printing in England in the Fifteenth Century: E. Gordon Duff's Bibliography with Supplementary Descriptions, Chronologies and a Census of Copies.* London: Bibliographical Society; British Library, 2009.

Hobson, G. D. *Blind-Stamped Panels in the English Book-Trade, c. 1485–1555.* Transactions of the Bibliographical Society, Supplement 17. London: Bibliographical Society, 1944.

Hodnett, Edward. *English Woodcuts, 1480–1535.* Rev. ed. London: Oxford University Press for Bibliographical Society, 1973. Orig. publ. 1935.

Hogg, James. "The Contribution of the Brigittine Order to Late Medieval English Spirituality." *Spiritualität Heute und Gestern, Analecta Cartusiana* 35,3 (1983): 153–174.

———. "Richard Whytford." In *Studies in St. Birgitta and the Brigittine Order,* vol. 2. *Spiritualität Heute und Gestern, Analecta Cartusiana* 35,19 (1993): 254–266.

Holbrook, Sue Ellen. "Margery Kempe and Wynkyn de Worde." In *The Medieval Mystical Tradition in England: Exeter Symposium IV: Papers Read at Dartington Hall, July 1987,* edited by Marion Glasscoe, 27–46. Cambridge, UK: D. S. Brewer, 1987.

Horobin, Simon. "A Manuscript Found in the Library of Abbotsford House and the Lost Legendary of Osbern Bokenham." In *English Manuscript Studies 1100–1700.* Vol. 14, *Regional Manuscripts 1200–1700,* edited by A. S. G. Edwards, 130–162. London: British Library, 2008.

Horsfield, Robert A. "*The Pomander of Prayer*: Aspects of Late Medieval English Carthusian Spirituality and Its Lay Audience." In *"De cella in seculum": Religious and Secular Life and Devotion in Late Medieval England: An Interdisciplinary Conference in Celebration of the Eighth Centenary of the Consecration of St Hugh of Avalon Bishop of Lincoln, 20–22 July, 1986,* edited by Michael G. Sargent, 205–213. Cambridge, UK: D. S. Brewer, 1989.

Hutchison, Ann M. "Devotional Reading in the Monastery and in the Late Medieval Household." In *"De Cella in Seculum": Religious and Secular Life and Devotion in Late Medieval England: An Interdisciplinary Conference in Celebration of the Eighth Centenary of the Consecration of St Hugh of Avalon Bishop of Lincoln, 20–22 July, 1986,* edited by Michael G. Sargent, 215–227. Cambridge, UK: D. S. Brewer, 1989.

———. "*The Myroure of Oure Ladye:* A Medieval Guide for Contemplatives." In *Studies in St. Birgitta and the Brigittine Order,* vol. 2. *Spiritualität Heute und Gestern, Analecta Cartusiana* 35,19 (1993): 215–227.

———. "What the Nuns Read: Literary Evidence from the English Bridgettine House, Syon Abbey." *Mediaeval Studies* 57 (1995): 205–222.

Katajala-Peltomaa, Sari. *Gender, Miracles, and Daily Life: The Evidence of Fourteenth-Century Canonization Processes.* History of Daily Life 1. Turnhout, Belgium: Brepols, 2009.

Keiser, George R. "The Mystics and the Early English Printers: The Economics of Devotionalism." In *The Medieval Mystical Tradition in England: Exeter Symposium IV: Papers Read at Dartington Hall, July 1987,* edited by Marion Glasscoe, 9–26. Cambridge, UK: D. S. Brewer, 1987.

———. "Patronage and Piety in Fifteenth-Century England: Margaret, Duchess of Clarence, Symon Wynter and Beinecke MS 317." *Yale University Library Gazette* 60 (1985): 32–46.

King, Patrick. "Martin Dature: London Bookbinder, 1526–1556." *Antiquarian Book Monthly Review* 5, 2, 46 (February 1978): 59–61.

Leuze, Otto, "Zwei unbekannte Drucke der Wynkyn de Worde (1506)." *Zeitschrift für Bücherfreunde* n.s., 22 (1930): 101–104.

Liber usualis missae et officii pro dominicis et festis I. vel II. classis cum cantu gregoriano. Paris: Typ. Soc. S. Joannis Evang., Desclée, 1928.

Needham, Paul. "*Res papirea:* Sizes and Formats of the Late Medieval Book." In *Rationalisierung der Buchherstellung im Mittelalter und in der frühen Neuzeit: Ergebnisse eines buchgeschichtlichen Seminars, Wolfenbüttel 12.–14. November 1990,* edited by Peter Rück and Martin Borghardt, 123–145. Elementa Diplomatica 2. Marburg an der Lahn, Germany: Institut für Historische Hilfswissenschaften, 1994.

Oldham, J. Basil. *Blind Panels of English Binders.* Cambridge, UK: Cambridge University Press, 1958.

Orme, Nicholas. *Medieval Schools from Roman Britain to Renaissance England.* New Haven, CT: Yale University Press, 2006.

———. "Whittington, Robert (c. 1480–1553?)." In *Oxford Dictionary of National Biography.* Oxford: Oxford University Press, 2004. http://www.oxforddnb.com/view/article/ 29331.

Painter, George D., Dennis E. Rhodes, and Howard M. Nixon. "Two Missals Printed for Wynkyn de Worde." *British Library Journal* 2 (1976): 159–171.

Pezzini, Domenico. "'The Meditacion of Oure Lordis Passyon' and Other Bridgettine Texts in MS Lambeth 432." In *Studies in St. Birgitta and the Brigittine Order,* vol. 1. *Spiritualität Heute und Gestern, Analecta Cartusiana* 35,19 (1993): 276–295.

Pfaff, Richard W. *The Liturgy in Medieval England: A History*. Cambridge, UK: Cambridge University Press, 2009.

————. *New Liturgical Feasts in Later Medieval England*. Oxford: Clarendon Press, 1970.

Phelps, Wayne H. "Some Sixteenth-Century Stationers' Wills." *Studies in Bibliography* 32 (1979): 48–59.

Plomer, Henry R. *Wynkyn de Worde & His Contemporaries from the Death of Caxton to 1535: A Chapter in English Printing*. London: Grafton & Co., 1925.

Powell, Susan. "Cox Manuscript 39: A Rare Survival of Sermons Preached at Syon Abbey?" *Medieval Sermon Studies* 52 (2008): 42–62.

————. "Lady Margaret Beaufort and Her Books." *The Library* 6th ser., 20 (1998): 197–240.

————. "Preaching at Syon Abbey." *Leeds Studies in English* n.s., 31 (2000): 229–267.

————. "Syon Abbey and the Mother of King Henry VII: The Relationship of Lady Margaret Beaufort with the English Birgittines." *Birgittiana* 19 (2005): 211–224.

————. "Syon, Caxton, and the *Festial*." *Birgittiana* 2 (1996): 187–207.

————. "What Caxton Did to the *Festial*." *Journal of the Early Book Society* 1 (1997): 48–77.

Procter, F., and E. S. Dewick, eds. *The Martiloge in Englysshe after the Vse of the Chirche of Salisbury and as It Is Redde in Syon with Addicyons: Printed by Wynkyn de Worde in 1526*. Henry Bradshaw Society 3. London: Henry Bradshaw Society, 1893.

Reed, A. W. *Early Tudor Drama: Medwall, the Rastells, Heywood, and the More Circle*. London: Methuen & Co., 1926.

————. "The Regulation of the Book Trade before the Proclamation of 1538." *Transactions of the Bibliographical Society* 15 (1917–1919): 157–184.

Rhodes, Dennis E. "A Lost Romance Printed by Wynkyn de Worde." *Transactions of the Cambridge Bibliographical Society* 11,4 (1999): 463–467.

Rhodes, J. T. "Religious Instruction at Syon in the Early Sixteenth Century." In *Studies in St. Birgitta and the Brigittine Order*, vol. 2. *Spiritualität Heute und Gestern, Analecta Cartusiana* 35,19 (1993): 151–169.

————. "Syon Abbey and Its Religious Publications in the Sixteenth Century." *Journal of Ecclesiastical History* 44 (1993): 11–25.

Roth, Francis. *The English Austin Friars, 1249–1538*. Vol. 1, *History*. Vol. 2, *Sources*. Cassiciacum: Studies in St. Augustine and the Augustinian Order 6–7 (American Series). New York: Augustinian Historical Institute, 1961 (vol. 2), 1966 (vol. 1).

Sargent, Michael G. "The Transmission by the English Carthusians of Some Late Medieval Spiritual Writings." *Journal of Ecclesiastical History* 27 (1976): 225–240.

———. "Walter Hilton's *Scale of Perfection:* The London Manuscript Group Reconsidered." *Medium Ævum* 52 (1983): 189–216.

Sayle, Charles. "Cambridge Fragments." *The Library* 3rd ser., 2 (1911): 338–355.

Shipley, A. E. "The Master's Lodgings, Christ's College, Cambridge." *Country Life* 40,1030 (30 Sept. 1916): 378–385; 40,1031 (7 Oct. 1916): 406–412.

A Short-Title Catalogue of Books Printed in England, Scotland, and Ireland and of English Books Printed Abroad, 1475–1640, first compiled by A. W. Pollard and G. R. Redgrave, 2nd ed. begun by W. A. Jackson and F. S. Ferguson, completed by Katharine F. Pantzer. 3 vols. London: Bibliographical Society, 1976–1991.

Steele, Robert. *The Earliest English Music Printing: A Description and Bibliography of English Printed Music to the Close of the Sixteenth Century* Illustrated Monographs 11. London: Bibliographical Society, 1903. Repr. Mansfield Centre, CT: Martino, 2005.

Stubbings, Frank. "A New Manuscript of *Generydes*." *Transactions of the Cambridge Bibliographical Society* 10,3 (1993): 317–339.

Sutton, Anne F. "William Bretton, Publisher of Fine Books, 1506–10." *The Library* 7th ser., 14 (2013): 3–17.

Vaissier, J. J., ed. "*A Deuout Treatyse Called the Tree & xii. Frutes of the Holy Goost*" Edited from MS. McClean 132, Fitzwilliam Museum, Cambridge. Groningen, Holland: J. B. Wolters, 1960.

Williams, Franklin B., Jr., ed. "*The Gardyners Passetaunce*" (c. 1512). Notes by Howard M. Nixon. London: Roxburghe Club, 1985.

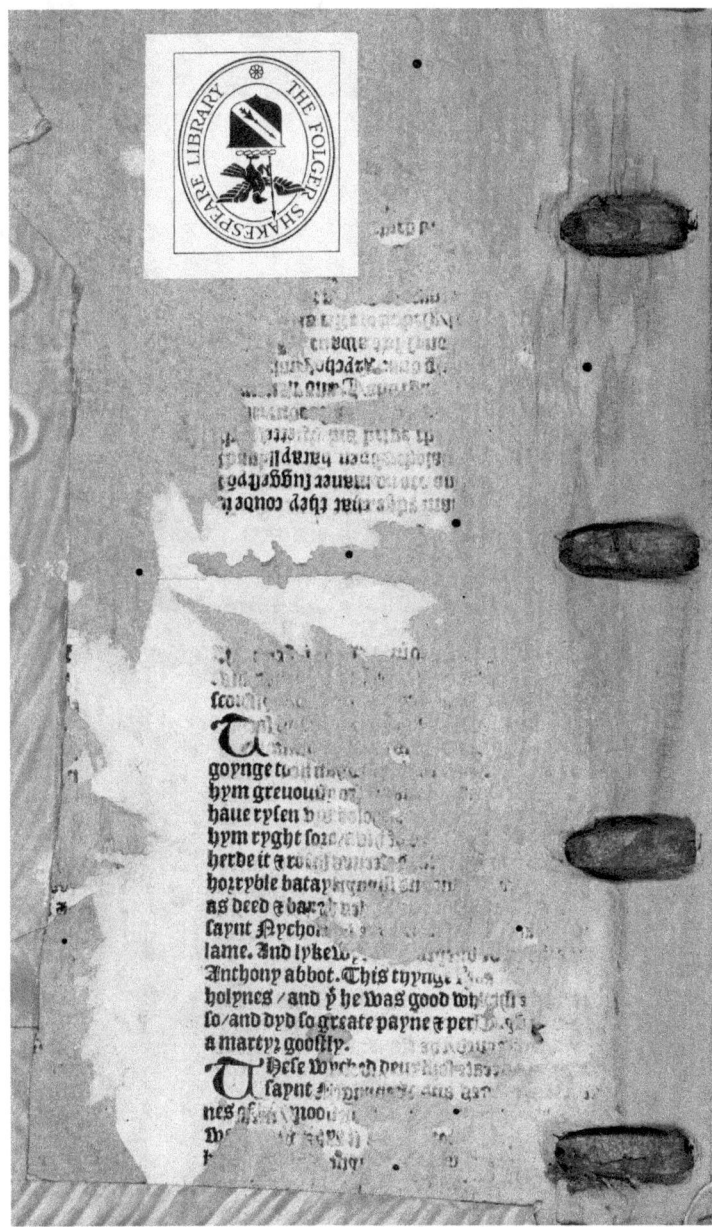

Figure 1. Folger Shakespeare Library, STC 2866: *The First Tome or Volume of the Paraphrases of Erasmus vpon the Newe Testament* (London: Edward Whitchurch, 1551). Printed waste pasted on the inside of the back board showing sigs. A5v and A6r of STC 18528.5, *Saynt Nycholas of Tollentyne* (London: Wynkyn de Worde, c. 1525). By permission of the Folger Shakespeare Library.

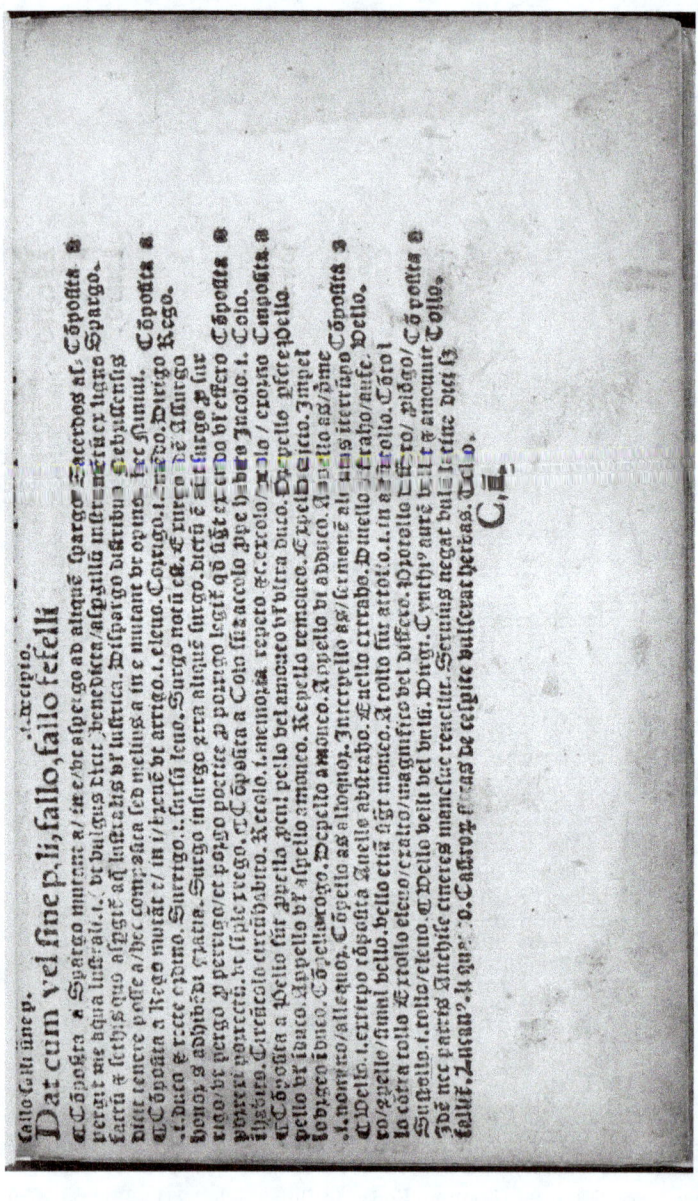

Figure 2. Folger Shakespeare Library, STC 12201: Dionis Gray, *The Store-House of Breuitie in VVoorkes of Arithemetike, Containyng Aswell the Soundrie Partes of the Science in Whole and Broken Numbers* (London: John Kingston for William Norton and John Harrison, 1577). Endpaper showing the lower half of sig. C2r of STC 25566.7, Robert Whittington, *Verborum praeterita et supina* (Southwark: Peter Treveris, 1531?). By permission of the Folger Shakespeare Library.

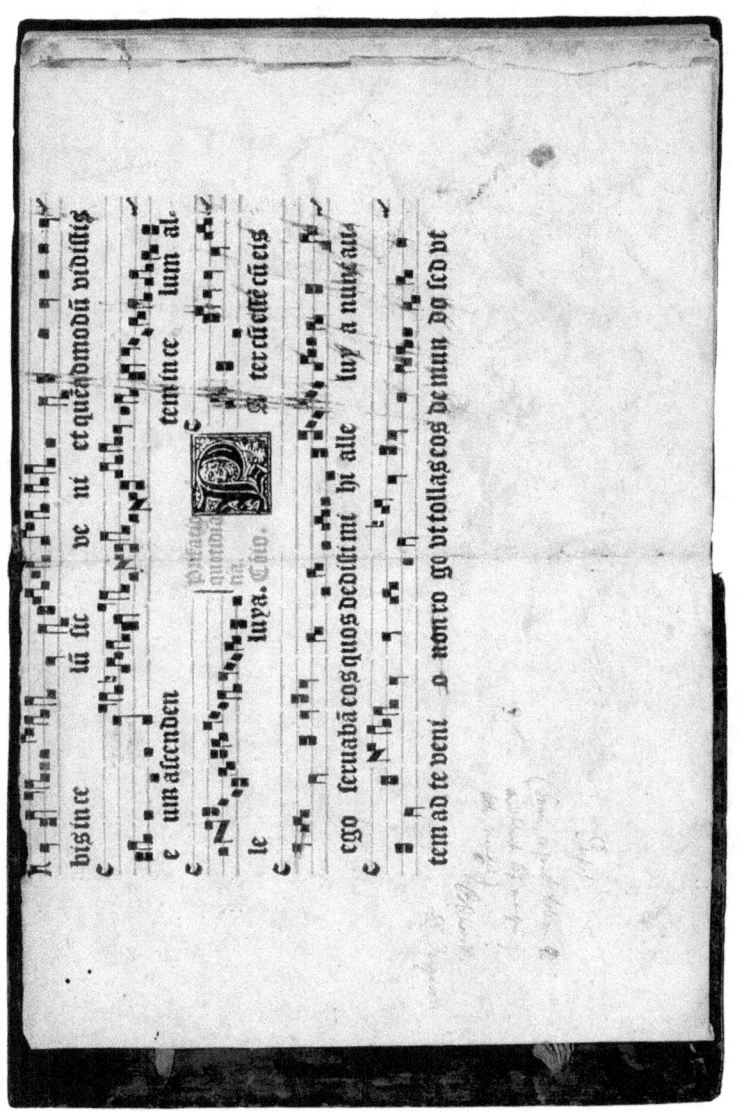

Figure 3. Folger Shakespeare Library; STC 19906: William Langland, *The Vision of Pierce Plowman* (London: Richard Grafton for Robert Crowley, 1550). Endpaper showing the lower half of sig. r1v of STC 15863, *Graduale secundum morem et consuetudinem preclare ecclesie Sarum* (Paris: Nicolas Prévost for Wynkyn de Worde, John Reynes, and Lewis Suethon [Sutton], 17 Cal. Jan. 1527). By permission of the Folger Shakespeare Library.

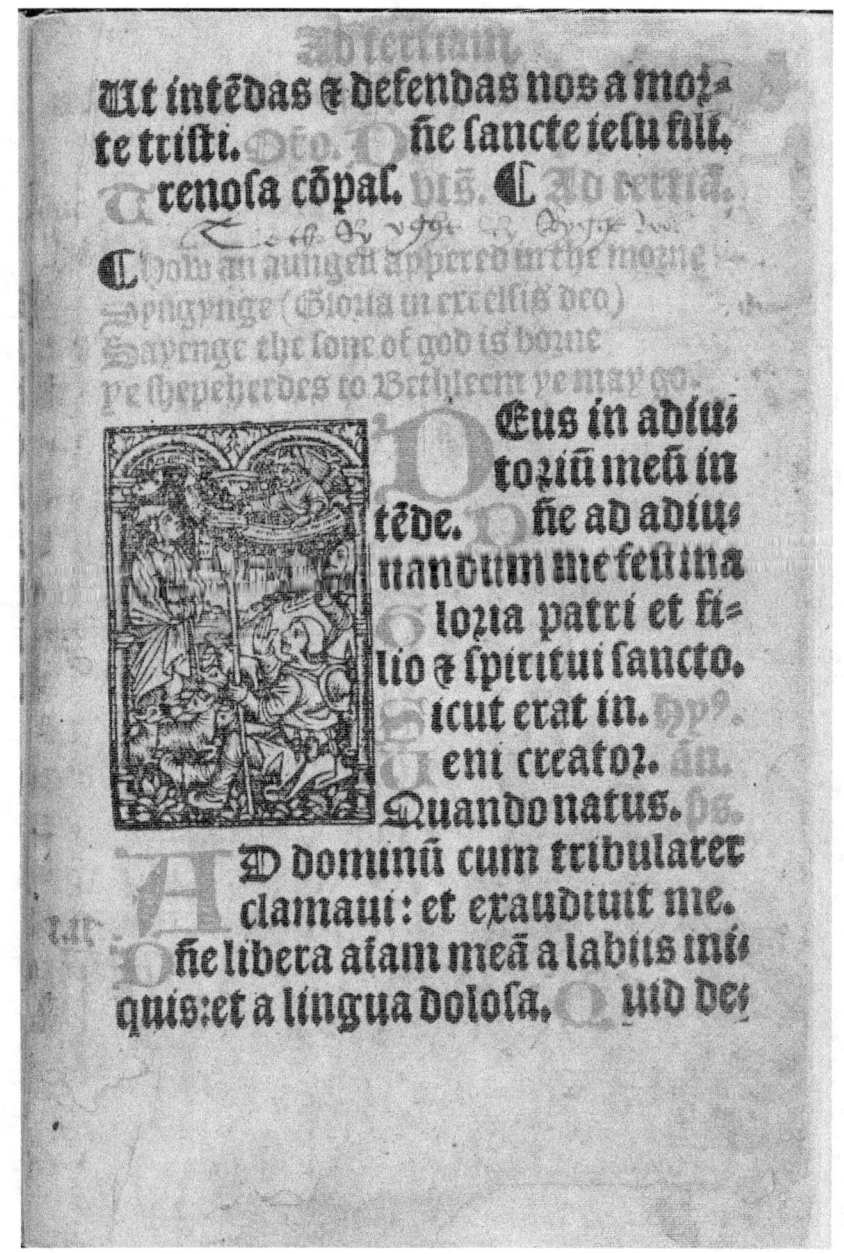

Figure 4. Folger Shakespeare Library, STC 3803 copy 1: John le Breton, *Britton* (London: Robert Redman, 1533?). Endpaper showing sig. E2r of an octavo Sarum Book of Hours (London: Wynkyn de Worde, [after 1531?]). By permission of the Folger Shakespeare Library.

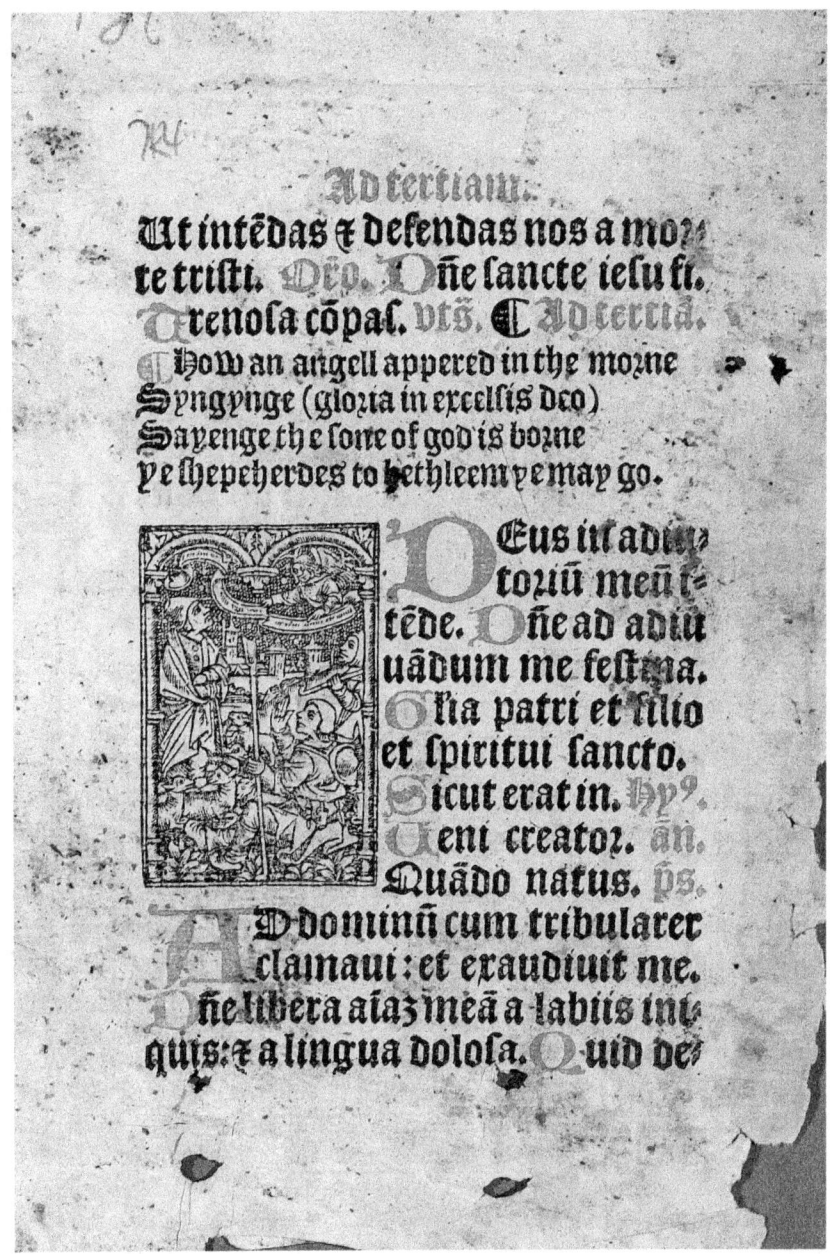

Figure 5. College of Arms, London. Sig. E2r of STC 15932.5 [c. 1525–1530?], one of several Wynkyn de Worde editions of an octavo Sarum Book of Hours removed from the binding of the *Ordinary of the Whyte Book of Trykes* of Christopher Barker (d. 1550), Garter King of Arms. By permission of the College of Arms.

Mandeville Rediscovered: Examining Beinecke MS Osborn a55, the "Lost" Manuscript of *Mandeville's Travels*

KATHERINE HINDLEY

When M. C. Seymour compiled his edition of the Defective Version of *Mandeville's Travels*, published in 2002 for the Early English Text Society, two manuscripts of the text were held by private collectors. One of these, MS 64 in the collection of Toshiyuki Takamiya, was included in Seymour's edition thanks to its owner's willingness to check its text.[1] The other manuscript was not available for study, and Seymour was able to comment only that it was "last seen" at the auction of manuscripts belonging to Sir R. Leicester Harmsworth. It was purchased by Maggs Bros for £100 on October 16, 1945, the twelfth day of the sale of Harmsworth's manuscripts.[2] This copy was offered for sale at Christie's on June 2, 2010. It was bought by the Beinecke Rare Book and Manuscript Library, Yale University, in 2011 and assigned the shelfmark MS Osborn a55.[3] Now that the manuscript belongs to a public institution and is available for study for the first time, I report upon its existence, history, and relationship to the other surviving manuscripts of the Defective Version of *Mandeville's Travels*.

Mandeville's Travels, as it is now known, or *The Book of John Mandeville*, as it was known to its medieval readers, was one of the most widely circulated texts of its time and survives in approximately three hundred manuscripts.[4] As C. W. R. D. Moseley writes, by 1600, it was "in the very warp of the age," influencing writers, mapmakers, and explorers alike.[5] It was originally written some time between 1356 and 1366, although whether it was written in French on the Continent or in Anglo-Norman in England is still debated.[6] By about 1400, it was available in every major language in Europe.[7]

It is perhaps not surprising that such a frequently copied text survives in multiple versions. The Defective Version contained in the Beinecke Osborn manuscript is so called because it was translated into English from a copy of the Anglo-French Insular Version that had either lost its own second quire or derived from a manuscript from which that quire had been lost.[8] It is the dominant English form, surviving in thirty-three manuscripts and six fragments.[9] It was also the first English version to be printed, by Richard Pynson in 1496, and remained the only English version in print until 1725.[10]

MS Osborn a55 consists of sixty-four folios and has been quite heavily cropped. It contains two texts. *Mandeville's Travels* runs from folio 1r to folio 63r. From folio 63v to folio 64v is a contemporary or near-contemporary list of biblical quotations, discussed below. As this text finishes in the middle of a word, it is clear that the manuscript must originally have been longer than it is now, although it is impossible to say by how much. The manuscript contains the bookplates and monograms of several collectors, allowing its history to be reconstructed in some detail. The earliest identifiable owner of the manuscript was the antiquary John Theyer (?1598–1673) of Cooper's Hill, Gloucestershire, whose monogram can be found on the first page of the manuscript along with the number 5 and the foliation "f³j."[11] His collection contained some eight hundred manuscripts, many of which he had inherited from his grandmother's brother, Richard Hart.[12] After John Theyer's death, his grandson Charles Theyer inherited the collection and sold it to the London bookseller Robert Scott, who later sold 312 of its manuscripts to King Charles II.[13]

At some time in the late eighteenth or early nineteenth century, MS Osborn a55 was owned by John Barwick of Charing, whose name is written on the front flyleaf. This was probably the Rev. John Barwick, who became vicar of Charing, Kent, in 1799.[14] He matriculated at Corpus Christi College, Cambridge, in 1784 and became a curate at Charing in 1790. He died in 1834 as the vicar of Charing as well as rector of Boughton Malherbe and perpetual curate of Egerton.[15]

The manuscript next appears in the library of the Rev. Walter Sneyd (1809–1888), who is named in Seymour de Ricci's *English Collectors of Books and Manuscripts* and whose bookplate appears on the manuscript's inside front cover.[16] It is presumably the copy listed at number 276 in the 1837 catalogue of Sneyd's collection: "Syr John Maundeville's Travayles. 8*vo*. Vel. S. xiv."[17] It appears as lot 495 in the sale of his manuscripts at Sotheby's, on the third day of the sale beginning December 16, 1903, when it was sold to the bookseller Ellis for £54.[18] Ellis subsequently sold the manuscript to one of his best customers, the bibliophile Sir Thomas Brooke (1830–1908) of Armitage Bridge, whose bookplate is on the first flyleaf.[19] When Thomas Brooke died, his library was divided and auctioned in several sales. *Man-*

deville's Travels was among the manuscripts that passed to Thomas's younger brother, Sir John Arthur Brooke (1844–1920), on whose death it was sold at auction at Sotheby's. It was bought by Maggs for £91 on the fifth day of the auction starting on May 25, 1921.[20]

It next appears in the auction of manuscripts sold on the death of another major bibliophile, Sir R. Leicester Harmsworth.[21] As mentioned above, it was sold on October 16, 1945, and did not appear for sale again until it was advertised at Christie's in 2010.[22]

MS Osborn a55 contains two texts: *Mandeville's Travels*, and a list of biblical quotations with some similarity to the Later Version of the Wycliffite Bible. The list of biblical quotations breaks off at the end of folio 64v with the words "he þat haþ my coman-." This is presumably the beginning of John 14:21, which reads: "He that hath my commandments, and keepeth them; he it is that loveth me. And he that loveth me, shall be loved of my Father: and I will love him, and will manifest myself to him."[23]

The quotations seem to be grouped roughly by theme. For example, there are short series of quotations dealing with speech and truth and with the raising of children, perhaps intended for a preacher to consult in his sermon preparation. Each quotation is accompanied by a biblical reference that should, according to the placement of the paraph marks, refer to the quotation preceding the reference. Some, however, apply to the quotation following. I am grateful to Anne Hudson for her observation that such misplacements might arise when copying from an exemplar with references in the margins rather than in the text itself.

Although only two folios of this second text survive, they have been written by at least three different hands. One hand wrote the first three quotations on folio 63v, before a second hand took over. This hand wrote the rest of folio 63v and the whole of 64r. A third hand, perhaps comparable to the hand of London, British Library MS Arundel 327, folio 28v, a manuscript written in Cambridge in 1447, wrote folio 64v.[24] A striking difference between the second and third hands is in the shape of *d*, which on folios 63v and 64r is unlooped, with a curving stem and broken lobe. On folio 64v, by contrast, the *d* has a lozenge-shaped bowl with a short, sloping ascender.

Mandeville's Travels was written by a different scribe, using an Anglicana script heavily influenced by Secretary forms, including 2-shaped *r* and a simplified *w*. He also used a single-compartment *a*, although this form becomes predominant only after folio 41v. His use of looped Anglicana *d* also changed as the manuscript goes on, with the form being rare at the beginning of the manuscript but more common from about folio 7r onwards. Most significant, however, is the consistent use of unadorned ascenders. Similar ascenders occur in Plate 13 (i) of Malcolm Parkes's *English Cursive Book Hands*, prompting him to comment that: "The most striking feature of the hand is the presence of simple upright ascenders which have not been furnished with loops or hooks. This feature is found in numerous manuscripts written in Secretary from 1470 onwards."[25] This hand therefore seems more likely to date from the second half of the fifteenth century than from the first.

Most of the textual divisions within *Mandeville's Travels* are marked with blue two-line initials with red penwork flourishes. The initial letter of the manuscript is more heavily decorated, with gold ivy leaves forming a spray border, which is defined as a border "composed of a large initial and of spraywork across most or all of a margin."[26] The waving vines with branches looping back to form circles are one of the later types described by Kathleen Scott, with examples dating from the 1420s to the end of the fifteenth century.[27] Based on a photograph of the manuscript, Scott dates this initial to the 1470s, probably the earlier part of the decade, and compares it to London, Guildhall MS 8695, a charter of incorporation of the Pewterers' Company dated 1473 or 1474.[28] Although the date of the initial should not heavily influence the dating of the manuscript as a whole because it could have been added later, the fact that it seems to come from the last decades of the fifteenth century does support the slightly later dating indicated by the script.

The manuscript also includes three contemporary marginal drawings illustrating themes from the text. On folio 7r, a small, green dragon with a red tongue is shown emerging from a yellow chalice. This symbolizes St. John the Evangelist, who is mentioned just below, in the description of "þe Ile of patmos whare seint jon ewangelist wrot þe apocalips." The text goes on to give St. John's age at the death of Christ and the number of years he lived after that. On folio 7v, the outline of a dragon's head is drawn in pen, accompanied by the word "no*ta*." The illustration refers to the accompanying text, which describes Ypocras's daughter who was "chaungid fro a damesell to a dragon*n*." On folio 36v is drawn the head of an ox to go with the phrase "in this contre men wurschypyþ þe oxe for his grete symplesse." Finally, there seems to have been a fourth illustration on folio 13v. The word "rosis" is visible, along with part of a flower and some leaves, alongside a portion of text describing how roses first appeared in the world. The rest of the image has been cropped away. Also in the margins of the manuscript are manicula and annotations in several hands, including corrections to the text.[29] The correcting hand is contemporary with the main scribe but uses looped ascenders, which the main scribe does not.

This text ends on folio 63r with a scribal colophon reading "qu*o*d Berstede." This is presumably the scribe's family name, and perhaps suggests a connection to Bearsted in Kent or to Bersted in West Sussex. I have been unable to find any colophons giving a similar name in other manuscripts.[30] Below the colophon are two couplets written in a different but contemporary hand using a mixture of Anglicana and Secretary letterforms. The first of these couplets reads:

truste in god thys say hys the tyex whan
bale hys moste byote hys next Amen.

Although the text is a little garbled, it appears to be a couplet from the fifteenth-century poem "This Worlde Is but a Vanyte," incorporating an older proverb.[31] This fifty-line poem survives in full in one fifteenth-century manuscript, San Marino, California, Henry Huntington Library MS HM 183, folio 3v.[32] The second of the two couplets is more common, appearing in eight different manuscripts as listed in *A New Index of Middle English Verse*.[33] This second couplet reads:

A man with hote marcy of marcy schall myse
And he schall have marcy that marcyfull hyst.

Having discussed the history, script, and appearance of the manuscript, I now move on to consider its text. Seymour's edition divides the surviving manuscripts of the Detective Version into five subgroups, with subgroups 1 and 2 deriving independently from the lost archetype. Subgroup 3 derives from subgroup 2, subgroup 4 from subgroup 3, and subgroup 5 from subgroup 4.[34] As he was unable to examine the manuscript itself, Seymour was able to state only that the date in the Prologue of MS Osborn a55—which was reported in the 1945 sale catalogue—was characteristic of manuscripts in subgroups 3, 4, and 5.[35] On closer examination of the text, it is clear that the manuscript is not a member of subgroups 4 or 5, according to the distinguishing features laid down by Seymour. However, it is also not fully a member of subgroup 3, a fact that raises larger issues about the validity of Seymour's subgroups.

According to Seymour, manuscripts of subgroup 3 avoid the characteristic features of subgroup 1, share the characteristic features of subgroup 2, and include four other distinctive features.[36] As listed by Seymour, these are:

1. they omit the Hebrew alphabet;
2. they corrupt the date in the Prologue and the Epilogue;
3. they variously corrupt the phrase *wel lowe in Ethiope*;
4. they corrupt an earlier *3e schal wite þat þe deed see* to *þe falle of þe deed see* and omit by eyeskip the next sentence *and þat see lastiþ fro Sora to Arabie*.[37]

The Beinecke Osborn manuscript avoids the features of subgroup 1 and shares the characteristic features of subgroup 2, but it does not include all of the features of subgroup 3.[38] This does not make it unique. As Seymour notes:

> The subgroup is not homogeneous. The imperfect and con-flated Rugby School manuscript and T[rinity] C[ollege] C[Cambridge] MS R. 4. 20 only partly reflect the characteris-tic features of this subgroup ... and so presumably derive from copies anterior in the scribal tradition to the lost common ancestor of the other five manuscripts of the subgroup.[39]

Both the Rugby and Trinity manuscripts come from the South East Midlands and are dated by Seymour to between 1425 and 1450.[40] Although the Beinecke Osborn manuscript is not closely related to either Rugby or Trinity, it seems plausible that it should be grouped with them.

The first major characteristic of subgroup 3 manuscripts listed by Sey-mour is the omission of the Hebrew alphabet. In MS Osborn a55, this sec-tion of the text appears on folio 24r. It reads "3yf 3e wille wete þe lettris of iewis þay beth suche Alpha beta A L P H A B E T A." Unlike the manuscripts in subgroups 1 and 2, the Beinecke Osborn manuscript does not give the Hebrew alphabet, or anything approximating to it, and it omits the subgroup 1 reference to the names of the letters.[41] However, it also avoids the more extreme corruptions that can occur in manuscripts of subgroup 3. Bodleian MS Douce 109, for example, reads "it is clepid the welle of the Iewis to ben clepid as þe namys ben as þay clepen Alphabe," omitting any mention of let-ters at all.[42] Although other manuscripts in subgroup 3 retain the reference to letters, only one does so while also omitting subgroup 1's reference to names. This is the Rugby School manuscript, whose reading is almost identical to that of MS Osborn a55. It reads, "if 3e wolle wite þe letres of iewes þei buþ siche Alpha Betha et cetera."[43] Like MS Osborn a55, it omits both the names of the letters and the characters themselves.

The second major characteristic of subgroup 3 manuscripts is their cor-ruption of the date in the Prologue and Epilogue. Where subgroup 1 manu-scripts give Mandeville's date of travel as 1332 in the Prologue, on folio 2r MS Osborn a55 gives 1300. This corruption is very common, occurring, ac-cording to Seymour, in twelve other manuscripts. Less usual is the corruption of the date in the Epilogue, which on folio 62v of MS Osborn a55 reads: "I Johan Maundevyle þat wente out of my contre *and* passid þe see þe 3ere of oure lord Mill CCC lxvi at xxxiiij 3ere after my departynge fro my contre." The first *x* in the number thirty-four is visible under ultraviolet light but has been erased, leaving a figure of twenty-four. Where the Beinecke Osborn manuscript gives only one date, the usual subgroup 1 reading gives two different dates in this section—one, 1332, as the year of travel and the other, 1366, as the year in which the text was compiled. Only one other manuscript of the Defective Version, London, British Library MS Arundel 140 part 1, a manuscript in Seymour's subgroup 2, shares this particular corruption of the text. Just like the original reading of MS Osborn a55, it reads: "I Iohan Maundevyle þat wente oute of my contre and passede þe see þe 3eere of oure lorde m¹. ccc. lxvi at xxxiiii. yeere aftre my departynge fro my contree."⁴⁴ It does not, however, include the erasure changing the number of years after Mandeville's departure from thirty- to twenty-four.

Two manuscripts do include the number twenty-four, although both also preserve the original form of the text, giving both the date of travel and the date of the text's compilation. One of these is the Rugby School Manuscript, which gives 1356 as the year of writing and which at this point is conflated with subgroup 1.⁴⁵ The other is London, British Library MS Royal 17 C. xxxviii, which derives "from a place in the scribal tradition immediately superior to the common ancestor of the five manuscripts of subgroup 2."⁴⁶ Here, then, the Beinecke Osborn manuscript's reading is unrelated to any of those in Seymour's subgroup 3.

The third variation characteristic of subgroup 3 manuscripts is the corruption of the phrase "wel lowe in Ethiope." MS Osborn a55 does corrupt the reading, on folio 16r, to "vell lawe in ethiope." However, as with the text dealing with the Hebrew alphabet, this reading is less corrupted than those of other manuscripts in subgroup 3. Oxford, Bodleian Library MS Douce 109, for example, has "he distroyid þe lawe in Egipte," while London, British Library MS Additional 33758 has "he felle low into Ethiope."⁴⁷ However, it is possible that the scribe of MS Osborn a55 had some difficulty with this phrase in his exemplar. After writing "vell" the scribe wrote two letters—perhaps an *l* and an *a*—before scribbling them out and starting the word again. It is particularly unusual for the scribe to scribble out a mistake. Other errors are corrected using a single line, as with the deletion of the word "Synay" on folio 11v. This section of the text is missing in the Rugby manuscript, while the Trinity manuscript reads, "Weltlawe in Ethiopie."

The fourth and final major feature of manuscripts in subgroup 3 is the corruption of "3e schal wite þat þe deed see" to "þe falle of þe deed see," with the omission through eyeskip of the next sentence, "and þat see lastiþ fro Sora to Arabie."⁴⁸ At this point, on folio 22r, MS Osborn a55 reads: "3e schal wete þat þe dede see departiþ þe lond of ynde and arabey *and* þe wat*er* of þat see is ful bitt*er*." The Beinecke Osborn manuscript, therefore, avoids the corruption of the sentence but does have the eyeskip. This is not the case for any other manuscript of subgroup 3, although this section of the text is lacking in the Rugby School manuscript. Cambridge, Trinity College MS R. 4. 20, the other manuscript that does not fully share the features of subgroup 3, has neither the corruption of the text nor the eyeskip. However, there is a strong similarity between the Beinecke Osborn manuscript's reading and that of Richard Pynson's printed edition of around 1496, assigned by Seymour to subgroup 2, which has: "ye shall wete the dedde see departeth the londe of Indee/ and of araby/ and the water of that see is full bytter/."[49]

Three other texts of *Mandeville's Travels*, therefore, share at least one reading with the Beinecke Osborn manuscript. These are the Rugby School manuscript, Pynson's printed text, and British Library MS Arundel 140. As well as listing the common features of each subgroup, Seymour's edition lists the unique features of each of the manuscripts of the Defective Version. MS Osborn a55 avoids all of the corruptions unique to individual subgroup 2 manuscripts, with the exception of the omission of text in the epilogue mentioned above as being common to MS Osborn a55 and to British Library, MS Arundel 140. They are the only two manuscripts that contain the reduced Epilogue but do not include the phrase "I came again" at the end of this passage.[50] They also share several minor textual variations. For example, on folio 45v MS Osborn a55 changes the word "philosofris" to "maystris" in the discussion at the court of the Great Khan. Of the manuscripts collated by Seymour, only MS Arundel 140 makes a similar alteration, changing the word to "mastirs."[51] However, MS Osborn a55 does not share the other unique feature of MS Arundel 140, the omission of the account of the island of Tracota. As MS Arundel 140 dates from the first quarter of the fifteenth century and MS Osborn a55 appears to date from the second half, these two manuscripts cannot be directly related, although it does seem possible that they are descendants of the same close antecedent.[52]

It is more difficult to compare the Beinecke Osborn manuscript with Pynson's printed text, because Seymour's edition is unclear about how exactly the printed version differs from other copies of the text. Seymour writes that Pynson "omits the rest of chapter 15 after the common loss of the account of *Sylha*" in the manuscripts of subgroup 2.[53] In his edition, however, the account of Sylha comes at the very end of chapter 15, leaving nothing extra for Pynson's text to omit.[54] A comparison of Seymour's edition with Tamarah Kohanski's edition of the Pynson text and with another manuscript of subgroup 2, London, British Library Royal MS 17 B xliii, confirms that Pynson's printing of *Mandeville's Travels* omits nothing from this section other than the commonly omitted account of Sylha.[55] Other factors, however, make it unlikely that Pynson's text could be related to MS Osborn a55. For example, Pynson preserves the correct reading for the passage describing the Hebrew alphabet, including the names of the letters.[56]

The remaining manuscript to share unusual features with MS Osborn a55 is the Rugby School manuscript. Seymour discusses the characteristics of this manuscript and of Cambridge, Trinity College, MS R. 4. 20 at some length:

The two aberrant manuscripts, 3R [Rugby] and 3T [Trinity], give different dates in Prologue and Epilogue: 3R has 1300, the common corruption, and 1356, the palmary reading; 3T has 1332 and 1366, as in subgroups 1 and 2; 3T avoids the corruptions [of *3e schal wite þat þe deed see*]; 3R lacks the leaf. Both manuscripts lack the extended initial rubric found in [London, British Library MS Additional 33758] and [Oxford, Bodleian Library MS Rawlinson B 216] ([Oxford, Bodleian Library MS Rawlinson D 100] and [Oxford, Bodleian Library MS Douce 109] lack leaf); avoid corrupt forms of names, like *Steven* for the better *Sophe* [in the discussion of Constantinople], which occur elsewhere in the subgroup; and avoid the *ile turne* corruption and give the Epilogue in full. Uniquely in its subgroup 3R is conflated with subgroup 1 for its last four leaves, ff. 33–7.[57]

As discussed above, the Rugby School manuscript uses the same dates in the Prologue and Epilogue as MS Osborn a55 although, unlike the Osborn MS, it gives both the year of travel and the year of writing. Also discussed above is the corruption of the phrase dealing with the Dead Sea: MS Osborn a55 omits part of the sentence through eyeskip but otherwise preserves the correct reading. Like the Rugby School and Trinity manuscripts, the Beinecke Osborn manuscript also does not include an extended initial rubric and it has *Sophe* rather than *Steven* when describing Constantinople on folio 3r. It does, however, differ from them in other ways. Like them, it avoids the reading "ile turne," but its reading on folio 2v, "þe yle of tyne," is not similar to that of either manuscript. The Trinity manuscript has the subgroup 1 reading "ile toun," while Rugby has "hille Tune."[58] Also unlike both Trinity and Rugby, MS Osborn a55 gives a reduced Epilogue. Despite these differences, there seem to be enough similarities between these manuscripts to place MS Osborn a55 with the Rugby and Trinity manuscripts, standing between subgroups 2 and 3.

MS Osborn a55 may also have a unique omission of its own. On folio 37r, it lacks a sentence which in Seymour reads, "And yf þe wyf dei3e first, men brenne hure and here housbande yf he wile."[59] When discussing the features of the surviving manuscripts of *Mandeville's Travels*, Seymour at no point mentions this omission, implying that none of the surviving manuscripts from later subgroups were derived in any way from MS Osborn a55. Other unique omissions may also be present that could be identified with further study.

On the basis of its text, MS Osborn a55 can be placed with the Rugby and Trinity manuscripts on the boundary between subgroups 2 and 3. Like these manuscripts, it does not fully reflect the characteristics of this subgroup. However, it also does not seem to be closely related to either of them, nor to the surviving manuscripts in later subgroups. This is, perhaps, to be expected: the impossibility of drawing close connections between the manuscripts of this text serves to emphasize the phenomenal popularity of *Mandeville's Travels* in the medieval period.

APPENDIX:
NEW HAVEN, BEINECKE LIBRARY, MS OSBORN a55
Extracts from the Beinecke Osborn manuscript for comparison with the appendix in Seymour, *The Defective Version*, 185–215:

> 1. fol. 2r: Jon de Maundevyle knyht þawh þat y be noht wordi þat was borne in inglond in þe town of Seint albonis and passid þe se in þe 3ere of owre lord ihesu crist M¹ CCC 3ere on þe day of Seint Michelle
> 2. fols. 2r–v: with many lordis and good company . . . and þorw þe castelle off newborwh and by þe yle of tyne to þe ende of hungry
> 3. fol. 11r: also he holdith calafes het ys a gret thyng to be sowdan hit is to say among hem Roys iles and þis vale is fulle colde
> 4. fol. 16r: and oþer kyngdomis many unto velle lawe in ethiope
> 5. fol. 22r: Also ii myle fro iericho is flum Iordan and 3e schal wete þat þe dede see departiþ þe lond of ynde and arabey and þe water of þat see is ful bitter . . . and som men calle þat þe lake of feutted
> 6. fol. 23r: a strong castel þat men calle garras oþer Sercinos þat is to say a real mount in frensche
> 7. fol. 24r: and in þis contre dwelliþ many Iewis paying trebut alle as cristyn men doth and 3yf 3e wille wete þe lettris of iewis þay beth suche Alpha beta A L P H A B E T A
> 8. fol. 31v: þerfore larschenyn whan he resevyth ham he sayþ þus
> 9. fol. 38r: þedir brengyþ marchandis childir to selle and þese þat beþ fat þey ete ham and þay kepe þe lene tyl þay be fat and þan þay beþ y ete. Besyde this yle ys anoþer yle þat is y callyd Somobere
> 10. fol. 57v: We have no king among us noht for to lawe ne deme no man for þer is no trespasoar among

us but al only to h lere us to be obedyent to god *and*
þou may noht take fro us but oure good pees
11. fols. 57v–58r: Anoþer yle ys callyþ Synophe
where also ben goode folke *and* ful of goode feyþ . . .
and alysaundir was gretly a stonyd *with* þis answere
12. fol. 62v: I Johan Maundevyle *þat* wente out of
my contre *and* passid þe see þe 3ere of oure lord
Mill CCC lxvi at xxiiii 3ere af*ter* my departynge fro
my contre[60]

NOTES

1. Professor Takamiya's Middle English manuscripts are currently housed
at the Beinecke Library in New Haven. For a brief description of this manuscript, see Toshiyuki Takamiya, "A Handlist of Western Medieval Manuscripts in the Takamiya Collection," in *The Medieval Book: Glosses from Friends
and Colleagues of Christopher De Hamel*, ed. James H. Marrow, Richard A.
Linenthal, and William Noel (Houten, Netherlands: Hes & De Graaf, 2010),
434. Seymour refers to the manuscript as Takamiya MS 63. See M. C. Seymour, ed., *The Defective Version of Mandeville's Travels*, Early English Text
Society o.s. 319 (Oxford: Oxford University, 2002), 200.
2. Seymour, *Defective Version*, xiv, n.2; S. C. Sotheby (1), October 16, 1945,
lot 2023.
3. S. C. Christie, June 2, 2010, lot 206.
4. Iain Macleod Higgins, *Writing East: The "Travels" of Sir John Mandeville*
(Philadelphia, PA: University of Pennsylvania, 1997), vii.
5. C. W. R. D. Moseley, "*Mandeville's Travels*: A Study of the Book and Its
Importance in England, 1356–1750," PhD diss., University of East Anglia,
1971, 179.
6. See, e.g., Moseley, "Book and Its Importance," 9, 26, and 32; Seymour,
Defective Version, xi; Higgins, *Writing East*, vii.
7. Moseley, "Book and Its Importance," 162.
8. Seymour, *Defective Version*, xi.
9. Ibid., xii.
10. Moseley, "Book and Its Importance," 168–169.
11. Irvine Gray, *Antiquaries of Gloucestershire and Bristol* (Bristol, UK: Bristol
and Gloucestershire Archaeological Society, 1981), 43.
12. Ibid., 43.
13. Charlotte Fell-Smith, "Theyer, John (bap. 1598, d. 1673)," rev. Robert
J. Haines, in *Oxford Dictionary of National Biography*, ed. H. C. G. Matthew
and Brian Harrison (Oxford: Oxford University Press, 2004), http://www.
oxforddnb.com/view/article/27178 (accessed December 30, 2013).

14. "Addenda and Corrigenda to Volume 7," in *The History and Topographical Survey of the County of Kent: Volume 8* (1799), 537–549, http://www.british-history.ac.uk/report.aspx?compid=63526 (accessed December 30, 2013).
15. "Barwick, John (1790–1834)," *CCEd: Clergy of the Church of England Database*, http://www.theclergydatabase.org.uk/jsp/persons/DisplayCcePerson.jsp?PersonID=8841 (accessed July 18, 2013).
16. Seymour de Ricci, *English Collectors of Books and Manuscripts (1530–1930) and Their Marks of Ownership* (Cambridge, UK: Cambridge University Press, 1930), 136–137.
17. "Catalogue of MSS in the Possession of the Rev. Walter Sneyd of Cheverels, Co. Herts. 1837," in *Catalogus Manuscriptorum in Bibliothecis Angliæ, Cambriæ, Scotiæ, et Hiberniæ* (England, 1833–1838?), possibly compiled by Sir Thomas Phillipps, 16, no. 276.
18. S. C. Sotheby (1), December 16, 1903, lot 495.
19. De Ricci, *English Collectors*, 167.
20. S. C. Sotheby (1), May 25, 1921, lot 921. See also de Ricci, *English Collectors*, 167–168.
21. De Ricci, *English Collectors*, 41, 110.
22. S. C. Sotheby (1), October 16, 1945, lot 2023; S. C. Christie, June 2, 2010, lot 206.
23. Douay-Rheims version.
24. Andrew G. Watson, *Catalogue of Dated and Datable Manuscripts c. 700–1600 in the Department of Manuscripts, the British Library* (London: British Library, 1979), 2:pl. 488b.
25. Malcolm B. Parkes, *English Cursive Book Hands, 1250–1500*, Oxford Palaeographical Handbooks (Oxford: Clarendon Press, 1969), 13.
26. Kathleen L. Scott, *Dated and Datable English Manuscript Borders c. 1395–1499* (Dorchester, UK: Henry Ling for Bibliographical Society, 2002), 11.
27. See, e.g., ibid., 47, pl. X (1421–1422), and 108–109, pl. XXXVI (1492).
28. Kathleen Scott, e-mail message to author, May 16, 2013.
29. Corrections can be seen, e.g., on fol. 19v.
30. Berstede, Burstede, Bersted, Bursted, Barstede, and Barsted are all absent from *Colophons de manuscrits occidentaux des origines au XVIe siècle*, 6 vols. (Fribourg, Switzerland: Éditions universitaires, 1965–1982). There is also no similar name in the index of N. R. Ker, *Medieval Manuscripts in British Libraries*, 5 vols., ed. I. C. Cunningham and A. G. Watson (Oxford: Clarendon, 2002).
31. R. H. Bowers, "Hichecoke's 'This Worlde Is but a Vanyte' (HM 183)," *Modern Language Notes* 67 (1952): 331–333. The text has been attributed to Hichecoke because it ends with the words "quod Hichecoke," but it is also possible that this refers to the scribe of the manuscript. Versions of the second line of the couplet dating from ca. 1275 are listed in *Middle English Dictionary*,

http://quod.lib.umich.edu/cgi/m/mec/med-idx?type=id&id=MED5609 (accessed December 27, 2013).

32. Julia Boffey and A. S. G. Edwards, ed., *A New Index of Middle English Verse*, (London: British Library, 2005), no. 1261.

33. Ibid., no. 77. It is also found on fol. 38v of New Haven, Beinecke Library MS Osborn fa50, where a sixteenth-century hand has written it three times onto the back flyleaf of a manuscript of Peter Idley's "Instructions to His Son."

34. Seymour, *Defective Version*, xv.

35. Ibid., xiv, n.2.

36. Ibid., xxi–ii.

37. Ibid., xxii.

38. The distinctive features of manuscripts of subgroup 1 are given in ibid., xvii. The distinctive features of subgroup 2 are given in ibid., xix–xx.

39. Ibid., xxii. The other five manuscripts of the subgroup are London, British Library MS Additional 33758; Oxford, Bodleian Library MS Rawlinson B 216; Oxford, Bodleian Library MS Rawlinson D 100; Oxford, Bodleian Library MS Douce 109; and New Haven, Beinecke Library MS Takamiya 61.

40. Seymour, *Defective Version*, 201–202. The Rugby MS has the shelfmark MS Bloxam 1008 and is dated by N. R. Ker to the second half of the fifteenth century. See N. R. Ker and A. J. Piper, *Medieval Manuscripts in British Libraries* (Oxford: Clarendon, 1992), 4:222. The Trinity manuscript is dated by M. R. James to the early fifteenth century. See M. R. James, *The Western Manuscripts in the Library of Trinity College, Cambridge* (Cambridge, UK: Cambridge University Press, 1901), 2:147. Both are also described in M. C. Seymour, "The English Manuscripts of *Mandeville's Travels*," *Edinburgh Bibliographical Society Transactions* 4 (1966): 169–210, nos. 16 and 18. MS Osborn a55 is described at no. 32.

41. For example, the subgroup 1 manuscript Oxford, Queen's College MS 383 reads "And if 3e wole wite þe lettris, þei beþ siche in þe names of þe lettris as þei clepiþ hem: *alph, beth, gimel, he, vau, 3ay, ex, ioth, karph, lamp, meu, nun, samech, ey, phe, lad, corth, fir, soun, thau, lours.* Now shal 3e haue þe figures of þe Iewis lettre." See Seymour, *Defective Version*, 45.

42. Oxford, Bodleian Library MS Douce 109, fol. 27r, as transcribed in Seymour, *Defective Version*, 199.

43. Rugby School Manuscript, fol. 9r, as transcribed in Seymour, *Defective Version*, 202.

44. London, British Library MS Arundel 140 part 1, fol. 41r, as transcribed in Seymour, *Defective Version*, 187–188.

45. Seymour, *Defective Version*, xxii and 204.

46. Ibid., xxi and 190–191.

47. Oxford, Bodleian Library MS Douce 109, fol. 18r, and London, British Library MS Additional 33758, fol. 15v, as transcribed in Seymour, *Defective Version*, 199 and 194.

48. Seymour, *Defective Version*, xxii.
49. Tamarah Kohanski, *The Book of John Mandeville: An Edition of the Pynson Text with Commentary on the Defective Version*, Medieval and Renaissance Texts and Studies 231 (Tempe, AZ: Arizona Center for Medieval and Renaissance Studies, 2001), 29. This corresponds to page d1r in the unique copy, which is housed at the British Library, pressmark 6173.
50. See "Appendix Reading 12" in Seymour, *Defective Version*, 185–215.
51. See ibid., 100.
52. Ibid., 187.
53. Ibid., xx.
54. See ibid., 88.
55. See Kohanski, *Book of John Mandeville*, 59.
56. Ibid., 32.
57. Seymour, *Defective Version*, xxii.
58. Ibid., 201–203.
59. See ibid., 75, ll. 20–21.
60. The text seems to have read "at xxxiiii 3ere," but the first *x* has been erased.

WORKS CITED

"Addenda and Corrigenda to Volume 7." In *The History and Topographical Survey of the County of Kent: Volume 8*, 537–549. 1799. http://www.british-history.ac.uk/report.aspx?compid=63526.
"Barwick, John (1790–1834)." In *CCEd: Clergy of the Church of England Database*. http://www.theclergydatabase.org.uk/jsp/persons/DisplayCcePerson.jsp?PersonID=8841.
Boffey, Julia, and A. S. G. Edwards. *A New Index of Middle English Verse*. London: British Library, 2005.
Bowers, R. H. "Hichecoke's 'This Worlde Is but a Vanyte' (HM 183)." *Modern Language Notes* 67 (1952): 331–333.
"Catalogue of MSS in the Possession of the Rev. Walter Sneyd of Cheverels, Co. Herts. 1837." In *Catalogus Manuscriptorum in Bibliothecis Angliæ, Cambriæ, Scotiæ, et Hiberniæ*, possibly compiled by Sir Thomas Phillipps. England, 1833–1838?
Colophons de manuscrits occidentaux des origins au XVIe siècle. 6 vols. Fribourg, Switzerland: Éditions universitaires, 1965–1982.
de Ricci, Seymour. *English Collectors of Books and Manuscripts (1530–1930) and Their Marks of Ownership*. Cambridge, UK: Cambridge University Press, 1930.
Fell-Smith, Charlotte. "Theyer, John (bap. 1598, d. 1673)," rev. Robert J. Haines, in *Oxford Dictionary of National Biography*, edited by H. C. G. Matthew and Brian Harrison. Oxford: Oxford University Press, 2004. http://www.oxforddnb.com/view/article/27178.

Higgins, Iain Macleod. *Writing East: The "Travels" of Sir John Mandeville.* Philadelphia, PA: University of Pennsylvania Press, 1997.

James, M. R. *The Western Manuscripts in the Library of Trinity College, Cambridge.* Cambridge, UK: Cambridge University Press, 1901.

Ker, N. R., A. J. Piper, I. C. Cunningham, and A. G. Watson, eds. *Medieval Manuscripts in British Libraries.* 5 vols. Oxford: Clarendon Press, 1969–2002.

Kohanski, Tamarah. *The Book of John Mandeville: An Edition of the Pynson Text with Commentary on the Defective Version.* Medieval and Renaissance Texts and Studies 231. Tempe, AZ: Arizona Center for Medieval and Renaissance Studies, 2001.

Marrow, James H., Richard A. Linenthal, and William Noel, eds. *The Medieval Book: Glosses from Friends and Colleagues of Christopher de Hamel.* Houten, Netherlands: Hes & De Graaf, 2010.

Middle English Dictionary. Ann Arbor: University of Michigan, 2007. http://quod.lib.umich.edu/m/med/.

Moseley, C. W. R. D. "Mandeville's Travels: A Study of the Book and Its Importance in England, 1356–1750." PhD diss., University of East Anglia, 1971.

Parkes, Malcolm B. *English Cursive Books Hands, 1250–1500.* Oxford Palaeographical Handbooks. Oxford: Clarendon Press, 1969.

S. C. Christie, June 2, 2010.

S. C. Sotheby (1), December 16, 1903.

S. C. Sotheby (1), May 25, 1921.

S. C. Sotheby (1), October 16, 1945.

Scott, Kathleen L. *Dated and Datable English Manuscript Borders c. 1395–1499.* Dorchester, UK: Henry Ling for Bibliographical Society, 2002.

Seymour, M. C., ed. *The Defective Version of Mandeville's Travels.* Early English Text Society o.s 319. Oxford: Oxford University Press, 2002.

Takamiya, Toshiyuki. "A Handlist of Western Medieval Manuscripts in the Takamiya Collection." In *The Medieval Books: Glosses from Friends and Colleagues of Christopher De Hamel*, edited by James H. Marrow, Richard A. Linenthal, and William Noel. Houten, Netherlands: Hes & De Graaf, 2010.

Watson, Andrew G. *Catalogue of Dated and Datable Manuscripts, c. 700–1600 in the Department of Manuscripts, the British Library.* 2 vols. London: British Library, 1979.

An Early Sixteenth-Century Lutheran Dialogue and its Wycliffite Excerpt

DAVID LAVINSKY

1.

In her seminal work on Wycliffism and the Reformation, Margaret Aston afforded heresy a central role "in moulding or preparing the minds of new reformers," a judgment both enriched and complicated by recent scholarship on the history of the book.[1] As a result, questions about the dissemination of Wycliffite thought and its affiliation with other reform movements now routinely extend to the networks of production and use in which Wycliffite writing was embedded. Nevertheless, these questions are rarely pursued in transcultural and transhistorical contexts, my interest here.[2] The case I will address concerning an early sixteenth-century Lutheran dialogue and its Wycliffite excerpt offers a vantage point for considering affiliation across the temporal, geographic, and material boundaries separating a medieval sermon tract from its fragmentary redeployment in a printed document.

My discussion will center on Lambeth Palace Library MS 551.[3] A variant version of a longer sermon on Matthew 15:13 (*omnis plantatio quam non plantavit Pater meus caelestis eradicabitur*) found in British Library MS Egerton 2820, the Lambeth tract first appeared in F. D. Matthew's 1880 *EETS* edition of Wycliffite texts.[4] Since that time, and despite Anne Hudson's authoritative 2001 edition of these and a third text by the same (anonymous) Wycliffite author, critical and historical focus has remained squarely on the version found in Egerton.[5] This imbalance seems at least in part due to the nature of their respective references. Allusions to Arundel's *Constitutions* attest to the obvious topicality of the Egerton sermon, while also dating it to sometime after 1409, when the archbishop's restrictions on vernacular preaching and religious instruction were promulgated; references in Lambeth, by contrast, are more difficult to trace, though Hudson suggests a *terminus ad quem* of about 1410, making it the earlier of the two.[6]

These are not the only differences between them, however. Although the two advance similar (though not identical) arguments against mendicant spirituality, secular lordship of the clergy, and clerical possessions, they diverge in some important formal respects. Lambeth consists of many fewer folios and has the qualities of a tract rather than a sermon, lacking as it does the pervasive first-person voice that makes Egerton so distinctive, including several moments when the sermon writer draws attention to his own signifying practices.[7] Lambeth also includes two appendices not found in Egerton, one of which is a catalogue of Latin authorities buttressing the tract's argument "a3ens þe seculer lordeschip of prestis" (ll.1053-1054).[8] Despite indications that it was intended for use in pedagogical or instructional settings, a copy of the tract caught the eye (if not necessarily the ear) of early evangelical reformers in the Low Countries, who included an excerpt from it in an anticlerical text known as *A proper dyaloge betwene a Gentillman and an Husbandman* (Fig. 1).[9]

A proper dyaloge, as I refer to it here, first appeared in 1529 as part of a compilation of Lutheran materials associated by its typographical characteristics with the work of one Hans Luft, a printer working in Marburg.[10] Like many other reformist texts printed in the Low Countries during this period, it is anonymous.[11] Nor do we know much about the circumstances of its printing. In her pioneering work on early Reformation publications in Dutch and English, M. E. Kronenberg argued that "Hans Luft of Marlborow" was one of two false ascriptions regularly employed by the Antwerp printer Johannes Hoochstraten, the other being "Adam Anonymous of Basel."[12] Kronenberg's conclusions have been challenged in recent years on the grounds that Hoochstraten's press used implements and typographical ornaments from a stock traced to signed works by Martin de Keyser, Tyndale's publisher in Antwerp, strongly suggesting it was in fact the latter who employed the pseudonyms—and whose press was therefore responsible for a large number of early Protestant publications, including *A proper dyaloge*, a second edition of which appeared in 1530 with the Marburg ascription.[13] If, as John D. Fudge has explained, "it remained largely up to an author or translator to approach a publisher or printer with new material," it is easy to imagine anticlerical texts coming into the possession of a press associated with imprints by the preeminent exiled English reformer.[14] All this underscores the significance of de Keyser's press both as a source of English Protestant books printed abroad, and as a point of contact between Wycliffite materials and Lutheran readers in the period.[15] Through such means, Wycliffite writing found a ready audience in early modern reformers who wanted to register similar complaints about clerical greed and corruption. At least in this respect, then, the printed editions produced in Antwerp during this time are evidence of a certain kind of cultural continuity, especially in securing what David Loades has referred to as "the Lollard inheritance." Grievances common to Protestant printers and their Wycliffite precursors, Loades writes, pointing to the "Hoochstraten" press in particular, "could make the voices of the early fifteenth century speak directly to the audience of the 1530s."[16]

2.

To evaluate this claim we first need to look more closely at the texts themselves. *A proper dyaloge* unfolds as a conversation between two speakers who complain in turn about oppression at the hands of a covetous and hypocritical clergy. The dialogue touches on familiar reformist themes—the doctrine of purgatory, practices such as tithing, increases in rents and fees, the trade in pardons, biblical censorship—before refuting the view that Lutherans lacked precursors for their opposition to clerical possessions and worldly dominion.[17] "By seynt mary syr," says the Husbandman, or farmer, responding to this familiar objection, "that is a starcke lye" (656). He then mentions a precedent for Lutheran views in a book "aboue an hundred yere olde / As the englishe selfe dothe testifye" (661-662). Although it has survived only as a "remenant," he says, the remaining chapters of this book speak directly to the problem of clerical temporalities (672). What follows, of course, are several pages of Wycliffite material, introduced here as an "olde treatyse made aboute the tyme of kinge Rycharde the seconde" (685-687).

Before proceeding, I want to assume for a moment that Lambeth represents an earlier stage of work on what would become the sermon in Egerton, in which case even this very brief account of how *A proper dyaloge* frames its Wycliffite excerpt reveals fault lines between different adaptations of a medieval source.[18] Egerton, for instance, significantly expands both the argumentative and formal registers of the tract through explicit appeals to the social setting of preaching. Having spent over a hundred folios vigorously condemning clerical temporalities, the sermonist pauses to propose leaving a written copy with the audience—who are presumably listening at this moment—so that "whoso likiþ mai ouerse [look over] it" (2941). But if we are inclined to think of the written copy as the authoritative image of the spoken, a stable or determinative textual record undergirding the preacher's verbal performance, what follows next is surprising. Rather than simply urging his listeners to read the sermon, he solicits their help to identify anything he may have said "amys," so that he can then emend the written copy before he departs (2945). And, looking ahead to his next visit, he adds that

> if ony aduersarie of myn replie a3ens ony
> conclusioun þat I haue shewid to 3ou at þis tyme,
> reportiþ redili hise euydencis, and nameli if he take
> ony euydence or colour of hooli scripture, and, if
> almy3ti God wole vouchesaaf to graunte me grace
> or leiser to declare mysilf in þese poyntis þat I haue
> moued in þis sermoun, I shal þoru3 þe help of him
> in whom is al help declare me, so þat he shal holde
> him answerid (2949-2955).

This moment is remarkable on a number of levels; for one, it underscores the point that while "voice" is a form of mimesis in literary narrative, the same is not necessarily true in sermon texts, where the first person speaker is something more than a mere conceit. Indeed, a whole range of Wycliffite texts—not just sermons, but trial transcripts, interpolated biblical commentary, testimonies like those of Oldcastle or Thorpe—sometimes prevail upon their readers in starkly interpersonal terms, turning our reading into the kind of engaged overhearing dramatized in the Egerton sermonist's gestures towards his own listening audience.[19] "[I]t is the function of preaching to reverse the relation from written to spoken," Paul Ricoeur writes, in a claim perhaps most interesting for its ethical corollaries.[20] Produced from within a context that includes not only its immediate audience but also potential audiences over time, including future adversaries, the sermon resists any single affiliation. It addresses whoever "mai ouerse it" (2941). We might say, then, that it emerges dialogically, that it comes into being through the polemical countersigning of other readers and listeners. To be its audience is to be inscribed in the social space of vernacular writing and hence alert to the ethical singularity of other speaking subjects.

A different model of intertextuality and affiliation governs the use of the sermon tract in *A proper dyaloge*. Although Lambeth already lacks the hermeneutic reflexivity of the Egerton sermon, here it is explicitly signified as an "olde treatyse," demarcated all that much more by its formal contrast with the dialogue's rhyming couplets (685).[21] Marked not only by its antiquity but also its residual status, the language of this Wycliffite "remenant" is "rude," "nothing eloquent," and "set out curiously" in comparison to that of the dialogue's two speakers (672, 678, 683, 684). The redeployment of heretical material here thus occurs in a way that permits no play, no polysemy, no productive friction with the semantic structure enclosing it.[22] Unlike the Egerton sermon, which discursively expands the material in Lambeth, *A proper dyaloge* constructs a medieval precedent for its views by casting the same material into a finite and monologic form. If the term "remenant" signifies loss, it also suggests the recuperation of the past in the form of cultural artifacts, and this is indeed the attitude both speakers take towards their peculiar textual object; they relate to it as one might a museum exhibit.

Of course, we need to consider the possibility that the author or editor of *A proper dyaloge* chose to include the Wycliffite excerpt only because a complete version of the tract was unavailable, which may indeed have been the case given the perils involved in transporting and obtaining reformist writing in this period. The years leading up to its publication in 1529 were ones of increased scrutiny for the book trade in England and the Low Countries; by the mid-twenties, according to A. G. Dickens, "the situation in the London diocese had become so notorious that Tunstall and his successor Stokesley were forced to attempt an extensive purge."[23] It is in this context that one name in particular gains prominence, that of Richard Bayfield, a monk and chamberlain of Bury St. Edmunds who became an active figure in the overseas book trade during the latter half of the decade.[24] Brought up on charges during Bishop Tunstall's anti-heresy proceedings in 1528, he was sentenced as a relapsed heretic in 1531 and burnt at Smithfield that same year after his traffic in books by exiled English reformers became known to More, whose list of Bayfield's seized inventory includes *A proper dyaloge* (Fig. 2).[25]

The issue I want explore here, however, concerns Bayfield's reputed Wycliffite contacts, John Stacy and Lawrence Maxwell, both of whom, according to Foxe (whose account is the major source for Bayfield's movements during this period) facilitated his travel to Antwerp.[26] The two first come to light in connection to John Hacker, a Wycliffite teacher whose interrogation by the bishops' authorities in 1531 revealed the rather extensive activities of a dissenting "sect" centered on a house of a tailor who lived near St. Stephen's Church, in Coleman Street. Wardens of the London Brickmakers' company, Stacy and Maxwell seem to have been ardent members of this sect, the former even entering into a financial agreement with a local grocer, John Sercot, to pay for an associate to copy a vernacular version of Apocalypse.[27] These two, according to Foxe, "once a year, of their own cost, went about to visit the brethren and sistern scattered abroad." Encountering Bayfield in the course of his duties as chamberlain of the abbey, Maxwell and Stacy "gave him Tyndale's Testament in English, with a book called 'The Wicked Mammon,' and 'The Obedience of a Christian Man:' wherein he prospered so mightily in two years' space, that he was cast into the prison of his house, there sore whipped, with a gag in his mouth, and then stocked." His release having been orchestrated by Robert Barnes, Bayfield, again according to Foxe, "went to London to Maxwell and Stacy, and they kept him secretly a while, and so conveyed him beyond the Sea." Once abroad, Bayfield proved himself "beneficial to Master Tyndale, and Master Frith; for he brought substance with him"—that is, books.[28]

Bayfield's movements, obscure though they are, suggest the lines of communication and commerce by which Wycliffite texts changed hands—and crossed borders—in this period. His position within this particular network of London readers, teachers, and missionaries afforded him unusual access to illicit books; and if we are to follow out one of the general implications of the accounts summarized above, it is not inconceivable that once in Antwerp Bayfield supplied Wycliffite material to the author of *A proper dyaloge* in the process of negotiating a consignment of heretical books to smuggle with him back into England—especially if Jerome Barlowe, a lapsed Franciscan and *A proper dyaloge*'s putative author, was abroad working on the production of reformist texts at the same time, as Tyndale's account of him in the *Parable of the Wicked Mammon* suggests he was.[29] At the very least, the details of this scenario fit the pattern of forbidden activities of which Bayfield was accused; these, according to Foxe's rendering of the bishop's sentence, included "commending and studying, reading, having, retaining, publishing, selling, giving and dispersing the books and writings, as well of the said Martin Luther, his adherents and disciples, as of other heretics before named."[30]

It is impossible to know whether the Antwerp press responsible for printing *A proper dyaloge* had access to more of the Wycliffite text than what is represented in the excerpt, or what editorial choices individual authors, compilers, and printers would have made if working from a longer version of the same text. But if one quality about Bayfield and the somewhat mysterious figures of Maxwell and Stacy comes through in the records, it is their determined *mobility*, even under the trying circumstances of state and ecclesiastical scrutiny. The conventional idea of a network does not quite capture the nature of this activity; Bayfield and his associates seem to have functioned less as fixed points within a system than as agents whose constant transit established a wide variety of pathways for the exchange and distribution of books.[31] It is almost certainly the case that the full scope of textual circulation is not reflected in the number of English Wycliffite texts actually printed in the early Reformation.[32] Yet the gap between these might be especially pronounced given the patterns of dissemination made possible through networks like Bayfield's.

Although the Husbandman's reference to a surviving Wycliffite "remenant" suggests that the authors of *A proper dyaloge* were constrained to use an incomplete or fragmentary exemplar for their publication, the substance of which now only survives in the variant form of Lambeth, it seems just as likely that the excerpt represents a selective and highly self-conscious treatment of a medieval source made available to them by any number of book agents in the period.[33] Enough Wycliffite writing seems to have travelled between England and the Low Countries on the threshold of the Reformation that many other texts besides the source for the excerpt could have been used to support the case for reform, if not to make the same points about clerical temporalities put forth in *A proper dyaloge*. Indeed, a version of the compilation printed later that same year incorporates a different Wycliffite text—namely, *The examinacion of Master William Thorpe*—and, in one printed a year later, a treatise by Richard Ullerston in support of vernacular biblical translation.

If these examples are in any way representative, then de Keyser's press had access to a fair range of English Wycliffite material. The "growing market" for evangelical books also likely afforded de Keyser opportunities to collaborate with authors or their representatives on the adaptation, use, and display of manuscript sources in its imprints.[34] As I have suggested, this picture accords fairly well with what we know about the book trade in early sixteenth-century Antwerp.[35] But this is also significant because it demonstrates how an English tradition of reform was shaped by the conjunction of different modalities of writing and book production. If texts such as *A proper dyaloge* seem to speak directly to the audiences of the 1530s, to recall David Loades' assertion, that is in part because historical and evangelical continuity is also an *effect* of how printed documents appropriate—and thus refashion, rather than passively inherit—the material and cultural forms of the past.

3.

Arguments "against the lordshippes and rentes / Of the clergye possessed wrongfully," to quote the Husbandman's summary of the interpolated Wycliffite material, may indeed have resonated with early sixteenth-century reformers sympathetic to Luther's attacks on monasticism and the landed endowments of the church (664-665).[36] In making this connection explicit, however, Lutheran materials do not simply reiterate an established theme within religious history; the self-conscious and strategic performance of affiliation in *A proper dyaloge* also constructs that history on the level of the material text itself. Hence a question specific to my own affiliative moves in this essay: how do we constellate materials across different contexts without forcing them into deterministic relation or reproducing the affiliative logic by which real differences of emphasis—for example, in anticlerical discourse—are effaced?[37] For if the Lambeth tract looks ahead to the 1530s, it also situates anticlerical ideas within a developed late medieval ecclesiology, at the center of which are interlocking ideas about scriptural authority, divine law, and the structure of God's church. In this context, the argument against worldly lordship is not always offered solely as a critique of contemporary clergy; the Lambeth tract also frames its concern about the issue as part of a larger effort to conform the clergy to "þe perfeccyon of þe gospell," and to chastise secular rulers who, acting contrary to the virtuous "ensaumple" of King David, "presume to ouerturne all þe gloriouse ordinance of God abowte siche temperaltes and make þe state of presthode lordis" (71, 117, 119-121).

Bayfield's admission that he had read *A proper dyaloge* "among company," to cite Foxe's account of his abjuration, is intriguing, all the more so alongside references by the dialogue's own characters to the "ornate speache" of the Wycliffite excerpt (684).[38] It would have taken an exceptionally adroit reader to negotiate the challenging formal and linguistic variety of this text. But this detail likely refers to Bayfield's use of *A proper dyaloge* for religious instruction rather than any attempt at public preaching, performance, or continuous reading. Many medieval sermons, including those in the long Wycliffite sermon cycle, served functions beyond preaching (if they were preached at all), and several details suggest this was the case with the Lambeth tract as well. As I mentioned earlier, the appendix of Latin authorities lent itself to expansion in exegesis and commentary, and hence suggests an instructional context differing from everyday gospel preaching.[39] In keeping with this observation, however, we can also note the careful attention Lambeth devotes to the substance and methods of arguments meant to defend worldly dominion—and how to answer such arguments with reasoning grounded in scripture (609-634). So, for instance, in the absence of any scriptural justification for worldly dominion, the tract argues, clergy instead point to "þe lyuynge of her patrons and sayntis, and sayen þus: 'Seynt Thomas ['Thomas Becker], and seynt Hwo [Hugh, bishop of Lincoln] and seynt Swithune [Swithin, bishop of Winchester] wer þus lordis, and in þis þai suyd Cristis lyuynge and his lore; þerfor we may lefulli be þus lordis'" (629-632). This reflection marks the beginning of the material excerpted in *A proper dyaloge* but the technique of imagining, anticipating, and even revoicing clerical counterarguments is a constant feature of the section appearing in that later text.

This pattern sometimes turns on quite technical matters of canon law, as, for instance, when chapter viii of Lambeth begins by refuting the anticipated objection among clerks and "religious folke" that they

> occupien not siche lordeschipis in propir as seculer
> lordis done but in comoun, like as þe apostles and
> þe perfite peple diden in þe begynnynge of Cristis
> chirche, þe whiche hadden alle þinge in comoun,
> like as suche clerkis and religious saien þai han nowe
> (670-675).

The argument from clergy anticipated here involves a defense of lordship based on notions of shared or "comoun" church property, and the closely related but equally technical idea of "perpetual almes," mentioned a few lines later in the same discussion. The latter refers to the holding of property or temporalities that originated as a donation to a church or religious house.[40] Both Lambeth and Egerton imagine their clerical opponents invoking such concepts under an appeal to apostolic models of shared or common possession. In both versions, Lambeth and Egerton, the Wycliffite writer rejects the clerical argument as a subterfuge for "a maner of propre possession, contrary to þe comounynge of þe comon goodis in tyme of þe perfyte men in þe begynnynge of Cristis chirche" (711-713). In rebutting arguments for "comoun" ownership and "perpetual almes," Lambeth lacks formal reference to the same verse from Acts 4 (verse 32) noted in Egerton as the basis for invalidating clerical claims of lordship (1922).[41] But the scriptural reference in Egerton only reinforces the unmistakable appeal to apostolic authority already in Lambeth, signaled by redundant mention of "perfite" people "in þe begynnynge of Cristis chirche" (673-674, 713). Indeed, both valorize "'þe forme of þe apostles liife,'" which enjoins (according to St. Bernard, the authority quoted here) a strict rejection of the temporalities associated with lordship, just as a lord himself is unfit for "apostilhede" (666-667, 659).[42]

By rehearsing clerical arguments against disendowment to the extent that it does, even going so far as to conjure up the voices of imagined opponents, the Lambeth tract accommodates itself to the dialogic context of vernacular preaching and religious instruction in surprising ways. More so, perhaps, even than the Egerton sermon, where the tract is expanded to include the charismatic voice of the sermonist himself, Lambeth locates its audience in a discourse community where different voices variously claim the attention of its readers; and this quality, I have suggested, is especially evident in the chapters making up the Wycliffite excerpt in A proper dyaloge. In this respect, the sermon tract resists the inert and monologic anteriority according to which it is framed as an "olde treatise" in its Lutheran sponsor text. But it is also possible to bend the particulars of this argument towards the larger question of affiliation and ask how we might approach a manuscript source which refuses to rest complacently in its Protestant reinscription—a manuscript which, in other words, emerges into singularity when considered from the perspective of book history. The afterlife of Lambeth invites us to adjust our models of religious descent and affiliation—of Lollard survivals and inheritances—to account for the various discontinuities that emerged as English Wycliffite texts took their place in the discursive economy of early Reformation printing.[43]

The material quoted above concerning what we might refer to as an apostolic form of life, with its injunctions against lordship and temporalities, extends to one final issue, which I offer here as an example of just such a discontinuity. The ideal of "apostilhede" espoused and defended in Lambeth was no nostalgic notion in the late 1520s and early 1530s. Despite the lingering orthodoxy of the political establishment under Henry, the king himself "could lean to the view that it would serve God's purpose to deprive the clergy of their temporal wealth," in R. W. Hoyle's analysis.[44] Within the scope of an incipient Protestant religiosity, however, the ethical example of life as it had been at "þe begynnynge of Cristis chirche" competed with a new emphasis on "nacion" as a vehicle for historical and cultural renewal, a tension already evident in the gentleman's impassioned condemnation of Henry V's reign:

> In kinge Henryes dayes of the name the fyft
> The clergye their pride aboue to lyft
>   Persecuted christen brothers haynously.
> The gospell of Christ a syde to cast
> Which at that tyme prospered fast
>   With all their puysaunce they dyd conspyre.
> Euery where they threwe theym in presones
> In sharp gayles and horrible doungeones
>   Causynge many to be brent in fyre.
> Their furious malice neuer stentyd
> Tyll they had the light oute quenchyd
>   Of the gospell and holy scripture.
> Wher of all bokes that they could get
> They caused on a fayre fyre to be set
>   To expell goddes worde doynge their cure.
> But consyder what ther of did chaunce
> Moste terrible plages of fearfull vengeaunce
>   And endles sorowe to oure nacion (586-603).

The gentleman goes on to lament the king's campaigns in France and the many "stronge batayles" resulting in a "great effusyon of englisshe bloode" (608-609). This recent history "is nowe a dayes clene oute of mynde," the Husbandman responds sympathetically, offering yet one more rationale for the recovery of Wycliffite texts and history while also anticipating the memorializing gestures of later evangelical writers such as John Foxe and John Bale (614). But, from this perspective, it is the more recent past, not a biblical one and only narrowly a Wycliffite one (since the gentleman's speech very specifically concerns events of the early fifteenth century), that frames the travails of the present; for the characters of *A proper dyaloge*, no less, perhaps, than for their various sixteenth-century audiences, the historical moment with the greatest foundational pathos and urgency was not the *ecclesia primativa* or the life of Christ as recorded in the Gospels but rather the book burnings and the spilling of English blood under Lancastrian rule. When the gentleman earlier criticizes an idle clergy for preferring prayer to physical labor—even the "gostely" apostles had to work for their living, he stresses—the Husbandman concurs but adds that this was "so longe ago / That their lyuynge is oute of memorye" (397, 399-400). These lines speak with unwitting candor to the contingencies of cultural memory and the material forms through which it was constructed in the early sixteenth century.

Yeshiva University

Acknowledgments

A version of this essay was presented at the Early Book Society's 2013 conference in St. Andrews, Scotland. I wish to thank the conference organizers, Margaret Connolly and Martha Driver, as well as those in attendance for their perceptive questions and comments. I am especially grateful to Matti Peikola for generously taking the time to comment on an early draft. My thanks as well to Yitzchak Honick for his many contributions in research and editing. Finally, I thank my colleague, Adam Zachary Newton, erstwhile medievalist, for his trenchant insights at different stages of this essay's composition.

NOTES

1. Margaret Aston, *Lollards and Reformers: Images and Literacy in Late Medieval Religion* (London: Hambledon Press, 1984), 232. For relevant methodological observations, see Arthur Bahr and Alexandra Gillespie, "Medieval English Manuscripts: Form, Aesthetics, and the Literary Text," *The Chaucer Review* 47.4 (2013): 346-360, especially their view that "new formalism deserves attention as one way of encouraging the book historian to treat manuscript 'material' or manuscript 'form' in careful, dynamic, and theoretically nuanced ways" (352).
2. Relevant in this context are the various essays published recently in Mishtooni Bose and J. Patrick Hornbeck II, eds., *Wycliffite Controversies*, Medieval Church Studies 23 (Turnhout: Brepols, 2012), especially Kantik Ghosh, "Wycliffite 'Affiliations': Some Intellectual-Historical Perspectives" (13-32); Anne Hudson, "'Who Is My Neighbour?' Some Problems of Definition on the Borders of Orthodoxy and Heterodoxy" (79-96); Maureen Jurkowski, "Lollard Networks" (261-278); and Peter Marshall, "Lollards and Protestants Revisited" (295-318). See, too, Michael van Dussen and Pavel Soukup, eds., *Religious Controversy in Europe, 1378-1536: Textual Transmission and Networks of Readership* (Turnhout: Brepols, 2013).
3. For a survey of Lambeth's contents, see Oliver Pickering and Veronica O'Mara, *The Index of Middle English Prose Handlist XIII: Manuscripts in Lambeth Palace Library* (Cambridge: Cambridge University Press, 1999), 52.
4. F. D. Matthew, ed., *The English Works of Wycliffe Hitherto Unprinted*, Early English Text Society 74 (London: Kegan Paul, Trench, Trübner, 1880, revd. edn. 1902), 362-404.
5. Anne Hudson, ed., *The Works of a Lollard Preacher: The Sermon "Omnis plantacio," the Tract "Fundamentum aliud nemo potest ponere," and the Tract*

"De oblacione iugis sacrificii," Early English Text Society 317 (Oxford: Oxford University Press, 2001). Cited parenthetically by line number. Suppositions about the Lambeth tract and its relation to the Egerton sermon as well as to the printed versions are based on Hudson's research, *Works of a Lollard Preacher,* xxxi-xliv. Unlike the tract in Lambeth, both "Omnis plantacio," the sermon found in Egerton 2820, and "De oblacione," a tract by the same Wycliffite author and the third text included in Hudson's EETS edition, have received sporadic treatment in recent scholarship, the former in Rita Copeland, *Pedagogy, Intellectuals, and Dissent in the Later Middle Ages: Lollardy and Ideas of Learning* (Cambridge: Cambridge University Press, 2001), 127-129, and Glending Olson, "Measuring the Immeasurable: Farting, Geometry, and Theology in the Summoner's Tale," *The Chaucer Review,* 43.4 (2009): 418-419; the latter in two essays by Kantik Ghosh, "Logic and Lollardy," *Medium Aevum* 76 (2007): 251-267, and "Wycliffite 'Affiliations': Some Intellectual-Historical Perspectives," 18-30. See, too, Anne Hudson, "A Wycliffite Scholar of the Early Fifteenth Century," in *The Bible in the Medieval World: Essays in Memory of Beryl Smalley,* ed. Katherine Walsh and Diana Wood (Oxford: Blackwell, 1985), 301-315.

6. Hudson, *Works of a Lollard Preacher,* lii.

7. See, e.g., 160. For Hudson's discussion of authorship and audience, see *Works of a Lollard Preacher,* lii-liv.

8. On catalogues and lists of authorities in Wycliffite tracts, see Matti Peikola, "The Catalogue: A Late Middle English Lollard Genre?," in *Discourse Perspectives on English, Medieval to Modern,* ed. Risto Hiltunen and Janne Skaffari (Amsterdam: John Benjamins, 2003), 105-135. Although Peikola's examples of prototypical usage do not exactly fit the current case, his remarks on form and genre are broadly relevant.

9. *A proper dyaloge betwene a Gentillman and an Husbandman,* ed. D. H. Parker (Toronto: University of Toronto Press, 1996). Cited parenthetically by line number. Noting agreements between the excerpt from the tract printed in the 1529 and 1530 editions of *A proper dyaloge* and the sermon as attested in its four manuscript versions (British Library MS Egerton 2820; Cambridge, University Library, MS Dd.14.30(2); Cambridge, University Library, MS Ff.6.2; and Huntington Library, San Marino, HM 503), Hudson argues that Lambeth MS 551 "seems likely to represent a defective copy of the tract version." Nevertheless, the source used as the basis for the printed versions "was plainly in the general form" of Lambeth, as the manuscript is very close to the tract as excerpted in both the 1529 and the 1530 versions of *A proper dyaloge.* Hudson, *Works of a Lollard Preacher,* xxxvii-xxxix. (This echoes Hudson's earlier conclusions concerning the overall fidelity of the printed version of *A proper dyaloge* to the Lambeth tract despite the fact that Lambeth itself is not the exemplar. Hudson, "'No Newe Thyng': The Printing of Medieval Texts in

the Early Reformation Period," reprinted in Hudson, *Lollards and their Books* [London: Hambledon Press, 1985], 233-234.) On print culture, religious reform, and early Protestant publications in the Low Countries, see the following important discussions: Paul Arblaster, "'Totius Mundi Emporium': Antwerp as a Centre for Vernacular Bible Translations, 1523-1545," in *The Low Countries as a Crossroads of Religious Belief*, ed. Arie-Jan Gelderblom, Jan L. de Jong, and Marc van Vaeck (Leiden: Brill, 2004), 9-31; Paul Valkema Blouw, "Early Protestant Publications in Antwerp, 1526-30: The Pseudonyms Adam Anonymous in Basel and Hans Luft in Marlborow," in *Quaerendo* 26.2 (1996), 94-110; Andrew G. Johnston and Jean-François Gilmont, "Printing and the Reformation in Antwerp," in *The Reformation and the Book*, ed. J.-F. Gilmont, trans. Karin Maag (Aldershot: Ashgate, 1998), 188-213; and, from the same collection, David Loades, "Books and the English Reformation prior to 1558," 264-291. More generally, see *Agent of Change: Print Culture Studies after Elizabeth L. Eisenstein*, Studies in Print Culture and the History of the Book, ed. Sabrina Alcorn Baron, Eric N. Lindquist, and Eleanor F. Shevlin (Amherst: University of Massachusetts Press, 2007); John Fudge, *Commerce and Print in the Early Reformation* (Leiden: Brill, 2007); *The Cambridge History of the Book in Britain*, Volume 3: 1400–1557, ed. Lotte Hellinga and J. B. Trapp (Cambridge: Cambridge University Press, 1999); Adrian Johns, *The Nature of the Book: Print and Knowledge in the Making* (Chicago: University of Chicago Press, 1998); and Andrew Pettegree, *The Book in the Renaissance* (New Haven: Yale University Press, 2011).

10. *A proper dyaloge*, it should be noted, is sometimes entitled *A. B. C. ayenst the Clergye* after the brief alphabetical poem with which the compilation itself begins (lines 6-98 in Parker's edition).

11. On anonymity and clandestine printing in the Low Countries, see Johnston and Gilmont, "Printing and the Reformation in Antwerp," 191. "The lack of factual evidence in this domain," Blouw reminds us, "is the rule rather than the exception; in the world of clandestine publications secrecy was literally a matter of life and death." Paul Valkema Blouw, "Early Protestant Publications in Antwerp," 95-96. Concerning possible authorship, see Parker, ed., *A proper dyaloge*, 22-50.

12. M. E. Kronenberg, "De geheimzinnige drukkers Adam Anonymus te Basel en Hans Luft te Marburg ontmaskerd," in *Het Boek*, 8 (1919): 241-280. See, by the same author, "Notes on English Printing in the Low Countries," in *The Library*, 4th ser., 9 (1929): 155-159, and "Forged Addresses in Low Country Books in the Period of the Reformation," in *The Library*, 5th ser., 2 (1948), 85-87.

13. Blouw, "Early Protestant Publications in Antwerp," 100, 104; on *A proper dyaloge* in particular, see 107-108. Blouw's research indicates that de Keyser "appears to have played a still greater part in the spread of Protestantism in

various countries than he has so far been credited with on the basis of an impressive series of Protestant publications in Latin, French, and, from 1530 onwards, in English" (104-105). See, too, Johnston and Gilmont, "Printing and the Reformation in Antwerp," 198-199. For more on de Keyser, see Arblaster, "'Totius Mundi Emporium,'" 9-30, esp. 21. More generally, see David Daniell, *William Tyndale: A Biography* (New Haven: Yale University Press, 1994); Daniell, "William Tyndale, the English Bible, and the English Language," in *The Bible as Book: The Reformation*, ed. Orlaith O'Sullivan (London: The British Library and Oak Knoll Press, 2000), 44; and Guido Latré, "William Tyndale in Antwerp: Reformer, Bible Translator, and Maker of the English Language," in *Antwerp, Centre of Dissident Printing: The Role of the Antwerp Printers in the Wars of Religion in England (16th Century)*, ed. Dirk Imhof, Gilbert Tournoy, and Francine de Nave (Antwerp: Plantin-Moretus en Stedelijk Prentenkabinet, 1995), 55-66.

14. Fudge adds that while "a printing house or publisher had to believe there was commercial potential" in what authors or translators brought to them, "by the late 1520s Martin de Keyser and other Antwerp printers Ruremund, Graphous, and Michiel Hillen van Hoochstraten—probably required little persuading to issue work by Tyndale and the English exiles," even paying for "revised and corrected texts" (Fudge, *Commerce and Print in the Early Reformation*, 241).

15. The volume of this output has been documented by Anthea Hume, "English Protestant Books Printed Abroad, 1525-1535: An Annotated Bibliography," Appendix B, in Sir Thomas More, *The Complete Works*, Yale Edition, vol. 8, pt. ii (New Haven: Yale University Press, 1973), 1065-1091. For items ascribed to "Hans Luft" or linked to the same series via *schwabacher* type, see nrs. 6, 7, 10, 11, 13, 15-19.

16. Loades, "Books and the English Reformation prior to 1558," 265. For Wycliffism in early Reformation contexts, see the following: Aston, *Lollards and Reformers*; Hudson, "'No Newe Thyng'"; William Clebsch, *England's Earliest Protestants, 1520-1535* (New Haven: Yale University Press, 1964); Brian Cummings, "Reformed Literature and Literature Reformed," in *The Cambridge History of Medieval English Literature*, ed. David Wallace (Cambridge: Cambridge University Press, 2002), 821-851; John F. Davis, *Heresy and Reformation in the South-East of England, 1520-1529* (London: Royal Historical Society, 1983); A. G. Dickens, *The English Reformation*, 2nd ed. (College Park: Pennsylvania State University Press, 1989), 49-60, especially regarding arguments in support of what Dickens refers to as a "Lollard survival," redeployed in reference to *A proper dyaloge* by Parker, who writes in his introduction to the edited text that heresy "came to the aid of the movement that would eventually truly challenge the prevailing version of Christian truth" (101); J. A. F. Thomson, *The Later Lollards, 1414-1520* (Oxford: Oxford University Press, 1965); and, more recently, Alec Ryrie, *The*

Gospel and Henry VIII: Evangelicals in the Early English Reformation (Cambridge: Cambridge University Press, 2003). For a recent consideration of Wycliffism within the historiography of the Reformation, including many studies referred to here, see Peter Marshall, "Lollards and Protestants Revisited," 295-319.

17. As Loades argues, citing lines from *A proper dyaloge*, the antiquity of Wycliffite works "served a useful purpose" to Protestant editors and publishers who sought to counter charges of religious novelty. (*Books and the English Reformation prior to 1558,*" 265). To Annabel Patterson, who briefly discusses the dialogue's Wycliffite excerpt, the Husbandman's argument "in favor of an unbroken tradition of anticlerical protest is supported by the survival of this text, which accrues authority precisely because of its antiquity." Annabel Patterson, "Sir John Oldcastle as Symbol of Reformation Historiography," in *Religion, Literature, and Politics in Post-Reformation England, 1540–1688,* ed. Donna B. Hamilton and Richard Strier (Cambridge: Cambridge University Press, 1996), 21. In Steven Justice's view, Wycliffite works adapted into print in the early sixteenth century "had little theological usefulness; they were valued above all for their mere survival, as living proof that reform was no novelty, but a proud English tradition." Steven Justice, "Lollardy," in *The Cambridge History of Medieval English Literature,* 688. Commenting on this concern about novelty as a motivation for "repackaging" late medieval texts for Tudor audiences, Greg Walker notes, however, that in every instance but the reprinting of Ullerston's treatise "the supposed origins of these books were in the very late fourteenth or early fifteenth centuries, the one period in history during which English literary and intellectual culture could be said to have been flourishing on a par with those of the best of the Continental monarchies." Walker, *Writing Under Tyranny: English Literature and the Henrician Reformation* (Oxford: Oxford University Press, 2005), 49. See, too, incisive comments on this topic by Walsham, who nevertheless omits the Lambeth/Egerton material from her list of printed texts implicated in the construction of a "Lollard past." Alexandra Walsham, "Inventing the Lollard Past: The Afterlife of a Medieval Sermon in Early Modern England," in *Journal of Ecclesiastical History,* 58.4 (2007): 640-641.

18. For the view that the Lambeth and Egerton manuscripts are related in this way, see Hudson, *Works of a Lollard Preacher,* xliv.

19. This point has a suggestive tangency to Peikola's recent arguments about voice in Wycliffite texts. M. Peikola, "Individual Voice in Lollard Discourse," in *Approaches to Style and Discourse in English,* ed. Risto Hiltunen and Shinichiro Watanabe (Osaka: Osaka University Press 2004), 51-77.

20. Paul Ricoeur, "The Sacred Text and the Community," from *Figuring the Sacred: Religion, Narrative, and Imagination,* ed. Mark Wallace, trans. David Pellauer (Minneapolis: Augsburg Fortress, 1995), 71.

21. Parker, in his introduction to the edited text, rightly refers to its rhyming pattern (*a a b c c b*) as "relentless" (6).

22. The critical context in which I invoke the term "play" and related concepts comes from Bakhtin's reflections on authoritative discourse in the novel. Bakhtin, "Discourse in the Novel," from *The Dialogic Imagination: Four Essays*, ed. Michael Holquist, trans., Caryl Emerson and Michael Holquist (Austin: University of Texas Press, 1982), 340-343.

23. Dickens, *The English Reformation*, 29. See, as well, A. W. Reed, "The Regulation of the Book Trade Before the Proclamation of 1538," in *Transactions of the Bibliographical Society*, 15 (1918): 157-184. More recent accounts of English anti-heresy strategies, including restrictions on London printers, can be found in Susan Powell, "After Arundel but Before Luther: The First Half-Century of Print," in *After Arundel: Religious Writing in Fifteenth-Century England*, Medieval Church Studies 21, ed. Vincent Gillespie and Kantik Ghosh (Turnhout: Brepols, 2011); Craig W. D'Alton, "The Suppression of Lutheran Heretics in England, 1526-1529," in *The Journal of Ecclesiastical History*, 54.2 (2003): 228-253; and Christopher Haigh, *English Reformations: Religion, Politics, and Society Under the Tudors* (Oxford: Oxford University Press, 1993), 56-71.

24. John Foxe, *Acts and Monuments* (London: G. Seeley, 1870), IV.680-688, as well as John Strype, *Ecclesiastical Memorials* (Oxford: Clarendon Press, 1822), vol. 1, pt. 1, 253-256. For a summary of the bishops' tribunals as represented in Foxe, see Phillip Hughes, *The Reformation in England* (London: Hollis and Carter, 1950-1954), vol. 1, 127-133. Hughes categorizes the "religious opinions" of many heresy suspects as "survivals from the Lollard movement" (126).

25. Details of Bayfield's inventory can be found in Foxe, *Acts and Monuments*, IV.683. On Bayfield's career and abjuration, see More's *Confutation*, in *The Collected Works of Thomas More*, 8/1: 17-18, as well as useful notes in 8/3: 1247-1248. For Bishop Stokesley's register, which includes a list of "heretical books" but does not mention Bayfield himself, see *Letters and Papers, Foreign and Domestic, of the Reign of Henry VIII*, ed. J. S. Brewer, 21 vols. (London: Longmans, 1862--), vol. 5, appendix 18, 768-769. See, too, Aston, *Lollards and Reformers*, 220, 233. I leave aside the question of authorship; in his introduction to the edited text, Parker suggests some combination of writing and editing by Jerome Barlowe and William Roye on the basis of their work in *Rede Me and Be Nott Wroth* (25).

26. As is well known, Foxe's account is impossible to verify, as his information about Bayfield included material transcribed from parts of Bishop Tunstall's courtbook, now lost. Rupp, working from Foxe's papers, refers to Maxwell and Stacy as "book agents" (8) and includes a brief account of Bayfield's activities under the auspices of the so-called Society of Christian Brethren,

which, he claims, "subsidized scholars, ordered the translation and arranged the printing, transportation and sale of forbidden books and employed agents in an adventurous traffic which passed to and from the Rhine and the ports of the Low Countries to the ports of London, Lynn and Bristol, and from there to the Universities and to certain large religious houses like Reading and Bury St Edmund." Bayfield was "one of the most active agents of the society." E. G. Rupp, *Studies in the Making of the English Protestant Tradition* (Cambridge: Cambridge University Press, 1947), 198. According to Parker, such a group "doubtless was responsible for getting *A proper dyaloge* into England" (110n11). Also worth consulting is James Davis, "The Christian Brethren and the Dissemination of Heretical Books," in *The Church and the Book: Papers Read at the 2000 Summer Meeting and the 2001 Winter Meeting of the Ecclesiastical History Society*, Studies in Church History 38, ed. R. N. Swanson (Woodbridge: Boydell, 2004), 190-200. For a more measured assessment of the Brethren's influence, though not specifically in relation to Bayfield, see *The Premature Reformation: Wycliffite Texts and Lollard History* (Oxford: Oxford University Press, 1988), 482-483; see, too, 476 (for Maxwell), 486 (for Stacy), and 488 (for Bayfield). In his extensive introduction to the edited text of *A proper dyaloge*, Parker does not mention Bayfield's contacts with Stacy and Maxwell, and neither is extensively attested in surviving records, despite Dickens' assertion that the two were "prominent members of the Tilers' and Bricklayers' Company and had wide contacts both inside and outside London" (*The English Reformation*, 28). McSheffrey cites Foxe's account in a passing mention of Stacy and Maxwell as examples of Wycliffites who "travelled extensively" in the process of recruiting others to the sect, "probably using an underground network" as they did so. Shannon McSheffrey, *Gender and Heresy: Women and Men in Lollard Communities, 1420-1530* (Philadelphia: University of Pennsylvania Press, 1995), 76. Davis also briefly mentions Maxwell and Stacy, speculating that Bayfield "became an agent for Tyndale through their good offices." (*Heresy and Reformation in the South-East of England, 1520-1529*, 54-55 [at 55]).

27. BL, MS Harleian 421, fos. 11b-12b (Foxe papers, Harleian Collection, British Library). D'Alton describes the material relating to Hacker's examination as "an amalgamation of proceedings." Craig W. D'Alton, "Cuthbert Tunstal and Heresy in Essex and London, 1528," in *Albion: A Quarterly Journal Concerned with British Studies*, 35.2 (2003): 210-228 (at 216). For Hacker and his circle, see, most extensively, Hudson, *Premature Reformation*, 464-465; 474-483; 486-487. On the implications of the word "sect" in this and other cases described by Foxe, see Patrick Collinson, "Night schools, conventicles and churches: continuities and discontinuities in early Protestant ecclesiology," in *The Beginnings of English Protestantism*, ed. Peter Marshall and Alec Ryrie (Cambridge: Cambridge University Press, 2002), 221-225.

28. Foxe, *Acts and Monuments*, IV.681. For difficulties with the chronology of Foxe's account of Barnes' interaction with Bayfield, see 768 (notes for 681, lines 16, 23).

29. William Tyndale, *Parable of the Wicked Mammon*, in *Doctrinal Treatises and Introductions to Different Portions of The Holy Scriptures*, vol. 42, ed. Rev. Henry Walter, The Parker Society (Cambridge: Cambridge University Press, 1848), 38-39.

30. Foxe, *Acts and Monuments*, IV.685.

31. Foxe notes, for instance, that Bayfield varied which ports he used for importing his prohibited inventory, finally being apprehended following a shipment into Colchester.

32. Hudson provides an index and discussion of printed Wycliffite materials in "'No Newe Thyng,'" 229-231.

33. I note the telling remark from the Husbandman concerning the missing half of the book (671), suggesting that the author or authors were not only aware of its full scope but had also perhaps seen a more complete version and from there made choices about what to excerpt.

34. Andrew G. Johnston, "Printing and the Reformation in the Low Countries, 1520-c.1555," in *The Reformation and the Book*, ed. Gilmont, 159. My point about de Keyser here is an extrapolation of Johnston's more general discussion concerning different motivations for printing and circulating evangelical books.

35. As a point of reference in this respect, see Fudge, *Commerce and Print in the Early Reformation*, 150-164, 233-243.

36. For such attitudes, see Dom David Knowles, *The Religious Orders in England*, vol. 3: *The Tudor Age* (Cambridge: Cambridge University Press, 1961), 165-172. According to Knowles, there was little in Luther's *De votis monasticis* "that had not been said before by Wycliffites, Hussites and others," though perhaps not so "powerfully massed" or "pungently expressed" as in Luther's own writings (165-166). On disendowment see, more recently, Keith Wrightson, *Earthly Necessities: Economic Lives in Early Modern Britain* (New Haven: Yale University Press, 2000), 141-145.

37. For the diversity of anticlerical discourse during this period, see articles in Peter A. Dykema and Heiko O. Oberman, eds., *Anticlericalism in Late Medieval and Early Modern Europe*, Studies in Medieval and Reformation Thought 51 (Leiden: Brill, 1993). Affiliation in the sense I intend here draws on Edward Said's discussion of the term in "Secular Criticism," where he describes how affiliative relationships naturalize hierarchies of authority and power—in other words, reproduce *filiation*. Crucially, he adds that criticism itself is complicit in such a process when it fails to recognize how these concepts work together in the construction of social and cultural reality. Hence his call for a secular critical consciousness "opposed to the produc-

tion of massive, hermetic systems," and for a renewed emphasis on the essay itself—"a comparatively short, investigative, radically skeptical form"—as a venue for practicing such criticism. Edward Said, "Secular Criticism," from *The World, The Text, and the Critic* (Cambridge: Harvard University Press, 1983), 24, 26 (at 26).

38. Foxe, *Acts and Monuments*, IV.683.

39. As Hudson notes, however, there is no evidence of such expansion in Egerton itself (*Works of a Lollard Preacher*, lv).

40. On grants in alms, see J. M. Kaye, *Medieval English Conveyances* (Cambridge: Cambridge University Press, 2009), 164-184. For Wyclif's critique of perpetual alms, see John Wyclif, *Sermones*, ed. Johann Loserth (London: Wyclif Society, 1888), 2.403-404.

41. The practice of adding formal notations to biblical passages already in Lambeth suggests that Egerton represents a later stage of revision. In addition to the instance here discussed, see, for example, the quotation from Matthew 7:12 in Lambeth (769) and the notation for "Mt. 7" added to the Egerton manuscript at the same place (2096).

42. Wyclif's own discussion of clerical temporalities in the *Trialogus* bears mentioning here inasmuch as it, too, reverts back to an apostolic ideal in which the clergy is called to uphold the words of Christ in Matthew 10:10: "'*nihil tuleritis in via neque peram neque baculum neque calceamenta in pedibus habeatis*' etc. Non enim debent viri apostolici tardari cum aliquo temporali, quod vel eorum affectionem vel occupationem quo ad suum officium impediret; nuda autem et moderata habitio per virgam gestam in manibus potest intelligi. Unde sicut oneratus multiplici vestimento est saepe per hoc indispositior ad iter, sic oneratus temporalibus est saepe indispositior ad prodessendum ecclesiae. Et ad istum sensum dixit Christus ubi supra, 'neque duas tunicas habeatis,' et ista lex Christi est fundata in lege naturae, cum qua nemo poterit dispensare." Wyclif, *Trialogus*, ed. G. V. Lechler (London: Wyclif Society, 1869), 305. Wyclif similarly connects the faith of the primitive church to the argument against clerical temporalities in *Sermones*, ed. Loserth, 2.293-300. For the centrality of apostolic life as a model in Wyclif's thinking, see Michael Wilks, "Royal Priesthood: The Origins of Lollardy," reprinted in Wilks, *Wyclif: Political Ideas and Practice* (Oxford: Oxbow Books, 2000), 108.

43. Genealogical analysis of this kind situates the history of the book in the domain of what Nietzsche described as the quest for *Herkunft*, memorably distilled by Foucault in his own essay on historical methodology and meaning. "The search for descent," Foucault writes, " is not the erecting of foundations: on the contrary, it disturbs what was previously considered immobile; it fragments what was thought unified; it shows the heterogeneity of what was imagined consistent with itself." Michel Foucault, "Nietzsche, Genealogy,

History," in *Language, Counter-Memory, Practice: Selected Essays and Interviews by Michel Foucault,* ed. Donald F. Bouchard, trans. Donald F. Bouchard and Sherry Simon (Ithaca: Cornell University Press, 1977), 139-64 (at 147).
44. R. W. Hoyle, "The Origins of the Dissolution of the Monasteries," in *The Historical Journal,* 38:2 (1995): 275-305 (at 281). Greg Walker notes that the opening session of the Reformation Parliament was "notoriously 'anticlerical' in its tone and direction," occurring shortly after "rumours" in October 1529 that "all the temporal possessions of the church would be seized." Walker, *Writing Under Tyranny,* 36, 38. T. M. Parker also documents the circulation of English Lutheran materials at the royal court in 1529-1530 apparently insisting that the King "'undertake to reduce the ecclesiastical state to the condition of the primitive Church, taking from it all its temporalities.'" T. M. Parker, *The English Reformation to 1558,* 2nd ed. (Oxford: Oxford University Press, 1966), 42-43.

WORKS CITED

Manuscripts
London, British Library, MS Harleian 421
London, British Library, MS Egerton 2820
London, Lambeth Palace Library, MS 551

Primary Sources
Brewer, J. S., ed. *Letters and Papers, Foreign and Domestic, of the Reign of Henry VIII.* London: Longmans, Green, Reader, & Dyer, 1862.
Foxe, John. *Acts and Monuments.* London: G. Seeley, 1870.
Hudson, Anne, ed. *The Works of a Lollard Preacher: The Sermon "Omnis plantacio," the Tract "Fundamentum aliud nemo potest ponere," and the Tract "De oblacione iugis sacrificii."* EETS 317. Oxford: Oxford University Press, 2001.
Matthew, F. D., ed. *The English Works of Wycliffe Hitherto Unprinted.* EETS 74. London: Kegan Paul, Trench, Trübner, 1880, revd. edn. 1902.
Parker, D. H., ed. *A proper dyaloge betwene a Gentillman and an Husbandman.* Toronto: University of Toronto Press, 1996.
Schuster, Louis A., et al., eds. *The Yale Edition of the Complete Works of St. Thomas More,* vol. 8. New Haven: Yale University Press, 1973.
Strype, John. *Ecclesiastical Memorials.* Oxford: Clarendon Press, 1822.
Tyndale, William. *Parable of the Wicked Mammon.* Ed. Rev. Henry Walter. Cambridge: Cambridge University Press, 1848.
Wyclif, John. *Trialogus.* Ed. G. V. Lechler. London: Wyclif Society, 1869.
———. *Sermones.* Ed. J. Loserth. London: Wyclif Society, 1886-1889.

Secondary Sources

Arblaster, Paul. "'Totius Mundi Emporium': Antwerp as a Centre for Vernacular Bible Translations, 1523-1545." In *The Low Countries as a Crossroads of Religious Belief*. Ed. A.-J. Gelderblom, J. L. de Jong, and M. van Vaeck. Leiden: Brill, 2004, 9-31.

Aston, Margaret. *Lollards and Reformers: Images and Literacy in Late Medieval Religion*. London: Hambledon Press, 1984.

Bahr, Arthur, and Gillespie, Alexandra. "Medieval English Manuscripts: Form, Aesthetics, and the Literary Text." *The Chaucer Review* 47.4 (2013): 346-360.

Bakhtin, Mikhail. *The Dialogic Imagination: Four Essays*. Ed. M. Holquist, trans., C. Emerson and M. Holquist. Austin: University of Texas Press, 1982.

Blouw, Paul V. "Early Protestant Publications in Antwerp, 1526-30: The Pseudonyms Adam Anonymous in Basel and Hans Luft in Marlborow." *Quaerendo* 26.2 (1996): 94-110.

Clebsch, William. *England's Earliest Protestants, 1520-1535*. New Haven: Yale University Press, 1964.

Collinson, Patrick. "Night schools, conventicles and churches: continuities and discontinuities in early Protestant ecclesiology." In *The Beginnings of English Protestantism*. Ed. P. Marshall and A. Ryrie. Cambridge: Cambridge University Press, 2002, 209-235.

Copeland, Rita. *Pedagogy, Intellectuals, and Dissent in the Later Middle Ages: Lollardy and Ideas of Learning*. Cambridge: Cambridge University Press, 2001.

Cummings, Brian. "Reformed Literature and Literature Reformed." In *The Cambridge History of Medieval English Literature*. Ed. D. Wallace. Cambridge: Cambridge University Press, 2002, 821-851.

D'Alton, Craig W. "Cuthbert Tunstal and Heresy in Essex and London, 1528." *Albion: A Quarterly Journal Concerned with British Studies*, 35.2 (2003): 210-228.

————. "The Suppression of Lutheran Heretics in England, 1526-1529." *The Journal of Ecclesiastical History*, 54.2 (2003): 228-253.

Daniell, David. "William Tyndale, the English Bible, and the English Language." In *The Bible as Book: The Reformation*. Ed. O. O'Sullivan. London: The British Library and Oak Knoll Press, 2000, 25-38.

————. *William Tyndale: A Biography*. New Haven: Yale University Press, 1994.

Davis, James. "The Christian Brethren and the Dissemination of Heretical Books." In *The Church and the Book: Papers Read at the 2000 Summer Meeting and the 2001 Winter Meeting of the Ecclesiastical History Society, Studies in Church History* 38. Ed. R. N. Swanson. Woodbridge: Boydell, 2004, 190-200.

Davis, John F. *Heresy and Reformation in the South-East of England, 1520-1529*. London: Royal Historical Society, 1983.

Dickens, A. G. *The English Reformation*, 2nd ed. College Park: Pennsylvania State University Press, 1989.

Foucault, Michel. "Nietzsche, Genealogy, History." In *Language, Counter-Memory, Practice: Selected Essays and Interviews by Michel Foucault*. Ed. and trans., D. Bouchard, S. Simon. Ithaca: Cornell University Press, 1977, 139-164.

Fudge, John. *Commerce and Print in the Early Reformation*. Leiden: Brill, 2007.

Ghosh, Kantik. "Wycliffite 'Affiliations': Some Intellectual-Historical Perspectives." In *Wycliffite Controversies*. Ed. M. Bose and P. Hornbeck. Turnhout: Brepols, 2012, 13-33.

———. "Logic and Lollardy." *Medium Aevum* 76 (2007): 251-267.

Haigh, Christopher. *English Reformations: Religion, Politics, and Society Under the Tudors*. Oxford: Oxford University Press, 1993.

Hoyle, R. W. "The Origins of the Dissolution of the Monasteries." *The Historical Journal* 38:2 (1995): 275-305.

Hudson, Anne. *The Premature Reformation: Wycliffite Texts and Lollard History*. Oxford: Oxford University Press, 1988.

———. "'No Newe Thyng': The Printing of Medieval Texts in the Early Reformation Period." In *Lollards and their Books*. London: Hambledon Press, 1985, 227-248.

———. "A Wycliffite Scholar of the Early Fifteenth Century." In *The Bible in the Medieval World: Essays in Memory of Beryl Smalley*. Ed. K. Walsh and D. Wood. Oxford: Oxford University Press, 1985, 301-315.

Hughes, Philip. *The Reformation in England*. London: Hollis & Carter, 1950.

Hume, Anthea. "English Protestant Books Printed Abroad, 1525-1535: An Annotated Bibliography." In *The Yale Edition of the Complete Works of St. Thomas More*, vol. 8, pt. ii. New Haven: Yale University Press, 1973, 1065-1091.

Johns, Adrian. *The Nature of the Book: Print and Knowledge in the Making*. Chicago: University of Chicago Press, 1998.

Johnston, Andrew G. "Printing and the Reformation in the Low Countries, 1520-c.1555." In *The Reformation and the Book*. Ed. J.-F. Gilmont, trans. K. Maag. Aldershot: Ashgate, 1998, 155-183.

Johnston, Andrew G., and Gilmont, Jean-François. "Printing and the Reformation in Antwerp." In *The Reformation and the Book*. Ed. J.-F. Gilmont, trans. K. Maag. Aldershot: Ashgate, 1998, 188-213.

Justice, Steven. "Lollardy." In *The Cambridge History of Medieval English Literature*. Ed. David Wallace. Cambridge: Cambridge University Press, 2002, 662-689.

Kaye, J. M. *Medieval English Conveyances*. Cambridge: Cambridge University Press, 2009.

Knowles, David. *The Religious Orders in England*. Cambridge: Cambridge University Press, 1961.

Kronenberg, M. E. "Forged Addresses in Low Country Books in the Period of the Reformation." *The Library*, 5th ser., 2 (1948): 81-94.

———. "Notes on English Printing in the Low Countries." *The Library*, 4th ser., 9 (1929): 139-163.

———. "De geheimzinnige drukkers Adam Anonymus te Basel en Hans Luft te Marburg ontmaskerd." *Het Boek* 8 (1919): 241-280.

Latré, Guido. "William Tyndale in Antwerp: Reformer, Bible Translator, and Maker of the English Language." In *Antwerp, Centre of Dissident Printing: The Role of the Antwerp Printers in the Wars of Religion in England (16th Century)*. Ed. D. Imhof, G. Tournoy, and F. de Nave. Antwerp: Plantin-Moretus en Stedelijk Prentenkabinet, 1995, 55-66.

Loades, David. "Books and the English Reformation prior to 1558." In *The Reformation and the Book*. Ed. J.-F. Gilmont, trans. K. Maag. Aldershot: Ashgate, 1998, 264-291.

Marshall, Peter. "Lollards and Protestants Revisited." In *Wycliffite Controversies*. Ed. M. Bose and P. Hornbeck. Turnhout: Brepols, 2012, 295-319.

McSheffrey, Shannon. *Gender and Heresy: Women and Men in Lollard Communities, 1420-1530*. Philadelphia: University of Pennsylvania Press, 1995.

Olson, Glending. "Measuring the Immeasurable: Farting, Geometry, and Theology in the Summoner's Tale." *The Chaucer Review* 43.4 (2009): 414-427.

Parker, T. M. *The English Reformation to 1558*, 2nd ed. Oxford: Oxford University Press, 1966.

Patterson, Annabel. "Sir John Oldcastle as Symbol of Reformation Historiography." In *Religion, Literature, and Politics in Post-Reformation England, 1540–1688*. Ed. D. Hamilton and R. Strier. Cambridge: Cambridge University Press, 1996, 6-26.

Pettegree, Andrew. *The Book in the Renaissance*. New Haven: Yale University Press, 2011.

Peikola, Matti. "Individual Voice in Lollard Discourse." In *Approaches to Style and Discourse in English*. Ed. R. Hiltunen and S. Watanabe. Osaka: Osaka University Press, 2004, 51-77.

———. "The Catalogue: A Late Middle English Lollard Genre?" In *Discourse Perspectives on English, Medieval to Modern*. Ed. R. Hiltunen and J. Skaffari. Amsterdam: John Benjamins, 2003, 105-135.

Pickering, Oliver S., and O'Mara, Veronica. *The Index of Middle English Prose Handlist XIII: Manuscripts in Lambeth Palace Library*. Cambridge: Cambridge University Press, 1999.

Powell, Susan. "After Arundel but Before Luther: The First Half-Century of Print." In *After Arundel: Religious Writing in Fifteenth-Century England*,

Medieval Church Studies 21. Ed. V. Gillespie and K. Ghosh. Turnhout: Brepols, 2011, 523-541.

Reed, A. W. "The Regulation of the Book Trade Before the Proclamation of 1538." *Transactions of the Bibliographical Society* 15 (1918): 157-184.

Ricoeur, Paul. "The Sacred Text and the Community." In *Figuring the Sacred: Religion, Narrative, and Imagination.* Ed. M. Wallace, trans. D. Pellauer. Minneapolis: Augsburg Fortress, 1995, 68-72.

Rupp, E. G. *Studies in the Making of the English Protestant Tradition.* Cambridge: Cambridge University Press, 1947.

Said, Edward. "Secular Criticism." In *The World, The Text, and the Critic.* Cambridge: Harvard University Press, 1983, 1-30.

Thomson, A. F. *The Later Lollards, 1414-1520.* Oxford: Oxford University Press, 1965.

Walker, Greg. *Writing Under Tyranny: English Literature and the Henrician Reformation.* Oxford: Oxford University Press, 2005.

Walsham, Alexandra. "Inventing the Lollard Past: The Afterlife of a Medieval Sermon in Early Modern England." *Journal of Ecclesiastical History,* 58.4 (2007): 628-655.

Wilks, Michael. "Royal Priesthood: The Origins of Lollardy." Reprinted in *Wyclif: Political Ideas and Practice.* Oxford: Oxbow Books, 2000, 101-116.

Wrightson, Keith. *Earthly Necessities: Economic Lives in Early Modern Britain.* New Haven: Yale University Press, 2000.

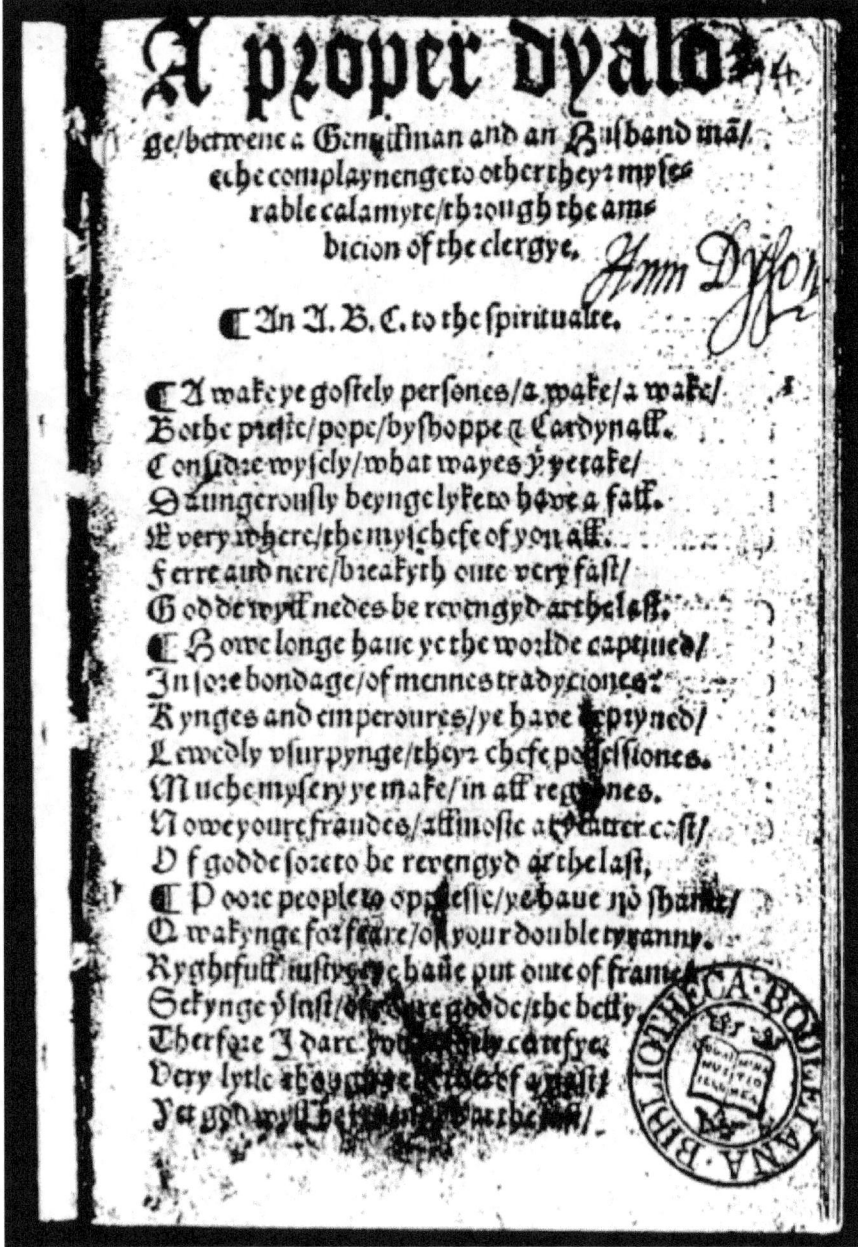

Figure 1. Title page from the 1529 edition of *A proper dyaloge*.

Figure 2. Woodcut depicting Bayfield's martyrdom, from the 1570 edition of John Foxe's *Acts and Monuments*.

Nota Bene: Brief Notes on Manuscripts and Early Printed Books

Highlighting Little-known or Recently Uncovered Items or Related Issues

The "1689 Chaucer": A Reissue of the Last Black-Letter Chaucer Edition

ARNOLD SANDERS

A recently discovered copy of the *Collected Works* of Chaucer contains a title page that claims it was printed in 1689, but it has not yet been recorded in the electronic English Short Title Catalogue (ESTC). The "1689 Chaucer" has been known to scholars at least since 1963, but it appears that until this year no descriptions were made based upon actual examination of a copy.[1] Now the 1689 Chaucer can certainly be identified as a reissue of leaves from the 1687 printing with a new title page.[2] The only point that distinguishes its title page from copies of the 1687 edition is the booksellers' description. Based on the evidence in the booksellers' lozenges on the title pages, this Chaucer edition may have been issued in four different states over the course of two years by a consortium of at least five booksellers and the printer, one J.H., generally believed to be John Harefinch.[3] The 1689 title page represents the last campaign to sell copies of the 1687 resetting of Speght's 1602 edition with a hybrid typographic style that put contemporary commentary in Roman type and Chaucer's text in Gothic, with some modernized spelling. This is a compelling visual indicator of late-seventeenth-century readers' reverence for Chaucer's poetry and of their failing ability to construe his Middle English and to read black-letter text. Though the 1687 Chaucer has little to tell scholars about Chaucer's text, the variant issues of the title page may reveal useful insights about readers' reception of Chaucer's works in the transition from the Renaissance to the modern era.

Many of the booksellers named on the title page bearing the 1689 date also seem to have participated in an emerging English rare-book market for bibliophiles. Beginning just ten years before the 1687 Chaucer printing, these same booksellers distributed numerous free auction sale catalogues describing book and art collections to promote book collecting, apparently a profitable side business to selling these same customers newly printed editions.[4] The auction catalogues' titles emphasized the learned disciplines of the books' subjects and the "antique" status of their editions. Simultaneously, older black-letter Chaucer editions, especially the 1602 Speght, appear to have become both rare and sought-after. For instance, Samuel Pepys' 1684 diary entry records his visit to St. Paul's to direct the deliberately archaic binding of his 1602 Chaucer, a volume he may have sought for as much as a year: "they were not full neate enough for me, but pretty well it is; and thence to the clasp-maker's to have it clasped and bossed."[5] This emerging market for collectable copies of old Chaucer editions may have been one factor motivating the printer and booksellers to produce this new, hybrid Speght edition in black letter with modernized apparatus which could be sold as a bargain to customers unable to acquire or to afford its rarer ancestors.

Derek Pearsall described the 1687 resetting of Thomas Speght's 1602 edition of Chaucer's collected works as the last in "what might be called a spate of Chaucerian publication" beginning in 1532.[6] The title page of the only issue recorded in ESTC listed the place of publication as London and gave the date in Roman numerals as 1687. The only evidence of the printer's identity was a one-page Advertisement signed J.H. To identify J.H. as John Harefinch, Pearsall referred to Charles Muscatine's Book of Geoffrey Chaucer, a 1963 monograph. Neither Pearsall nor Muscatine had seen a copy of the 1687 edition with the "John Harefinch" title page, however. For this, they both depended upon William Alderson's research from the 1960s, though this identification also was based upon a secondhand description of a copy that was apparently never seen again.[7]

William Alderson wrote that P. L. Heyworth, the University of Toronto medievalist, had sent him the collation of a 1687 volume described in the 1956 catalogue of Folio Books, Oxford, whose title page listed no booksellers but specified that the books were "Printed and are to be sold by John Harefinch in Montague Court in Little Britain."[8] Neither Alderson nor any other scholar appears to know what became of this book. Alderson was the first to suggest that the 1687 reimposition of Speght's text was produced by a consortium of commercial interests as a "publisher's venture."[9] He thought they may have been attempting to establish a profitable copyright to the Speght Chaucer; that right had lain fallow since the deaths of the heirs of Adam Islip and George Bishop, the original publishers, at some point between 1611 and 1625.[10] Pearsall agreed with Alderson's assertion, but the sheer size of such a "collected works" edition in folio suggests the printer's and sellers' ambitions to profit by selling the printed leaves. Each copy is composed of 600 pages, most of it Chaucer in Gothic type, plus 60 pages of Roman type apparatus, along with Lydgate's *Siege of Thebes*, John Speed's engraved Chaucer portrait, and the coat of arms attributed to Chaucer.

Although survival rates alone do not yield conclusive evidence about print runs or sales, the ESTC records fifty-five copies of the "London: 1687" issue in public and national libraries in Britain and North America, plus five copies recorded in Australia and New Zealand. This suggests that a wide readership for the edition may have been desired and achieved. Moreover, the existence of two different title pages, distinguished only by absence or mention of the printer, indicates active attempts to sell the books. The existence of a copy with a third title page listing the booksellers clearly shows signs of a continuing marketing campaign to recover the edition's cost in paper, press time, and labor.

Charles Muscatine's 1963 monograph, drawing upon Alderson's as-yet-unpublished notes, was the first published news of the existence of the 1689 title page. He described the edition as "again entered in the [booksellers'] *Catalogue* as being sold by S. Crouch in Cornhill; Math. Gilliflower, and W. Hensman in Westminster Hall; and A. Roper, and G. Grafton, in Fleet Street."[11] This description, depending, like Alderson's, on Edward Arber's transcription in the 1911 *Term Catalogues*, has been the only evidence of the 1689 Chaucer's existence.[12] Alderson and Henderson cautiously described the booksellers' title page as coming from "among the works 'reprinted' during the Easter term of 1689."[13] Alderson's note advises that the 1689 "'reprint' probably should be understood as a reissue," and that "No known copies carry the 1689 imprint."[14] Because Alderson was not actually able to examine a 1689 copy, and because Muscatine and Pearsall based their conclusions upon Alderson, the reappearance of the 1689 Chaucer gives us an opportunity to discover whether it included previously unknown text rather than conforming exactly to the content and layout of the 1687 copies. That opportunity presented itself in an eBay auction in January 2013, when I purchased the book in question with a fourth version of the title page.[15]

In a side-by-side comparison with a copy of the "London: [1687]" edition, I have confirmed that the 1689 book is a reissue of the 1687 edition with a reprinted title page; nothing else has been changed.[16] Even the title pages of both books are exactly alike to the millimeter, including all type heights outside the publication lozenge, and spacing between types and between type and ornaments. The booksellers' information was set in five millimeter capitals for the 1687 copy and in four millimeter capitals for the 1689. The gatherings of the 1687 and 1689 copies are identically signed, including signature "c" missigned as "d," and are identical in all page numbers, headers, and catchwords. In addition, I noted two identical typesetting peculiarities on different leaves that would be highly improbable to reproduce with a new setting of the type. These include a battered capital "W" beginning the first line of the poem, "Upon the Picture of Chaucer" (sig. a1v), and low-set printer's ornaments on the bottom right row at the top of the first numbered page. Three of the last four ornaments at the right end of the lower row produced lighter ink deposition on both copies.

I also attempted to compare paper watermarks, but in most cases the black-letter type on both sides of each leaf frustrated my efforts. In one stroke of luck, however, on the first leaf of the missigned gathering, both the Johns Hopkins University copy with the 1687 title page and my copy with the 1689 title page reveal a distinctive portion of what appears to be the same watermark, three touching circles below a shieldlike shape. The three circles depending from a single line can be seen within millimeters of each other in the same blank space below the "bend countercharged" of Chaucer's coat of arms.[17] This suggests that the two sheets may have been printed from the same batch of paper.[18]

The basic content of the publisher's information for my 1689 copy largely conforms to Arber's description, but its spelling differs in so many points that it indicates yet another setting of the type in this contested piece of title-page real estate. The printer and publishers' information reads:

LONDON,

Printed by *J.H.* and are to be *ſold by Samuel Crouch* in *Cornhill, Mat-thew Gelliflower* and *William Henſhman* in *Weſtminſter-Hall, Abel Roper* and *George Grafton* in *Fleet-Street*, MDCLXXXIX.

Along with the trivial change from Arber's "Gillyflower" to "Gelliflower" and the provision of the first names of Crouch, Roper, and Grafton, the last name of the third seller indicates one of William Hensman's two variant spelling of his name. According to Henry Plomer, who identifies Hensman as having "a share in most of the large ventures of his time, notably a folio edition of Chaucer," Hensman also spelled his name "Henshman" and "Hinchman."[19] The ESTC indicates that Hensman was an active bookseller at Westminster from 1671 until at least 1704, and on two other occasions he collaborated with Matthew Gillyflower (also spelled "Gilliflower") in 1678 to sell the anonymous *The Refined Courtier, or a Correction of several Indecencies crept into civil conversation*, and in 1685 to sell Charles Cotton's English translation of Montaigne's essays. In effect, these men are using the reissued Chaucer edition to promote their bookstores, and further examination of titles they published may yield insights about their role in the literary market for such books.

In addition to the occurrence of "Henshman" on the second state of the 1689 Chaucer issue title page, the same spelling appears on three other editions found in the ESTC. There, some years before the main leaves of the 1687/1689 Chaucer edition were printed, the bookseller "William Henshman in Westminster-Hall" partners with members of a different consortium of booksellers to distribute three catalogues promoting the auction of individual collectors' libraries of "antique and modern" books.[20] These are among the dozens of auction sale catalogues for collections of paintings and books distributed by London booksellers that included the sellers of the 1687/1689 Chaucer edition. This may have given them the means and the motive to estimate the market for a black-letter type Chaucer in an era during which some readers still sought Renaissance, Middle English, black-letter editions as collectable rarities and other readers were beginning to prefer new printings of modern English in Roman type.

Goucher College

NOTES

1. See Charles Muscatine, *The Book of Geoffrey Chaucer* (San Francisco, CA: Book Club of California, 1963), 33; William Alderson and Arnold C. Henderson, *Chaucer and Augustan Scholarship* (Berkeley, CA: University of California Press, 1970), 40–48; and Derek Pearsall, "Thomas Speght (ca. 1550–?)," in *Editing Chaucer: The Great Tradition*, ed. Paul G. Ruggiers (Norman, OK: Pilgrim Books, 1984), 90–92.
2. Philip Gaskell, *A New Introduction to Bibliography* (Oxford: Oxford University Press, 1972, rpt. 1995), 316–316.
3. Alderson and Henderson, *Chaucer and Augustan Scholarship*, 48. Harefinch has been identified as a printer who collaborated with William Hensman. Henry R. Plomer, "Westminster-Hall and Its Booksellers," *The Library* N.S. (1905): 386; and Henry R. Plomer, *A Dictionary of the Printers and Booksellers Who Were at Work in England, Scotland and Ireland from 1668–1725*, ed. Arundel Estaile (Oxford: Oxford University Press, 1922), 152.
4. A search of ESTC for the subject "Book auctions—England—Early works to 1800" yielded 203 entries, the earliest of which (1634) was printed by John Janson in Amsterdam with four pages of titles in English (ESTC 006206333). The next entry recorded occurs forty years later, when the Widow Page sells a broadsheet listing "A Catalogue of Mathematical Books" for sale (ESTC 006171062). Moses Pitt's 1675 sixteen-page octavo offer to purchase copies of Janson's "great atlas" to be sold at an Amsterdam auction is the first of these catalogues to record that the catalogue will be given away (ESTC 006157300). Beginning in 1680, ESTC records five such free catalogues for book auctions, most written by Edward Millington, who had previously entered the trade as a bookseller but seems to have served London booksell-

ers as an early professional bibliographer to develop interest in the auctions. According to Antony Griffiths, he was also one of the most ambitious of the art auctioneer/booksellers. Antony Griffiths, "Early Mezzotint Publishing in England II: Peter Lely, Tompson and Browne," *Print Quarterly* 7:2 (1990): 132–134.

5. Muscatine mentions this event (Muscatine, *Book of Geoffrey Chaucer*, 35) but does not point out that Pepys may have had to seek for as long as a year to acquire the volume he called "my Chaucer." Samuel Pepys, *The Diary of Samuel Pepys: A New and Complete Transcription*, ed. Robert Latham and William Matthews (Berkeley, CA: University of California Press, 1970–1983). The entry for July 8, 1684 is almost thirteen months after the entry for June 14, 1663, which first records Sir John Minnes's praise of Chaucer. Six months later, on December 10, 1663, Pepys describes his visit to St. Paul's Churchyard to select books for purchase, including a "Chaucer" that he had bound in July of the next year. Pepys' November 21, 1666 entry mentions his having read "something from Chaucer" to his wife and brother, possibly from his copy of the 1602 edition

6. Pearsall, "Thomas Speght," 90–91. Although this "last of the black-letter Chaucers" has little to recommend it as an example of Chaucer editing, it has interested scholars such as Alderson, Muscatine, and Pearsall because it divides the work of the earnest but sometimes credulous printer-publishers, who enhanced Chaucer's canon with apocrypha, from the later, scholarly editors of Chaucer, who applied the principles used to edit classical literary texts to the first English author with claims to classic status.

7. Alderson's work was brought posthumously to press by Arnold Henderson in 1970, but Alderson had previously shared his research with Muscatine while *The Book of Geoffrey Chaucer* was being prepared (64).

8. Alderson and Henderson, *Chaucer and Augustan Scholarship*, n. 17, 253, 47.

9. Ibid., 44–48.

10. Ibid., 45–60. Alderson points out that the last link in that commercial and hereditary chain appears to be one George Hebb, to whom Thomas Adams's widow, Elizabeth, sold the rights to many works (not specifically the works of Chaucer) on May 6, 1625. After this date, no further evidence of copyright claims for Speght's edition of Chaucer's works has been found. It seems noteworthy that by 1652 Elias Ashmole already believed he was safe in publishing both the Speght text of the "Canon's Yeoman's Tale" and the Westminster tomb engraving made for Speght's edition in *Theatrum Chemicum Britannicum*, an anthology of otherwise anonymous and pseudonymous alchemical works. The right to print Speght's Chaucer edition, if anyone seriously cared to contest it, was already "in play" by the middle of the seventeenth century.

11. Muscatine, 33.

12. Edward Arber, *The Term Catalogues, 1668–1709 A.D.; with a Number for Easter Term, 1711 A.D.*, vol. 2 (London: Edward Arber, 1905), 261.
13. Alderson and Henderson, *Chaucer and Augustan Scholarship*, 41. Alderson's evaluation of the 1721 Urry Chaucer was used for Chapter 5 of *Editing Chaucer: The Great Tradition*, ed. Paul G. Ruggiers on that edition. Later researchers have been extremely dependent upon Alderson, whose untimely death kept him from seeing publication of this work.
14. Alderson and Henderson, *Chaucer and Augustan Scholarship*, n. 16, 253.
15. J & J Fine Books (Indian Land, SC) reported to me on February 10, 2013, that they had purchased the book at a 2006 auction of the collections of Jack Palance, a television and movie star of the 1950s and sixties, but they were mistaken. On November 24, 2012, about a month before the eBay auction, Merrill's Auction Gallery (Williston, VT) advertised and sold what appeared, based on the auction house's title-page image, to be an identical copy of this issue (see "Lot 229: 1689 Works of Jeffrey Chaucer—London printed by J.H.," *Invaluable: The World's Premier Auctions*, available at http://www. artfact.com/auction-lot/1689-works-of-jeffrey-chaucer-london-printed-by-229-c-d1807a01ad). Duane Merrill & Co. would not confirm the sale of this Chaucer edition to J & J Fine Books, but digital images of the spine and pages 32–33, kindly provided by Adam DeMasi of Duane Merrill & Co., match perfectly the spine wear marks and two stains on pages 32 and 33 of my copy. The only other provenance information is contained on the front pastedown, which carries the undated bookplate of Colonel Thomas Glyn, who may be the same man mentioned in Burke's *Annual Register* for August 28, 1778 (115). In addition to Alderson's description of the 1689 copy with the abbreviated booksellers' names, a third copy bearing the 1689 date but without bookseller information is recorded in the *Catalogus van de boeken der Nationale Bibliotheek* (The Hague, Holland: Lands Drukkerye, 1700), 295, as entry 3312 under "English Dichters": "The Works of our ancient, learned and excellent English Poet, Jeffrey Chaucer: &c. to which is adjoyn'd the Story of the Siege of Thebes, by J. Lidgate, Monk of Bury. London 1689. in fol. 2.28." This information can be retrieved from a GoogleBooks image http://books.google.com/books?id=DDdWAAAAYAAJ&pg=PA295&l pg=PA295&dq=Chaucer+Works+1689+%22Nationale+Bibliotheek%22 &source=bl&ots=YlMd_xddST&sig=TIOS_aVvR7TLisGEZvR9EqDi7 pw&hl=en&sa=X&ei=j0osU4icA6KGyAGFl4H4DA&ved=0CDkQ6AE wAg#v=onepage&q=Chaucer%20Works%201689%20%22Nationale%20 Bibliotheek%22&f=false. The current online catalogue of the *Bibliotheek* contains no record of this volume (http://www.kb.nl/).
16. I thank Earle Havens, Amy Kimball, and the Johns Hopkins University Library for granting me access to one of two Johns Hopkins copies of the 1687 Chaucer, shelf mark PO 1850 1687. Digital images for comparison are

available at "Links to Parallel Comparison Images: '1687' Issue vs. '1689' Issue," http://faculty.goucher.edu/eng241/links_to_parallel_comparison_images_1687_1689.html.

17. Based on a comparison with Briquet watermarks, this partially visible watermark most closely resembles the "arms of Basel with three circles" seen in types 656, 12103, 12122. Briquet attributed paper with this mark to the firm of Düring, which is first noted in Swiss and French books printed in the sixteenth century and was active into the seventeenth century. Charles-Moïse Briquet, *Les filigranes: Dictionnaire historique des marques du papier dés leur apparition vers 1282 jusqu'en 1600* (Paris: A. Picard & fils, 1907), 106, 109.

18. Because of the edition's heavy use of Gothic type on both sides of most leaves, no more than the slightest traces of watermarks could be discovered with the aid of a Zelco lamp and shade. The coat-of-arms page of each copy is the only leaf with enough blank space to allow the watermark to be seen.

19. Plomer, "Westminster-Hall and Its Booksellers," 386; and Plomer, *Dictionary of the Printers and*, 152.

20. *Catalogus librorum, in quavis lingua & facultate insignium instructissimarum bibliothecarum Reverendi dm lissimiq[ue] domini D. Doctoris Gulielmi Outrami* (1681), *Bibliotheca Smithiana* (1682), and *Catalogus variorum librorum quavis facultate insigniorum bibliothecarum instructissimarum Rev. Doct. Amb. Atfield* (1685). The 1681 auction catalogue describing the libraries of Dr. William Outrami and Thomas Gataker was distributed by booksellers William Cooper, Richard Chiswel, Christopher Wilkinson, William Nott, Robert Horn, and William Henshman. Richard Smith's library, described in the 1682 catalogue, was distributed by nearly the same syndicate of booksellers, with Sam[uel] Tidmarsh taking Robert Horn's place. Ambrose Atfield's 1685 library sale catalogue was distributed by Henshman/Hensman, Nott, and Wilkinson, together with William Miller, a Mr. Southby and a Mr. Stephens. Southby was probably John Southby, active as a bookseller from 1684 to 1691, and Stephens may have been Anthony Stephens, active in 1685 in Oxford, according to the *Dictionary of the Printers and Booksellers*, 277, 280.

WORKS CITED

Alderson, William L, and Arnold C. Henderson. *Chaucer and Augustan Scholarship*. Berkeley, CA: University of California Press, 1970.

Arber, Edward. *The Term Catalogues, 1668–1709 A.D.; with a Number for Easter Term, 1711 A.D.* Vol. 2. London: Professor Edward Arber, 1905.

Briquet, Charles-Moïse. *Les filigranes: Dictionnaire historique des marques du papier dès leur apparition vers 1282 jusqu'en 1600*. Paris: A. Picard & fils, 1907.

Catalogus van de boeken der Nationale Bibliotheek. [The Hague]: Lands Drukkerye, 1700.

Chaucer, Geoffrey. *The Works of our Ancient, Learned, and Excellent, English Poet Jeff [e] ry Chaucer, as they have lately been compared with the best Manuscripts; and several things added never before in print. To which is adjoined, The Story of the Siege of Thebes, by John Lydgate, Monk of Bury. Together with the Life of Chaucer; shewing his Country, Parentage, Education, Marriage, Children, Revenues, Service, Reward, Friends, Books, Death. Also a Table wherein the old and obscure Words are explained; and such words (which are many) that either are by nature or derivation, Arabick, Greek, Latin, Italian, French, Dutch, or Saxon, mark'd with particular Notes for the better understanding their original.* London: [1687].

————. *The Works of our Ancient, Learned, and Excellent, English Poet Jeff [e] ry Chaucer, as they have lately been compared with the best Manuscripts; and several things added never before in print. To which is adjoined, The Story of the Siege of Thebes, by John Lydgate, Monk of Bury. Together with the Life of Chaucer; shewing his Country, Parentage, Education, Marriage, Children, Revenues, Service, Reward, Friends, Books, Death. Also a Table wherein the old and obscure Words are explained; and such words (which are many) that either are by nature or derivation, Arabick, Greek, Latin, Italian, French, Dutch, or Saxon, mark'd with particular Notes for the better understanding their original.* London: Printed by J.H. and are to be sold by Samuel Crouch in Cornhill, Matthew Gelliflower and William Henshman in Westminster-Hall, Abel Roper and George Grafton in Fleet-Street, [1689].

Editing Chaucer: The Great Tradition, ed. Paul G. Ruggiers. Norman, OK: Pilgrim Books, 1984.

Gaskell, Philip. *A New Introduction to Bibliography*. Oxford: Oxford University Press, 1972. Rpt. 1995.

Griffiths, Antony. "Early Mezzotint Publishing in England II: Peter Lely, Tompson and Browne." *Print Quarterly* 7:2 (1990): 130–145.

Muscatine, Charles. *The Book of Geoffrey Chaucer*. San Francisco, CA: Book Club of California, 1963.

Pearsall, Derek. "Thomas Speght (ca. 1550–?)." In *Editing Chaucer: The Great Tradition*, ed. Paul G. Ruggiers. Norman, OK: Pilgrim Books, 1984, 71–92.

Pepys, Samuel. *The Diary of Samuel Pepys: A New and Complete Transcription*, ed. Robert Latham and William Matthews. Berkeley, CA: University of California Press, 1970–1983.

Plomer, Henry R. *A Dictionary of the Printers and Booksellers Who Were at Work in England, Scotland and Ireland from 1668–1725*, ed. Arundel Estaile. Oxford: Oxford University Press, 1922.

————. "Westminster-Hall and Its Booksellers." *The Library*, n.s. (1905): 380–390.

Book Forensics: The Analysis of Material Evidence Found in Book Conservation

DOROTHY AFRICA

Our current awareness that books carry important physical and historical evidence aside from their textual content seems to us to be mere common sense, so it is sobering to note that until fairly recently books were routinely rebound or discarded with no thought given to their value as evidence of material culture or historical practice. Excellent studies were made of particular surviving ancient codices, illuminated manuscripts, and fine bindings, but these tended to focus on the texts or artistic value rather than the physical structures and constituent materials of the books themselves.[1] The disregard for such things is famously illustrated by the disbinding of the bindings of the Coptic Nag Hammadi books following their discovery in 1945, the use of adhesive tape to connect Dead Sea Scroll fragments (also in the 1940s), and the 1972 rebinding of a surviving ninth-century manuscript book from the monastery at Reichenau which was probably a significant witness to the origins of Western binding structures.[2] We will never know now what discarded evidence might have told us.

It is hard to determine an exact time or particular perception that marked a new sensibility about the value of physical evidence inherent in book structures and materials. Like the invention of the wheel or the discoveries of fire and yeast, it has had many points of independent genesis. One of them was certainly in 1955, when the noted English bibliographer H. Graham Pollard delivered an address to the Bibliographic Society in which he advanced what was then a startling thesis about the physical value of book bindings: "[I]t is important," Pollard asserted, "that we should be able to date and localize bindings, because it may contribute to problems of text and authorship. This can only be done by selecting certain features that change and recording all that we can find about them."[3]

No doubt Pollard would be pleased to know that his perceptive address was in the vanguard of what has become the academic field of the History of the Book, one that has gone on to embrace not only his questions of text and authorship but also the material culture and technical evolution of the physical book and its social and economic context.[4] The technological advances of our times are unlikely to diminish interest the field. On the contrary, the advance of the digital age, it seems to me, is likely to increase the importance of academic studies of books as the experience of reading old books and manuscripts becomes for young scholars increasingly a digital one, by its nature visual and nontactile. Older scholars are not often aware of how much their own experiences in libraries and with handling books and manuscripts collectively inform what they see when they go online.

Book forensics—the examination and investigation of the physical evidence preserved in any given book for information on its material culture and construction—requires an observant eye but also an educated mind. Yes, a digital image can be worth a thousand words, but only if you recognize what the image is. An example came to my attention at the Harvard Law Library more than a dozen years ago. It was extremely humble, laced, limp, vellum binding of a small Italian notary's manual, a sixteenth-century imprint, as I recall.[5] As I examined the book, I became aware of an odd bump on the spine. Since the two tanned leather sewing supports holding the book to the cover were broken, it was an easy matter to gently pull the text away from the vellum wrapper to see the spine. On the lowest sewing support, about two-thirds to three-quarters of the way up the stitching, was a protruding bit of leather with a single long, vertical stitch down its center. Some closer examination with a magnifier led me to the following interpretation.

The binder had almost finished sewing (it was customary to sew from the last gathering forward toward the beginning of the book) when the lower sewing support snapped off just above the sewing. The book was too cheap to be worth the time it would have taken to start over, so the binder pared one end of the piece of the support that had broken off, shaping it to a thin, neat point. He then inserted his needle into this point from behind and used the thread to make a long, vertical stitch downward, thus pulling the thinned point of the support over the thread wraps below the break. From there, he ran his needle back up toward the break through the thread wraps to anchor the point in place over the lower completed sewing and to return his needle to the point he had reached when the break occurred. With the sewing support now anchored back in place, he resumed sewing—a very neat save indeed. And though the supports had all broken eventually where they laced across the joints to hold the vellum cover on, the sewing on the text block was still intact some four hundred years later.

Sometimes an important feature is more deeply concealed, escaping all notice until the passage of time or misuse causes a tear or the concealing material wears through, and the secret comes again into light. Such an instance is presented by Harvard Law School Library MS. 54, one of many books of English statutes in the Law School collection. The manuscript dates to about 1350 and is in a handsome, English, full-leather binding dated to the fifteenth century. The spine of that binding had failed at some point, and the book had been rebacked, but the repair was an old one. It came into the Law School collection with many other books purchased from the library of George Dunn (1864–1912) in 1913. At some point, the leather of the reback on the spine split vertically and tore across the lower spine.

Figure 1. Lifted and cleaned original spine view of MS 54. *Magna carta cum statutis,* HLS MS 54, Historical and Special Collections, Harvard Law School Library.

The book was sent down to me with the request that I tack down the torn leather at the heel to prevent further damage, but what caught my eye immediately was the bright white material showing through the split. It could only be alum taw, but the use of alum taw as a spine-lining material was most uncommon. Such a sturdy cover material is quite unsuitable for such a purpose, but there it clearly was, under the leather of the rebacked spine. I

Figure 2. Inner board view of MS 54. *Magna carta cum statutis*, HLS MS 54, Historical and Special Collections, Harvard Law School Library.

proceeded to clean off the residue of leather suede and fiber under the lifted leather and found myself looking at a damaged but surviving medieval alum-taw binding, complete with a neatly sewn end band.

The later tanned-leather binding had been applied wholesale over the original alum-taw binding, and the person who did the reback had also left it in place. Thanks to the lifting of the pastedowns on the inner board surfaces, we can ascertain that indeed, the whole medieval binding is intact under the later binding.

The problem for the library is that given the age of the fine later leather binding, we should not remove it, despite the greater value of the medieval binding underneath. These two examples illustrate, I hope, the importance of both direct observation of an evident phenomenon—the odd bump, a flash of white—and the observer's own understanding of the evolution of the Western codex to "read" the evidence.

My own interests center upon the material and technical study of the Western codex form, which goes back to the pioneering studies of early bindings and astute bibliographers such as Pollard, Howard Nixon, and Dorothy Miner, among others, in the mid-twentieth century whose work expanded the investigation from fine bindings into bookbinding in general.[6] In 1966 a tremendous impetus to these investigations arose from the work of conservators present in the aftermath of a damaging flood in Florence, Italy. The salvage and recovery efforts in the wake of that disaster brought together conservators and binders from all over the world. Their collaborations and shared observations led to great advances in conservation techniques but also brought attention to the differences that binding structures and materials made in the durability and survival rates of books damaged in the flood.

The conservation work emerging from the Florence flood recovery, in addition to its contributions to academic study of book history, transformed the field of book conservation in the following decades. For recent monographs of the technical and structural history of the book, see the masterly work of J. A. Szirmai, the festschrift for the noted English binder Roger Powell, and Julia Miller's book on the importance of incorporating physical evidence into bibliographic records.[7]

This potted history of the evolution of the formal study of book history is absurdly brief, but it provides context for the contemporary examination of an historical book by a scholar, conservator, curator, or librarian. The rest of this paper concentrates on how the forensic investigation of an early printed book or manuscript can discover evidence of its past.

One of the most informative structural features of a book is its sewing, which is also the aspect that seems to be least understood by researchers and book lovers of all stripes and descriptions, including many librarians. Sewing is the most crucial element in the structure of the preindustrial book and the most time-consuming part of the manual binding process. The sewing stations—points by means of which the individual gatherings are connected either directly to each other or by means of supports—distribute the movement of the text block throughout the structure, preventing acute and repeated concentrations of stress on any single point. In early books and manuscripts, the number of sewing stations is a useful indicator, therefore, of the expense (time, money, or both) of the binding. Sadly, especially for the early medieval period, when the supported sewing that is the distinctive hallmark of the Western codex was being developed, holes are often the only remains we have of earlier binding structures in old books and manuscripts. The estimate offered by Szirmai is that we have "no more than one to five percent of original bindings on the surviving medieval books."[8] Furthermore most of our surviving early codices have been rebound many times, and the more significant the book or manuscript, the likelier it is to have been frequently rebound. It was estimated by Roger Powell, for example, in his report on the rebinding of the Book of Kells in 1953, that Kells had been rebound "at least five times and possibly more."[9]

The number of sewing stations as evidence of solid structural work is less reliable as evidence of good sewing after the mid-fifteenth century, especially in the sixteenth century, when the rapid increase in book production after Gutenberg presented binders with an enormous challenge. Johann Gutenberg's invention provided the binders with no assistance whatsoever, but their customers continued to expect that binding would be cheaper than the text itself, although the cost of the text was dropping rapidly. As Nicholas Pickwood aptly observes, "it is a story of the binding trade facing the realities of increasing demand and financial pressure, sometimes with ingenuity, sometimes with shoddy work and sometimes with straightforward deception."[10] Anyone trying to rebind an old book or manuscript must turn to book forensics to try to identify which of those possibilities is before him or her, in order to determine how to rebind the book in the manner most historically sympathetic that is also compatible with its present use.

Since sewing took most of the binder's time, it is hardly surprising that from the sixteenth century on, binders developed an ingenious array of ways to make the sewing faster while still providing their esteemed customers with the familiar appearances they expected. The evolution of the most common sewing patterns is hard to study, since most early manuscript and printed books, as noted above, have been rebound many times. In a most counterintuitive manner, innovations in sewing styles and abbreviated methods of sewing, such as "sewing up" and "skip sewing,"[11] led to an increased number of sewing stations. This increased number remained the fashion for false bands, narrow strips of cardboard across the back of the spine, which continued the look of traditional supported sewing long after its disappearance in favor of sunken cord and machine sewing.

In the nineteenth century it was common, as an economic measure, to cut off the spine folds of older books, especially those with thin signatures or gatherings, and create artificially thicker gatherings by the simple expedient of running wads of single folios under a sewing machine, then notching the ravaged margins for sunken cord sewing or simply oversewing the wads. Cutting off the spine folds eliminated the valuable historical evidence the sewing holes would have provided for many old books and manuscripts. However, in addition to frequent rebinding, the evidence provided by sewing holes cannot always give clear testimony since binders would reuse any old holes they found useful, leaving a confusing maze of overlapping patterns to confront the bemused modern binder attempting to recover the original structure.

How does one go about this recovery process? For a scholar trying to collate and describe the present binding on his or her manuscript or early printed book, there are practical limitations on what can be observed. Rare-book reading rooms are somewhat reluctant to allow readers to force open fragile binding spines to investigate sewing buried deep in shadowy depths of their gutter margins, if visible at all. For reasons already given, simply counting and measuring what is visible on the spine is scarcely reliable on bindings from the sixteenth century on. Sometimes lacing patterns can be discernible on the surfaces of the boards, but rarely were all the sewing stations laced into boards after the late-medieval period, even after the switch from wooden boards to cardboard. As is so often the case, one does the best one can with what circumstances and conditions allow.

It is somewhat easier when a book or manuscript comes in for extensive conservation and repair. For one thing, the current binding is often badly broken and in many cases has to be removed anyway. When a book is to be rebound, as opposed to simply recased, the binding has to be pulled entirely, that is, the current sewing must be removed as well as the binding and spine linings. This affords considerable opportunity for detailed study and, if possible, recovery of previous sewing structures. My approach to rebinding early books and manuscripts has evolved over time; my current practice is first to study and record as much as I can about the book in its present state, especially its sewing. For books sewn through the fold, I do this by assigning numbers to the sewing stations and the kettle-stitch beginning at the head. I then record the locations of the visible threads in the gutter between the various stations. The emerging pattern gives some indication of the binder's concern for the structural whole, depending, of course, on the thickness of the book in question.

A volume of statutes of the region around Naples, *Placita principum seu constitutions Regni Neapolitani cum glossis*, printed in Lyon in 1533 and now in the collection of the Harvard University Law School Library, can act as a case study. The work consists of twenty-nine gatherings and was bound together at a later point, probably in the eighteenth century, with a smaller work, a *Tractatus* (*Treatise*) of only six gatherings but sewn in a completely different fashion. The two works were kept bound together when the work was rebound at some point in the recent past. It is impossible to describe that modern binding, because when the volume came to me for rebinding in 1998, it had been removed and discarded already, but the modern sewing remained. My first step was to record the modern sewing before taking the text block apart for examination. The larger work had been sewn two-on, i.e. the attachment of two gatherings with one pass of thread, but there are several sections of all-along sewing interspersed to strengthen the quick but inherently weaker sewing of the other sections.

Once the existing sewing has been recorded, it can be removed to release the individual gatherings. At this point, tears and losses in the folios can be most easily mended, but this stage also allows for a careful examination of the evidence of the sewing holes. On a large sheet of paper, I draw a series of parallel vertical lines, one line for each gathering of the book, marked off at top and bottom to the height of the text block. For very large and/or thick books, this is not always possible, but for most small formats and short works, a complete record can be made. Above and below the height marks, I mark each vertical line to correspond to the signature system used by the printer. This is usually a lettering sequence, a, b, c, and so forth, but the initial matter may have Roman numerals or symbols. I then take the center sheet of each gathering, center its spine fold over its assigned line on my paper, and make a small prick through each visible hole along the spine and onto my paper with a fine awl. I then remove the sheet and darken the prick mark on the paper with a pencil point. When I have finished this process for the entire book, I use my record of the most recent sewing to mark it on the prick pattern I have created, usually in red ink to separate it from the other marks. At the end of the process, I have a diagram of the entire text block.

The following diagram is based on my prick pattern for the *Placita* gatherings K through P. The holes recorded for each gathering appear as circles

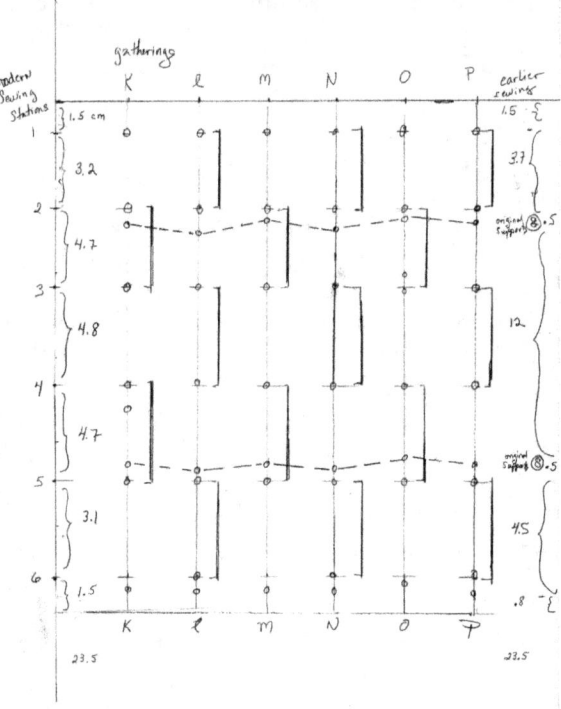

Figure 3. *Placita* Diagram. Naples (Kingdom). Laws, statutes, etc. *Placita principium seu constitutions Regni Neapolitani cum glossis.* (Lyon: Dionysius de Harsy dor Symon Vincent, 1533), Historial and Special Collections, Harvard Law School Library.

on the diagram. The modern sewing is indicated by short vertical lines to the right of the gathering lines. On the left side are the approximate measurements for the spacing between sewing stations of the modern sewing structure.

The hard part now comes with the analysis of what the holes mean. Some random holes will appear throughout, perhaps accidental needle stabs or mistakes. In some cases one cannot be sure if a hole was made by a needle, an insect, or a later tear. However, since few sewing structures were done completely at random, in most instances patterns are discernible, if not always intelligible. In this example for the *Placita*, the modern sewing shows a sewn two-up pattern interspersed with all-along sewing on the first two gatherings and the gatherings i, V, and D. The feature of greater importance, however, is the pattern of zigzag lines that emerge just below station two and just above station five. Clearly they represent sewing stations from an earlier sewing, but the regular formation of the zigzag is distinctive.

I return again to the article cited above by Pickwoad on a French library collection of sixteenth-century books now at the Morgan Library in New York.[12] In this article, he examines the various sewing innovations displayed by these volumes, noting the economies these changes evince. According to Pickwoad, sewing all along was the common method of sewing until the 1540s in almost all European countries, but the 1550s saw the appearance of what he calls "sewing economies," at least in France. The first of these is skip or by-pass sewing, "where the binder leaves out the attachment to some of the sewing supports within each gathering, though the thread still runs in an unbroken line from head to tail of each gathering." The second economy was the appearance of sewing two-up, or two-on, which appeared within a decade after the first.[13] A further impetus for the expansion of cheaper kinds of bindings came from the ever-expanding book trade. Some books certainly traveled as printed sheets packed in barrels or bales, but many traveled cheaply bound as a way of protecting the text; this also allowed the books to be sold for immediate use.[14]

When looking at the *Placita* sewing pattern, I recalled Pickwoad but also Christopher Clarkson, whose class I took years ago at the Rare Book School of the University of Virginia. Clarkson noted the wish of many book buyers to have bindings that looked expensive but were not. To oblige them, binders would provide the appearance of double sewing supports but make them cheaper by using skip sewing and sewing on alternating cords of the double supports. That, I believe, is what we have here in the distinctive zigzag lines discernable in the *Placita* prick pattern. This book is rather tall for only two stations in addition to the kettles, but as seen in the case of the notary book, two supports placed near the ends were not uncommon, especially in "economy" work, which the abbreviated sewing structure suggests this was.

The presence of periodic all-along sewing, in which the sewing thread forms a figure eight around both cords of each support, indicates that it was utilitarian, not shoddy, work. Since the *Placita* is only twenty-nine signatures, the abbreviated pattern would have been quite adequate to secure it as a single work. The abbreviated sewing could mean that it was originally bound with other works in a thicker book even before it was bound with the *Tractatus.*

It remained for me in rebinding the volume to restore the earlier sewing pattern of the *Placita*, but also to preserve the different sewing structure of

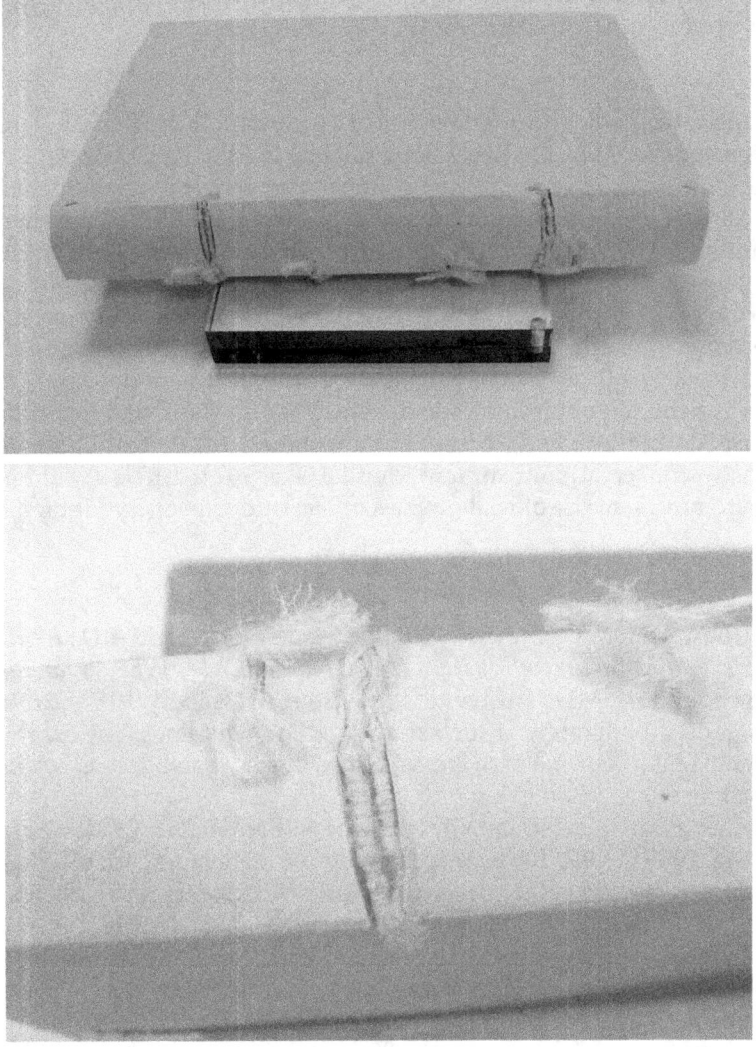

Figure 4. Two Views of *Placita* spine. Naples (Kingdom). Laws, statutes, etc. *Placita principium seu constitutions Regni Neapolitani cum glossis.* (Lyon: Dionysius de Harsy dor Symon Vincent, 1533), Historial and Special Collections, Harvard Law School Library.

its companion, the *Tractatus*. I chose to rebind the work in a tough cover-stock paper binding, as the value of this item to our library collection did not merit the use of parchment. In the sixteenth century, such titles could have been bound in either paper or vellum, so the paper binding was within reason. In order to preserve the evidence of the originally separate circulation of the two works, I constructed an open spine over the sewing stations to keep this evidence visible. A future researcher may or may not take an interest in the historical features of the book, but I hope my rebinding has restored these historical features to the book in such a way as to make them visible to future researchers.

Author's Note

This article is an expanded version of a presentation made at a Kalamazoo session sponsored by the Early Book Society in May 2012. For publication in the *Journal*, I have expanded the contextual material but retained the focus of the article on the particular treatment given to a specific book rather than expanding on the various approaches that could have been taken within current conservation practice and other decisions that could have been made regarding the treatment of similar materials. Such decisions are often made according to resources, available finances, and the particular circumstances obtaining at the time. I do not suggest that the treatment described in this paper is a model for all similar instances, but I do think that some kind of forensic description and documentation should always be done when an extensive conservation treatment is undertaken. This article should not be taken to represent the official policies of Harvard University Library.

NOTES

1. Dorothy Miner, ed., *The History of Bookbinding 525–1950 A.D.: An Exhibition Held at the Baltimore Museum of Art, November 12, 1957, to January 12, 1958* (Baltimore, MD: Trustees of the Walters Art Gallery, 1957), 269–270, has a good bibliography of such studies of book bindings. The exhibit was an important milestone in that it set out to illustrate an historical evolution of bindings.
2. J. A. Szirmai, *The Archaeology of Medieval Bookbinding* (Aldershot, UK: Ashgate, 1999), 7, 97. The use of adhesive tape on fragments of the Dead Sea Scrolls is noted in a video presentation on the discovery and early research as part of a traveling exhibit, *Dead Sea Scrolls: Life in Ancient Times*, at the Museum of Science, Boston, August, 2013. The resulting damage to these fragile pieces had to be laboriously corrected, but some loss is inevitable when dealing with such corrections to earlier practice.
3. Graham Pollard, "Changes in the Style of Bookbinding, 1550–1830," *The Library* 5th ser., 11.2 (1956): 71.

4. An example is Robert Darnton, *The Case for Books: Past, Present and Future* (New York: Public Affairs, 2009).

5. Unfortunately I could not locate my note on the call number, but I do have some images of the spine and the repair to the broken support. The book is in the Historical and Special Collections of the Harvard Law School Library.

6. I cite these three as examples but not as the most significant writers: see Howard Nixon, *Five Centuries of English Bookbinding* (London: Scolar Press, 1978); Miner, *History of Bookbinding*; Pollard, "Changes." Nixon's book centers on particular bindings but includes a great deal of information on the publishers, printers, and owners of the books as well. Miner's book is the catalogue of an exhibit of historic bindings. For a study of the craft (as opposed to a technical manual), see Bernard C. Middleton, *A History of English Craft Bookbinding Technique*, 3rd ed. (London: A. Wheaton & Co, 1988; 1st ed. 1963).

7. J. A. Szirmai, *The Archaeology of Medieval Bookbinding* (Aldershot, UK, and Brookfield, VT: Ashgate, 1999); John L. Sharpe, ed., *Roger Powell, The Compleat Binder: Liber Amicorum*, Bibliologia 14 (Turnhout, Belgium: Brepols, 1996); Julia Miller, *Books Will Speak Plain: A Handbook for Identifying and Describing Historical Bindings* (Ann Arbor, MI: Legacy Press, 2010).

8. Szirmai, *Archaeology*, ix.

9. Roger Powell, "Report on the Repair and Rebinding of the Book of Kells", typescript copy from the Conservation Education Programs, Columbia University, School of Library Service, 14.

10. Nicholas Pickwoad, "Onward and Downward: How Binders Coped with the Printing Press before 1800," in *A Millennium of the Book: Production, Design and Illustration in Manuscript and Print 900–1900*, ed. Robin Myers and Michael Harris (Winchester, UK: St. Paul's Bibliographies; and New Castle, DE: Oak Knoll Press, 1994), 61–106, at 61.

11. Sewing up, or on, allows the binder to sew two or more gatherings onto the text block in one pass from the kettle stitch at one end of the book to the other by alternating among them. Skip sewing simply bypasses some of the sewing stations during the pass between kettle stations. Both methods allow the binder to sew more quickly but produce a text block with a weaker structure than one sewn all along, in which each gathering is attached at each sewing station. See also Nicholas Pickwoad, "Books for Reading: Commercial Bindings in Parchment and Paper in the Era of the Handpress," in *Great Bindings from the Spanish Royal Collections, 15–21st Centuries*, ed. María Luisa López-Vidriero (Madrid: Patrimonio Nacional, Ediciones el Viso, 2012), 96–123.

12. Pickwoad, "Onward and Downward," 75–78.

13. Ibid, 77.

14. Pickwoad, "Books for Reading," 96–97.

Interplay between Text and Text Collection: The Case of Augustijnken's *Dryvoldicheit*

GERARD BOUWMEESTER

The awareness of the dynamic nature of medieval literature is one of the most significant accomplishments of modern-day philology.[1] Nowadays, scholars, both in and outside medieval textual criticism, are aware that searching for *the* meaning of a text is treading on thin ice. A similar thing can be said about the audience of a text, as we have become aware that the intended audience of a text does not "predict" or necessarily match the audience of the manuscripts containing that text. Rather, the repeated copying of a text in different codices results in a plurality of audiences. In this essay, these general statements about the instability of meaning, interpretation, and audience of a text traveling from one manuscript to another are illustrated by discussing Augustijnken's short verse narrative, "Van der Heiliger Dryvoldicheit Vader Soen Heilge Geest Eyn Schoen Gedichte" ("On the Holy Trinity, Father, Son and Holy Spirit: A Beautiful Poem"; henceforward, "Dryvoldicheit").[2]

Introduction: Augustijnken and (Intended) Audience

There are seven texts attributed to the fourteenth-century itinerant storyteller Augustijnken.[3] They have in common that they are all in Middle Dutch and relatively short, but otherwise there are considerable differences between them. In this corpus we find, for instance, a song, a riddle, and two predominantly religious texts. The first of the religious texts is a rather elaborate exegesis of the prologue of St. John's Gospel. This text amounts to around a thousand lines and is Augustijnken's longest and most learned text.

The second "Dryvoldicheit" is much shorter: 316 lines in the most extensive version. This text consists of two parts. In the first part, the Creation is explained as coming from a tree, which is rooted in God the Father, the Son, and the Holy Spirit. Everything comes in sevens: there are seven Sacraments, the tree has seven branches and seven flowers, there are seven days, seven planets, seven liberal arts, and so on. The second part of "Dryvoldicheit" combines two lists of seven: seven religious authorities (from pope and cardinal down to monk) and seven secular authorities (from emperor and king down to squire). The two lists are combined seven times: an emperor and a pope are placed at the same level to enlighten Christianity, as are a king and a cardinal, and so on. Both parts of the text contain different sevens, but whereas the first part of "Dryvoldicheit" focuses on the Creation, the second part is devoted to exegesis of the Bible.[4] Both parts of the text are enriched with Bible quotations from different books of Scripture but especially from Genesis, the Apocalypse, and St. John's Gospel.

Little is known about Augustijnken's intended audience. None of his texts explicitly addresses anyone identifiable. All we know is based on archival records. As the name "Augustijnken" does not occur very often, it is assumed that the Augustijnken referred to in the records is the same person as Augustijnken the author. The oldest records in which this name occurs are from the County of Holland.[5] This "archival" Augustijnken initially provided his (literary?) services at the count's court at The Hague in 1358. Soon thereafter, Augustijnken seems to have moved to a place where he stayed for a longer time: the court of Jan of Blois in Schoonhoven (also in Holland). Having inherited most of his grandfather's possessions, Jan was a nobleman of significant standing and, like many others in this circle, he became involved in the Teutonic Order. The members of this order had a hobby in which he participated: Jan spent his winters traveling to Prussia, where, according to the Teutonic Order, people were waiting to be converted to Christianity, often violently.

The participants in these "Prussian Crusades" or "*Preussenreisen*" (especially popular in the fourteenth century) not only marched and fought but were entertained as well.[6] In 1362 and 1363, we encounter Augustijnken in Jan's retinue, traveling east. In the records, he is called a storyteller, but they also mention that at some point he was involved in a bar fight and as a result was in need of medical and legal assistance. If we assume that this Augustijnken is indeed our author, we know that his primary audience was among the higher ranks: the circles of nobility around Jan of Blois and perhaps wider, the Teutonic Order. The second part of "Dryvoldicheit," which makes secular and religious authorities equally important in their teaching of Christianity, could therefore have been appreciated by this audience. The problem with this line of reasoning, however, is that it is hypothetical; it starts from various assumptions that are not supported (so far) by any factual evidence. Before turning to the matter of interplay between text and text collection and the interpretation of this interplay, I therefore first discuss the four manuscripts in which "Dryvoldicheit" is preserved.

"Dryvoldicheit": Real Audiences

"Dryvoldicheit" is, with some variance, preserved in four manuscripts: Brussels, Bibliothèque Royale Albert 1er, 15.642–651; Berlin, Staatbibliotheek zu Berlin—Preussischer Kulturbesitz (SPK), ms. germ. fol. 1027; New York, Pierpont Morgan Library, M. 385; and Nijmegen, Gemeentearchief, Archief van de Beide Weeshuizen, 953 (see Tables 1 and 2 for detailed information on these manuscripts; I refer to them by their place of preservation). No audience or user is mentioned in the Brussels and New York manuscripts, but hypotheses for these manuscripts have been derived from other information.

The Brussels manuscript was probably made in an urban setting; both the material features and at least one of the ten texts points in that direction.[7] The manuscript contains the only complete Middle Dutch verse translation of Honorius of Autun's *Elucidarium*.[8] The second text is a mirror of sins that has a clear emphasis on the pitfalls of living in a city.[9] The eight texts (including "Dryvoldicheit") following these two all explain or elaborate on issues raised in the first two texts. They often do so by applying relatively simple, mnemonic, and explanatory imagery. These features make the manuscript fit for educational purposes for an urban audience.

The New York manuscript containing "Dryvoldicheit" is devoted to the *Speculum humanae salvationis*; Augustijnken's text served as a filler on the last folio, 51v.[10] These texts both explain theological matters in a rather accessible way. The combination of these texts led Geert Warnar to connect this manuscript to the Teutonic Order: the *Speculum* was a popular text in this order, and both Augustijnken's choice of topic and course of life, as mentioned above, point in that direction.[11] As most of the members of this order were noblemen, a noble ownership of this manuscript seems plausible. However, Bernadette Kramer's recent study of the *Speculum* makes clear that not all the members of the order were indeed noblemen; Hinrich Westhof, owner of a vernacular *Speculum* manuscript, was a merchant who became a member of the order but does not seem to have had any rank in the nobility.[12] Thus, although they do not contain any concrete marks of ownership, the Brussels and New York manuscripts containing "Dryvoldicheit" can tell us something about Augustijnken's reception. In one case, the text was received by a probably urban audience; in the other case, a noble audience seems plausible but not certain.

Whereas the Brussels and New York manuscripts do not feature any explicit owner or audience marks, the other two manuscripts do: the Berlin and Nijmegen manuscripts contain colophons with explicit dating and localization.[13] The Berlin manuscript was made by two scribes who finished their work in 1436 and 1437. The manuscript was made for or in the Nazareth Convent in Geldern, in the eastern part of the Low Countries (east of Arnhem). The Nijmegen manuscript is slightly younger: it was made in 1445. Like the Berlin manuscript, the Nijmegen manuscript was initially used and probably made in a convent in the eastern part of the Netherlands, probably in Nijmegen (south of Arnhem) in the convent of Hessenberg or Bethlehem. Similarly, each of these manuscripts was made by two (different) scribes. As both manuscripts contain the same texts in nearly the same order and with only minor textual variation, and given the geographical proximity of the convents, it is very likely that Nijmegen is a copy of Berlin.

The preservation of Augustijnken's "Dryvoldicheit" illustrates the general statement made in the introduction of this article: the intended audience of a text does not "predict" or necessarily match the audience of the manuscripts containing it. Whereas a noble audience for Augustijnken's text seems plausible at the time it was written, we can be sure that at least the Brussels, Berlin, and Nijmegen manuscripts do not contain any indication that they were made for that social class. The presence of a known audience for two of these manuscripts makes them attractive for further analysis of another variable mentioned in my introduction: how are new interpretations of a text created by its inclusion in a text collection?

Table 1. General Information on Manuscripts Preserving "Dryvoldicheit"

Manuscript	Date	Locale
Brussels, Bibliothèque Royale Albert 1er, 15.642–651	1400–1450	Brabant
Berlin, SPK, ms. germ. fol. 1027	1436–1437	Geldern
New York, Pierpont Morgan Library, M. 385	ca. 1440	Bruges
Nijmegen, GA, Archief van de Beide Weeshuizen, 953	1445	Nijmegen

Table 2. Length of "Van der Heiliger Dryvoldicheit Vader Soen Heilge Geest Eyn Schoen Gedichte"[14]

Manuscript	Length (lines)
Brussels, Bibliothéque Royale Albert 1er, 15.642–651, fols. 99r–102r[15]	316
Berlin, SPK, ms. germ. fol. 1027, fols. 153a–154vb[16]	262
New York, Pierpont Morgan Library, M. 385, fols. 51v[17]	152
Nijmegen, GA, Archief van de beide Weeshuizen, 953, fols. 275rb–279vb[18]	259

"Dryvoldicheit": Text, Collection, and Interpretation

The Berlin and Nijmegen manuscripts both contain Augustijnken's "Dryvoldicheit" and share the same collection of texts. One item is present in the Berlin manuscript but omitted in the Nijmegen manuscript: on folios 169r to 171v of Berlin, we encounter a contemporary table of contents. This table of contents was probably very useful for the medieval user, as it lists all the preceding texts in the manuscript with the folio number where the text begins.[19] At the same time, the contents gives the modern researcher a tool to dissect the text collection, as it gives insight into the principles of organization, creating a hierarchy of three levels of inclusion. The highest level is indicated by a rubricated title that stands out because there is some blank space before and/or after it and because the title is written on two or more lines. The second level is indicated by (generally) shorter rubricated titles that do not stand out from the third level apart from their coloring. At the third level, one encounters short titles written in black ink.

Presented on the first level (Level 1 in Table 3) are the longest texts in the text collection, the "Zielen Troist" and "Ander Sielen Troist" ("Consolation of the Soul" and "Second Consolation of the Soul"; henceforward, "Zielentroost" and "Andere Zielentroost").[20] The text collection opens with the "Zielentroost." The author positions his text in opposition to secular texts about, for example, Perceval, Tristan, Arthur, Alexander, and Apollonius, because *men en vint dar nicht der sele trost* ("one will not find consolation of the soul in there").[21] Instead, other stories should be read and heard, especially those found in the Scriptures. The most profitable ones are collected in this work, according to the narrator. What follows is a framing story in prose that gathers 239 exempla. These exempla are structured according to the Ten Commandments: ten times a child asks his father to teach him a Commandment. The father does so by citing the Commandment in Latin, translating it into the vernacular, and explaining it by several exempla, the number of which varies from one Commandment to another (see Table 3). This structure is visible in the table of contents, because the Commandments are presented at the second level (rubricated titles) and the titles of the exempla at the third (black titles).

In the table of contents, the Commandments are presented at level 2 as well as another text: "Spigel der Mynschen" ("A Mirror of All Man"). This is the title not only of this text but also of a cluster of nine consecutive texts (I aim to visualize this aspect in Table 3 by giving this title both in the "level 2" and "level 3" columns).[22] Some of these texts also circulated separately, not in single-text manuscripts but as individual texts rather than as sections of a larger text (albeit often incorporated in text collections). The sixth text of this cluster, for example, entitled "Dit Sijn Teyken des Aenstaenden Dodes" ("These Are the Signs of Impending Death"), can be found in a medical manuscript.[23] The compiler of the Berlin manuscript thus creates a cluster of otherwise independent or individual texts, presenting them as if they belonged together and as if they had a fixed relation to the long text they accompany, the "Zielentroost." The nine short texts are embedded in three layers of inclusion parallel to the three levels of hierarchy in the table of contents: 1) they are part of a newly formed cluster, 2) which forms a dyad with the "Zielentroost,"[24] 3) which is part of a text collection.

The same process of inclusion occurs in the second half of the text collection. Here the anchor text is the "Andere Zielentroost." This text, too, collects many example stories (92 exempla), but this time the structuring element is not the Ten Commandments but the Seven Sacraments. However, this structuring element is not visible in the table of contents. In addition to the exempla, this text also contains extensive instruction for confession (added to the fourth sacrament) and a "Monastery Mirror" (added to the sixth sacrament).

After this anchor text follows "Hier na Volgen Voel Leren der Heilger Meisteren Bescreven" ("After This Follow Many Lessons from the Holy Masters, Written Down").[25] Just as in the first part of the manuscript and as can be derived from the table of contents, this is the title both of a text and of the text cluster attached to the "Andere Zielentroost." The text itself collects dicta of several classic and religious authorities, such as Augustine, Seneca, and Gregory. The collective title covers five texts. As before, at least some of these texts also have an independent existence elsewhere. That is shown, for example, by the third text, "Van Drie Doden Konyngen" ("About Three Dead Kings"), which has a widespread tradition.[26] Another of these similarly independently preserved texts is the one central to this contribution, Augustijnken's "Dryvoldicheit." Thus the reader of Berlin encounters this text embedded in three layers of inclusion: part of a cluster entitled *Lessons*, which forms a dyad with the second *Consolation*, which is part of a text collection including both *Consolations* and the attached clusters. In this final part of my contribution, I discuss the consequences of this embedding.

At the first level of inclusion, Augustijnken's text is presented as part of a larger unity entitled "Hier na Volgen Voel Leren der Heilger Meisteren Bescreven," in the text itself abbreviated to "Dit Sijn Heilge Leren" ("These Are the Holy Lessons," fol. 148v). As a result of the positioning of "Dryvoldicheit" in a cluster with this title, the text gains authority, as the reader finds Augustijnken's text not as a separate item but under the same heading and thus part of (or at least closely related to) various dicta from authorities. Likewise, the author (who refers to himself in the text: "Now I, Augustijnken, wish to expound this matter," ll. 107–108) becomes as authoritative as the other masters quoted in the "Dit Sijn Heilge Leren."

At the second level, the text is part of a cluster attached to the "Andere Zielentroost." This dyad foregrounds for example the importance of confession. This effect is achieved by combining the inserted confession instruction in the first text of the dyad, the "Andere Zielentroost," and the six confession poems at the very end of the dyad. The confession poems are six short texts, three of which are to be read before and three after one goes for confession. A second focus in the whole dyad is the importance of sevens. As noted above, the "Andere Zielentroost" is structured by the Seven Sacraments, and comparable with that, the passion treatise "Van der Passien Ons Heren Jhesus Christus" ("About the Passion of Our Lord Jesus Christ") is structured around the seven canonical hours. This importance of sevens is also found in "Dryvoldicheit," which, as discussed above, is almost completely organized by lists of seven.

At the third level, "Dryvoldicheit" is part of the text collection as a whole. Surveying that text collection, some general tendencies can be distinguished. First, the text collection has a marked preoccupation with (the proximity of) death. This theme is foregrounded in the first cluster by, for example, the inclusion of the aforementioned "Dit Sijn Teyken des Aenstaenden Dodes," but also by the incipit of "Spigel der Mynschen": "I advise you to turn to [the right thing], and that you learn how to die, because God did not tell us how long we would live."[27] The second cluster achieves the same effect by including the short verse narrative in which three living kings are reminded by three dead kings of how little importance they should attach to material, earthly possessions, as upon death, which is always closer than one assumes, everyone is judged on their spiritual credentials.

A second theme across texts from various parts of the manuscript is giving practical tools for a life in a Christian world; throughout the manuscript, lists of important things are given and often repeated. A reader of this manuscript, for example, will never forget what the Ten Commandments are, as they structure the "First Consolation" and are again the main topic in the short verse narrative in the first cluster entitled "Van der X Gebaden Gaets te Ryme" ("About the Ten Commandments in Rhyme"). Likewise, the twelve degrees of humility from the Rule of Benedict are introduced ("Twellef Sijn Graden der Oitmodicheit"), the six prayers around confession ("Hoe Sich Eyn Bereiden Sal te Ontfangen dat Heilge Sacrament Ende dan van Gude Gebede Ist") and the Sacraments. In that context of practical Christian guidance through the presentation of lists, it is exactly that aspect of Augustijnken's "Dryvoldicheit" that stands out: by addressing the matter of the Trinity, listing secular and religious authorities, and ordering Creation in clear lists of seven, the text correlates constantly with the mnemonic form of much that can be found in the Berlin (and Nijmegen) text collection.[28]

Table 3. Contents of Berlin According to Table of Contents

Level 1: Large Initial	Level 2: Small Initial	Level 3: Black Ink
In Deser Tafelen Salmen te	"Dat Ierste Gebot Gades"	26 exempla
vynden Mennich Mirakel	"Dat Ander Gebot Onses Heren"	34 exempla
dat Voir Bescreuen Steet yn	"Dat Derde Gebot"	52 exempla
Desen Boeke dat Men Heit	"Dat Vierde Gebot Gades"	40 exempla
der Zielen Troist Ende Is al	"Dat Vijfte Gebot"	27 exempla
Seer Nut Gelesen Allen	"Dat Seste Gebot"	18 exempla
Mynschen die Gerne Toe	"Dat Sevende Gebot Gades"	4 exempla
Gade Weren	"Dat Achte Gebot Gades"	10 exempla
	"Dat Negende Gebot Gades"	23 exempla
	"Dat Tiende Gebot Gades"	5 exempla
	"Hier Is Uyt der Sielen Troest"	
	"Spigel der Mynschen"	"Spigel der Mynschen"
		"Twelf Graden der Oit-modicheit"
		"Ordel dat die Scepen Wysen"
		"Van Boesheit der Woek-eners"
		"Van Teyken des Dodes"
		Van der X Gebaden Gaets te Ryme"
		"Van Geistliker Mynnen"
		"Woe Lude Sanck die Lerer Up"
		"Nu Sterck Ons Got yn Onser Noit"
		92 exempla
"Eyn Ander Sielen Troist van den Seuen Sacramenten"	"Hier na Volgen Voel Leren der Heilger Meisteren Bescreven"	"Hier na Volgen Voel Leren der Heilger Meisteren Bescreven"
		"Van der Heilger Drievol-dicheit"
		"Van Drie Doden Konyn-gen"

		"Van der Passien Ons Heren Jhesus Christus"
		"Hoe Sich Eyn Bereiden Sal te Ontfangen dat Heilge Sacrament Ende dan van Gude Gebede Ist"

Conclusion

Medieval texts are dynamic, and aspects such as their form, audience, and interpretation vary when a text "travels" from one manuscript to another. An example of that is Augustijnken's "Dryvoldicheit." This Middle Dutch short narrative is preserved in four manuscripts, and whereas it is plausible to assume a noble intended audience for the *text*, at least 75 percent of the surviving *text carriers* cannot be connected to that audience. Instead, we encounter "Dryvoldicheit" in manuscripts made for urban (Brussels) and conventual (Berlin, Nijmegen) audiences. In the last part of this essay, I focus on one particular case, namely the preservation of "Dryvoldicheit" in three levels of inclusion in the Berlin text collection: 1) the text is included in an authoritative dicta collection as part of a cluster of short texts, 2) which was added to the exempla frame of the "Andere Zielentroost," 3) which was in turn part of a text collection that contains both *Zielentroost* texts and two clusters of shorter texts. Each of these levels influences the way Augustijnken's text can be read: the text becomes authorial by its placement under the "Dit Sijn Heilge Leren"; by being part of a dyad with the "Andere Zielentroost," the sevens in "Dryvoldicheit" are foregrounded; and within the text collection as a whole, all the mnemonic and instructive lists in the "Dryvoldicheit" come to our attention.

This case of Augustijnken's "Dryvoldicheit" thus illustrates what has been put in a general sense before: what is important about a text—how it is read and interpreted—is not prescribed or determined by how it was once intended by the author but first and foremost by the manuscript context in which a text is copied. In the eloquent words of Stephen G. Nichols: "The bookish text casts itself adrift from a particular historical moment to make its way among other texts, from other periods, to which it contributes new meanings and from whose association it derives new senses."[31]

Utrecht University

Acknowledgments

This article arises from the project "The Dynamics of the Medieval Manuscript: Text Collections from a European Perspective" (available at http://www.dynamicsofthemedievalmanuscript.eu), which is financially supported by the HERA Joint Research Programme (http://www.heranet.info) and the European Community FP7 (2007–2013). I would like to thank Daniël Ermens, Paul Wackers, Bart Besamusca, and the editors of the *Journal of the Early Book Society* for their comments on earlier drafts of this piece. Before publication, this paper was read at the Early Book Society conference in St. Andrew's; I thank the participants in that session for their questions and comments.

NOTES

1. The number of studies that could be mentioned here is long, but see, e.g., several essays in the programmatic Stephen G. Nichols and Siegfried Wenzel, eds., *The Whole Book. Cultural Perspectives on the Medieval Miscellany* (Ann Arbor: University of Michigan Press, 1996).

2. This text is often referred to as "De Schepping" ("The Creation"), but "Dryvoldicheit" makes more sense; the author refers to his text with these words, and two of the four manuscripts preserving the text use this title. "De Schepping" as a title probably finds its origins in the fact that the *editio prin-ceps* refers to the text with these words (which in turn is probably caused by the fact that the title is missing in the manuscript used by the editor, while a modern hand wrote "*Schepping van de mens*" ("Creation of men") in the blank space. This might be motivated by a quick reading of the opening part of "Dryvoldicheit," which summarizes the Creation.

3. Brief information on Augustijnken in English is in Frits Pieter van Oostrom, *Court and Culture: Dutch Literature 1350–1450*, trans. Arnold J. Pomerans, foreword by James H. Marrow (Berkeley: University of California Press. 1992), 12, 83, 85, 109–110, 278, 310, and 341; and Gerard Bouwmeester, "Connecting the Dots: Thoughts on MS Brussels, Royal Library, 15.642–51" (provisional title), in A. A. M. Besamusca, A. D. Putter, et al., eds., *Dynamics of the Medieval Manuscript* (Göttingen, Germany: Vandenhoeck & Ruprecht, forthcoming 2014).

4. The Bible exegesis consists of an interpretation of the candleholders and seals from the Apocalypse (Rev. 1:13–15, 5:1–8:5).

5. Many relevant parts of the records are in W. J. A. Jonckbloet, *Geschiedenis der Middelnederlandsche Dichtkunst*, 3 vols. (Amsterdam: Kampen, 1854), 3:595–652.

6. The Prussian Crusades are extensively discussed in Werner Paravicini, *Die Preussenreisen des europäischen Adel*, Beihefte der Francia 17 (Sigmaringen, Germany: Thorbecke, 1989).

7. See Bouwmeester, "Connecting the Dots."

8. The Middle Dutch *Lucidarius* tradition (including international relations) is studied in Nolanda Klunder, *Lucidarius: De Middelnederlandse Lucidarius-*

teksten en Hun Relatie tot de Europese Traditie (Amsterdam: Prometheus, 2005).

9. Herman Brinkman, "De Stedelijke Context van het Werk van Jan de Weert," in Herman Pleij, et al., *Op Belofte van Profijt*, vol. 4 of *Nederlandse Literatuur en Cultuur in de Middeleeuwen*, ed. F. P. van Oostrom and W. van Anrooij (Amsterdam: Prometheus, 1991), 101–120.

10. Bert Cardon, *Manuscripts of the Speculum Humanae Salvationis in the Southern Netherlands (c. 1410–c.1470): A Contribution to the Study of the 15th Century Book Illumination and of the Function and Meaning of Historical Symbolism* (Leuven, Belgium: Peeters, 1996), 131, 408–409.

11. Geert Warnar, "Augustijnken in Pruisen: Over de Drijfveren van Een Middelnederlandse Dichter en Literatuur binnen de Duitse Orde," *Jaarboek voor Middeleeuwse Geschiedenis* 8 (2005): 101–139.

12. Bernadette Kramer, *Een Lekenboek in Woord en Beeld: De Spegel der Minschliken Zalicheid* (Hilversum, Netherlands: Verloren, 2014), 84–85.

13. This was first noted by Jan Deschamps, who for a very long time was the only scholar who paid attention to these manuscripts, see Jan Deschamps, "De Middelnederlandse Handschriften van de Grote en de Kleine Der Sielen Troest," *Handelingen der Koninklijke Zuidnederlandse Maatschappij voor Taal- en Letterkunde en Geschiedenis* 17 (1963): 111–167. More recently, a description of the Berlin manuscript was part of an attachment in Monika Costard, *Spätmittelalterliche Frauenfrömmigkeit am Niederrhein: Geschichte, Spiritualität und Handschriften der Schwesternhäuser in Geldern und Sonsbeck* (Tübingen, Germany: Mohr Siebeck, 2011), 346–353.

14. Dini Hogenelst, *Sproken en Sprekers: Inleiding op en Repertorium van de Middelnederlandse Sproke*, XVI of *Nederlandse Literatuur en Cultuur in de Middeleeuwen*, ed. F. P. van Oostrom and W. van Anrooij, 2 vols (Amsterdam: Prometheus, 1997). Information on this text comes from 2:22–23 (R11).

15. In Ph. Blommaert, *Oudvlaemsche Gedichten der XIIe, XIIIe en XIVe Eeuwen: Derde Deel* (Ghent, Belgium: L. Hebbelynck, 1851), 120–123.

16. This text has not been published.

17. This text has not been published.

18. This text has not been published.

19. "Preceding texts" is used deliberately, because there are three texts in the folia following the table of contents. These texts are not discussed in this article but will be part of the analysis in my forthcoming dissertation.

20. The texts are commonly referred to as the "Big Consolation of the Soul" and the "Small Consolation of the Soul" ("Grote Zielentroost" and "Kleine Zielentroost"), but these titles 1) are not used in these manuscripts (see Table 3); and 2) are incorrect and deceiving, as the so-called "Small Consolation" is actually more extensive than the "Big Consolation," as is shown below.

21. Margarete Schmitt, *Der grosse Seelentrost: Ein niederdeutsches Erbauungs-*

buch der vierzehnten Jahrhunderts, Niederdeutsche Studien 5 (Cologne, Germany: Böhlau, 1959), 1.

22. Costard, *Spätmittelalterliche Frauenfrömmigkeit,* 347–353, gives an extensive overview of the contents, including all the titles, incipits, and excipits of the "subtexts."

23. MS Brussels, Bibliothèque Royale Albert 1er, 15.624–41, fol. 8v.

24. I use "dyad" in the way Sarah Westphal applies it: "Dyads seem to be the textual equivalent of the couplet rhyme; as words are bound by related sounds, so poems are bound by related themes or meanings." Sarah Westphal, *Textual Poetics of German Manuscripts 1300–1500* (Columbia, SC: Camden House, 1993), 12.

25. In the text collection, this title is abbreviated to "Dit Sijn Heilge Leren" ("These Are Holy Lessons").

26. An excellent introduction to this tradition is Helmut Tervooren and Johannes Spicker, eds., *Die Begegnung der drei Lebenden und drei Toten: Eine Edition nach der maasländischen und ripuarischen Textüberlieferung,* Texte des späten Mittelalters und der frühen Neuzeit 47 (Berlin: E. Schmidt. 2011).

27. Costard, *Spätmittelalterliche Frauenfrömmigkeit,* 350: "Ick rade v allen dat ghi dair toe keert, ende ghi alle daghe steruen leert, want got en heft ons nyet te weten gegeuen woe lange wu sullen leuen."

28. An issue that is not discussed here but will be a part of my forthcoming doctoral dissertation is how the contents of the exempla in the "Zielentroost" texts illustrate these general trends.

29. In the table of contents, the titles of the exempla are given, e.g., first exemplum of First Commandment: "Doe Adam ende Eua" ("When Adam and Eve"); for convenience in Table 3, I do not include all those titles here, but only the number of exempla. Note the significant differences in the numbers of exempla between the different Commandments.

30. In the table of contents, the exempla are not divided into seven.

31. S. Nichols, "Why Material Philology? Some Thoughts," in *Philologie als Textwissenschaft: Alte und neue Horizonte,* ed. Helmut Tervooren and Horst Wenzel, Zeitschrift für deutsche Philologie 116 (Berlin: Erich Schmidt, 1997), 10–30, 23.

The Middle English *Melusine*: Evidence for an Early Edition of the Prose Romance in the Bodleian Library

The French prose and poetic *Mélusine* romances, composed in the late fourteenth and early fifteenth centuries respectively, enjoyed widespread popularity in manuscript across the later Middle Ages, while revised versions of the prose text in print continued to attract romance audiences throughout the early-modern period.[1] From the mid-1400s onward, the works were also translated into many European languages and disseminated throughout the Continent.[2] However, evidence for the circulation of the prose romance, written by Jean d'Arras in the early 1390s, is limited in Middle English to a single manuscript located in the British Library (MS Royal 18.b.II, ca. 1500–1515),[3] and to a small collection of printed fragments of a work entitled *Melusyne*, attributed to Wynkyn de Worde around 1510, located in Oxford's Bodleian Library under the shelfmark Vet. A1 d.18.[4] This collection of fragments is not entirely unknown to scholars, having been cited in the revised *Short Title Catalogue* (no. 14648), noted in H. S. Bennett's handlist of publications printed by de Worde, and included in the Early English Books Online (EEBO) database.[5] However, EEBO reproduces only two of the surviving six fragments (4–5), while the Bodleian's own catalogue refers only to those fragments to which it attributes signatures Q2 and 5 (frags. 2–3), and R1 and 3 (frags. 4–5), thus omitting reference to the first and last fragments in the collection. This note offers an updated descriptive and stylistic appraisal of the fragments and, in so doing, locates the English *Melusyne* within the wider context of early Tudor romance literature. By thus drawing scholarly attention to these fragments, this paper also highlights the value of such serendipitous survivals for enhancing our understanding of early-modern book production and reception.

Vet. A1 d.18 is a guard-book collection containing six numbered paper fragments from the Middle English edition of *Melusyne*. While the original source of fragments 1 and 5 is uncertain, the pieces were gleaned from the bindings of assorted volumes located elsewhere in the Bodleian's collections.[6] Due to cropping and the exigencies of binding, the fragments vary in size and condition. Fragment 2, the largest and most complete leaf, is still adjacent to the other half of its original bifolium (frag. 3), and measures around 182 millimeters at its widest point near the bottom of the folio, and around 265 millimeters along the inner vertical edge.[7] Fragments 1 and 2 each reveal pricking along their original inner edges to mark lines of text; fragment 1, cropped along the bottom third of the leaf, measures around 186 to 190 millimeters wide, which may be closer to the original page width than fragment 2 in view of the uneven cropping evident on the outer vertical edge of the second piece. Fragments 1v and 2r reveal printed foliation ("Fo. lxxxxviii" and "Fo. lxxxxix," respectively) in the upper right corners, while printed signatures are located on fragments 2r (Q2), 4r (R1), and 5r (R3).[8] The surviving fragments do not contain any catchwords. Formatted as a folio volume, the edition may have contained quires originally consisting of three or four bifolia.[9] A watermark is partially visible on fragment 1; it is possible to discern what may be horns or the vertical spokes of a crown, but the greater portion of the mark is otherwise obscured. No colophons or printer marks survive. The printing of the fragments has been widely assigned to Wynkyn de Worde. I have seen no scholarly discussion exploring this attribution, but in view of the fact that the other main London printer in this period, Richard Pynson, is thought to have printed few, if any, popular romances after 1506, de Worde remains the most likely candidate.[10] Further, as becomes clear below, many of the production and stylistic features of the fragments are consistent with de Worde's output.

Aside from those leaves that have been cropped along their upper register (frags. 4–6), the romance is laid out in two columns of continuous prose beneath a single-word, centered, running headline, "Melusyne." The text is structured by means of numbered chapter titles, capital initials of assorted sizes and designs, paraphs, decorative line fillers, and illustrations of differing sizes. Columns are around 71 to 72 millimeters in width; the number of lines they contain varies according to the inclusion of images, headings, line fillers, and so forth, but the greatest number of text lines is forty-one lines in a column that also includes one line of ornamentation and two blank lines between paragraphs (frag. 3vb). Each line is allocated around 5 millimeters in height. The typeface used in the body of the text closely resembles the 95

Textura (Duff 8) type illustrated in Frank Isaac's *English and Scottish Printing Types*, Figure 3, which depicts a leaf from *Thordinary of Crysten Men* (E2v) printed by de Worde in 1506 (STC 5199); the type of the *Melusyne* fragments appears sharp in comparison with the type of *Thordinary* reproduced both in Isaac and on EEBO, and may reflect a set of letters cut after this date.[11]

The narrative is organized by chapter titles, of which eleven survive in whole or in part. The titles are preceded by paraphs, and those that are complete include numbers at the end.[12] These headings are separated from their surrounding paragraphs by means of one or two blank lines. The preceding paragraph and the line immediately following a title typically conclude with combinations of one or more small blocks of ornamentation in the form of vines/foliage, loose or tightly interwoven waves, or woven angular shapes, which may occupy one or two lines. Ordinary paragraphs may also conclude with such decoration, and one or two blank lines often precede a new passage of text. Capital initials of three distinctive sizes and types commence different sections of a chapter. Large, five-line bold and often grotesque capitals of the sort identified with de Worde typically introduce a paragraph immediately after a title or large woodcut and incorporate anthropomorphic, avian, or foliate designs (frags. 2va, 4va–b).[13] Less often, three-line singleton Ws open up chapter paragraphs, and they occasionally alternate with two-line singletons to introduce subsequent paragraphs within a chapter (e.g., frags. 4vb and 1va respectively for three-line W; frags. 2–6 passim for two-line singletons). The W, the ascenders of which are incised with decoration, closely resembles the W in Set 1 of the initials that de Worde recast from the set identified as Caxton's Set 1, portions of which he used sporadically after 1498.[14] The two-line singletons are virtually identical to those in the de Worde initials Set no. 11 discussed by Lotte Hellinga, which the printer used regularly from 1497 onward.[15]

The printed *Melusyne* edition is illustrated, and the fragments include the remains of four woodcuts, three of which are identifiable. The first and largest set of imagery laid across the top of two columns comprises a composite triptych using three interchangeable blocks, a method that de Worde pioneered in England (frag. 1r).[16] The illustration is primarily made up of a central panel of around 88 millimeters in width by 113 to 115 millimeters in height enclosed in a black line border between 1 and 2 millimeters thick. This woodcut depicts a giant on the left raising a battle-ax over the head of an armed man wielding a similar weapon in the center; a town forms the background, from which a male spectator watches from an overhead window in the upper right register (Hodnett 1234).[17] A border block on each side of the main panel measures between 20 and 30 millimeters wide; these scenes are not enclosed within an external frame, and each depicts a different example of cityscape architecture between half and two thirds of the height of the main panel. Scant evidence for the second illustration survives on fragment 3va, which has suffered cropping to the outer vertical edge, removing around one third of the leaf; the surviving fragment reveals only a thin portion of an image in which a building, plants, and hills can be discerned within a column. The remaining two images are set within individual columns on fragment 4. Although cropped along the top, the first of these shows the bottom two thirds of an armed man in front of a castle with arms raised overhead on the left; he faces the right toward a larger figure dressed in more ornamental armor, whose arms are also upraised (Hodnett 902; frag. 4ra); the last depicts an armed man with a protruding tooth in the center-right placing a spear or lance downward into a hole; he faces rocks and hills to the left, and his horse is behind him on the right margin (Hodnett 1218; frag. 4va).

To the best of my knowledge, only Edward Hodnett has examined these illustrations.[18] He suggests that alongside number 1218 above, woodcut numbers 1219 and 1220 comprised a "Melusine Series," in other words, a set of specific images that de Worde (or his woodcut designer) probably copied from a French edition, as was the case with de Worde's edition of *Helyas, Knighte of the Swanne* in 1512 (STC 7571).[19] Certainly, number 1219, a cut of a man on horseback riding toward the right, identified by Hodnett only in de Worde's *Olyuer of Castylle* of 1518 (STC 18808; P7r), derives from the French *Mélusine* corpus. Not only did the earliest French edition of the romance, published by Adam Steinschaber in 1478, include an illustration of Raymondin riding toward the right with his arms crossed over his chest, a dead boar and the uncle he has inadvertently killed on the ground to the left, as Hodnett describes for number 1219,[20] but this image was also reproduced in a sequence of early French editions. Of particular interest here are the Lyonnais editions of the *Roman de Mélusine* published by Guillaume le Roy around 1487 and Martin Husz around 1479 and around 1493 to 1494.[21] As studies of de Worde's iconography show, the printer used woodcuts strongly influenced by images included in, for example, Le Roy's *Ponthus et la belle Sidoine* (Lyon, 1483) and Husz's editions of *De proprietatibus rerum* (Lyon, 1482, 1485, and 1491 or 1492) in his own *Kinge Rycharde Cuer de Lyon* (1509, STC 21007) and his 1495 edition of Trevisa's translation of Bartholomaeus Anglicus's encyclopedia (STC 1536).[22] Although Raymondin is depicted riding toward the left in the Lyonnais editions, the reversal in composition might suggest that de Worde's cutter simply traced and so inverted the image when it was cut, if in fact a Lyonnais edition was a direct source.[23]

The design of image number 1218 in *Melusyne*, which illustrates Geffray's pursuit of the giant Grimault into a cave, further points to the transnational influences acting upon early Tudor book production. The likely source of this woodcut can also be identified in the Lyonnais editions of *Mélusine*;

in contrast with the scene depicted in Steinschaber's Genevan edition, the composition of the image in the English edition closely reproduces that in the volumes printed by Le Roy and Husz, albeit in a simplified form that is less weighted with line shading.[24] As Hodnett notes, this cut was also re-printed in at least two separate de Worde editions of the St Albans *Chronicle of England* between 1515 and 1520.[25] Image numbers 1218 and 1219 from the "Melusine Series" each draw attention to the complex processes of European book production and transmission in this period. As Laurence Harf-Lancner demonstrates, the iconography of the Lyonnais editions was closely modeled on the program of woodcut decoration identified in an edition of the German *Melusine* translation printed by Bernard Richel in Basel around 1473 or 1474.[26] Although number 1219 no longer survives in the English *Melusyne*, along with number 1218 it bears witness to the transcontinental circulation and dissemination of woodcut iconography in which de Worde participated.

In contrast with woodcuts numbers 1218 and 1219, it is unclear why Hodnett assigned 1220, an image depicting two men on a shore, one of whom carries a money purse on the right, while a woman sits on a boat watching them from the left, to the "Melusine Series," as the scene does not correspond with any episode within the prose romance and is not, as far as I am aware, located in any contemporary French editions; the scene (or a variant thereof) is reprinted in the Caxton translations of Raoul le Fèvre's *Recuyell of the Hystoryes of Troye* printed by de Worde in 1502 and 1503, and in several of his *Chronicle of England* editions.[27] Hodnett omits number 902 from the aforementioned "Melusine Series," and its appearance in at least three separate de Worde editions of the *Chronicle of England* between 1515 and 1528 suggests that it may have an alternative line of descent, the pursuit of which is beyond the scope of this discussion.[28]

Also of interest among the *Melusyne* fragments is the image corresponding to Hodnett's number 1234. This illustration correlates with a woodcut included in de Worde's *Troye* romance editions of 1502 and 1503, and subsequently reproduced in other printers' editions of such texts as *Guy of Warwick*, indicating that he supplemented the woodcuts specific to the *Melusyne* romance with additional iconography.[29] The *Melusyne* copy of this image is similar in design to that of the *Troye* woodcuts, the *Melusyne* variant producing a cleaner, more aerated effect for the viewer, as the newly cut block did not fill the ground behind the two armed combatants with white line shading. The heavy eyelids of the figures in the *Melusyne* variant and the strong border recall the work of the *Morte d'Arthur* cutter, who contributed several designs to the *Troye* editions.[30]

Coupled with the evidence of the typefaces discussed above, the use of composite imagery and the reuse of images located in the *Melusyne* fragments among editions produced by de Worde before and after 1510 support the identification of de Worde as the printer of the Middle English romance.

How does the Middle English translation of the prose *Melusyne* romance accord with de Worde's known printing output? If we reflect that the printer probably produced between nine hundred and a thousand individual titles between 1491 and his death in 1535, then his prose and verse romances constitute a minor proportion of his catalogue, numbering between around thirty to forty titles excluding the works of Lydgate and Chaucer.[31] Nonetheless, as Jordi Sánchez-Martí notes, de Worde was "the most prolific printer of Middle English romances" during the early Tudor period, especially after 1500.[32] As Norman Blake shows, following Caxton's death in 1492, de Worde initially moved away from his former master's emphasis on prose romance translations, although he did republish Caxton's 1485 edition of the *Morte d'Arthur* in 1498 (STC 802). Throughout his career, de Worde evinced a preference for English verse, especially religious or spiritual works, and he also published extensively in the area of schoolbooks, including grammars, and liturgical works.[33] However, after 1500, de Worde ventured seriously into romance publication, and Carol Meale argues that it was de Worde, rather than his rival and colleague Richard Pynson, who led the way in recognizing the market potential of both prose and verse romances among printers in the early sixteenth century.[34] For example, between 1500 and 1510 de Worde published the Middle English metrical romances *Bevis of Hampton, Sir Eglamour,* and *Rycharde Cuer de Lyon,* with *Guy of Warwick* possibly having been printed in 1500 or a little earlier.[35] Doubtless maximizing his Continental commercial links to identify trends abroad, which he would have monitored carefully as an importer of books from 1503 as well as a printer, de Worde also employed translators who proposed and/or translated French and, in at least one instance, Italian romances.[36] For example, in this same period Robert Copland translated *King Appolyn* (1510, STC 708.5) from a French edition apparently owned by de Worde, while Henry Watson, who preferred translating in prose, produced English texts of the French works *Valentine and Orson* (ca. 1510, STC 24571.3) and *The Noble History of King Ponthus,* the latter of which was first printed around 1509 (STC 20107) and subsequently reprinted by both Pynson and de Worde around 1510 and in 1511 respectively (STC 20107.5, 20108).[37] The production of an English edition of the French prose *Mélusine* romance is thus consistent with de Worde's printing output to around 1510 and beyond; translated romances after this date included Copland's translation of *Helyas, Knight of the Swan,* mentioned above (1512, 1522), and Watson's translation of *Olyuer of Castylle* (1518).

Thematically and technically, *Melusyne* coincides and contrasts with de Worde's romance publications in different ways. Up to two thirds of the prose romance is focused upon chivalric adventure and crusading activity represented by the Lusignan sons and their exploits, whether they were combating giants close to home or fighting the infidel across the Mediterranean. The convergence of history, heroic action, and concerns with the fate of Eastern Christendom in *Melusyne*, reflected in Hodnett 902 (frag. 4ra), an image in which a small-statured Geffray battles a giant with orientalized weaponry and exoticized armor, virtually assured its appeal to early Tudor audiences of crusade romances in a period when the European West was refocusing its gaze on the Ottoman empire.[38] In this context, *Melusyne* sat closely alongside de Worde's verse *Rycharde Cuer de Lyon* (1509) and *Capystranus* (first printed ca. 1515, STC 14649), while the work's penitential themes have been compared with those in *Robert the Deuyl*, printed by de Worde around 1500 and 1517 (STC 21070, 21071).[39] Equally, *Melusyne*'s blend of the dynastic with the magical coincided with the primary tropes of its contemporary, *Helyas, the Knight of the Swan*, an account of the crusader Godefroy de Bouillon's legendary metamorphic ancestor, while *Melusyne*'s fairy ambiance aligned it with Julian Notary's edition of *Huon of Bordeaux* (ca. 1515, STC 13998.5), in which the fairy king Oberon plays his first leading role in English.[40] On the other hand, alongside the *Morte d'Arthur*, *Historyes of Troye*, and Caxton's translation of *Four Sons of Aymon* (1504–1505, STC 1008), *Melusyne* stands out among de Worde's publications in having been produced as a folio volume, a feature that contrasts with early criticism of Wynkyn's catalogue as having been predominantly comprised of popular quarto volumes.[41] From a practical perspective, however, formatting *Melusyne* as a quarto volume would have produced a bulky volume, especially in view of de Worde's preference for heavily illustrated editions. Moreover, as Joseph Dane and Alexandra Gillespie suggest, the folio volume could offer printers a more economical format in terms of words per page and overall sheet usage, depending on the layout adopted. In this regard, Meale's suggestion that de Worde was simply adapting his method to suit the material in question is highly plausible and reflects de Worde's commercial acuity.[42]

As studies of his romance editions show, de Worde's printing house, which included his editors, translators, designers, and compositors, introduced considerable editorial novelty into his publications.[43] To reflect on this point, this note considers the surviving textual fragments of the *Melusyne* romance in relation to the contemporary English manuscript and relevant French editions. In what follows, I am less concerned with pronouncing aesthetic judgments on the philological quality of de Worde's text, such as those articulated by Nicolas Jacobs with respect to the "deterioration" of *Sir Degare* across manuscript and print, than with the main stylistic and linguistic features of the printed edition and their influence upon the narrative.[44]

The portions of text represented in the *Melusyne* fragments belong to a sequence of narrative events that surround the romance's climax. Fragments

1 and 2 (Q[1]–2) recount Geffray of the Grete Toeth's battle with and defeat of the giant Guedon of Guerrand and delivery of Guedon's head to his father; the profession of Geffray's brother, Froymond, as a novice at the monastery of Maillezais; the approach of an embassy from Northumberland to Geffray to seek aid in ridding the region of another giant, Grimault; and Geffray's agreement to this but deferral of his journey in order to punish Maillezais for his brother's monastic profession, which he does by incinerating the monks in the abbey.[45] Fragment 3, from which the outer vertical third of the leaf has been cropped, narrates the immediate aftermath of Raymondin's climactic denunciation of Melusyne as a treacherous serpent, the court's grief, and Melusyne's departure and serpentine transformation.[46] Fragment 4 (R1) recounts Geffray's encounter with Grimault and discovery of the subterranean tomb where lay King Elinas, Geffray's grandfather.[47] The death of the Earl of Forest at Geffray's instigation, the latter's forgiveness by Raymondin, and Raymondin's pilgrimage to Rome and decision to enter a hermitage on Montferrat occupy fragment 5 (R3),[48] while Geffray's own pilgrimage to visit his father and the shocked response of the local monks to his presence make up fragment 6.[49]

In analyzing the text of the printed *Melusyne*, it is difficult to determine the precise relationship between the printed edition's copy and the sole surviving manuscript of the Middle English romance in BL, MS Royal 18.b.II. Robert Nolan's study of watermarks in the Royal manuscript suggests that they resemble marks 3637 and 3638 in Charles-Moïse Briquet's compendium, each of which depicts a "Chien avec un collier." The earliest example of these marks is 3637, which was noted in Cologne in 1515, a date that follows that assigned to the Bodleian fragments but does not preclude the paper from having circulated earlier.[50] As Meale and Nolan each note, the *Melusyne* edition omits passages of considerable length; Nolan estimates that up to a quarter of the romance may have been excised from the edition, in comparison with the narrative in the Royal manuscript and French editions. Meale also observes the edition's inclusion of unique portions of text while conceding that "these additions are insubstantial compared with the passages which are omitted." Despite probably having had access to only fragments 4 and 5, these scholars also observe that the numbers allocated to the printed rubrics, of which eleven survive in varying degrees across the six fragments, consistently diverge from the headings included in the manuscript by a difference of seventeen titles.[51]

Irrespective of the likely influence of early French *Mélusine* editions on the iconography of the fragments, it is difficult to ascribe the revised textual organization indicated by the enlarged number of rubrics to the seven extant French editions printed before 1517, as the rubrication across these versions closely aligns with that in the Middle English manuscript.[52] Moreover, the surviving titles in the edition correspond with those in the Middle English manuscript and French editions; they serve as both chapter titles with specific relationship to the subsequent text, as indicated by the "Ca. + no." that accompanies them, and as captions explicating the content of those images with which they are in proximity.[53] Beyond surmising that de Worde's editor added new chapter headings to draw attention to narrative action omitted from other headings, perhaps to balance approximate chapter lengths, as Watson may have done in his translation of *Valentine and Orson* for de Worde, or to provide captions for new images, it is not possible to ascertain where or on what principles the additional titles were added.[54]

However, Nolan and Meale are divided as to the order in which the printed and manuscript *Melusyne* texts were produced. Nolan suggests that the "fragment is too closely parallel" with the manuscript "to represent a separate translation," speculating that the edition "is probably an abridgement of the British Museum [now Library] manuscript." Meale approaches the issue from the reverse position, concluding that while the "differences make it virtually certain that the manuscript could not have been copied from the printed text, . . .given the fidelity of the two translations in some respects, derivation from a common exemplar seems a distinct possibility."[55] This suggestion implicitly leaves open the question of whether the surviving Middle English copies derived from an English or a French exemplar; ultimately, only further research into the philological relationship between the Middle English fragments and manuscript in relation to each other and to those contemporary editions and manuscripts produced in French will shed greater light on this issue.[56]

Several of the *Melusyne* fragments' linguistic and stylistic features distinguish them from the Royal manuscript and reshape the narrative in different ways. The orthography adopted in the fragments coincides broadly with patterns noted by Mark Aronoff in his analysis of de Worde's publications.[57] In particular, we see a tendency to use a y in place of i in verbs, nouns, adjectives, and adverbs, especially where the use of i would lead to consecutive minims, a feature that was particular to de Worde's output;[58] the frequent, often indiscriminate, addition of a silent final e;[59] the doubling of vowels;[60] and the repetition of the final l in shorter words.[61] Such features are not applied uniformly but they are commonly used. In addition, many of the linguistic and stylistic variations in the printed *Melusyne* correspond with those observed in Sánchez-Martí's comparative study of de Worde's two editions of the *Ipomedon* romance and the known manuscript exemplar.[62] In particular, when compared with the Royal manuscript, the printed *Melusyne* bears evidence of syntactical glossing,[63] lexical substitution,[64] semantic clarification,[65] intensification,[66] and the elimination of repetition,[67] as well as the occasional error.[68] Overall, these editorial practices standardize and often modernize the text, producing a clearer and more directly expressed narrative.[69]

In addition to such technical emendations, the *Melusyne* fragments also reveal editorial practices that subtly offer possibilities for new readings of the romance. Significant among such practices are instances of "[s]mooth-ing or flattening," whereby precise narrative details are omitted from the text, simplifying passages of prose and blunting their specificity.[70] Important examples of this occur when Froymond and the abbot defend the former's decision to join Maillezais Monastery. After Geffray claims that the monks "enchaunted" his brother (a term used in both the manuscript and the printed edition), the abbot and Froymond seek to appease him. "Halas my lorde sayd thabbot haue pyte on vs for it was not thrughe vs" that the decision was made, proclaims the printed edition, while Froymond himself declares: "Dere broder by the body and soule whiche I haue gyuen to god / it was by none but thrugh myn owne deuocion" (frag. 2vb). These succinct explana-tions diminish the detail, strength, and emotion of the claims expressed in the manuscript: "Helas my lord said thabbot for the loue of god haue mercy on vs / and suffre you to be enfourmed of the trouth & rayson ffor on my Creatour I nor none of vs all counseylled hym neuer therto" (182r). Further, Froymond's manuscript declaration reads:

> By [*sic*] dere brother / by the body & sowle which
> I haue gyuen to god here is no personne nor within
> this place that euer spake ony word to me touching
> my professyon ffor I haue it doon of myn owne free
> wylle & thrugh deuocion. (182r)

The printed text considerably flattens Froymond's claims to have made his decision independently of external influences, while the abbot's fear of Gef-fray's retribution and his more detailed justification that neither he *nor* his monastic colleagues influenced Froymond's decision is suppressed. While such redaction conveys the essence of Froymond's and his abbot's protesta-tions, their rhetorical and affective force in the narrative is reduced.

Stylistic flattening also occurs throughout the climactic scene where Raymondin repents his denunciation of Melusyne. Whereas in the manu-script, we read that "[T]hystorye sayth that Raymondyn was right dolaunt and for trouth the true cronykle testyfyeth that neuer no man suffred so grete dolour without he of his lyf expired" (186v), the printed edition nar-rates more concisely "Here sayth thystorye þat Raymondyn was soo so-rowfull þat he almoost deyed" (frag. 3ra). Later in the same passage, in the manuscript Melusyne "saw the grete habundaunce of teerys fallyng fro his [Raymondin's] eyen" (186v), whereas in the printed edition she merely sees "his grete repentaunce" (frag. 3ra). Emotionally expressive speech also undergoes modification in this scene, whereby the grief experienced by the

Lusignan courtiers after the simultaneous swoon of Melusyne and Raymondin is abridged: after the court commences crying, they declaim "Ha false fortune we shall lese this daye þe best lady that euer gouerned ony lande / and þe moost vertuous" (frag. 3ra). The Royal manuscript (and French editions) offered extensions upon this:

> Ha fals ffortune We shal lese this day þe best lady
> that euer gouerned ony land / the moost sage / most
> humble / moost charytable & curteys of all other
> lyuyng in erthe[.]And they al lamented & bewaylled
> so pyteously & rendred teerys in habundaunce in so
> moche that it was a pyteous syght. (187r)[71]

The printed edition acknowledges the courtly sorrow and tributes to the fairy but omits the heightened pathos attending the laments and tones down the eulogistic acclaim accorded to Melusyne in the Royal manuscript. Condensing these passages by removing the details that specify the emotional experience of individual characters, the printed edition offers a more prosaic and potentially less (melo)dramatic interpretation of the narrative action than is suggested by the manuscript text.[72] Helen Cooper notes an interest in sentiment within late-medieval prose romances such as *Paris and Vienne,* and certainly emotional intensification is evident in some later French *Mélusine* manuscripts in prose and verse.[73] However, as Cooper and Meale point out, the greater proportion of Middle English romance owners were men; the evidence suggests that English women tended to prefer French romances.[74] Given that the English romances that enjoyed the greatest longevity in print in the sixteenth century and beyond, such as the metrical *Bevis of Hampton* and *Guy of Warwick* and prose *Hystoryes of Troye* and *Morte Darthur,* were focused more on heroic action than on personal affect, the textual variance evident in the *Melusyne* edition may well reflect the editor's or translator's understanding of contemporary literary trends and the demographics of the edition's primary readership.[75]

Perceptions about audiences and their expectations may also have informed a smaller yet suggestive textual modification, one that corresponds with what has been termed "ideologically motivated" variance.[76] During the emotional scene preceding Melusyne's serpentine departure from her family and court, the manuscript tells us that on seeing Melusyne and Raymondin swoon in distress, "There wept & bewaylled barons / ladyes & damoyseltes [*sic*]" (187r), while in the printed edition, the scene is rendered as "bothe more and lesse wepte" (frag. 3ra). Similarly, when the fairy says farewell to her court, the manuscript reports her speech as "ffarewel my lord / barons / ladyes & damoyselles" (188v), while the printed edition awkwardly offers the syntactically erroneous "Farewell my lorde / and all the assystentes" (frag. 3vb). The printed *Melusyne* thus effaces the social distinctions among courtly attendants present in the manuscript redaction.

Although the modification of this particular passage cannot be attributed to the surviving contemporary French editions or manuscripts,[77] the removal of passages in de Worde's edition that drew attention to the elite social levels to whom the *Roman de Mélusine* was originally addressed is consistent with similar evidence of *mouvance* between French *Mélusine* manuscripts and editions identified by Harf-Lancner. She attributes the expurgation from printed editions of episodes that drew on elite cultural practices and ideals, such as Jean d'Arras's nostalgic reflection on the period when education in the arts and sciences was the exclusive domain of a privileged nobility, to printers' astute recognition that their audiences were rapidly expanding beyond the courtly elite to encompass a more diverse demographic.[78] Similar editorial practices have also been identified in other late-medieval English translations, including, for example, fifteenth-century redactions of the French *Partenopeu de Blois*.[79] In view of the breadth of de Worde's publishing output and his known commercial relationships with merchants, scholars, clerics, and members of the court, Wynkyn's appreciation of the varied tastes of his audiences plausibly contributed to the nature of these textual emendations.[80]

The *Melusyne* fragments also show evidence of textual interpolations and omissions that do not readily fit within precise categories of scribal emendation but which reshaped particular episodes to varying degrees. Comparison of the printed *Melusyne* text with the copy in BL, MS Royal 18.b.II suggests that de Worde's editor prioritized details focusing on deeds and actions that expedited the overall plot, frequently by abridging or omitting passages of speech, emotion, and internal reflections that do not contribute to this end. The account of Geffray's battle with the giant Guedon of Guerrand in fragment 1 includes both textual omissions and insertions that draw attention to Geffray's chivalric qualities and the combat itself. For example, Guedon's direct question about Geffray's identity in the manuscript ("What art thou knight that art so bold to com hither," 177r) is compressed into a short piece of indirect discourse (he "demaunded of Geffray what he was," frag. 1va). The oblique rendering and compression of speech is a technique that has been identified in translations printed by de Worde, including, for example, Watson's *Valentine and Orson*, and it allows the focus to be placed more directly upon Geffray's bold identification of himself and his challenge to the giant's tyranny.[81] The battle itself is subject to extended interpolations that enhance perceptions of Geffray's valor and prowess. For example, at the commencement of the combat, in place of reading that Geffray "descended lyghtly from hys hors & came toward the geant the swerd drawen and thenne cam the geaunt toward hym" (178r), the reader of the printed edition encounters the following lengthy passage:

> he auoyded the deed hors quyckely and dilygently
> and stope vp vpon his fete / and after drew oute
> his swerde lyke a valiaunt and hardy knighte in
> marchynge forthe towarde þe gyaunt with a fyers
> countenaunce / sayenge in hymselfe that he sholde
> auenge the dethe of his good hors vpon the giaunt /
> and in lykewyse the gyaunt Guedon came towarde
> hym. (frag. 1vb)

Geffray's agility, bravery, and motivations (vengeance) are underlined in
the printed edition, significantly extending the portraits of him as a worthy
warrior in both the English manuscript and French editions. However, not
all opportunities to underline Geffray's qualities are adopted. For instance,
the printed edition omits the Guerrand lords' praise for Geffray's having
imperiled himself to defeat Guedon (frag. 2ra, 179r) and abridges a passage
in which the spread of news about Geffray's conquest ellcits a wondrous
preption (frag. 1va, 180r). Nevertheless, it might be argued that while
such passages build Geffray's diegetic reputation, they do not in themselves
forward the narrative action, which may explain their modification in the
printed edition.

The *Melusyne* editor's concern with action over rhetoric has particular
consequences for the romance's portrayal of Geffray's character, a point
that may be illustrated with two examples. On their return from delivering
Guedon's head to Raymondin, two envoys inform Geffray that his brother
Froymond had entered the monastery of Maillezais as a novice, news that
deeply provokes his ire. The manuscript records that Geffray displays:

> so fel & cruel semblaunt that there ne was so hardy
> that durst abyde the syght of hym. But þey all voyded
> the place. . . . Whan Geffray knew the tydynges of
> Ffroymonds professyon he was so dolaunt that
> almost he went fro his wyt. (181v)

In his rage, Geffray blames the Maillezais monks, declaring that they have

> enchaunted my lord my fader & haue drawen
> Ffroymond with them for to fare þe better by hym
> / but by the feyth that I owe to god I shal pay them
> so therfore that they shal neuer haue neyther lust
> ne talent to withdraw no noble man to be shorne
> monke with them. (181v)

In contrast, the printed edition relates only the bare facts of the message. While acknowledging that Geffray "was almoost mad for angre," that he was critical of his parents, and that he planned to punish "these flaterers monkes" (frag. 2vb), *Melusyne* diminishes the intensity of Geffray's emotional response and the fear he engenders in his companions.[82] A similar type of redaction occurs when Geffray observes the body of his uncle, the Earl of Forest, who has fallen to his death fleeing his nephew. The manuscript narrates:

> And thenne Geffray loked out of the wyndowe &
> sawe hym al to rent & brusid lyeng deed on the
> erthe / but therof he toke no pyte / But sayd. Ffalse
> traytour by thyn euyl report I haue lost my lady my
> moder / now haue I quyted the therfore. / And
> thenne he cam doun ayen to þe halle. (195v)

In contrast, the printed edition comments only "Whan Geffray sawe that [i.e., his fallen uncle] he came downe in to the halle" before explaining why he sought Forest's demise (frag. 5ra).

In each of these passages, *Melusyne* omits details that shed light on Geffray's motivation and the rationale for his behavior, an editorial feature that has implications for the resultant text and consequent interpretive possibilities. In the first instance, Geffray is portrayed as nearly witless from grief while also presenting a harsh countenance to his companions. Geffray's mental condition in the manuscript serves to explain his mistaken attribution of malign influences to the Maillezais monks, whom he accuses of using underhand supernatural forces to sway Froymond for personal gain before incinerating the monastery. In the printed edition, Geffray is also portrayed as nearly mindless with rage but his anger lacks the vehemence of the manuscript copy and, aside from flattery, readers are not offered any justification for his anger at this stage of the narrative. The printed edition thus diminishes the audience's insight into Geffray's mind, with the result that his characterization is weakened.

The elimination of passages that underline the extreme nature of Geffray's ire may have had indirect implications for understanding the thematic and narrative significance of irrational anger as a sin within the *Melusyne* romance. As Barbara Wahlen and Jean-Claude Mühlethaler suggest, in the French versions, when mindless anger is experienced and then acted upon by both Geoffroy à la Grand Dent and his father at sequential stages of the plot, the enraged act functions as a turning point marking the characters' subsequent shock, repentance, and journey toward spiritual enlightenment.[83] Alterations to Geffray's internal disposition in *Melusyne* may thus have partially downplayed the thematic connections between ire and sin for its audiences. On the other hand, perhaps consistent with the earlier discussion of passages that enhance the English Geffray's knightly presentation, rather than shifting the thematic emphasis of the work, the printed edition's diluted portrait of Geffray at this point may have been intended to minimize passages that did not reflect well on the character or that did not actively advance the narrative. Similarly, in the second example, the manuscript draws attention to Geffray's mercilessness and ruthlessness as he looks upon his uncle's broken body. However, it also offers some insight into his rationalization for Forest's death, that is, that he holds Forest responsible for his mother Melusyne's departure. The *Melusyne* fragment eliminates these unchivalrous qualities and Geffray's explanation of vengeance from the printed edition's portrait. It effectively flattens the romance's presentation of Geffray's character while excising those unflattering traits.

Cumulatively *Melusyne*'s editor/translator excludes passages that would otherwise offer audiences a greater understanding of Geffray's motivation and character, thereby presenting an attenuated portrait of Geffray in which his own malign qualities are downplayed. However, beyond observing this tendency, the surviving evidence does not permit generalizations about the narrative aims of the editor/translator, who may well have been more concerned to promote action than to dwell on reflection or to prioritize Geffray himself. Notably, the editorial practice surrounding the presentation of Geffray of the Grete Toeth in the Middle English *Melusyne* is consistent with that in the French editions published from 1478 onward. As Harf-Lancner and Hélène Bouquin show, these editions offered a more favorable presentation of Geoffroy à la Grand Dent than preceding manuscripts. This trend developed to the point where the French Geoffroy's heroic status and intrinsic appeal were recognized by the division of the *Roman de Mélusine* into two separate romances around 1520, one focused on the tale of Mélusine, the other centered upon Geoffroy's chivalric adventures.[84] Given the ongoing popularity of chivalric romances, it is reasonable to speculate that similar interests guided the editorial hand behind de Worde's edition of the Middle English *Melusyne*.

On the basis of these six fragments, then, we can suggest that the Middle English prose *Melusyne* edition offered audiences a more streamlined, action-driven narrative than either the contemporaneous manuscript or earlier French editions. Consistent with the editorial practices applied to fifteenth-century prose translations and contemporary editions, the printed *Melusyne* was subject to a range of stylistic modifications and broader textual revisions that, as a result of reducing the number and nature of various rhetorical and reflective passages, privileged the romance's chivalric adventure narrative, often at the expense of its characterization.

While we can hypothesize that the prioritization of the adventure story was consistent with evolving tastes among Tudor audiences of romance literature, in the absence of significant evidence about the sixteenth-century circulation and reception of *Melusyne*, it is difficult to draw firm conclusions. Complementing the Middle English prose *Melusyne* manuscript and the printed edition, we know that the tale was transmitted in at least one English manuscript copy of the poetic redaction, the *Romans de Partenay*,[85] and that the French prose and poetic romances were also disseminated in two early-fifteenth-century manuscripts circulating in Tudor England.[86] Alongside these copies, there is some additional evidence of early Tudor audiences' awareness of the romance. *Melusyne* is included in a list of pernicious and "ungracious" literary influences on women in Juan Luis Vives's *Instruction of a Christen Woman*, which was translated into English by Richard Hyrd and first printed around 1529 or 1530. Additionally, the eponymous fairy was ambivalently referred to as *mystical* in Wilfrid Holme's Protestant polemic, *The Fall of Rebellion*, written around 1537 and published in 1572.[87]

Notwithstanding the apparent absence of further evidence of later Tudor reception of the *Melusyne* romance, many of the technical features of the Bodleian fragments, such as the fonts, iconography, and orthography, point to their production by Wynkyn de Worde, whose commercial perspicacity has been increasingly recognized in recent years. Moreover, the conjunction of the themes of magic and marvels alongside crusade and heroic action in *Melusyne* aligned it closely with de Worde's romance catalogue, even if it shortly preceded what Douglas Gray terms the "last flowering of the French romance of wonders."[88] In this context, even if the *Melusyne* romance faded from the mainstream of romance audience consciousness in early modern England, we can reasonably assume that in the early 1500s, de Worde's edition of this medieval French tale found a ready audience among at least some English readers.

Beyond the *Melusyne* romance itself, through comparative analysis of the text, paratext, and iconography in the Vet. A1 d.18 fragments with related manuscripts and Continental editions, this essay also suggests how study of such literary ephemera can shed light on transnational processes of book production and reception in the early sixteenth century. Indeed, the *Melusyne* fragments not only underscore de Worde's ongoing exploitation of French iconography but highlight the complex interrelationship of early book production networks and influences across early modern Europe. As Meale notes, fragments often provide our only evidence for some romance works having been published in English at all in the period to 1535, as is the case for de Worde's editions of *Torrent of Portyngale* (?1510, STC 24133.5) and *Generides* (?1506, STC 11721.5).[89] While this note is only a modest contribution to the scholarship on the literary remains of the *Melusyne* edition, it is hoped that its findings will encourage specialists to return to collections of fragments with a view to enriching our understanding of early modern literary production and transmission.

Australian National University

Acknowledgments

I would like to acknowledge with thanks the valuable assistance of Sarah Wheale, the Head of Rare Books at the Bodleian Library, in the preparation of this essay, and I am grateful to Merridee Bailey and Mark Wilson for their comments on earlier drafts.

NOTES

1. The premodern printing history of the French *Mélusine* romances is limited to the prose romance, the poetic redaction not having been printed until 1854.

2. Laurence Harf-Lancner, "Le *Roman de Mélusine* et le *Roman de Geoffroy a la grand dent*: Les éditions imprimées de l'œuvre de Jean d'Arras," *Bibliothèque d'Humanisme et Renaissance* 50 (1988): 349–366, 349 and n. 31; *Incunabula Short Title Catalogue* (hereafter ISTC), http://istc.bl.uk (accessed November 3, 2013); *Universal Short Title Catalogue* (hereafter USTC), http://www.ustc.ac.uk (accessed November 3, 2013).

3. George H. Warner and Julius P. Gilson, *Catalogue of Manuscripts in the Old Royal and King's Collections*, 4 vols. (London: Trustees of the British Museum, 1921), 2:279; Harry L. D. Ward and John A. Herbert, *Catalogue of Romances in the Department of Manuscripts in the British Museum*, 3 vols. (London: Trustees of the British Museum, 1883–1910), 1:690–692; Jayne Sears and Francis R. Johnson, eds., *The Library of John, Lord Lumley: The Catalogue of 1609* (London: Trustees of the British Museum, 1956), 132, no. 1036. For an edition, see Jean d'Arras, *Melusine: Compiled (1382–1394 A.D.) by Jean d'Arras*, ed. A. K. Donald, EETS e.s. 68 (London: Kegan Paul, Trench, Trübner, 1895).

4. *Search Oxford Libraries Online* (SOLO), http://solo.bodleian.ox.ac.uk/primo_library/libweb/action/dlDisplay.do?vid=OXVU1&docId=oxfaleph014867999 (accessed February 19, 2014). I hope to address the reasons for this apparent divergence in taste among English and Continental, specifically French, audiences in future research.

5. A. W. Pollard and G. R. Redgrave, *A Short-Title Catalogue of Books Printed in England, Scotland, & Ireland, and of English Books Printed Abroad, 1475–1640*, 2nd ed., rev. W. A. Jackson and F. S. Ferguson, compl. Katharine F. Pantzer, 3 vols. (London: Bibliographical Society, 1976–1991) (hereafter STC); H. S. Bennett, *English Books and Readers, Being a Study in the History of the Book Trade from Caxton to the Incorporation of the Stationers Company*, 2nd ed. (Cambridge, UK: Cambridge University Press, 1969), 255; *Early English Books Online*, http://rp.nla.gov.au/login?url=http://eebo.chadwyck.com/home (accessed November 25, 2013).

6. Sarah Wheale kindly provided advice concerning the most recent sources of these fragments. She notes that frags. 2–3 were removed from shelfmark

C 10.13 Th (Gonçalo Cervantes, *In librum Sapientiae commentarii, et theoriae* [Seville: Hispali, 1614]); frag. 4 from BB 69 (Michele Zanardi, *Disputationes de vniuerso elementari* [Cologne, 1620]); and frag. 6 from DD 30 Th. (Ludovicus Crocius, *Apologeticus pro Augustana . . . contra collationem ac defensionem Anti-Pierianam Balthasaris Mentzeri* [Bremen, 1621]). Frag. 5 was recorded as coming from the Aubrey manuscripts collection, but no further information about it or frag. 1 is available. Sarah Wheale, e-mail message to author, October 30, 2013.

7. Dimensions of individual fragments to nearest millimeter, taken at the widest and longest points (w. x h.), are as follow: 1) 190 x 187; 2) 182 x 265; 3) 83 x 265; 4) 195 x 226; 5) 191 x 291; 6) 184 x 183.

8. The cropping along the lower register of frag. 1 has removed what would have been Q1 on frag. 1v. Note that the signatures in the fragments themselves use lowercase roman numerals. However, since the Bodleian's SOLO catalogue uses Arabic numerals to denote the signatures, this format has been retained here.

9. The Bodleian catalogue appears to assume that quires were made up of three bifolia, since frag. 3 is identified as signature Q5 in the online catalogue. However, it seems uncertain whether the original quires would have contained three or four bifolia; in the absence of other evidence, frag. 3 *may* have equated with Q7.

10. See, e.g., Bennett, *English Books and Readers*; James Moran, *Wynkyn de Worde, Father of Fleet Street: With a Chronological Bibliography of Works on Wynkyn de Worde Compiled by Lotte Hellinga and Mary Erler, and a Preface by John Dreyfus* (London: British Library/Oak Knoll Press with the Wynkyn de Worde Society, 2003), 49. In his dissertation on the Middle English manuscript, Robert Nolan suggests that based on the dating of the fragment, "it is likely that de Worde was its printer." See Robert J. Nolan, "An Introduction to the English Version of *Mélusine*: A Medieval Prose Romance" (PhD diss., New York University, 1970), 22.

11. See Francis Swinton Isaac, *English and Scottish Printing Types* (Oxford: Oxford University Press for the Bibliographical Society, 1930), [1–2], and figs. 1 (for different lettering types) and 3. Fig. 3 shares with the *Melusyne* fragments the use of s^2, v^3, w^2, and y^2, lowercase d's share similarly angled ascenders, and the tail of the lowercase g is also alike; the texts also share close resemblances with respect to the following uppercase characters: A; the T with two central vertical bars; I/J; S. The Tironian *et* used in each work is also very similar, with a slight flourish kicking upward to the right from the base of the character and a flourish curved downward from the top horizontal bar. The type used may well be a later derivation of de Worde Type 4 and its subsequent recastings; see Lotte Hellinga, "Printing Types and Other Typographical Material," in *Catalogue of Books Printed in the XVth Century*

now in the British Library, vol. 11, *England* ('t Goy-Houten, Netherlands: Hes & Der Graaf, 2004), 335–417.

12. Surviving rubrics read as follow: "¶How Geffray with the grete toeth dide [...]" (cropped horizontally along second line; frag. 1vb); "¶How Froymont brother to Geffray was professed monke at Mayllerez by consentement of his fader and moder. Ca. lvi." (frag. 2ra); "¶How the two messengers of Raymondyn came to Geffray in Guerrend. lvii." (frag. 2va); "¶How Raymondyn and Melusyne felle bothe in a swowne. Ca. lxi." (frag. 3ra); "How Melu [...]" (frag. 3rb); "[...] e of a serpent [...] lxiii." (frag. 3va); "¶How the gyaunt fledde and geffra [...] lowed hym. Ca. [...]" (frag. 4rb); "¶How Geffray wente and entred in to þe hoole for to fyght with the gyaunt. lxviii." (frag. 4vb); "¶How Geffray founde the sepulture of þe kynge of Albanye his graundfader Helynas within the mountayne. ca. lxix." (frag. 4vb); "¶How Geffray was the dethe of the erle of Forestz his vncle. Ca. lxxi." (frag. 5ra); "¶Howe Raymondyn came towarde the pope of Rome and confessed his sinnes to hym. Ca. lxxiii." (frag. 5va). Here and throughout in manuscript and edition quotations, thorns have been retained but long *s*'s rendered as short *s*'s; capitalization is modernized, and expansions are rendered in italics; double *virgula* marking line ends, diacritical marks, and references to line fillers are omitted; physical damage to the text is indicated by [...]; and Tironian *et* is represented with an ampersand.

13. Isaac, *English and Scottish Printing Types*, fig. 48, reproduction from Henry Pepwell's 1521 edition of Christine de Pizan's *Cyte of Ladies* (STC 7271), Oo.4r, with a bold four-to-five-line W with a crowned face in the interior between the central and right ascender that Isaac labels a "de Worde grotesque." The capital A in *Melusyne*, frag. 1ra, is five lines high and formed of bold strokes with a face appended to the exterior of the left ascender and an angular frill on the interior; it is identical to that used in de Worde's edition of *Chronicle of England* of 1515 (STC 10000.5), e.g., 94rb. On early printed initials and de Worde's use of grotesques, see also Charles Sayle, "Initial Letters in Early English Printed Books," *The Library* 7 (1904): 15–48, 21–22.

14. See Hellinga, "Printing Types," 361, 378.

15. Ibid., 378–379. In particular, compare the flourishing and thickness of lines in the uppercase T, I, H, and A (frag. 2ra–2vb) and R (frag. 4ra) with the set reproduced in ibid., 378.

16. Martha W. Driver, "The Illustrated Wynkyn de Worde: An Overview," *Studies in Iconography* 17 (1966): 349–403, 350.

17. Hodnett numbers in the text refer to the catalog listing of woodcuts in Edward Hodnett, *English Woodcuts, 1480–1535*, rev. ed. (Oxford: Oxford University Press, 1973).

18. The first fragment depicting no. 1234 may not have been collated into the guard-book at the time of Hodnett's research; Sarah Wheale suggests

that most of the items had been collated by the 1970s (frags. 2–5 probably having been gathered in the 1950s, according to notation visible on the pieces themselves) and that nothing has been added since 2001. E-mail message to author, October 30, 2013.

19. Hodnett, *English Woodcuts*, 23.

20. Ibid., 302; Jean d'Arras, *Roman de Mélusine* (Geneva: Adam Steinschaber, 1478), 12r (hereafter Steinschaber); for a facsimile reproduction of this volume, see Jean d'Arras, *L'histoire de la belle Mélusine de Jean d'Arras*, ed. W. J. Meyer (Bern, Switzerland: Société Suisse de Bibliophiles, 1923–1924). On Steinschaber's edition, see ISTC ij00218380; USTC 71174.

21. ISTC nos. ij00218400, ij00218385, and ij00218405. I have consulted the first and third of these: the Le Roy edition is located in Paris, Bibliothèque de l'Arsenal, shelfmark Fol. B. 95 (hereafter Le Roy), the later Husz edition in Chantilly, Musée Condé, VI.I 30 (hereafter Husz 1493–1494). On the history of the French Mélusine woodcuts, see Laurence Harf-Lancner, "L'illustration du *Roman de Mélusine* de Jean d'Arras dans les éditions du XVe et du XVIe siècle," in *Le livre et l'image en France au XVIe siècle*, Cahiers V. L. Saulnier 6 (Paris: Presses de l'École Normale Supérieure, 1989), 29–55; and Hélène Bouquin, "Éditions et adaptations de *L'histoire de Mélusine* de Jean d'Arras (XVe–XIXe siècle): Les aventures d'un roman médiéval," 3 vols. (PhD thesis, École Nationale des Chartes, 2000), 1:62–85.

22. Jordi Sánchez-Martí, "Illustrating the Printed Middle English Verse Romances, c. 1500–c. 1535," *Word and Image* 27 (2011): 90–102, 94, fig. 8, and 95 for de Worde and Le Roy; Martha W. Driver, *The Image in Print: Book Illustration in Late Medieval England and Its Sources* (London: British Library, 2004), 40–46 for de Worde and Husz.

23. Le Roy, B4v; Husz 1493–1494, B1r.

24. Steinschaber, 162r (Geoffroy and his horse are oriented to the right); Le Roy, V3v and Husz 1493–94, V3v (Geoffroy and his horse are oriented to the left); see also a fourth Lyonnais edition, *Roman de Mélusine* (Lyon, France: Gaspar Ortuin and Peter Schenck, 1485–1486), Paris, Bibliothèque Nationale de France, Rés. mY2. 31; hereafter Ortuin-Schenck), also V3v. As Harf-Lancner notes, the Parisian edition published by Thomas du Guernier for bookseller Jehan Petit (ca. 1503, ISTC ij00218415) contains the same scenes as the Lyonnais editions (Harf-Lancner, "L'illustration du *Roman de Mélusine*," 35).

25. 1515 (STC 10000.5) and 1520 (STC 10001), 94rb in each. The image illustrates an episode discussing William Wallace's rebellion. The face on the newly cut image in these *Chronicles* appears to have lost the tooth that protrudes from Geffray's cheek in *Melusyne*, suggesting an effort on the part of the new woodcut designer or printer to accommodate the image to the textual episode without including the monstrosity of the original. The figures in the *Chronicles* are also positioned centrally in the image, whereas in the

Lyonnais *Mélusine* editions, the figure of Geoffroy is both oriented toward and positioned on the left.

26. Harf-Lancner, "L'illustration du *Roman de Mélusine*," 33–36; Thüring von Ringoltingen, *Melusine (1456)*, ed. André Schnyder and Ursula Rautenberg, 2 vols. (Wiesbaden, Germany: Reichert, 2006), 1:18, 152 for color plates of source images influencing the design of Hodnett nos. 1218–1219. Thüring von Ringoltingen's German *Melusine* of 1456 was a prose translation of the French poetic version, the *Roman de Parthenay*, composed by Couldrette ca. 1400–1401.

27. See, e.g., *Recuyell of the Hystoryes of Troye* of 1502 and 1503 (STC 15376 and 15377), H1rb and H4va in each printing; see also the *Chronicle of England* of 1515 and 1520 cited above, 65vb, as well as a 1528 edition (STC 10002), also fol. 65vb. This listing is by no means exhaustive. Hodnett may have identified the very narrow vertical edge of the woodcut on *Melusyne* frag. 3va with no. 1220 (see his fig. 87) on the basis of the visibility of a few landscape features (mountain, tree, grass) that are present in the *Chronicle* prints, but they are differently distributed along the vertical edge and do not seem sufficient grounds to make a judgment either way.

28. See 17vb in each of the three *Chronicle* editions cited above.

29. It is reproduced twice in the *Hystoryes of Troye*, 1502 and 1503, P8vb and X1v in each; also William Copland's 1565 edition of *Guy of Warwick* (STC 12542), Ii1v. See also the argument in Sánchez-Martí, "Illustrating the Printed Middle English Verse Romances," 98, that de Worde preferred to seek images from his extensive stock of cuts before deciding whether to have new designs cut. The evidence provided here and Sánchez-Martí's argument both counter the proposal in Hodnett, *English Woodcuts*, 23, that *Melusyne* was likely to have been "fully and appropriately illustrated with copies from a French edition," although frag. 1 was probably not included with the fragment collection to which he had access.

30. Hodnett argues that this designer produced around a dozen blocks for the *Troye* editions, but he does not include no. 1234 among these; see Hodnett, *English Woodcuts*, 14, 17, 302–304.

31. See Driver, *Image in Print*, 33–34 and 222 n. 4, for an estimate of complete output. The number of romances, a genre that has been understood inclusively but from which the courtly writings of Lydgate, Chaucer, and Boccaccio have been excluded, is estimated from "Handlist of Publications by Wynkyn de Worde, 1492–1535," in Bennett, *English Books and Readers*, app. 1, 239–276.

32. Jordi Sánchez-Martí, "The Textual Transition of the Middle English Verse Romances from Manuscript to Print: A Case Study," *Neuphilologische Mitteilungen* 110 (2009): 497–525, 522.

33. N. F. Blake, "Worde, Wynkyn de (*d.* 1534/5), printer," *Oxford Dictionary of National Biography* (Oxford: Oxford University Press, 2004), http://

www.oxforddnb.com/view/article/29968 (accessed September 9, 2013); N. F. Blake, "Wynkyn de Worde: The Early Years," *Gutenberg Jahrbuch* (1971): 62–69; and the follow-up, N. F. Blake, "Wynkyn de Worde: The Later Years," *Gutenberg Jahrbuch* (1972): 128–138; Lotte Hellinga, *William Caxton and Early Printing in England* (London: British Library, 2010), 131–155.

34. Carol M. Meale, "Caxton, de Worde, and the Publication of Romance in Late Medieval England," *The Library* 6th ser., 14 (1992): 283–298, 289; cf. Blake, "Wynkyn de Worde: The Early Years," 66.

35. *Bevis of Hampton*, first printed ca. 1500 (STC 1987), *Sir Eglamour*, ca. 1500 (STC 7541), *Rycharde Cuer de Lyon*, 1509 (STC 21007); de Worde's *Guy of Warwick* (STC 12541), is dated 1497? by the STC, and ca. 1500 in Jennifer Fellows, "Printed Romance in the Sixteenth Century," in *A Companion to Medieval Popular Romance*, ed. Raluca L. Radulescu and Cory James Rushton (Cambridge, UK: D. S. Brewer, 2009), 67–78, 72.

36. Julia Boffey, "Wynkyn de Worde, Richard Pynson, and the English Printing of Texts Translated from French," in *Vernacular Literature and Current Affairs in the Early Sixteenth Century: France, England and Scotland*, ed. Jennifer Britnell and Richard Britnell, Studies in European Cultural Transition 6 (Aldershot, UK: Ashgate, 2000), 171–183; Hellinga, *William Caxton and Early Printing*, 150; Dennis E. Rhodes, "A Lost Romance Printed by Wynkyn de Worde," *Transactions of the Cambridge Bibliographical Society* 11 (1999): 463–467.

37. Blake, "Wynkyn de Worde: The Later Years," 130. For a slightly earlier dating of *Valentine and Orson* to 1503–1505, see Henry Watson, trans., *Valentine and Orson*, ed. Arthur Dickson, EETS o.s. 204 (London: Oxford University Press, 1937), xi.

38. Although Hodnett 902 is cropped in *Melusyne*, the full image can be seen in de Worde's 1515, 1520, and 1528 editions of the *Chronicle of England*, 17vb. Geraldine Heng, *Empire of Magic: Medieval Romance and the Politics of Cultural Fantasy* (New York: Columbia University Press, 2003); Catherine Gaullier-Bougassas, *La tentation de l'Orient dans le roman médiéval* (Paris: Champion, 2003); Debra Hassig Strickland, *Saracens, Demons, & Jews: Making Monsters in Medieval Art* (Princeton, NJ: Princeton University Press, 2003); Norman Housley, *Religious Warfare in Europe, 1400–1536* (Oxford: Oxford University Press, 2002), 62–85; Harf-Lancner, "*Roman de Mélusine*," 366.

39. Harf-Lancner, "*Roman de Mélusine*," 366.

40. Douglas Gray, *Later Medieval English Literature* (Oxford: Oxford University Press, 2008), 210, 212–214; Meale, "Caxton, de Worde," 286 n. 12.

41. Henry R. Plomer, *Wynkyn de Worde & His Contemporaries from the Death of Caxton to 1535* (London: Grafton, 1925; repr. Folkestone, UK: Dawson, 1974), 60.

42. Joseph A. Dane and Alexandra Gillespie, "The Myth of the Cheap Quarto," in *Tudor Books and Readers: Materiality and the Construction of Meaning*, ed. John N. King (Cambridge, UK: Cambridge University Press, 2010), 25–45; on the efficiency of folio formatting, see also Steven K. Galbraith, "English Literary Folios, 1593–1623: Studying Shifts in Format," in *Tudor Books and Readers: Materiality and the Construction of Meaning*, ed. John N. King (Cambridge, UK: Cambridge University Press, 2010), 46–67; Meale, "Caxton, de Worde," 292.

43. Some examples from a growing field of studies include Sánchez-Martí, "Textual Transition"; Sánchez-Martí, "Illustrating the Printed Middle English Verse Romances"; Tsuyoshi Mukai, "De Worde's 1498 *Morte Darthur* and Caxton's Copy-Text," *Review of English Studies* 51 (2000): 24–40; Watson, *Valentine and Orson*.

44. In this, I follow the approach to woodcut analysis in Sánchez-Martí, "Illustrating the Printed Middle English Verse Romances," 90; cf. Nicolas Jacobs, *The Later Versions of Sir Degarre: A Study in Textual Degeneration*, Medium Ævum Monographs n.s. 18 (Oxford: Society for the Study of Medieval Languages and Literature, 1995).

45. Corresponds with BL, MS Royal 18.b.II, 177r–182r (Jean d'Arras, *Melusine*, 301–309). Note that frag. 1 has been pasted into the guard-book with the recto side down, so frag. 1v should precede frag. 1r.

46. Corresponds with BL, MS Royal 18.b. II, 186v–189r (Jean d'Arras, *Melusine*, 316–320).

47. Corresponds with BL, MS Royal 18.b. II, 191r–193r (Jean d'Arras, *Melusine*, 324–327).

48. Corresponds with BL, MS Royal 18.b.II, 195r–198r (Jean d'Arras, *Melusine*, 331–336).

49. Corresponds with BL, MS Royal 18.b.II, 201r–203r (Jean d'Arras, *Melusine*, 340–344); frag. 6 has been placed recto side down in the guard-book, so the fragment should be read 6v–6r.

50. Nolan, "Introduction to the English Version," 18–19; Charles-Moïse Briquet, *Les filigranes: dictionnaire historique des marques du papier dès leur apparition vers 1282 jusqu'en 1600. A facsimile of the 1907 edition with supplementary material contributed by a number of scholars*, ed. A. Stevenson, 4 vols. (Amsterdam: Paper Publications Society, 1968), 1:223.

51. Nolan, "Introduction to the English Version," 21; Meale, "Caxton, de Worde," 287 n. 15. Frag. 2ra includes the title "How Froymont brother to Geffray was professed monke at Mayllerez by consentement of his fader and moder. Ca. lvi," which corresponds with the thirty-ninth (nonrubricated) heading in BL, MS Royal 18.b. II, 179r ("How Ffroymond brother to Geffray was professed monke at Mayllezes by consentement of hys fader & moder"). Nolan and Meale both comment on passages corresponding with frags. 4–5

alone, which may suggest that they had access only to the University Micro-films International collection, now on EEBO; this supposition is reinforced by Meale's attribution of signatures H1 and H3 to the fragments consulted, the smudged signature on frag. 4 perhaps resembling an H rather than the actual R on the scanned microfilm on EEBO.

52. Rubrication changed radically only once the *Roman de Mélusine* was divided into two narratives, around 1520; see discussion below. Harf-Lancner, "*Roman de Mélusine*," 360; Bouquin, "Éditions et adaptations," vol. 1.

53. E.g., the depiction of the knight fighting a giant in armed combat on frag. 1r was preceded by a partially surviving rubric, "❡How Geffray with the grete toeth dide [...]" (frag. 1vb), which corresponds with "How Geffray slough Guedon the geaunt in Garande" (BL, MS Royal 18.b. II, 178r); on frag. 4rb at the base of the column, the title "❡How the gyaunt fledde and Geffra [...] lowed hym. Ca. [...]" precedes the in-column image on frag. 4va of an armed knight with protruding tooth placing his spear down the hole through which the giant flees into the mountain, and down which Geffray follows him (Hodnett 1218).

54. Watson, *Valentine and Orson*, xix.

55. Nolan, "Introduction to the English Version," 21; Meale, "Caxton, de Worde," 287 n. 15.

56. It seems less likely, although not impossible, that the Middle Dutch edition published by Gerhardt Leeu in Antwerp, 1491 (ISTC ij00218420) or the Castilian edition published in Toulouse by Johannes Parix and Stephan Cleblat on July 14, 1489 (ISTC ij00218430) contributed to the Middle English edition of *Melusyne*.

57. Mark Aronoff, "The Orthographic System of an Early English Printer: Wynkyn de Worde," *Folio Linguistica Europeana* 8 (1989): 65–96.

58. Ibid., 85. This is most common in verbal forms. Compare, e.g., frags. 2ra, *dyde, sayd, trybute,* 3ra, *touchynge,* with BL, MS Royal 18.b. II, fols. 179r, *dide, said, tribut,* 186v *touching.*

59. E.g., compare frags. 2rb, *sente* x 2 (also *sent*), *wente, trouthe, gyaunte* (also *gyaunt*), 4va, *hurte, wyste, valeye,* 6va, *lorde* x 3, *daye* x 2, with BL, MS Royal 18.b. II, fols. 179v, *sent, went,* 180r, *trouth, sent, geaunt,* 192r, *hurt,* 192v, *wyst, valey,* 201v, *lord* x 3, *day* x 2.

60. E.g., compare frags. 1va, *poore foole, fooles, hoole,* 2ra, *countree* x 2, 4rb, *noo,* 4vb, *hoole* x 2, with BL, MS Royal 18.b. II, fols. 177r, *poure fole,* 177v, *foles, holl,* 179r, *countre, Countre,* 191v, *no,* 192v, *holl* x 2.

61. E.g., compare frags. 1va, *shall, wyll well* (one phrase), 2rb, *shall* x 4, *well* x 2, *joyfull,* 3ra, *lytell, wyll,* 5ra, *castell,* 5rb, *sorowfull, all,* with BL, MS Royal 18.b. II, fols. 177v, *shal, wyl wel,* 179v, *shal* x 2, 180r, *shal* x 2, *wel* x 2, *joyful,* 186v, *lytel, wyl,* 195r, *Castel,* 195v, *sorowful, al.*

62. Sánchez-Martí, "Textual Transition." Sánchez-Martí adapts the classification of scribal variations outlined in Jacobs, *Later Versions of Sir Degarre.*

63. Sánchez-Martí, "Textual Transition," 502–503. This term describes modifications to the choice or order of words that do not produce significant semantic differences. Compare the edition's "his fader made there [at Narbonne] many habytes" (frag. 6va) with the Royal manuscript: "he dide do make there many habytes" (201r), the perfect *made* simplifying and modernizing the complicated locution *did do make*. Similarly, Geffray "made theym [the barons of Forest] do hommage to Raymond his brother" (frag. 5ra), while in the manuscript Geffray "dide make them to doo hommage" (195v). In a simpler rearrangement of word order, another passage from the edition prefers "than the gyaunt came towarde Geffray" (frag. 4ra), to "thenne cam the geaunt toward Geffray" (191v), a phrase whose syntax in the manuscript lacks the resemblance to modern English carried by the printed text; similarly "towarde þe chirche" (frag. 6ra) is preferred to "to chirch ward" (202v).
64. Sánchez-Martí, "Textual Transition," 500–501. This is typically demonstrated by single words of French or Anglo-Saxon origin replacing single words of either derivation or short phrases; e.g., *unhappy* is preferred in the edition (frag. 1va) to the manuscript's *Meschaunt* (177v; this is also used in Steinschaber, 143v), *secretely* (frag. 6rb) condenses the manuscript's "in secret wyse" (203v); "aualed the brydge" (frag. 1va) is the printed *Melusyne* editor's choice in contrast with the manuscript's "came to the brydge and lete it fall" (177r). In this last example a simple verb of French origin (OF *aualer*) is preferred to the lengthier multiclause English "came to the brydge and lete it fall"; interestingly, it is not the word used in either Steinschaber or two of the Lyonnais editions, which prefer *baissa* (Steinschaber, 143r; Le Roy 1493–94, S2v; Ortuin-Schenck, S2v), and thus may have been chosen as a more economical phrase in view of the reduced number of characters.
65. Sánchez-Martí, "Textual Transition," 503–504. Passages are occasionally clarified with the addition of articles, pronouns, and/or added detail. Thus the printed edition chooses "smyten Geffray at the herte" (frag. 2ra), compared with the potentially more metaphorical "trowed to haue smyte Geffray at herte" (BL, MS Royal 18.b.II, 178v); and in the same passages, Geffray "smote the gyaunt with his swerde vpon the legge" in the printed edition, lending depth to the manuscript's "smote the geaunt vpon the legge."
66. Sánchez-Martí, "Textual Transition," 511. Amendments in this mode typically insert adjectives to enhance narrative impact, such as the use of "moche grete douloure" (frag. 2rb) in place of the manuscript's "trystefull doleur" (180r), or "kneled downe on bothe his knees" (frag. 3ra), compared with "kneeled doun on his knees" (186v).
67. Sánchez-Martí, "Textual Transition," 515. Conversely, the printed *Melusyne* also frequently subdues the narrative intensity created by the practice of synonymy, the pairing of adjectives. Compare the manuscript's use of "the patiz or trybut" (177r) with the edition's "the trybute" (frag. 1va); "thy

grete hardynes & the grete enterprise of thyn herte" (177r–177v) becomes "thy grete hardynes" (frag. 1va); "recounted & shewed" (195v), becomes *recounted* (frag. 5ra).

68. See, e.g., *vnpossyble* in place of *impossible* (frag. 3ra; BL, MS Royal 18.b.II, 186v); "embrased & kyssed" (frag. 3ra) for "embraced & kyssed" (187r). In the latter example, the printed *Melusyne*'s editor or compositor seems to have confused the ME *embrasen* ("To set on fire; *fig.* to inflame with passion, to warm [one's heart]") for *embracen* ("To embrace [someone] affectionately, to clasp in ones arms"). For definitions, see "*embrasen* (v.)" and "*embracen* (v.)" in the online *Middle English Dictionary*, http://quod.lib.umich.edu/m/med/ (accessed November 18, 2013). Alternately, it may be a mistranslation of the French "lembrascha de ses bras et sentrebaiserent" (Steinschaber, 153v), which is modified to "lembrassa en ces bras et sentrebaiserent" in Le Roy 1493–94 (T4r), and to "lembrassa de ces bras & sentrebaiserent" in Ortuin-Schenck (also T4r).

69. Aronoff, "Orthographic System," 91–96; on the archaic language of the translation in the Royal manuscript, see Nolan, "Introduction to the English Version," chap. 4.

70. Sánchez-Martí, "Textual Transition," 510, where he draws on Demelza Curnow, "Five Case Studies on the Transmission of Popular Middle English Verse Romances" (PhD Diss., University of Bristol, 2002). I have not been able to access this work.

71. See also Steinschaber, 153v:

> Faulce fortune comment es tu si faulce et si peruerse que tu tes entremise de ces deux loyaulx amans / et en ce disant sescrierent tous a vne voix / Nous perdons au iourduy la meilleure dame qui oncques gouuenast terre la plus saige la plus humble la plus charitable la plus priuee de ses gens qui oncques fut sur terre / Adonc commencerent tous a plourer et a plaindre & a mener si grant douleur quilz entreoublierent les deux amans qui gisoient par terre.

For equivalent passages, see Le Roy 1493–94 and Ortuin-Schenck, T4r in each.

72. Nolan makes similar observations regarding the diminution of emotional content in this scene in the Middle English manuscript copy of the romance compared with earlier French versions. See Nolan, "Introduction to the English Version," 28–31.

73. Helen Cooper, "Prose Romances," in *A Companion to Middle English Prose*, ed. A. S. G. Edwards (Cambridge, UK: D. S. Brewer, 2004), 215–229,

226–227; on *mouvance* in selected French prose and poetic Mélusine manuscripts, see Tania M. Colwell, "Reading Mélusine: Romance Manuscripts and their Audiences, *c.* 1380–*c.* 1530" (PhD diss., Australian National University, 2009), chaps. 3–4.

74. Helen Cooper, "Romances after 1400," in *The Cambridge History of Medieval English Literature,* ed. David Wallace (Cambridge, UK: Cambridge University Press, 1999), 690–719, 703; Carol M. Meale, "'All the Bokes that I Haue of Latyn, Englische, and Frensch': Laywomen and Their Books in Late Medieval England," in *Women and Literature in Britain, 1150–1500,* ed. Carol M. Meale (Cambridge, UK: Cambridge University Press, 1993), 128–158, 139–141.

75. Fellows, "Printed Romance," 67–78; A. S. G. Edwards, "William Copland and the Identity of Printed Middle English Romance," in *The Matter of Identity in Medieval Romance,* ed. Philippa Hardman (Cambridge, UK: D. S. Brewer, 2002), 139–147, 146–147; more generally, Alex Davis, *Chivalry and Romance in the English Renaissance* (Cambridge, UK: D. S. Brewer, 2003).

76. Sánchez-Martí, "Textual Transition," 516; Jacobs, *Later Versions of Sir Degarre.*

77. Interestingly, the contemporary French editions retain the phrasing evident from the earliest complete French *Roman de Mélusine* manuscript to note the different social grades in attendance ("dames et damoiselles cheualiers et escuiers"; Steinschaber, 153v), even if Mélusine bids farewell to "tous et toutes" in her chamber (156r); they thus do not provide a ready source for the Middle English printed copy. For these passages in the oldest French prose *Mélusine* manuscript (Paris, Bibliothèque de l'Arsenal, MS 3353, ca. 1420s), see Jean d'Arras, *Mélusine ou La noble histoire de Lusignan,* ed. Jean-Jacques Vincensini (Paris: Libraire Générale Française, 2003), 696, 702.

78. Harf-Lancner, "*Roman de Mélusine,*" 355–356.

79. Brenda Hosington, "*Partenopeu de Blois* and Its Fifteenth-Century English Translation: A Medieval Translator at Work," in *The Medieval Translator II,* ed. Roger Ellis, Westfield Publications in Medieval Studies 5 (London: Centre for Medieval Studies, Queen Mary and Westfield College, University of London, 1991), 231–252, 242–243.

80. Gavin Bone, "Extant Manuscripts Printed from by W. de Worde with Notes on the Owner, Roger Thorney," *The Library* 4th ser., 12 (1931–1932): 284–306; Susan Powell, "Lady Margaret Beaufort and Her Books," *The Library* 6th ser., 20 (1998): 197–240; A. S. G. Edwards and Carol M. Meale, "The Marketing of Printed Books in Late Medieval England," *The Library* 6th ser., 15 (1993): 95–124; Hellinga, *William Caxton and Early Printing,* 139–155.

81. "I am Geffray with þe grete toethe sone to Raymondyn of Lusygnen that come hether to chalenge the trybute that thrughe thy pryde thou takest of

my faders people" (frag. 1va), which compresses the manuscript's phrasing: "And Geffray ansuered in this manere. I am Geffray with the grete toeth sone to Raymondyn of Lusynen that commeth hither to chalange the patiz or trybut that thou takest thrugh thy grete pryde of my lord my faders peple" (177r). On speech compression, see also Watson, *Valentine and Orson*, xix.

82. "And whan Geffray vnderstode it / he was almoost mad for angre / and sayd in this manere / how deuyl hadde not my fader and my moder ynough for to entreteyne and kepe thestate of Froymonde my brother / and hym to haue maryed some noble lady of the lande and not to haue made hym a monke / by god omnypotent these flaterers monkes shall repent them therof /" (frag. 2vb).

83. See Barbara Wahlen and Jean-Claude Mühlethaler, "Dépasser le modèle arthurien: Geoffroy la Grand' Dent, chevalier de la fin des temps," in *550 Jahre deutsche Melusine—Coudrette und Thüring von Ringoltingen / 550 ans de Mélusine allemande—Coudrette et Thüring von Ringoltingen. Beiträge der wissenschaftlichen Tagung der Universitäten Bern und Lausanne vom August 2006 / Actes du colloque organisé par les Universités de Berne et de Lausanne en août 2006*, ed. André Schnyder and Jean-Claude Mühlethaler (Bern, Switzerland: Peter Lang, 2008), 343–362, 351; I discuss this in Colwell, "Reading Mélusine," chap. 3, and briefly in Tania M. Colwell, "Gesture, Emotion, and Humanity: Depictions of Mélusine in the Upton House Bearsted Fragments," in *The Inner Life of Women in Medieval Romance Literature*, ed. Jeff Rider and Jamie Freedman (New York: Palgrave Macmillan, 2011), 107–127, 110–111.

84. Harf-Lancner, "*Roman de Mélusine*"; Bouquin, "Éditions et adaptations," 1.2; Ana Pairet, "Medieval Bestsellers in the Age of Print: *Melusine* and *Olivier de Castille*," in *The Medieval Author in Medieval French Literature*, ed. Virginie Greene (New York: Palgrave Macmillan, 2006), 189–204, 196–197.

85. Cambridge, Trinity College Library, MS R. 3. 17; Montague Rhodes James, *The Western Manuscripts in the Library of Trinity College, Cambridge. A Descriptive Catalogue*, 4 vols. (Cambridge, UK: Cambridge University Press, 1900–1904), 2:66–67, no. 597; catalogue available online at http://sites.trin. cam.ac.uk/james/index.php as *The James Catalogue of Western Manuscripts* (accessed November 15, 2013). For the printed edition, see Couldrette, *The Romans of Partenay, or of Lusignen: Otherwise Known as the Tale of Melusine*, translated from the French of La Coudrette (before 1500 A.D.), ed. Walter W. Skeat, EETS o.s. 22 (London: Kegan Paul, Trench, Trübner, 1899).

86. British Library, MS Cotton Otto D.II, a compilation produced in the 1400s containing the *Roman de Mélusine*, was autographed by Jacquetta of Luxembourg who probably inherited the volume on the death of her first husband, John, Duke of Bedford, in 1435; Oxford, Bodleian Library, MS Bodley 445, also a compilation, contains the *Roman de Parthenay* and includes marginal annotations in English dating from the mid-sixteenth century. I have

consulted each of these volumes; see also Meale, "Caxton, de Worde," 296; T. Smith, *Catalogue of the Manuscripts in the Cottonian Library 1696 (Catalogus librorum manuscriptorum bibliothecae Cottonianae), Reprinted from Sir Robert Harley's copy, annotated by Humfrey Wanley, together with documents relating to the fire of 1731*, ed. Colin G. C. Tite (Cambridge, UK: D. S. Brewer, 1984), 74–75; Falconer Madan, et al., *A Summary Catalogue of Western Manuscripts in the Bodleian Library at Oxford*, 7 vols. in 8 pts. (Oxford: Clarendon Press, 1895–1953), 2.1:342, no. 2386; Eleanor Roach, "La tradition manuscrite du *Roman de Mélusine* par Coudrette," *Revue d'histoire des textes* 7 (1977): 185–233, 189–192.

87. Juan Luis Vives, *Instruction of a Christen Woman*, trans. Rychard Hyrd (London: Thomas Berthelet, ca. 1529) (STC 24856.5), E4r; Wilfrid Holme, *The Fall and Euill Successe of Rebellion* (London: Henry Binneman, 1572) (STC 13602 and 13603), I4r. On these, see Helen Cooper, *The English Romance in Time: Transforming Motifs from Geoffrey of Monmouth to the Death of Shakespeare* (Oxford: Oxford University Press, 2004), 175–176, 423; A. G. Dickens, *Lollards and Protestants in the Diocese of York*, 2nd ed. (Oxford. Hambledon Press, 1982), 114–131.

88. Gray, *Later Medieval English Literature*, 216–217.

89. Meale, "Caxton, de Worde," 286.

An English *Owain* Prophecy: The Influence of Welsh Prophetic Material in Oxford, All Souls College, MS 33

VICTORIA FLOOD

I print here a new transcription of a unique witness of a late-medieval political prophecy found in Oxford, All Souls College, MS 33:

Cadwalladyr sall Owan call	
and walys sall busk yai*m* forto ryse	
And allbayn sall to yai*m* fall	*Scotland*
and ky*n*dyll bale apon yair wyse	
yan ryse vnro tyll alyens all	*trouble*
Owen grondyn glayus gers yai*m* gryse	*sharpened spears, makes them fearful*
and Bretons chullys yai*m* als a ball	*kick*
and setts to yaim ou*er* sary assyse	*harsh judgement*

The prophecy appears in a late-fourteenth-century hand on the final parchment folio of a twelfth-century copy of William of Malmesbury's *Gesta regum anglorum* with other Latin chronicle material.[1] The text is in a typical late-fourteenth-century Anglicana script, with descending *r*s, double-compartment *g*s, and barred double *l*s, and employs the same graph for *y* and *þ*. Although it was once understood to be a fragment lifted from the fifteenth-century *Metrical Chronicle of John Harding*, in 1980 Clifford Peterson put forward the hypothesis that the prophecy is an independent derivative of Geoffrey of Monmouth's *Prophetiae Merlini*.[2] The question of the All Souls prophecy has since remained unconsidered, and it has yet to be oriented within the broader historical milieu in which we can locate All Souls MS 33.

As far as we can trace the late-medieval provenance of the manuscript, its earliest owner appears to have been the Cistercian abbey of Merevale in Warwickshire; folio 136r has an *ex libris* of the house recoverable under ultraviolet light.[3] The origin of the text itself, however, cannot be located in the West Midlands. On such a slight sample it is difficult to position the dialect with any precision, but it is consistent with features that the *Linguistic Atlas of Late Medieval English* locates in northern England and Scotland ("sall" for shall, "yaim" for them).[4] The circulation of northern English or Scottish prophetic material in the West Midlands is by no means unprecedented. There are important examples of northern prophecies extant only in West Midland witnesses, for example, Thomas of Erceldoune's prophecy as it is found in British Library, Harley MS 2253 (ca. 1336–1340).[5] However, the All Souls prophecy indicates not simply one geographical movement but two. A number of allusions in the prophecy strongly suggest the acquaintance of its author with Welsh prophetic material mediated through sources other than Geoffrey of Monmouth.

The eight-line prophecy details the marshaling of a British (Welsh and potentially Breton) and Scottish army. A Cambro-Scottish alliance is figured by the joining of Cadwaladr, a familiar hero of Welsh political prophecy generally held to be representative of the northern Welsh kingdom of Gwynedd, with Alban, a conventional figure representing Scotland in fourteenth- and fifteenth-century northern English and Scottish political prophecy. This alliance is derived indirectly from the anti-English confederation that appears as a long-lived theme of Welsh political prophecy. The best-known and oldest datable articulation of this is the British, Scottish, and Norse anti-Saxon confederation led by Cadwaladr and his Breton counterpart Cynan in the tenth-century *Armes Prydein Vawr* ("Great Prophecy of Britain"), a prophecy preserved in the fourteenth-century Book of Taliesin (National Library of Wales, Peniarth MS 2) envisaging Saxon slaughter and the exile of survivors from the British Isles.[6]

In England and Scotland for the greater part of the Middle Ages, the primary source for this material was Geoffrey of Monmouth's reworking of this Welsh theme in *Prophetiae* 110: "Cadualadrus Conanum uocabit et Albaniam in societatem accipiet" ("Cadualadrus will summon Conanus and make Scotland his ally").[7] As we find it in All Souls 33, this formulation bears a strong resemblance to an immensely popular English vernacular reimagining of *Prophetiae* 110 originally of Scottish origin, in circulation on both sides of the Anglo-Scottish border roughly contemporary to the All Souls prophecy "When Rome Is Removyd," dated to the 1380s.[8] As it appears in the fifteenth-century Anglo-Scottish border witness Cambridge University Library, MS Kk. I. 5, the A-text of "When Rome Is Removyd" prophesies:

> Tatcalders sall call on Carioun the noyus
> And than sall worthe up Wallys and wrethe othir landis
> And erth on tyll Albany, if thai may wyne. (ll. 23–25)[9]

Although the text presents a corruption of the heroes' names (Cadwaladr and Cynan, or the Galfridian Cadualadrus and Conanus), the reference to the Cambro-Scottish alliance is preserved here. The All Souls prophecy can be understood as a variation on the A-text in which Owain is substituted for Cynan. Lines 1 to 3 rework this passage; and the allusion to "bale" that follows in line 4 very plausibly draws on the assertion in the fourth line of the "When Rome" A-text that "Mekyll baret ande bale shall fall in Brutis lande." Similarly, the movement of this Cambro-Scottish force against "alyens" (the English), echoes not only the meaning but the terms of line 26 of the A-text: "Herme wnto alienys, anever thai sall wakyne." The All Souls prophecy is almost certainly descended from this northern derivative of *Prophetiae* 110 rather than the *Prophetiae* directly. However, the replacement of Cynan with Owain presents an important innovation. To my knowledge, this is the earliest recorded English vernacular example of an Owain prophecy, suggestive of the direct transmission of Welsh material to northern England or Scotland or to a northern English or Scottish scribe working in the West Midlands, incorporating Welsh elements that could not possibly have been taken from Geoffrey of Monmouth.

Owain appears as a national deliverer, analogous to Cynan or Cadwaladr, in pre- and non-Galfridian Welsh political prophecy and is also a hero of Welsh prose tales and poetry.[10] A figure of the legendary British Old North, he was identified as Ewein ap Urien, son of Urien Rheged, who appears in the *Historia Brittonum* as a northern king engaged in the late-sixth-century British defense against the Anglo-Saxon kingdom of Bernicia.[11] In Wales a number of tales grew up around Ewein or Owain, the son of Urien, who was said to have fought the Saxons alongside his father. This reputation almost certainly formed the basis for the national deliverer Owain as he appears in Welsh prophecy. This is precisely the context in which we must understand the use of his name in the All Souls prophecy, a feature that depends on some level of acquaintance with Welsh prophecy.

This use of Owain could not have been mediated through Geoffrey of Monmouth, in whose writings Owain (named only in a single, oblique allusion in the *Historia*) is never identified as a prophetic hero.[12] Although Owain's name may have plausibly been known in English and Scottish clerical culture through his brief appearance in the *Vita Kentigerni* produced for Herbert Bishop of Glasgow around 1147 to 1164 (extant only in fragmentary form), where Ewein ap Urien is identified as the father of the British Saint Kentigern, this stands outside a network of prophetic meaning, and Ewein's conduct is decidedly unheroic (he enters the scene for the rape of Kentigern's mother, Thaney).[13] Indeed, if the name Owain meant anything in England it would have been through the French romance by Chrétien de Troyes, *Yvain*, but again the most important innovations in this material, for the purposes of understanding the All Souls prophecy, occur in a Welsh context.

In Chrétien's tale Yvain is given a "lance,"[14] described as a spear in the Welsh prose version of the same: *Chwedl Iarlles y Ffynawn* ("The Story of the Lady of the Fountain"), where Owain defends the fountain "o waew a chledyf" ("with spear and sword").[15] Owain's association with the spear (among other weapons) assumed a long life in Welsh literary-political culture. In his poem "Iarll y Cawg" ("Earl of the Basin"), addressed to Sir Rhys ap Thomas (a reputed descendant of Owain ap Urien), the sixteenth-century Denbighshire poet Tudur Aled wrote: "Owain oedd, ni wyddym, / Â chawg a llêch a gwayw llym" ("Owain, we know, had a basin and a stone and a keen spear").[16] Owain's prowess with a spear is also notable in texts firmly outside the romance tradition. In the elegy to Owein ap Urien in the *Book of Taliesin*, "Marwnat Owein" ("Owein's Elegy"), we read of the hero's work on the battlefield: "escyll gawr gwaywawr llifeit" ("[like] the rays of dawn the whetted spears," l. 6), referring to spears wielded against a number of enemies including the English.[17]

This broader cultural context almost certainly stands behind Owain's activities in the All Souls prophecy with his spears, which induce terror in his enemies. However, in the All Souls prophecy (as we find in a Welsh prophetic context), the name Owain, like Cadwaladr, signifies not simply a historical individual but a British army, and notably the spear functions as a weapon of choice in a number of Welsh prophecies of British restoration (two important examples are given below). The All Souls prophecy presents material fundamentally consistent with Owain's place in Welsh romance and elegiac traditions alongside broader prophetic commonplaces. This combination of material most plausibly entered northern English or Scottish circulation through Welsh lines of influence that associated Owain's spear, or rather the spears of Owain's army, with an act of British restoration.

Another very strong claim to a Welsh influence is found in the enigmatic seventh line of the prophecy: "and Bretons chullys yai*m* als a ball" ("the Britons [or Bretons] kick them like a ball"). The "yaim" in question here can only be the "alyens," that is, the Saxons—the English. This allusion corresponds very closely to a figure preserved in the *Book of Taliesin* in a prophecy beginning "Rydyrchafwy Duw ar plwyff Brython" ("May God rise up over the people of the Britons").[18] The prophecy stages an anti-English alliance between the Welsh kingdoms of Gwynedd and Powys, and envisages Welsh forces around Chester exacting a bloody vengeance on the English for the death of Gwynedd ruler Idwal Foel in 942. In a scene that Marged Haycock, the most recent editor and translator of the prophecy, notes as "bringing to mind the split heads and heaving corpses in the more savage lines of *Armes Prydein*," we read of the Welsh cavalry, "gware pelre a phen Saesson" ("playing ball with the heads of the Saxons").[19]

The allusion appears to have been a stock one. It is also found in the prophecy "Yr Afallennau" ("The Apple Tree Verses") as it is preserved in the *Black Book of Carmarthen* (NLW, Peniarth MS 1, compiled ca.1250), where in a description of the carnage of a battle at a location identified as Cyminawd, we read of "Aer o saesson ar onn verev / A guarwyaur pelre ac ev pennev" ("the slaughter of Saxons on ashen spears / and players of a ball-game with their heads").[20]

It makes little difference to the meaning of this phrase in the All Souls prophecy whether the "Bretons" to whom this activity is ascribed are the Welsh or the Bretons of Brittany. The Bretons are conventionally participants in the confederation against the English, as we find in *Armes Prydein*. In this context the Bretons are the British diaspora returning from exile in mainland Europe. In Welsh prophecy the Breton contingent is generally understood to be signified by the presence of Cynan, commonly identified as Cynan ap Eudaf, or Meiriadoc, a figure associated with the British settlement of Brittany in the fourth century—a legend reworked by Geoffrey of Monmouth in his *Historia*.[21] This position is implied by Geoffrey in *Prophetiae* 110, and made explicit in his later reworking of this material in his *Vita Merlini*, where Conanus's return from Brittany is prophesied.[22] Importantly, the macabre ball game of the Britons appears in "Yr Afallennau" as part of a trajectory that concludes with the return of Cynan and Cadwaladr and the establishment of British rule. Read in the similar context of the All Souls prophecy as a whole and with this background tradition in mind, whether British or Breton, this field of allusion frames a powerful statement of opposition to English claims to insular hegemony, grounded in a long-lived Welsh political prophetic discourse.

During the last quarter of the fourteenth century, the name Owain became the focus of fresh nationalist ambitions in Wales. Owain ap Thomas ap Rhodri (d. 1378), also known as Owen of Wales or Owain Lawgoch (Owain of the Red Hand),[23] a great-nephew of Llywelyn ap Grufffydd and a soldier in the French wars against the English, became a new focus for hopes for Welsh independence.[24] The All Souls prophecy potentially belongs to the period of Owain's claims to independent Welsh sovereignty, declared in May 1372. The attack Owain launched upon Britain from France with the help of the French fleet was ultimately unsuccessful, foundering at Guernsey. It is possible that if we can regard the "Bretons" of the prophecy as of Brittany, potentially we see a conflation of the French supporters of Owain with the returning Bretons of Welsh political prophecy. However, this connection remains purely speculative. The last living heir to the kingdom of Gwynedd, Owain became the object of Welsh political expectations both at home and for the Welshmen who accompanied him into exile. His assassination by the English agent John Lambe in Poitou in 1378 left a vacuum into which Owain Glyn Dŵr stepped in the early years of the fifteenth century: another heroic Owain lauded by the Welsh bards.[25]

The age of the revolt of Owain Glyn Dŵr was also a period of renewed prophetic expectation in Scotland, and it has been argued that the early 1400s saw the direct transmission of prophetic materials from Wales to Scotland as the old prophetic motif of an anti-English confederation came to assume a new political utility in both places.[26] We might even attempt to press the All Souls prophecy into the early fifteenth century, but this remains uncertain (the scribal hand does not show any obvious fifteenth-century features). Yet, certainly, the appeal in Scotland of an anti-English Cambro-Scottish union, and its English circulation as we find in the A-text of "When Rome is Removyd," can be observed as early as the final decades of the fourteenth century.

Whether Scottish or English in its extant form, the All Souls prophecy must not be understood as a translation from Welsh: other than the heroes' names, there is no obvious trace of Welsh linguistic influence. Rather it is an English language composition influenced by Welsh themes. The only way to explain this phenomenon is to isolate a point at which Welsh material might have become familiar to a northern English or Scottish scribe. The broader Cistercian milieu provides a persuasive context for the meeting of these insular elements. In the centuries following Edward I's conquest of Wales, Cistercian houses (already well integrated into the native milieu) continued to play an important part in the preservation of Welsh culture and manuscript production, and by the mid-fourteenth century, Cistercian abbots were patrons of politically minded Welsh poets.[27] The Cistercian foundation at Whitland was particularly active in its prophetic interests; this was a movement that reached its apex during the revolt of Owain Glyn Dŵr but may well have been in place earlier.[28] It has been suggested as the site of the compilation of the *Black Book of Carmarthen*, one of the earliest surviving Welsh prophetic manuscripts.[29] Another candidate for the collection and dissemination of prophetic material is the Cistercian house of Cwm-hir in Maelienydd, where, it has been suggested, the *Book of Taliesin* was produced.[30]

The manuscript circumstances of the All Souls prophecy suggest that during the late fourteenth century Welsh prophetic material, or at the very least fragments of Welsh prophetic themes, circulated between Cistercian houses across the Welsh border. Whether the prophecy traveled in a complete form from the north to Warwickshire as a movement supplementary to an earlier northward transmission of Welsh prophetic material, or whether we find a northern scribe with access to Welsh prophetic materials working in Warwickshire, remains uncertain. In either case the movement of Welsh material through pan-insular Cistercian networks presents the most plausible hypothesis for this English-language reuse of Welsh prophetic motifs, particularly in a dialect localized so far from the Anglo-Welsh border. We might understand this as a movement analogous to the better-noted involvement of Franciscan monasteries across the British Isles in the circulation of anti-Lancastrian rumors and prophecies during the reign of Henry IV.[31] Although almost certainly not a statement of political intent or affiliation in the same sense as we find in Franciscan anti-Lancastrianism, the All Souls prophecy is representative of a literary interest in anti-English prophetic material within a Cistercian context, resting on a similar cross-border network.

Philipps-Universität Marburg

Acknowledgments
With thanks to the librarians and staff of the Codrington Library, All Souls College, Oxford, and Helen Fulton for her comments and suggestions.

NOTES

1. Oxford, All Soul's College, MS 33, fol. 136v (my transcription). The contents of the manuscript are catalogued in Andrew G. Watson, *A Descriptive Catalogue of the Medieval Manuscripts of All Souls College* (Oxford: Oxford University Press, 1997), 65–67.
2. Clifford Peterson, "John Hardyng and Geoffrey of Monmouth: Two Unrecorded Poems and a Manuscript," *Notes and Queries* 27.3 (1980): 202–204.
3. Watson, *Descriptive Catalogue*, 66–67.
4. Andrew McIntosh, M. L. Samuels, Michael Benskin, Michael Laing, and Keith Williams, *A Linguistic Atlas of Late Medieval English*, 4 vols. (Aberdeen, Scotland: Aberdeen University Press, 1986).
5. For the most recent scholarship on British Library, Harley MS 2253, see Susanna Fein, ed., *Studies in the Harley Manuscript: The Scribe, Contents, and Social Contexts of British Library MS Harley 2253* (Kalamazoo, MI: Medieval Institute Publications, 2000). For a discussion of the provenance of Thomas of Erceldoune's prophecy, see Victoria Flood, "Imperfect Apoca-

lypse: Thomas of Erceldoune's Reply to the Countess of Dunbar in MS Harley 2253," *Marginalia* 11 (2010): 11–27.

6. I. Williams, ed., *Armes Prydein*, trans. Rachel Bromwich (Dublin: Dublin Institute for Advanced Studies, 1972). For the most recent dating of the poem, see T. M. Charles-Edwards, *Wales and the Britons, 130–1064* (Oxford: Oxford University Press, 2013), 519–535. For a discussion of the antiquity of the prophecy's Cynan-Cadwaladr material, see David Dumville, "Brittany and *Armes Prydein Vawr*," *Études Celtiques* 20 (1983): 145–159. For another recent translation of the poem, see G. R. Isaac, "'Armes Prydein Fawr' and St David," in *St David of Wales: Cult, Church and Nation*, ed. J. Wyn Evans and Jonathan M. Wooding (Woodbridge, UK: Boydell Press, 2007), 161–181. For the most recent discussion of material from the Book of Taliesin and the manuscript's provenance, see Marged Haycock, *Legendary Poems from the Book of Taliesin* (Aberystwyth, Wales: CMCS, 2007); Marged Haycock, *Prophecies from the Book of Taliesin* (Aberystwyth, Wales: CMCS, 2013).

7. Geoffrey of Monmouth, *The History of the Kings of Britain: An Edition and Translation of De gestis Britonum (Historia regum Britanniae)*, ed. Michael D. Reeve and trans. Neil Wright. Arthurian Studies 69 (Woodbridge, UK: Boydell Press, 2007), vii.

8. For an overview of the manuscripts, see *DIMEV* no. 6398, The DIMEV: An Open-Access, Digital Edition of the *Index of Middle English Verse*, http://www.dimev.net. Peterson, "John Harding," 204, also briefly suggests this as an analogue to the All Souls prophecy.

9. Printed in Reinhard Haferkorn, ed., *When Rome Is Removed into England* (Leipzig, Germany: Verlag von Bernhard Tauchnitz, 1932), 92–103; J. Rawson Lumby, ed., *Bernardus de Cura Rei Famuliaris with Some Early Scottish Prophecies* (London: Oxford University Press, 1870), 32–34; Rossell Hope Robbins, ed., *Historical Poems of the XIV and XV Centuries* (New York: Columbia University Press, 1959), 118–120; James M. Dean, ed., *Medieval English Political Writings* (Kalamazoo, MI: TEAMS, 1996), 13–15.

10. M. E. Griffiths, *Early Vaticination in Welsh with English Parallels* (Cardiff: University of Wales Press, 1937), 93, 99–100; Rachel Bromwich, *Trioedd Ynys Prydein* (Cardiff: University of Wales Press, 2006), 467–472.

11. *Historia Brittonum*, in *Nennius: British History and the Welsh Annals*, ed. and trans. John Morris (London: Philimore, 1980), §63; Bromwich, *Trioedd*, 479–483; J. Macqueen, "Yvain, Ewein, and Owain ap Urien," *Transactions of the Dumfriesshire and Galloway Natural History and Antiquarian Society* 33 (1956): 107–131.

12. Geoffrey of Monmouth, *History*, xi, 23–25.

13. Printed in Alexander Penrose Forbes, ed., *Lives of Saint Ninian and Saint Kentigern* (Edinburgh: Edmonston and Douglas, 1874), 243–252, 245; Macqueen, "Yvain, Ewein," 122–128.

14. "Yvain ou le Chevalier au Lion," in *Chrétien de Troyes, Œuvres complètes,* ed. Daniel Poirion, et al. (Paris: Éditions Gallimard, 1994), 340–503. For recent discussion of the relationship between the French and the Welsh versions, see Ceridwen Lloyd-Morgan, "Migrating Narratives: *Peredur, Owain,* and *Geraint,*" in *A Companion to Welsh Arthurian Literature,* ed. Helen Fulton (Oxford: Wiley-Blackwell, 2009), 128–141.

15. *Owein or Chwedyl Iarlles y Ffynnawn,* ed. R. L. Thomson (Dublin: Dublin Institute for Advanced Studies, Four Courts Press, 1968), 450.

16. Bromwich, *Trioedd,* 471.

17. Ifor Williams, ed., *The Poems of Taliesin* (Dublin: Dublin Institute for Advanced Studies, 1968), 12, 114–115.

18. Haycock, *Prophecies,* 109–125.

19. Ibid., 13, l. 22.

20. A. O. H. Jarman, *Llyfr du Caerfyrddin* (Cardiff: University of Wales Press, 1982), 26–28, ll. 9–10.

21. Bromwich, *Trioedd,* 316–318, 292–293; Bromwich, *Armes Prydein,* 46; Rachel Bromwich, "Cynon fab Clydno," in *Astudiaethau ar yr Hengerdd: Studies in Old Welsh Poetry,* ed. Rachel Bromwich and R. Brynley Jones (Cardiff: University of Wales Press, 1978), 151–164. The last article is an argument against M. E. Griffiths's hypothesis that the prophesied Cynan was not originally associated with Brittany but was Cynan, son of Clydno Eiddyn, whom she regards as the only survivor of the northern British battle of Gododdin, for which see Griffiths, *Early Vaticination,* 110–118. Geoffrey of Monmouth, *History,* v, 310–330.

22. Basil Clarke, ed. and trans., *Geoffrey of Monmouth: The Life of Merlin* (Cardiff: University of Wales Press, 1973), 967.

23. E. Owen, "Owain Lawgoch / Yeuain de Galles: Some Facts and Suggestions," *Transactions of the Honourable Society of Cymmrodorion* (1899–1900): 6–105; A. D. Carr, *Owen of Wales: The End of the House of Gwynedd* (Cardiff: University of Wales Press, 1991); "Owain of Wales," in *Oxford Dictionary of National Biography* (Oxford: Oxford University Press, 2004), http://www.oxforddnb.com/view/article/20983?docPos=1 (accessed February 9, 2014).

24. R. R. Davies, *The Age of Conquest: Wales 1063–1415* (Oxford: Oxford University Press, 2000), 438, discusses the possibility of Owain Lawgoch as a Welsh messianic *mab darogan.*

25. Ibid., 448.

26. Juliette Wood, "Where Does Britain End? The Reception of Geoffrey of Monmouth in Scotland and Wales," in *The Scots and Medieval Arthurian Legend,* ed. R. Purdie and N. Royan (Cambridge, UK: D. S. Brewer, 2005), 9–24, 19–20; G. W. S. Barrow, "Wales and Scotland in the Middle Ages," *Welsh History Review* 10 (1981): 302–319, 316–318.

27. Daniel Huws, *Medieval Welsh Manuscripts* (Cardiff: University of Wales Press, 2000), 12, 29, 52–53.

28. Davies, *Age of Conquest*, 197; Glanmor Williams, *The Welsh Church from Conquest to Reformation* (Cardiff: University of Wales Press, 1976), 19–20, 242.

29. Jarman, *Llyfr du Caerfyrddin*, li. However, an originally Augustinian site of composition is also suggested in Huws, *Medieval Welsh Manuscripts*, 72.

30. Haycock, *Prophecies*, 1; Huws, *Medieval Welsh Manuscripts*, 79.

31. L. D. Duls, *Richard II in the Early Chronicles* (The Hague, Holland: Mouton & Co, 1975), 192–193; Peter McNiven, *Heresy and Politics in the Reign of Henry IV* (Woodbridge, UK: Boydell and Brewer, 1987), 95–96, 99; Peter McNiven, "Rebellion, Sedition, and the Legend of Richard II's Survival," *Bulletin of the John Rylands Library* 76 (1994): 93–117, 95–96; Ralph Griffiths, "Some Secret Supporters of Owain Glyn Dŵr?," *Bulletin of the Institute of Historical Research* 37 (1964): 77–100, 79, 86; Davies, *Age of Conquest*, 450–451. Franciscan uses of anti-Lancastrian prophecy are recorded in Frank Scott Haydon, ed., *Eulogium historiarum sive temporis Chronicon ab orbe condito usque ad annum domini M.CCC.LXVI., a monacho quodam Malmeburiensi exaratum*, 3 vols. Rolls Series 9 (London: Longman, 1858–1863), 3:389–394.

A Blessed Burgh, Fasting, and Filthy Lucre: Middle English Bits from Merton College, MS 249

RALPH HANNA

Whenever I visit the manuscripts at Merton College, Julia Walworth, the librarian, always asks what I'm doing there. "We don't have any English in our books," she says. Of course, English medievalists ought to pay a great deal more attention than they usually do to contemporary Latin books. These customarily include considerably more intellectually demanding texts than do vernacular manuscripts and, given the excessive familiarity with books that typifies Latinate culture, considerably more interesting codicological problems as well.

I had a variety of reasons for visiting Julia for a look at Merton College, MS 249, none of them including any expectations about English.[1] The book stands on a particularly interesting intellectual fault line. It was compiled, certainly in communal circumstances, perhaps as a sequence of units to be joined, sometime in the period from 1215 to 1230. As it is now bound (which may be a later conjunction of pieces produced quite independently of one another), the volume shows more than an awareness of the fourth Lateran Council (1215), whose decrees form item 4 of the ensemble. Yet the hands writing the book (and there are quite a number, none of them repeated across the separable units that comprise the whole) all look as if their training, at least, had occurred s. xiii in., that is, from 1200 to 1230.[2] However, although the team(s) responsible for these booklets knew Lateran IV, the book shows no awareness of what is taken as the customary fallout of that council, the concerted interest in training clerics to meet the demands of an aggressive *cura animarum*. Clearly the book emerged from a situation in which the implications of the council had not been fully absorbed. With but a single exception, the composition dates of all the texts presented here cluster in the period roughly from 1170 to 1200, and the exception, the one text addressing pastoral duties directly, is the suitably antique *Regula pastoralis* of Gregory the Great (text 9).

Here I simply report some observations about a single, small piece of the whole, the end of the book, folios 175–185. This segment, quasi-independent of everything else, contains a fairly widely copied *ars praedicandi*, Richard of Thetford's *Ars dilatandi sermones* (here called *De dilatatione sermonum*), William de Montibus's ubiquitous *Peniteas cito* with gloss, and two sermons.[3] For this occasion, I ignore William, although his is the culturally most important text here (printed, probably for continuing grammar school use, by Wynkyn de Worde as late as 1516), in order to concentrate upon the sermons and Richard's *Ars dilatandi*. The first sermon, for the Rogation Days, expounds Genesis 12:8, "on the east side . . . , he [Abra(ha)m] there pitched his tent"; the second, for Pentecost, treats Lamentations 1:13, "From above he hath sent fire into my bones."

As texts, these prove intriguing because they show signs of emerging from that same transitional moment as do the remaining texts here. Neither sermon follows the plan of the traditional *sermo antiquus*, most typically devoted to a reading of the daily gospel, cited in full with a summary narration, succeeded by straightforward development of a single moral message inherent in that text. But, equally, neither shows the developed forms of the *sermo modernus*, with attention to a single verse, a "protheme," a tripartite division of the verse that provides the teacher's text, and development of that verse through three "principals," argumentative divisions. Like the other texts of Merton MS 249, the form of these sermons is decidedly that of the period just before and around 1200, poised somehow between old and new. As we see below, in these features both sermons may respond vitally to another transitional text, Richard of Thetford's *Ars dilatandi*, whose principles they may well have been composed to exemplify.

Both sermons are strongly guided by their texts, although in different ways. The sermon on Abraham, which seems to include one moment where it consciously shifts from one "principal" to another (fol. 182vb), pursues its basically penitential argument by taking up the individual words of the text (the cited "Abraham tetendit tabernaculum suum ab occidente") in turn—first "ab occidente," then "tetendit tabernaculum" (noting that one needs *servi* to do this, and that they might be *amici* or *inimici*, the latter—following considerable development—*servi diaboli*), next "Abraham," finally "tabernaculum" (connected forcefully with the tabernacle of the covenant, mainly from Exod. 27:16). The Pentecost sermon, which has a formal "protheme," concluding with the customary injunction that the audience repeat with the preacher a Pater Noster, is much more tautly constructed, aided by a concordance or perhaps just concordance thinking, the elaboration of a sequence of triads that develop the word *ignis*.[4] In both sermons, amplification of the topics discussed depends upon finding appropriate "proof texts," nearly all of them biblical statements that support the connections between the preacher's ideas and the words of his chosen text. Both sermons avoid the direct narrative and holistic moralization of the older model yet know some rhetorical prescriptions for composing sermons that typify "modern" usage.

In the course of reading the first of these sermons, I ran across a little surprise for Julia Walworth. On folio 182vb, as part of his discussion of the *servi* I mention above, the preacher comments:

> Those who accede to the devil's suggestions are turned from the good, and these suggestions are actualized in two ways, either through gluttony or through lechery. It is obvious that this happens through gluttony because, in the language of an English phrase, these three days are called *fles halidauues* [holidays from meat/holy days for fasting]. Seneca says about these, "In this feast, the bellies of connoisseurs reach the point that they can not bring themselves to taste a fish, unless they have first seen it quivering in its death-throes. It's not just their teeth, belly, and mouth that are gluttonous, but their very eyes." And don't you in my audience know that Adam was thrown out of paradise for gluttony? And also that Queen Vashti was divorced on account of gluttony? And that John the Baptist was beheaded because of gluttony? And many other evil deeds come about through gluttony as well.[5]

From a strictly philological point of view, one might point out that the English cited here is itself transitional, caught in its development from late Old English to more familiar Middle English forms. The phrase shows customary difficulties, particularly in clerical surroundings, over how to handle the Old English grapheme /sc/. Given the date of the manuscript, the text obviously precedes the usual Middle English development of Old English ā to "long open o" (usually dated ca. 1250). Further, *halidauues* represents Old English *hālidagas*, showing the potential development of the Middle English diphthong here (cf. modern "dawn"), but the scribe has, as yet, no ready substitute for the Old English letter *wynn*.

But surely more striking is the juxtaposition the passage establishes. The preacher resorts to English at precisely that point at which he then turns to make his most excessively learned move, a classical citation (not elsewhere paralleled in this text), and at which he summons his audience's recall of relevant biblical analogues. These include the relatively obscure—and unusually literal—evocation of Esther 1.[6] Julia Walworth does not expect to find English in Merton manuscripts, because these are typically books associated with Latinate learned men. But it is worth recalling that all of these men, whatever their Latinity, were native anglophones, and they engage in a continuity of linguistic usage that allows English to pop up in circumstances that customary views of language politics would see as surprising. Here Latinate "Rogation Days" does not communicate clearly any salient feature of the observance at issue, but an apparently unparalleled bit of English slang for the occasion offers a neat encapsulation of a primary responsibility at this season, the unusual holiday observance that does not encourage stuffing yourself. Bilingualism here means not that languages are grammatically distinct (although the preacher's "in nominiu Anglici interpretatione" tends to imply that) but that all are actively in play simultaneously and that from the mélange one can select the most evocative term to fit the immediate situation, regardless of its grammatical origins.

I turn now to consider briefly a second textual moment in this portion of Merton MS 249. This comes late in Richard of Thetford's instructions to preachers on how to elaborate their topics. This text indeed seems to me integral to the two sermons here, since Richard actually lays down the precepts that both sermons are striving to instantiate (the Pentecost sermon more effectively, I think, than the one I discuss above). Richard's arguments in this context are worth a summary review, since they reveal a text poised in the same transitional moment as most of the other contents of the manuscript.

First of all, unlike a wide range of other well-known examples of *artes praedicandi*, Richard is completely uninterested, if not implicitly opposed, to the customary emphasis upon sermon structure. Unlike, say, Robert of Basevorn and his ilk, Richard offers no advice on how to divide the text of a sermon or how to display those various parts in a three-part development; his tract "does exactly what it says on the tin": teaches preachers only how to expand a discussion appropriately, under eight carefully delimited headings.[7] Moreover, Richard loads the tract with warnings against excessive intricacy in the sermon, particularly as the preacher goes about developing a "dilated" and extensive reading. He emphatically opposes the entertaining flights of invention that became normal in the course of the thirteenth century. In his account, preachers are persistently reminded that they need to be clear teachers; they should stick to the point, understand what is digressive (and what might not be), avoid anything that looks like obscurity, strive for transparent language.

Indeed, Richard's entire tract instantiates his teaching. Like a sermon, it has a text, in this case (as frequent allusions scattered through his discussion remind his reader), Paul's 1 Corinthians 14:12: "So you also, forasmuch as you are zealous of spirits, seek to *abound* unto the edifying of the church." Although the usual title of his tract promises instruction in "dilation" (even this term is slightly *retardataire* in a context where the rhetorical term "amplification" usually holds sway), this is training in a double abundance. First, and most obviously, Richard instructs in ways of saying the same thing more than once in order to clarify and exfoliate the implications of a bare statement. Secondly, Richard is aware of Paul's slightly earlier statement (1 Cor. 14:10), "There are, for example, so many kinds of tongues in this world." Most normally, for Richard, this statement signifies an abundance of situations for preaching, for each of which the preacher should specifically temper his skills.[8]

However, at one point (Merton MS 249, fol. 179ra), the issue of "tongues" as Paul conceives it—multiple languages—emerges fully in Richard's argument. At least in its fullest copies (of which Merton 249 is one), the *Ars dilatandi* ends with two sections of *recapitulaciones*, mainly addressing Richard's first two "modes of abundance." In the second of these reformulations, whilst addressing (for the third time!) his first mode of dilation, Richard suggests that the preacher should vary (or expand abundantly upon) proper names by substituting for them (and then developing) epithets. On this occasion, he offers a series of arguments and examples about the power of etymology as such a tool of abundance and continues:

> Let us add that on many occasions, one should attempt to explain or lay open names, insofar as they may edify, and not just the ones that are Greek and Latin but French and English ones, too. For example, *monachus* 'monk' is understood to mean 'the guardian of a monad,' that is of one or, more powerfully, of unity. *Episcopus* 'bishop' is understood to mean 'overseer.' *Sacerdos* 'priest,' either 'giving holy things' [*sacra dans*] or 'holy leader' [*sacer dux*]. 'Agnes' is understood to mean 'ewe-lamb + bronze' [*agna es*], so that her innocence may be imitated through *agna*, and her constancy through *es*. Similarly, the explanation of 'Eadburg' is as if it were *Eaddi burg*, the same as 'blessed city.' Similarly, in French, one should explain 'treasure' as if it were *tresord* ['very dirty'; or 'filthy lucre'?], to which the word accords, since holy men call

temporal things shit. Hence it says in Lamentations
4:5, 'They that were brought up in scarlet have
embraced the dung.'[9]

Richard of Thetford's customary examples, those that rely on Latin and
Greek, are of course largely commonplace and easily paralleled in ancient
Latin tradition. Yet there may be surprises here, since neither "sacer dux" nor
"agna es" is particularly usual.[10] Indeed, the latter, associated with the saint's
persistence in virtue, may, like the Seneca citation above, wittily demonstrate
the preacher's familiarity with classical literature, if only through a collection
of *flores*. At the least, the etymological suggestion resonates with Horace's
proverbial "aere perennius" (a monument more long-lasting than bronze;
Odes 3.30).

Thus, just as in the Rogation Days sermon, a smattering of classics is
immediately collocated with vernacular language. Rather than seeing the
standard "learned languages" as offering an exclusive outlet for etymological thinking, Richard insists on occasions when the practice might extend
to vernaculars as well. These do not exist qualitatively outside the learned
thinking that sees etymology as offering a convincing argument for the inherent likeness of things. The English example, of course, is rather banal,
although it does indicate reasonably sophisticated linguistic thought, the
ability to connect the onomastic element *ēad-* with parallel adjective *ēadig*.
But Richard's discussion simply gestures toward usual pre-Conquest naming
practice and only reiterates those hopes Eadburh's parents had invested in
her.[11] However, the French example is vastly more sophisticated than any of
the others, with its clever pun *tresor/tres sord* and its precise bilingual linkage
(predicated, as this form of "abundance" is supposed to be, on synonyms,
sord/stercus) to a locus in the Vulgate. In this regard, it is worth noting that
Merton MS 249 includes two French texts (numbers 1 and 10), and that the
second of these is far and away the most overtly learned and sophisticated
piece of writing in the entire volume.[12]

Certainly, Julia Walworth is right about Merton manuscripts; two English words in 185 folios of Latin could scarcely be presented as a triumphant
haul. But the implications here for vernacular usage might well cause one to
rethink some old chestnuts about medieval English language relations. The
immediate juxtaposition of classical allusion (whatever the degree of actual
contact with full texts) and "rude" English, not to mention Richard of Thetford's insistence that one might perform comparable "textual" maneuvers in
the course of oral delivery in any of three (or four) languages while moving
freely among them, is both startling and provocative.[13]

Keble College, Oxford

NOTES

1. For a description, which might be amended in many details, see R. M. Thomson, *A Descriptive Catalogue of the Medieval Manuscripts of Merton College, Oxford* (Cambridge, UK: Boydell, 2009), 192–194. Thomson's unsubstantiated assertion that the volume is "probably" mostly of common origin must rest on similarities of ruling systems in various portions and repeated initials in the same (commonplace and anonymous) style.

2. Communal production is marked by alternation of hands in very short stints, particularly in text 11, and by such features as three later-thirteenth-century hands collaborating in adding a short note at fols. 74vb–75ra (text 7[c]). There are six separate production units, not the five that Thomson identifies (text 9 is independent of texts 10–15, and at least one now-missing quire followed it). In addition, the concluding portion of the book, my subject here, although within the same expansive quire as the conclusion of the preceding text, appears a distinct assay—usually below topline (not above), with a different handling of initials, the preceding text breaking off fragmentarily at a folio boundary. As Thomson points out, the first incontrovertible evidence of the volume as the set unit that survives comes from its 1374 donation to Merton.

3. For manuscripts of Richard's treatise, see Richard Sharpe, *A Handlist of Latin Writers of Great Britain and Ireland before 1540*, Publications of the Journal of Medieval Latin 1 (Turnhout, Belgium: Brepols, 1997), 514–515. As Sharpe notes, a printed version appears as part 3 of a pseudo-Bonaventuran *Ars concionandi*, in the Quaracchi *Opera*, 9:16–21. This edition is generally usable; its omissions include Richard's prologue and the two *recapitulaciones* (so-called in the copy in MS Bodley 848) at the end, but it does include a certain amount of intruded later material (e.g., in 3.51, 20b–21b).

4. The second possibility resonates with the behavior of the lecturer responsible for text 6, much earlier in the volume. In calling attention to the "habundancia spiritualium sensuum" (fol. 50va), a phrase reminiscent of Richard of Thetford (see below), he comments that he has gathered fourteen mystical "powerful senses of 'the word of God' from holy Scripture, but eager readers are able to collect a great many more" ("potentias . . . diuini sermonis ex sacra scriptura collegimus, set plures alie a studiosis lectoribus colligi possunt"; fol. 51ra). This sounds as if this author has access to some set of biblical *distinctiones*, a tool coming into prominence in the later twelfth century; see Richard H. and Mary A. Rouse, "Biblical *Distinctiones* in the Thirteenth Century," *Archives d'histoire doctrinale et littéraire du moyen âge* 41 (1975 for 1974): 27–37.

5. "Uertuntur qui eius [diaboli] suggestionibus adquiescunt, que fiunt duobus modis, per gulam scilicet et per luxuriam. Per gulam, quod bene patet in no-

minis Anglici interpretatione, quia isti tres dies dicuntur *fles halidauues*. De quibus dicit Seneca, 'Ad hoc festum deuenerunt uentres delicatorum, ut gustare non possint piscem, nisi prius uiderint palpitantem. Non enim tantum dentibus, uentre, et ore, set occulis gulosi sunt.' Et nescitis quod per gulam eiectus fuit Adam de paradiso? Per gulam autem Uasti regina repudiata? Per gulam Iohannis Baptista decollata est? Et alia multa mala per eam fiunt." The citation, well known to classicists interested in excessively cultivated Roman dining habits (the freshest fish one can imagine), represents *Natural questions* 3.18.3, 7, "festum" replacing Seneca's "fastum." The second sermon includes similarly literate materials: three references to commonplace lore from Aristotle.

6. The customary interpretation does not, as here, present Assuerus as a bumptious, drunken lout but reads the text allegorically, with Assuerus as a type of Christ and Vashti as a sinner reluctant to heed his call; cf. the "Glossa ordinaria," *Patrologia Latina* 113:740 (hereafter *PL*).

7. Interestingly, text 6, which I cite in note 4, also presents an eightfold division, in this case reading Zachary in the temple (Luke 1;9ff.) as an eightfold ascent from worldly thoughts to contemplation. For the force of this number, cf. the most influential discussion, Augustine, "De sermone Domini in monte" 1.11–12 (*PL* 34:1234–1236).

8. Cf. his immediate explanation of the Pauline text (fol. 175ra): "Moreover, because there are differing degrees in the church, it is impossible to follow a single kind of argument when addressing everyone. Hence it is necessary, for the benefit of the whole church, to have diverse ways of preaching.... There are many ways by which a preacher can abound and expand his sermon." ("Quoniam autem in ecclesia uarii sunt ordines, impossibile est modum unum tenere ad omnes. Unde ad utilitatem tocius ecclesie necesse est uarios modos predicandi habere.... Sunt plures modi quibus potest abundare predicator et sermonem dilatare.") As one example of attentiveness to audiences, cf. his statement that *exempla* (which, with customary restraint, he limits to references to biblical or hagiographic narratives only) "are of great strength when addressing laypersons, who are delighted by similes drawn from things extraneous to the text" ("multum ualet laicis, qui similitudinibus gaudent externis"; edn 3:38, 9:18a; fol. 175vb).

9. I cite here not Merton fol. 179ra, its variant readings provided parenthetically, but the slightly more accurate version at MS Bodley 848, fol. 11va (a book also of s. xiii in., from Reading OSB): "Superaddamus quod multociens conandum est nomina exponere uel excoriare, non solum Greca et Latina [*adds* lingua M], set eciam Gallica et Anglicana [*trs. adjs.* M] secundum quod edificare poterunt. Verbi gracia, *monachus* interpretatur 'custos monadis,' id est unius, uel pocius [melius M] unitatis. *Episcopus*, 'superintendens.' *Sacerdos*, 'sacra dans' uel 'sacer dux' [*trs. phrs.* M]. *Agnes*, 'agna es,' ut per 'agnam'

imitetur [inmitatur ? M] eius innocencia, per 'es' [*as one word* peres *in both*] eius constancia. Similiter *Eadburg* exposicio [*om.* M; read 'exponitur'?] quasi 'eaddi [edi M] burg,' quasi 'beata ciuitas.' Similiter in Gallico, *tresor* quasi 'tresord,' cui consonat quod temporalia a sanctis dicuntur stercora. Vnde in *Trenis* (Lam. 4:5), 'Qui nutriebantur in croceis amplexandi sunt stercora.'" My translation of *excoriare* might well be improved upon; the verb usually means "to flay" (hence "display the innards [of]"?) but also at least once "to make a distinction." Notice, as well, Bodley's spelling *eaddi*, philologically another transitional form; unlike Merton's *edi*, the spelling indicates retained association with the Old English diphthong (*ēadig*), rather than its development to Middle English "long open e."

10. For "*monachus,*" "*episcopus,*" and "*sacerdos*" ("*sacrum dans*" only), all examples blending Latin and Greek, as Richard says, see Isidore of Seville, *Etymologiae* 7.13.1, 7.12.11, and 7.12.17, respectively (*PL* 82:293, 291, 291–292). For Agnes, cf. Augustine, *Sermo de sanctis* 273.6 ("Agnes Latine agnam significat; Graece, castam. Erat quod vocabatur: merito coronabatur," *PL* 38:1250). Jerome, *epistula* 130.5 (ad Demetriadem), "Agnes quae et aetatem vicit et tyrannum" (*PL* 22:1110), may seek to imply that *Agnet-* should be associated with *aetat-* (thus implying, like Richard, a youth who persists).

11. This is not the occasion to take up issues of provenance, but one should note that Eadburh provides the dedication for the Benedictine house at Pershore (Worcester), which had in the tenth century removed some of her relics from Winchester.

12. For description and discussion, see Stuart Gregory, "The Twelfth-Century Psalter Commentary in French Attributed to Simon of Tournai," *Romania* 100 (1979): 289–340, esp. 295–304, 328; for the only printed portions (exemplifying the quality of the commentary but none of the selections from materials copied here), see Charles J. Liebman, ed., *The Old French Psalter Commentary: Contribution to a Critical Study of the Text Attributed to Simon of Tournai* (Geneva, NY: W. F. Humphrey Press, 1982), 124–145.

13. This is not the first occasion on which I have addressed features like this. See, for example, Ralph Hanna, "Jolly Jankin Meets Aristotle," *Journal of the Early Book Society* 11 (2008): 223–229; Ralph Hanna, "Lambeth Palace Library, MS 260 and the Problem of English Vernacularity," *Studies in Medieval and Renaissance History* 3rd ser., 5 (2008): 131–199 (perhaps especially the trilingual bit of etymologizing discussed at 139–140); and Ralph Hanna, "Performing Exegesis: Lyric and Sermon in CUL, MS Gg.vi.26" (forthcoming).

Old Age and Economic Practices: Court of Chancery Cases Involving Richard Pynson, King's Printer

MERRIDEE L. BAILEY

Two Court of Chancery documents, both at the National Archives, re-count the commercial transactions of the London printer Richard Pynson during the final years of his life and add to our knowledge of Pynson's business affairs and finances. This article looks to supplement the important work of S. H. Johnston, who was the first to bring to light these two Chancery cases referring to Pynson's later years. Johnston suggests that these two documents hint at Pynson's senility and the increasingly important role of Pynson's daughter and her successive husbands. This article expands upon this analysis by exploring how the mix of family and business ties involving apprenticeships can be integrated into the study of old age and economic practices.[1]

The early sources for Pynson record him working in London as a glover in 1482, but by 1490 he was described as a bookseller and by 1496 as a printer. It is the latter for which Pynson is best known, and he became king's printer in 1506. From then until 1529, Pynson was responsible for printing numerous legal works, statutes, and proclamations.[2] The first of the two Early Chancery Proceedings in question, C1/680/45, is dated from the period 1529 to 1532, but given that it refers to Pynson as still being alive, it can be more precisely dated to the period between December 1529 and February 1530, when Pynson died. The second of the Early Chancery Proceedings, C1/649/32, is dated to the period immediately following Pynson's death.

On the surface, both Chancery cases deal with the contentious issue of debt. However, if one looks more closely, one sees that both shed light on

Pynson's final years and, poignantly, on his relationships with his daughter and former apprentices. These two court records show that age and feebleness, probably linked to dementia, were responsible for two apprentices independently claiming that Pynson had forgiven them their debts. It is valuable to find two bills in Chancery that address an almost identical issue but are presented by two different plaintiffs in independent lawsuits. In this way, they resemble the scarce bill-pairs that Timothy Haskett has uncovered in mid-fifteenth-century Chancery records. Haskett's examples include multiple bills on the same case or bills on the same matter drawn for two petitioners. The two cases concerning Pynson are slightly different as they concern nearly identical cases and arguments but do not refer to the same debt.[3]

Both cases extend our understanding of interactions between sixteenth-century printers and apprentices and of the nature of master-apprentice relationships in the years immediately following the completion of an apprentice's term in the Stationers' Company. The latter is especially valuable, since records for the Stationers' Company prior to 1557 are uncommon, particularly in relation to apprenticeship.[4] As master to apprentices, Pynson would necessarily have been a freeman member of the Stationers' Company, as London regulations forbade anyone other than a freeman from formally taking on apprentices.[5]

In each case the recipients of the loans allegedly pardoned by Pynson were initiating the actions in Chancery, and for reasons that are stated in the petitions: they had no written evidence of what they said Pynson had done, and therefore they were without a defense at common law if they were sued for the money. Henry Tabbe is named as the sole plaintiff in the suit in the earlier document, C1/680/45. He identifies himself as Richard Pynson's former apprentice and later as his servant. The petition deals with Tabbe's plea to the chancellor, at that time Sir Thomas More, over a debt Tabbe owed to Pynson. The original obligation is not disputed, and it is clear that Tabbe had entered into a bond of £20 with Pynson. However, Tabbe deposes that after he had repaid 53s 4d, Pynson had freely forgiven the remainder. Part of the substance of Tabbe's argument is that he had served Pynson well as his apprentice and later as his servant. Further, it appears that Pynson had received goods as the executor of Jane Crabbe (Tabbe), Henry Tabbe's aunt. Tabbe's connections to Pynson therefore comprised business and family ties. The sum of money loaned by Pynson was to ensure his former apprentice's future as a printer. This was written down, or perhaps phrased, by the clerk using the common expression "to sett the same Henry fourth so thatt he myght begynne the work and soe to gain competent levyng yn hys age." In the second document, C1/649/32, we see the same phrase used in relation to Thomas Kele, another of Pynson's former apprentices.

There were numerous reasons for masters to loan or even give money to their apprentices and journeymen to set them up in business, usually at the end of the apprentice's term.[6] Such loans or gifts may have been intended to secure the future of a trusted and well-beloved apprentice. They could also have been part of an economic strategy to retain apprentices, although small sums of money offered at the end of apprentice terms do not seem to have positively affected apprentice retention rates.[7] However, in both cases discussed below, the sums are substantial and indicate the reliance of these young men on previously established master-apprentice relationships as a crucial way of securing capital. Such connections between masters and apprentices were likely to be deeply rational in the sense of being economically motivated, although certainly the nature of emotional ties developing between apprentices and masters over the seven- to ten-year period of an apprenticeship should not be discounted. In addition, Pynson had acted as executor to Tabbe's aunt. This kind of interdependency of business and family ties appears frequently in London wills.

Perhaps the most significant insight these cases provide about Pynson's state before his death relates to his old age and how this could be brought into consideration in legal matters. In each case Pynson's age is recorded with a phrase, "consyderyng hys grett age & Impotence." The language used to characterize and describe old age in medieval England borrowed from classical authors such as Galen, who wrote of dementia in terms of the coldness and dryness of old age.[8] Medieval writers such as Bartholomew the Englishman drew on the writings of Aristotle to describe the ages of man, suggesting that old age began between the years of forty-five to fifty, after which followed dotage.[9] Pynson's birth around 1449 means he would have been around eighty years of age at his death, considerably past Bartholomew's notion of old age (forty-five to fifty), Isidore of Seville's notion of fifty as the turning point, and Augustine's limit, which was set at sixty.[10] Although there was no clear consensus in medieval writings on when life stages began or ended, certain ideas about old age were usually expressed. One of these was that the elderly returned to a state of childishness in which a loss of control, poor judgment, and lack of intelligence became the dominant characteristics of the aged individual.[11]

We can gain insight in connections between old age and its undesirable characteristics in the additional details cited in Tabbe's case. Here, the bill refers to forgetfulness and feebleness: "the same Rychard is very agyd and feble and also as nowe nott perfitt of remembrauns & so nott able yn the lacke to make aquitance or releas." Forgetfulness and feebleness were two commonly named signs of old age in medieval medical and religious texts. Vincent de Beauvais, for example, referred to four characteristics of age-related mental decline: lack of energy, forgetfulness, gullibility, and foolishness.[12] Pynson's age and feebleness are unambiguously connected to his imperfect memory. The weight placed on memory is significant because of the legal ramifications it had for Pynson being unable "yn the lacke [of memory]" to forgive the debt. Tabbe is also unable to call on the witnesses to the earlier acquittal as they were equally old and unreliable in court: "& also Suche wytnes as then was ther present be yn leke case agyd." If his associates were men of contemporary age, it is likely that Pynson's business networks were largely dormant by this stage.

One question scholars have raised is why Pynson's output declined so much in his later life, with only three books printed in his workshop between 1528 and his death in 1529 or 1530.[13] As Johnston hints, the apparent decline in both Pynson's physical and his mental condition described in these documents explains why this occurred. It may also explain why Tabbe and Kele pursued funds to establish themselves in independent business instead of remaining in a workshop that was in decline.

C1/649/32 reinforces the apparently significant deterioration in Pynson's faculties. According to the initial bill, Thomas Kele had previously been lent £24. There is some uncertainty about whether Kele repaid any of this debt, for the Chancery official crossed out a reference to Kele repaying money that had been noted in his "bok of Rekenyng." As with Tabbe, Kele deposed that Pynson forgave the debt before his death. Again, Pynson's age is a significant factor in the case, although Kele is more circumspect in describing Pynson's mental condition, merely commenting once on Pynson's "grett age & Impotence," perhaps because by the time Kele brought the case to Chancery, Pynson had already died.

These two documents allow us to flesh out Pynson's final years. He appears to have been an elderly man who had begun losing his mental faculties. His memory was commented upon, "nowe nott perfitt of remembrauns," and given legal weight via the pragmatic acknowledgment that he could no longer, by law, make acquittance of his previous declaration. The same reason was also given in C1/680/45 to explain why the testimony of the witnesses was invalid. We can also note that in both C1/680/45 and C1/649/32, Tabbe and Kele comment that Pynson had lost the original obligation. Nevertheless, Pynson had ongoing, although increasingly ineffectual, interactions with his former apprentices, Tabbe and Kele, up to the moment of his death and he still figures as an important figure in their lives due to his past status as master and benefactor. The ongoing nature of these legal proceedings reinforced these connections.

The chancellor may have taken both cases at face value. Pynson may have forgiven the debts of both Tabbe and Kele, with his old age genuinely preventing either of his former apprentices from relying on his verbal promises. It is also possible that both plaintiffs were deliberately misleading the court, meaning Tabbe and Kele's ongoing relationship with Pynson was exploitative, with both abusing the culturally and medically popular trope that senility was a trait of old age. A commonly cited characteristic of old age referred to in medieval documents was gullibility. If Pynson had been suffering from dementia, his two former apprentices may have been playing on an aged man's gullibility. They may even have been drawing on the strong cultural assumptions about old age and feebleness shrewdly to press their claims at this time. Recent study of old age in the medieval period shows that in many ways the connection between old age, helplessness, and senility blinds us to the wider views held. For instance, old age could be depicted as a time of wisdom and experience. The depiction of Pynson's old age in these two Chancery cases accords with the more negative view of mental decline and decay.[14]

Pynson's relationships with others, namely his daughter and executor, Margaret, and her husband, John Hawkyns, appear to be significant in these years. After Pynson's death in 1529 or 1530, Hawkyns finished printing Pynson's *Lesclarcissement de la langue francoyse compose par maistre Iehan Palsgraue Angloyse natyf de Londres, et gradue de Paris* (July 1530).[15] Duff suggests that Hawkyns would have been Pynson's assistant at the time of his death.[16] Hawkyns's marriage to Margaret may thus be explained. Hawkyns's marriage may also be the cause of the imprint appearing under their joint names. No other books appear to have been printed by Hawkyns, and nothing else is known of him.

The glimpse into the relationship between Pynson and two of his former apprentices also makes us rethink Pynson's will, dated November 18, 1529, and probated February 23, 1530. Pynson specifically named his two apprentices, John Snowe and Richard Withers, bequeathing 6s 8d to the former and 40s to the latter upon the completion of their apprenticeships.[17] No other apprentices, former or current, are named, and there is no mention of the recovery of any outstanding debts. Of Pynson's two former apprentices, Tabbe and Kele, we know some further details. Henry Tabbe was a member of the Stationers' Company, and his will, dated March 1, 1549, shows he was moderately successful, leaving £10 to his daughter, Johan Goodman, £20 to his granddaughter, Mary Goodman, and a further £10 to Johan's unborn child. The remainder of his estate was left to his executor John Goodman, his son-in-law. Thomas Kele remained a stationer, and there is a brief record of him renting part of a shop next to St. Paul's gate in about 1526 from printer John Rastell, who sublet parts of these premises to various small printers. Richard Kele, printer, and John Kele, stationer, were probably Thomas's sons.[18] These two Chancery documents connect two former apprentices to Pynson's ongoing business affairs and present a complex and nuanced picture of his final years. C1/680/45 and C1/649/32 offer revealing and poignant glimpses into the life and death of one of England's earliest printers.

The Two Chancery Cases

Both documents are laid out in the fashion typical to Chancery documents. Each of the cases concerning Pynson is addressed to the chancellor, Sir Thomas More, with the text written in a single block.[19] Each document is written in a clear, upright, Chancery hand and was adjudicated by John Skewys. Richard is written as both Richard and Richerd. In C1/649/32 the scribe frequently, but not always, abbreviates Richard to Rich. In places the text has been corrected by adding further information. All corrections and other additions to the text are enclosed in square brackets. Deletions are explained in notes and contractions have been expanded.

C1/680/45
To the Ryght Worshypfull Sir Thomas More
knyght lorde Chaunslere of yngland

Shewyth and complayneth vnto your good lordshypp your dayly orator Henry Tabbe. that wher as your seyd orator was prentys and aft seruant wyth Rycherd pinson of London prenter by the space of viij yere and afterwardes the seyd Rychard to thentent to sett the same Henry fourth so thatt he myght begynne the work and soe to gain competent levyng yn hys age. delyvred vnto the same Henry a stoke of xxiiii li for repayment therof the same Henry was bounden by hys sede oblygacon vnto the seyd Rych in the some of xx ^{li} payable at certayn dayes..............nowe past/ wherof your seyd orator hath repayed liij s iiii d/ so yt was good lorde that the [^{seyd}] Rych aboute the fest of all saynts last past consyderyng hys grett age & Impotence. & the good and trew longe seruice that your seyd orator had done onto hym. & pretendyng to doe good dedes of charyte in hys lyf & consyderyng also the substance in the goodes that the same Rychard had by Jane Crabbe Aunt vnto yor seyd orator by reason that the same Rych was hyr executor/[20] the same Rych of hys owne goodnes in presens of diuers honest men frely for gave vnto your seyd orator the seyd obligacion and all the dette in the same contaynyd and wold haue them delyvryd vnto your seyd orator the seyd obligacion yf he coud have founden it/ And by cause that the same Rychard is very agyd and feble and also as nowe nott perfitt of remembrauns & so nott able yn the lacke to make aquitance or releas/ & also Suche wytnes as then was ther present be yn leke case agyd/ And weder the seyd oblygacon may be fond in the seyd Rycherd is lyf or not it is adoute And yf the seyd wytnes shuld deces byfore the seyd Rychard & the seyd oblygacon shuld come to hys executors handes your seyd orator shuld be dryvyn to paye the seyd dette contrary to the mynde of the seyd Rychard, and against all good concyense In consyderacion whereof that it may please your seyd lordshype thatt all suche wytnes as your seyd orator shall here after bryng vnto this court uppon the premisses may be ther sworne and examynyd *ad perpetuam rei memoriam* And thys for the loue of god and in the waye of Charyte.

———Johis Skewys[21]

C1/649/32
To the ryght honorable sir Thomas more
kynght Lord chaunsler of ynglond

Showyth and complayneth vnto your good lordshype your dayly orator Thomas Kele of London stacioner that wher as your seyd orator was prentes & afterwardes servant with Rych pynson of London prenter by the space of viii yeres/ And afterwarde the seyd Rych to thentent to sett the same your orator fourth soe that he might begynne the worke & soe to have a compe-tente levynge in hys age delyured vnto the same your orator a stoke of xxiiij [li] for repayment[22] wherof the same your orator was bounden by hys dede obligatocon vnto the seyd Rych in the some of xxiiij [li] payable att curtayn dayes [23] Soo it is good hinde that the seyd Rych pynson consyderlng hys great age & ympotence & the good & trewe longe seruys that your seyd orator hath done vnto hym & intendyng to doe goode dedes of charyte in hys lyf thesame Rich of hys owne goodnes yn presens of dyues honest persons frely forgave vnto your seyd orator the seyd obligation & all the dette in thesame contaynyd & wold then & ther have delyvyred the same oblygacon vnto your seyd orator yf he coude [then] have found the same/ which Rich afterwardes made one Margarett[24] hys daughter hys sole execu-trix [& dyed]/ syth when the same Margarett hath takyn to husbond one John Hawkyns whych John Hawkys [and Margarett] sith the deyth of the seyd Rych pynson your seyd orator hath many & dyues tymes requyryd delyuas of the seyd obligacon whych to delyre thesame John & Margett hys wyf have att alle tymes refusyd & yette refusyth thretenyng to sewe your seyd orator uppon the seyd oblygacon contrary to all ryght & good concyence & con-trary to the mynde of the seyd Rych pynson/ And bycause that your seyd orator hath noe specyalce prouyng the seyd remyssyon & forgauyng of the seyd dette but only the bare worde of the seyd Rych pynson he is wyttout remedy by the courts of the comon lawe/ In concsyderacon whereof please it [your] good lordshype to graunt a wryt of suppena to be durectyd to the seyd John [and Margarett] comaundyng them [by the same] to apper byfore the kyng yn hys channcery att a certayn daye & uppon a certayn payn by your seyd lordshype to be lymittyd ther to answer to the premysses & on that to abyd & obey all such dyrecyons & Juggementes as shalbe thought by your seyd lordshyppe most resonable yn the premysse & thys for the loue of god & yn the waye of Charite

———Johis Skewys

University of Adelaide

NOTES

1. Transcripts of these two cases appear in S. H. Johnston, "A Study of the Career and Literary Publications of Richard Pynson" (PhD diss., University of Western Ontario, 1977), 530–531. My transcript differs slightly from Johnston's. He has transcribed the final line of each case with "in the name of Christ," whereas Chancery cases from this period conclude with "in the waye of Charyte." Johnston transcribed "Jane Crabbe" as "Tabbe," whereas the National Archives catalogue and my own close study show that the scribe wrote "Crabbe." I include a footnote that puts "Tabbe" in parentheses, as it is likely the scribe made an error here.

2. Pamela Neville-Sington, "Pynson, Richard (c. 1449–1529/30)," *Oxford Dictionary of National Biography* (Oxford: Oxford University Press, 2004).

3. T. S. Haskett, "The Presentation of Cases in Medieval Chancery Bills," in *Legal History in the Making: Proceedings of the Ninth British Legal History Conference*, ed. W. M. Gordon, et al. (London: Hambledon, 1991), 11–28.

4. This was not the case in the seventeenth century. See D. F. McKenzie, *Stationers' Company Apprentices 1605–1640* (Charlottesville: Bibliographical Society of the University of Virginia, 1962).

5. Peter W. M. Blayney, *The Stationers' Company before the Charter, 1403–1557* (London: Worshipful Company of Stationers, 2003), 23–24.

6. Farley Grubb, "The Statutory Regulation of Colonial Servitude: An Incomplete-Contract Approach," *Explorations in Economic History* 37 (2000): 42–75. Steve Rappaport, "Reconsidering Apprenticeship in Sixteenth-Century London," in *Renaissance Society and Culture, Essays in Honor of Eugene F. Rice, Jr.*, ed. John Monfasani, et al. (New York: Italica, 1991), 239–261, 251.

7. Patrick Wallis, "Apprenticeship and Training in Premodern England," *Journal of Economic History* 68 (2008): 832–861.

8. Karen Cokayne, *Experiencing Old Age in Ancient Rome* (London: Routledge, 2003), 70.

9. Joel T. Rosenthal, *Old Age in Late Medieval England* (Philadelphia: University of Pennsylvania Press, 1996), 97–98.

10. Ibid., 98.

11. Shulamith Shahar, *Growing Old in the Middle Ages: "Winter Clothes Us in Shadow and Pain,"* trans. Yael Lotan (London: Routledge, 1997), 4.

12. Ibid., 56.

13. E. Gordon Duff, *The Printers, Stationers and Bookbinders of Westminster and London from 1476–1535* (New York: B. Blom, 1971), 165.

14. Albrecht Classen, ed., *Old Age in the Middle Ages and the Renaissance: Interdisciplinary Approaches to a Neglected Topic* (Berlin: Walter de Gruyter, 2007).

15. The colophon reads "The imprintyng [by Richard Pynson, ca. 1524] fynysshed by Iohan Haukyns the. xviii. daye of July."

16. E. Gordon Duff, *A Century of the English Book Trade: Short Notices of All Printers, Stationers, Bookbinders, and Others Connected with It from the Issue of the First Dated Book in 1457 to the Incorporation of the Company of Stationers in 1557* (London: Bibliographical Society, 1905), 69.

17. National Archives, Kew, PROB11/23 sig. 15.

18. Duff, *Century*, 83–84, 129.

19. Haskett, "Presentation of Cases," 12.

20. Jane Crabbe (Tabbe) must have made a will, as Pynson is identified as her executor. However, no will for either Jane Crabbe or Tabbe appears in the Prerogative Court of Canterbury, the Court of Hustings, or the London Consistory Court. The scribe has presumably misspelled the surname of Tabbe in this document.

21. John Skewys (d. 1544) made a career at law and, after Cardinal Wolsey's fall from grace in 1529, adjudicated all cases in Chancery. Peter Sherlock, "'Skewys, John (d. 1544),'" *Oxford Dictionary of National Biography* (Oxford: Oxford University Press, 2004).

22. xx^{li} has been crossed out.

23. Accompanied by crossing out, "nowe past/ Wherof your seyd orator hath repayd to the seyd Rych...as aperyth by hys owne bok of Rekenyng."

24. Margaret was Pynson's only living child. She had been married to William Campion, by whom she had two daughters, Amye and Joane. Duff suggests Campion was probably William Campion, stationer. Margaret later married Steven Warde, also deceased, with whom she appears to have had no children. She subsequently married John Hawkyns after Pynson's will had been made on November 17, 1529. On Campion, see Duff, *Century*, 127.

Early Printed Chaucer Editions in the Harry Ransom Center's George A. Aitken Collection

HOPE JOHNSTON

The Harry Ransom Center at the University of Texas in Austin is well known for its fine collection of manuscripts and rare books, but perhaps less well known is that it has one of the largest collections of early printed Chaucer editions in the world. Its complement of thirty-six volumes plus a Caxton fragment is remarkable by any standard; keeping in mind that fewer than five hundred copies of Chaucer survive based on English Short Title Catalogue records, it is perhaps even more remarkable that at least seventeen of them come from the library of one collector, George A. Aitken (1860–1917).[1] His collection of books is decidedly eclectic, ranging from copies still bound in sixteenth-century blind-tooled calf over oak boards to more than a few soiled, mismatched, and badly deteriorated copies that have seen better days. What follows is a brief introduction to this little-known collector who gathered multiple copies of each edition of Chaucer's *Works* printed between 1532 and 1602.

George Atherton Aitken was born in Barkingside, Essex, on March 19, 1860, to John and Mary Ann Aitken (née Salmon). After studying English at University College London, he entered the English civil service in 1883 with the Secretary's Office of the General Post Office.[2] Reforms of the postal system included the provision of a private library and reading room for its employees to encourage intellectual development, and Aitken lived up to the reformers' expectations: in 1889, he published *The Life of Richard Steele*, a two-volume biography, and he continued pursuing his interest in eighteenth-century English literature after transferring to the Home Office in 1892, publishing *The Life and Works of John Arbuthnot* in the same year.[3] Aitken also edited works by Andrew Marvell (1892, 1898), Robert Burns (1893), Thomas Parnell (1894), Daniel Defoe (1895, 1898), Richard Sheridan (1897, 1911), Jonathan Swift (1901), and multivolume editions of Joseph Addison and Richard Steele's *Spectator* (1898) and *Tatler* (1898–1899). In addition to these efforts, he published criticism on Matthew Prior (1897) and Alexander Pope (1914), and contributed numerous entries to the *Dictionary of National Biography*.

While Aitken had an avid interest in literary biographies, his own life remains relatively obscure. He was an only child and had no children of his own, but he dedicated a substantial part of his career to improvement of child welfare. This might in part be a reflection of his experience growing up in a reformatory. Census records indicate that by 1871, when he was eleven, his mother was a widow who earned their keep as matron of the Hull, East Riding, and North Lincolnshire Female Penitentiary, established in 1811 "for the reclamation of fallen women," with a jail, a convent, a workhouse, and an insane asylum located in the same vicinity,[4] Aitken's career in civil service appears to follow naturally from his childhood exposure to Victorian reform efforts. He became the secretary of the Reformatory and Industrial Schools Departmental Committee at the Home Office in 1895 and of the Inebriate Reformatories Committee in 1898.[5]

On April 18, 1903, when he was forty-three, Aitken married Emma Cawthorne, former headmistress of Coborn School, who was forty-five at the time.[6] He played a key role in assisting Home Office Secretary Herbert Samuel in the passing of the Children Act of 1908, which consolidated and simplified existing legislation on child welfare and, most significantly, created a separate juvenile justice system.[7] Aitken received a series of promotions, rising to the rank of assistant secretary, and he became head of the Children's Department at the Home Office when the division was created in 1913.[8] For his efforts, he was honored as a Member of the Royal Victorian Order (MVO) in 1911 and as a Companion of the Order of Bath (CB) in 1917.[9] He died unexpectedly on November 16, 1917, when he was fifty-seven.

Aitken left a record of notable achievements in his civil service career and literary pursuits despite his premature death; likewise, as a book collector, his scholarly dedication earned the respect of his peers. The *Publishers' Circular* reports that at a dinner celebrating the centenary of the bookseller Hodgson & Co. in 1907, Aitken raised a toast, saying that "he supposed there were collectors who bought rare books merely because it was the fashion, but it was not true, on the whole, that collectors were not real book lovers."[10]

On the other side of the Atlantic, Chicago banker John H. Wrenn was actively collecting books during the same period, and at the time of Aitken's death, Wrenn's son, Harold Wrenn, was in the process of selling his father's library of 5,300 items to the University of Texas. The sale fetched $225,000, with the funds supplied by Major George W. Littlefield, a significant benefactor of the university and member of the board of regents. Meanwhile, Harold Wrenn acquired Aitken's library of some five thousand items for $20,000, paid to Aitken's widow before the collection went to auction.[11] The love of a good deal might have been a stronger motive in this case than the love of books. Carl L. Cannon recounts how the topic of Aitken's library came up in a discussion between Harold Wrenn and Dr. Reginald Griffith, the English faculty member who initiated the acquisition of the Wrenn library:

> [O]n a visit to Austin, [Wrenn] confided to Dr. Griffith that he had bought the Aitken books at a bargain, expecting to sell them at a profit. Dr. Griffith replied that he should, rather, give them to the University as a supplement to his father's collection, but Wrenn rejoined that while he could not do that he would let the Aitken books go at the price he paid for them plus transportation and storage. The offer was generous enough, but the university had no funds for the purchase.[12]

With this goal in sight, the curator of the nascent rare books collection, Fannie Ratchford, worked to secure a $10,000 appropriation from the Texas state budget for the purchase, which the Board of Regents matched with another $10,000. Wrenn held true to his word, selling the Aitken library to the University of Texas in 1921 for the same price he had paid for it.[13] Four years later, Miriam Lutcher Stark donated another significant private collection to the university, and the combination of the Wrenn, Aitken, and Stark libraries provided a strong core for the rare books collection, which in the late 1950s evolved into the Humanities Research Center under the guidance of Harry Ransom.

If one wished for proof of Aitken's claim at Hodgson's centenary that book collectors are emotionally invested in their pursuit of rare editions, the outcry in the wake of the Thomas J. Wise scandal demonstrates just how high passions could run. John Carter and Graham Pollard revealed in 1934 how the rare book dealer Wise had snookered wealthy collectors with forgeries and corrupted books; more damning information came to light between 1959 and 1961, when David Foxon and William B. Todd discovered that Wise had stolen leaves from copies at the British Museum to complete imperfect copies in his possession and fetch a higher sale price for them.[14] Carter expresses his feelings about the duplicity in no uncertain terms: "in bibliography, as in any science, the one ultimate necessity is a genuine desire for the truth at all costs," he writes, and "that Wise should have prostituted bibliography to his own profit was a disgraceful thing."[15] A similar vehemence simmers in a chapter on the early history of the University of Texas rare books collection by John B. Thomas, III. He reports that "the Aitken and Wrenn collections proved to have more than a hundred of [Wise's] corrupted copies, which suffered a much diminished value for research. Many public and private libraries on both sides of the Atlantic were similarly infected with these tarted-up books."[16] Evidently it proved to be too complex a task to reunite Wise's stolen leaves with their original codices, but one could argue that the affected copies are not entirely bankrupted of research value. Indeed, the Thomas Wise affair has become an area of research interest in its own right.[17]

The Aitken library arrived at the University of Texas without a comprehensive catalogue, though Aitken did maintain files of typed records on his books of varying length and detail. The University of Texas sought assistance in creating thousands of entries for the Aitken library in the university's card catalogue through the U.S. government's Federal Emergency Relief Administration (FERA) program, which was intended to create employment opportunities during the Great Depression. The two-year Aitken project began in 1934 with one full-time and four part-time typists working under Ratchford's supervision. She reports that "[b]y actual count on 22 Feb. 1935 over 4,200 volumes are completed and on the shelves, with cards filed" and adds that if the university wished to extend the scope of the project to include an official catalogue of the Aitken collection, additional resources would be necessary: "I think we can provide a good part-time typist (FERA) through May to work on it, but another typewriter will have to be provided . . .After May, when the FERA closes, other means for carrying on must be worked out."[18] The effort concluded without pursuing the production of a published catalogue.

The original parameters of Aitken's collection were already changing by the time of the card catalogue initiative. Materials continued to be added to the collection bearing his name, growing from five thousand items to more than eight thousand by 1934.[19] Writing in 1941, Cannon raises the estimate to ten thousand volumes, explaining that, "[t]he Aitken collection forms the basis of a growing rare book collection, since the Wrenn library cannot be increased, and the Stark collection is open only to additions from the collector's son."[20] Twenty copies of Chaucer editions printed before 1700 contain a standard bookplate reading "Library of the University of Texas George A. Aitken Collection," but some uncertainty exists as to whether they were accumulated during or after Aitken's lifetime due to the practice of adding new acquisitions to the Aitken collection and the incomplete nature of Aitken's typed notes at the time of his death.[21]

However, Aitken clearly had a lively interest in early printed Chaucer editions, even though this was not his chief area of literary study. H. F. B. Wheeler reports in a note published in 1909 that "Mr. Aitken's library contains many editions of *The Works of Chaucer*, including the undated issue *circa* 1550, and those of 1561 and 1598."[22] Aitken continued to collect copies after 1909, and in a 1974 reprint of Wheeler's piece it in the *Library Chronicle*, Todd adds a footnote:

> Of this author, quite beyond his normal scholarly pursuits, Aitken had many important exemplars, e.g. a fragmentary copy of 1525, three specimens each of 1532, 1542, 1545 (in text cited as *circa* 1550), five of 1561, and two of 1598. To support this grand array of printed editions the University has since added one other significant text, the Brudenell-Cardigan manuscript of the *Canterbury Tales* [*ca.* 1450].[23]

Todd's note identifies seventeen copies as being from Aitken's original library. The typed inventory sheets that came with the library are not entirely reliable, but they do list two entries for books printed in 1602 that are not mentioned by Todd. Cannon makes reference to Aitken's "run of printed Chaucers from 1532–1602, all notable copies," though he goes on to say that "[t]he condition of the Aitken books is in general not so good as the Stark and Wrenn, for they were gathered by a scholar with limited means."[24]

The fashion for "clean" books, with marginalia assiduously washed away, is not what it was at the beginning of the twentieth century. Indeed, the messiness of Aitken's collection is a large part of its attraction from a bibliographic perspective because he did not automatically discard heavily used quires as irredeemable. Scholars turn with interest to marked-up books as a potential source of evidence regarding patterns of ownership in the secondhand book trade, the reception of specific authors over time, and the history of reading.

One unprepossessing copy of the 1542 edition contains copious sixteenth-century annotations that signpost names and themes, as one would expect. In addition, evidence of rereading in the layering of writing by the same hand in different shades of ink provides a striking example of how the process of copying can be a means of processing information. The cumulative result is that individual passages no longer stand out at a glance, in rather the same way that an overly highlighted modern book ceases to highlight specific points effectively. A later owner of the 1542 edition, James Danis, adds a few more annotations in a tidy hand and gives the date 1604 beside his name.[25] At least two more early hands make contributions, including a partially cropped passage in French at one point in Chaucer's translation of *Le roman de la rose*, and "Lassemble de dames" above the running title of "The assemble of ladyes."[26] This unprepossessing copy of the 1542 edition provides multiple points of interest for the modern bibliographer, and it is not the only one: Aitken's library is an Aladdin's cave of annotated wares, offering caustic polemical commentary by a seventeenth-century Protestant, a medicinal recipe, and inscriptions witnessing to an early female audience for Chaucer's writing.[27] They also provide moments of levity in a careful thank-you note or a doodled elephant.[28]

It would be a mistake to conclude that Aitken swept up unwanted copies at a moment's whim. The typed sheets in the Aitken collection file that accompanied his books and notes in the books themselves indicate that he invested methodical research into the tracking of Chaucer editions. For example, a tipped-in note details his investigations into the known copies of the 1532 edition:

> The copy in the Ashburnham Library (1897), with title and 3 end leaves in laid, sold for £45; another copy, wanting first 4 and last 4 leaves, for £18; and a third copy, wanting first and last leaves, 4, for £19.10/–. All were in modern binding.
>
> A copy in the Hoe Library (1912) in modern binding, sold for $565. It measured 12½ x 8½ inches; the last two leaves had been in laid.
>
> There was no copy in the Huth Library; and there seem to be none in Trinity College, Dublin, Advocates, Guildhall or Ryland Libraries. The B.M. has two copies, one complete (Grenville Library), the other with the first four leaves in facsimile. There is a copy at the Bodleian (Douce Collection).
>
> A copy (half morocco) sold for £50 at Sotheby's in 1891; another (title in laid) for £45 in 1888. A copy (morocco) with title and 5 other leaves in facsimile sold for £21.10/–. The Amherst copy (wanting title and 5 other leaves; wormed stained, +c; old oak boards, no back) fetched £30 in 1908.

Aitken could therefore congratulate himself on a good bargain when he purchased an imperfect copy in blind-tooled brown calf over oak boards for £16 and ten shillings during the auction of George Dunn's library in 1913. Its price and binding seem to have been of key interest to him. Some of the embedded hardware remains, though the clasps are gone, and four of six leather thongs remain intact. A reinforcing strip of manuscript can be seen near the spine of the rear board, and the paper pastedowns are covered in sixteenth-century writing, partly obscured where the edge of the binding leather has been affixed to the front and rear boards. Aitken also purchased a copy of the edition of around 1550 in an early blind-tooled binding, though it had been mended and rebacked by a subsequent owner.[29] Other fairly plain but serviceable contemporary bindings remain intact, with fillets in blind or in gilt, perhaps with a center ornament or fleurons in the corners, and several have decorated edges. One also finds modern craft bindings by Sangorski and Sutcliffe or Riviere. In any event, while Dunn's 1532 copy is special in part because of its binding, it seems safe to say that Aitken generally cared more about the book than its display value. His professional success would mean that he had moderately more than modest means, but if he had to choose between rebinding a shabby volume or acquiring a new find, his unusually large collection of Chaucer editions seems to answer that question in favor of the find.

Aitken's library includes more than one association copy. He writes the following in his notes about a copy of the 1602 edition:

> Inscriptions on the fly-leaves show that this fine copy belonged to Sir Robert Dudley (1574–1649) Duke of Northumberland and Earl of Warwick in the Holy Roman Empire, who was the son of Robert Dudley, Earl of Leicester. At his death in Florence in 1649 the book was bought by Mr. J. Abdy, ancestor of the late Judge Abdy. Contemporary sheepskin.

This is certainly the version of history that Sir Robert Dudley would endorse, but Simon Adams writes in his *Oxford Dictionary of National Biography* entry that questions about Dudley's paternity became a defining aspect of his life.[30] He established a name for himself as a sixteenth-century explorer, but at home in England, he was unsuccessful in his legal bid to be recognized as the legitimate son of Robert Dudley, earl of Leicester. Adams remarks that "he destroyed the sympathy he had previously enjoyed" as the claimant to the Dudley legacy when he abandoned his wife Alice and their daughters in 1605 to live in Florence with Elizabeth Southwell, with whom he had twelve children. He proved valuable to the Spanish court because of his naval expertise and styled himself as the earl of Warwick and Leicester; after 1620, he also claimed the title of duke of Northumberland.[31] The Italian agent who handled the sale of Dudley's Chaucer must have hoped to capitalize upon this connection: an inscription on the first front flyleaf reads "Il Duca di Northumbria Inglese di Poesia an lingua Inglese." Aitken seems quite as happy to note its association with "Judge Abdy," referring to John Thomas Abdy (1822–1899), Regius Professor of Civil Law at Cambridge University from 1854 to 1873.[32] The book contains few marginalia, but Dudley's colorful life lends the book a noteworthy provenance.

The jewel of Aitken's collection is an association copy of John Stow's 1561 edition purported to have belonged to Stow himself and afterward to members of Matthew Parker's circle; a note by Joseph A. Dane and Alexandra Gillespie explains its history.[33] Aitken himself was skeptical about the authenticity of this attribution, inscribed by a former owner of the book

on a front flyleaf, but he concedes that "it is pleasing to think that this may
have been the editor's own copy. This theory receives some support from
the initials I. S. and from the fact that the copy belongs to an early issue."[34]
The main focus of his note concerns the variants found in copies of the 1561
edition due to its publishing history, which he reprises briefly in his own file
on the Stow Chaucer:

> Copies of the 1561 Chaucer are found with two en-
> tirely different title-pages, one with Chaucer's arms in the
> centre, the other with a picture of a King in council at the
> top. Copies differ also as regards the Prologue, some having
> wood cuts of the characters and others not. These wood-
> cuts had been used in Pynson's edition of the Canterbury
> Tales, 1526; by 1561 several of the blocks seem to have been
> lost (e.g. the Wife of Bath is represented by the picture of
> the Prioress); for this reason and because the blocks were
> worn and out of date, it was evidently decided, after a few
> copies of the leaves had been struck off, to dispense with
> the illustrations. The saving of space caused the number
> of introductory leaves to be reduced from fourteen to ten.
> This is the only recorded copy in which the Prologue with
> illustrations is found with the Title bearing Chaucers Arms.
>   On the back of the title in an Elizabethan hand is a pas-
> sage from the peroration to the Parsons Tale which does not
> appear in the printed text, and on the last leaf, is a note re-
> specting Chaucer's Monument. The initials I. S. are stamped
> on the sides, and it may be (as a former owner thought) that
> this copy belonged to John Stow, the editor of the book.
>   For notice of this book, see *Athenaeum* Ap. 7. 1906.
>   Calf, part of original binding inlaid. Some edges uncut.

Aitken continues to posit at greater length what combinations might
result from these variants:

> If the title with Chaucer's arms is called A, the title with the
> king in Council B, the introductory leaves with the woodcuts
> C, and the leaves without them D, the combinations usually
> found are A+D (by far the commonest) and B+C; these are
> the forms described in the 1893 catalogue of the Grolier Club.

However, he reports, other combinations could and do exist, "which,
from their condition, have clearly not been 'made up.'" He refers to an ex-

ample of B plus D in Robert Hoe's library and then concludes that "the copy now before me [the Stow Chaucer] is the only example I can trace with the title with Chaucer's arms and the 'Prologue' with the woodcuts (i.e., A+C)."

His excitement as a collector and lover of books rises from the copy's printing history rather than its possible status as an association copy. Such attentiveness to variants in Chaucer's black-letter editions indicates that his interest in collecting early printed editions involved much more than the ebb and flow of chance. His pursuit of specific editions—and variant states of the same edition—shows an intentionality informed by scholarly study. Aitken, it would seem, approached his hunt for Chaucer editions avidly and personally, ferreting out items from libraries much more modest than Hoe's, including those of James Bromley (1839–1925), George Dunn (1864–1912), Percy Hetherington Fitzgerald (1834–1925), and William Harcourt Hooper (1834–1912). The edition formerly owned by this last collector might be considered an association copy of sorts, too, since Hooper, an engraver, worked on the Kelmscott Chaucer.

But are the seventeen-plus copies in the Aitken library all "real" copies of Chaucer's writing, or are some simply "tarted-up books" of dubious authenticity? Ratchford's publications on the Wise issue point out that the majority of the holdings in the Wrenn and Aitken collections are authentic and valuable. She particularly defends Aitken, writing that he "was a far better scholar and more astute bibliographer than Wise," and states that "[t]he most careful examination of available records fails to find even a scrap of evidence involving him in the fraud."[35] Maybe, as she suggests, he was deliberately kept in the dark or knew better than to get involved, but Aitken certainly did not hesitate to tear apart his honestly acquired copies. Wise reports in a letter dated November 28, 1909, that he had recently sold numerous plays to Aitken, adding that "poor though their condition is. . .he is always open to buy such copies, for he has time to hunt them up; and then he breaks them up, and out of two or three bad copies makes up one good one."[36]

This comment is in retrospect perhaps a little ironic coming from Wise, considering his recourse to theft as a means of completing imperfect copies. Yet the practice of supplying the leaves wanting in a particular copy is not of itself unusual for the period. The Morgan catalogue record for a copy of Caxton's second edition (ca. 1483) notes with respect to its provenance that it was given in 1838 by "Lord Fitzwilliam to the Earl of Ashburnham, who improved it from three other copies."[37] The Huntington Library reports, tersely, that a number of its early printed Chaucers are "made-up copies." Aitken similarly endeavored to "improve" certain copies at the expense of others in accordance with practices of the time, though he did not summarily discard the remnants: he writes, for example, on the verso of a detached front board that "the three leaves wanting in my other copy was taken from this copy."[38] However, he does not appear to have kept meticulous notes about every book with foreign leaves the addition of which might predate his acquisition. An "individual" copy, as it stands now, might well be a hybrid of two or more volumes.

Quantity of volumes provides one way of measuring the significance of the Harry Ransom Center's collection of early printed Chaucer editions, but the even more important factor in terms of research value is the individual histories of books that have largely been spared by the fashion for sanitized books at the beginning of the early twentieth century. The "poor condition" of the copies George A. Aitken acquired makes them a fascinating resource, and a recataloguing initiative (no typewriters required) will greatly improve the usefulness of the Aitken library for future research. While wealthy collectors sought one fine copy of each edition for their extensive libraries, Aitken scoured the catalogues persistently; it is pleasing to think that someone who worked in the civil service on behalf of overlooked members of society also looked out for Chaucer editions that others might have missed. By seeking out original bindings and examples of printers' variants, he demonstrated a love not only of books but of book history.

University of Texas Harry Ransom Center Early Printed Chaucer Editions

Year	Collection	*Short Title Catalogue*, rev. ed.	Current Shelfmark
ca. 1477	Incunable	STC 5082 (Caxton)	Incun 1478 C393c
1526	Aitken	STC 5086 (Pynson)	PR 1865 1526
1532	Stark	STC 5068 (Godfray)	PR 1850 1532 cop. 1
1532	Aitken	STC 5068 (Godfray)	PR 1850 1532 cop. 2
1532	Aitken	STC 5068 (Godfray)	PR 1850 1532 cop. 3
1532	Aitken	STC 5068 (Godfray)	PR 1850 1532 cop. 4
1532	Pforzheimer	STC 5068 (Godfray)	PFORZ 173
1542	Aitken	STC 5070 (Grafton for Reynes)	Ad C393+C542a cop. 1
1542	Aitken	[acephalous]	Ad C393+C542a cop. 2
1542	Aitken	[acephalous]	Ad C393+C542a cop. 3
ca. 1550	Stark	STC 5072 (Hill for Kele)	STARK+6453
ca. 1550	Aitken	STC 5071 (Hill for Bonham)	Ad C393+C545t cop. 1
ca. 1550	Aitken	STC 5071 (Hill for Bonham)	Ad C393+C545t cop. 2
ca. 1550	Aitken	STC 5073 (Hill for Petit)	Ad C393+C545taa
ca. 1550	Pforzheimer	STC 5073 (Hill for Petit)	PFORZ 174

ca. 1550	Pforzheimer	STC 5074 (Hill for Toye)	PFORZ 175
ca. 1550	Wrenn	STC 5073 (Hill for Petit)	Wd C393+C545taa
1561	Aitken	STC 5075 (*Workes*, Kingston for Wight) B+C*	Ad C393+C561s
1561	Aitken	STC 5076 (*Woorkes*, Kingston for Wight) A+C*	Ad C393+C561sa
1561	Aitken	STC 5076 (*Woorkes*, Kingston for Wight) A+D*	Ad C393+C561saa cop. 1
1561	Aitken	STC 5076 (*Woorkes*, Kingston for Wight) A+D*	Ad C393+C561saa cop. 2
1561	Aitken	[acephalous] [A?]+D*	Ad C393+C561saa cop. 3
1561	Aitken	[acephalous] [A?]+D*	Ad C393+C561saa cop. 4
1561	Aitken	[acephalous] [A?]+D*	Ad C393+C561saa cop. 5
1561	Pforzheimer	STC 5075 (*Workes*, Kingston for Wight) B+C*	PFORZ 176
1561		[detached copy of Astrolabe only]	71-51
1598	Aitken	STC 5078 (Islip for Norton)	PR 1850 1598
1598	Aitken	STC 5077 (Islip for Bishop)	PR 1850 1598b cop. 1
1598	Presbyterian	STC 5077 (Islip for Bishop)	PR 1850 1598b cop. 2
1598	Pforzheimer	STC 5077 (Islip for Bishop)	PFORZ 177
1602	Stark	STC 5080 (Islip)	STARK+6452
1602	Aitken	STC 5081 (Islip for Bishop)	Ad C393+C602s cop. 1
1602	Aitken	[acephalous]	Ad C393+C602s cop. 2
1602	Pforzheimer	STC 5080 (Islip)	PFORZ 178
1635	Wrenn	STC 5097.3 (Lichfield)	Wd C393 482dd WRE
1687		Wing C3736	PR 1850 1687
1687	Pforzheimer	Wing C3736	PFORZ 179

* Aitken on the variant states of the 1561 edition: "If the title with Chaucer's arms is called A, the title with the king in Council B, the introductory leaves with the woodcuts C, and the leaves without them D, the combinations usually found are A+D (by far the commonest) and B+C." (*Athenæum* 4093, April 7, 1906, 432).

Baylor University

Acknowledgments
The Carl P. Pforzheimer Endowment provided generous support for this study during a short-term fellowship at the Harry Ransom Center in 2013. I am extremely grateful to Jack Blanton and Richard Oram for their kind advice and feedback on an earlier draft of this article; any faults are my own. I am also thankful to Kevin Auer, Pat Fox, Michael Gilmore, Bridget Gayle Ground, and Margaret Tenney for their assistance.

NOTES

1. For an earlier census of early printed Chaucer editions, see Alison Wiggins, "What Did Renaissance Readers Write in Their Printed Copies of Chaucer?" *The Library*, 7th ser., 9 (2008): 3–36, which examines the entire collection of pre-1700 printed Chaucers at the Folger Shakespeare Library (30), Cambridge University Library (15), and the Library of Congress (8) and Gabriel Harvey's heavily annotated copy of the 1598 edition at the British Library, Additional MS 42518. Regarding the Caxton fragment at the Harry Ransom Center (HRC), see Daniel Mosser, "William Caxton's First Edition of the Canterbury Tales and the Origin of the Leaves for the Caxton Club's 1905 Leaf Book," in *Disbound and Dispersed: The Leaf Book Considered*, ed. Susan F. Rossen (Newcastle, DE: Oak Knoll Books, 2005), 24–50. Seven more copies of Chaucer's *Works* (1532–1687) came to the University of Texas with the purchase of the Pforzheimer library in 1986.

2. "Mr. G. A. Aitken," *The Times*, November 19, 1917, 6.

3. Laura Rotunno, *Postal Plots in British Fiction, 1840–1898: Readdressing Correspondence in Victorian Culture* (New York: Palgrave Macmillan, 2013), 34–35; Michael Mandelkern, "George A. Aitken," *Dictionary of Literary Biography*, vol. 149, *Late Nineteenth- and Early Twentieth-Century British Literary Biographers*, ed. Steven Serafin (New York: Gale, 1995), 3–8.

4. National Archives, *Census Returns of England and Wales, 1871* (Kew, UK: Public Record Office, 1871), class RG10, piece 4795, folio 86, page 55, GSU roll 847350, http://www.ancestry.co.uk; GB Historical GIS/University of Portsmouth, "History of Myton, in Kingston upon Hull and East Riding: Map and Description," *A Vision of Britain through Time*, available at http://www.visionofbritain.org.uk/place/25973. See also "Institutions & Charitable Agencies of the City of Hull" (Hull, UK: Rotary Club, 1928), http://www.carnegiehull.co.uk/the-anlaby-road/history/anlaby-road-history-08.html.

5. "Aitken, George Atherton, MVO," in *Who's Who* (London: A. & C. Black, 1916), 20.

6. London Metropolitan Archives, Saint Barnabas, Kensington, Register of Marriages, P84/BAN, item 008, http://www.ancestry.co.uk.

7. Christine Piper, "Children Act 1908," in *Dictionary of Youth Justice*, ed. Barry Goldson (Devon, UK: Willan Publishing, 2008); Kate Bradley, "The

Children Act 1908: Centennial Reflections, Contemporary Perspectives," *History Workshop Journal* 68 (2009): 303–305.

8. Regarding Aitken's appointment, see "Care of Children," *The Times*, November 12, 1913, 8; "Social Work of the Home Office," *The Times*, July 9, 1914, 5.

9. *London Gazette*, July 25, 1911, available at http://www.london-gazette. co.uk/issues/28516/pages/5548; *London Gazette*, June 4, 1917, available at http://www.london-gazette.co.uk/issues/30111/supplements/5456.

10. "The Centenary of Hodgson's," *Publishers' Circular and Booksellers' Record*, October 5, 1907, 390–394, at 393.

11. Clara Sitter, "Librarian, Literary Detective and Scholar: Fannie Smith Elizabeth Ratchford," in *Reclaiming American Library Past: Writing the Women In*, ed. Suzanne Hildenbrand (Norwood, NJ: Ablex, 1996), 135–162, at 139, 142.

12. Carl L. Cannon, *American Book Collectors and Collecting from Colonial Times to the Present* (New York: H. W. Wilson, 1941), 204.

13. Sitter, "Librarian," 142.

14. John Carter and Graham Pollard, *An Enquiry into the Nature of Certain Nineteenth Century Pamphlets* (London: Constable & Co. and New York: Scribner's, 1934), repr. with essay by Nicholas Barker and John Collins (London and Berkeley, CA: Scolar Press, 1983); David F. Foxon, *Thomas J. Wise and the Pre-Restoration Drama: A Study in Theft and Sophistication* (London: Bibliographical Society, 1959); David F. Foxon and William B. Todd, "Thomas J. Wise and the Pre-Restoration Drama: A Supplement," *The Library*, 5th ser., 15 (1961): 287–293.

15. John Carter, *Books and Book-Collectors* (London: Rupert Hart-Davis, 1956), 18–19.

16. John B. Thomas, III, "Beginnings: The Rare Books Collection, 1897–1955," in *Collecting the Imagination: The First Fifty Years of the Ransom Center*, ed. Megan Barnard (Austin: University of Texas Press, 2007), 1–17, at 11.

17. For further discussion of the Wise scandal, see John Carter, "Thomas J. Wise and 'Richard Gullible,'" *Book Collector* 8 (1959): 182–183; John Collins, *The Two Forgers: A Biography of Harry Buxton Forman & Thomas James Wise* (Aldershot, UK: Scolar Press, 1992); Donald C. Dickinson, *Dictionary of American Book Collectors* (Westport, CT: Greenwood Press, 1985), 345; Thomas J. Gearty, Jr., "Thomas J. Wise: A Brief Survey of His Literary Forgeries," *Courier* 11 (1973): 51–64; Lyle H. Kendall, Jr., "The Not-So-Gentle Art of Puffing: William G. Kingsland and Thomas J. Wise," *Papers of the Bibliographical Society of America* 62 (1968): 25–37; Roger C. Lewis, "Thomas J. Wise and the Trial Books of Rossetti's Poems (1870)," *Journal of Pre-Raphaelite Studies* 2 (1989): 73–87; James Morgan, "Thomas J. Wise and His Printers," *Black Art* 3 (1965): 67–80; Wilfred Partington, *Forging

Ahead: The True Story of the Upward Progress of Thomas James Wise, Prince of Book Collectors, Bibliographer Extraordinary, and Otherwise (New York: Putnam's, 1939), rev. ed. retitled as *Thomas J. Wise in the Original Cloth: The Life and Record of the Forger of the Nineteenth-Century Pamphlets* (London: Robert Hale, 1946); Katharine Greenleaf Pedley, *Moriarty in the Stacks: The Nefarious Adventures of Thomas J. Wise* (Berkeley, CA: Peacock Press, 1966); Fannie E. Ratchford, *Between the Lines: Letters and Memoranda Interchanged by H. Buxton Forman and Thomas J. Wise* (Austin: University of Texas Press, 1945); Fannie E. Ratchford, *Letters of Thomas J. Wise to John Henry Wrenn: A Further Inquiry into the Guilt of Certain Nineteenth-Century Forgers* (New York: Knopf, 1944); Fannie E. Ratchford, "Thomas J. Wise to John Henry Wrenn on Nineteenth Century Bibliography," *Papers of the Bibliographical Society of America* 36 (1942): 215–228; W. O. Raymond, "The Forgeries of Thomas J. Wise and Their Aftermath," *Journal of English and German Philology* 44 (1945): 229–238; William B. Todd, ed., *Thomas J. Wise: Centenary Studies* (Austin: University of Texas Press, 1959).

18. Aitken manuscripts inventory, Harry Ransom Center collection files, 3, 5.

19. Aitken manuscripts inventory, 1.

20. Cannon, *American Book Collectors*, 204.

21. Information about changing cataloguing practices kindly provided in private correspondence from Margaret Tenney (October 31, 2013) and Jack Blanton (November 26, 2013).

22. Harold F. B. Wheeler, "Notable Private Libraries, No. 6: The Library of Mr. G. A. Aitken," *Bibliophile* 3 (1909): 282–286, at 284.

23. William B. Todd, "Unfamiliar Collections: I, The Aitken Library," *Library Chronicle of the University of Texas at Austin*, new ser. 7 (1974): 58–64, at 61. The colophon of the Pynson edition, wanting in this fragment, gives the date as 1526 (STC 5086). H. P. Kraus acquired the Cardigan Chaucer on February 23, 1959, before the book found its current home in the HRC collection. Regarding its history, see Daniel Mosser, "Two Scribes of the Cardigan Manuscript and the 'Evidence' of Scribal Supervision and Shop Production," *Studies in Bibliography* 39 (1986): 112–125; and Daniel Mosser, "The Cardigan Chaucer: A Witness to the Manuscript and Textual History of the *Canterbury Tales*," *Library Chronicle*, new ser. 41 (1987): 82–111; A. S. G. Edwards, "The Case of the Stolen Chaucer Manuscript," *Book Collector* 21 (1972): 380–385.

24. Cannon, *American Book Collectors*, 204.

25. Ad C393+C542a cop. 2; the hand of the main annotator might belong to the owner who signs his name "et per me Johanem Savadge" in the top margin of sig. 2S6r. The Danis owner inscription appears on sig. 2C4v; at least two other hands make contributions to the book's cumulative marginalia.

26. "The Romaunt of the Rose," sig. 2E5r; "The Assemble of Ladyes," sig. 3F2v.

27. Protestant commentary appears in PR 1850 1532 cop. 3 beside the Summoner's and the Pardoner's Prologues, e.g., "Chaucer in this *prologue* (as in dyverse other places) veray excellently descryves the greate crafft & abhominable disceyts of all the popush prela*tes*, vernyshed over *with* a fayre face & color of fayned religion & fals pretended holynes" (sig. P4v). Medicinal recipe in Ad C393 + C542a cop. 2 begins "Take 3 pintes of muskedell and pegeon of 3 weeks old and make all the bones and seeth it in the wyne," then proceeds to list measures of various herbs, concluding "Boyell them all to gather and drink it morning and euening" (sig. Ss6r). Inscriptions of female names occur, among other places, on the pastedowns of PR 1850 1532 cop. 2: Helen Byrd, Elizabethe Druit, and Katerynne Leke.
28. Ad C393 + C542a cop. 2: "master gorge manninge i thinke you ʃ ffor your bocke | Mary buckmor" (sig. Ii5r).
29. Ad C393+C545t cop. 2.
30. Simon Adams, "Dudley, Sir Robert (1574–1649)," in *Oxford Dictionary of National Biography* (Oxford: Oxford University Press, 2004), http://www.oxforddnb.com/view/article/8161.
31. Ibid.
32. "Abdy, John Thomas," in *A Cambridge Alumni Database*, http://venn.lib.cam.ac.uk/, comprising, among other sources, John Archibald Venn, *Alumni Cantabrigienses. . .from 1752 to 1900*, 6 vols. (1940–1954).
33. Joseph A. Dane and Alexandra Gillespie, "Back at Chaucer's Tomb: Inscriptions in Two Early Copies of Chaucer's *Workes*," *Studies in Bibliography* 54 (1999): 89–96. A note about the book's provenance is signed "W. H. Goldwyer—Bristol, 1807," which can be identified as the Bristol surgeon William Henry Goldwyer (1763–1820).
34. George A. Aitken, "Chaucer Bibliography," *Athenæum* 4093, April 7, 1906, 432.
35. Ratchford, *Letters*, 33, 111.
36. Ibid., 548.
37. Morgan Library ChL1783.
38. Note appears in Ad C393 + C545t cop. 1; two other ca. 1550 copies are in the Aitken library: Ad C393+C545t cop. 2 and Ad C393+C45taa.

Lefèvre d'Étaples and the Politics of Plato: The *Hecatonomiae* (1506)

JEAN MARIE FLAMAND

In 1506 Jacques Lefèvre d'Étaples was around fifty years old. This great and dedicated professor had been teaching for twenty years at the college of Cardinal Lemoine in Paris. He had introduced into the Faculty of Arts new translations of Aristotle from the Greek made recently by Italian humanists. Lefèvre had thus become the renovator of the teaching of Aristotle at the University of Paris, and by quietly distancing himself from scholasticism, he had become a celebrity across Europe. He was highly regarded as a scholar (*eruditissimus*) because of his many philosophical publications, which were centered on Aristotle but branched out in many directions, toward mathematics, music, and religious authors. His translations and commentaries on the Bible would be the crowning achievement of his editorial work, because Lefèvre was also, and above all, a priest. His thinking is profoundly religious and—in the manner of his predecessor, the great Florentine Platonic scholar, Marsilio Ficino—he was very attached to Christianity and wanted to lead the faith back to the purity and fervor of the apostolic period.[1]

I. What is the *Hecatonomiae*?

The editorial work of Lefèvre is immense. His textual editions and commentaries are so numerous that they form a veritable labyrinth.[2] For all its richness, sorting out his work poses a huge challenge to historians of the early book. Recently the department devoted to humanism at the Institut de Recherche et d'Histoire des Textes in Paris (IRHT) has undertaken the systematic identification of all the editions of all the texts, both ancient and medieval, that Lefèvre wrote or compiled—in the form of editions, translations, explanations, and commentaries. Within this vast project, I would like to draw attention to one particular publication that fills fewer than forty leaves in a folio volume printed in Paris by Henri Estienne, senior, on August 5, 1506. The work was composed by Lefèvre, who coined its peculiar title: *Hecatonomiae.*[3]

Where can one read the *Hecatonomiae*? The work is difficult to find, which explains in part why it has been neglected, except in the unfinished writings of Professor Jean Boisset (1909–1978), an historian of the Reformation at the University of Montpellier, who specialized in the writings of John Calvin.[4] The *Hecatonomiae*[5] is incorporated into an edition of Aristotle.[6] In the first and greater part of this book, Lefèvre published Leonardo Bruni's Latin translation of the *Politica* of Aristotle in 135 folios. Between the chapters of this vast treatise in eight books, Lefèvre placed his own commentary in the manner of Marsilio Ficino. Next came the *Hecatonomiae* (folios 135v–168r). Lefèvre then resumed his edition of Aristotle (fols. 168v–178 plus 16 supplementary fols.) with the text of the *Œconomica*, a work attributed to Aristotle that treats domestic economy and for which Lefèvre wrote a commentary (for the title page of this edition, see Figure. 1).

What, then, is the *Hecatonomiae*? This is a collection of laws (in Greek, *nómoi*), grouped in sections of one hundred (*hecatón*) excerpts. The title thus means "Groups of one hundred laws." The work has seven sections, giving a total of seven hundred excerpts from Plato. The first one hundred excerpts are drawn from the *Republic*, and the six hundred others come from the *Laws*, the last dialogue written by Plato. These are not abstract philosophical reflections. They are realistic and very concrete dispositions—or laws. But these laws are not those of a city or a country that exists in reality. They are virtual laws, "desirable" laws, by which Plato, within the framework of a political and metaphysical vision, regulates in minute detail every aspect of life in an ideal civil community; the *Laws* describes the fictive constitution of an ideal and perfect city made up of virtuous citizens, the Magnetes. In the *Republic*, Plato makes a model for a city where the common good and justice are the objectives, at once the "principle and the synthesis of the virtues of the soul and of the city."[7]

The text is a *Plato latinus*, the fruit of a recent discovery. Lefèvre owned a copy of Marsilio Ficino's translation of Plato's *Opera omnia*, printed in Florence in 1484.[8] It was thanks to this monumental and masterful translation that the Latin world discovered the entire works of Plato, saved from oblivion by Ficino like Orpheus leading Eurydice out of the underworld. Most importantly, Ficino brought to light the *Republic* and the *Laws*, two works unknown in the West in the Middle Ages. Lefèvre read the volume with great care. His excerpts do not always cite the text of Plato verbatim

Figure 1. Title Page of [Aristotelis,] *Politicorum libri octo*, etc. (Paris: Henri Estienne, 1506). Title: Aristoteles ; Lefèvre d'Etaples, Jacques, Paris 1506. *Bayerische StaatsBibliothek München 2 A.gr.b. 373.*

but give a condensed version following the text quite closely. He uses many imperatives, because this is a collection of laws, even if the laws are fictional. Neither the *Republic* nor the *Laws* of Plato is a juridical treatise. They are philosophical dialogues in which the speakers are searching for truth; they seek the nature of justice (in the *Republic*) and ways of assuring the construction of a virtuous city (in the *Laws*). But in order that the citizens accept the constraints of the laws, they must understand the rationale behind them. In the *Laws*, Plato is constantly trying to convince us of the merits of the laws that will be decreed.[9] This heuristic aspect, so important for Plato, has disappeared in the excerpts of Lefèvre, who concentrates above all on the result to which the philosophical reflection or dialogue leads, without repeating the sometimes meandering demonstration.

Lefèvre constantly uses the imperative mood for his ideal laws, and gerundives expressing obligation are also frequent. For example:

> 1.17. *Pueri, maxime qui custodes futuri sperantur, instituantur in gymnastica et musica* (*Rep.* 2:376e). ("Children, especially those who will become 'guardians,' should be taught gymnastics and music.")
>
> 1.18. *Sint qui fictoribus fabularum praesint: et si quas bonas fecerint eligant, reliquas abjiciant* (*Rep.* 2:377b–d). ("There should be magistrates in charge of supervising the inventors of fables; the magistrates ought to retain the good fables they have made and reject the others.")
>
> 1.27. *Sermonis summopere vitetur inhonestas* (*Rep.* 3:400d). ("Inappropriate language is to be absolutely avoided.")
>
> 1.28. *Cauendum est ne quid circa musicam et gymnasticam innouetur* (*Rep.* 4:424b). ("One must make sure that no novelties are introduced in music or gymnastics.")
>
> 1.39. *Juniores principes metuant, et seniores reuereantur* (*Rep.* 5:465a). ("The youngest should be fearful of the leaders, and show respect toward the eldest.")

Lefèvre offers this vast collection of formulas in order to express the core of Plato's political doctrine. In 1506, very few people in France knew Greek.[10] One of Lefèvre's self-appointed tasks was to make known, in Latin translation, Greek texts that were unknown at that time in France.[11] The 1506 edition of the *Hecatonomiae* was reprinted in Paris in 1512, 1515, 1526, 1535, and 1543.[12] For printer-booksellers all over Europe, Lefèvre was a blessing. The editions, issues,[13] and/or re-editions of his works, not only of Aristotle but of a host of ancient and medieval authors and, of course, the Bible, were a true publishing phenomenon and illustrate in a particularly remarkable fashion the rapid diffusion of texts in the early years of the printed book.

II. The Content of the *Hecatonomiae*

Lefèvre adopted the method of the Italian humanists, which was new and radically different from the methods of medieval commentators. He does not substitute himself for Plato; he explains Plato by Plato, just as he explains Aristotle by Aristotle.[14] He does not intend to edit all of the *Republic* and the *Laws*: he limits himself to large extracts. When Lefèvre cuts up the text in *excerpta*, he is not appropriating selected ideas of Plato to serve his own purposes; his aim is to offer an honest, objective overview of the doctrine of Plato on the constitution of a just city. Thus he goes into all aspects of communal life, describing the moral implications for the individual and the political implications for the city.

In *Hecatonomiae* 1 (folios 136r–142r in the edition of 1506), the first group of one hundred excerpts is entitled by Lefèvre *leges Socraticae*, "the laws of Socrates," because they are excerpts from the *Republic*, in which Socrates is the principal speaker in the dialogue. Lefèvre uses books I to VII of the *Republic*, leaving aside books VIII to X. He also makes an index of the excerpts, which is printed at the beginning of his work:

> *De legislatore* (On the legislator)
> *De nuptiis* (On weddings)
> *De educatione* (On education)
> *De disciplina* (On discipline)
> *De moribus* (On customs)
> *De artificibus* (On craftsmen)
> *De regione* (On the country [where you live])
> *De victu et necessariis* (On food and necessities)
> *De militia* (On military duties)
> *De re sacra* (On religion)
> *De magistratu* (On magistrates)
> *De legislatore* (On the legislator)

The last entry repeats the first: one can see the importance Lefèvre gives to the legislator, whose role is to insure the unity of the city.

Lefèvre did not compile an index for *Hecatonomiae* 2 to 7, by far the longest section of the work, but he notes that the excerpts taken from the *Laws* treat matters similar (*consimiles fere materias*) to those in *Hecatonomiae*

1. I have begun indexing these six hundred excerpts, but it is a long and tedious task. The excerpts contain rules for all sorts of things: the education of children, the distribution of wealth, the necessary limitation of individual wealth, provisioning of the city, for example, with rain water (2.93) and fountains (2.94), and surveillance by guardians of the city (3.9) and guardians of the countryside (*custodes agrorum*; 3.5). Many measures concern penal law, which is not surprising, since Plato in the *Laws* considers that only a city with political constraints can be virtuous. Once the laws are laid down, Plato gives considerable space to the courts of justice (3.37), age for marriage (4.1), rules of conduct for nannies (4.5–7), moderately stringent rules imposed on young children (4.11), and controls on commerce, distribution of land, housing conditions, and travel. The extracts vary in length. Many are one or two lines long:

> 4.49. (*Laws* 7:824a) *Sacros venatores: ubicumque venari velint, nemo prohibeat.* ("Sacred hunters [i.e., very courageous hunters] may hunt where they like and no one should stop them.")
>
> 5.4. (*Laws* 8:847b) *Vectigal importandarum aut exportandarum rerum: nullum sit penitus.* ("No one will be taxed for importing or exporting merchandise.")
>
> 5.44. (*Laws* 9:865b) *Omnes medici qui curantes non sponte occiderint: mundi sint.* ("Medical doctors who are not at fault when the patient dies should be exempt from legal action.")
>
> 7.97. (*Laws* 12:960a) *Lachrymis mortuos decorare aut non: legum lator non prohibeat. Plangere vero et extra domum vociferare prohibeat.* ("The dead may be mourned with or without tears, but lamentations and cries are prohibited outside the home.")

But some extracts have as many as fifteen lines or more. For example, extract 4.72 condenses *Laws* 8:838e, 839a, 837c, 838a–d, and 840d. Extracts 1.97, 1.98, and 1.100, at the end of the first group of the *Hecatonomiae*, are very long. The length of these passages, which Lefèvre could have cut up into smaller pieces, can doubtless be explained by his formal decision to limit the number of extracts from the *Republic*. Before going on to the *Laws*, he obviously wanted to load as much of the *Republic* text as possible into the first group of hundred extracts.

For the most part, the extracts follow the order of Plato's text.[15] But sometimes several extracts are taken from a single passage,[16] or an excerpt is taken from an earlier passage,[17] or the order of presentation within a passage is reversed, which can distort or color the interpretation, so that Lefèvre decrees as a principle what Plato formulated as a conclusion.[18] For example, in 7.12, we read that Plato refuses to tolerate the presence of beggars in the ideal city. But before formulating his refusal, he begins with an important preamble, which has a powerful moral: the person to be pitied is not the beggar, but he who sees *what is good* and turns away. Moral deprivation is more serious than material deprivation. Plato says that a well-regulated city allows no one to behave in such a fashion, turning his back on what is good and looking for evil. Lefèvre, however, inverts the presentation. He begins by saying that, according to Plato, mendicants ought to be banished without pity. He does not give the reason until afterward, and this inversion leads to his condemnation of Plato's position, which he probably judges as "uncharitable." By inverting Plato's text, Plato's preamble becomes in Lefèvre's text a sort of justification a posteriori, and the true sense of Plato's thought is lost. Lefèvre's text reads as follows:

> 7.12 (Laws 11:936c; b) [936c] *Nullus in civitate nostra mendicus sit: sed quicumque id tentauerit victumque inexplebilibus precibus colligere coeperit, a rerum venalium curatoribus e foro pellatur, ab aedili vero magistratu ex urbe eiiciatur, ex tota denique regione ab agri magistratu exterminetur. Ut ab huiusmodi animali: omnino uniuersa regio munda sit. [936b] Nam mirum profecto esset: eum qui temperans esset, et virtute alia aut virtutis parte praeditus, in extremam paupertatem deuenire, ut fame vel re alia consimili premeretur et ita neglectum esse, siue liber siue seruus in ciuitate moderate gubernata. Talis profecto si calamitate vel sorte aliqua vexatur, misericordia dignus existimandus est. Non qui fame vel re consimili pressus: precibus victum quaeritat.*
>
> [936c] "In our city, there should be no beggars. If someone should do so and go about collecting his means of subsistence by endless supplications, the guardians of the public place will chase him away from the public place, the guardians of the city will chase him from the city, and the guardians of the countryside will chase him from the countryside and expel him from the territory, so that the entire country be rid of this kind of person. The man who is worthy of pity is not he who is hungry or who

suffers from some similar woe. It is he who, although
he practices temperance, another virtue, or a part
of that virtue, is no less a victim of misfortune.
[936b] Therefore it would be strange if a man of
this kind were abandoned to the point of falling into
profound indigence in a city that is well regulated
and provided with good institutions."

The question arises as to whether Lefèvre has given some internal logic
to the *Hecatonomiae*. The end of one of the seven sections of *Hecatonomiae*
does not necessarily mark the end of a book in Plato; the same material from
Plato is distributed across sections 6 and 7, for example. At this point in my research I would say that the construction appears arbitrary, with little thematic
grouping. What philosophical point of view governs the choice of excerpts?

Lefèvre provides no commentary for the *Hecatonomiae*. This marvel-
ous teacher who wrote so many very clear explanations for his students on
the works of Aristotle (on physics, logic, and ethics) offers no explanatory
text for Plato. Nor does he give a systematic description of Plato's political
doctrines. One looks in vain for explanation of the underlying principles of
Plato's ideal city, for example his distribution of the population into three
groups in the *Republic*—guardians, warriors, and artisans—corresponding
to the three parts of the soul (*logistikón, thumoúmenon, epithumętikón*).[19] The
reader may also wish for a commentary in Lefèvre's long extract from Book 5
of the *Laws*, which defines the conditions that should govern the distribution
of land and the installation of citizens in colonies. Plato limits the population of the city of the Magnetes to 5,040 households. This perfect number
("perfect" because it is divisible by every number up to ten) ought to allow
for the best distribution of goods and duties in the ideal city. Lefèvre, however, offers no such explanation, despite his appetite for mathematics. Nor
does he provide his usual type of paraphrase, a short, pedagogical precis.[20]

However, Lefèvre prints his negative evaluations of certain laws in the
margins of his text: *Stultitia* or *Stul.*, *Semist.* (*Semistultitia*), and *Gentilis.* (*Gen-
tilitas*) (see *Hecatonomiae* 4.14, 4.18, 4.19, 4.21, fol. 150v; see also Figure 2).
Here he castigates customs and beliefs he sees as pagan. These brief formulae
thus convey some commentary.

⸿Heca.

gant mulieres nuptiarũ curatrices / in vnaquaꝗ tribu/que ipſis etate ſit equa=
lis.⸿Ad hunc magiſtratum aſſumpta/in ſacrum quotidie eat/ iniuriantemꝗ 13
puniat/ſeruũ quidem et ſeruam/peregrinũ et peregrinã per vrbanos quoſdam
miniſtros.ciuem vero cuius animaduerſio in cõtrouerſia ſit:ad edilium trahat
iudicium.de quo autem non ſit controuerſia:puniat ipſa.⸿Poſt ſex annorum 14
Semiſt.   etatem:femina a maribus ſecernant/pueriꝗ deinceps cũ equalibus maioribus/
et puelle cum feminis equalibus conuerſentur. et ad ſcientias vtriꝗ ſe vertant:
mares quidem ad magiſtros equorũ/arcuum/telorum/et funde/ſemine quoꝗ
ad eadem ſi cõcedatur vſꝗ ad ſcientiam tantum/et maxime ad armorũ vſum.
⸿Iuxta ſcytharum legem /non ſolũ ſiniſtra arcu et dextra ſagitta vtantur:ſed 15
vtriſꝗ ſimiliter ad vtrũꝗ.⸿Principes curam habeãt:vt mulieres ludos/alimẽ 16
taꝗ cõſiderent/viri vero diſciplinas/ quibus omnes pedibus manibuſꝗ vtrinꝗ
eque potentes facti per conſuetudinem/ nature non noceant.et diſciplina cor=
poris in ſaltatiõe et lucta/gymnaſtica dicitur:animi vero muſica. ⸿Luctatio= 17
nem et diſcentes et docẽtes alteri beniuole largiantur/alteri ſuſcipiat gratioſe.
nã que in recta luctatione:a collo/ manibus laterũꝗ motu/ cũ victorie ſtudio
honeſtoꝗ adhibentur/ et ad ſanitatem vireſꝗ conducũt/ et vtilitatem non mo=
Stul.   dicam habent. ⸿Saltationes in choreis:tam viris ꝗ̃ mulieribus armatis/ſiant/ 18
imitẽturꝗ curetarum armatorũ ludos/et minerue.nam minerua ludis choree
delectata:non nudis manibus ludendum cenſuit/ ſed arnis tota ornata ſaltã=
Gentilis.   di officio eſt perfuncta.⸿Pueri et puelle anteꝗ in bellum ꝓdire poſſint : armis 19
equiſꝗ oportet in deorũ omnium pompis ornatos/modo velociores modo tar=
diores in chorea et itinere ſupplicationes fundere.quia hec in pace et bello vti=
lia ſuntꝉetere vero corporis exercitationes que horũ gratia non fiunt/nõ ſunt
liberales. ⸿Iiſdem ludis et geſtibus iiſdem homines quos leges ſtatuerũt / eiſ= 20
dẽ tẽꝗ apparatibus et ſupellectile ſemper vtantur. nam cũ mutantur:iuuetus
occulte mores mutat.facitꝗ id:vt priſca vilia noua vero in honore habeantur.
ſicꝗ priſce leges pereũt irrite. quare:nulla ciuitati peſtis eſt pernicioſior.⸿Sũ= 21
mopere cauedum eſt:ne pueritia in cãtibus/ et ſaltationibus noua vnꝗ̃ audeat
Gentilis.   imitari/ neue vllos pueros voluptatum blandimẽtis alliciat. Sed Egyptiorum
more:tripudiorum cantuũꝗ genera dijs omnia conſecrentur.quod ſi quis ali=
ter ꝗ̃ cõſtitutum ſit/hymnis/ choreiſꝗ vtatur:ſacerdotes tam viri ꝗ̃ mulieres cũ
legum cuſtodibus/eum ſancte ac legitime arceant.et qui repulſus fuerit:niſi li=
benter obtemperauerit/ per totã vitam volẽti cuiꝗ penas impietatis perſoluat.
⸿Nemo audeat ꝓter publicos/ſacroſꝗ cãtus aliquid canere/ et ꝓter cõſtitutã 22
iuuẽtutis choreã moueri tripudio.qui paret:indemnis abeat.qui minus:legũ
cuſtodes/ſacerdoteſꝗ tam viri ꝗ̃ mulieres/puniãt.⸿Si quer ula oratione a ciui 23
bus audire quãdoꝗ oporteat:nõ fauſtis diuinarũ ſolemnitatũ diebus/ ſed ne=
faſtis potius conueniant/ eantꝗ tunc conducti chori externiꝗ cantores/ quem
admodum in funeribus fieri videmus/vbi quidã mercede conducti/cum flebi=
les melliꝗ ſint/ lugubris quoꝗ veſtis Carice gẽtis inſtar/ miſere defunctũ ipſũ
deplorant.⸿Cantuũ genus omne:in benedicendo/et feliciter ominando ver= 24
ſetur/ſitꝗ hec prima lex. ſecũda:vt cantu preces dijs quibus libamus effundã=

Figure 2. *Hecatonomiae* 4.14, 4.18, 4.19, 4.21, in [Aristotelis,] *Politicorum libri octo*, etc. (Paris: Henri Estienne, 1506), fol. 150v. Title: Aristoteles ; Lefèvre d'Etaples, Jacques, Paris 1506. *Bayerische StaatsBibliothek München 2 A.gr.b. 373.*

Stultitia   3.51. (*Laws* 6:771e–772a) [regulations for games and danc-
             ing] *Ludi chorique puellorum et puellarum simul fiant, nudatis*
             corporibus quatenus modestus pudor patiatur. ("May there be
             games and dancing where young men and women participate,
             their bodies left bare within the limits acceptable to a temper-
             ate modesty.")

Stultitia   3.71. (*Laws* 6:775b) *Bibere ad ebrietatem, neque alibi unquam*
             decet, praeterquam in solennitatibus euis dei qui largitus est vinum.
             ("Drinking to the point of drunkenness is never acceptable,
             except at feasts of the god [Bacchus] who gave the gift of
             wine.")

Semist.   4.67. (*Laws* 8:833d–834a) [armed combat for men and for
             women] *Vnius ad unum, duorum ad duos, et usque decem ad*
             decem armis pugna fiat ad robur augendum: et id commune sit tam
             viris quam mulieribus, ad aetatem usque nubilem. ("One against
             one, two against two, or even ten against ten; and it should be
             the same for both men and women, until the age of marriage.")

Stul.   6.86. (*Laws* 11:929d–e) *Liceat filiis parentes morbis vel senio*
             turpiter affectos: amentiae accusare. ("Let it be permitted for
             children of parents who are [mentally] ill or senile to accuse
             them of dementia.") [Lefèvre defends the idea of absolute
             respect for parents]

These negative judgments concerning dress, drunkenness, combat, and
parental respect express a certain distrust of Plato. For Lefèvre, Plato's philosophy must not contradict the fundamental verities of Christianity. Thus,
in *Hecatonomiae* 2 to 7, one observes an "almost general adaptation of pagan
divinities to Christianity, by different means of expression."[21]

The negative comments culminate in a collection of rejected passages
(*Reiectitia*) placed at the end of the *Hecatonomiae* (fols. 167–168), "as in the
most faraway and abject place" (*in fine collocavimus ut in ignobiliori extremo,*
quo cetera intelligantur digniora et potiora a deterioribus secernantur) (fol. 167,
see Figure 3). Lefèvre rejects the right of magistrates to lie to citizens, communal nudity while exercising, the communal status of women and children
and the proscription of family ties, the banishing of beggars, and the practices
of divorce, eugenics, and abortion.

VII
167

190 bent.verum virtus vnicum est:ad quod semper respiciendu.⸿Sanciat legisla=
tor que discenda erunt.namque discenda sunt:ea nec discere facile/ et inueto=
ris discipulum fieri arduu/et quando, non enim possunt qui discunt/cognosce
re:quid et quado opportune discatur.id naq officium est coru: in quorum ia
animo/rei ipsius scientia est.Igitur his legibus qui paret/non modo indemnis
sed et laudabilis esto:qui vero non paret/ab omnibus vt communiter videbi=
tur/puniatur.

⸿REIECTITIORVM CAPVT/FINI HECATONOMIARVM ADIECTVM.

Rodunt medici corpus humanum quatuor humores continere necessarios: pitui=
tam/sanguinem/biles duas flauam atq atra, pituita que et flegma digentur in sa=
guinem.sanguis autem:nutricat.flaua bilis:quod hebes est et obtusu acuit:et de=
sum subtiliat. atra vero bilis:egerendis subministrat ac subseruit. nos itaq atre bi=
lis/virulentiq fellis/aut excrementoru loco/hec reiectitia Socratis Platonis et Aristotelis in
fine collocamus vt in ignobiliori extremo.quo cetera intelligantur dignora:et potiora a de=
terioribus secernantur.Prima igitur reiectitia lex socratis hec esto.

1 ⸿Fas esto magistratum gerctibus mentiri.⸿Liceat nudas ceu vetulas tum iu=
2 uenes/cum viris ad palestre certamen descendere,vt solet viri in gymnasijs : cu
vna exercentur/licet rugosi veternosiq sint, et ita circa armatura /equestremq
facultatem se habeant.cum enim ratiõe id iudicatu fuerit optimum: oculis ri=
diculum minime videbitur.Sed sane inanis is homo est:qui deridendu quicq
3 preterq quod malum est/existimat.⸿Custodu mulieribus nudandu erit cor=
pus:quandoquidem pro vestibus virtutem induent/comunicanduq in bello/
et alia omni ciuitatis custodia/atq tutela/neq aliud agendu, horu tamen of=
4 ficiorum:leuiora/propter generis imbecillitatem/mulieribus tribueda.⸿Mu=
lieres he/horum viroru omnes omniu comunes sint/ nullaq priuati alicui ad=
hereat:ac rursus filii comunes/neq pater filium noscar meq filius patrem
5 ⸿Comunes habeant edea comessationes comunes:nichil habetites proprium
6 ⸿Vbi vero ex comuni habitatione cogressioneue in gymnalijs/ac reliquo cõ=
uictu ex innata necessitate ad mutuam trahentur comixtionem: se sine ordine
denudari/inter se/aliudue quippiam tale facere/neq sanctu sit in beatoru ciui=
7 tate/neq iudices permittant.⸿Optimoru proles nutriatur:deterrimoru vero
minime.et dum hec aguntur omnes ignorent/preter principes.sic enim arme=
tum custodu:seditione carebit.et deteriores illi:fortunam/ non principes cul=
8 pabunt.⸿Quare necessariu fore videtur:vt frequenti mendacio et deceptione
vtantur principes ad subditoru vtilitatem.huiusmodi enim omnia:pharmaci/
9 medicineq loco necessaria sunt. ⸿Qui nascentur ex deterioribus/aut ex qui=
busuis sed membro aliquo manci:in abditis vt decet locis abscondantur. nam
10 purum decet esse custodum genus.⸿Cum mulieres et viri etatem generatio=
ni aptam egressi fuerint:liceat viris cuicunq voluerint/preterq filie atq matri/
et filiaru natis/matrisq maioribus commisceri,sed et mulieribus liceat copula=
ri preterq filio aut patri/ac superioribus atq inferioribus eorudem.sed partus
si quis contigerit:prohibeatur in lucem educi,si aute prodatur:ita ponatur vt
11 eius nulla nutritio sit.⸿Qui egregie sese exercens/excelluerit:primo qui=
dem in ipsa expeditione/ab ijs qui vna militant adolescentibus ac pueris/sigil=
latim a quolibet coronetur/et illi dexteras iungat/et a quolibet osculum accipi
at/atq det,vt quoad in expeditione fuerit:nemini renuere liceat/ quemcumq

SO
CRA
TI
CE
LE
GES
AB
SVR
DE

Figure 3. *Hecatonomiae*, REIECTITIORUM CAPUT FINI HECATONOMIARUM ADIECTUM, in [Aristotelis,] *Politicorum libri octo*, etc. (Paris, Henri Estienne, 1506), fol. 167r. Title: Aristoteles ; Lefèvre d'Etaples, Jacques, Paris 1506. *Bayerische StaatsBibliothek München 2 A.gr.b. 373.*

REIECT. 1. (*Republic* 3:389b) [rejecting the government's right to lie] *Fas esto magistratum gerentibus mentiri.* ("A magistrate has the right to lie to those he governs.")

Plato restricts this prescription to a very limited context, which Lefèvre ignores:

It is thus for those who govern the city, if indeed it is necessary, that there exists the right to lie, whether with regard to enemies or with regard to citizens, when it is in the interests of the city. For all others, it is out of the question that they resort to lying.[22]

REIECT. 2. (*Republic* 5:452a–c) [rejecting communal physical education or exercise of females and males in the nude] *Liceat nudas cum vetulas tum juvenes cum viris ad palestrae certamen. Ut solent viri in gymnasiis.* ("Let nude females, young and old, enter the palestra [area for wrestling and physical exercise] with the men, as men have a habit of doing in the gymnasia.")

REIECT. 4. (*Republic* 5:457d) [rejecting the community of women and children and repudiation of private family ties] *Mulieres hae, horum virorum omnes omnium communes sint nullaque priuatim alicui adhaereat: ac rursus filii communes neque pater filium noscat neque filius patrem.* ("Let women be communally available to all men, and let no woman cohabit privately with a man; let children also be looked after communally, and may no parent know which are his progeny, nor the child his parent.")

REIECT. 12. (*Republic* 5:468e–469b) [rejecting divine honors accorded to warriors who die in combat] *Eorum sepulchra, veluti daemonum, colentes atque adorantes.* ("We will care for their graves and we will bow down as on the tombs of divine spirits.")

This is a rejection of practices linked to pagan religion, as with the *Stultitia* quoted above that rejects drinking at feasts of Bacchus.

7.12. REIECT. 16. (*Laws* 11:936c) [rejecting beggars]
Nullus in civitate nostra mendicus sit. ("There will be
no beggars in our city.")

Even more important is Lefèvre's rejection of divorce,
eugenics, and abortion:

divorce REIECT. 14 (= *Hecatonomiae* 6.89-90) et
15 (= *Hecatonomiae* 6.90-91 from *Laws* 11, 930a)

6.88 *Si vir et uxor, propter morum acerbitatem invicem
non conveniant : decem viri de legum custodibus
qui medii sint, et decem mulieres de connubiorum
curatricibus prouideant. Quorum sententia : si ita
conciliati fuerint, valida et stabilis habeatur.*("If the
incompatibility of their characters prevent a man
and woman from finding harmony, ten men of
medium age, picked from among the guardians
of the laws, [930a] and ten women who provide
counsel for marriages should deal with the matter.
If they succeed in obtaining a reconciliation, that
decision will prevail.")

6.89 *Si autem illorum animi vehementius etiam
iracundia fluctuant : facto diuortio, illos pro viribus
quaerant, qui utrisque conueniant. Et acerbioribus
ingeniis : maturiora mitioraque ingenia accomodentur.*
("But if the storm that shakes the soul is too violent,
a divorce will be pronounced and persons will
be sought out who are suitable for each. As such
people are likely to be rather prickly, they should
be accommodated with partners who are more
constant and gentle.")

6.90 *Qui sine filiis sunt, aut paucos procreauerunt,
dissentiuntque procreandorum liberorum causa :
coniugium rursus quaerere compellantur.*("If the
couple has no children, or too few, or does not agree
about the procreation of children, they should be
compelled to seek out a new union.")

6.91 *Si filios non paucos habeant atque dissentiant :
senectutis curandae gratia (diuortio facto) aliud*

coniugium ineant.("If their children are not too few and they have fallen out, they should care for one another in their old age, having divorced and remarried.")

eugenics REIECT. 7 (from *Rep.* 5, 459d-e ; 460c) *Optimorum proles nutriatur: deterrimorum vero minime. Et dum haec aguntur omnes ignorent, praeter principes. Sic enim armentum custodum : seditione carebit et deteriores illi: fortunam, non principes culpabunt.* ("The progeny of those who are of greater worth should be nourished, those of lesser worth not at all. And this shall be done unbeknownst to all, save the leaders. Thus the 'herd' of guardians will be free of internal discord, and men of lesser value will blame fate and not the leaders.")

REIECT. 9 (from *Rep.* 5, 460c) *Qui nascentur ex deterioribus aut de quibusuis sed membro aliquo manci: in abditis ut decet locis abscondantur. Nam purum decet esse custodum genus.* ("As to the progeny of those of lesser value, and in the case of malformed children that they bear, they will be hidden as appropriate in a secret and isolated place... if one wants the race of guardians to be pure.")

Perhaps most emphatic is his rejection of abortion, which Plato admits and which Aristotle tolerates, and even recommends in certain cases:

REIECT. *in fine* (Arist. *Polit.* VII 16, 1335b19-26): ... *determinanda profecto erit procreandorum multitudo. Quod si quibusdam ad procreandum copulatis praeter haec euenerit : priusquam sensus vitaque insit, abortionem procreare oportere.* ("... a numerical limit must be imposed on procreation, and if the couples conceive beyond that limit, an abortion must be made before the foetus has received its senses (i.e., life)."

What is Lefèvre's position on Plato? He knows Plato by way of Marsilio Ficino, the remarkable Hellenist, great Platonic scholar, and sincere Christian whom he met in Florence in 1492 and whom he calls "very honored father" (*pater reverendissimus*). Soon after Lefèvre's return from his first trip to Italy, when he met Ficino, he expressed his great admiration for the eminent Florentine translator by publishing, with the printer Johann Higman, Ficino's edition of the *Poimandres* of Hermes Trismegistus in July 1494, accompanied by brief *Argumenta*. But his admiration slowly became tainted by distrust: in 1505, he published a new Parisian edition of *Poimandres*, printed this time by Henri Estienne, which shows that Lefèvre's enthusiasm for Ficino had waned. The *Argumentum* for book 3 of *Poimandres* is a modified version of the one in the 1494 edition and shows a much more prudent Lefèvre, who warns the reader that this book "should be read with caution" (*caute legendum*). In the margins of this work are printed scholia denouncing pagan beliefs (*gentilissime*), exactly parallel to those found in the *Hecatonomiae* of 1506.

It is evident that by 1505 Lefèvre did not share Ficino's Platonic enthusiasm or even the same attraction to Plato's work. But it is important to remember that Lefèvre only "transmits" Plato in aid of better comprehension of Aristotle, as he wrote in his dedication to his friend Joan de Ganay, First President of the Parliament of Paris.²³ Indeed, Aristotle strongly criticizes some of Plato's political views, such as the communal status of women. Lefèvre judges Plato to be inferior to Aristotle, or "more dangerous." And while Lefèvre admires Aristotle, he places him on a low rung of his *scala studiorum*, or ladder of scholars. Aristotle is the "best guide to our knowledge of the senses,"²⁴ and can be relied on for the study of logic; further, he established fine principles for ethics. Concerning the knowledge of higher realities, Lefèvre thinks that one should be guided by Christian authors, those who lived in apostolic times, as well as by the Fathers of the Church and mystics such as Dionysius the Areopagite, who offers a *theologia vivificans, cibus solidus*—the solid food of a vivifying theology.²⁵ But access to the highest truth ultimately comes only through knowledge of Holy Scripture. In fact, Lefèvre never really wanted to publish or explain Plato. Even the *Phaedo*, on the immortality of the soul, did not interest him, nor did Plato's eschatology, as expressed in the Myth of Er in book 10 of the *Republic*. Lefèvre probably admired it, but he kept it at a distance.

What place does the *Hecatonomiae* have in studies of Plato? The answer is: a modest one at best, with most influence at the beginning of the early modern period. Lefèvre's "transmission" of his author is limited, serious, and honest; in doing this, he made known certain of Plato's political ideas for the first time in France. Philosophers and scholars interested in Plato would wait another fifty years for Loys Le Roy, known as Regius (ca. 1510–1577), to publish—this time in French—and comment on the most important and significant parts of the *Republic* and the *Laws*.²⁶ Lefèvre was an attentive reader in a time and place when Plato was still largely unknown, and he circulated Platonic ideas in an academic community still in the grip of the medieval scholastic tradition. Lefèvre's role in his commentaries on Plato was to subordinate an untamed wild beast to Christianity.[27] What appealed to Lefèvre was the ideal regulation of a city, which, in order to be just, had to be founded on metaphysical and religious values: the divine office, the common good, and justice. Lefèvre prudently notes that Plato's reflections have both a religious and a moral basis but that they correspond to the vanished world of antiquity, not the Christian world. He further raises the question as to whether Plato might be influential in a Christian world.

It is difficult to measure any direct influence by the *Hecatonomiae* because the work is buried as a sort of appendix in an edition of Aristotle, and the few steps that Lefèvre takes toward Plato are embedded in his transmission of Aristotle. A case of formal resemblance exists in a work entitled *Tres hecatonomiae de conceptibus* by Nicolaus Francus, known as Vimacuus, published in Paris in 1509 by Jean Barbier for Jean Joncour.[28] Apparently only one copy of this book is preserved at the University of Cambridge. The author was a student of Philippe Prévost of Arras, himself a teacher at the college of Cardinal Lemoine at the same time as Lefèvre. The title of the work is obviously a direct echo of Lefèvre's collection, but its essentially academic content has nothing to do with Plato.

The political ideas of Plato, and especially the project for the ideal city developed in the *Republic* and the *Laws*, had much more resonance with the utopian tradition than the strictly philosophical tradition. More important, therefore, are the resemblances to Thomas More's *Utopia*, published in 1516, which is awash in Platonic ideas[29]—and yet it is quite different from Lefèvre's work. More's work, so important in the history of political thought, was certainly not inspired by Lefèvre's collection of excerpts; More had a complete text of Plato and did not need Lefèvre's excerpts.

The idea of the "philosopher king"[30] could have seduced some religious reformers, convinced that rigorous regulation was necessary if one were to govern a city according to purely religious values. Such is the case with Jean Calvin, who submitted the entire city of Geneva to strict ecclesiastical discipline in the 1540s and 1550s. The many Platonic themes in Calvin's thought are often overlooked. Their importance is emphasized by Jean Boisset, the only scholar to my knowledge who has studied the *Hecatonomiae*. Did the *Hecatonomiae* inspire Calvin to read Plato? I leave this to the historians of Protestantism.[31]

To read Plato is—and will forever be—a great intellectual pleasure, but we know that his ideas are impracticable. This caveat was already apparent during the Roman Empire when, six centuries after Plato, his distant successor Plotinus planned to found an ideal city, which he called Platonopolis, in 268 A.D. The philosopher and founder of Neoplatonism was aided, it seems, by the support of the Emperor Gallienus and his wife, Cornelia Salonina, but the project (which was intended to give new life to a community of philosophers already imagined in the time of Cicero) came to nothing because of opposition in the circle of the emperor.[32] Plato himself was conscious of the impossibility of ever finding practical conditions that would be favorable to the realization of his discourse. He is the first to say it: the legislator cannot model a particular city "as in wax."[33] The demonstration in the *Laws* presents a model[34] and proposes nothing more than a reasoned fiction.[35] Renaissance readers were utterly sure that the type of ideal city described by Plato in the *Republic* was a paradigm, even if it was given a more concrete meaning in the *Laws*.

Ficino, in the *argumenta* and the *epitomai* that accompany his translation of the *Republic* and the *Laws*, agrees with Plato's affirmation of the superiority of the contemplative life over the active life. But he keeps his own counsel in the face of ideas he finds scandalous, such as eugenics or the communal status of property, women, and children. Lefèvre, in his limited selection of political ideas, is far more critical, considering that on many points the Platonic city transgresses the law of God. This "fundamental criticism" is repeated by many French scholiasts at the end of the sixteenth century, such as Jean de Serres in his commentary accompanying his Latin translation of Plato (1578), or the Hellenist and translator Loys Le Roy who, like Lefèvre, produced a commentary on the *Politics* of Aristotle (Paris, 1568), emphasizing Aristotle's criticisms of Plato in book 2.[36] At the dawn of the sixteenth century, when Platonic thought was being widely rediscovered, Lefèvre was the pathfinder for all these readers with his *Hecatonomiae*.

Institut de Recherche et d'Histoire des Textes (CNRS), Paris

Acknowledgments
An earlier version of this text was read at the 48th Medieval Congress (Western Michigan University, Kalamazoo, May 10, 2013). I thank my colleague at the Institut de Recherche et d'Histoire des Textes (IRHT, Paris), Patricia Stirnemann, who translated the paper into English and gave aid and support that were indispensable and generous, elegant and light-hearted.

NOTES

1. The two fundamental studies on Lefèvre are still Augustin Renaudet, *Préréforme et humanisme à Paris pendant les premières guerres d'Italie (1494–1517)*, rev. 2nd ed. (Paris: Librairie d'Argences, 1953), 130–158; and Guy Bedouelle, *Lefèvre d'Étaples et l'intelligence des écritures* (Geneva: Droz, 1976).

2. See Eugene F. Rice, "Bibliography," in Jacques Lefèvre d'Étaples, *The Prefatory Epistles of Jacques Lefèvre d'Étaples and Related Texts*, ed. Eugene F. Rice (New York: Columbia University Press, 1972), 535–568.

3. Ibid., 553, no. 198.

4. Jean Boisset, *Sagesse et sainteté dans la pensée de Jean Calvin: Essai sur l'humanisme du réformateur français* (Paris: Presses Universitaires de France, 1959).

5. Jean Boisset was preparing a critical edition of the *Hecatonomiae*. The posthumous publication is sadly inadequate: Jacques Lefèvre d'Étaples, *Hecatonomiarum libri: Texte latin des Hécatonomies de Lefèvre d'Étaples, en parallèle avec la traduction latine de Platon par Marsile Ficin*, ed. Jean Boisset, revised Robert Combès (Paris: J. Vrin, 1979).

6. [Aristotelis,] *Contenta. Politicorum libri octo. Commentarii. Economicorum duo. Commentarii. Hecatonomiarum Septem. Economiarum publ. unus. Explanationis Leonardi in oeconomica Duo* (Paris: Henri Estienne, August 5, 1506); Rice, "Bibliography," 553, no. 198. The *Hecatonomiae* occupies only folios 135v–168r of this volume, that is, only thirty-four folios out of nearly two hundred ([5] +178 + 16).

7. G. Leroux, "Introduction," in Plato, *Platon: La République*, 2nd rev. ed., trans. G. Leroux (Paris: Flammarion, 2005), 15.

8. Plato, *Platonis Opera omnia* (Florence: Lorenzo Veneto [and San Iacopo di Ripoli, 1484]), two volumes; see Sebastiano Gentile, et al., eds., *Marsilio Ficino e il ritorno di Platone: Mostra di manoscritti stampe e documenti, 17 maggio–6 giugno 1984: Catalogo* (Florence: Le Lettere, 1984), no. 91, 117–119. See also P. O. Kristeller, "The First Printed Edition of Plato's Works and the Date of Its Publication," in *Science and History: Studies in Honor of Edward Rosen* (Wrocław: Ossolineum, 1978, 1978), 35–35. This *editio princeps* was full of errors and displeased Ficino, who declared it spoiled by *neglegentia impressorum vel potius oppressorum* (untranslatable pun in Latin: "through the negligence of printers or rather of oppressors"); Marsilio Ficino, "Letter to Francesco Bandini," in *Marsilii Ficini opera* (Basel, Switzerland: 1576), 872. It was followed by a second edition, Venice, August 13, 1491, printed by Bernardino de Cori and Simone da Lovere.

9. A "persuasive" discourse should precede the establishment of the law in order to convince the citizens of its utility and obtain their assent: Plato, *Laws* 4:723a–b. See Luc Brisson, "Les préambules dans les *Lois*," in *Lectures de Platon* (Paris: Vrin, 2000), 235–262.

10. Jean-Marie Flamand, "Les écoles de grec à Paris au XVe siècle," paper read at the Institut de recherche et d'histoire des textes (Paris: March 26, 2010).

11. On this point, Lefèvre's views coincide exactly with those of Leonardo Bruni, who declared: "*Quid enim opera mea utilius, quid laude dignius efficere possim, quam ciuibus meis primum, deinde ceteris, qui Latina utuntur lingua,*"

ignaris Graecarum litterarum, facultatem praebere, ut non per enigmata ac deliramenta interpretationum ineptarum ac falsarum, sed de facie ad faciem possint Aristotelem intueri et, ut ille in Graeco scripsit, sic in Latino perlegere" (see Rice, 153). See Jacques Lefèvre d'Étaples, *The Prefatory Epistles of Jacques Lefèvre d'Étaples and Related Texts*, ed. Eugene F. Rice (New York: Columbia University Press, 1972), 153.

12. Paris: Henri Estienne, March 31, 1511/1512; Paris: Ponset le Preux, 1515 (edition shared with François Regnault and Jean Petit); Paris: Simon de Colines, April 30, 1526; Paris: Simon de Colines, 1535; Paris: Simon de Colines, 1543. See Rice, "Bibliography," 553–554, nos. 197–203.

13. See Isabelle Pantin, s.v. "émission," in *Dictionnaire encyclopédique du livre*, ed. Pascal Fouché, Daniel Péchoin, and Philippe Schuwer, vol. 2 (Paris: Édition du Cercle de la Librairie, 2005), 48–49.

14. See Charles H. Lohr, "Renaissance Latin Translations of the Greek Commentaries on Aristotle," in *Humanism and Early Modern Philosophy*, ed. Jill Kraye and M. W. F. Stone (London: Routledge, 2000), 24–40; and Luca Bianchi, "From Jacques Lefèvre d'Étaples to Giulio Landi," in *Humanism and Early Modern Philosophy*, ed. Jill Kraye and M. W. F. Stone (London: Routledge, 2000), 41–58. Lefèvre adhered to the fundamental approach of the Italian humanists, which consisted of finding the texts themselves and refusing the burden of interpretation that led to accumulation of "delirious commentaries" (see n. 11).

15. One of the merits of Boisset's edition (Lefèvre d'Étaples, *Hecatonomiae*, ed. Jean Boisset, revised Robert Combès) is that it has a "Table of Concordance" (pp. 248–253) between the extracts retained—and often remodeled—by Lefèvre and the passages of Plato identified by cross-reference to the Estienne edition (Genève, 1578; column number, followed by letters a, b, c, d, e), which is today the universally accepted norm in studies on Plato. By consulting the table, one easily notes that the order of the extracts chosen by Lefèvre generally corresponds to a continuous reading of Ficino's text of Plato.

16. For example, the six extracts numbered by Lefèvre 2.30–2.35 on the use of money all come from the same passage of the *Laws* (5:742a–742c); elsewhere, the five extracts in Lefèvre as 4.49–4.53 concerning the hunt come from the *Laws* 7:824a.

17. For example, Lefèvre's extract 7.57 refers to *Laws* 12:950a–c, while the preceding extract, 7.56, refers to a later passage in the *Laws*, 12:952a–b.

18. On Lefèvre's inversions within certain of Plato's passages (e.g., in *Hecatonomiae* 1.38), see "Introduction," in Lefèvre d'Étaples, *Hecatonomiae*, ed. Jean Boisset, revised Robert Combès, 29–30.

19. Plato, *Republic* 4:427e–445e, a long passage devoted to the dialectic of justice in the individual and in the city, with a discussion of the role of wisdom, courage, moderation, and justice.

20. Lefèvre's celebrity throughout Europe is due above all to his "Paraphrases" of Aristotle. The first series concerned natural philosophy: *Totius Aristotelis philosophiae naturalis*, (Paris: Johann Higman, 1492). This work, intended for his students at the University in Paris, was followed by thirty-six reissues, either complete or partial (some accompanied by the commentaries of his student Josse Clichtove) up to 1540 in Paris, Lyons, Alcalá de Henares, Freiburg im Breisgau, Strasbourg, Leipzig, Kraków, Salamanca, and Nuremberg; see Rice, "Bibliography," 535–539, nos. 1–37.

21. See "Introduction," in Lefèvre d'Étaples, *Hecatonomiarum libri*, ed. Boisset, revised Combès, 30.

22. For this theory of the "noble lie," cf. REIECT. 8 (= *Rep.* 5, 459c-d): *Quare necessarium fore videtur: ut frequenti mendacio et deceptione utantur principes ad subditorum utilitatem. Huiusmodi enim omnia pharmaci medicinaeque loco necessaria sunt.* ("This is why it seems that it will frequently be necessary for the leaders to use lies and subterfuges for the good of their subjects. All procedures of this kind are necessary, if they act as remedies and medical treatments.")

23. On Jean de Ganay (ca. 1450–June 3, 1512), who was very open to humanist ideas, see Ernest de Ganay, *Un chancelier de France sous Louis XII, Jehan de Ganay* (Paris: Plon, 1932). See also Lefèvre d'Étaples, *Prefatory Epistles*, 17–20, ep. 5, 155–157, ep. 50: *cum suscepissem Politicorum Aristotelis recognitionem et commentarios meditatus fuissem, occurrebant Socrates et Plato frequenter in jus ab Aristotele vocati, quos si adducerem et ad politicen facere visi sunt, et ne falso videretur Aristoteles illos pro veritatis defensione insimulavisse ; adducere autem dispersim et in singulo quoquie loco et longum et onerosum visum est, at legentibus multo conducibilius si sua serie pro rei magnitudine in uno volumine collecti pariter ederentur ; sicque magis insuper posse prodesse, praesertim iis qui prima legum tyrocinia aggrediuntur, si post lectam Ethicen et Politicen ... ex philosophicis legibus, ut ex quibusdam praeludiis, ad illas sacrosanctas, augustas et imperatorias leges surgerent.* ("As I had undertaken a critical rereading of the *Politics* of Aristotle and thought about glossing the text, Socrates and Plato have come to me, frequently invoked by Aristotle in judicial matters; if I wanted to cite them, it was because they not only seemed adapted to the politic, but also because I wanted to make clear that Aristotle was not making untruthful accusations against them. But to cite them helter-skelter in the course of my text seemed labored, and I found it much more practical for my readers to edit them in order, given their extent, in one volume. In so doing, I intended to be useful to those apprehending the very rudiments of law so that after having read the *Ethics* and *Politics* ... they might progress from the laws of the philosophers to the sacrosanct august and imperial laws.")

24. *Summum Aristotelem omnium vere philosophantium ducem* ("the great Aristotle, the guide of all those who are really philosophers"), from Lefèvre

d'Étaples, *Prologus in Paraphrasin librorum Physicorum Aristotelis, in Totius Aristotelis philosophiae naturalis paraphrases*, Paris, Johann Higman, 1492 (Rice, 5).

25. Heb. 5:14. Cf. Lefèvre's edition of Dionysius the Areopagite, *Dionysii Areopagitae opera omnia: Theologia vivificans. Cibus solidus. Dionysii Celestis hierarchia. Ecclesiastica hierarchia. Mystica theologia. Undecim epistole. Ignatii undecim epistole. Polycarpi epistola una* (Paris: Johann Higman & Wolfgang Hopyl, February 6, 1498/1499), fol.; Rice, "Bibliography," 549–550, no. 155.

26. Plato, *Le premier, second et dixiesme livre de Iustice, ou de la Republique de Platon . . . traduict de grec en françois* [par Loys Le Roy] (Paris: Sébastien Nyvelle, 1555); Plato, *Discours de Platon extraict du troisiesme de ses Loix, sur le royaume de Perse* (Paris: F. Morel, 1562). Moreover, Loys Le Roy also translated into French and commented on Aristotle's *Politics*; Aristotle, the *Politiques d'Aristote*, trans. Loys Le Roy (Paris: Michel de Vascosan, 1568; new ed. 1576).

27. Fifty years after Lefèvre, Loys Le Roy would cautiously try to reconcile Plato with Christianity in France; see Raymond Lebègue, "La *République* de Platon et la Renaissance française," *Lettres d'Humanité* 2 (1943): 141–165, esp. 150–151.

28. See [Philippe Renouard], *Imprimeurs et libraires parisiens du XVIe siècle*, t. III (Paris: 1979), 110–111, no. 149: *Tres hecatonomiae Nicolai franci Vimacui* [= du Vimeu] *de conceptibus. Prima de potentia cognitiua, obiecto cognoscibili, et medio cognoscendi ; deque tribus signis doctrinalibus (scriptura inquam voce et conceptu) in generali: correspondens primo capiti tractatus summularum Petri hispani. Secunda de conceptus incomplexis eorumque speciebus ac proprietatibus: subordinata prohemio primi perihermeneias Aristotelis. Tertia de conceptibus complexis ac eorumdem appaehensione* [sic] *dubitatione, assensu et dissensu, actu, dispositione, et habitu, subseruiens primo capiti posteriorum eiusdem Aristotelis* (copy in the University Library, Cambridge). Signature a i v°: dedicatory epistle from the author to his teacher Philippe Prévost d'Arras (*Philippus Prepositus Attrabatensis*), on whom see Lefèvre d'Étaples, *Prefatory Epistles*, 111.

29. See Jean-Yves Lacroix, *L'Utopia de Thomas More et la tradition platonicienne*, De Pétrarque à Descartes 74 (Paris: Vrin, 2007).

30. Plato, *Republic* 5:473d.

31. See Boisset, *Sagesse et sainteté*, 253–314, esp. 277–284 on political themes.

32. Porphyrius, *Vita Plotini*, 12; see Lucien Jerphagnon, "Platonopolis ou Plotin entre le siècle et le rêve," in *Néoplatonisme: Mélanges offerts à Jean Trouillard*, Les Cahiers de Fontenay 19–22 (Fontenay-aux-Roses, France: E.N.S., 1981), 215–229.

33. Plato, *Laws* 5:745e–746a.

34. Ibid., 3:702d; 5:739e1; 5:746b7.

35. See Jean-François Pradeau, *Platon, les démocrates et la démocratie: Essai sur la réception contemporaine de la pensée politique platonicienne* (Naples: Bibliopolis, 2005), 66–73.

36. Jean Céard, "Le modèle de la *République* de Platon et la pensée politique au XVIe siècle," in *XVIe Colloque International de Tours: Platon et Aristote à la Renaissance* (Paris: Vrin, 1976), 175–190.

Queen Mary I's Books at Lambeth Palace Library

VALERIE SCHUTTE

Lambeth Palace Library has recently published a research guide listing manuscripts and books within its collection that are relevant to Queen Mary I.[1] This research guide briefly lists each manuscript in its holdings and explains its relevance, from the Shrewsbury and Talbot papers belonging to important Roman Catholic families, to grants of land given by Mary, to papers relating to bishops of London, Durham, and Winchester. The library also has a large collection of printed books associated with Mary, including four books that were written in support of Mary, ten Protestant books written during her reign, four devotional books possibly owned by Mary, as well as others.

The four books identified as possibly owned by Mary are a Latin breviary printed in Lyon in 1556,[2] a Latin missal printed in Lyon in 1550,[3] Ludolphus de Saxonia's *Vita Christi* printed in Paris in 1534,[4] and Luigi Lippomano's *Vitarum sanctorum* printed in Venice in 1554.[5] *Vitarum sanctorum* and *Vita Christi* were both bound by the so-called King Edward and Queen Mary Binder. *Vitarum sanctorum* is bound in brown leather with gold inlay, with both the front and back covers featuring an ornate border with the arms of Queen Mary in the center. The spine contains six gold-embossed roses. The book is written entirely in Latin, and it begins by explaining rites and sacraments of the Catholic Church, then moves on to tell the life of Jesus as well as the lives and miracles of many other biblical and church figures, such as Joseph and Moses. Overall, it is in excellent condition and looks as if it were barely used. There are no marginalia or indications of readership, and even the corners of the binding are in good condition. The only evidence that this book was owned by Mary is the binding, which can clearly be identified as by the King Edward and Queen Mary Binder. Therefore, this book can be identified as likely having been owned by Mary.

Ludolphus of Saxony's *Vita Christi* can also be identified as having likely been owned by Mary. Like many of Mary's books, there are no marginalia within the text, but the corners of the binding are worn, suggesting that someone actively read this book but was careful not to leave marks in it. The binding is comprised of the traditional brown leather and gold inlay of the King Edward and Queen Mary Binder, with Mary's coat of arms and crown in the center of both the front and back covers. However, Mary is known to have owned two copies of this book during her lifetime, and it cannot be confirmed which copy Lambeth Palace Library has. Sometime in early 1534, Katherine of Aragon, Mary's mother, sent Mary a letter commenting that both had been reduced in status by the position of Anne Boleyn as King Henry's second wife. Katherine implores Mary to regard God above all things, always to obey the king, and to continue her reading and recreation to give herself pleasure since so much had been taken away from them. Also in the letter, Katherine promises to send two books to Mary, writing, "I will send you two books in Latin: one shall be *De Vita Christi,* with the declaration of the Gospels, and the other the Epistles of Hierome, that he did write always to St. Paula and Eustochium; and in them I trust you shall see good things."[6] The approximate dating of this letter to early 1534 fits with the 1534 print date of the copy of *Vita Christi* held by Lambeth Palace Library. In fact, the research guide postulates that the library's copy may have been the exact one sent by Katherine to Mary.

Nevertheless, Mary did receive a second copy of *Vita Christi*. Printer John Cawood gave Mary two books as New Year's gifts in 1557, which her gift roll reflects were a book in "laten entitled vita Christi and a little boke of exhortation to young men."[7] In return, Cawood received an eleven-ounce gilt cruse from Mary. James Carley suggests that the copy of *Vita Christi* in Lambeth Palace Library is more likely the copy given to Mary by Cawood rather than the one sent to her by her mother.[8] I suspect that Carley's suggestion is correct for several reasons. *Vita Christi* was printed many times from the late fifteenth through the mid-sixteenth centuries. If Katherine owned a copy in early 1534 and sent it to her daughter, it was probably not a copy that had just been printed in Paris of that same year; it most likely would have been an earlier edition. Also, when Cawood gave Mary *Vita Christi* for New Year's in 1557, he probably had it bound by the King Edward and Queen Mary Binder for her. So it is not likely that he took her old copy and had it bound and gave it back to her for a present. His gift to her must have just happened to have been a 1534 edition that he was able to find and have bound for her, because according to the Universal Short Title Catalogue, *Vita Christi* was never printed in England. There is a possibility that Cawood knew of Mary's appreciation of the book when he sent her a second copy. No matter how Mary came to acquire the copy held by Lambeth Palace Library, the binding suggests that Mary was already the queen when it came into her ownership.

The Latin breviary and the Latin missal, however, are more difficult to establish as linked to Mary. According to the research guide, both were possibly presentation copies for Mary. The breviary is a recension of the Quignon version, which was written by Francis de Quiñones, a Spanish Franciscan, for the purpose of simplifying the existing Roman breviary. Neither was printed in England, and both are bound in red morocco leather and have inlays of black, white, brown, and green with gold toolmarks. The missal's front and back covers appear to be the same, and its spine has the same engravings as on the covers, but there are no initials or coat of arms to identify ownership. The breviary has nearly the same pattern and decoration as does the missal, and also has no initials or coat of arms to identify the owner or intended recipient. The toolmarks on the bindings of the books are not the same as those of the King Edward and Queen Mary Binder's work. Both texts are printed in red and black inks. Within these two books, I was unable to find any marginalia or written indications of ownership by Mary.

Perhaps these two books were presented to her, but that does not seem likely, as there is a place in the center of the binding of the missal that would have typically held a coat of arms or at least initials but does not have either. If this book really was presented specifically to Mary, it would probably have some toolmarks or inlays specific to her. I have not found any other books in her personal collection with this type of binding. Moreover, the suggestion in the research guide that these were possibly presentation copies to Mary came from the old catalogues of Lambeth Palace Library and was simply repeated in the research guide, so there is no way to corroborate why they were identified with Mary in the first place. For these reasons, the Latin breviary and Latin missal cannot be confirmed as having been owned by Mary.

Lambeth Palace Library's research guide for Mary Tudor, along with all of their research guides, is an incredibly useful tool to catalogue all of their collection materials related to Mary. However, of the four devotional works listed as possibly belonging to Mary, only two can be likely identified as having been owned by her, while the other two were almost certainly not.

University of Akron

NOTES

1. This research guide is available through the Web site of Lambeth Palace Library at http://www.lambethpalacelibrary.org/files/Mary_Tudor.pdf.

The library has also published many other research guides on topics such as archbishops of Canterbury, kings and queens, and church history that make its collection very accessible.
2. H2000.Q8.
3. H2015.(A2 1550).
4. F298.(L8).
5. H4654.(L5).
6. London, British Library, Arundel 151, fol. 194r. The letter is written in English. Here I quote the modern spelling as provided by the reprint of the letter in James Gairdner, ed., *Letters and Papers, Foreign and Domestic, of the Reign of Henry VIII*, vol. 6 (London, 1882), entry 1126. The letter has no date but appears among letters dated September 1633 in the British History Online catalogue (http://british-history.ac.uk/report.aspx?compid=77568).
7. Taken from Mary's New Year's gift roll of 1557, as reprinted in David Loades, *Mary Tudor: A Life* (Oxford: Basil Blackwell, 1989; rev. 1992), 365.
8. James Carley, *The Books of King Henry VIII and His Wives* (London: British Library, 2004), 110.

Another New Fragment of *Speculum Vitae*

ERIC WEISKOTT

In the Beinecke Library, the printed book with the shelfmark 2008 2479 is a copy of the *De regulis iuris* of Dinus de Mugello (b. 1254) printed at Lyons in 1562. Two strips of vellum cut to about 25x165mm were used as endpaper guards in this copy. The front endpaper guard contains fragments of a Vulgate Bible in a fifteenth-century Gothic book hand. The back endpaper guard contains fragments of a hitherto unrecorded copy of the fourteenth-century Middle English poem *Speculum vitae*. The text is copied in a workmanlike late fifteenth-century anglicana script, in prose format rather than in verse lineation. A somewhat inelegant two-line blue initial Þ with red flourishing appears at the beginning of the fragmentary text. The first line of each couplet is closed with a red virgule, and, after the opening initial, each couplet is headed by a red paraph and a red slashed-line initial.

The recent *editio princeps* of *Speculum vitae* by Ralph Hanna lists forty-five complete or fragmentary copies of the poem.[1] In addition to its intrinsic value as a new copy of *Speculum vitae* and the only one written as prose, the Beinecke fragment suggests that this copy of the *De regulis* was imported to England and bound there.[2] The Beinecke text corresponds to lines 4039 to 4046 and 4097 to 4111 in Hanna's edited text, with scribal omission of lines 4103 to 4108, apparently due to eyeskip between two lines with identical openings, Hanna's 4105 and 4109 Þe meke him lawes to serue. Extrapolating from the dimensions of the strip and the lines lost between recto and verso gives an original writing area of about 150x120mm, thirty-six to thirty-seven manuscript lines in one column, noticeably squatter than all of the other extant copies.

The Beinecke text preserves four substantial variants not found in any of the five texts collated by Hanna: line 4045 has *dysese* for Hanna's *and assayse*; line 4097 has *dung* for Hanna's *barly*; l. 4098 omits Hanna's *gase*; and line 4102 has *semely* for Hanna's *semy*. The first alteration simplifies the syntax of Hanna's lines 4045 to 4046 and renders the sense redundant, replacing "He suffers for the love of God and makes trial of/ Hunger and cold and other hardship" with "He suffers hardship for the love of God/ Hunger and cold and other hardship." The substitution may also have a metrical explanation, for Hanna's line 4045 must be scanned with the more innovative monosyllabic *Goddis*, whereas the line in the Beinecke fragment shows the more conservative disyllabic *Goddis*.

The second alteration may likewise have a metrical explanation if a scribe missed the elision between Hanna's 4097 *barly*, "barley," and *als*, "as," and scanned a metrically difficult two-syllable dip there. The substitution also serves to intensify the contrast between the two hypothetical loads carried by "þe asse þat beres oft heuy," "the ass that often bears heavy (loads)" (Hanna's l. 4096; cp. Hanna's 4099 *stanes*, "stones," and *brede*, "bread"). The third alteration may also have been made *metri causa*, since Hanna's line 4098 begins with a metrically difficult two-syllable dip (*And als*). The verb for the quasi-adverb *fast* in line 4098 (both texts) must be *beres*, "bears," understood from the previous line (l. 4097, both texts). The fourth alteration, *semely*, "seemly," for *semy*, "?quick," probably indicates confusion with the online *Middle English Dictionary*'s "sēmī" (a) ('seemly'), but compare with the *Middle English Dictionary*'s "sēmī" (b), glossing *subtilis*, and Hanna's note on line 4102.

In the following diplomatic edition, lineation, capitalization, and (lack of) punctuation are editorial; manuscript line boundaries are indicated by a vertical stroke (|); italics indicate the expansion of scribal abbreviations, including the Tironian note as *and*; and illegible or partly legible letters are enclosed in angled brackets. In order to achieve the correct textual sequence, I pair 4) the lines visible after the endleaves, on the outside of the strip, with 1) those visible before the endleaves, on the outside of the strip; and 3) those visible after the endleaves, on the inside of the strip, with 2) those visible before the endleaves, on the inside of the strip. The numbering 1), 2), 3), 4) represents the physical order of the fragments as they now exist in Beinecke 2008 2479, front to back.

Beinecke 2008 2479, back endpaper guard

	4)
	Þe fowrte b<r>aunche as men ma<y> proue
4040	Is when a | man will povert³ loue
	So <d>ooþe þe verray mek | in hert
	On fowre maneres he loues pouert
	He loues | <. . .> co<. . .>
	And haldis <þ>e manere of <. . .> h<a>lly |
	1)
4045	<H>e tholes for goddis loue dysese⁴
	Hunggyr *and* cald and. . ..
	3)
	. . . .beres as blythly dung as whete
	And as <f>ast for smale | as for grete
	And as blythly beres stonys as brede
4100	And | l<ee>d and irne as gold rede
	Þe meke hym lowes to *serue* | w<y>ghtly
4102	As he þat is lyght and semely
4109	Þe meke hym low |
	2)
4109 cont'd	es to ser<u>e lastandly
4110	As he þat is neu*er*more wery
	To bow|. . .

Acknowledgments

Thanks are due to Christopher Clarkson, Ralph Hanna, Aaron Pratt, and Barbara Shailor for consultation on paleographical and codicological matters and to *JEBS* editors Linne Mooney and Daniel Wakelin for helpful suggestions.

Boston College

NOTES

1. Ralph Hanna, ed., with Venetia Somerset, *Speculum Vitae: A Reading Text*, 2 vols., Early English Text Society Original Series 331 and 332 (Oxford and New York: Oxford University Press, 2008), 1:xiv–lx. Ibid., lx–lxii, express-

ing serious skepticism about the traditional attribution of *Speculum vitae* to William of Nassyngton (d. 1349). For two other fragments, see Ralph Hanna, "Two New Manuscript Fragments of *Speculum Vitae*," *Journal of the Early Book Society* 16 (2013): 193–198.

2. The copying of verse in prose format was the norm in England before 1250 and persisted sporadically afterward. See A. S. G. Edwards, "Editing and Manuscript Form: Middle English Verse as Prose," *English Studies in Canada* 27 (2001): 15–28, 17–19, reporting that the copying of verse in prose format was rather more common in the West Midlands than elsewhere 1250–1400, but rare overall by the fifteenth century. Ibid., 21–2, notes that considerations of space could lead to prose format. The format of the Beinecke *Speculum vitae* fragments thus gives no secure evidence for the provenance of the lost codex. The binding decoration of Beinecke 2008 2479 closely matches David Pearson, *English Bookbinding Styles, 1450–1800: A Handbook* (London: British Library, 2005), 62, Fig. 3.46 (a book printed 1575). An *ex libris* note in English secretary script, name blotted out, appears on the title page, and other notes in secretary script appear on the endleaves. The latter are brownish and speckled, of poor quality, with no discernible watermarks.

3. An indistinct letter form follows *p*, perhaps a correction.

4. Erasure after *y*.

Descriptive Reviews

KATHERINE ACHESON
Visual Rhetoric and Early Modern English Literature.
Material Readings in Early Modern Culture.
Burlington, VT: Ashgate, 2013. 174 pp., illus.

Katherine Acheson's inspired and inspiring book, *Visual Rhetoric and Early Modern English Literature*, will be welcomed with both delight and admiration by a wide variety of readers: here is material of interest to scholars in fields ranging from the history of the book to early modern English literature, as well as politics and religion, intellectual history, graphic design and informatics. The book had its genesis in Acheson's fascination with the diagrams and technical illustrations that are ubiquitous in early printed books; her extensive study of this material led to her identification of the types of diagrams and illustrations that form the backbone of each of the book's four chapters. Chapter one concerns illustrations of garden design, military strategies, and sundials; chapter two, dichotomous tables; chapter three, illustrations in manuals of drawing and writing and in advertisements for the tools of both; chapter four, visual representations in books of natural history, comparative anatomy, and copies of *Aesop's Fables*.

But as the term "visual rhetoric" in its title announces, this book is much more than a survey of this truly fascinating array of visual artifacts. Its core argument is that "diagrams and illustrations of a technical nature insinuated ways of thinking in their audiences, and that those ways of thinking could migrate ... from the images themselves and affect concepts and communication in other forms" (2). In developing this argument, Acheson draws upon work by Gunthur Kress and Theo Van Leeuwen to identify the "representational codes" (4) upon which each of her genres of illustration depends along with the assumptions—about subjectivity, genealogy, war, peace, race, and relations between humans and animals—they both imply and produce.

She finds proof of her images' capacity to migrate in their verbal reflections in the work of Andrew Marvell, John Milton, and Aphra Behn. Proof of their persuasiveness is apparent in her analyses of those reflections, which disclose a fresh panorama of early modern English culture's ideas on the topics announced in the first words of each chapter: space, truth, art, and nature.

As its title forecasts, Acheson's first chapter, "SPACE: 'The description of the worlde': Military, Horticultural, and Technical Illustration and Andrew Marvell's Gardens," brings together a set of illustrations that would seem to be unrelated. As we quickly learn, however, these illustrations are all founded upon an abstract "analytical coding orientation" (26), arraying letters to represent soldiers and dots for trees in a "uniform flattened space" (8), thereby suggesting a shared territory between the ostensibly disparate realms of garden design and military strategy. As Acheson points out, that shared territory is also discoverable in the emerging concept in seventeenth-century England of land as a commodity coupled with a notion of "dominion" as a matter of both cultivation and conquest (41). Turning to Marvell's gardens, and particularly to those of *Upon Appleton House*, Acheson discerns in his integration of military and horticultural imagery the influence not only of these cultural shifts but also of the "radical abstraction" (20) that characterized the illustrations of garden design and military strategy. That abstracted point of view is employed in *Upon Appleton House* to convey the "vigilant subjectivity" (45) necessitated by life in a "militarized garden" (45). The persuasiveness of the images Acheson examines in this chapter thus resides less in their content than in the way of seeing they mandate.

Acheson begins chapter two, "TRUTH: The 'Way of Dichotomy': Dichotomous Tables and John Milton's *Paradise Lost*," with an overview of dichotomous tables published as appendices to the Bible in early modern England, arguing that they serve both to represent its matter, in the form of genealogies, tables of contents, and reading guides, and to model a way of thinking through relational and hierarchized categories. She goes on to analyze Milton's treatment of key tenets of Protestant theology in *Paradise Lost* in terms of three dichotomies that these tables emphasize: cause versus effect, whole versus part, and plot versus narrative. In this way, the amenability of genealogical diagrams to being "read forwards or backwards" (61) is reflected in Milton's use of genealogical terms in his representation of Christ's role as both "the effect of God . . . and . . . the cause of faith" (62). Similarly, in giving Adam and Eve a genealogical account of the future, the archangel Michael weaves their individual lives into the whole of salvation history and implies at the same time that "genealogy is the *method* of providence" (72, emphasis in text). Finally, the capacity for dichotomous tables to represent both plot and narrative is seen in *Paradise Lost* in the numerous instances of its contrasting the divine plan (or plot) with the human tendency to become caught up in story and thus to lose sight of "the providential thread" (79).

The materials Acheson examines in chapters three and four are progressively more pictorial than diagrammatic. In the first two sections of chapter three, "ART: 'Speculatory Ingenuity': Painting, Writing, and Andrew Marvell's 'Last Instructions to a Painter,'" she describes a contest between the skills of painting and drawing on the one hand and those of penmanship on the other as that contest was played out in manuals devoted to teaching these skills. Title pages of painting and drawing manuals tend to display an array of precision instruments, linking these skills "with the new science and empiricism" (112); title pages of writing manuals answer with calligraphic displays that not only have a pictorial aspect but convey an engagement with science and technology as well. The third section of the chapter examines these illustrations' "migration" into ekphrastic poetry, Marvell's "Last Instructions to a Painter" in particular, where the pictorial arts' reliance on technology becomes its weakness, linking it with "market-forces, foreign influences, and individual greed" (92).

While the agents of verbal and pictorial domains are in competition in chapter three, they work in partnership in Acheson's final chapter, "NATURE: 'Surveying Nature, with too nice a view'. Naturalistic, Realistic, Anatomical, and Allegorical Animals in Aphra Behn's *Oroonoko*." Here Acheson begins with a discussion of three early modern genres dealing with animals: natural history, comparative anatomy, and "the illustrated Aesopic fable" (128). In Aphra Behn's *Oroonoko*, she then argues, the influence of these genres is apparent not only in the novel's content but also in its blend of the realistic depiction and naturalistic narrative, in which Behn favors the "values of natural historical representations" (129). Those "values" include a keen regard for the specificity both of a given animal's physical features and of its behavior, the first supplied in drawings and the second in narrative. As Acheson points out, Behn's description of Oroonoko himself exemplifies the natural historical mode: "While his features may help us identify him, we can only know him through his behaviour in the contexts in which he finds himself" (150).

As this review will have suggested, Acheson's book not only raises the curtain on a type of visual material in early modern books that has so far been neglected but also, and more importantly, demonstrates its persuasive presence in early modern literature. It will surely inspire further exciting work in the field it has opened.

Martha Rust, New York University

CRAIG E. BERTOLET
*Chaucer, Gower, Hoccleve and the Commercial Practices
of Late Fourteenth-Century London.*
Surrey, UK: Ashgate, 2013. 168 pp.

Craig Bertolet's book provides a fascinating snapshot of the commercial practices of late fourteenth-century London as reflected in the literary output of its principal authors. Bertolet uses examples from the works of Chaucer, Gower and Hoccleve, relates them to documentary evidence found in London custumals and court records, and interprets them within the framework of the sociological theories of Pierre Bourdieu.

Bertolet's "Introduction" (1-15) sets the scene of his investigation by suggesting that aspects of the commerce of the medieval city "shape the literary personalities" of some of Chaucer's Pilgrims (2), demonstrate the anxieties of Hoccleve with regard to his out-of-control spending which excludes him from the society in which he wishes to participate (6) and underpin Gower's belief that a commercial polity encouraged fraud which in turn provided a "negative outcome" for the citizens of London (14).

The focus is on late fourteenth-century London, a city still recovering from the ravages of the Black Death. Bertolet demonstrates that all three poets were part of an increasingly urbanized environment in which "church time" had been co-opted by a merchant culture whose "trading time" began with the ringing of the bell for Prime. The city gates were opened; trading of every kind began, and business hours ended at curfew (24). Thus the move from an agricultural to an urban economy involved a commodification of time. At the same time the shift in economic power, a result of the Statute of Laborers (1351), produced a ripple effect whereby market forces dictated new employment possibilities but was a source of anxiety for the elite classes. As a result, every aspect of life became a commodity to be traded as the citizens jostled to acquire what Bertolet describes as Bourdieu's "social capital." Bertolet shows how, apart from the obvious trade in goods, other aspects of life—such as time, space, personal relationships including marriage, the hospitality trade as well as religious life—were all part and parcel of the same commodification. An economy was created based on "emulation," a fundamental element in the pursuit of Bourdieu's social and political capital.

The work of the three poets includes incisive assessments on different aspects of commercial life and its trading practices as they impinge on the lives of London citizens. Examples from the tales of the Pardoner, the Shipman and Sir Thopas are used by Bertolet to demonstrate how the influence of a market culture permeated and shaped the thinking of London citizens. The church had become a profit-based institution, providing a market in benefices. In marriage, women became the property, and marriage itself was the market in which trading rather than love was the principal factor. The increasingly important role of the merchant saw him establishing a more solid place in society's hierarchy, and the development of the guild structure served to support and protect the rise of the individual merchant trader. Gower's writings in the *Mirour de L'Omme* and the *Confessio Amantis* support the development of the trading culture of the city but include reflections on the concomitant rise of baser human instincts involving fraudulent dealings and deception, part and parcel of an increasing mercantile polity with no one apparently responsible for its regulation. The whole of life was a market with the need to purchase for the purposes of survival, overtaken by the desire to purchase, a feature of a society in the process of monumental change as London's citizens became increasingly concerned with buying and selling (62-63). In *Male Regle* and *Regiment of Princes*, Hoccleve reflects on personal problems as he struggles to combat the temptations of overspending and makes his way up the slippery slope to preferment and consequent wealth accumulation. Debt and credit were a part of life, but management of debt was essential in order to thrive and prosper (81), and according to Bertolet, "Debts have nothing to do with virtue and everything to do with social inclusion" (150). Bertolet shows how the need to acquire Bourdieu's "symbolic capital," or wealth, was often based on credit, necessary to move up the social ladder to raise status or "social capital" (51, 60). Social capital enabled access to positions of authority and the opportunity for land and property acquisition, a further step up the ladder to ultimate noble status and political influence in the city (53).

However, the reflections in the narrative outputs of the three authors also suggest that the pursuit of wealth, by whatever means, destabilizes a city and its citizens in the throes of such momentous social change. The purchase of luxuries rather than necessities, often used for foolish purposes, demonstrates that the elevation of an individual to "worthiness" cannot, of itself, guarantee the "social capital" required (62, 80), and reflects on the fragility of human nature. The same destructive qualities of consumerism in which "Getting and spending we lay waste our powers" are noted by Wordsworth more than 400 years later. Wordsworth's conclusion that "We have given our hearts away, a sordid boon" resonates in more or less the same way from the fourteenth-century to the present-day culture of the city of London, lately evident in the trading and banking crises.[1] It is worth reflecting therefore that Bertolet highlights universal and timeless truths on the human condition noted by poets and authors over the centuries, which he has filtered through the lens of Bourdieu's theories. Perhaps it is in the work of the late fourteenth-century authors, Chaucer, Gower and Hoccleve that these "truths," distinctive traits of the human condition, are first observed by writers of the period and reiterated in the work of writers of succeeding generations.

Estelle Stubbs, University of Sheffield.

---

[1] William Wordsworth wrote the sonnet "The World is too much with us" in 1802. The poem was first published in *Poems, In Two Volumes* (1807).

VIRGINIA BLANTON, VERONICA O'MARA AND PATRICIA STOOP, EDS.
Nuns' Literacies in Medieval Europe: The Hull Dialogue.
Medieval Women: Texts and Contexts.
Turnhout: Brepols, 2013
xviii +367, 19 figures (with subdivisions), 6 tables.

This important collection of seventeen essays had its origins in the conference of the same title held at the University of Hull in June 2011. "Medieval Europe" is a strength of this volume: it has taken a long time for scholars in England sufficiently to recognize medieval religion as a European religion, and the willingness of European scholars to travel to England and speak in English is much to our benefit. The slightly odd subtitle is justified, in that a dialogue (perhaps "conversation" would be a more accurate word) does appear to have emerged at the Hull conference among a range of scholars of European women's orders and houses.

The volume is divided (perhaps unnecessarily, given that nuns' literacy is the topic of each essay) into four sections. "Literacy and Nuns: Finding and Interpreting the Evidence" includes five essays, three relating to Europe and two to England: "Reading Women at the Margins of Quedlinburg Codex 74," by Helene Scheck; "Making History at Fontevraud: Abbess Petronilla de Chemillé and Practical Literacy," by Bruce L. Venarde; "'Mathild de Niphin' and the Female Scribes of Twelfth-Century Zwiefalten," by Alison I. Beach; "Rendering Accounts: The Pragmatic Literacy of Nuns in Late Medieval England," by Marilyn Oliva; and "The Late Medieval English Nun and her Scribal Activity: a Complicated Quest," by Veronica O'Mara. The arrangement appears to be chronological, with the first three essays specific (and outside this *Journal's* remit, being early medieval) and the final two more general. Literacy covers a range of issues: a much studied manuscript of the letters of Jerome at elite Quedlinburg (Scheck), a political campaign conducted through the written word in unorthodox Fontevraud (Venarde), a female scribe at upper-class Zwiefalten (Beach), English nuns as administrator-managers (Oliva), and English nuns as (or not as) copyists (O'Mara).

Marilyn Oliva undertakes one of the less explored literacies, the keeping of accounts. Convents appear, unsurprisingly, to have been run as any other institution, with the obedientiaries taking on the same roles as household servants on a secular estate. Just as nuns were kitcheners, cellarers, bursars, and so on, they were also accounting obedientiaries. It is at this point (53) that the reader may wish that Oliva provided the actual term used for such accountants (and other obedientiaries), especially since, firstly, her footnote (n. 5) indicates a variety of titles (gendered and not gendered). Secondly, all the accounts she deals with (except for Barking) are in Latin (55, n. 9), and, thirdly, she displays later in her essay an interest in the languages used in the accounts. More than one account was kept, and more than one obedientiary was involved in the keeping of accounts, whether in the form of journals, daybooks, "papers," books of provision, books of the household, accounts books, or whatever (Latin terms are not given). Outside auditors seem usually to have prepared the final accounts, but the nuns themselves prepared the intermediary accounts. Oliva suggests that the code-switching between Latin, French and English is the result of the nuns' interventions: "Latin is the formal language of business documents drawn up by the auditors, and the French and English words the language of the women rendering their accounts, which the auditors saw and examined" (62-3). I wonder whether this is true; if so, it nevertheless needs modification, since household accounts from indisputably male households regularly display the features she suggests ("lez saltfisshe," to take one example). Nevertheless, this is an important essay and provides considerable food for thought. A nunnery was a business, managed as efficiently as its abbess or prioress was efficient (Petronilla de Chemillé, the twelfth-century abbess of Fontevraud, was formidably efficient, "an expert property manager,"as Venarde's essay demonstrates). Nuns had to handle administration and management and were not left entirely to follow their vocation without interference from secular matters.

Veronica O'Mara's essay attempts to explain and remedy the paucity of evidence for female scribes as copyists in England in contrast with the abundant European information (some evidence for which is found in Beach's essay which focusses on the twelfth-century female scribe Mathilde von Neuffen at Zwiefalten and even proposes a scriptorium for each sex at this double monastery). Only two indisputable cases of nuns as scribes are known from medieval England (one, at Syon, discovered by O'Mara herself), and her zealous attempt to add to this number offers a potential three more (Margery Byrkenhed of Chester, Elizabeth Trotter of Ickleton, and Alice Champnys of Shaftesbury), and a fourth for later consideration. O'Mara's research is meticulous, and her arguments are weighed and balanced to such an extent that hers is indeed "a complicated quest," as her subtitle suggests. Such careful work is essential, and tenuous results are better than tendentious ones.

The second section ("Language and Literacy: Latin and the Vernacular") is self-explanatory. Its three essays consider the level of Latin literacy in Vadstena and Vienna, and the use of Dutch prayer books in the diocese of Utrecht: "Nuns and Latin with Special Reference to the Birgittines of Vadstena," by Monica Hedlund; "Vernacular and Latinate Literacy in Viennese Women's Convents," by Cynthia J. Cyrus; and "Praying in the Vernacular: Middle Dutch Imitative Forms of the Divine Office from the 1370s to 1520s," by Thom Mertens. Hedlund and Cyrus concur on the level of Latin understood by their respective nuns. As the former points out, with great common sense, medieval nuns were constantly exposed to Latin, and an ability to read Latin should not be compared with an ability to read Cicero (her example) today. (One might add that medieval Latin was syntactically much easier than classical Latin, and the nuns never had to read Latin poetry.) Hedlund suggests that Vadstena sisters were trained in Latin and that literacy in Latin was the norm; at least half of the thirty-four nuns who are known in a book-related context must have had some such literacy, of whom most are recorded as scribes, mostly of Latin as well as Old Swedish texts. Hedlund demonstrates their competence in copying the Latin material and notes that almost half of the thirty (at least) manuscripts extant from the sisters' convent are in Latin.

In her essay Cyrus reviews the extant manuscripts from the seven main Viennese convents in order to assess what monastic literacy entailed. Nuns understood the Latin of the liturgy and were provided with aids to do so, and they were able to read and comment on the texts. Literacy entailed access to liturgical and vernacular books, which were the focus of study as well as performance, and the standards required of performance encouraged careful and deliberate study. Reading was a communal activity and might be in the vernacular or Latin, but the division between the two was not complete: German rubrics in Latin service books established "a bivalent literacy, one in which the materials of one linguistic culture overlapped with and informed their reading in another" (132). Finally, in this section, Mertens discusses Middle Dutch versions of the monastic office which developed for the use of the various female communities of the *Devotio moderna* movement: "In the private prayer of less-educated people, as most of the religious women were, the *Devotio moderna* preferred competent vernacular literacy to superficial Latin literacy. This is a striking difference to other language areas, where the less-educated people said their hours in Latin" (143).

Mertens's essay leads naturally into the discussions of the next, and largest, section, "Literate Nuns: Reading and Writing in the Convent." Arranged chronologically, the first two are outside the *Journal's* time-period: "Conceiving the Word(s): Habits of Literacy among Earlier Anglo-Saxon Monastic Women," by Lisa M.C. Weston ("absence of evidence should not be read as evidence of absence," 167) and "The Literary Culture of the Anglo-Saxon Royal Nunneries: Romsey and London, British Library, MS Lansdowne 436," by Stephanie Hollis. Virginia Blanton ("The Devotional Reading of Nuns: Three Legendaries of Native Saints in Late Medieval England") also deals with Romsey in her survey of the twenty-two legendaries associated with English nunneries, "six written in Latin, four in French, and twelve in English" (188)—perhaps "recorded" in such languages would be more accurate here, since only six of them are extant. The three she discusses and analyzes by tables are the Latin legendary from Romsey dealt with by Hollis, one in Anglo-Norman used at Campsey Ash, and one in Middle English from East Anglia currently being edited by Blanton and O'Mara. The remainder of the essays in this large section deal with Europe. These include Bohemia in "Between Court and Cloister: Royal Patronage and Nuns' Literacy in Medieval East-Central Europe," by Alfred Thomas; Germany in "Books in Texts – Texts in Books: The St. Georgener Predigten as an Example of Nuns' Literacy in Late Medieval Germany" by Regina Dorothea Schiewer; and two complementary essays on Sweden, "The Birgittine Sisters at Vadstena Abbey: their Learning and Literacy, with Particular Reference to Table Reading" by Jonas Carlquist and "Vadstena Abbey and Female Literacy in Late Medieval Sweden" by Ingela Hedström.

Finally, with "Authorship and Nuns: Writing by the Nun for the Nun," we at last reach undisputed writing (perhaps not exactly "authorship") by nuns in just two essays, "Writing, Editing, and Rearranging: Griet Essinchghes and her Version of the Sister-Book of Diepenveen" by Wybren Scheepsma and "Nuns' Literacy in Sixteenth-Century Convent Sermons from the Cistercian Abbey of Ter Kameren" by Patricia Stoop. Scheepsma's essay is interesting and wide-ranging, dealing with not just the sixteenth-century editor and scribe herself but the interesting genre of sister-books and the phenomenon of the *Devotio moderna* from which the convent at Diepenveen (and hundreds of others) sprang. In such a milieu "one's literacy determined whether a new postulant could become a choir nun or lay sister" (285), and one nun was so overwhelmed by the burden of literacy that she appealed for prayers to help her master cases and tenses. Stoop in turn deals with the genre of convent sermons at a slightly later period, specifically, the fifty-seven sermons delivered by the popular preaching friar Johannes Mahusius, which were copied as he delivered them ("from the mouth") in the 1560s by the Cistercian nuns of Ter Kameren near Brussels.

This book, with its excellent reproductions of several of the manuscripts discussed, offers full and important coverage of a topic for which there can be no final conclusions, other than to say that nuns were more literate than has previously been thought, particularly in certain convents and in the Low Countries and Germany. Not surprisingly, like all institutions, some were more competent, more academic, and more literate than others.

Susan Powell, University of Salford

EMMA CAYLEY AND SUSAN POWELL, EDS.
Manuscripts and Printed Books in Europe 1350-1550:
Packaging, Presentation and Consumption.
Liverpool: Liverpool University Press, 2013. xx + 327.

This collection of essays edited by Emma Cayley and Susan Powell (the latter being the Reviews Editor of this journal) arises from papers presented at the 2009 conference of the Early Book Society. The foreword by Derek Pearsall offers members of the Society, especially newer ones, a useful reminder of its history. Pearsall reflects on the growing strengths not only of the Society but also, interestingly, of certain aspects of scholarship over the last few decades, noting some improvements, particularly in greater precision in more recent work (x). It is pleasing to hear this variation on the usual laments that all has gone downhill, and it is more pleasing to see some proof of that in the ensuing chapters.

Unusually for a book reviewed in this *Journal*, a few of the chapters focus more on literary texts than the books in which they travel. Emma Cayley's chapter interprets references to fleas in some fifteenth- and sixteenth-century French texts. John Block Friedman's chapter surveys references to table manners in Geoffrey Chaucer's *The Canterbury Tales* and Heinrich Wittenweiler's *Der Ring* and speculates whether Wittenweiler knew Chaucer's text or vice versa; he is wisely wary of espying direct knowledge (186), as the case is not yet convincing. There is a return to the history of the book, or to the history of ideas about reading at least, in Anna Lewis's chapter about one of the so-called "common profit" books that is associated with John Colop. As well as taking quotations from the manuscript itself and reflecting on the titles which works are there given (88-89), Lewis elucidates some ideas about reading and textual "consumption" which provide the background to codicological and bibliographical research.

There is a yet stronger connection between literary criticism and the history of the book in Kate Maxwell's chapter on collections of Machaut's lays, which relates textual arrangements to the poems' meaning. Likewise, Sonja Drimmer explores how illustrations in different copies of Lydgate's *Saints Edmund and Fremund* present it in new ways. She draws well on theories in art criticism about illustration and framing (52-57). Anamaria Gellert's chapter draws on the wider iconography of fools (153-64) in order, finally, to interpret the addition of a fool to a woodcut of Chaucer's pilgrims. She demonstrates how the analysis of a woodcut, which one might be tempted to explain by purely technical or economic motives (which she duly considers, 152), can be improved by considering its artistic inheritance with similar precision.

There are similar challenges to utilitarian explanations in two of the best chapters in the book. Carrie Griffin studies the manuscripts of recipes, considering their layouts and accompanying texts, alongside an interpretation of their wording, in a pleasingly holistic manner. She thereby argues that recipes might be best analyzed not only as utilitarian writing but also "as fictions, narrative wish-lists" (142, 144). Her combination of literary and codicological analysis makes this convincing; we might well start rethinking our explanations of the genre along lines that she suggests. There are similar directions for future travel in Matti Peikola's survey of ruling patterns, one of the best researched essays in the collection and perhaps that which suggests the most intriguing questions for future research. He asks what determines the different patterns of ruling used in copies of the Wycliffite Bible and *Pore Caitif*. He mentions but then goes beyond the usual generic explanations for page layout (24) to consider instead scribal motives and agency. He has some surprising findings: not only the expected tendency to simplify ruling patterns, as one scribe follows another, but also to reproduce it (17), even when complex; this suggests that "scribes only rarely opted for the simplest and least time-consuming pattern" (19). That offsets the usual explanations for scribal practice as limited by efficiency and economy. He makes this case convincing by his own painstaking labor with a large quantitative survey of books, some examined first-hand, and some from a judicious survey of the best published catalogues, showing what one can do with such secondary sources, even at a distance from the manuscripts (25). Anglophone manuscript scholarship needs more work like this, which moves beyond case-studies to clarify patterns across books in a methodologically rigorous way, and which then thinks through the rationale for such patterns in an imaginative way.

Two other very strong chapters also draw on impressively large bodies of evidence, but this time about the use of books. Yvonne Rode surveys records of imports of printed books into London in the late fifteenth and early sixteenth centuries. She offers tables of her thorough evidence, for those who would like to take her research further, and she draws out some interesting patterns, such as the possibility that some merchants were specializing in importing books (75). Her sources also yield the terms in which people took account of books; this is extremely valuable, as they, perhaps unsurprisingly but nonetheless chasteningly, are almost entirely vague and focused on their physical properties or their value as commodities. There is a similar body of evidence presented in Anne F. Sutton's survey of references to books in the wills of the mercers. This chapter draws on wide-ranging and precise research to present hard-won information about the books actually owned but also, incidentally, about how people described and so perhaps thought those books. Their terms again often identify the books as material artefacts – whether they are "written" or printed, large or small, bound in various styles, as executors seek to identify books. Peikola's, Griffin's, Rode's and Sutton's chapters show the benefits of more extended and extensive research, for yielding fuller data and richer ideas.

There are other highlights in the collection, of diverse and often charming sorts. Mary Morse describes the layout of prayer-rolls used to protect women in childbirth, to see what the visual presentation of these fascinating artefacts might tell us about their use. There are two interesting "group biographies," so to speak. Martha Driver has an illuminating overview of female printers in the mid-sixteenth century, which reveals them engaged in some contentious editions (116-17). She also, like Rode and Sutton, offers informative close readings of people's passing comments on books, this time of female printers' descriptions of themselves in colophons (118). Shayne Husbands has an account of the early years of the Roxburghe Club, often condemned as a bastion of anti-intellectual bibliophily, which Husbands argues could have been considered a radical group in the early nineteenth century for bringing aristocrats and self-made men into close connection. And the collection begins with Anne Marie Lane's chapter about ways to identify bindings of different periods; this would be useful for the novice to this subject, such as Master's students.

If the Early Book Society can continue to be the place where people share such diverse and often excellent scholarship, the Society should continue to thrive as it has over the previous decades.

Daniel Wakelin, University of Oxford

SABRINA CORBELLINI, ED.
Cultures of Religious Reading in the Late Middle Ages:
Instructing the Soul, Feeding the Spirit, and Awakening the Passion.
Utrecht Studies in Medieval Literacy, 25. Turnhout: Brepols, 2013.
vi + 295 pp., 11 color plates.

For a time-pressed reviewer it is often fairly easy to get the measure of a volume without feeling obliged — or inspired — to read every word. Each essay in the present collection has something worthwhile and so the whole volume (albeit with a somewhat long-winded title) more than repays close attention from the first page to the last. There are four sections: "Latin and Vernacular — Orthodoxy and Heterodoxy," "Print and Public: The Impact of Printing on the Dissemination of Orthodoxy," "Socio-Cultural Contexts of Production, Acquisition, and Reading of Vernacular Religious Books," and "Religious and Sacred Texts in the Vernacular: Methodological Aspects of a Social History of Reading." There is a degree of freedom about the categorization of some essays, but these titles give some definition to the twelve essays that follow a useful introduction by the editor. Corbellini also provides a lively and engaged essay, "Beyond Orthodoxy and Heterodoxy: A New Approach to Late Medieval Religious Reading," which would have worked very well as an informative opening chapter.

While invidious to choose specific examples, no self-respecting reviewer can bypass the following essays without the highest praise: Eyal Poleg (on Wycliffite Bibles), Koen Goudriaan (on religious printing in the Low Countries from 1477 to 1540), and Kristian Jensen (on the printing of the works of Augustine — mostly pseudo-Augustine — in the fifteenth century). In each case these contributors manage to accommodate what are book-length studies within the confines of a single essay. Focusing on some two hundred and fifty Wycliffite Bibles, Poleg carefully shows their indebtedness to the standardized layout of the Latin biblical tradition. He further demonstrates that in their addenda, most importantly the tables of lections, and their omissions, especially the *Interpretationes nominum Hebraeorum*, the Wycliffite Bibles became dissociated from fraternal and university preaching, and in their enhanced applicability to the Latin liturgy, were made more acceptable — and useful — to the orthodox, both religious and secular. Covering a span of some sixty years of early printed religious books in the Low Countries and with detailed statistical examples to hand, Goudriaan's essay provides a thoughtful overview. By arguing that the authorities lacked an overall strategy and that the effects of the *Devotio moderna* may have been overestimated, he focuses instead on the part played by the Franciscans, who realized the potential of the new printing medium. Jensen's essay makes even greater use of statistical methods with its colorful charts, lists, and tables that are like a whole essay in themselves. It is a measure of his thoroughness that in his quest "to gain greater understanding of fifteenth-century reading communities for which Augustinian texts were of central importance" (141) he has identified 103 tract volumes with at least one Augustinian text produced in a German-speaking area and containing 506 copies of books owned by those who bought an Augustinian text; thirty-six of these are manuscripts. Both the quantity of material and the sheer detail are very impressive. Jensen works through geographical distribution; analyzes the number of editions, the number of sheets in one copy, the average number of sheets per edition; discusses the other works in the volumes; disaggregates the genuine Augustinian from the spurious; identifies owners; and so on and so forth.

Set beside the above are other interesting essays rather narrower in range: Else Marie Wiberg Pedersen on the thirteenth-century works of Beatrice of Nazareth and Margarete Porete, and Andrew Taylor on devotional reading at the Burgundian court of Margaret of York, sister of Edward IV and wife of Charles the Bold. Others are more restricted in focus, for example, John Thompson's essay based on the now familiar Belfast "Geographies of Orthodoxy" project on Middle English pseudo-Bonaventuran lives of Christ.

Besides the essays commented on already, the chief merit of the volume — for this reviewer at least — has been in extending her range of knowledge, and even more excitingly, in being introduced to material not so well known to scholars in the Anglophone world. In the first category I would include the essay by Werner Williams-Krapp on the life of St James in German tradition. Williams-Krapp displays his characteristic understanding of the area based on an in-depth knowledge of hagiography in Germanic lands. Even the brief synthesis of Dutch and German legendaries (202–205) provides an excellent background. In the second might be included the essays of Mart van Duijn on the Delft Bible of 1477; Suzan Folkerts on lay urban readers and the New Testament in the northern Low Countries; Anna Adamska on the reading of two Polish queens, Hedwig of Anjou (1374–1399) and Zofia Holszańska (*c.* 1405–1461); and Margriet Hoogvliet on religious reading in the French vernaculars. Adamska explores the specific bookish interests (particularly biblical volumes) and the complicated linguistic mix of two East Central European pious women, the first raised in Hungary and Vienna and the second a former Lithuanian Orthodox Christian, who became wives of the same Polish king. Hoogvliet combines a synthesis of modern theoretical approaches to reading with a judicious understanding of the material text, with its various "navigation tools" (258). Van Duijn provides an insight into the variation in the fifty-one (out of sixty-one) known copies of the first printed Dutch book, a diversity that was already evident when this first printed Bible in the Low Countries was produced. By providing only a copy of the Old Testament (minus the Psalms) and by allowing buyers to choose which books were included and in which order, the Delft Bible, which was read from the fifteenth to the early twentieth century, was not a "fixed cultural object" (140) but part of a negotiation between printer and owner. Complementing this essay is Folkerts's on the translations of parts of the New Testament in the northern Low Countries by such well-known writers as John Scutken (d. 1423), who was part of the *Devotio moderna*. Like the Delft Bible (or rather Bibles), these New Testament translations were adopted by lay and religious alike.

Indeed what stands out from this collection again and again is a definite focus on the biblical tradition (alongside the issue of orthodoxy). There is the germ here of another collection of equally good essays concentrating on one or other or a combination of the two. While it is possible to wonder why some areas or countries have been omitted (there is a decided concentration on the Low Countries), reviewers can always ask for more, and there is often a pragmatic explanation for a particular focus. Editors do not live in an ideal world where every potential contributor is able or willing to participate in a current project. For now, Sabrina Corbellini is to be much congratulated on bringing together this thought-provoking collection of material, for allowing her contributors to range widely and deeply, and in encouraging the publisher to supply so many (mainly) color plates.

Veronica O'Mara, The University of Hull

MARTHA W. DRIVER AND VERONICA O'MARA, EDS.
Preaching the Word in Manuscript and Print in Late Medieval England.
Essays in Honour of Susan Powell.
Turnhout: Brepols, 2013.
xv + 393 pp., 24 B&W illustrations.

This handsomely produced collection of essays provides ample evidence of the surprisingly diverse intersections between medieval sermon studies and the wider reaches of medieval literary and historical research. As a festschrift in honor of Susan Powell, it is only to be expected that the central unifying thread between most of the essays is their reference to Powell's major work, her edition of Mirk's *Festial* (EETS OS 334, 335, 2009-2011); Ronald Waldron discusses the importance of this edition "for the study of the medieval sermon and of Middle English language and literature in general" in the preface (xiv). The editors of the volume assist the reader with an exceptionally informative introductory synopsis of the contents, which is particularly helpful in relation to the more technical studies: Joseph J. Gwara's minute analysis of Wynkyn de Worde's textura fonts in use from 1501 to 1511, with resultant suggestions for re-dating the "Devotional, Homiletic, and Other Texts" that de Worde produced during those years, and Stephen Morrison's detailed scrutiny of "Scribal Performance in a Late Middle English Sermon Cycle" (Bodleian MS e Musaeo 180 and related manuscripts).

The collection is framed by a pair of essays that look back to the work of early editors and scholars in the field: Derek Pearsall's discussion of "G. R. Owst and the Politics of Sermon Studies" and Veronica O'Mara's account of the Boy Bishop sermon in "A Victorian Response to a Fifteenth-Century Incunabulum," focused on the edition by John Gough Nichols. Pearsall gives Owst due credit for his "greatest achievement" in initiating the discipline of medieval sermon studies by bringing the almost unknown manuscript collections of popular English sermons to public awareness (14), while at the same time exposing the limitations of Owst's eccentric historical and cultural interpretations with many aptly chosen quotations, and an explanatory account of his unhappy experience of academic life. O'Mara has a narrower scope but draws out of the available documentation a vignette of Nichols the antiquarian bibliophile basing his edition of the early printed text upon "flimsy" preferences, "airily" unsupported choice (369), and an "impressionistic" account of textual spelling (373). Both Owst and Nichols are thus characterized by a certain amateurish enthusiasm that can make their work engaging and illuminating as a period piece, but somewhat unreliable as a scholarly tool. In the case of the Boy Bishop sermon, O'Mara proceeds to demonstrate the best of modern editorial practice with her careful re-edition of the re-dated second edition (*c.* 1497-1498, STC 283), noting each variant from the first edition (*c.* 1496, STC 282) and from Nichols's edition (1875), in the process revealing a greater degree of "orthographical rigour" and typographical consistency in the work of the fifteenth-century compositors than had previously been allowed. Between their two essays, then, Pearsall and O'Mara indicate both the debt owed by sermon studies to the work of nineteenth- and twentieth-century pioneers in this subject, and the continuing need for rigorous modern scholarly investigation, while the rest of the contributions to the volume offer varied examples of just such investigations.

The contributions are divided into two sections, "Studies" and "Texts," though the editions of texts are accompanied by very substantial interpretive and contextual studies: besides O'Mara's essay the section contains Oliver Pickering's "Preaching in the *South English Legendary*: A Study and Edition of the Text for All Souls' Day" and Kari Anne Rand's "The Syon Pardon Sermon: Contexts and Texts." Pickering notes that while "*All Souls* cannot be considered a sermon," its style and mixture of materials have "strong preaching characteristics," intended to create an illusion of oral delivery (283); conversely, Rand argues that despite being written "in the form of a sermon," the Syon Pardon sermon is "patently unpreachable" and its function is rather that of a repository of information from which extracts circulated as "advertisements for the Syon indulgences" (335).

These concerns with the purpose and function of homiletic texts are reflected in most of the other essays. R. N. Swanson, in "A Cycle Recycled," examines the role of a set of Latin sermons from Carolingian Italy incorporated into a fifteenth-century English pastoral miscellany (MS Bodley 123) and argues that they served as a quarry to be exploited by the owner composing his own sermons. Anne Hudson, in her study of the relative fidelity of English and Bohemian copies of Wyclif's Sunday epistle sermons, notes that the two Wolfenbüttel manuscripts, one of which formed part of an *opera omnia* (MS 565), indicate by their "remarkable fidelity" the importance attached to Wyclif's works in central Europe in the early fifteenth century (57). In "The Devil as Narrator of the Life of Christ and the *Sermo literarius*,"

William Marx discusses the unique revisions in the B-version of *The Devils'
Parliament* in light of the modern understanding of written sermons as "essentially readerly" and reads the text as "an imagined discourse" in the same
mold as Chaucer's Pardoner's Prologue and Tale (64). Margaret Connolly
considers the interdependency of medieval sermons and the devotional
manuals used by the writers, preachers and hearers of sermons through the
lens of one teaching text, *The Seven Gifts of the Holy Ghost*, to demonstrate
that preaching was not confined to the pulpit but might be "more quietly"
conveyed in memorizing and meditating on such texts (97). In "Preaching
with a Pen," John J. Thompson takes a similar view of the reception of Mirk's
Festial and Love's *Mirror of the Blessed Life of Jesus Christ*, preaching by providing "essential safe reading" in the vernacular for parish clergy and literate
laity (105) while Jeremy J. Smith, in "Punctuating Mirk's *Festial*," examines
an early sixteenth-century Scottish manuscript copied from a printed edition
(Cambridge St John's College MS G.19) to argue that its "sophisticated punctuation aligned with periodic, 'rhetorical' structures" indicates the beginning
of those private reading practices termed "godly reading" in Reformation
contexts (188-189). Vincent Gillespie's discussion of "The Lections in the
Latin *Martiloge* of the Syon Brethren" gives an insight into medieval preaching
ideals: the set of daily readings added to the martyrology exhorts the brethren to preach plainly, to adapt their preaching to their audience's needs, and
above all, to practice what they preach (recalling Chaucer's Parson). As he
concludes, the lections transform the *Martiloge* into "an embodiment of the
values and ideals of the order, a sort of mission statement" (156).

Two essays take a more general approach: in "Middle English Sermon
Verse in Manuscript and Print," Julia Boffey considers the problems of
categorizing verse texts incorporated in sermons and shows that the transition to print, with its potential "to fix and make stable" their "characteristic
slipperiness," seems to have had no such effect (269), while Martha W. Driver,
surveying late medieval representations of preaching in her study of "Preachers in Pictures From Manuscript to Print," draws on secular and religious
material to illustrate the visual conventions used to convey both preaching
events and authorship, including serious and satirical usages.

This impressively wide-ranging collection of essays is witness to the
lively status of sermon scholarship at the present time, and it also points to
an equally fruitful future, as many of the essays conclude by looking forward
to opportunities for further investigations in their particular field of sermon
studies.

Phillipa Hardman, University of Reading

LUCIE DOLEŽALOVÁ AND KIMBERLY RIVERS, EDS.
Medieval Manuscript Miscellanies: Composition, Authorship, Use.
Krems, Österreich: Medium Aevum Quotidianum Sonderband XXXI,
2013.
x + 300 pp., 28 B&W figures and 25 color plates.

Lucie Doležalová and Kimberley Rivers, the editors of this nicely produced and well-illustrated volume, point out two truths about medieval
manuscript miscellanies: that they are ubiquitous in modern manuscript
collections and that they have not attracted much scholarly interest in their
own right. Now, it seems, their day has definitely come: the editors cite a
number of recent publications and on-going projects that focus on this topic
(several, like the current volume, stem from conference gatherings), and the
list that they give is far from exhaustive.

The volume's introduction and the identically-titled conference in which
these papers had their origins (Charles University, Prague, 24–26 August
2009) take a good deal of inspiration from an illustrious predecessor in the
field: *The Whole Book: Cultural Perspectives on the Medieval Miscellany*, edited
by Stephen G. Nichols and Siegfried Wenzel (Ann Arbor: The University of
Michigan Press, 1996). In their efforts to define a useful approach to miscellanies, Doležalová and Rivers highlight three concerns raised by Nichols and
Wenzel (codicology, thematic unity, and intentionality), and employ these
to inform their own collection's threefold division into composition, authorship, and use. Within each of these sections they aim to organize material
chronologically, though this aim is not always achieved.

Doležalová and Rivers rightly note that one factor that has inhibited the
study of miscellanies is "the sheer difficulty of defining them" (1). Nevertheless, this is where all who venture into these waters are obliged to start,
and accordingly the first three of the volume's essays are grouped under the

heading "Taxonomy and Methodology." Two of these contributions, by Greta Dinkova-Bruun, "Medieval Miscellanies and the Case of Manuscript British Library, Cotton Titus D.XX," and by Adam S. Cohen, "The Art of Regensburg Miscellanies," explore the particular complexities of the composite miscellany, and suggest using the terms "primary" and "secondary" to define volumes that did or did not have structural integrity from their conception. Eva Nyström's essay in this section, entitled "Looking for the Purpose behind a Multitext Book: The Miscellany as a Personal 'One-Volume Library'," scrutinizes the internal codicological minutiae of her fifteenth-century Greek miscellany to determine its homogeneity. Yet the flagging of these three essays as dealing principally with composition is misleading since each has other merits, too, and as the editors admit, all of the contributions engage to some extent with the vexed issue of taxonomy, as indeed it would be impossible for them not to do.

The four essays in the second part of the volume are judged to deal more directly with questions of authorship and with "how the meaning of texts may be altered in a manuscript by the presence of other texts" (7). These essays, by Diana Müller (on a collection of saints' lives), Siegfried Wenzel (on the "artes praedicandi"), Kimberly Rivers (on meditational texts), and Lucie Doležalová (on texts copied by an itinerant Benedictine monk), are also well-placed together because of their broadly religious subject material.

The third section of the volume covers the idea of "use." Unsurprisingly, this is both the largest section, with six essays, and also the most wide-ranging in terms of content. Religious material is again very well-represented, and both chronological and geographical coverage is formidably broad, beginning with Alessandro Zironi's study of what he calls "An Educational Miscellany in the Carolingian Age: Paris, BNF, lat. 528," a late eighth- or early ninth-century manuscript. Next both Stéphane Gioanni and Csaba Németh discuss volumes which are compilations of extracts from patristic or theological sources, while Kees Schepers explores the so-called Wiesbaden miscellany, a voluminous early fifteenth-century collection of Middle Dutch devotional texts. The last two essays take a slightly different direction. Dario del Puppo's contribution, "Recasting Meaning About the World for a Different Age: Italian Medieval Texts in Renaissance Manuscripts," focusses on Brunetto Latini's *Tresor* and leads us into the realms of fifteenth-century science. Finally, Elizabeth Watkins discusses the badly burnt British Library, Cotton Vitellius D.III, suggesting that its unique juxtaposition of both Middle English and French romances might not date from before Cotton's handling (and dismembering) of it; her analysis makes thought-provoking reading and reminds us of the necessity for painstaking attention to these complex codices, especially those that we already think we know very well.

A large part of the brief introduction by the editors is given over to summaries of the essays, to which this brief review can scarcely do justice. The desiderata underlined at the end of the introduction by Doležalová and Rivers are depressingly familiar. This is a subject area where there is still, after at least a quarter of a century's debate, no general agreement about terminology. Overall this is a collection of particular case studies, which is both a strength and a weakness. We will only achieve a better understanding of medieval manuscript miscellanies as a whole by finding out more about individual miscellanies, and the studies gathered here are valuable additions to existing knowledge; the focus on religious miscellanies is particularly welcome. Yet, despite the accumulation of information about individual miscellanies, we are still left rather in the dark when it comes to understanding the nature of the miscellany itself; this wood is becoming more and more populated by individual trees, but its geography and boundaries continue to elude us.

Margaret Connolly, University of St Andrews

MARY C. ERLER
Reading and Writing during the Dissolution:
Monks, Friars, and Nuns 1530-1558.
Cambridge: Cambridge University Press, 2013. 211 pp., 6 illus.

A new book by Mary Erler is always a cause for celebration, since her work is so meticulous, reasoned and instructive. This slim volume is no exception. Two of the chapters admittedly have seen a previous form of publication, the first, on Simon Appulby, and the fifth, on William Peryn, but their inclusion is important in a book which begins with Appulby, hermit of All Hallows London Wall, whose *Fruyte of Redempcyon* was published first in 1514 and last in 1532, to William Peryn, Dominican, whose *Spirituall Exercyses* was published in 1557, and beyond, to Richard Whitford, whose last publication, in 1541, of his *Dyvers Holy Instrucyons* post-dated the dissolution of Erler's title.

After Appulby, chapter 2 deals with the *Greyfriars Chronicle*, specifically the manuscript account of the years 1538 (the dissolution of the London Franciscan house) to 1556. Chapters 3 and 4 both deal with the letters sent by nuns on the eve of the dissolution, the first with Katherine Bulkeley, last abbess of Godstow, Morpheta Kingsmill, last prioress of Kingsmill, and Joan Fane, last prioress of Dartford, and the second with Margaret Vernon, last abbess of Malling. One might query whether, chronologically, Whitford should appear next, since he spans the pre- to post-dissolution period, but Whitford is someone who tends, by the force of his still-evident personality and his relative prolificness, always to get the last word. Hence Chapter 5 deals with Peryn and Chapter 6 Whitford.

The heart of this book is, for me, the chapters on nuns, on whom Erler has always written so persuasively and sensitively. Chapters 3 and 4 are revelatory in their insight into the reactions of the female communities at the impending dissolution. As is always the case in crises, some capitulated at once; some bought time; some left early and happily; some stayed to the bitter end and left reluctantly; some continued their communal life outside their former houses. The letters that Erler has disinterred (from an 1846 edition of *Letters of Royal and Illustrious Ladies of Great Britain* and from the *Letters and Papers of Henry VIII*) are gems, and the chapters are also revelatory in their display of the relationship between these nuns and, particularly, Cromwell, the "onlie begetter" of the dissolution that was to change their lives forever. In each case Erler places the letters in context, critiques them with wisdom, and—most noticeably—frequently overturns datings or conclusions previously reached, simply by dint of careful scrutiny and common sense.

Margaret Vernon, in particular, is a fascinating case study. A career nun, she was successively prioress of Sopwell, St Mary de Pré near St Albans, and Little Marlow, before, at the projected dissolution of Little Marlow, unsuccessfully suing for St Helens Bishopsgate in London and eventually securing head of house at Malling in Kent. Twenty-one of her letters to Cromwell survive, indicative of what Erler calls "a friendship that may have been based on shared religious perspectives" (88), but which to me show little evidence of spirituality. Erler is wise but also kind—her verdict is of "a powerful and attractive personality," drawn to Cromwell as another "ambitious and rising" person (105), whereas mine is of a rather stupid but sly, pushy and manipulative woman. The blatancy of her letters suing (with financial inducements) for St Helen's, in one of which she begs Cromwell's favor "that all men may see that I am your prioress" (162,8), is astonishing but probably not untypical (Katherine Bulkeley thanks Cromwell who has brought her "of nothing … to all that I have by your mere goodness, never deserved of me in any part," 68). She makes much in several letters of her concern for Cromwell's son Gregory who was in her schooling at Little Marlow for a few years from (presumably) the death of his mother in 1528, when he was seven or eight years old. (At the imminent closure of Little Marlow, her concern for her future is evident in her pestering of Cromwell, both by letter and in attempts to see him personally, and in one letter there is an interesting lacuna which only an inspection of the document itself might explain: "if it will please your goodness to take this poor house into your own hands, either for yourself or for mine own... your son" (165,13). Her relationship with Cromwell led to her promotion after Little Marlow was dissolved in 1536 to become abbess of Malling (presumably for the pension, since Malling itself, Cromwell clearly knew, would be dissolved in 1538). Her last but one letter sets out a financially advantageous settlement for herself, and the final letter agrees that she will visit Cromwell to discuss it. Erler notes that "the abbess did not get quite what she asked for" (104), but she drew her pension until 1546, six years after the execution of her more prominent friend. She was no longer then living as a religious, although still with her junior nun, Rose Moreton.

The fascination of Vernon's story has perhaps overshadowed the rest of Erler's book in this review. This it should not do, as the whole is full of insight and wisdom, not just local but general. In some ways the subtitle of Erler's work is more accurate a reflection of its contents than the rather all-embracing title. However, writing is the focus of the book (and reading an inevitable corollary), and the narrow period of 1530 to 1558, from the first murmurs of dissolution to the death of Mary Tudor and the final demise of monasticism in England, is an excellent one to focus on. Erler investigates a range of writing—the printed publications of Appulby, Peryn and Whitford, the personal record (probably of a Franciscan, but, if so, a remarkably detached one) of events after the dissolution of the London Greyfriars, and the letters of four nuns. While the book focusses on individuals (including, for example, other London Franciscans and the two nuns who were the dedicatees of Peryn's book), rather than offering a broad overview of "reading and writing during the dissolution," much can be learned from these individuals, and Erler's forte has long been detailed and skilfully argued dissection of the written word in order to display the individual in the climate of her or his times. As she herself says, "I have regularly thought of bibliography as a way of exploring lives" (2).

The volume is furnished with some telling and some useful illustrations, and it concludes with valuable appendices. Some are based on published sources (Appulby's will of 6 June 1537, the letters of the nuns), but others are Erler's own work: a list of anchorites of All Hallows; a life of Elizabeth Woodford, referred to only briefly in the text, but whom Erler rightly signals as "important but little-known" (109) and who might have deserved an article in her own right; and an excerpt from Richard Whitford's sermon "On Detraction" from his *Dyvers holy instrucyons*, which Erler has critiqued with skill and insight in her final chapter. The latter is important in that no vernacular sermon preached *ad populum* at Syon now exists (in that the Syon pardon sermon is arguably unpreachable), but Erler's eagle eye has noticed Whitford's comment on "On Detraction": "This draft that followeth was a piece of a sermon that I spoke unto the people years ago" (175). Whitford, as usual, gets the last word.

Susan Powell, University of Salford

VINCENT GILLESPIE AND ANNE HUDSON, EDS.
Probable Truth: Editing Medieval Texts from Britain
in the Twenty-First Century.
Texts and Transitions, 5.
Turnhout: Brepols, 2013. xiv + 549 pp.

This volume, the proceedings of an Oxford Early English Text Society conference held in 2010, opens with an engaging account of EETS between 1930 and 1950 in which Helen Spencer rightly emphasizes the heroic part played by Mabel Day, the Society's principal officer from 1921 to 1949, who "has tended to be overshadowed by the great men by whom she was surrounded" (19). One irony of this is that in the list of EETS non-executive Council members (xii) fifteen of the eighteen are male (two sadly now deceased). At the beginning of the twenty-first century, surely it should be possible to find more than three great women with an expertise in editing and a willingness to serve?

Following an editorial introduction and Spencer's survey, there are twenty-eight further contributions in a collection that borrows a quotation by Eleanor Hammond for the title, overlooks Celtic sensitivities in the subtitle, and says as much about editing in the twentieth century as it does about the twenty first. It is divided into: "From Script to Print to HTML: Electronic Editions," "Practices, Habits, Methodologies," "In Praise of the Variant: Why Edit Critically?," "Editing British Texts in Latin, Anglo-Norman, Celtic, and Scots," "Scientific Texts," and "Middle English Case Studies." Much of the collection concerns medieval English (mostly Middle English), despite reference to "British" Irish-language and Welsh-language texts (two essays); there is also one essay each on Latin and Anglo-Norman and two on (non-Gaelic) Scottish works.

It may seem strange that the editors chose to begin with digital editions but, on reflection, this is an inspired move. Bella Millett's excellent overview of the perils of electronic editing in terms of technological changes, the constraints of impact, and the need for sustainability should be required reading for anyone thinking of doing such an edition. In his equally thoughtful essay focusing on the Society for Early English and Norse Electronic Texts (SEENET) and the *Piers Plowman Electronic Archive* (PPEA), Thorlac Turville-Petre, while acknowledging the freedom afforded by an electronic edition, stresses the tedium of computer tagging and notes the problems of the need to develop browsers and the difficulties of access when libraries are reluctant to buy CDs and students expect free downloads. There is, too, the often unrecognized reluctance of readers to use online editions: he gives the salutary example of how a print version of *The Destruction of Troy* (2010) appeared *after* the electronic one, produced eight years previously by the same editor, had been overlooked.

Thereafter, the volume encompasses a range of junior and senior contributors, without any correlation between the commonly perceived importance of a text and the degree of effort expended on it. Possibly the best examples of the latter disjunction are David Moreno Olalla's dedicated listing of seventy-one texts of botanical *Synonyma*, something to which many will never have given a second thought; Peter Grund's plea for the editing of alchemical texts, "the largest corpus of writings that remain largely untouched by editors" (428); and Helen Fulton's equally expert discussion of the neglected medieval Welsh prose history of the destruction of Troy, *Ystorya Dared*. Essays on major writers, such as Langland (A. V. C. Schmidt on textual "contamination") and Chaucer (Orietta Da Rold on stratigraphical analysis of early Chaucerian manuscripts), take their place with other discussions of the editing process rather than being allowed to dominate. Indeed, Derek Pearsall (on variants and *variance* in general) argues that despite "all the fanfare of Chaucer editors" (202), neither the works of Chaucer — nor Gower — provide evidence of the need for critical editions.

In a sense editors are born not made, though exposure to conversations such as those in the current volume has the potential to improve us all. Contributors engage thoughtfully from their own experience of editing difficult cases (for example, Susan Powell on substantive variants in the *Festial* because "[w]ithout such information an edition is a dead text" [282]). Various test cases are put forward. Katherine O'Brien O'Keeffe weighs up the relative merits of the *Old English Boethius* by Malcolm Godden and Susan Irvine which, in their decision to print two full editions of some 1200 pages, allows the user "to collaborate with the editors" (85), against Daniel O'Donnell's dual-medium *Caedmon's Hymn* which is an "invitation to the reader ... to publish her own edition" (90). Other essays examine the part played by memory and/or extemporized performance in the editing process: Ardis Butterfield and Helen Deeming on a song of six or seven stanzas that survives in three trilingual manuscripts, or Rosamond Allen in her daring defense of superior readings, "even if unprovably 'authorial' rather than surmised 'original' readings" (308).

Elsewhere we encounter aspects about which we might have become complacent (Malcolm Godden disturbs any simplistic assumptions about the textual stability of Old English prose texts), lack information (Richard Newhauser lays the foundations for a critical edition of Peter of Limoges's *Tractatus moralis de oculo*, an unacknowledged source in much homiletic literature), need instruction (Michelle Doran discusses the inadequacy of a uniform editorial approach for medieval Irish texts often preserved in much later manuscripts), or require reminders (Sally Mapstone in her overview of editing Older Scots texts in manuscript and print notes that this period stretches from *c.* 1375 to *c.* 1700).

In other cases, the same issue, text or topic crops up in various guises: Matthew Fisher explores authors such as Thomas Hoccleve and Ranulph Higden as scribes; Richard Beadle investigates scribal accuracy in a text shown years ago by Ian Doyle to be by one scribe (in Cambridge, Magdalene College, MS Pepys 2125) imitating the hand of another (in London, British Library, MS Harley 2398); Stephen Morrison examines specific types of scribal error in a sermon collection; and Daniel Wakelin provides statistical evidence from the Huntington Library on general scribal corrections in some fifty volumes and various snippets ("9220 corrections over 11,876 pages," 245). There are two essays on the *Brut*, a general one by John Thompson that rhetorically asks "Why Edit the Middle English Prose *Brut*?," although, like Marie Stansfield, who investigates the so-called "Peculiar Version to 1437," he is really interested in *how* it might be done.

Again and again, dedicated editors struggle with the critical variants of some intractable manuscripts that can behave like bindweed, threatening to strangle text and editor alike. Michael Sargent, the final contributor to the volume, describes the intricate textual relationships of the sixty-seven manuscripts (and five incunables) of the *Scale of Perfection*. In the course of attempting this edition, which Sargent describes in forensic detail, three well-known medievalists, T. P. Dunning, Alan Bliss (responsible for Book I), and Stan Hussey (Book II), have already expired. This is not to blame the project for their demise but sometimes — much as the purists among us might not wish to do so — it might be no harm to consider (even if not to emulate exactly) the jaunty advice of Ralph Hanna (now an evangelical promoter for the joys of editing), gained from his work on the *Speculum vitae* and *The Prick of Conscience*, which is effectively to produce an edition "with expectations reduced" (123). If there is anything to be learned from some of the considered essays here, it is that we editors must recognize at an early stage what we are up against, as Emily Wingfield does in her exploration of the intriguing relationship of the fragmentary *Scottish Troy Book* with Lydgate's *Troy Book* in preparation for a new edition.

Inevitably there are gaps in this collection. The absence of drama may be overlooked, given the excellent editions available, but there is little on sermon study even less on short devotional texts or the problems of composite manuscripts (only William Robins's study of composite texts that function as independent works or as a larger compilation). Early printed material creeps in only when connected with manuscripts, and there is virtually nothing on language (except for Laura Esteban-Segura and Teresa Marqués-Aguado on software tools for the analysis of computerized historical corpora, and Heather Pagan and Geert De Wilde on editorial policy in the Anglo-Norman dictionary). Other areas such as hagiography are completely neglected. But, of course, one cannot have everything. Yet there is one unfortunate repetition. It is a pity that the editors did not curtail the retelling of the same recent history of editing in essay after essay (as a brief glance at the many entries for Bernard Cerquiglini and his *Éloge de la variante* in the index will show). Even if the individual contributors thought this reiteration necessary, a summary in the introduction would have been sufficient.

Yet this is an important collection of conversations about editorial conundra. To what extent its significance is dependent on EETS as a national institution is a moot point, even if an EETS edition confirms a certain status. As Spencer says, EETS editorial policy was a bit vague in the early days: "'transcribe a good manuscript, collate it with as many others as you can find, emend sparingly and *ad hoc* where the copy-text seems to be at fault, and furnish it with a short introduction, a few notes, and a very brief glossary'" (23). Things have improved since then, but EETS editions can still be of variable quality. Similarly it is no longer the sole outlet for editions, and it would have been no bad thing had it been recognized that there are other possibilities, primarily the Middle English Texts series (published by Winter in Heidelberg) which has several members of its editorial/advisory board on the EETS Council (the work of the Scottish Text Society *is* acknowledged in Mapstone's essay).

The volume also raises important larger questions about editing as the bedrock of scholarship and its neglect in funding terms and otherwise. While mindful of the huge amount of labor expended, for instance, by Sargent in "The Case for a Rhizomorphic Historical Edition" of the *Scale*, we may have to be more pragmatic than we would like in the editing of larger, more complicated projects because few of us have the time or energy of Furnivall or Horstmann — or Sargent — who has long struggled alone with this huge burden. Indeed, if there was ever a case for cooperative teams of editors (like medieval *pecia* production), this is it.

In the introduction Gillespie and Hudson mention that Dr Johnson's description of the lexicographer as a "harmless drudge" is often transferred to the editor of manuscripts. This definition might also be applied to editors of collections. In the same way as the world is divided into those who edit for the good of the scholarly community and those who do not, so it may be classified into those who trouble themselves to edit the work of others and those who are not minded to do so. It is always possible for reviewers to find fault in an editor's work — whether it is the editorial approach in a complicated edition or the nature of an extensive collection of essays. Anyone who has done both editorial tasks is tempted to tell such reviewers to try it for themselves and see how well they get on. In the current instance, while one might hesitate to refer to Gillespie and Hudson as "harmless drudges," they must be greatly praised for timely seeing to press — with all the frustrating difficulties that usually entails — no fewer than twenty-nine essays on some very varied topics in over 550 pages, together with a nicely designed list of manuscripts and a brief but helpful index. Those interested in editing should be much in their debt.

Veronica O'Mara, The University of Hull

VINCENT GILLESPIE AND SUSAN POWELL, EDS.
A Companion to the Early Printed Book in Britain 1476–1558.
Cambridge: D. S. Brewer, 2014
xviii + 385 pp., 32 illus.

This collection of sixteen essays edited by Vincent Gillespie and Susan Powell offers a dedicated study of the early printed book in the later medieval and early modern periods. Attention is focused on the material artefact itself (paper, type, bindings, woodcuts), and on its distribution through the book trade (printers, publishers, stationers). Its readers are investigated largely through groups of patrons or purchasers (clergy, laity) or institutions (universities, colleges). Finally, a section that treats what is termed the "cultural capital of print" considers how printing affected the spread of ideas, humanism, censorship, and religious change (both Lutheran Protestantism *and* the restoration of Catholicism under Mary Tudor).

The three essays in the first section consider the printed book trade, with Julia Boffey given the opening position and the opportunity to stress continuities and crossovers between manuscript and print. Tamara Atkin and A. S. G. Edwards divide their account of printers, publishers, and promoters into three – a sort of early, middle, and late chronology of print that foregrounds the dominance of particular individuals (Caxton, then de Worde and Pynson) and which shows very clearly how the early history of printing in England was dominated by aliens. Both of these essays concentrate on vernacular printing and on printing in England. Alan Coates's contribution rounds out this section by focussing on imported books, and specifically on Latin texts, though the larger part of his discussion confines itself to examples from before 1500.

The second section considers physical and material aspects of printing. Pamela Robinson deftly demystifies many of the mechanics of printing, explaining both the process of production and the use of paper and type. Alexandra Gillespie considers the rise of the new fashion of blind-stamping in bookbinding while emphasizing that old and new were merged in book-binding as in other aspects of book production. Martha Driver discusses woodcuts and decorative techniques in a copiously illustrated essay (in fact all three essays in this section are generously illustrated) that relies largely on literary texts for its examples; it would have been good to know whether all kinds of texts are similarly decorated, or if this is an aspect particularly connected with literary works.

The third section, devoted to a consideration of patrons and purchasers, is subdivided into studies of merchants (Anne Sutton), the laity (Mary Erler), the secular clergy (Susan Powell), the regular clergy (James G. Clark), and universities, colleges, and chantries (James Willoughby); the lack of refer-ence to lawyers is a striking omission here. Anne Sutton's essay is centered on London and offers a review of the evidence of wills; her observation that there is very little testamentary evidence of ownership of printed books is a salutary reminder of just how much of the picture is obscured. Fortunately Mary Erler expands our sense of the printed book itself by noting the kinds that were printed in vast numbers but which now tend to be overlooked: indulgences, almanacs, calendars, and—perhaps less neglected—Books of Hours. The clergy are well-served by the very substantial chapters by Susan Powell and James G. Clark, both of which contain a wealth of detail. James Willoughby's otherwise Anglocentric chapter also takes in the English hospi-tal in Rome and pays much attention to the imported (Latin) books desired by his educated audience.

The five essays in the final section take a broader perspective. Daniel Wakelin shows how humanist printing in England grew out of and then away from Continental printing. Brenda M. Hosington considers the importance of translation in relation to printing, choosing to focus on the little-known phenomenon of the female translator: she identifies seven who were active in the first half of the sixteenth century. Andrew Hope's account of English books printed abroad is the first of three essays that deal specifically with the evolving religious environment of the period: his essay focuses on English responses to Lutheran reform. Thomas Betteridge then considers the chang-ing nature of censorship after the introduction of printing, ending with the specific example of Thomas More. Finally Lucy Wooding reconsiders how print was used during the Marian restoration. The volume concludes with various indexes including, unusually and helpfully, a very extensive index of early printed books.

The collection is furnished with a preface by Susan Powell and a short introduction by Vincent Gillespie. Both use the opportunity to foreground a point that quickly becomes apparent when reading the essays: the date range chosen for the volume not only allows a generous assessment of early print history, but also necessarily engages with a period of tumultuous religious change in England. There is consequently a much greater emphasis in this collection on religious printing, an aspect that distinguishes it from earlier studies that have concentrated largely on William Caxton and on secular literature, especially romances. Close attention is paid to ecclesiastical markets and makers, and as a result this volume more accurately reflects the reality of the market for printed books in England before 1558. This is a positive result, but one that highlights a deficiency: while 1558 (the year of the death of Mary Tudor and the accession of Elizabeth) may be a significant date in English history, it does not resonate north of the border. Arguably a better endpoint might have been 1603 and the accession of James VI and I, which would have allowed consideration of the whole of the sixteenth century and of the firm establishment of Protestantism under Elizabeth I—the end of one strand of the story, as it were. It might also have prompted contributors to pay more attention to what was going on (or even to what was not) in terms of early print history in Scotland: only the essays by Atkin and Edwards and by Coates make any kind of gesture towards this, which in a volume that promises to cover Britain is regrettable. Admittedly this extension of the time covered might have resulted in a volume of unwieldy size (at 385 pages, this companion to the subject is already substantial), or instead the volume might have been correctly labelled as a history of the early printed book in *England*, a brief that it fulfills admirably.

This dedicated study of the early printed book is very much overdue and will be welcomed by readers of *JEBS*. Since the material culture of medieval literary texts became a central focus of scholarly endeavor, the detailed investigation of manuscripts has flourished rather more than that of printed books, despite the stated interest of the Early Book Society and *JEBS* in the study of both. It seems that the majority of scholars who are comfortable with manuscript study are less at home with the study of the early printed books and early print history; it is still only a minority who successfully link the two areas. This is very much to the detriment of understanding, as many of the essays in the present volume make clear. A point made repeatedly by various contributors is that during this period of the "long Middle Ages," change was gradual: manuscripts were not discarded overnight; print did not replace manuscripts; and print did not change the way that books were read. These essays are full of much informative detail and collectively provide a robust account of the history of the early printed book that *JEBS* readers will learn from and enjoy.

Margaret Connolly, University of St Andrews

CARRIE GRIFFIN, ED.
The Middle English Wise Book of Philosophy and Astronomy:
A Parallel-Text Edition.
Middle English Texts, 47. Heidelberg: Winter, 2013.
lxxv + 74 pp.

According to the introduction, "The *Wise Book of Philosophy and Astronomy* has the distinction of being one of the most widely circulated pieces of instructional prose in English surviving from the late medieval period and, paradoxically, the most consistently over-looked tract of its kind in terms of textual scholarship relating to Middle English" (xv). Thus begins Carrie Griffin's edition of a text that few of us, except for specialists in medieval sciences, have even heard of — let alone read. This liminal text, a hard-to-define combination of the instructional, philosophical, and scientific, is extant in two recensions, A and B, along with a fragment that combines part of both. It is found in thirty-four manuscripts that range from the early fifteenth to the late sixteenth century, although many are incomplete, abridged, or damaged.

The first part of the introduction is devoted to manuscript descriptions. Of the thirty-four manuscripts, fourteen are in London (in three different libraries), nine in Oxford, six in Cambridge (in four libraries), and one each in New Haven, New York, San Marino, Tokyo, and Woking. Only those of us accustomed to laboring and fretting over descriptions can appreciate the amount of time and effort — not to mention the logistical travel difficulties and great financial outlay — that will have gone into making these twenty-one pages. Although scholars always want more from manuscript descriptions (for instance, in some cases I would have liked a little more about other contents), Griffin is to be much congratulated on the degree of useful information fitted into a small compass. The detail shows that she has not taken shortcuts by relying on existing online descriptions or getting hard-working librarians to answer her questions but has made the effort to study all the manuscripts thoroughly.

The rest of the introduction works through the usual aspects: broadly, scholarship past and present, structure and content (including an excursus on *The Book of Destinary*, a text only found with the *Wise Book* but distinct from it), analogues, audience, and editing policy. The book is completed by a commentary, glossary, and bibliography. Taking full cognizance of previous scholarship, Griffin sets out a clear idea of the options for a base text, noting that even with such a surfeit of manuscripts, the choice is limited as only seven "contain the fullest version of the 'text' as it survives" (lxvii). Selecting the one to use is "a matter of judgement" (lxvii), and Griffin wisely chooses a professionally produced full exemplar for A, which in its "workmanlike" way "is typical of the context in which the majority of *Wise Books* circulated throughout the fifteenth century" (lxvii), and the earliest of the three manuscripts of B. In the absence of a digital edition that would represent all thirty-four manuscripts, she understandably opts for a parallel-text edition of the A and B recensions (plus an extensive variant to A and the fragment in separate appendices), with full critical apparatus (neatly set out on 22–42) — no mean feat even for a short text of 381 or 337 lines each. The general editors are to be equally congratulated on helping her to devise a format that works so well.

The work presented here is based on Griffin's doctoral dissertation of 2006. She has clearly thought extensively about the topic in the interim, having given various papers, as well as publishing some four articles on the *Wise Book* or related fields. The present tendency (virtually enforced by our audit culture) is for younger scholars to rush their dissertations into print at the earliest opportunity; the current instance demonstrates what can be achieved when ideas are allowed to ripen and develop. This is particularly necessary for an edition of a text that has not been published in full before. Modern readers may only be amused by learning that people born on a Thursday (at least those who are male) are said to be "sangueyn of kynd, lovely, benyvoile, wise, dileitabull, & worschipfull" (21/371) or that those born in February are all "gracius and happy" (6/75). Yet it is texts like the *Wise Book*, taken as a whole rather than in selected quotations, which in some respects can do more to inform us about the general medieval worldview, as it were, than many of the more *central* texts that we study today. Griffin has admirably discharged her responsibilities to the wider scholarly community by providing an approachable and thorough edition of a text that many of us might not otherwise encounter if left to our own devices.

Veronica O'Mara, The University of Hull

INA KOK
Woodcuts in Incunabula Printed in the Low Countries.
Bibliotheca Bibliographica
Neerlandica Series Maior, 2. Trans. Cis van Heertum. 4 vols.
Houten, Netherlands: HES & DE GRAAF, 2013.
x-xxxi + 898 pp., 4000+ B&W illustrations.

The four volumes of this handsome catalogue comprise "an exhaustive inventory of the incunabula woodcuts of the Low Countries and all the [Dutch and Flemish] editions in which they occur, including repeats" and analysis "of the woodcuts used by every printer as well as a survey and analysis of any business relations existing between printers," again of the Low Countries (xv). The catalogues are drawn from Kok's dissertation, an inventory and bibliographic analysis of the 2229 incunabula now known from this area, a number that is greatly increased over those catalogued in William Martin Conway's nineteenth-century surveys. Kok lists both the book in which the woodcut (or woodcut series) appears first and all the repetitions of the woodcut that occur in books printed in the Low Countries prior to 1501. This catalogue will be useful not only to scholars studying woodcuts that illustrate incunables produced in the Low Countries but also to those interested in related woodcuts in books printed later and/or in other countries, in relationships between woodcuts and other media, and more generally in iconography and book illustration.

Volume 1 includes thirty-seven chapters organized by printer with comprehensive descriptions of books and prints. The printers include Gerard Leeu, Arend de Keyser, Jacob Bellaert, Colard Mansion, Richard Pafraet, and Johan Veldener, whose books and woodcuts (and in the case of Veldener, types) were influential or indirectly influential on English and French printing. Colard Mansion, for example, initially worked as a calligrapher and bookseller in Bruges and made "the most sumptuous incunabula to have been produced in the Low Countries" (60). In Mansion's French edition of the *Ovide Moralisé*, the woodcuts were "printed independently of the text, in a separate printing" (63). Though not within the purview of Kok's study, Mansion's illustrations were later copied in France for the publisher Antoine Vérard; the reproduction of all the prints used by Mansion here makes for ready comparison with Vérard's illustrations. Mansion is also of interest, of course, to English print historians for his collaboration with William Caxton. Kok further cites the illustrated edition of *De ludo scachorum* printed in 1483 in Delft by Jacob Jacobszoon van der Meer which was preceded by Caxton's English translation *The Game and Playe of Chesse* first published in 1474 and perhaps produced with Mansion; the woodcuts in the Delft version look to have influenced the illustrations in Caxton's later edition of 1483. A woodcut of the Man of Sorrows (Hodnett 380) printed by Caxton about 1490, and here "probably a galley proof" (479), mysteriously turns up in an edition printed by Mathias van der Goes in Antwerp, also in 1490. There is no previously known connection between the two printers. Jacob Bellaert, working in Haarlem, not only published an illustrated Dutch translation of *Le Recueil des histoires de Troyes* in 1485, but the highly influential *De Proprietatibus Rerum* of Bartholomaeus Anglicus the same year; the illustrations in this latter book were later used as models by French, English and Spanish printers. Both works were published earlier by Caxton as well, the *Recuyell* in Bruges between 1473 and 1474, and *De Proprietatibus Rerum* printed in 1472 with Johan Veldener's Cologne type. Veldener worked in many other cities, including Louvain, Utrecht, and Culemborg. He was a type cutter, printer, publisher and is also thought to have supplied two presses with woodcuts, himself using "some three hundred different woodcuts, occurring in thirteen of well over forty editions" (36). His influential *Fasciculus Temporum*, which appeared in 1475, was the first illustrated book printed with movable type in the Low Countries; he was also likely the compositor and book designer for Arnold Therhoernen who printed the first edition of this work by the German Carthusian Werner Rolewinck in 1474. As scholars who study early English books know, the *Fasciculus* would be partially incorporated by Caxton into his *Polychronicon* and finds its way as well into later editions of printed English chronicles.

Volume 2 comprises five indexes, four concordances, bibliographies and lists. These include an index of printers, an index of reference numbers to items as catalogued in *Incunabula Printed in the Low Countries. A census*, edited by Gerard van Thiennen and John Goldfinch (1999), an iconographical index, an index of other names, and several bibliographies including lists of reference works and libraries and editions consulted.

Volumes 3 and 4 are plates, which reproduce illustrations originating in the blockbook *Biblia Pauperum* and *Speculum Humanae Salvationis* as they appeared in Dutch incunables, images that continued to illustrate numerous European and English books well into the sixteenth century. All of the woodcuts that illustrate Dutch and Flemish incunabula are reproduced in these two volumes, including their various states; these are organized by the names of the printers who produced the books in which the woodcuts appear. Printers' devices and border work are also reproduced here, along with figurative initials.

The pictures themselves are not of the highest quality (as one also finds in *Dutch and Flemish Woodcuts of the Fifteenth Century* by M. J. Schretlen, 1925, for example) and have been taken from microfilm but are perfectly adequate for purposes of iconographic reference. For scholars interested in picture sources, this is an excellent and comprehensive reference work. For example, there is an earlier model for the scene in Richard Pynson's edition of *Troilus and Criseyde* in which a letter is delivered (Hodnett, item 1625) in the edition of the *Historia van Parys ende Vienna* printed in Antwerp by Gerard Leeu in 1487 (item 168.20), the first edition printed in the Low Countries. Leeu subsequently published in June 1492 an English language edition of *Paris and Vienne* as well as an English translation of Raoul Lefèvre's *Histoire de Jason* also in June 1492, both of which books were illustrated with the same woodcuts.

Print historians, literary scholars, and experts in related fields who study a variety of texts from Aesop to the *Legenda aurea* as they appear in the earliest printed books published in the Low Countries will find their images laid out and catalogued completely here. In *The Fifteenth-Century Printing Types of the Low Countries* (1966), Wytze and Lotte Hellinga called for a bibliographic study of woodcuts. Kok's monumental catalogue answers that call by providing every detail about the woodcuts including "when and where they appear and which printers used them" (xv).

Martha W. Driver, Pace University

LINNE R. MOONEY AND ESTELLE STUBBS
*Scribes and the City: London Guildhall Clerks
and the Dissemination of Middle English Literature, 1375-1425.*
University of York, UK: York Medieval Press, 2013.
ix + 155 pp. 53 B&W illus.

Our view of later medieval book production has changed over the years from the notion of scribes working in an organized bookshop (as proposed by L.H. Loomis for the Auchinleck manuscript) to the concept of independent craftsmen working on an *ad hoc* basis in fulfilment of a particular commission, as persuasively argued by Ian Doyle and Malcolm Parkes in their seminal article on the Trinity Gower. Doyle and Parkes established that the copy in Cambridge, Trinity College MS R.3.2 of John Gower's *Confessio Amantis* was produced by five different scribes, whom they labelled A to E, and identified the handwriting of three of them, B, D and E (the poet Thomas Hoccleve), in other manuscripts. Linne Mooney and Estelle Stubbs now build on this work to produce a handsome, well-illustrated volume in which they suggest that these scribes were employed in the City of London's Guildhall where they copied literary manuscripts for dissemination as a sideline. That the Guildhall clerks may have played a crucial role in the dissemination of Middle English literature, in particular the works of five major authors, Chaucer, Gower, Trevisa, Langland, and Hoccleve, and hence the introduction of English as the language of commerce and government, is an attractive hypothesis.

Following an introductory chapter on the roles of the clerks employed in the Guildhall, the authors set out to prove this hypothesis by "matching the idiosyncratic elements" (1) of the handwriting of certain scribes who appear in the City's *Liber Albus* and its Letter Books with the handwriting of contemporary literary manuscripts. None of these scribes signs his work; the attribution to each of the copying attributed to him is deduced from circumstantial evidence. Thus they are identified as Richard Osbarn, Chamber Clerk (1400 to 1437); John Marchaunt, Chamber Clerk (1380 to 1399), Common Clerk (1399 to 1417), also Doyle and Parkes' Scribe D; Adam Pinkhurst, scrivener (Doyle and Parkes' Scribe B); and John Carpenter, Common Clerk (1417 to 1437), each of whom warrants a chapter to himself and his *oeuvre* (Chapters 2 to 5). Chapter 6 discusses further scribes including Richard Frampton and Thomas Hoccleve, clerk of the Privy Seal, who may have been employed at the Guildhall at some time in their careers.

The "idiosyncratic elements" of an individual's handwriting have been established by constructing graphic profiles for the scribes, focussing on the key letter forms **a d g h r s w** and **y** (42). This approach can lead to a consideration of letter forms out of context, looking *for* rather than looking *at*. The aspect of an individual's hand should also be considered, the angle of the pen nib, the slant of the pen, and the weight of the letter. Moreover, features of style may be common in a script, not features by which a scribe can be readily recognized. In the case of Chancery scribes a model was there to be studied and practiced, and they were trained to write in a uniform style, while Hoccleve presumably followed the conventions of the Privy Seal Office. Few allowances were made for a writer's personality. Can one surmise that the Guildhall clerks had an office style? They seem to have used "a special variant of **A** when writing the words 'Alderman' and 'Anglia'" (43). As Doyle and Parkes remarked of Scribe D, a number of contemporary scribes wrote a very similar form of Anglicana Formata, and it is difficult to distinguish one from another.

The hand detected writing finding aids throughout the *Liber Albus*, an important task, can be identified as Osbarn's, since responsibility for the upkeep of that volume was shared between the Common Clerk (Carpenter) and the Chamber Clerk (Osbarn). As it is not the hand known to be Carpenter's, it must be Osbarn's. The same hand is that of the scribe formerly known as the "HM 114 scribe" (after his work in San Marino, Huntington Library, HM 114, one of three manuscripts he copied). Other identifications, however, seem less happy.

Mooney's earlier identification of Adam Pinkhurst, signatory to the Scriveners' Company Common Paper, with the subject of Chaucer's poem to "Adam his owen scryveyne" and hence as the scribe of the Hengwrt and Ellesmere manuscripts of the *Canterbury Tales* has already been challenged, the unconvinced including Malcolm Parkes. The Hengwrt scribe does not appear to have had a particularly clear sense of where all the items he was copying were supposed to fit. While the *Tales* are unfinished, if Pinkhurst were Chaucer's amanuensis, would he not have had a better idea? Here Pinkhurst's hand is said to occur in Letter Books H and I covering the years (1375 to 1399 and 1400 to 1423), and he is assumed to have been a Guildhall clerk who flourished c.1378 to 1410. Adam's name, however, has not been found in the City's own records, unlike those of Osbarn and Marchaunt. Nor is Adam such "a relatively unusual given name" (69), as the Indexes of Christian names in A.B. Emden's *Biographical Registers of the Universities of Oxford and Cambridge* establish, while Paul Christianson's *Directory of London Stationers* (1990) lists two other contemporary Adams if we must treat Chaucer's Adam as historical fact.

If Pinkhurst's *oeuvre* can be questioned, what of that claimed by the authors for John Marchaunt, also known as Doyle and Parkes's Scribe D, whom they characterize as an independent craftsman? The authors argue D/Marchaunt's hand appears in Letter Books G, H and I and thirteen manuscripts (eight of the *Confessio Amantis*, two of the *Canterbury Tales*, and one each of Trevisa's *De proprietatibus rerum*, Langland's *Piers Plowman*, and the anonymous prose *Brut*). Eight of these manuscripts were copied by D/Marchaunt on his own. It seems scarcely credible that a busy clerk, who had no need to moonlight since not only was he paid £10 a year but was also able to collect fees for enrollments in the Hustings' and Mayor's Court Rolls as well as for writs drawn up for the assizes (8), would have the time to act as a literary copyist. The authors recognize that their readers may have this difficulty ("Remarkable as it seems, these busy clerks found time to prepare copies of vernacular literary writings," 16) and seek to establish that it would be possible. But their estimate of the time it would take for Marchaunt to copy all the manuscripts attributed to him seems wildly over-optimistic, even assuming he was copying full-time. His contemporary Richard Frampton took five to six years between 1402 and 1407 to copy the two volumes of the Duchy of Lancaster's Great Cowcher (964 folios), and between four and five years between 1413 to 1416 a transcript of it (620 folios), nine years at least. The authors have allowed Marchaunt a six-day week for forty-eight weeks of the year (132-133), based on an average rate of copying of two to four folia a day. (In addition to the article they cite by Peter Gumbert, the authors should also look at E.A. Overgaauw, "Fast or slow, professional or monastic. The writing speed of some late-medieval scribes," *Scriptorium*, 49 (1995): 211-27.) Yet as a general rule the longer the job the slower the speed and the more formal the hand, the slower the copying. What we cannot know of any medieval scribe is the number of hours worked per day nor the number of days worked, excluding Sundays and holy days. The texts Marchaunt is supposed to have copied are long, often written many lines to a column, in careful Anglicana Formata. Copying literary manuscripts must have come second to Marchaunt's professional duties as a clerk at the Guildhall. How much free time would he have had? And copying in the evening after work would be tiring in an age of candle light. (Wax was expensive, and tallow candles smell.)

The quality of the manuscripts produced by Richard Osbarn would suggest he was copying for his own library rather than providing exemplars for other people's use, a possibility the authors recognize (35). But a scribe copying eight manuscripts of the same text (the *Confessio*) suggests to me a full-time literary scribe who in the age before printing specialized in a certain kind of text for sale. As the late Jeremy Griffiths once observed, specialization would be one of few ways in which a freelance copyist could improve his chances of a consistent supply of work. His "forked **t** scribe" appears in at least nine manuscripts of the *Nova Statuta*, while Kathleen Scott has identified a single hand she dubbed the "Considerans scribe" working on a group of chronicle rolls. Scribes such as these seem to have developed a specialist skill and reputation for copying certain kinds of texts. There is also documentary evidence from London, Oxford, and Paris of independent scribes working in their own lodgings, even if we cannot always associate a particular manuscript with them.

This book is provocative, and despite my criticisms, I have enjoyed reading it.

Pamela Robinson, University of London

NICOLE R. RICE, ED.
Middle English Religious Writing in Practice:
Texts, Readers, and Transformations.
Late Medieval and Early Modern Studies, 21.
Turnhout: Brepols, 2013. 278 pp. 2 illus.

Several important texts and interesting manuscripts are considered in this meticulously edited volume, and the essays on them are correspondingly detailed and thorough. Each essay is provided with its own works cited, which comprises not only primary sources and secondary works, but also a list of manuscripts and archival documents. These lists form the index of manuscripts at the end of the volume.

After a comprehensive introduction by Rice, the book is divided into three parts: Continental Religious Women in English Practice, Manuscript Compilation and the Adaptation of Religious Practice, and (an awkward and not entirely apposite title) Negotiating Orthodoxy: Revision, Circulation, Annotation. The continental religious women of Part I are Catherine of Siena, Marguerite Porete, and St Bridget of Sweden. In "From the Charterhouse to the Printing House: Catherine of Siena in Medieval England," Jennifer N. Brown looks at the transmission and circulation of three of Catherine's works among the Carthusians and Bridgettines and then into the seventeenth century, and in "Poetry as Prayer: John Audelay's 'Salutation to St Bridget,'" Martha W. Driver looks at Audelay's verse and imagery in the context of salutation poetry. Between these two essays, Michael G. Sargent considers "Medieval and Modern Readership of Marguerite Porete's *Mirouer des Simples Âmes Anienties*: The French and English Traditions." Sargent tackles Marguerite Porete and her modern critics head-on, arguing that the Free Spiritism she is said to have promoted is more an academic construct than reality: readers of the *Mirror* read what they saw as "a compelling, esoteric, but fundamentally orthodox work" (63). His analysis of the Middle English transmission is particularly interesting, drawing as it does on his work with Father Edmund Colledge in the 1970s, and showing a deep familiarity and understanding of the historiography of the *Mirror*. As with Brown's texts of Catherine, all three extant Middle English manuscripts, as well as the Latin translation, have strong Carthusian connections – "and there is no evidence that either text had any other readers" (77). In other words, it was not orthodox but it was read by the orthodox, and there was no Free Spiritism in England. The essay is furnished with an appendix of textual agreements among the French and Latin translations.

Part II consists of just two essays, both weighty. In "From 'Companion to the Novitiate' to 'Companion to the Devout Life': San Marino, Huntington Library, MS HM 744 and Monastic Anthologies of the Twelfth-Century Reform," Mary Agnes Edsall seeks to relate this mercantile family anthology (the "Fyler MS") to a tradition of "companions to the noviate" and to show how such works developed into "companions to the devout life." Edsall's careful analysis and comparison is furnished with three appendices: the first presents the contents of the manuscript (with quiring and booklet division), the second details of anthologies containing the works of Hugh of Fouilloy, a novitiate author, and the third Edsel's comparison manuscripts. Nicole R. Rice's "Lay Spiritual Texts and Pastoral Care in two Fifteenth-Century Priests' Collections" places both her manuscripts (Cambridge, Jesus College Q.D.4 and Cambridge University Library Ii.4.9) in their religious and spiritual context, analyzing the two texts shared by the manuscripts (*The Abbey of the Holy Ghost* and *The Charter of the Abbey of the Holy Ghost*) in order to emphasize their relevance and appeal to the clergy, both the individual priest and the lay and clerical inhabitants of a medieval hospital, Rice's preferred context for the CUL manuscript.

Part III opens with "Women, Tales, and 'Talking Back' in *Pore Caitif* and *Dives and Pauper.*" Here Moira Fitzgibbons argues that two tracts of the former are incorporated into the latter in such a way as to allow the sort of dialogic encounters (the "spirit of pragmatic negotiation," 207) which the *Dives* author favors. An appendix compares the Ten Commandments in the two texts. Next, in their essay, "'Citizens of Saints': Creating Christian Community in Oxford, Bodleian Library, MS Laud Misc. 23," Stephen Kelly and Ryan Perry discuss the contents of the three booklets that make up this manuscript, suggesting the focus and contexts of some of the twenty-seven texts it contains and pointing up the hybridity of a collection which can marry the orthodox with the doubtfully orthodox. The doubtfully orthodox (indeed, Lollard) is the unedited and unique sermon which features in their essay title ("Citizens of Saints") about which we hear disappointingly little and an edition of which would have been very desirable. Finally, Margaret Connolly considers "Sixteenth-Century Readers Reading Fifteenth-Century Religious Books: The Roberts Family of Middlesex." Eight books can be traced to this mercantile family, five of which Connolly discusses (two Books of Hours and three devotional works). Connolly explains the nature of the annotations, mostly by Edmund Roberts (1520-1585), some indicative of engagement with the texts and others using the books as repositories of family records, and looks at the family's connections with religious houses in order to explain how these fifteenth-century books ended up in sixteenth-century hands.

Susan Powell, University of Salford

**JUANITA FEROS RUYS, JOHN O. WARD, AND
MELANIE HEYWORTH, EDS.**
*The Classics in the Medieval and Renaissance Classroom: The Role of Ancient
Texts in the Arts Curriculum as Revealed by Surviving Manuscripts and Early
Printed Books*
Brepols: Turnhout, 2013.
ix + 420 pp., 2 B&W plates.

This book, developed from a conference held at the Centre for Medieval Studies, University of Sydney, in 2006, seeks to examine the role of the
classics in medieval and Renaissance arts curricula by relating the physical
evidence of manuscripts, incunables and cinquecentine with contemporary
responses to the classical texts, such as commentaries and notes. The emphasis on what actually happened in the classroom distinguishes this book
from other studies: it approaches the fundamental, yet admittedly ultimately
unanswerable, question of how the manuscripts were used.

Starting in the Anglo-Saxon period and just reaching the seventeenth
century, and taking English and Continental case-studies into account, *The
Classics in the Medieval and Renaissance Classroom* is wide-ranging in scope.
Indeed, by including late antique commentaries, such as those of Servius
on the *Aeneid* and Macrobius on Cicero's *Dream of Scipio,* in its definition of
"Classics" (4), this range is extended to produce a sophisticated and complex view of classical reception. Ward's introduction leaves the question of
the definition of the "classroom" open to allow for scope among the essays
as they navigate the many different contexts and settings in which learning
took place across the early medieval and Renaissance periods.

The chapters are arranged chronologically, which allows different approaches
to be juxtaposed, as well as providing a coherent overview; however, this also
means that when the volume is read as a whole, resonances can be traced across

the centuries and between the essays. Comparable methodologies are repeated in studies of varied time frames, leading to fascinatingly diverse results.

Both Birger Munk Olsen and Marjorie Curry Woods survey commentary traditions and challenge current perceptions, as Munk Olsen concludes that the seemingly simple twelfth-century *Accessus* to classical poets in fact implies sensitive awareness of pedagogical trends (141) and Curry Woods calls for a comprehensive re-thinking of the distinctions between "classical, medieval and Renaissance" in terms of the approach of each period to classical texts (338).

Gabriele Knappe studies the extant Anglo-Saxon manuscripts pertaining to the liberal arts and calls for closer attention to be focused on features such as glosses and additions to texts in order to ascertain if they are the result of classroom use (40). In contrast, Robert Black focuses on manuscripts used or produced in the schoolroom in Florence at the other end of the medieval period and through them generates a picture of pupils' composition and reading. Dugald McLellan uses printed editions to shape a picture of the values and importance of one Renaissance figure, Antonio Mancinelli (288), while Martin Camargo examines English manuscripts of the *Poetria nova* of Geoffrey of Vinsauf to ask questions about how the text was used in various teaching contexts (146). Moving away from material evidence, Beth Bennett and Lucia Calboli Montefusco examine the works of single medieval and Renaissance authors, namely, Anselm de Besate and George of Trebizond, both pioneers far ahead of the schools of their own times.

Coming back to the schoolroom, several essays are concerned with the reception of a single classical author. Lola Sharon Davidson traces the reception of Aristotle's *De sompno* in the schools via the surviving manuscripts and considers the place of Aristotle in the medieval sciences curriculum; Craig Kallendorf, on the other hand, highlights how Virgil was studied for moral truths in the Renaissance classroom by way of the *Observations on the Works of Vergil* by Orazio Toscanella, a sixteenth-century schoolmaster in Venice. Ursula Potter combines a study of the statutes of Tudor grammar schools with the views of contemporary commentators on pedagogical practice, especially Erasmus and Vives, to explore the applications of the ideological debate surrounding censorship of Terence's plays in the grammar school context, where performance of these texts was a central feature. Steven J. Williams takes an opposite perspective, analyzing the part played by students in steering the curriculum towards the inclusion of Aristotle in the schools of Paris in the twelfth and thirteenth centuries.

The shape of the curriculum is considered more widely in another group of papers. Rita Copeland examines Thierry of Chartres's *Heptateuchon* and uses it to divine Thierry's ideal of a liberal arts curriculum in the early twelfth century; she then goes further, via Thierry's preface to his commentary on

Cicero's *De inventione*, to consider the value placed on the rhetorical arts in the twelfth century for their function, morality and utility (98). Karin Margareta Fredborg reconstructs the curriculum of Chartres and Paris in the 1130s and 1140s, following John of Salisbury's educational path, and notes that it mirrors William of Conches's claim that a close grounding in major classical works by figures such as Cicero, Plato and Boethius was intended to initiate understanding of the world and truth-finding (115). The classics as a mode of training for moral, religious and political debate also feature at the center of George Buchanan's revision of the curriculum in St Andrew's University in sixteenth-century Scotland, as outlined in C. Jan Swearingen's paper.

Finally, two essays extend the scope of interest even further, at either end of the chronological span and beyond the boundaries of the curricula or conventional classroom. Manfred Kraus interrogates the survival of the ancient *progymnasmata* system of rhetorical exercises beyond late antiquity and into the medieval classroom, while, in the final paper, Brian Taylor examines how the teachings of the German Mastersingers in the fifteenth and early sixteenth centuries promoted rhetorical and poetic arts among the culturally aspiring lay urban middle classes.

In his introduction Ward emphasizes the foundational importance of this volume by outlining directions for future research, such as the necessity of producing preliminary compilations of manuscripts to enable further work in the area of classical reception (5). Indeed, some of the essays provide the first contributions to these collections of primary sources, such as Gabriele Knappe's appendix listing "Manuscripts Written or Known in England from the Eighth Century to *c.* 1130 Containing Works for Instruction in the Language Arts" (41–56); Beth Bennett's comprehensive listing of sources used by Anselm of Besate in his *Rhetorimachia* (69–71); Karin Margareta Fredborg's edition, from the manuscripts, of extracts of Petrus Helias's commentary on the *De inventione* (116–125); Manfred Kraus's list of manuscripts containing works by Priscian which include the *Praeexercitamina*, demonstrating their chronological and geographical distribution (177–179); and Martin Camargo's four appendices on Geoffrey of Vinsauf's *Poetria nova*, including a list of English manuscripts and editions and translations of additions to manuscripts of the text (156–172).

This collection of essays has a wide significance within the field, as, with its emphasis on the historical and material contexts in which the classics were read, it provides a bridge between purely codicological studies and investigations with a more literary focus.

Kirstie McGregor, University of Oxford

WENDY SCASE, ED.

The Making of the Vernon Manuscript. The Production and Contexts of Oxford, Bodleian Library, MS Eng. poet. a. 1. Texts and Transitions, 6. Brepols: Turnhout, 2013. 331 pp., with 40 plates, 60 figures, and 2 tables.

This book marks a significant point in a large-scale research project on the Vernon manuscript initiated and overseen at the University of Birmingham by Wendy Scase. Conceived with the aim of enhancing knowledge and understanding of this huge repertory of texts for "sowlehele," spiritual health, the Vernon Manuscript Project has already generated an electronic facsimile of the manuscript and a range of informative online resources. *The Making of the Vernon Manuscript: The Production and Contexts of Oxford, Bodleian Library, MS Eng. Poet. a. 1* draws together the fruit of research undertaken by project members and other scholars in the form of linked essays. It offers a detailed and up-to-date account of the manuscript's physical features, of the processes by which it was compiled, copied, and decorated, and of the range of possible patrons and readers for whom it might have been produced. Wendy Scase's role as orchestrator of the overall project is fittingly reflected in her multiple appearances in this book: as well as providing editorial oversight, she supplies five chapters of her own on aspects of the manuscript's production, its analogues, and its functions and commissioning.

Scholarly interest in the Vernon manuscript has rightly recognized its significance as a mighty compendium of some of the most important late Middle English works, both prose and verse. Weighing in at 22 kg (approximately 48 pounds), it contains copies of *The Northern Homily Cycle, The South English Legendary, The Prick of Conscience, Speculum Vitae, Ancrene Riwle,* Hilton's *Scale of Perfection, Piers Plowman,* and a number of other works. Vernon's main scribe was also responsible for the copying of the Simeon manuscript (London, British Library Add. MS 22283), which duplicates many of its contents, and the two manuscripts share further connections, both scribal and textual, with a number of other compilations. *The Making of the Vernon Manuscript* is a new contribution to an already long history of research into these West Midlands compilations, research which was given new stimulus when a facsimile of the Vernon manuscript was published by D. S. Brewer in 1990, along with a volume of studies edited by Derek Pearsall. The new collection of essays preserves continuities of various kinds with this earlier volume, in some cases developing suggestions made there, and elsewhere revising or modifying its arguments. A. I. Doyle's opening essay on "Codicology, Palaeography, and Provenance," for example, offers new reflections on findings about Vernon and Simeon which were first published in 1974, then reshaped and extended in an introduction to the facsimile and in a contribution to the 1990 volume of studies.

Doyle's essay in the new volume sets out evidence and a series of hypotheses which one way or another remain central to the other contents of this book. His account of the vital statistics of the manuscript, of the materials that went into its production (no fewer than 211 calf-skins), the scribal labor (four years for copying both Vernon and Simeon), and the likely cost for the patron make clear both the ambition of the undertaking and the apparently rich cultural resources of the area around Lichfield in which the manuscript seems to have taken shape. Doyle's identification in other manuscripts and documents of one of the scribal hands of Vernon, together with his findings about Dominus Thomas Heneley and a scribe named John who seem to have had access to texts copied in both Vernon and Simeon, point to a production context (if not necessarily an early readership) which may have involved secular clergy rather than religious. (A number of earlier accounts of the manuscript have related it to religious houses in the area, with Bordesley Abbey as a strong contender.) The possibilities raised in Doyle's essay are further explored in Simon Horobin's discussion of "The Scribes of the Vernon Manuscript." Horobin adduces still more documentary evidence that the scribes associated with Vernon were more likely to have been professional scriveners than monks and that they worked on a freelance basis in the area around Lichfield (probably with connections to the cathedral) from 1373 to around 1414.

Vernon was made to be both visually pleasing and usable, equipped with an extensive program of decoration, two cycles of miniatures, and a table of contents. Five of the essays explore features of its layout and artwork, in some cases exploiting the magnification possibilities opened up by the digital facsimile. Wendy Scase investigates the sequence of rubrication and decoration, and uses the relationship between scribal rubrics and the titles used in the table of contents to reconstruct the likely stages in which the table took shape; she suggests that this part of the manuscript might have been originally designed for separate use and not necessarily bound together with the other contents. Scase writes also on the artists of the initials, studying relationships between guide initials and scribal hands through graphemic profiling, and proposes that there are some clear divisions of practice between different teams of artists. Rebecca Farnham's work on the border artists, of whom she identifies nine, confirms the likelihood that the manuscript's production was complex and involved a large personnel. If this was so, then the mixture of styles and influences in the illumination which are outlined in Lynda Dennison's essay on "The Artistic Origins" seems quite plausible: Dennison's identification of similar work from artists known to have had associations with Norwich Cathedral Priory and Westminster Abbey suggests to her the existence of a Benedictine monastic circuit, with peripatetic artists who spent periods of residence in different locales as and where work presented itself. The miniature artists were certainly skilled and innovative, as Alison Stones argues in an essay on the two Vernon miniature cycles, one in the context of the *Estorie del Evangelie,* the other in a series of Marian miracles. Stones develops a suggestion made by Carol Meale in the 1990 collection of *Studies in the Vernon Manuscript,* and finds for these Marian scenes a number of analogues in French manuscripts of the *Vie des pères* and Gautier de Coinci's *Miracles de Nostre Dame.*

Vernon was evidently a large-scale and lavish commission, using local scribal resources over a long period, and drawing on the work of several, possibly even many, manuscript artists. It was conceived with care and its contents presumably took some seeking out. It was costly – but not so costly that it could not in part be replicated in the form of Simeon. Why would such volumes be produced? And who might have commissioned and paid for them? Jeremy Smith's essay on "Mapping the Language of the Vernon Manuscript" presents detailed evidence of a significant amount of linguistic modernization in the Vernon text of *Ancrene Riwle,* intimating that the compilers planned a comprehensive repertory of "sowlehele" which would give new life to older works as well as incorporating new ones. Ryan Perry's exploration of "Editorial Politics" sets the production of the manuscript in its historical moment, asking whether it constituted a retreat into orthodoxy or rather an active, dynamic textual response to Wycliffite ideas. His scrutiny of the interpolation of a section on the seven sacraments from Robert Mannyng's *Handlyng Synne* into the Vernon and Simeon texts of *The Northern Homily Cycle* develops and explicitly answers suggestions in an essay by Thomas J. Heffernan in the 1990 *Studies in the Vernon Manuscript.*

The last words on the origins of the manuscript, appropriately enough, are the editor's, in the form of three linked essays by Wendy Scase. These offer a thoughtful and wide-ranging review of the forms of pious statement that a manuscript might make, and point out that the years in which Vernon took shape might well have been ones in which the commissioner of a collection of religious works understood the wisdom of silent, anonymous patronage. In seeking analogues to Vernon, Scase moves beyond English books and makes the case for large-scale compilations of primarily Anglo-Norman material: manuscripts such as Cambridge University Library Gg. 1. 1, and Cambridge, Trinity College R. 14. 7, which match the scope and general lavishness of Vernon, if not quite its weight and scale. In this company, she sees Vernon as the likely product of a patronage nexus involving both lay bibliophiles and secular clergy. Her candidate as the lay representative of such a partnership is William Beauchamp, brother of Thomas Beauchamp, Earl of Warwick: a supporter of writing in the vernacular (his will was made in English) whose estates, connections and residences in both the Lichfield area and London suggest contexts hospitable to the compilation and production of a manu-script like Vernon. Scase is properly tentative about the case for Beauchamp, stressing that he is the kind of patron we should be considering, rather than the precise candidate, but her outline of his credentials provides a fitting end to an informative and attractively illustrated collection of essays, and moves forward our understanding of the cultural and other contexts in which this important manuscript was produced.

Julia Boffey, Queen Mary, University of London

About the Authors

Dorothy C. Africa is an Associate in the Celtic Languages and Literatures department of Harvard University, and is also employed in the Harvard Library in the Preservation, Conservation and Digital Imaging Unit, with a primary assignment to the Harvard Law School Library. Her major research interests are Irish history and hagiography (fifth to the twelfth century) and the early history of the book in the West. She has a doctorate from the Centre for Medieval Studies, University of Toronto, and a certification in bookbinding from North Bennet Street School, Boston, Massachusetts.

Merridee L. Bailey is a Senior Research Fellow with the ARC Centre of Excellence for the History of Emotions at the University of Adelaide. She has previously published on ideas about virtue and courtesy in fifteenth- and sixteenth-century England and more recently has begun working on morality and emotions in merchant practices in London. She has recently published a book on childhood in late medieval and early modern England, *Socialising the Child in Late Medieval England c. 1400-1600* (Boydell and Brewer, 2012).

Julia Boffey is Professor of Medieval Studies in the Department of English at Queen Mary, University of London. Her most recent book *Manuscript and Print in London c.1475-1530* (British Library, 2012) was reviewed in *JEBS* 16.

Gerard Bouwmeester is a Ph.D. candidate at the University of Utrecht (Netherlands), researching Middle Dutch texts and text collections. His research is part of the HERA-project "The Dynamics of the Medieval Manuscript: Text Collections from a European Perspective" (www.dynamicsofthemedievalmanuscript.eu), which is financially supported by the HERA Joint Research Programme (www.heranet.info) and the European Community FP7. He has Master's degrees from York (Medieval Studies) and Utrecht (Dutch Language & Literature).

James P. Carley is a Distinguished Research Professor (Emeritus) at York University and a Professor of the History of the Book at the University of Kent. His most recent book (with the assistance of Carolin Brett) is an edition and translation of John Leland's *De uiris illustribus* (Toronto/Oxford: PIMS/Bodleian Library, 2010), and he is working on a second commentary volume to the edition.

Tania M. Colwell completed her PhD on the French *Mélusine* manuscripts and their audiences at the Australian National University, Canberra, where she is currently a Visitor in the School of History. She is extending her doctoral research for monograph publication while working on a new project mapping emotions of encounter within manuscript and early printed collections of ethnographic texts compiled and translated into French by Jean le Long in 1351.

Margaret Connolly teaches at the University of St Andrews and is a general editor of the Middle English Texts series. Her most recent publication is *Index of Middle English Prose, Handlist XIX: Manuscripts in the University Library, Cambridge* (Dd-Oo) (2009). She has also published editions of Middle English religious prose texts; the monograph *John Shirley: Book Production and the Noble Household in Fifteenth-Century England* (1998); and, jointly with Linne Mooney, a collection of essays, *Design and Distribution of Late Medieval Manuscripts in England* (2008). She is a co-editor of *The Mediaeval Journal* published by Brepols and the St Andrews Institute of Mediaeval Studies.

Martha W. Driver is Distinguished Professor of English and Women's and Gender Studies at Pace University in New York City. A co-founder of the Early Book Society for the study of manuscripts and printing history, she writes about illustration from manuscript to print, book production, and the early history of publishing. In addition to publishing some 55 articles in these areas, she has edited nineteen journals over seventeen years, including *Film & History: Medieval Period in Film* and the *Journal of the Early Book Society*. Her books about pictures (from manuscript miniatures to woodcuts to film) include *The Image in Print: Book Illustration in Late Medieval England* (British Library Publications and University of Toronto), *An Index of Images in English MSS*, fascicle four, with Michael Orr (Brepols), and *The Medieval Hero on Screen* and *Shakespeare and the Middle Ages*, with Sid Ray (McFarland). She contributed to and edited *Preaching the Word in Manuscript and Print in Late Medieval England: Essays in Honour of Susan Powell* with Veronica O'Mara (Brepols, 2013).

Jean-Marie Flamand is a member of the "Section de l'humanisme" at the Institut de Recherche et d'Histoire des Textes (CNRS) in Paris. He has been collaborating on various works on Greek Neoplatonism (mainly translations into French of Plotinus and Porphyrius). His research on the beginnings of the study of Greek in sixteenth-century France has been published in *La France des humanistes: Hellénistes II* (Turnhout, Brepols, 2010). He is now preparing a volume dedicated to Jacques Lefèvre d'Étaples and a bio-bibliographical dictionary of some 600 European humanists.

Victoria Flood is an Alexander von Humboldt postdoctoral fellow in the department of Keltologie at Phillips-Universität, Marburg and is working on the relationship between late medieval English and Welsh political prophecy. A former student at the Centre for Medieval Studies at the University of York, she wrote her PhD thesis on the development of political prophecy in medieval Britain. In May 2015, she will join the Department of English Studies at the University of Durham as a Leverhulme Early Career Fellow

John Block Friedman is Emeritus Professor of English at the University of Illinois at Urbana-Champaign and currently Visiting Scholar at the Center for Medieval and Renaissance Studies, The Ohio State University. In 2010, he published *Brueghel's Heavy Dancers: Transgressive Clothing, Class, and Culture in the Late Middle Ages*. With Kristen Figg and Kathrin Giogoli, he has also written the commentary volume for *Libro de las Maravillas del Mundo*, an edition and translation of *Les Secrets de l'Histoire Naturelle*, a Middle French geographical and encyclopedic compendium now in press from Siloé, Burgos. His present research is on animal fashion in the late Middle Ages.

Kathryn Kerby-Fulton is The Notre Dame Professor of English at University of Notre Dame. She has published on Middle English literary manuscripts, reception history and censorship, including *Books Under Suspicion: Censorship and Tolerance of Revelatory Writing in Late Medieval England* (University of Notre Dame Press, 2006) and *Opening Medieval English Manuscripts: Literary and Visual Approaches*, co-authored with Maidie Hilmo and Linda Olson (Cornell University Press, 2012). She has also edited *New Directions in Medieval Manuscript Studies and Reading Practices: Essays in Honour of Derek Pearsall*, with John Thompson and Sarah Baechle, forthcoming from University of Notre Dame Press in 2014.

Joseph J. Gwara is Professor of Spanish at the United States Naval Academy. In 2014, the Bibliographical Society awarded him the Katharine F. Pantzer Research Fellowship in the History of the Printed Book. He is currently researching the sixteenth-century output of Wynkyn de Worde and his circle.

Phillipa Hardman recently retired as Reader in Medieval English Literature at the University of Reading. Her primary research interest is in Middle English metrical romances and their manuscript contexts, particularly miscellany collections. Her current research project focuses on the Charlemagne romances.

Ralph Hanna is Senior Research Officer, Faculty of English Language and Literature, at the University of Oxford. His recent publications include editions for the Early English Text Society, *Richard Rolle: Uncollected Verse and Prose, with Related Northern Texts* (o.s. 329, 2007) and *Speculum Vitae: A Reading, Editions I and II* (o.s. 331-2, 2008).

Katherine Hindley read English at the University of Oxford and is now a PhD candidate in the Program in Medieval Studies at Yale University. She is currently researching the use of text for protection and healing in medieval England. Her publications include a chapter in *An English Prayerbook of the Fifteenth Century in Vercelli* (Vercelli: Gallo, 2012).

Ann Hutchison is Academic Dean at the Pontifical Institute of Mediaeval Studies and a member of the Department of English at Glendon College, York University. She studies St Birgitta of Sweden and the English House of her Order, Syon Abbey, with particular interest in the books the nuns shared and read. She is currently editing *The Myroure of oure Ladye*.

Hope Johnston is an Assistant Professor of Medieval Literature in the Baylor University English Department. She has edited Christine de Pizan's *Boke of the Cyte of Ladyes* for Medieval and Renaissance Texts and Studies (ACMRS, forthcoming). Her current book project discusses reader annotations in Tudor Chaucer editions.

David Lavinsky is Assistant Professor of English at Yeshiva University. He publishes on late medieval vernacularity and material culture, and is working on a book tentatively entitled *Inscription and Sacred Truth: Wycliffite Biblical Scholarship, 1380-1450*.

Kirstie McGregor is a DPhil student in the English Faculty at the University of Oxford, working on the manuscript reception of Gildas's *De excidio Britanniae*. She was formerly a member of the Department of Anglo-Saxon, Norse and Celtic at the University of Cambridge.

Linne R. Mooney is Professor in Medieval English Palaeography at the University of York and an Officer of the Early Book Society. Her research focuses on late medieval English literature and the scribes who copied it. She is PI for a major Arts and Humanities Research Council-funded project to study the scribes who copied works by Geoffrey Chaucer, John Gower, John Trevisa, William Langland and Thomas Hoccleve (working with Simon Horobin and Estelle Stubbs), of which the website is http://www.medievalscribes.com; and also co-author, with Daniel Mosser and Elizabeth Solopova, of the iMEV, a freely accessible web-based version of The Index of Middle English Verse, available in prototype at http://www.cddc.vt.edu/host/imev/index.html. As the editor of *Nota Bene: Brief Notes on Manuscripts and Early Printed Books*, she is a regular contributor to *JEBS*.

Susan Powell is Emeritus Professor of Medieval Texts and Culture at the University of Salford, a Research Associate at the Centre for Medieval Studies, University of York, and a Visiting Research Fellow at the Institute of English Studies, University of London. As review editor for *JEBS*, she regularly contributes several reviews to each issue. Her research interests are in manuscripts and early printed books, with particular relation to late medieval and Tudor preaching and devotional texts. With Emma Cayley, she edited *Manuscripts and Printed Books in Europe 1350-1550: Packaging, Presentation and Consumption*, the 2009 EBS conference proceedings at the University of Exeter (2013). Her most recent publication, edited with Vincent Gillespie, is *A Companion to the Early Printed Book in Britain 1476-1558* (2014).

Veronica O'Mara is a Senior Lecturer in the Department of English at the University of Hull. Her main research areas are Middle English religious literature, female literacy, preaching, and the relationship between manuscript and print. She is currently involved in a project on medieval nuns and literacy. She has recently edited (with Virginia Blanton, University of Missouri-Kansas City, and Patricia Stoop, Universiteit Antwerpen) *Nuns' Literacies in Medieval Europe: The Hull Dialogue, Medieval Women: Texts and Contexts*, 26 (Turnhout: Brepols, 2013) and (with Martha W. Driver) *Preaching the Word in Manuscript and Print in Late Medieval England: Essays in Honour of Susan Powell*, Sermo, 11 (Turnhout: Brepols, 2013), both reviewed in this issue.

Pamela Robinson is a Senior Research Fellow at the Institute of English Studies, University of London. She is author of *A Catalogue of Dated and Datable Manuscripts c.888-1600 in London Libraries* (British Library, 2003), *A Catalogue of Dated and Datable Manuscripts c.737-1600 in Cambridge Libraries* (D.S. Brewer, 1988), and co-editor of *The Making of Books, Medieval Manuscripts, their Scribes and Readers: Essays presented to M.B. Parkes* (Scolar Press, 1997).

Martha Dana Rust is Associate Professor of English at New York University. She is the author of *Imaginary Worlds in Medieval Books: Exploring the Manuscript Matrix* (Palgrave 2007) as well as articles on a broad range of topics, from teaching intertextuality using Umberto Eco's *The Name of the Rose*, to the metaphorics of paper and parchment, to the space of the page in comics and medieval manuscripts. Her current book project is entitled "Item: Lists and the Poetics of Reckoning in Late-Medieval England."

Arnold Sanders is Associate Professor of English at Goucher College. He also teaches in the Book Studies Minor and serves on the Brooke and Carol Peirce Center advisory board. His research interests include medieval and early modern English literature, interpretive theory, and the history of the book. He has published on Malory, Spenser, Chaucer and early Chaucer editions, Margery Kempe, authorship in medieval compilations, and teaching early modern literature to undergraduates using rare books and archives. He is currently completing an article on the Middle English *Pearl* using evidence from the digitized facsimile of BL MS Cotton Nero A.x.

Valerie Schutte recently received her PhD in history from the University of Akron. Her research focuses on book dedications directed to Queen Mary I and on cataloguing Mary's personal library. She has published on Shakespeare, printer patronage by early Tudor royal ladies, and a book dedication by Erasmus to Katherine of Aragon.

Estelle Stubbs is Honorary Research Fellow in the Humanities Research Institute at the University of Sheffield. She has recently co-authored *Scribes and the City* with Linne Mooney (reviewed in this issue), completed a Mellon-funded project with the University of Toronto on Book Networks in the medieval period and is acting as a consultant on the Yale University project, "Digitally Enabled Scholarship with Medieval Manuscripts."

Daniel Wakelin is Jeremy Griffiths Professor of Medieval English Palaeography in the University of Oxford and a Fellow of St Hilda's College. He has recently been appointed as a co-editor of *JEBS* and has worked with Linne Mooney on the Nota Bene section of this issue. His recent publications include *Scribal Corrections and Literary Craft: English Manuscripts 1375-1510* (Cambridge University Press, 2014) and "When Scribes Won't Write: Gaps in Middle English Books," *Studies in the Age of Chaucer*, 36 (2014), 249-78. He has also contributed essays to *Probable Truth: Editing Medieval Texts from Britain*, edited by Vincent Gillespie and Anne Hudson (Brepols, 2013) and to *A Companion to the Early Printed Book in Britain*, edited by Susan Powell and Vincent Gillespie (D. S. Brewer, 2013), both of which are reviewed in this issue.

Eric Weiskott is Assistant Professor of English at Boston College. His research concerns the metrical form, cultural meaning, and manuscript contexts of Old English and Middle English poetry. His recent publications include "Lawman, the Last Old English Poet and the First Middle English Poet," in *Laȝamon's Brut and other Medieval Chronicles: 14 essays*, ed. Marie-Françoise Alamichel (2013), and "Phantom Syllables in the English Alliterative Tradition," in *Modern Philology* (2013).

www.ingramcontent.com/pod-product-compliance
Lightning Source LLC
Chambersburg PA
CBHW060305100726
47907CB00002B/296